THE COMMUNITY

A Comparative Perspective

THE
COMMUNITY

A Comparative Perspective

EDITED BY

Robert Mills French
Florida State University

F. E. PEACOCK PUBLISHERS, INC.
ITASCA   ILLINOIS

Preface

As the following pages demonstrate, the community has been studied by many researchers in many different societies. To attempt to present a comprehensive collection of existing community studies in a single volume would be impossible. Even to attempt to cover the studies within a given society would be difficult if not impossible. This collection makes no pretense to comprehensiveness, rather, it is representative of the rich variety of materials that are available to the student of the community.

The comparative perspective of this volume takes the reader to American, Canadian, and several European societies and in so doing, demonstrates the variations and similarities among communities and their problems. The comparative base could be extended to studies of Asian, African, and Latin American communities but this would be the subject of another volume. Comparability of the communities in this volume is simplified inasmuch as all share some facets of European culture.

The book is divided into three major subject categories. The first section: "The Community as an Object of Study" deals with definitions of community and how to study it. The comparative perspective which guides this book is spelled out in the introduction, and the differing perspectives of anthropologists and sociologists are presented in several readings. The object of this presentation is not to argue who has the

v

proper methods of study, but rather, to demonstrate how each approach adds a special dimension to our understanding of the community.

The second section: "Bases of Community Organization" presents a variety of studies that show differing dominant themes of communities. What creates "community," or perhaps, what holds a group of people together in a certain pattern which we identify as a community, is the subject of this section. Family ties are important for some communities but actually tend to destroy the basis of other communities' existence. Similar cultural heritage draws many people together, but rancorous ethnic conflict between groups can also create "community." What this section demonstrates is that any simplistic explanation of "why communities" must fail, for just as Durkheim discovered that differing causes of suicide in fact indicate different kinds of suicide, so too an examination of the bases for communities indicates that there are several kinds of community. This presentation is intended to be a modest step toward the creation of a typology of communities. This does not mean that similarities among communities of several types are to be overlooked; indeed, such similarities would be the true "universals" that students of the community seek.

The final section: "The Community and the Larger World" deals with the changes that have affected all mankind. The awakening to larger cultural horizons of men who have been introduced to other ways is a common theme of social scientists—this theme takes on more meaning when it is presented in the context of what Serbian peasants or a French–Canadian community experience. That change has some costs to traditional ways and communities is attested to by the selections on economic pressures from the outside world and those that deal with migration. Certainly no student of the traditional community should be unaware of the threat to its very existence. More than any other single factor, the threat to the existence of the small community from pressures exerted by outside forces (metropolitan, national and even international) makes all the communities presented in these pages similar. The intention of the editor is not to call to arms the champions of small community life, but rather, to bring attention to, and illustrate, the great change taking place in society. The study of the community is important if only because it enables us to observe this transformation more readily than any other approach.

Contents

Part One

———————

The Community

as an

Object of Study

CHAPTER I

Perspectives on Community Study

"What is a community" is a question that has had many answers. In his work *The Community—An Introduction to a Social System*[1], Irwin T. Sanders listed four ways of viewing the community: "The Community as a Place to Live" (qualitative approach), "The Community as a Spatial Unit" (ecological approach), "The Community as a Way of Life" (ethnographic approach), and "The Community as a Social System" (sociological approach). Examples of all of these ways of viewing the community are contained in this volume with most selections presenting either the ethnographic or sociological approach.

Just as the community appears to be different things depending upon one's perspective in viewing it, so too the boundaries of community are unclear and variable. The difficulty that writers have had in attempting to derive satisfactory definitions illustrates this problem. Robert A. Dentler states that ". . . a modern community is a nexus—a point in a terrain where society, culture, and individuals meet" and takes great pains to spell out the need to conceptualize a "full community" that

---

[1] Irwin T. Sanders, *The Community—An Introduction to a Social System* (New York: The Ronald Press Co., 1966), pp. 11–24.

3

would be representative of society.[2] This is suggestive of Arensberg and
Kimball's definition:

> Communities do not exist *in vacuo*. Each one occupies its own physical
> setting and is spatially surrounded by other communities more or less
> similar in organization, culture, and function. Institutional arrangements
> provide the framework within which various members of these separate
> communities relate to each other in transitory or in permanent cooperative
> activities. Within each community one finds the economic, political, re-
> ligious, social, even familial activities which create cohesion among its
> members, and which also extend to or include those of other communities.
> Taken as a whole, these linkages between communities make up the net-
> work called 'society'.[3]

The same necessary elements for community are found in Warren's
definition: "One thinks of communities, large or small, as clusters of
people living in close proximity in an area which contains local stores
and other service facilities for the sustenance of local people, and also
industries whose produce is distributed throughout a much wider area
. . . . Various criteria thought to characterize communities include a
specific population, living within a specific geographic area, amongst
whom there are present shared institutions and values and significant
social interaction."[4]

In all of these definitions we see the requirement for a perspective on
community that presents it as not simply a local place with a unique way
of life; rather, it must be both a part of the larger society and an entity
unto itself that can be identified and studied as such. In the article by
Arensberg reprinted in the first section of this volume, we see his attempt
to spell out this twofold conceptualization of what the community is.
Redfield approached the problem another way by viewing any given
community as part of a number of overlapping communities. In the
excerpt from *The Little Community* reprinted here, he points out that
the difference between primitive and modern, simple and complex societies, is that as societies grow their complexity increases by the web of
overlapping communities expanding. Thus a primitive community has
elements in common with the modern community; it differs in that it has
fewer elements linking it to outside, or extralocal, institutions. Warren

---

[2] Robert A. Dentler, *American Community Problems* (New York: McGraw-Hill Book
Company, 1968), p. 16.

[3] Conrad M. Arensberg and Solon T. Kimball, *Culture and Community* (New York:
Harcourt, Brace & World, Inc., 1965), pp. 3–4.

[4] Roland L. Warren, *The Community In America* (Chicago: Rand McNally & Co.,
1963), p. 2.

has provided a fitting terminology for these differing dimensions of community. He has labeled the local dimension the *horizontal community*, the extralocal dimension the *vertical community*—they are spelled out in the article by Warren in the first section.

Our definition of the community by necessity must be complex and difficult to spell out. The meaning of community is not just a place, not just a social system, not just a way of life that is shared by a number of people that identify themselves with a sense of *we*–ness. All of these elements must be contained in our conceptualization of community, for it is a most complex entity. At one and the same time it is an important building block of society, and it is society itself. It represents the culture to the individual and as such shapes him, and it is subject to the will of the individual who as a citizen can enact changes in his community.

Difficult though it may be to define, nevertheless, the community has been and continues to be the focus of much study. How to approach this study has been the subject of a good deal of controversy; the article by Simpson reviews much of the literature on communities and presents the differing points of view. Anthropologists, who generally employ the ethnographic approach, are often criticized for failing to derive general statements of community. The popular notion of the anthropologist as one who lives with "his tribe" cataloging every aspect of life yet failing to relate any of what he finds to the larger world could possibly be supported if one selected examples from the numerous ethnographies. This is not a fair evaluation, however, as the works of Arensberg, Redfield, Halpern, and others contained in this volume demonstrate. Because they have focused on the life of a single community does not mean that ethnographers are unaware of the role that the larger world plays.

The criticism of those who approach the community as a social system is almost the opposite of the charges leveled at the ethnographer. In his quest to derive systems, the sociologist is often portrayed as a distant, cold researcher who conceives of persons as "carriers of variables," and of the community as a code number on an IBM card. The perceptive analyses of community characteristics and problems presented by sociologists in this volume should quell this stereotype. The community is often portrayed as a "real place with real people," and traditions and the dimension of time are often essential elements in describing the social system of the community.[5]

The question of which approach is best is unanswerable, for each

---

[5] For an excellent discussion of why it is important that community analysts be aware of traditions and temporal dimensions of community decisions, see Stephan Thernstrom, "Yankee City Revisited: The Perils of Historical Naivete," *The American Sociological Review*, XXX (April, 1965), 234–242.

provides us with different information, all of which aids us in gaining an understanding of the community. The ethnographic accounts cited in this volume illustrate community life as no amount of detached discussion could; however, no ethnography can provide the insights that one gets from reviewing a number of different accounts. What is needed, as Simpson suggests, are comparative tests on controlled variables of community characteristics. The ethnographic material can provide the cases for our tests, but the very nature of the comparative approach forces us to summarize data and approach the community from a social systems perspective.

Although selected variables are not systematically tested out in the following selections, due to the fact that researchers have not focused on similar facets of community, the readings do demonstrate the variability of community types. The goal of community research is to arrive at more general statements of community organization; however, the complexity of the community may lead to a variety of types so that a key variable in one community, e.g., family ties, would not be crucial in another community. Unless we proceed cautiously and derive our selected variables on the basis of a wide variety of communities, we may test "universals" that are true for only a given community type or a single culture. A cross-cultural perspective insures that we will not suffer this type of myopia.

1. The Community
as Object
and as Sample

CONRAD M. ARENSBERG

One of the encouraging points of convergence in the various empirically based social sciences is the growing power and sophistication of the community-study method (Arensberg 1954; Hollingshead 1948; König 1956; Chiva 1958; Redfield 1955). The method has come to be much and ably used in ethnography. There it has added much to the emerging possibility of an at-last meaningful comparative sociology of the world's peoples (Steward 1950). The method, of course, has long roots in social surveys, in rural and agricultural sociology and economics, and in human geography (Young 1949; Wilson 1945; Taylor 1945; Utermann 1952; Maget 1953). It has not been confined to small and rural communities alone. It has as well been employed in urban sociology and in the studying and planning of *urbanisme* (Bott 1956; Young and Willmott 1957; Shevky and Williams 1949; Simey 1954; Balandier 1955).

This convergence upon the community-study method signals the growing use of the community for many purposes. The community has served as a sample or unit of observation for the study of a culture or society, as

SOURCE: Reproduced by permission of the author and the American Anthropological Association from the *American Anthropologist 63:241–264* (April, 1961).

a locus or local embodiment of a wider or general social problem or
phenomenon, as a testing ground for plans of change, amelioration, or
development (Batten 1957; Ruopp 1953; Ware 1952) . Convergence upon
the community-study method thus marks a re-entrance of the community,
small and large, into the forefront of social science activity. We say re-
entrance because much of the earliest social science, in the seminal period
of the late decades of the last century, was also focused on the community. Such seminal work explored the repeated, often widespread,
elementary or simple forms of the local commonwealth; the village, its
land-use and settlement pattern, its village constitution; the *polis,* the
early city (Maine 1871; Maurer 1854; Peake 1854; Fustel de Coulange
1905; Meitzen 1895). Problems were different then, of course, but the
community as field for their study or sample of their universe was even
then the workplace.

Despite the long and now renewed history of the community as a
center and workplace of social science interest, much confusion about it
still persists. The thing-in-itself, the community as object, is imperfectly
separated, in concept and in practice, from the use of it, as field or
sample, where the community is that within which work is done, observations made, relationships traced out. The separation of the problems is
clear enough in the abstract; it is clearly a necessary one. To study a
problem in a community, in its natural setting, or in an exemplification
in one well chosen community rather than in all its endless local occur-
rences, one must first recognize and mark off one community among the
many. Only later, and after one's field work or local survey or experiment, must one next ask: In what way is what I find here representative?
In what way is this community and the place of my problem data in it
capable of standing for, and leading me to explanation of, the universal
occurrence of the problem and its place and reasons in the whole culture
or society of its occurrence? Identification and definition is the first step;
a theory of sampling and of part-whole relationships is the second.

Let us review the obvious separateness of the questions about community. On the one hand, one asks what a community is. One asks as well
what kinds there are of them; how and why these kinds developed; what
functions they perform. One asks how functions change or shift in their
identities, or how they succeed or fail in their execution, as the form, life,
or viability and cohesiveness of the community changes, with the emergence and the succession of one variety of community upon another, in
response to differing economic, political, religious, or demographic influences. One can ask as well about the pathology of the community, the
effect of its falling away, or of its overgrowth, upon human welfare or
performance or security; one can ask about its success, even its necessity,

in supporting or perfecting these human results, individual or collective. However far one goes, the questions are about the nature of the community as a thing (Brownell 1950; Stein 1960; Sanders 1958).

On the other hand, the questions are different when one asks about the community as a field or a sample in which to study something else than the community itself. How far can one trust what one finds to be general? Or, turning it around, how far can we trust the general to show up in one, or this, community? How is any particular community, so local and unique in place and time, also standard, "average," representative? How does any one stand for all the others, or for the whole of, a society, culture, civilization, or epoch? Can one legitimately see in any one community, even the best chosen one, a microcosm of a whole society, or of a particular, but much wider and more populous, national, religious, or epochal whole? Will what we see in it mirror faithfully what we might see in any and all other unseen parts of that whole? Will what we see in it teach us surely about that whole? Other figures of speech and thought provide us tentative models of the part-whole connection that seem to justify using the community as field or sample? Are they capable of refinement into justifiable and rigorous scientific method? How far can we use a known community of persons as a portrait, an epitome, a witness of the life, nature, fate, character, and spirit of the unknown others of the people of their age and civilization? Granted we know some things about these others, or about the collectivity, like their works or art products, their social and psychological problems, their common national character or ethos, what is the new light about these things that intimate and detailed knowledge of a community of their fellows in local interaction will throw?

The re-entry of the community into central social science interest which we are witnessing today continues to demand solution of the conceptual and methodological problems corresponding to the two lines of questioning about community as object and community as sample or field which we have distinguished here. The first step toward a better theory of the nature of the community as object cannot be forever left untaken; the second step of a rationale for the community-study method, toward a better theory of the part-whole relations of findings in a community and explanations of a problem of a larger universe of many communities, cannot continue to be taken in the dark of vague models of the mirrorings or sampling of reality derived from unspecified and unsystematized canons of art and literature.

What one can do in a single short chapter, however summary, cannot be much. Nevertheless, in the space at our disposal here, we would like to take up some of the main difficulties that have been pointed out by critics or practitioners of community studies[1] and suggest answers to these difficulties which derive from a possible, already emergent theory of community as thing and as a sample. Space will not, of course, permit full exposition, let alone full proof, of such a theory; nor am I sure I have it fully complete. But enough of its outline seems already to be arguable to allow us to resolve some, if not all, of the conceptual and methodological difficulties to be cited.

Difficulties raised against the method or about its execution in one study or another can be roughly, if badly, summarized under a very few heads. They are four:

  1. Representativeness? Which community shall be chosen? The matter is very difficult in countries without seemingly uniform peasant villages, with strong regional differentiation, stratified and segregated classes, ethnically mixed, religiously composite, perhaps racially "plural" societies. It is no easier where economic or administrative or other functional specialization exists among population centers, or where great ranges in size and density separate metropolises from towns and towns from hamlets and dispersed countrysides.

  2. Completeness? When is a community a whole one? How is it to be bounded when, usually, one settlement or circle of human interest and contact grades off into and articulates with neighboring or overlapping ones? How, as well, when often one community, at one level, seems to be part of another larger one, or subdivides, below, into still smaller ones?

  3. Inclusiveness? How far must a community contain in it the institutions, the culture traits, the forces of the whole society or civilization for which it is to serve as a part, sample, or mirror? If it has too few cosmopolitan or external features or influences working locally or extending into it, can it serve as a sample of the world in which they penetrate universally? If it has too many, can it still be counted a viable community?

  4. Cohesiveness? And last, when is a community integrated enough, common-minded enough, cooperative or sharing enough, first, to be a community at all? Second, to mirror, but not over- or underrepresent, the fissions normal to its society? Communities, especially from close up and within, are as often divided into estranged groups, factions, sects as they are harmonious or concerted. What of limits, balances, unities here?

Communities seem to be basic units of organization and transmission within a society and its culture. The definition is suggested both by their repetitive character and by their characteristics of personnel, form, and function. The definition can only be won by modeling and structuring the comparative ethnographic and historical record of human and ani-

---

[1] What can be said here can only be a small push forward beyond the already excellent recent summaries of König (1956; 1958).

mal communities, with proper attention to their evolutionary variation in biological and human evolution and to their organizational, sociological, and political constitutions *in addition to* their ecological, economic, and human-geographical aspects.

To date a much too limited understanding of the community and its variations has prevailed. On the one hand ecological factors have been appealed to almost exclusively. The community has been seen—a legitimate and useful view but not a complete one—solely as a land-use pattern, a form of settlement, or a territorial unit or range of environmental exploitation. Or, on the other hand, definitions have taken a psychologistic or collective-sociological turn. They have appealed to the putative need of human beings to belong, or to the survival necessities of cooperation and solidarity, or even to consciousness of kind, or the gregarious spirit. One standard definition combines locality with a sociological criterion, calling the community "the maximal group of persons who normally reside together in face-to-face association" (Murdock 1949). All of these definitions, traditional or learned, are limited, restricted, and unspecific. They are quite insufficient to deal with the known varieties of the human community, to cope with its known functions and processes, and to separate it properly from other local, geographical, or associational phenomena of human life. A moment's reflection will suffice to remind one that none of them except the last ("maximal group of coresidents") addresses itself to the structured and repetitive character of communities in society. The last, while making a start at it, imposes an unnecessary and unrealistic confinement of community life and association to face-to-face contacts. Not all community members need touch one another; a baby's or a slave's contacts are not those of an honored grandfather or a magnate.

Now the undoubted territorial or geographical character of the community as a human grouping, providing a range of land use and a particular ecological resource-base, gives us only our initial comparative datum about communities. Without additional elements of definition, we do not know why such land use is repeated in fairly standard, similar form throughout the occurrence of populations both animal and human, at no matter what level of cultural or biological evolution. No bees have only one hive, nor peasants only one village, nor metropolitans of today only one metropolis. Nor can we distinguish the community from the region, the province, the administrative district, the nomadic band, the farm, the plantation, the *sovkhoz*, the land-use corporation, the parish, the manor, the monastery, etc. All of these may use and bound a tract of land, may even divide the landscape into like tracts, but they may or may not be usefully treated as communities.

Now what distinguishes communities from other human associations based upon territoriality and land use is precisely their repetitive character and their wholeness and inclusiveness. They are like units not so much only as collections of culture traits or social institutions repeated again and again, but first of all as population aggregates. A demographic criterion is part of the definition which allows us to recognize the thing; it is also that part of the definition which makes the thing useful as a sample.

Thus the unit minimum population aggregate, the community, is a structured social field of interindividual relationships unfolding through time. The community is not only a territorial unit and a unit table of organization; it is also an enduring temporal pattern of coexistences, an ordered time-progress of individuals, from their births to their deaths, through roles and relationships of each kind known to their species or their culture. In short, it is the minimal common cast of characters supporting the drama of the biogram, in biology, or, in social science, its analogue, of the way of life. This is its character as thing subsistent in space and time: an enduring natural unit of both process and organization in living phenomena. Where the drama of living is done by and with culture, in a particular ethnographically differentiable human way of life, a community is a natural sample, too, because it is a natural unit of the drama of successive repetitions of the life of an enduring culture or society.

Thus it is that modern community study, whether addressed to social problem or to cultural comparisons, has forced us to the steps in definition we have made. It makes it imperative that the definition of community be expanded to include populational and temporal dimensions in addition to the original spatial and ecological ones.

By the same reasoning, it forces us to see that there is a contentual, a behavior-inventory component to the definition of community as well. We must include the cultural, the institutional, the learned aspect of behavior as well as that genetically determined in the "natural" criterion in our definition of the community as a natural unit of organization in the life and the way of living of man and animal. The community is the natural unit, as well, of cultural transmission, in man, as it is the natural unit, like the gene-pool, of genetic transmission in the animal. It is a "natural" collection of the inventory of behaviors and culture patterns, or institutions, known to the persons of the species—here the culture—too, because it is the natural field and its content which a child learns in becoming a man of his people (Whiting 1941; Kluckhohn 1951).

It is a truism, of course, that the biogram of *homo* involves not only individual learning of inherited capabilities as with the animal, but also the learning, in culture, of the roles and the institutions that mark off the society of one human culture or civilization from another. The community is the minimal unit table of organization of the personnel who can carry and transmit this culture. It is the minimal unit realizing the categories and offices of their social organization. It is the minimal group capable of re-enacting in the present and transmitting to the future the cultural and institutional inventory of their distinctive and historic tradition. And *from* it, *in* it, the child learns, from peers and the street as well as from parents and teachers, the lore of his people and what must be learned to become one of them.

It is here, indeed, that we must look to functional reasons for the community's universal existence even in man, so different from lower animals. Communities collectivize in their territories, among their members, through their lives (which are generations long and thus longer than those of their members) many gains for individual and for social survival or advantage. These are provision of mates, of defense, of cooperative resource exploitation, of sociability, etc. They have been long and often appealed to, both in ecology and in sociology, to account for community, from the beginning of social and political speculation onward, even with Aristotle's initial derivation of community and political life from the nature of man as *politikon zoon,* so often quoted. But we can now see that invoking the general functions of social life is as improper and unspecific as is relying on other received definitions.

These functions do not define communities. Any culture has other ways of defense, of mate finding, of socializing, of governing, that extend beyond the community's and may supplant the community's. Likewise, communities, like other things, can develop dysfunctions, pain and thwart members, gain and lose functions without losing identity. The broad functions appealed to neither distinguish the community from other social phenomena nor account for its structure and demography.

Yet some other functional reason, more specific, can well be found for the community. We know already, as we have said, that some local, continuing grouping of men or animals nearly always comes to exist. Bigger than the family or mating pair, smaller than the whole population, it insures continuity of the species. Where the species is human, to wit, one of the cultures of modern comparative ethnography and sociology, a characteristic minimal unit of personnel arises, as surely as among the animals, to subsist in a territory, to endure over its members' lives. It is this minimal unit, the community, which insures continuity of the now culturally defined species. For it is only in man that differentiation of kind takes not a genetic but a cultural, a taught-and-learned form.

Thus it is that we must recognize that a human community contains within it, specifically—and the content gives us both our definition and our license for sampling—persons and roles and statuses, or the transmitted and learned awarenesses of them, for every kind and office of mankind that the culture knows: husband, artisan, miser, mother, priest, criminal, aristocrat, heretic, etc. The list is different for every human culture. A human community does this as surely as does one of ants, which, too, provides a role for every kind of ant the species has evolved: queen, worker, egg, soldier, larva. The mechanisms, we know, are quite different; the lists are of various lengths; but the structuring of life process in the various species has important parallels.

It is plain, then, that with such a specific and structural definition of the community, many of the complexities of the social and cultural phenomena we must deal with in community study, like many of the questions about the use of the community as field or as sample for the study of other data, take on a new guise. First, of course, we have a justification for the perception of the rich and complex wholeness and separateness of the community, both for itself and as a field for other phenomena, already well won in international social science. We see why other social objects are not and cannot be communities, and why other institutions, however complex, offer a less rounded picture of human life. A monastery, whatever its spirit, cannot be a community. Its population has but one sex. A mining camp, an old age home, a children's village, an army, and so on, cannot serve as one, either in definition or in social science use. When we say a technology, a church, a political party pushes toward engulfing "the whole of the life" of its people, to try to grow from being one institution to dominating a community, we now know what we can mean.

With this insight, then, what answers have we for the four questions posed earlier? The four summed up the difficulties of the choice of community to serve as a sample, but they could not be answered until a fuller definition was assured. They were: (1) representativeness: which community of the many to choose? (2) completeness: how should we recognize we have a whole, a viable community before us in the object of our choice and how separate it off from others? (3) inclusiveness, how can we be sure the community as sample samples enough of the phenomena, trends, culture traits, institutions, problems, of the whole culture or society it is surrogate for? (4) cohesiveness, or how unitary, single-hearted, solidary must it be to save us from choosing a community divisive to the point of uselessness?

The newly won and many-faceted definition just achieved offers resolutions to all four of the questions. A better and fuller theory of the community, as of anything else, provides a better, fuller methodology of strategy and decision in research.

First, then, a community is representative, and any one so representative can probably be used as sample or field of study for a problem or a comparison, when it offers the personnel, the table of organization we have found to be the demographic component of the definition. If the culture knows two sexes, several ages, several classes, several sects, several ethnic groups including majority and minority ones, several or many professional or full-time specializations, of occupation or technical and economic function, then the community we choose must have some at least of all these people, enough to man at least minimally their roles and statuses.

Second, it must give us these people, this table of organization, in some repetition and continuance. The personnel must be joined, at least in minimal seriation, in a succession of lives. The table of organization must be refilled successively, in some minimal degree, for the continuation of existence of the community to be effected. Only thus is the second, temporal component of our new-won definition satisfied.

Thus we can choose as sample any community minimally "stratified" to offer us some minimal population of each kind of person our culture or society knows as long as that realization of the categories continues to repeat itself through the successive lives of the community's members. Mt. Athos is not a community, though monks have lived there, admitting no female thing, for nearly two thousand years; a dormitory suburb of young marrieds and their babies is not one, however intense neighborhood "togetherness," unless the old people and the bachelors are there too. Many an exogamous Indian village, we are now learning, is a land-use corporation and a residential segregation, in which wives marry in and daughters out and only some of the usual complement of castes may be present, but the Indian community, instead, is the circle of villages from which wives come and around which daughters move and in which all the castes, whether or not they have members in every village, have their councils (panchayat) and treat with one another. The North American city taken whole, then, not the suburb, the city into which bachelors disappear, or older couples retire after their time in the collective harem of the dormitory suburb is up, is thus itself the community of American modernity. These marrieds', bachelors', and old people's patterns repeat themselves, and individuals progress through such patterns in endless successive moves as they pass through their age roles in the structuring which students of modern urbanism are just beginning to lay clear.

The structure of the community thus involves both a full table of organization and a continuity in depth uniting the lives of the people of the table, repeating or reiterating, in the main, their experience from generation to generation. Our sample communities must have both these memberships and these depths.

We can thus spare ourselves the imperative of a fully "stratified" sample in choosing a community. The point distinguishes clearly community-study method from social survey methods. Indeed, too strict sampling may be supernumerary in the former case, though it is of the essence in the latter. Minimal, not ideal, numbers of our personnel identify our sample, not necessarily fully stratified, proportionate ones, as in a nationwide or other random sample survey, where we cannot rely on the natural structuring of the community. The rigor of exactly faithful proportions here is less important than is the fulfillment of the structural and the temporal criteria of our definition. It is less important that some controlled number of each category of personnel of the table of organization be present nicely measured against each other's share of the whole society's population than it is that the categoric subsamples of whatever number be together over time, across their lives, "longitudinally."

The reasons come clearly from our acquired experience with culture and society in research and in the theoretical understanding won from it. Roles, institutions, statuses, we have learned, are filled by *any* competent person. They may be undermanned or overmanned, of course, but some filling there must be if they are to exist. Futher, the learning of culture involves also the learning of behavior and attitude of one's culture vis-a-vis *any* filler of such role. It is a prefiguring, a "programming" in the individual for recognition of and reaction to the first such filler-of-role to appear. That some or one appear is enough to evoke prefigured expectation and response.

But the minimal, even the single, filler-of-role and role expectation and evoker of response, whose being is more important than his numbers, *must* both so appear and continue to do so. Roles, culture traits, patterned responses of cultural and social life, are habits of individuals needing at least some repetition if they are not to be extinguished; and they are transmissions to yet other individuals, cultural successors, in whom such repetition must also take place. Perhaps once a generation is enough for some such habits and transmissions of habits. Just as the life of the community is to be found first of all in its continuance from generation to generation of individual lives, so is the test for a cultural or institutional role or other pattern of behavior that it be transmitted, above accidents of personal characteristic and social event, from incumbent-enactor to incumbent-enactor. Succession of individuals through fixity of patterned behavior is of the essence here, not numbers. Structuring is independent of quantity in nature, whether we are dealing with a square, a jet stream, a cell, or a kingship. In *this*, social science does not differ. Numbers can measure and compare such structures once achieved; they do not define them.

The same consideration arises with social and economic stratification other than age-grading. All too many community studies have mistaken one-class or two-class segregations, from dormitory suburbs to peasant villages or proletarian slums, for communities. True, the life of a class, as a subculture, provides a way of life from birth to grave, as we have known from Max Weber down. True, it may provide an inventory of special traits of learned behavior, of value, of institutional and social-relational or associational action. The residential segregation of a slum, a peasant village, a nomad camp, a garden city of the rich, may mirror faithfully such a separated, encapsulated subculture. But the class is only part of a society; its culture only part of a larger order and civilization; its false community only a segregation. When one disputes the representativeness of community-study findings about, say, the class structure of the U.S.A., by confronting a rural village of small farmers containing only two classes with a metropolis showing six, as critics have argued against the Warner studies of American life through the six classes and their differences and complementarities in the middle-sized cities of Yankee City, Old South, and Jonesville, U.S.A., such a criticism betrays a naïveté about comparison, about structure, and about society which is close to obscurantism.

Nonetheless, the question of stratified sampling in community study is in point once again. A community chosen for study as a sample or a field of a societal problem need not reflect with complete fidelity the proportion of the classes in the over-all society, even here. Every Middle Eastern villager has experience of Bedouins as raiders, harvesters, or beggars; he knows mountaineers as laborers, landlords, or *shitiyyīn* (winterers). His village is a complete community, not because cityfolk or nomads or mountaineers are coresident with him, but because he knows of them, has relations with them, and passes his knowledge and his role (even his fear) down to his children. Thus a mining town or a farmers' market village are complete enough, too, however equal the vast majority may be in their common experience as miners or as farmers and in their common disdain or envy of their betters (and their inferiors) and of the other strangers to their local life, as long as they also know and tell their children how to recognize and to deal with these incursors: the squire, the lawyer, the "city-slicker," the tramp, the priest, the teacher, etc., who bring in the outer world. Just as cells can specialize within the body and can change form with function and anatomic position but still take part in the system of metabolism, communication, and excretion which unite them to the other co-inhabitant cells of their body, so can special and differently functioning communities exist and stand for their over-all societies and their cultures. But one must show the connections and treat the realities.

In the social science case, simply, that community is still representative which knows and deals with persons and things of its culture and society, as long as a minimal number, a minimal contact, and a minimal continuity connects them. Once again, pattern and awareness, structuring and relationships, not numbers, is of the essence.

With this referral of the question of representativeness to the points of our structural definition completed, we are ready now for the other difficulties of the community as sample and as field.

For completeness, the criteria are already foreshadowed. A community is whole when the table of organization and its successive filling is complete. Redfield, as we know, called the Little Community of his book among other things, a Community among Communities. This is, of course, a common figure of speech, and it is inescapable that the circles of relationship and concern of higher placed persons or local representatives strike out wider and higher in the social systems of region, province, nation, and *oikomene* than do those of children or menials. The people of any community, individually taken, may, some of them, range far and wide; they may have overlapping memberships in neighboring communities, communities of relatives, communities of sojourn nearby. *These* villages group round a market center or a seat of administration; *those* round still another. All these circles and placements of human communication and relationship, in and out from any center at which one begins observation, high and low and up and down any reaches of further and further interconnection, structure themselves out for us when we remember our criteria defining a community. The cell-like reiteration of our personnel and their interstructured lives break up these continua into systems and their boundaries; the repeated local, generation-long grouping and structuring of minimal fillers of the repeated roles tell us where the instant community ends, the next one begins, the line between inside and outside and insider and outsider falls.

One already mentioned part of the dynamic of the rhythm of community life in space and time gives us an easiest, most usable criterion. The community, we have learned, always shows an alternation of dispersal and assemblage of its personnel, though different cultures pattern these functions differently. The easiest criterion may well be: who come together and who separate again, characteristically speaking? When we find the people of our table of organization assembled or come together at one time and know the limit of their dispersal at another, only to meet them regathered with one another at a third time, we have found the range, the rhythm, the membership, and the identity of the community we seek.

Our last two questions fall into place quickly enough once such criteria are put to work. Inclusiveness? As we have defined and demarcated a community to serve as sample or as field by structural and systemic criteria, we need not use culture trait inventory or enumeration to guide our choice. Any Maori *hapu* (hamlet) of aboriginal New Zealand had a heraldic bard who might sing the local chief's genealogy and prowess, but Maori culture knew only one college of heralds. We avoid, certainly, the locus of that college, a pinnacle of specialization, but make sure the hamlet we choose has a herald of its own, or failing him, is looking for an incumbent for the post. A fortiori, we do not choose a capital city, an atomic-laboratory research station, or a Bohemia of artists and their hangers-on, to stand for modern life. But we make sure our sample town has felt the lure of the capital, knows the modern skills and the modern awe of powerful physical science in its schools and its press, wonders over and envies a little such bohemians. Specializations in both high culture ("The Great Traditions") and popular or local culture ("The Little Traditions") are not our concern; instead we seek out those persons who in their community stand at the joint between them and represent in their community and in their personal experiences the continuous mutual penetration the two sorts of specialization common to all complex societies everywhere display. Here again structure rules. The jointure, the mutual penetration of specialization of the unique sort the whole culture or civilization achieves and that the instant little community has acquired, is the thing we seek in a sample or a field of study. We need not drive ourselves to a rigorous exclusion of anything except the average, the mediocre, and the universally common and indistinguishable cultural possessions of all the citizenry everywhere within our universe. No harm is done if a sample community has local legends, nor if an occasional speciality appears, like a school or a monastery not duplicated exactly in every next town. As long as specialities do not dominate community experience and community culture, and as long as citizens are aware of and prepare their children to recognize, again at least minimally, the outer reaches of such specialization stretching away from their own lores and skills, the community will serve.

And, finally, cohesiveness? Our structural definition spares us deciding between a community of harmony and sweet affection and a bed of hate and fire. The formal sociology of Georg Simmel, or many another, rescues us here. The people of our table of organization, in their lives together, alternate between strife and accommodation, solidarity and antagonism; if they come together again, in their reassemblages, after dispersal, it matters not whether dispersal grew out of hatred, dissension, or flight, or merely out of the need to fan out over a space of sparse and dispersed resources. It matters not whether their coming together again was for massacre or for the headiest unity. The limits of our discrimination of their community, their pattern of alternation between dispersal and assemblage as a social system, are self-enforcing and self-insistent. A collective, assembled internecine fight that ends in full massacre of one part by another, or a dispersal that ends in full flight of one part from another, brings the community to an end and causes it to cease to be. The table of organization is broken; the continuance of lives interlaced has stopped. Here again structural criteria, turned into measures and used for at least minimal recognition, give us our guide. Just as whole societies, whole civilizations (after Toynbee) know civil war, religious schism, flight in emigration, times of troubles, so do communities. A sample community must reflect both the unities and the fissions of the parts it samples in its table or organization of the whole society it mirrors. But it need do that again only within the outer limits of its own continuance.

REFERENCES

ARENSBERG, CONRAD M. "The Community Study Method," *American Journal of Sociology* 60 (1954), 109–125.

BALANDIER, G. *Sociologie des Brazzavilles noires.* Paris: Foundation Nationale des Sciences Politiques, 1955.

BATTEN, T. R. *Communities and Their Development.* Oxford: Oxford University Press, 1958.

BOTT, ELIZABETH. "Urban Families: The Norms of Conjugal Roles." *Human Relations* 9 (1956), 325–343.

BROWNELL, BAKER. *The Human Community.* New York: Harper & Row, Publishers, 1950.

CHIVA, I. *Rural Communities: Problems, Methods, Types of Research.* Reports and Papers in the Social Sciences, Bulletin 10 (1958), UNESCO.

FUSTEL DE COULANGES. *La cite antique.* Paris: Hachette et Cie., 1905.

HOLLINGSHEAD, AUGUST B. "Community Research: Development and Present Condition." *American Sociological Review* 13 (1948), 136–146.

KLUCKHOHN, CLYDE. "The Study of Culture," in *The Policy Sciences,* Daniel Lerner and Harold D. Lasswell (eds.). Stanford: Stanford University Press, 1951.

KONIG, RENE. "Die Gemeinde im Blickfeld der Soziologie," in *Handbuch der Kommunalen Wissenschaft und Praxis,* Hans Peter (hrsg.). Berlin: Westdeutscher Verlag, 1956.

————. "Die Gemeindeutuntersuchung des deutschen Unesco-institutes," in *Handbuch der Kommunalen Wissenschaft und Praxis,* Hans Peter (hrsg.). Berlin: Westdeutscher Verlag, 1956.

————. "Soziologie der Gemeinde," in *Sonderheft I, Kolner Zeitschrift fur Soziologie und Sozialpsychologie* 8 (1956), 1–12.

MAGET, M. *Ethnographie metropolitaine.* Paris: Guide D'etude Directe des Comportements Culturels, Civilisations du Sud, 1953.

MAINE, SUMNER. *Village Communities in the East and West.* London: J. Murray, 1871.

MAURER, GEORG VON. *Einleitung zur Geschichte der Mark–, Hof–, Dorf–, und Stadtveriassung und der offentlichen Gewalt.* Munich: C. Kaiser, 1854.

MEITZEN, A. *Siedlung– und Agrarwesen der Westgermanen und Ostgermanen, der Kelten, Rober, Finnen und Slaven.* Berlin: W. Hertz, 1895.

MURDOCK, GEORGE PETER. *Social Structure.* New York: Macmillan Co., 1949.

PEAKE, HAROLD. "Village Community," in *Encyclopedia of the Social Sciences.* New York: Macmillan Co., 1954.

REDFIELD, ROBERT. *The Little Community.* Chicago: University of Chicago Press, 1956.

RUOPP, PHILLIPS (ed.). *Approaches of Community Development.* The Hague: W. Van Hoeve, 1953.

SANDERS, IRWIN T. *The Community: An Introduction to a Social System.* New York: Ronald Press Co., 1958.

SHEVKY, ESHREF, and WILLIAMS, MARYLIN. *Social Areas of Los Angeles.* Berkeley: University of California Press, 1929.

SIMEY, THOMAS S. (ed.). *Neighborhood and Community.* Liverpool: Liverpool University Press, 1954.

STEIN, MAURICE. *The Eclipse of Community.* Princeton: Princeton University Press, 1960.

STEWARD, JULIAN H. *Area Research.* New York: New York Social Science Research Bulletin 63, 1950.

TAYLOR, CARL T. "Techniques of Community Study and Analysis as Applied to Modern Civilized Societies," in *The Science of Man in the World Crisis,* Ralph Linton (ed.), New York: Columbia University Press, 1945.

UTERMANN, KURT. "Aufgaben und Methoden der gemeindlichen Sozialforschung," in *Beitrage zur Soziologie der industriellen Gesellschaft.* Walther G. Hoffmann (hrsg.). Dortmund: Ardey, 1952.

WARE, CAROLINE. *Estudio de la Comunidad.* Washington: Pan-American Union, 1952.

WHITING, JOHN. *Becoming a Kwoma: Teaching and Learning in a New Guinea Tribe.* New Haven: Yale University Press, 1941.

WILSON, LOGAN. "Sociography of Groups," in *Twentieth Century Sociology,* G. Gurvitch and W. G. Moore (eds.). New York: Philosophical Library, 1945.

YOUNG, MICHAEL, and WILLMOTT, PETER. *Family and Kinship in East London.* London: Routledge and Kegan, Paul, 1957.

YOUNG, PAULINE V. *Scientific Social Surveys and Research.* Englewood Cliffs, N. J.: Prentice-Hall, Inc., 1949.

2. A Community within Communities

ROBERT REDFIELD

How, in describing the little community, are we to include the fact that it is a community within communities, a whole within other wholes? Is it possible to describe as a whole a community whose life is modified by bits of other communities in whose local life we find institutions and offices recently imported into it? What forms of thought are available to us for conceiving and describing a whole that is both inclosed within other wholes and is also in some part permeated by them?

In trying to understand the concept of social structure we began with that idea as put forth by Firth, and then as by Fortes, and only after we had begun to understand the concept as a considered idea to guide systematic study did we attempt to make use of it in connection with facts from Yucatán. But now in beginning to think about the sequence and interrelations of communities, let us reverse this procedure. Let us begin with the facts as we find them in the simplest and most nearly self-contained of the four little communities that have been chosen for special attention here, adding then ideas and concepts as they are suggested either by these facts or by the anthropologists or sociologists who have reported these and other communities to us.

SOURCE: Reprinted from *The Little Community* by Robert Redfield by permission of The University of Chicago Press. © 1956 by The University of Chicago Press.

The band of Siriono Indians is easily the most distinct and self-contained of the four. Holmberg, who lived with these Indians for more than six months, had great difficulty at first even in finding the band with which he later associated, so secluded and shy were these Indians; and when he had gained admission to their group he was completely dependent for all material support and all human association upon this little group of about sixty people. This was such a little community as was all humanity could offer fifteen thousand years ago.

The Siriono band is composed of people all related to one another; it is made up of several matrilinear extended families, each embracing several nuclear families. The band camps together on high ground provided with trees with edible fruits during the rainy season. During the dry season the band breaks up into smaller familial groups. When settled at a camp, the band has a single house; the chief, an officer of very limited powers, occupies the center of this house.

We should find it difficult to write much about the social structure of the Siriono band; beyond the simple familial groups and relationships there is almost none. The people of the band occasionally combine into co-operative hunting parties. The band also provides wives and children. Furthermore, no doubt, it provides a certain amount of common defense against marauders, human or animal, and surely, even in this community where quarreling and indifference are common, a certain primary human warmth always acceptable to mankind.

Outside the band are other bands of Siriono Indians of the same culture and language. But relations with these other bands are very slight. Holmberg tells us that if an Indian wishes to visit such another band it may take him ten days to reach it. He is not sure where to look for it, because its location is frequently changed according to the necessities of the hunting and the weather. When members of two different bands do meet each other, relations are usually friendly, but there are no political or ceremonial institutions that bring the two bands together in any sort of even temporary common action.

Most marriages are made within the band; a man may find a wife in another band, but this occurs very rarely because of the distance between bands, the disposition of the men of a band to keep their women to themselves, and the rule of matrilocal residence which would compel a man if he married a woman from another band to move away from home. In short, there is very little concept of a tribe here, and no tribal institutions.

The Siriono recognize also the existence of other kinds of Indians, those with whom relations are unfriendly. The Siriono do not practice warfare, although they have occasionally killed white men and "missionized" Indians, either to get food or tools or in revenge for other killings. On the whole, the Siriono strive to avoid these other Indians. For the most part, they avoid also the white men of the mission stations and the Indians who have taken up life in connection with the mission.

This is a very simple arrangement of community within communities. Nothing inside the band represents the outside world at all. It is entirely self-contained, except as fears of hostile Indians or occasional thoughts about friendly bands of other Siriono may enter into the native's view of the world. A rare marauding expedition in which the band may be predator or prey slightly qualifies this self-containment of the community.

A simple diagram would represent the inclosure of this little community within others: a small circle, the circumference strongly marked, outside of which would be placed distant other circles, some perhaps colored green for "friendly" and some red for "hostile" with the faintest of lines of relationship between some of these and the band of our central interest.

The situation could be diagrammed differently. One could draw two large circles around the small circle denoting our band. The inner circle of these two would represent the less distant and more friendly outside world of other Siriono. The outside circle would represent the more distant and unfriendly world of other Indians and white men.

We have then two diagrams, one schematically cartographic, and the other diagrammatic, to represent this state of communities within communities as it appears most simply in the case of the Siriono. Let us take the system of concentric circles as our initial form of thought for taking account of the community within other communities. Let us see what becomes of it as we try to make use of it in describing little communities of greater complexity than the Siriono.

This is the form of thought employed by Evans-Pritchard in describing what he calls "structural distance" in the case of the Nuer of the Sudan. I present his diagram of thirteen concentric circles[1] in simplified form. His first four circles, representing nuclear family, homestead, and group of related families I combine into one circle: the village.

The nine circles, the nine successively outward communities which Evans-Pritchard recognizes as inclosing the village, are in the simplified diagram reduced to six. The principal fact for us now is that the first four circles or communities of these six are constituted of people of the same language and culture as the Nuer of the village at the center. They are four progressively remote communities of people bound to one an-

---

[1] E. E. Evans-Pritchard, *The Nuer* (Oxford: Clarendon Press, 1940), p. 114.

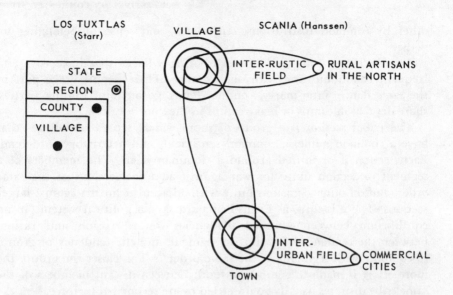

LOS TUXTLAS (Starr)

STATE
REGION ◉
COUNTY ●
VILLAGE ●

VILLAGE

SCANIA (Hanssen)

INTER-RUSTIC FIELD — RURAL ARTISANS IN THE NORTH

INTER-URBAN FIELD — COMMERCIAL CITIES

TOWN

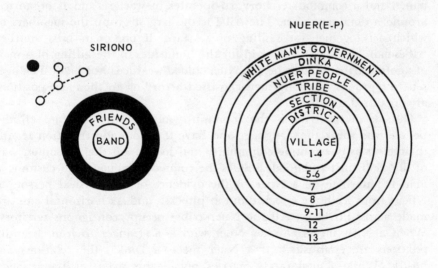

SIRIONO

FRIENDS
BAND

NUER(E-P)

WHITE MAN'S GOVERNMENT
DINKA
NUER PEOPLE
TRIBE
SECTION
DISTRICT
VILLAGE
1-4
5-6
7
8
9-11
12
13

other by common institutions, sentiments, and sense of belonging together.

The district is composed of neighboring villages that have easy and
frequent communication with one another. These people "take part in
the same dance, inter-marry, conduct feuds, go on joint raiding parties,
share dry-season camps or make camps in the same locality."[2]

The tribal section is a group of more widely separated villages that
have a common name, a common sentiment, and a territory to defend.
Each section is organized around a dominant clan. The members of a
segment or section unite for war against adjacent sections of the same
order, and on other occasions unite with adjacent segments against larger
sections. There is thus, as Evans-Pritchard says, a political system "in an
equilibrium between opposed tendencies toward fission and fusion,
between the tendency of groups to segment, and the tendency of groups
to combine with segments of the same order."[3] The closer the group, the
more effort is made to compose a feud; between distant members of the
same tribe disputes usually go unsettled or are reconciled by force.

Outside the section is the tribe. This community also has a common
name, and a common territory, co-operates in warfare and is organized
around a dominant clan. The tribe is the largest group the members of
which act together for raiding or warfare. If one man kills another
tribesman, blood-wealth is paid for the homicide. In the killing of a man
of another tribe, though he is a Nuer, blood-wealth is not paid. The age-
sets, the groups of young men classified according to their age-position,
are organized tribally.

Outside of the tribe is the community of the Nuer people: all the
people who speak that language and have that common tradition regard
themselves as one unique community and look upon their common way
of life as distinct and good. Besides the common language and customs, a
man is known to be a Nuer by the evidence of his physical person: a
Nuer's front teeth are knocked out at puberty, and six horizontal cuts are
made across his brow. All the Nuer tribes occupy contiguous territory.
When a Nuer meets another Nuer who is a stranger to him, friendly
relations are established. If a Nuer meets a Dinka, the relations are
hostile. While a man rarely marries outside his tribe, such marriages,
when they do occur, are recognized on both sides. When Nuer fights
Nuer, women and children are spared. But when Nuer fights Dinka, it is
war to the uttermost.

With the community of the Nuer people, we have reached the fifth

---

2 *Ibid.*, p. 116.
3 *Ibid.*, pp. 147–48.

circle of the simplified diagram. There are two more. The next to the last circle represents the community of the Dinka, a people similar to the Nuer in language and culture, yet different. They are the bitter enemies of the Nuer. To the Nuer, the Dinka exist in order to be their enemies. The Nuer raid the Dinka for cattle and slay them out of patriotism.

Finally, in the outermost circle, lies the white man's government. With this world the Nuer does not even share common understandings as to enmity. Evans-Pritchard does not tell us much about the relationships that Nuer have with this remote world. He refers to recently instituted government courts and to American church missions. If we were among the Nuer today, twenty or more years after Evans-Pritchard worked there, we should perhaps find more to say about the effects of this outermost circle upon the Nuer little community.

Let us review and simplify the inclosure of the Nuer village within outer communities. The village is inclosed first within a neighborhood of intimately known other villages. Outside this come two groups with political functions chiefly, the tribal section, organized around a leading clan, and the tribe, a more inclusive group and the largest unit that acts collectively. And outside this lie other tribes also of Nuer. Thus far, in these eleven concentric circles as Evans-Pritchard has them, or in five circles as I have simplified them, we recognize one moral world. At the borders of the Nuer territory the Nuer steps into a world of alien and hostile peoples, more hostile than alien in the case of the Dinka peoples, more alien than hostile in the case of the white man's government. Evans-Pritchard's first seven circles outside of the village correspond, in their essential nature, to the single band of the Siriono together with the friendly bands of other Siriono outside. In the case of the Nuer, the community of "my people" is subdivided into a whole series of communities inclosed within one another and characterized by a transition from intimate relations and functions and from domestic institutions to less intimate relations and functions and to political institutions.

With the Nuer as with the Siriono, there are two kinds of communities outside the larger community of "my people": traditional enemies and the relatively recent and almost completely alien interference of the white man and his civilization. The white man has no place within the Siriono band, and if he has in the Nuer village, we are not told about it in the book I quote.

In these two cases, the scheme of concentric circles seems almost adequate to represent the situation. As I have suggested, the diagram is most in need of some modification to indicate the important difference in quality between, on the one hand, all those concentric communities of the Nuer which share a common culture and some sense of belonging together, and, on the other hand, the hostile and alien people outside of Nuerland. There is perhaps a certain violence of transition between the community of Nuer and that of the Dinka that the scheme of circles does not fully express, and the transition must be even greater as one moves to the circle of the white man's government. Further I imagine that the peculiar kinds of relations of the Nuer with the white man's government and possibly the missions are not fully represented by a spatial scheme which simply puts the white man in the farthest circle beyond the Dinka. What if the white man, the alien government, puts its agents of influence directly into a little community with which we imagine ourselves to begin our work?

In describing the relations of the village of Chan Kom with other communities, in the book written in 1933, I, too, used a diagram of concentric circles,[4] except that I put the circles on a map, and so pulled them out of shape so that they might more or less correspond with the actual territories and settlements included within each area on the map. I recognized three communities concentric to Chan Kom. The first of these is a cluster of hamlets all within twenty kilometers of Chan Kom. This is that community of frequent personal contacts over which Chan Kom exercises economic, cultural, and political leadership. Next comes a wider community embracing villages of importance and influence similar to that exercised by Chan Kom. These villages are not economically or politically dependent upon Chan Kom. Relationships are frequently friendly within this zone. Wives are occasionally taken in a village that lies here. Visiting goes on, especially at times of festivals. The first zone is a political unit, but the second is not.

Outside of both, I recognized a third zone, perhaps a hundred kilometers in diameter, including many villages of similar culture and similar importance to Chan Kom. In this wider community intermarriage and visiting are much less common, and disputes between villages are not rare. Nevertheless, there is in this wider community, I wrote, "a larger polity, a consciousness of common interests that may, in emergencies, be fanned into flames of regional patriotism."[5] During the revolution of 1917, the villagers of this zone fought together. This third outer community corresponds in this part of Yucatán, if anything does, to the tribe of the Nuer. If I had thought of it, I might well have added a fourth zone to represent all Maya-speaking rural villagers, most of them very slightly known or quite unknown to the people of Chan Kom. Like the Nuer and

---

[4] Robert Redfield and Alfonso Villa Rojas, *Chan Kom, A Maya Village* (Washington, D.C.: Carnegie Institution of Washington, Pub. No. 448, 1934), p. 10.
[5] *Ibid.*, p. 9.

like the Siriono, the Maya villager recognizes in another Maya language, custom, and manners like himself, even if he has never seen him before, one of his own kind.

This comparison of Chan Kom with the Nuer village leads us, however, in a direction of thought which has serious consequences for the use of the diagram of concentric circles to describe the relations of communities in peasant villages such as Chan Kom. Let us look more closely at the situation in Chan Kom as compared with the situation reported by Evans-Pritchard for the Nuer.

First, the political and military organization of the Nuer villages is more complex and more regularly hierarchical than it is with the Maya, and among the Nuer the role of kinship in uniting villages and districts and tribal segments is much greater. Kinship connections decrease and political functions and institutions increase as one goes outward until a peak of political activity is reached in the tribal section; political action then declines while consciousness of common culture persists until one comes to the territories of the Dinka.

Second, in the larger territory within which the Maya lives his life are to be found town, small city, and larger city. These constitute a progressive series of urbanized communities in this order increasingly exterior to the life of the village. These are apparently lacking in Nuerland. In the Maya villages, the political organization, and the economic, are in large part controlled by authority and decision from outside the world of common cultural consciousness: from the world of the European or Europeanized townsman and cityman. The relations that the Chan Kom people have with townsmen and citymen, with people who are not thought of as their own kind of people, are much more numerous, influential, institutionalized, and immediately present in the village itself, than in the case of the Nuer. On the other hand, the difference in culture between the native of Chan Kom and the man of town or city is much less than the corresponding difference in the case of the Nuer—remote from the Nuer as town and city may be.

Thus the folk community of regionally united Maya is an aspect or dimension of the total society of Yucatán, and indeed of Mexico. The city, the town, and the villages considered all together present themselves to us as a new kind of larger whole of considerable distinctness and integrity. Looking at this other large whole, one would not see a series of concentric circles around one village, but rather a complex aggregation of settlements to which any one village such as Chan Kom would be related in a number of kinds of relationships and functions. Even if we put aside the possibility of describing this larger whole—the state of Yucatán, let us

say—how are we to describe such a single village in Yucatán as Chan-
Kom so as to take account of its relations with town, city, and national
state?

Among those who have addressed themselves to this problem is Dr.
Betty Starr, who has sought for a solution in connection with facts from a
part of Mexico not far from Yucatán: the region of Los Tuxtlas, in
southern Vera Cruz.[6] Like Evans-Pritchard, she begins with the family,
and she recognizes certain other groupings, concentric to one another,
within the village itself.[7] We will here consider her work as it relates to
the communities that inclose our little community, the village.

Dr. Starr describes the Mexican villager as related not only to his
village and its component subcommunities, but also to several communities outside of it at successive degrees of remove from it. One is the
municipio; the word "county" roughly suggests the nature of this community. Next is the region, a group of counties. Within these two successive communities the villager still finds people of his own kind; he has a
sense of in-group with respect to both county and region, but in lessening
degree. Thus in this respect Dr. Starr's region corresponds to Evans-
Pritchard's Nuerland and to my third zone, or perhaps to my missing
fourth zone, for the Maya. Outside of the region, as Starr describes it, are
other regions with which the villager feels little affinity.

How does Dr. Starr think of these successive social entities? She thinks
of them as a series of communities each of which is characterized by a
nuclear center with a depending surrounding rural area. The nuclear
center of the *municipio* or county is the head town *(cabeçera)*, that of the
region is the capital city.[8] She finds this kind of structure also in Japan,
and in rural Georgia, U.S.A. In a later and unpublished work[9] she makes
it plain that this kind of rural-urban structure requires for its realization
certain factors including rural settlement in villages rather than in scattered farms, the sort of compact and nucleated town-planning of Spanish
America and elsewhere, a uniform habitat, and an even spread of communication. More generally, I would add that its realization requires the
presence of urban centers of influence: towns and cities exercising widespread influence over the economies and governments of the people
round about.

Here, I think, the most interesting aspect of Dr. Starr's analysis lies in
her recognition of the important and regular qualitative differences in
the kinds of relationships that really prevail between the villager, on the

---

[6] Betty Starr, *Los Tuxtlas: A Study of Levels of Communal Relations*, Ph.D. thesis,
University of Chicago, 1951.

[7] *Ibid.*, pp.14–18.

[8] *Ibid.*, pp. 85 ff., 100 ff.

[9] Starr, "Levels of Communal Relations," manuscript.

one hand, and the people and institutions of the next outer or wider
community, the county or the region, on the other. For Dr. Starr does not
regard this ordered series of inclosing entities *simply* as a series of areas,
one within another. It is significant that she does not often use the word
"community" to denote them; she calls them "levels." Moreover, she does
not use a diagram of concentric circles. When she makes a diagram,[10] it
is a series of squares arranged so that the eye, moving from the village to
the symbols representing county and region begins in the lower lefthand
corner and moves up as well as out. The word "levels" suggests a series of
steps. The communities or levels of integration are different in kind of
relationship, and these changing kinds of relationship depend in part on
the fact that the townsmen and citymen have institutions, moral life, and
view of the world different from those of the villager, while at the same
time the villager's life is in long-established adjustment to controls and
influences coming from these more urban communities. Dr. Starr brings
this out when she tells us that as one moves up the levels, social relations
become more impersonal and come to be affected by the principle of
superordination and subordination. This is to say that as one moves out
of one's village, if one is an Indian of this part of Mexico, one enters into
relationships which draw upon only one interest one has, or one role—as
a buyer in a market or a litigant in a law court perhaps; and into
relationships which express the class or other status differences that prevail in that part of the world between Indian and non-Indian, city
person and rustic, laborer and white collar official, and so forth, distinctions which may not be apparent in observing only the day-to-day life of
the village itself.

This is a form of thought, expressed in words and in diagram, which
can take account not only of the relations of these Indian peasant villagers to one another within their own village, but also of their relations
to townspeople and city people who have a life that is only in part shared
with them. The series of steps suggests, better than would a simple
scheme of concentric circles, the change in the qualities of relationships,
the movement into a world wider and more complex than is a single local
community with one common set of conventional understandings. The
drawing I made of three ovals inclosed within one another, for Chan
Kom and its hinterland, is inadequate for the facts I myself reported in
the text of the book. Dr. Starr's eccentric series of squares better suggests
the viewpoint of the Mexican villager who looks outward from his village
and also upward to urban ways of life that are centered in the Spanish-
built town and then city which he knows about and occasionally visits.

We seem to need a recognition of a series or range of kinds of com-

---

[10] Starr, thesis, p. 11.

munities according to their degree of independence from city, manor, national state, or other center of a different or more developed mode of living. Dr. Starr recognizes this. There are societies without towns and cities "organized primarily upon the principle of extended kinship."[11] We think of the Nuer. Here almost all the relationships of the individual tend to be personal and many-sided. Here we think of the community within communities as a series of concentric circles. At the other extreme are the fully urbanized people who live in the city, or who live in the mind of the city while dwelling in the country or in the farther countryside. These people are in large part organized in terms of relationships, many of them impersonal, with distant people and institutions. Here no diagram of circles and no diagram of regular steps would help us very much. In between these two extremes are the societies in which rural people with long-established local cultures live in partly self-contained little communities; but these little communities are also involved with, and dependent upon, the town and the city. These are the societies of peasantry or of rural people yet distinct from townspeople. In societies of this middle type the form of thought represented by the concentric circles is insufficient to stand for the relations of communities within communities. The form of thought to be used must be one that will take account of the different qualities of relationships that prevail on the one hand as the villager looks inward toward his village, his neighborhood, his family, and, on the other hand, as he relates himself to those aspects of town and city or manor which he must use to sell his grain or his services, buy his hoe or his gun, pay his taxes, or try his lawsuit.

It is, I think, just to Dr. Starr's helpful analysis to say that it represents the system of communities from the point of view of the villager, and that it does not fully take into account the lines and patterns of persisting interaction between villager and townsman, townsman and villager. The diagram in the form of steps leading upward to higher levels of relationship does not quite represent the systems of relationships, economic, cultural, and personal, that compose the larger society of both town and country, and in that it fails to show the situation as it would appear to one viewing town and countryside equally from a point of view above and fair to both. It should be possible to look at a society of the middle kind—at a rural-urban society in which the economic and social relationships are still distinct and fairly stable—from a point of view inclosing equally both village and town, or manor and countryside, and to recognize the relationships and activities of the villager as one of the two

---

11 Starr, "Levels of Communal Relations."

reciprocal halves of a relationship and an activity of which the resident in the town or in the manor is the other half.

It seems to me that Dr. Börje Hanssen has done just this in one part of his recent study of rural-urban life in Scania at the end of the eighteenth century.[12] Dr. Hanssen's principal concept is the "activity-field." This is both an area and a pattern of acts and relationships. The activity-field is represented spatially, on a map or diagram, for Dr. Hanssen approaches his materials in the first instance ecologically—"ecologically" in the modified sense usual in urban sociology, meaning the spatial and temporal expression of human relationships.

When Dr. Hanssen represents the activity-fields of the villager they appear as concentric circles. His conception of fields inclosed within one another—household and family, friendly adjacent villages, and outer fields characterized by stranger-relations—is substantially that which is conceived by Evans-Pritchard for the Nuer. But the great advantage of Dr. Hanssen's activity-field for describing a rural community of peasant and townsman lies in the fact that it enables him to recognize differentiation of activities and relationships within a village or town, and to represent the different kinds of relationships and activities that certain groups within the village have with people outside of it. Dr. Hanssen puts this point in the following words:

> When investigating a certain town . . . , it would appear more realistic to regard each specific group as a separate behaviour-field, than to let the whole community in question represent one field. That goes for highly differentiated urban communities generally, but naturally not for relatively undifferentiated village communities. [The present investigation] shows how the result can be faulty if it is not remembered that groups distinct economically and in respect of social class comprise different fields, and if it is assumed instead that such juridical and administrative concepts as "towns" comprise a whole. Certain groups in the town of this area had much more intimate connections with the population of the surrounding countryside than with each other.[13]

The villages Dr. Hanssen studied in Scania were, however, differentiated. This sociologist was able to take account of the difference between the way of life of property-owning peasants in the village, on the one hand, and the unpropertied cotters on the other. The cotters took

---

12 Börje Hanssen, Osterlen (Stockholm: LT:s Forlag, 1952); Hanssen, "Fields of Social Activity and Their Dynamics," Translations of the Westermarck Society, II (Copenhagen: Ejnar Munksgaard, 1953), 99–133.
13 Börje Hanssen, "Fields of Social Activity and Their Dynamics," p. 110.

employment in parsonages and in manors as the landed peasantry did not often do. Further, Dr. Hanssen was able to recognize the trading activities between town and countryside, between one village and another, and between town and commercial city. The description of the rural-urban region is thus made from a viewpoint that is just to both town and country, and that sees the whole as interrelated activity-fields. Some of these fields are, for the villager, inclosed within one another; but even here the cotter and servant has a system of fields different from that of the land-owning farmer, and this consequence of the town and manor on the village is taken into account. Finally, the diagram Dr. Hanssen produces (which is given here considerably simplified) allows us to study the persisting patterned relationships of townsman and villager, manor dweller, and servant of the cotter class. Dr. Hanssen has given us a tool offering fresh advantages to students of communities in which town and country have interpenetrated one another.

We are not, of course, to lean too heavily upon any diagram in our effort to describe and analyze community life. No diagram tells us what words can. Each is a framework for thought, a plan of the possible significant relationships, to be tried and then qualified or perhaps rejected. Perhaps the series of diagrammatic forms considered in this ·chapter does show us again how it is that the concepts, verbal or diagrammatic, that we use in description and analysis undergo modification and development as the subject matter to be described and analyzed changes—in this case, changes from the almost isolated primitive community to the rural village in a national state.

In these pages too little attention has been given to the relationships that in many cases exist between the people of one band or village and those of another. Small communities are such convenient units for study and analysis that the eye of the anthropologist is not often enough lifted to view the larger community composed of a few or many bands or settlements linked in more or less stable relationships. The case of the Siriono, where each band is truly an isolate, is exceptional today. In many parts of even the uncivilized world the band or settlement is a part of a regional network of relationships. The band may be for the most part distinct and independent, but with latent relationships through kinship with many other similar groups; in parts of aboriginal Australia connections of people are open to extension through recognition of kinship connection between one man and another: the local society can expand outward almost indefinitely to provide for the occasional traveler. In West Africa there are peoples, like the Tiv of Nigeria, "who number well over half a million, and all of whom regard themselves as descended from an ultimate ancestor, Tiv. Every local settlement is, through its main body of male kinsmen, linked by ever widening, if weakening, ties of kinship and is ultimately associated with all the others."[14] Such ties make it possible for people to move safely over a wide area, "and there is a sense of unity among the whole population."

There is, then, even in societies without the added dimension of gentry, town, or city, a kind of community much wider than the little community. We may study more closely than has yet been done these far-flung networks of social relations. They have their structure too. And where the small community does form a part of a national state, the rural networks include not only town or manor, but also the relations of village to village. Dr. Hanssen's study takes some account of these. Those who have recently been studying rural India tell us that in parts of that country the village is plainly an insufficient unit of study; it is no isolate but rather a focus for understanding wide and complex communities. One village may have traditional relationships through marriage and caste with scores of or even with several hundred other villages. There the village is a unit in some senses; in others the unit is the rural network or lattice. As work proceeds, we shall come to study these, and perhaps to distinguish types of rural lattices. In western Guatemala the rural lattices are composed chiefly of relationships of primitive commerce, with travel to attend festivals or to visit shrines constituting a secondary basis of connection among settlements. In India the castes and exogamous marriages make for rural networks based on more personal, intimate, and hereditary kinds of connections.

In the case of civilized societies and national states, this review of some attempts to develop forms of thought for describing communities that are not isolates exposes a problem with a double aspect. The problem is how to understand a community that is not only a simple band or village but is perhaps many villages in important relationships with manors, towns and cities. Because no one village is really independent, but is a part of a much larger and more complicated system, our interest is drawn toward the description of the more complicated system. Detaching one's self, so to speak, from the village, one moves to consider the whole region or even the whole national state as the entity to be studied and understood. And how shall one study so large and complex an entity? On the other hand, in so far as one remains within the village or other local community and retains a determination to study just that village, one is required to find ways to describe what I have just called the penetration of manor or town into the village. There are now people in the village who have worked in

---

[14] Daryll Forde, "The Conditions of Social Development in West Africa, Retrospect and Prospect," *Civilisations, Revue Trimestrielle*, III, No. 4 (1953), p. 473.

the town or manor and have been thereby changed. And all the villagers are more or less affected by, perhaps, the school, the visiting trader, the missionary, and the more distant but perhaps significant example and suggestion manifest by the townsman or gentry-person known to them. And how shall we describe this interpenetration?

Among anthropologists, Professor Julian H. Steward has given great attention to the problems of describing a national state.[15] He makes the important distinction between two features of national state societies: those that function and must be studied on the national level; second, those that pertain to sociocultural segments or subgroups of the population. To understand the national state we must take account of national institutions such as schools, banking, and influences of the fully literate and the elite; the local differences among little communities; the effects of education and propaganda on villager and on townsman; and the relationships among all these things. The difficulties are great but not unsurmountable. Professor Steward has attempted to surmount them in the study he and his associates have made of Puerto Rico.

I turn away from the task of describing a national state and come back to the problem of describing a village community into which the manor or the town or the city has penetrated. The point of difficulty here is the fact that right there in the village things go on, acts are performed, thoughts are entertained, by the villager, which cannot be accounted for merely by referring to the several concentric spheres of activity of the local community and its traditional ways of life. These acts and thoughts of the villager have to be described as part of the changed village life and as qualitatively different from the acts and thoughts characteristic of the local tradition.

I recall the presence in Chan Kom of a school established for the people though decisions and policies with which the people had little to do. I recall the organization of villagers, brought about by townsmen, expected to vote the straight Revolutionary party ticket. I still wonder how to express, in words or perhaps in a diagram, the criminal hearing I observed in the village on an occasion when certain Indians were charged with killing cattle that had broken into their cornfields. Local people conducted the hearing, but a messenger had been sent off to tell the

---

15 Julian H. Steward, *Area Research: Theory and Practice,* Social Sciences Research Council, Bull. 63 (New York, 1950); "Levels of Sociocultural Integration," *Southwestern Journal of Anthropology,* VII, No. 4 (Winter, 1951), 374–90; Robert Manners and Julian H. Steward, "The Cultural Study of Contemporary Societies: Puerto Rico," *The American Journal of Sociology,* LIX, No. 2 (September, 1953), 123–30.

With regard to the description of peasant communities within states or civilizations: R. Redfield, *Peasant Society and Culture,* manuscript.

authorities of the city of the event, and while the investigation was taking place in the village the local officers who conducted it kept discussing among themselves what would be the attitude and action of the official from the city on the matters that they were at that moment concerned with. I cannot forget the long efforts of the Chan Kom villagers to persuade the national government to give them formal title to their communal lands, or the endless discussions over the merits of the school or about the trustworthiness of those strange people, the American archeologists, who were doing something mysterious in the ruined stone buildings of the ancients. All these things are a part of the life of such a little community. They happen right in the village, yet they are somehow outside of it. How shall we deal with the relative outsideness of these things that happen in the village?

Here, I think, we can return to Professor Steward's distinction between elements in the national state that represent the local and traditional way of life that was worked out there by those people out of the circumstances that immediately surrounded them; and, on the other hand, the elements that come from and represent the national state, state-wide or nation-wide, and that, to be understood fully, would have to be studied on the national level and studied largely in terms of explicit rules and deliberately created forms. We can consider the village of Chan Kom as a complex of folkways and stateways.

This complex of stateways and folkways is a needed dimension of the reality of such little communities as fall in the middle group of Starr's three groups along a range of difference that she imagines, a range on which the Siriono would occupy one terminus and the "Gold Coast and the Slum," or the people between Philadelphia and Wilmington, the other. We may come to conceive folkways and stateways more abstractly than does, I think, Professor Steward; we may conceive them as generalized qualities. To describe the whole within the wholes, we may use a form of thought which conceives of two kinds of organized human life as interpenetrating one another, right within the little community itself. The interpenetration is observable in certain frontiers between the two as these frontiers appear in the life of the village. When the villager adjusts himself to the visit of the tax collector or political organizer, when the village fathers discuss the newly introduced school, when the villager thinks of himself as a poor, hard-working peasant so regarded by the townsman to whom he goes or who comes to him—in all these moments and situations there is this frontier, the margin of adjustment between folkways and city ways. Some of these adjustments are old and stable, like the relationships of status between peasant and townsman.

Some are new and ill defined, as those that appear when a court or school or mission is first introduced by the national state into the little community.

So, in thinking about peasant communities or about partly urbanized rural communities, we begin to shape a form of thought that will conceive of primitive, folk, or peasant life as a general and abstract kind of living, as an imagined total structure, qualitatively different from the kind of living that comes to characterize towns and cities. We could perhaps see in the village two kinds of abstractly distinguishable kinds of life and kinds of communities, and see these, right in the village, in relationship to each other. The interpenetration of town and country can be conceived not only as a system of differentiated activity-fields but also, as Dr. Hanssen too has noticed, as an intermingling of two styles of life. This interpenetration, this intermingling, occurs within the village, within, indeed, the individual villager himself.

3. Toward a Reformulation
of Community Theory

ROLAND L. WARREN

INTRODUCTION

Few students of the community are satisfied with current theoretical approaches to this perplexing social group. Little advance has been made in the decades since MacIver gave theoretical formulation to the concept of the community; since Park, Burgess, and others of the Chicago school made their rich strike of valuable ore in the veins of the ecological approach; or since Wilson, Galpin, and Sanderson devised ways for operationally defining, delineating, and describing the rural community in a way which lent itself to useful research.

The MacIverian approach has long since proved inadequate to cope with the field described by the two coordinates of interest and locality. The ecological approach has failed to account for the data in as gloriously symmetrical a system as was first envisaged at Chicago, and has come, in addition, to be seen as only one of a number of facets of the community (which includes such other facets as the power structure and the relation to the larger society), all of which must be subsumed under

Source: Reprinted with permission of the author and publisher from *Human Organization*, XV, No. 2 (Summer, 1956), published by The Society for Applied Anthropology. This article was presented as a paper at the meeting of the Upstate Sociological Society, Syracuse, New York on May 8, 1956.

an adequate systematic theory of the community. And the pioneer work of Wilson, Galpin, and Sanderson has put out few new lush theoretical shoots to stand out among the proliferation of monotonously similar studies on the social organization of Grayhue County.

The inadequacy of the above-mentioned theories stems not only from their inability to deal coherently with the many aspects of community living which have been newly explored since these theories were first formulated (one thinks of recent work in stratification and informal group analysis, for example); the inadequacy is caused also by developments in community living which have become more markedly apparent in recent decades and which none of these formulations was adequate to accommodate in a systematic framework. These developments have been variously described as: the transition from Gemeinschaft to Gesellschaft, from sacred to secular, from folk culture to mass culture, from primary group association to secondary group association, from sympathetic contacts to categorical contacts, from locality groups to interest groups, from simple organization to complex.

However these polarities and processes are described, they cause some social scientists to wonder whether the very concept of community is not already a nonfunctional survival from earlier days, while others feel impelled to admonish the world that the community is going to hell because I don't know the name of the man across the street in apartment 4B.

This paper does not propose to sketch out a completely comprehensive theory of the community. But it will attempt to relate some concepts which in a modest fashion—on the level of Merton's "middle range," perhaps—may prove more adequate to cope with the data of the modern scene where interest is eclipsing locality as a central focus of association, where we know less and less about the man in apartment 4B, and yet where, far from disintegrating or vanishing, the interrelated cluster of people and facilities which we call a community is more delicately interdependent and more functionally vital than ever before.

THE CHANGING COMMUNITY

The community is not dying out as an effective locality group. Rather, it is changing structure and function to accommodate modern developments. This change is in the direction of greater specialization of function on the community level, a part of the overall process of social differentiation and increased specialization which our times embody.

The structural-functional changes in the community can be analyzed in terms of a horizontal axis and a vertical axis. The *horizontal axis* emphasizes locality. It involves the relationship of individual to individual or of group to group within the locality. It is illustrated by a group of citizens coming together to form a neighborhood association, and by the local community chest or welfare council. As will be indicated later, its principal task is coordinative, and its principal leadership role is that of the "permissive community organizer."

The *vertical axis* emphasizes specialized interest. It involves the relationship of the individual to a local interest group and of that local interest group to a regional, state, or national organization. It is illustrated by the relation of John Smith to his local Red Cross chapter and the relation of that Red Cross chapter to the regional and national Red Cross. As we shall see, its principal task is accomplishing some specific achievement, and its principal leadership role is that of the "problem area specialist."

This conceptual framework of a vertical axis of orientation and a horizontal axis is admittedly abstract, yet I believe we shall see that it is useful as we go along. Using these two terms, we can see that the progressive reorganization (rather than deterioration) of community living mentioned earlier is in such a direction that the horizontal axis becomes increasingly less important, the vertical axis increasingly more important. This is much more than to say that there has been a shift from locality grouping toward interest grouping. For the shift involves the whole structure of the community as a system of interdependent parts; it involves the types of problems which communities are pressed to solve, the types of associational life the people lead, and the types of leadership roles which are appropriate.

What occurs seems to be that as communities grow, or as they perdure through time under modern conditions, there is greater specialization of effort within the community, a reflection of the overall process of a progressive division of labor. This process is especially familiar to all of us in the gradual differentiation of older family functions and their assumption by such social agencies as the school, the church, governmental bodies, and commercial enterprises. Community development thus manifests a progressive differentiation of function and structure. As this process occurs, a more intricate network of interdependent, specialized parts forms the increasingly complex system and with this progressive fragmentation of function, the problem of community coherence arises. Can the increasingly specialized parts be kept in coordination? Can the increasingly specialized interest groups work together for common community goals?

NEED FOR MODERN FRAMEWORK FOR
COMMUNITY STUDIES

If the analysis so far is sound, then the major weakness of conventional community theory becomes apparent. Conventional community theory is set up to emphasize the horizontal axis, the factor of locality, the factor of common interests, common life, common associations, common institutions based on locality. And, it is just this factor which is becoming progressively weaker as time goes on.

It is perhaps for this reason that community sociologists have so characteristically fallen into the pattern of treating the community as if it were a desert island culture, almost completely cut off from the surrounding world. We do not have an adequate theoretical framework for analyzing the relations of the community to the surrounding society and culture, even though we realize that this is a great lack. "There are few studies," Steward points out, "which attempt to show how the larger society affects the community under investigation; and there are no studies which undertake to conceptualize fully and in detail the relationship between the community and the larger whole.[1] We do not have an adequate framework for such a conceptualization because our rudimentary community theory is adequate to a rural, sacred, primary-group-oriented, pre-industrial society, but is inadequate to accommodate the very changes which are transforming the nature of American communities in our time.

HORIZONTAL COORDINATION AND VERTICAL COORDINATION

As a system becomes more complex, there arises greater need for coordination. As a school, or a church, for example, take on many specialized functions, there is greater administrative need for holding all these differentiated functions together in an efficiently operating system. As the schools, churches, social agencies, business establishments, and other community facilities multiply and differentiate, there is need for keeping these facilities in some sort of adequate coordination with respect to each other. This coordinating function can be performed within the community, along the horizontal axis, through the community welfare council or various types of local planning agencies, or the coordinating function can be performed on a supercommunity level; that is, along the vertical axis. Thus, the national organization of the labor union, the Red Cross, the Methodist Church, or a state department of education, can lay down rules and procedures for the structure and function governing its particular community association or agency, thus fitting the community organization into the vertical system of local members, local units, district, regional, state, and national organization, and, in this way, the efforts can be coordinated along the vertical axis of common interest.

---

[1] Julian H. Steward, "Area Research: Theory and Practice," *Bulletin 63* (New York: Social Science Research Council, 1950), 22–23.

Putting the vertical coordination another way, supercommunity units, like state voluntary organizations or state and federal governmental departments, develop patterns for their local units in communities. For example, the size of the new post office door in Alfred, New York, was determined by a national policy of the United States Post Office Department. Similar decisions are made by the formal leadership structure of a Masonic Lodge, a Catholic Church, or the program set-up of a grange meeting. Thus, on this vertical axis, coordination of the local unit with the state or national unit becomes the important focus, guaranteeing that the total effort of the overall organization with respect to its special area of interest and operation will be brought to bear in coordinated fashion.

In addition, there is the problem of local coordination with other agencies of different types on the community level. Here, such questions are relevant as: How good a citizen of your community is the local heart or polio organization, or the local branch of a veterans' organization, or the local factory, or the local public welfare department, granted that each is pursuing its own interest as best it can?

VERTICAL AXIS VERSUS HORIZONTAL AXIS

The conflict between vertical and horizontal axis of orientation is nowhere more readily apparent in our communities today than in the two competing systems of fund raising for health and welfare. I am referring, of course, to the all-inclusive community chest campaign, on the one hand, and the special fund-raising campaigns, particularly of the various health groups, on the other. Here is the horizontal orientation of agencies getting together for fund-raising on a locality basis, and the vertical orientation of state and national organizations reaching into the local community through their individualized, task-oriented branches, to carry on fund-raising activities in little relation to what this adds up to on the local community level. Thus the local community quota for the problem-oriented health association is calculated with respect to the state and national program of the specialized organization, rather than in relation to the respective needs and services of other problem-oriented associations in the local community. We begin to gain perspective on this competition in fund raising once we realize that they are but a part of the over-all division of community activities into horizontal and vertical components, with the vertical components gradually increasing as communities become more differentiated.

Now it is the thesis of the present paper, to repeat, that providing sufficient horizontal coordination is becoming more of a problem as vertical orientation and coordination develop.

INDUCING COMMUNITY CHANGE AND
DEMOCRATIC VALUES

At this point, I would like to interrupt the analysis by introducing another problem, whose relationship to the main theme of this discourse will, it is hoped, become increasingly apparent. It is a problem which, though subject to dispassionate analysis, is fraught with ethical values, and is one which individual social scientists, participating in community endeavor, cannot side-step. It is the problem of the relation between deliberately induced community change, on the one hand, and democratic values on the other.

Anyone who knows something that is "good" for a community is faced with the dilemma of forcing this good, however subtly, on the community, or of running the risks that the community will not accept it, and that his efforts will be unsuccessful. Now one way to attempt to solve this dilemma is to ignore it. It is enlightening to see how many social scientists, who lay great stress on being value-free, often fail to raise questions about the basic value assumptions implicit in their action programs. We assume, tacitly, that the social scientists should take that horn of the dilemma which involves forcing the good, as defined by us in our infinite wisdom, on other less fortunate peoples, and of accomplishing this forcing process, if possible, without their realizing that they are being "taken." This applies in Syracuse or Southeast Asia.

Thus, as one technical assistance administrator puts it:

> What groups in particular areas are most influential in promoting or retarding economic change and development and what are the personality and culture traits of the groups that are favorable (or unfavorable) to particular changes required for economic development? If there are psychological or cultural barriers impeding desired types of development, what ways can be found to eliminate or surmount these barriers? . . . These are among the most important questions that social scientists might help program administrators to answer.[2]

The other horn of the dilemma also has its difficulties. It involves the idea of democratic self-determination, the respect for this principle coming before the importance placed on the value of the specific improvement, whether this be a new recreation program, a new heart clinic, or the establishment of a youth board. This emphasis is illustrated in the following succinct quotation: "Communities, like individuals, have a

---

[2] Samuel P. Hayes, Jr., "Personality and Culture Problems of Point IV," in Bert F. Howelitz, (ed.). *The Progress of Underdeveloped Areas,* (Chicago: University of Chicago Press, 1952), p. 207.

right to self-determination. In community organization, the worker enables the community to develop its own policies, plans, and programs. They are not super-imposed."[3] We can hear the harried public health official, or representative from the state mental health department, or from the state education department, saying:

> If I had to wait for the communities in my district to examine their various needs and decide which ones have most priority and then hope that my program was included, I would never get anything accomplished. As it is, look what I have done. Six new communities have fluoridated their water, or five new communities have established a mental health clinic, or six new districts have improved their pupil personnel facilities. Can you imagine any of these field workers hurrying back to the state mental health department and reporting: 'I invited them to assess their needs and formulate them and determine priority and to consider our program among others, and they decided on a new sewage system instead of our mental health clinic!'

I would like to leave this problem in its present state of irresolution and resume the thread of the theoretical analysis, which will rapidly catch up with it once more.

PROBLEM AREA SPECIALIST VERSUS DEMOCRATIC SELF-DETERMINATION

It was maintained above that coordination is becoming more and more effective along the vertical problem-area or interest-group axis, but that at the same time greater horizontal coordination is made necessary by the progressive differentiation of function and structure within the community.

We have all seen the important role in community differentiation played by the problem-area specialist. This is the man from the state education department, or from the mental hygiene department or from this or that national voluntary agency. His orientation is vertical, in that he is relating the state or national program to the local community unit. He is task oriented, focussing on the particular task to be accomplished— the new clinic, the new social service, etc.—he is likely to be highly specialized, and an expert in his own special field, having had experience with many, many communities in his particular subject. He is thus likely to have many of the answers before he reaches the community. He is likely, in other words, to "know better than the community does what the

---

[3] Ray Johns and David F. DeMarche, *Community Organization and Agency Responsibility* (New York: Association Press, 1951), p. 235.

community really needs." Thus, he is paternalistic. He may be demo-
cratically oriented with respect to group self-determination, but by the
very nature of his role he cannot encourage the community to consider
all the possible alternatives for community improvement. He is "selling"
a particular program. He thus tends to lean toward the ethical absolutist
side, toward the side which knows what is right and wants that right to
prevail. If he is successful in activating his program, that is, in inducing
the new school consolidation or in establishing the new clinic, the impact
of his work is bound to be disruptive, as the power structure, balance of
agency functions, and other nice relationships are disturbed by the institutional innovation. His loyal group who have helped put across the
improvement may have also created antagonisms in the process. We
might add that, in Riesman's terminology, this problem area specialist
comes very close to the ideal type of the "inner-directed" personality.

PROBLEM AREA SPECIALIST VERSUS COMMUNITY COORDINATOR

If what has been said is true, then it is reasonable to hypothesize that
as community solidarity weakens in favor of vertical articulation of
increasingly complex components, the role of the problem-area specialist
would not necessarily weaken, but would in many ways come to be
complemented by the emerging role of the local community coordinator.
(Significantly enough, this latter is himself a product of the increasing
trend toward differentiation of function.) It is interesting to note that
the above is just about what has happened. The results of the task-
oriented activity of the problem area specialists have been to produce
disalignments which have structural, functional, and emotional aspects.
It has become more difficult to keep this structurally differentiated
community "together," to keep effective horizontal relationships of
parts while vertical changes go on apace.

It is in this situation that the horizontally oriented permissive community organizer, the nonspecialist, the "process man," whose chief
concern is with what happens to the interrelated parts of the community
in planning, coordinating, and changing, comes into the picture. He is
permissive and equalitarian, rather than paternalistic. His orientation is
horizontal, toward the relationship of the parts of the community to each
other. His chief focus is on process, on what happens to interacting
people and groups in the community, rather than on the accomplishment
of this or that specific task. In this respect, since he places greater weight
on the rightness of whatever decision the community makes in a democratic, permissive context, he tends toward ethical relativism, being less
sure that he knows in advance what is "right," and being less willing to

impose his "right," as he sees it, on others. The overall impact of his function is tension-reducing. He tries to help ease tensions resulting from uneven developments and from the hostility engendered by the pulls and tugs to which the community is subjected by problem-area specialists and their local related vertical interest groups. Need we add that, in Riesman's typology, this man approximates the "other-directed" personality?

Thus we begin to see the community as a social system which undergoes stresses and strains but whose overall longtime process is one of increasing differentiation of function and structure, and whose chief orientation of interest and association is shifting from the horizontal to the vertical as defined above. We also begin to get a picture of the dynamics of induced community change, in which the problem-area specialist and his vertically-oriented interest group achieve accomplishments which in turn make for greater differentiation of function and also create tensions within the community. Complementing this function is that of the permissive community organizer with his horizontal focus of interest and his typical leadership functions of tension reduction and coordination among the parts of the system.

Those who have followed this analysis and who are familiar with the structural-functional analysis of social systems, as developed notably by Talcott Parsons, and of small groups, as developed by Robert F. Bales, will have noticed a striking relationship of this analysis to some of their findings.

Bales found that in those groups which had high consensus about leadership, leadership roles tended to polarize around two functions, that of the task-oriented leader, and that of the social-emotional specialist. The task-oriented leader pressed the group to make some adaptive change, the social-emotional specialist helped to ease the tensions and hostilities arising from the adjustive process.

Parsons, in his analysis of the nuclear family of the United States, makes a strong case for the father's role as instrumental leader, as task oriented, as relating the family to the socio-economic world, with the mother's role being closer to that of the expressive leader, the one who keeps peace in the family, the one who helps hold the family together as stresses and strains are engendered by adaptation and change.

The above analysis of the community is, on the one hand, a close parallel of the Parsonian-Bales analysis. I take note of this parallelism, but do not want to over-emphasize it. The analysis here given should stand on its own feet. On the other hand I do want to stress that this analysis provides a particularly helpful approach to the differentiation of the two roles about which there is the greatest controversy and misunderstanding in the field of community organization today—that of the problem-area specialist and that of the process-oriented permissive community organizer.

CONCLUSION

I return, in conclusion, to our ethical dilemma. There is, of course, no sociological solution to a problem of values. Each of us must make his own decisions as to the relative importance in our value hierarchy of the principle of self-determination of individuals and groups and of the principle of doing for others what we think is right for them. But I do think we are now in a position to see this moral dilemma in context. What we see, if the above analysis is sound, is a perpetual process of new achievement and consolidation, coupled with a process of tension induction and reduction, and we have seen that in this multiple process there are roles in our communities both for the man whose eye is on the task accomplishment, and for the man whose eye is on the relationships existing among people. It may be just as well, given these diverse needs and this pulsating process, that not all people choose the same way to serve. Perhaps here, some advice from St. Paul is appropriate:

> Having gifts that differ according to the grace given to us, let us use them: if prophecy, in proportion to our faith; if service, in our serving; he who teaches, in his teaching; he who exhorts, in his exhortation; he who contributes, in liberality; he who gives aid, with zeal; he who does acts of mercy, with cheerfulness.

4. Sociology of the Community: Current Status and Prospects

RICHARD L. SIMPSON

Community-centered research covers a broad range of topics. In such a large and diverse field, it is helpful to take stock occasionally. This paper is an attempt to assess the present status and prospects of community sociology by identifying and evaluating some main varieties of current efforts in the field.

In the sociological study of communities it is possible to identify three principal approaches or research foci. First, there are what might be called studies of *life in communities*. These are not really studies of communities as such, but of social life which happens to take place and be studied within community settings. Studies of social mobility, for example, often use cities as sources of their samples of workers—one thinks of Natalie Rogoff's Indianapolis mobility study[1] and of Lipset

SOURCE: Reprinted with permission of the author and publisher from *Rural Sociology*, Vol. 30, No. 2 (June, 1965).

[1] Natalie Rogoff, *Recent Trends in Occupational Mobility* (New York: The Free Press, 1953).

and Bendix's study of mobility in Oakland, California,[2] among others—but the object of study is not the community but its occupational structure, or its workers. Rural sociology offers similar examples, in which the behavior under examination takes place within a specified community which provides a sample of respondents, but the community as such is not the object of inquiry.

A second kind of community-oriented research is research on *social life as affected by community settings*. A sociologist might, for example, be interested in understanding juvenile delinquency, and he might conclude that some kinds of urban neighborhoods have characteristics which cause high rates of delinquency.[3] Or he might study race relations as influenced by residential segregation and by the interracial contacts taking place where racial enclaves meet.[4] In this second kind of research, behavior is explicitly explained on the basis of community characteristics, but the community as such still is not the object of study.

The third kind of research can genuinely be called *sociology of the community*. The community as such and its characteristics are the objects of study. It is with this kind of community sociology that this paper is concerned, not because the other two research foci are any less valuable, but to keep the topics to be covered within reasonable bounds. *Sociology of the community*, in turn, lends itself to a classification of approaches. We shall identify and discuss three such approaches which deal, respectively, with (1) communities as wholes, (2) communities as types, and (3) social processes and dimensions which are specific to the community and which distinguish it as a sociological category from other kinds of social structures.

RESEARCH ON COMMUNITIES AS WHOLES

Various holistic research emphases have in common the effort to understand the community as a totality. This does not mean that to be holistic one must try to describe everything, but it does mean that one should regard the community as an integrated whole and seek to under-

---

[2] Seymour Martin Lipset and Reinhard Bendix, *Social Mobility in Industrial Society* (Berkeley and Los Angeles: University of California Press, 1959). This study includes analysis of effects of childhood community size on mobility opportunities, and therefore might be considered in part an example of our second-named research focus (below).

[3] The best-known such study is reported in Clifford R. Shaw and Henry D. McKay, *Juvenile Delinquency and Urban Areas* (Chicago: University of Chicago Press, 1942).

[4] For example, St. Clair Drake and Horace R. Cayton, *Black Metropolis*, Vol. I (New York: Harper and Row, Publishers [Torchbook edition], 1962), pp. 174–213, esp. pp. 190–195.

stand what keeps it that way. Let us examine some varieties of holistic community research.

COMMUNITY ETHNOGRAPHY: DESCRIPTION OF THE ROUND OF LIFE

The anthropological tradition has produced many valuable case studies of American community cultures. The Middletown studies[5] may still be the most notable of these, even though subsequent researchers have been able to make use of improved research techniques and insights. The most obvious limitation these total community studies impose is that they can be made only in relatively small communities, where fewer and fewer of our people live. But it is still possible to study subcommunities within the big cities.[6] Some of the finest of the early Chicago studies were of this type, and include Wirth's study of the ghetto[7] and Zorbaugh's *The Gold Coast and the Slum*.[8] Subcommunity studies since the 1940's have paid even closer attention to ways in which subcommunities fit into the larger community matrix. Examples are Drake and Cayton's *Black Metropolis*,[9] Whyte's *Street Corner Society*;[10] works by J. Kenneth Morland and Hylan Lewis on the mill village and the Negro subcommunity of "Kent" in South Carolina;[11] and still more recently, Herbert J. Gans's *The Urban Villagers*, on an Italian-American area in Boston.[12]

In a sense, the social diversity of modern communities does not prevent holistic analysis of fairly unified cultures as long as subcommunities rather than total communities are studied. But in addition to diversity of culture, modern communities large and small are characterized by an expansion in social scale.[13] The social relationships even of villagers

---

[5] Robert S. Lynd and Helen Merrell Lynd, *Middletown* (New York: Harcourt, Brace and World, 1929); Robert S. Lynd and Helen Merrell Lynd, *Middletown in Transition* (New York: Harcourt, Brace and World, 1937).

[6] Holistic studies of urban subcommunities are urged by Conrad M. Arensberg, "The Community Study Method," *American Journal of Sociology*, LX (September, 1954), 109–124.

[7] Louis Wirth, *The Ghetto* (Chicago: University of Chicago Press, 1928).

[8] Harvey Zorbaugh, *The Gold Coast and the Slum* (Chicago: University of Chicago Press, 1929).

[9] Drake and Cayton, *op. cit.*

[10] William Foote Whyte, *Street Corner Society*, 2nd ed. (Chicago: University of Chicago Press, 1955).

[11] J. Kenneth Morland, *Millways of Kent* (Chapel Hill: University of North Carolina Press, 1958); and Hylan Lewis, *Blackways of Kent* (Chapel Hill: University of North Carolina Press, 1955).

[12] Herbert J. Gans, *The Urban Villagers* (New York: The Free Press of Glencoe, 1962).

[13] The concept of scale was developed by Godfrey Wilson and Monica Hunter Wilson in *The Analysis of Social Change* (London: Cambridge University Press, 1945).

extend far beyond the immediate localities where they live. More fundamentally, the forces which integrate modern communities are likely to lie
in organizations, both private and governmental, centered outside the
community, and any analysis which fails to take account of this has not
really analyzed the community social system as a whole.[14] Vidich and
Bensman, in their study of an upstate New York village and township,
build their analysis around this problem, showing how the local community is dependent on decisions made by outside organizations.[15] But
if the integration of a community's activities is accomplished from outside, and if the community is divided into subcultural groups and special-
interest groups which have relations, separately, to outside organizations
but not to each other, it may be questionable whether a modern community *is* a unified whole in any real sense except that of geography. The
moral may be that if the chief assumption of the holistic approach, that
of the community as a unified whole, has become inaccurate, we should
not put all our eggs in this basket though we need not give up the
endeavor entirely.

Another difficulty with community ethnographies is that they tend to
be noncumulative: each one is a case study of a single community. They
usually show little attempt to build explicit theory, though one investigator may use concepts and insights developed by his predecessors. The
answer to this charge is that many individual case studies can be drawn
upon as sources of data for comparative analysis, and this can be cumulative and can lead to the establishment of generalizations about different
kinds of communities. Maurice Stein, in his *The Eclipse of Community*,[16] for instance, shows that the work of Park and the early Chicago
school, of the Lynds in Middletown, and of Warner and Low in
their study of the Yankee City shoe strike reveal, respectively, the effects
of urbanization, industrialization, and bureaucratization—three distinct
processes which are hard to separate in a study of a single case because
they tend to be found together empirically, but can be separated
analytically by examining a wide range of studies.

---

[14] The dominance of local communities by outside organizations is shown in Albert
Blumenthal, *Small-town Stuff* (Chicago: University of Chicago Press, 1932); and Kenneth
MacLeish and Kimball Young, *Landaff, New Hampshire* (Washington, D. C.: Bureau of
Agricultural Economics, 1942).

[15] Arthur J. Vidich and Joseph Bensman, *Small Town in Mass Society* (Princeton,
N. J.: Princeton University Press, 1958). See also Roland L. Warren, "Toward a
Typology of Extra-Community Controls Limiting Local Community Autonomy," *Social
Forces*, XXXIV (May, 1956), 338–341.

[16] Maurice R. Stein, *The Eclipse of Community* (Princeton, N. J.: Princeton University Press, 1960), pp. 13–93.

STRATIFICATION STUDIES

These are anthropological in inspiration but focus on structural divisions of the community into social classes. In addition to describing the way of life in each class, they describe the relations between the classes. There have been many such studies, the best known probably being those by Warner[17] and by Hollingshead.[18] Recently Vidich and Bensman[19] have made a theoretical improvement over earlier stratification analyses by arguing that if classes are to be conceived as real entities—as status groups, to use Weber's term[20]—they must be conceived as two-dimensional rather than as a simple hierarchy. Vidich and Bensman note that communities have status groups which differ markedly in values and behavior though they may be equal in social rank; leaders of the town and gown segments of a college town would illustrate this phenomenon. Accordingly, Vidich and Bensman arrange their classes vertically, by social rank, and also horizontally, by dominant values and behavioral orientations. Taking this cue, perhaps future students should distinguish at the very least what Miller and Swanson[21] call the entrepreneurial and bureaucratic segments of the community. The nonvertical dimension of social class has been a central fact of history. The struggle between aristocracy and bourgeoisie, and the shift from a self-employed to a salaried middle class, are only two examples. It is time for sociologists to incorporate this commonplace knowledge into their systematic analyses.

The community stratification approach has died down somewhat. No stratification study in the past fifteen years has created nearly the stir in the field that followed the Warner and Hollingshead reports. Lenski[22] showed some years ago that people do not agree on the number of classes

---

17 The Warner studies include, among others, W. Lloyd Warner and Paul S. Lunt, *The Social Life of a Modern Community* (New Haven: Yale University Press, 1941); W. Lloyd Warner and Paul S. Lunt, *The Status System of a Modern Community* (New Haven: Yale University Press, 1942); W. Lloyd Warner and Leo Srole, *The Social Systems of American Ethnic Groups* (New Haven: Yale University Press, 1945); W. Lloyd Warner and J. O. Low, *The Social System of the Modern Factory* (New Haven: Yale University Press, 1947); W. Lloyd Warner and Associates, *Democracy in Jonesville* (New York: Harper & Row, Publishers, 1949); Allison Davis, Burleigh B. Gardner, and Mary R. Gardner, *Deep South* (Chicago: University of Chicago Press, 1941).

18 A. B. Hollingshead, *Elmtown's Youth* (New York: John Wiley & Sons, Inc., 1949).

19 Vidich and Bensman, *op. cit.*

20 Max Weber, "Class, Status, Party," in Max Weber, *From Max Weber: Essays in Sociology*, ed. and tr. by H. H. Gerth and C. Wright Mills (New York: Oxford University Press, 1946), pp. 180–195.

21 Daniel R. Miller and Guy E. Swanson, *The Changing American Parent* (New York: John Wiley & Sons, Inc., 1958).

22 Gerhard E. Lenski, "American Social Classes: Statistical Strata or Social Groups?" *American Journal of Sociology*, LVIII (November, 1952), 139–144.

in a community; Lenski, Landecker, and others have shown that the different status attributes of an individual are often inconsistent with each other, so that the class placement of individuals is often ambiguous,[23] many writers have questioned the adequacy of Warner's and (by implication) Hollingshead's research methods.[24] These criticisms have won wide acceptance among sociologists. No one, however, seems to have produced a better general treatment of community stratification if we may judge by the decisions on topical coverage made by the writers of textbooks. Quite commonly the stratification chapter of an introductory textbook will indicate that no clear-cut stratification system exists in American communities, but will then present the Warner scheme in rich detail anyway.

If not much has developed in community stratification analysis except criticism for more than fifteen years, the reason may be that the traditional stratification approach becomes less applicable as the society becomes more urban and heterogeneous. The traditional approach assumes that the community as such has a class structure which unambiguously includes all or nearly all inhabitants, that people use the community as a reference group in their status-striving, and that most people agree on the criteria of rank and can classify each other by them. None of these assumptions is as true of cities as of small towns,[25] and none is as true in a society with diverse occupational and ethnic subcultures as in an occupationally and ethnically simple society. Therefore, while social ranking goes on in cities just as elsewhere, it is less likely than in the communities of the past to produce genuine social classes in the sense of socially unified status groups distinguished from each other by social rank.[26]

---

[23] Gerhard E. Lenski, "Status Crystallization: A Non-Vertical Dimension of Social Status," *American Sociological Review*, XIX (August, 1954), 405–413; Werner S. Landecker, "Class Boundaries," *American Sociological Review*, XXV (December, 1960), 868–877.

[24] Criticisms of the Warner approach are summarized and discussed in Ruth Rosner Kornhauser, "The Warner Approach to Social Stratification," in Reinhard Bendix and Seymour Martin Lipset (eds.), *Class, Status and Power* (New York: The Free Press, 1953), pp. 224–255. See also Milton M. Gordon, *Social Class in American Sociology* (Durham, N. C.: Duke University Press, 1958), pp. 85–123.

[25] Gordon, *op. cit.* See also Neal Gross, "Social Class Identification in the Urban Community," *American Sociological Review*, XVIII (August, 1953), 398–404; Gregory P. Stone and William H. Form, "Instabilities in Status: The Problem of Hierarchy in the Community Study of Status Arrangements," *American Sociological Review*, XVIII (April, 1953), 149–162; and William H. Form and Gregory P. Stone, "Urbanism, Anonymity, and Status Symbolism," *American Journal of Sociology*, LXII (March, 1957), 504–514.

[26] For a heuristic model of urban stratification which assumes an unambiguous rank order but does not assume clearly demarcated classes, see James M. Beshers, *Urban*

STUDIES OF COMMUNITIES AS TYPES

The effort in this kind of research is to explain a wide range of behavior on the basis of a simple classification scheme. Once a concept like *Gemeinschaft,* or folk, is invoked, everything falls into place. The typological tradition can claim a long history of distinguished names: Maine, Tönnies, Spencer, Durkheim, Redfield, Odum, Becker, and others. Recently McKinney and Loomis[27] have surveyed the history of typological concepts, extracted some unities from the great morass of different words meaning the same things, and made use of their own refinements in a study of a Latin American community.

In addition to its use in studies of rural and folk communities, this approach is represented in theorizing about the Chicago studies by Louis Wirth in his "Urbanism as a Way of Life,"[28] which may be the most influential article ever to appear in a sociological journal. This approach reappears in literature of the 1950's by William H. Whyte, Jr., and others, on the suburbs as a new community type combining urban and folk qualities.[29]

Unfortunately, it is the essence of typologies that they exaggerate the facts on which they are based. Several bodies of empirical work suggest that in the community typological tradition, the exaggeration may have gone too far.

William Foote Whyte, in *Street Corner Society,*[30] and Lazarsfeld and his associates and followers in their research on the two-step flow of information from mass communication media to opinion leaders to rank and file,[31] have "rediscovered the primary group" in the city. As Katz indicates in comparing the Katz and Lazarsfeld research with rural soci-

---

Social Structures (New York: The Free Press, 1962), pp. 127–158. "Horizontal" ethnic divisions are emphasized by Milton M. Gordon, *Assimilation in American Life* (New York: Oxford University Press, 1964); he expands on earlier analyses by Ruby Jo Reeves Kennedy, Will Herberg, and Gerhard Lenski.

27 John C. McKinney and Charles P. Loomis, "The Typological Tradition," in Joseph S. Roucek (ed.), *Contemporary Sociology* (New York: Philosophical Library, 1958), pp. 557–582.

28 Louis Wirth, "Urbanism as a Way of Life," *American Journal of Sociology,* XLIV (July, 1938), 1–24.

29 William H. Whyte, Jr., *The Organization Man* (Garden City, N. Y.: Doubleday Anchor Books, 1957), pp. 295–434. See also Sylvia Fleis Fava, "Suburbanism as a Way of Life," *American Sociological Review,* XXI (February, 1956), 34–38. Prevailing views of the suburbs are discussed in William M. Dobriner, *Class in Suburbia* (Englewood Cliffs, N. J.: Prentice-Hall, Inc., 1963), pp. 5–28.

30 William Foote Whyte, *op. cit.*

31 See especially Elihu Katz and Paul F. Lazarsfeld, *Personal Influence* (New York: The Free Press, 1955); and Elihu Katz, "The Two-Step Flow of Communication: An Up-to-Date Report on an Hypothesis," *Public Opinion Quarterly,* XXI (Spring, 1957), 61–78.

ologists' studies of diffusion of new farm practices,[32] the primary group communication networks seem to work about the same in both urban and rural settings. Studies of urban family life by Sussman,[33] Litwak,[34] Willmott and Young,[35] and others and of informal sociability in cities by Greer and Kube,[36] by Smith, Form, and Stone, [37] and by Gulick, Bowerman, and Back[38] suggest that rumors of the death of primary group life in cities have been exaggerated. Most city dwellers do not live in isolation. In addition, Kollmorgen and Harrison have questioned whether rural communities in the United States, with their pattern of isolated farmsteads rather than rural villages, have ever been the close-knit groups which are sometimes portrayed by rural sociologists and other incurable romantics.[39] All of these writings have created doubt about our traditional notions of the supposed differences between the quality of rural and urban social life.

The idea of the suburb as a distinct community type has also been questioned. Berger's study of a California working-class suburb suggests that workingmen do not suddenly start behaving like middle-class organization men simply because they have moved to a suburb. The Republicanism, upward mobility, *kaffeeklatsching*, and organizational joining of

---

[32] Elihu Katz, "Communication Research and the Image of Society: Convergence of two Traditions," *American Journal of Sociology*, LXV (March, 1960), 435–440. On agricultural diffusion studies, see Everett M. Rogers, *The Diffusion of Innovations* (New York: The Free Press, 1962).

[33] Marvin B. Sussman, "The Isolated Nuclear Family: Fact or Fiction?" *Social Problems*, VI (Spring, 1959), 333–340; Marvin B. Sussman and Lee Burchinal, "Kin Family Network: Unheralded Structure in Current Conceptualizations of Family Functioning," *Marriage and Family Living*, XXIV (August, 1962), 231–240.

[34] Eugene Litwak, "Occupational Mobility and Extended Family Cohesion," *American Sociological Review*, XXV (February, 1960), 9–21; Eugene Litwak, "Geographic Mobility and Extended Family Cohesion," *American Sociological Review*, XXV (June, 1960), 385–394.

[35] Michael Young and Peter Willmott, *Family and Kinship in East London*, (London: Routledge and Kegan, Paul, 1957); Peter Willmott and Michael Young, *Family and Class in a London Suburb*, (London: Routledge and Kegan, Paul, 1960).

[36] Scott Greer and Ella Kube, "Urbanism and Social Structure: A Los Angeles Study," in Marvin B. Sussman (ed.), *Community Structure and Analysis*, (New York: Thomas Y. Crowell Company, 1959), pp. 93–112.

[37] Joel Smith, William H. Form, and Gregory P. Stone, "Local Intimacy in a Middle-Sized City," *American Journal of Sociology*, LX (November, 1954) 276–284.

[38] John Gulick, Charles E. Bowerman, and Kurt W. Back, "Newcomer Enculturation in the City: Attitudes and Participation," in F. Stuart Chapin, Jr., and Shirley F. Weiss (eds.), *Urban Growth Dynamics*, (New York: John Wiley & Sons, Inc., 1962), pp. 315–358.

[39] Walter M. Kollmorgen and Robert W. Harrison, "The Search for the Rural Community," *Agricultural History*, XX (March, 1946), 1–8. See also Walter L. Slocum and Herman M. Case, "Are Neighborhoods Meaningful Social Groups throughout Rural America?" *Rural Sociology*, XVIII (March, 1953), 52–59.

which we have heard so much in writings on middle-class tract suburbs were not prevalent among Berger's suburban factory workers.[40] Ernest Mowrer's research on the family in Chicago suburbs shows that the folksy, primary group quality of suburban life disappears after a few years of the suburb's existence; people then go back to their relatives and their specialized interest groupings and start ignoring their neighbors, like urban apartment dwellers (and like many farmers).[41] Meyersohn and Jackson reach a similar conclusion in their comparison of gardening norms in an old and a new suburb; the kind of hyperconformity Whyte has decried was found only in the new suburb where it would presumably disappear once people had lived there long enough to develop outside ties and stop worrying about what the neighbors might think.[42] William Dobriner in a survey of literature and a comparative study of several New York suburbs gives evidence that class and ethnicity, not suburban residence *per se,* explain many of the characteristics often attributed to suburbs.[43] Dobriner also finds reason to believe that a homogeneous, brand-new middle-class suburb like White's Park Forest—Dobriner's suburb was Levittown—becomes less homogeneous in age, class, and ethnicity after a few years.[44] These writings have cast serious doubt on the explanation of suburbanites' behavior on the basis of community type.

The strongest attack on the typological approach may have been Oscar Lewis's critique of Robert Redfield's work on the village of Tepoztlán.[45] Lewis asserted that the characteristics by which Redfield distinguished folk from urban communities can vary independently from each other, so that a place can be very urban in some ways and decidedly "folk" in others. Lewis's Tepoztlán findings suggest that instead of types under which many variables are subsumed, the separate variables ought to be the focus of study. The variables usually incorporated in the folk-urban distinctions fall into several clusters referring to (a) *interaction networks:* for instance, extensity of the range of close acquaintances, in-

[40] Bennett M. Berger, *Working Class Suburb* (Berkeley and Los Angeles: University of California Press, 1960).

[41] Ernest R. Mowrer, "The Family in Suburbia," in William M. Dobriner (ed.), *The Suburban Community* (New York: G. P. Putnam's Sons, 1958), pp. 147–164.

[42] Rolf Meyersohn and Robin Jackson, "Gardening in Suburbia," in Dobriner, *The Suburban Community, op. cit.* pp. 271–286.

[43] Dobriner, *Class in Suburbia, op. cit.*

[44] *Ibid.,* pp. 85–126. But see Reynolds Farley, "Suburban Persistence," *American Sociological Review,* XXIX (February, 1964), 38–47, for national data showing a tendency for the status levels of suburbs to persist.

[45] Oscar Lewis, *Life in a Mexican Village: Tepoztlán Restudied* (Urbana: University of Illinois Press, 1951).

tensity of primary group ties; (b) *values and mental orientations:* for example, cosmopolitanism *vs.* provincialism, rigidity *vs.* flexibility of outlook, moral absolutism *vs.* moral relativism or tolerance, degree of attachment to traditional beliefs and resistance to changing them; and (c) *quality of interaction:* for example, intrinsic *vs.* extrinsic motivation to enter into interaction, expressivity *vs.* manipulativeness of orientation to other people. Parsons's pattern variables[46] are a refinement of typological ideas into variables expressing the ways in which people relate to one another when they interact.

A good procedure might be to split up the global notions of the typologies into separate variables, examine their interrelationships through research, and then, insofar as possible, put them back together into theoretically coherent basic variables and perhaps (if the research findings warrant it) into new typologies. In this way the value of the typological tradition would be retained without our having to assume relationships which have not been demonstrated and may not exist. For example, instead of saying that in a folk community people lack secondary relationships, are provincial, and are resistant to innovation, the sociologist can take these characteristics as variables for research and see if they are in fact related. Does a lack of social contacts beyond the immediate primary group make people provincial? Do a provincial outlook and a lack of attachment to reference groups beyond the local community make people resistant to social change? These questions are raised in Daniel Lerner's study of modernization in the Middle East,[47] and also in the study by Emery and Oeser on the acceptance of innovations by Australian farmers.[48] Both of these studies try to see whether exposure to urban and nonlocal stimuli actually does broaden people's frames of reference, and whether a broadened frame of reference makes them more willing to accept change. (Both studies find that the answer to both questions is Yes.) These studies use insights from the typological tradition without trying to explain everything on the basis of global "types"; for example, both find great variation in the behavior of different individuals within the same communities, one of them (Lerner's) quite backward and "folklike." These studies carry the process urged above half way; the variables are split up for use in research but are not

---

46 Talcott Parsons, *The Social System* (New York: The Free Press, 1951), pp. 46–51, 58–67, 101–112, *et passim.* See also Talcott Parsons, "The Pattern Variables Revisited: A Response to Robert Dubin," *American Sociological Review,* XXV (August, 1960), 467–483.

47 Daniel Lerner, *The Passing of Traditional Society* (New York: The Free Press, 1958).

48 F. E. Emery and O. A. Oeser, *Information, Decision, and Action* (Melbourne: Melbourne University Press, 1958).

recombined. Another use of typological characteristics as variables is that by Freeman and Winch.[49] They show that eight polar typological characteristics form a Guttman scale, which suggests that the characteristics change from folk to "modern" in a predictable order as societies become increasingly complex.

A difficulty in the kind of revised approach we are suggesting is that it ultimately requires comparative community study, and in this kind of research it is not easy to isolate the variables empirically once the conceptual distinctions among them have been made. The logic of comparative study is the same as that of survey research, but surveys of samples of individuals are easier than comparative community studies. When it takes months or years to study a single small community properly, how can anyone get data on hundreds of communities so that their characteristics can be cross-tabulated to discover whether features of given communities are causally or only fortuitously found together? One answer is to use sources of comparative material like the Human Relations Area Files, or to do the same sort of comparative analysis less systematically but still using other people's work as data, as Stein did in *The Eclipse of Community*.[50] But the other people may not have gotten the data you need, because they may not have had your research question in mind. We will probably continue to rely in community research on less complete comparability of data than survey research can attain in order to keep the richness and depth which only intensive case studies can bring, and to count heavily on the creativity of the comparative analyst to classify the variables which parade under different names in different studies.

STUDIES OF COMMUNITY-SPECIFIC PROCESSES

The identification and examination of processes and dimensions which are specific to the community in the sense that they are not found in other social structures provide much of the rationale for regarding "community" as a distinct area of investigation apart from stratification, family life, and other aspects of behavior that may occur in communities.

DEFINING THE COMMUNITY AS A SOCIAL REALM

The concept of community has suffered, like some other sociological concepts, from vagueness stemming from the vernacular rather than

49 Linton C. Freeman and Robert F. Winch, "Societal Complexity: An Empirical Test of a Typology of Societies," *American Journal of Sociology*, LXII (March, 1957), 461–466.

50 Stein, *op. cit.* The work of George A. Hillery, Jr., is another useful beginning in comparative community analysis. See especially his "The Folk Village: A Comparative Analysis," *Rural Sociology*, XXVI (December, 1961), 335–353; and "Villages, Cities, and Total Institutions," *American Sociological Review*, XXVIII (October, 1963), 779–791.

scientific origin of the term. Some progress has been made, however, in winnowing a workable sociological meaning from the many everyday meanings of the term.[51]

Harold F. Kaufman has given a clear portrayal of the community as a distinct social realm.[52] He regards the community as a set of locality-oriented interactions: as goal-directed interaction processes engendered by the fact of people's common residence in a locality. Thus, family life is largely noncommunity, and only some aspects of stratification are "community" phenomena while most aspects of local government are "community" phenomena. This view is logically sound, is rather easily applied, and leaves less room than most definitions for hair-splitting about what is and what is not a community phenomenon.

Sutton and Kolaja have developed a notion of "community" almost identical to Kaufman's, and have worked out techniques for applying the concept in research.[53] To them, as to Kaufman, "community" is not identical with "local society" but involves only "the policy-deciding, self- or identity-maintaining social system of families residing in a particular area which confronts collectively problems arising from the sharing of the area."[54] Like Kaufman, they feel that such a view of community will be helpful in focusing research on the dynamics of action rather than on the statics of structure. Sutton and Kolaja have illustrated the feasibility of their approach by developing a scheme to measure the "communityness" of events reported in local newspapers. To give an over-simplified example, the meeting of a committee of local citizens to petition for improved air service to the local airport would be community-relevant, while an article advising gardeners to spray rosebushes for bugs every three weeks would not be community-relevant.[55] They illustrate the technique by applying it to newspaper articles, but there is no reason why it could not also be applied to other kinds of data on community events. They suggest that the overall degree of "communityness" of the events taking place within a locality, and of the events deemed newsworthy, may be an important characteristic of the community.

George Hillery has examined a number of ethnographic and socio-

---

51 See especially George A. Hillery, Jr., "Definitions of Community: Areas of Agreement," *Rural Sociology*, XX (June, 1955), 111–124; and George A. Hillery, Jr., "A Critique of Selected Community Concepts," *Social Forces*, XXXVII (March, 1959), 236–242.

52 Harold F. Kaufman, "Toward an Interactional Conception of Community," *Social Forces*, XXXVIII (October, 1959), 8–17.

53 Willis A. Sutton, Jr., and Jiri Kolaja, "Elements of Community Action," *Social Forces*, XXXVIII (May, 1960), 325–331; Willis A. Sutton, Jr., and Jiri Kolaja "The Concept of Community," *Rural Sociology*, XXV (June, 1960), 197–203.

54 Sutton and Kolaja, "Elements of Community Action," *op. cit.*, p. 325.

55 Sutton and Kolaja, *ibid.*, give less obvious examples and explain their classification of events on the basis of a formal scheme.

logical studies to see what attributes communities have in common—what social structures, institutions, and other characteristics are found in all of them.[56] He contrasts villages and cities with prisons and mental institutions, because the latter are sometimes called communities. He shows that the social organization of villages and cities is integrated around three foci—space, cooperation, family—which are quite different from the foci of organization in what Goffman has called "total institutions".[57] Hillery concludes that to equate vills (cities and villages) with total institutions and call them all, indiscriminately, "communities" loses sight of much that is important about cities and villages. This work, like Hillery's earlier efforts to find agreement in the definitions of community used by different writers and his earlier analysis of community characteristics,[58] should go a long way toward clarifying the nature of the community as an object of study. Like the writings mentioned previously, it is, however, just a beginning. These writings bring greater conceptual clarity, but the ways in which community research will be improved thereby will still need to be demonstrated.

In addition to the problem of defining what they mean by the community, sociologists who wish to analyze communities and systems face the problem of determining community boundaries: where one community stops and the next one starts. This is not much of a problem in very small towns, in peasant societies where people go out to the fields from a central village, or—for some purposes—in metropolitan suburbs where school district lines and psychological identifications coincide with political boundaries. It is a problem in rural areas where farm homes are widely spaced, and in cities, except for some of their ethnic enclaves.

Efforts to delineate rural community boundaries have met with fairly good success. Galpin's pioneering techniques[59] have been refined, brought up-to-date, and used by rural sociologists such as Sanderson,[60] Sanders and Ensminger,[61] and Mayo.[62] Despite the ingenuity of these

---

56 Hillery, "Villages, Cities, and Total Institutions," op. cit.

57 Erving Goffman, "The Characteristics of Total Institutions," in Symposium on Preventive and Social Psychiatry (Washington: Walter Reed Army Institute of Research, 1957), pp. 43–84.

58 Hillery, "Definitions of Community: Areas of Agreement," op. cit.; Hillery, "The Folk Village: A Comparative Analysis," op. cit.

59 Charles J. Galpin, The Social Anatomy of an Agricultural Community, (Madison: Wisc. Agr. Exp. Sta., Bull. 34, 1915).

60 Dwight Sanderson, Locating the Rural Community (Ithaca: Cornell University Press, 1939).

61 Irwin T. Sanders and Douglas Ensminger, Alabama Rural Communities: A Study of Chilton County (Montevallo: Alabama College, Quarterly Bulletin 136, 1940).

62 Selz C. Mayo, "Testing Criteria of Rural Locality Groups," Rural Sociology, XIV (December, 1949), 317–325; Selz C. Mayo and Robert McD. Bobbitt, "Biracial Identity of Rural Locality Groups in Wake County, North Carolina," Rural Sociology, XV (December, 1950), 365–366.

efforts, some nagging problems remain. Mayo finds in a southern county that the white and Negro community boundaries do not coincide; presumably the same is true wherever two relatively segregated ethnic groups are interspersed in an area. Trade area boundaries may not coincide with boundaries based on other criteria, and even trade areas are not always unambiguous as the area boundaries may be different for different kinds of purchases. The areas identified by the usual techniques may not coincide with political boundaries, and the latter must be taken into account in many types of action programs.

The situation is still more complex in cities. Several studies have concluded that urban residents do not agree on the names and boundaries of the subareas where they live.[63] Ross,[64] in a recent Boston study, finds that people do tend to agree on the names and boundaries of local areas, and that the names of areas have a status-ascriptive function but do not coincide with trade areas except for local convenience goods like groceries which people buy very close to home; the small neighborhood rather than the urban subcommunity or natural area seems to be the meaningful trade area for groceries, drugs, and the like. Early Chicago sociologists noted that even in the 1920's, urban natural areas were already losing ground to specialized interest groupings which cut across spatial boundaries.[65] Paul Hatt, finding the same sort of conflicting boundaries based on different criteria which have bedeviled the rural sociologists, felt that the concept of urban natural areas had no meaningful empirical referent and should be abandoned.[66] But sociologists writing in the late 1950's and early 1960's have argued that meaningful subcommunities do characterize large cities; they point to homogeneity of demographic characteristics[67] and to locally based organizations and

---

[63] Roderick D. McKenzie, *The Neighborhood: A Study of Local Life in the City of Columbus, Ohio* (Chicago: University of Chicago Press, 1923); Svend Riemer, "Villagers in Metropolis," *British Journal of Sociology,* II (January, 1951), 31–43; Donald L. Foley, "Neighbors or Urbanites?" (Rochester, N. Y.: University of Rochester, 1952 [mimeographed]); and Smith, Form, and Stone, *op. cit.*

[64] H. Laurence Ross, "The Local Community: A Survey Approach," *American Sociological Review,* XXVII (February, 1962), 75–84. Throughout this paragraph we are indebted to Ross's discussion.

[65] For example, Zorbaugh, *op. cit.; cf.* Mowrer, *op. cit.,* on the suburbs.

[66] Paul K. Hatt, "The Concept of Natural Area," *American Sociological Review,* XI (June, 1946), 423–427. See also William H. Form, Joel Smith, Gregory P. Stone, and James Cowhig, "The Compatibility of Alternative Approaches to the Delimitation of Urban Sub-Areas," *American Sociological Review,* XIX (August, 1954), 434–440.

[67] The mounting avalanche of urban studies using "social area analysis" and related methods gives evidence of this. A few early examples are: Eshrev Shevky and Marilyn Williams, *The Social Areas of Los Angeles* (Berkeley: University of California Press,

community newspapers[68] as evidence of the vitality of urban sub-communities.

From these conflicting arguments and partially successful attempts to identify community boundaries, it seems that for most Americans, except small town dwellers and some suburbanites, "community" has no hard and fast empirical referent. Interaction, organizational membership, psychological identification, and various types of service mapping produce differing community or subcommunity boundaries. Some of the most successful efforts to delineate communities are not congruent with the emerging definition of the community as an arena of goal-directed locality-based interaction exemplified in the writings cited earlier by Kaufman and Sutton and Kolaja. Despite its inevitable difficulties, however, the problem is important for both social theory and social action, and therefore should not be abandoned. How can we analyze something we cannot even identify? And how can we succeed in action programs which fail to take account of people's behavioral and psychological definitions of reality? Perhaps we should continue to attack the problem with old methods, until better ones are devised. If these methods bring success in identifying communities, well and good; if they do not, perhaps the locality under study simply is not a community with meaningful boundaries, and we should leave the matter at that.

COMMUNITY POWER STRUCTURE AND DECISION-MAKING

This is a community-specific phenomenon *par excellence* by the Kaufman and Sutton-Kolaja definitions. The topic has received great atten-

---

1949); Eshrev Shevky and Wendell Bell, *Social Area Analysis* (Stanford, Calif.: Stanford University Press, 1955); Robert C. Tryon, *Identification of Social Areas by Cluster Analysis* (Berkeley and Los Angeles: University of California Press, 1955); Maurice D. Van Arsdol, Santo F. Camilleri, and Calvin F. Schmid, "An Investigation into the Generality of the Shevky Social Area Indexes," *American Sociological Review*, XXIII (June, 1958), 277–284. These writings, and our discussion, are concerned with the contemporary United States. Small homogeneous areas are also evident, perhaps more so, in preindustrial cities; see Gideon Sjoberg, *The Preindustrial City* (New York: The Free Press, 1960), pp. 80–107. It is also clear, though our discussion does not go into it, that unassimilated ethnic groups and lower class rural migrants very often form identifiable subcommunities with relatively clear boundaries, in both industrial and preindustrial cities. For recent studies showing this, see Erich Rosenthal, "Acculturation without Assimilation," *American Journal of Sociology*, LXVI (November, 1960), 275–288; and Janet Abu-Lughod, "Migrant Adjustment to City Life: The Egyptian Case," *American Journal of Sociology*, LXVII (July, 1961), 22–32. The existence and delineation of subcommunity boundaries become problematic when ethnic groups are not residentially segregated.

[68] Morris Janowitz, *The Community Press in an Urban Setting* (New York: The Free Press, 1952); Scott Greer, "Urbanism Reconsidered: A Comparative Study of Local Areas in a Metropolis," *American Sociological Review*, XXI (February, 1956), 19–25.

tion from sociologists and political scientists during the past decade, since Floyd Hunter's *Community Power Structure*[69] was published. Unfortunately the subject has been dealt with increasingly as a dispute over research methods and over the differing theoretical implications of the competing methods.[70]

Hunter and many others following him have used the "reputational" technique: go into the community and ask knowledgeable people who the leaders are. This technique seems to imply a monolithic power elite theory of power, or at least studies using the reputational method have tended to report that small cliques are said to run communities. Exponents of the method, some of whom have made useful refinements of it, include Alexander Fanelli,[71] Robert Agger,[72] Delbert Miller,[73] William D'Antonio,[74] and Charles Bonjean.[75]

Robert A. Dahl and various others, chiefly political scientists among whom Dahl's former graduate students at Yale are prominently in evidence, argue that the reputational method incorporates a self-fulfilling prophecy: the sociologist goes into a community and asks who the bosses are, then comes out with the conclusion that the community has bosses.[76] This group prefers the "decisions" approach in which an issue is traced

---

[69] Floyd Hunter, *Community Power Structure* (Chapel Hill: University of North Carolina Press, 1953).

[70] For concise, nonargumentative sociological discussions of community power and decision-making, see Peter H. Rossi, "Community Decision-Making," *Administrative Science Quarterly*, I (September, 1957), 415–443; and Richard A. Schermerhorn, *Society and Power* (New York: Random House, Inc., 1961), pp. 87–105.

A fuller and also balanced treatment is that of Wendell Bell, Richard J. Hill, and Charles R. Wright, *Public Leadership* (San Francisco: Chandler Publishing Company, 1961). A general discussion which has harsh things to say about the "pluralist" approach of the political scientists *(vide infra)* is presented in Thomas J. Anton, "Power, Pluralism, and Local Politics," *Administrative Science Quarterly*, VII (September, 1963), 425–457; this article contains an extensive bibliography. For several papers arguing on both sides of the reputation *vs.* decisions controversy, see William V. D'Antonio and Howard J. Ehrlich (eds.), *Power and Democracy in America* (Notre Dame, Ind.: University of Notre Dame Press, 1961).

[71] A. Alexander Fanelli, "A Typology of Community Leadership Based on Influence within the Leader Subsystem," *Social Forces*, XXXIV (May, 1956), 332–338.

[72] Robert E. Agger, "Power Attributions in the Local Community," *Social Forces*, XXXIV (May, 1956), 322–331.

[73] Delbert C. Miller, "Industry and Community Power Structure: A Comparative Study of an American and an English City," *American Sociological Review*, XXIII (February, 1958), 9–15.

[74] D'Antonio and Ehrlich, *op. cit.;* William V. D'Antonio and Eugene C. Erickson, "The Reputational Technique as a Measure of Community Power: An Evaluation Based on Comparative and Longitudinal Studies," *American Sociological Review*, XXVII (June, 1962), 362–376.

[75] Charles M. Bonjean, "Community Leadership: A Case Study and Conceptual Refinement," *American Journal of Sociology*, LXVIII (May, 1963), 672–681.

[76] Raymond E. Wolfinger, "Reputation and Reality in the Study of Community Power," *American Sociological Review*, XXV (October, 1960), 636–644.

from inception to resolution to see who brought influence to bear, and how, at various stages. Students using the decisions approach have tended to find a wider distribution of power; on any important community decision many people enter into the process at one time or another, and different decision-making groups are involved depending on the issue, rather than the same small group deciding everything.[77] A difficulty with this technique is that it captures only the overt manifestations of power. Without allowing "reputation" to enter the picture it is hard to observe that a man who says nothing and does nothing may nevertheless be wielding power if those who make the decision tailor their actions to suit what they think he would accept. Another difficulty, noted by Anton,[78] is that those interested in maintaining the *status quo* sometimes do so by preventing any "issue" from coming up for resolution, as in the case of the village board described by Vidich and Bensman.[79] Both of these situations—the tailoring of decisions to meet the perceived wishes of people who do not become overtly involved, and the suppression of potential conflicts so that no overt issue or decision arises—will show up in reputations but not always in identifiable decision-making events.

The topic of community decision-making is plainly of the highest possible significance, as a practical matter and for the theory of community organization. Therefore, it is to be regretted that the subject has become embroiled in polemics. The sanest course of action may be to do what Elaine Burgess did in her study of Negro power structure in a North Carolina city.[80] She used both main techniques and demonstrated that they are complementary rather than competing if they are skillfully used; in her study each revealed facts the other might have missed and they did not contradict each other in any essential way. A similar eclectic approach is used by political scientists like Edward C. Banfield and James Q. Wilson, who go after the facts of urban power without becoming overly concerned about the claims and counter-claims of alternative research strategies.[81]

---

[77] Robert A. Dahl, *Who Governs?* (New Haven: Yale University Press, 1961); Nelson W. Polsby, *Community Power and Political Theory* (New Haven: Yale University Press, 1963); Wolfinger, *op. cit.*; and Benjamin Walter, "Political Decision Making in Arcadia," in Chapin and Weiss, *op. cit.*, pp. 141–187. The basic theoretical ammunition for these assaults on Hunter was developed in Robert A. Dahl, "The Concept of Power," *Behavioral Science*, II (May, 1957), 201–215; and Robert A. Dahl, "A Critique of the Ruling Elite Model," *American Political Science Review*, LII (December, 1958), 463–469.

[78] Anton, *op. cit.*, p. 453.

[79] Vidich and Bensman, *op. cit.*, pp. 111–139.

[80] M. Elaine Burgess, *Negro Leadership in a Southern City* (Chapel Hill: University of North Carolina Press, 1962).

[81] Edward C. Banfield and James Q. Wilson, *City Politics* (Cambridge, Mass.: Harvard University Press and M. I. T. Press, 1963). This is only a recent example of the studies by political scientists, studies which probably number in the hundreds, many of which if

An obvious next step, not yet pursued very far in a systematic way, is to see how decision-making structures vary in accord with other community characteristics. This makes power structure the dependent variable in comparative community study. Some efforts have been made in this direction. Ernest A. T. Barth, reporting a study of ten Air Force Base host communities, finds a pyramidal elite structure in the large, stable communities; a diffuse structure in smaller, rapidly growing communities; and an amorphous and poorly integrated structure in small, static communities.[82] Barth's findings seem, superficially, to contradict the results of David Rogers's analysis of published studies of community power. Rogers concludes that the more differentiated the social structure of a community is, the less monolithic its elite will be;[83] and one might suppose that Barth's large communities would tend to be more socially differentiated than his smaller though growing communities. Perhaps community size and rate of growth—hence, degree of social differentiation and rate of differentiation—need to be distinguished as variables influencing the shape of community power structure.

Studies of industrial communities by Hart[84] and McKee[85] lend support to Rogers's hypothesis that social differentiation leads to power differentiation. They report that in the heavy industrial cities of Windsor, Ontario and Lorain, Ohio, the local business leaders must share power with representatives of absentee-owned big business, labor, and the Roman Catholic Church. Their conclusions suggest that Hunter may

---

examined with the present distinction in mind would turn out to have used varying combinations of the reputational and decisions approaches. Just as political scientists until recently ignored the many sociological studies of community power from *Middletown* onward, current community power analyses in both disciplines largely ignore the great wealth of material in earlier writings by political scientists and muckraking journalists. Big-city machines came in for an especially large amount of attention beginning with that of Lincoln Steffens. A recent study which compares different methods and, unlike Elaine Burgess, finds that the method makes a considerable difference in the findings, is Linton C. Freeman, Thomas J. Fararo, Warner Bloomberg, Jr., and Morris H. Sunshine, "Locating Leaders in Local Communities: A Comparison of Some Alternative Approaches," *American Sociological Review*, XXVIII (October, 1963), 791–798.

82 Ernest A. T. Barth, "Air Force Base-Host Community Relations: A Study in Community Typology," *Social Forces*, XLI (March, 1963), 260–264. See also Ernest A. T. Barth, "Community Influence Systems: Structure and Change," *Social Forces*, XL (October, 1961), 58–63.

83 David Rogers, "Community Political Systems: A Framework and Hypothesis for Comparative Studies," in Bert E. Swanson (ed.), *Current Trends in Comparative Community Studies* (Kansas City, Mo.: Community Studies, Inc., 1962), pp. 34–47.

84 C. W. M. Hart, "Industrial Relations Research and Industry," *Canadian Journal of Economics and Political Science*, XV (January, 1949), 53–73.

85 James B. McKee, "Status and Power in the Industrial Community: A Comment on Drucker's Thesis," *American Journal of Sociology*, LVIII (January, 1953), 364–370.

have been led into overgeneralization by the relatively slight development of competing interest groups in Atlanta in view of its size. Negroes
were weak, at least when Hunter's field work was done; the city was
rather solidly Protestant and lacked sizable ethnic minorities other than
Negroes; and organized labor was weak. Small wonder, even apart from
his research method, that he found a more monolithic and business-
dominated power structure than one might find in, for example, Detroit
or Buffalo.

A related study is reported by Amos Hawley,[86] who presents evidence
that a city with numerous high status people can get things done more
effectively than one whose class structure is weighted toward the lower
end of the scale. Specifically, Hawley finds that cities with large percentages of relatively high status people have had the best success in getting
urban renewal programs into operation, the reason (he feels) being their
readily available sources of elite leadership. Combining the Rogers and
Hawley conclusions, one might infer that effective democracy—conflict
resolution—is most likely where there is a large but differentiated elite
representing differing interests and able to bring them into active controversy so that something will be done to resolve differences of interest
one way or another.[87]

These studies are a promising beginning. More work is needed to
explain the structure and dynamics of power, using it as a dependent
variable in comparative research rather than as something simply to be
described in one community after another. Of single-community power
structure descriptions we may have enough by now, except as data for
comparative analysis.

ECOLOGY, OLD AND NEW

The old Park and Burgess ecology with its concentric rings[88] was an
extremely useful descriptive rubric for Chicago and some other cities. But
its assumption of subsocial (biotic) competition as the determinant of

---

86 Amos H. Hawley, "Community Power and Urban Renewal Success," *American
Journal of Sociology*, LXVIII (January, 1963), 422–431.

87 For a systematic treatment of the idea of democratic government as the development and resolution of conflict issues, see David B. Truman, *The Governmental Process*
(New York: Alfred A. Knopf, 1951).

88 Ernest W. Burgess, "Urban Areas," in T. V. Smith and Leonard D. White (eds.),
Chicago, An Experiment in Social Science Research (Chicago: University of Chicago
Press, 1929), pp. 113–138. The concentric zone hypothesis was only a limited, empirical
aspect of a broadly and theoretically conceived field of ecological investigation; but in
its influence on research it may have been more important than the broader theoretical
framework. For a discussion of classical ecological theory, see Robert Ezra Park, "Human
Ecology," *American Journal of Sociology*, XLII (July, 1936), 1–15.

urban spatial structure was challenged by a number of writers, Alihan's and Firey's critiques[89] probably being the best known. Its generality for the United States was questioned by the sector theory of Homer Hoyt[90] and the multiple nuclei theory of Harris and Ullman.[91] An even more fundamental blow was struck at the concentric zone hypothesis by writers like Gist,[92] the Dotsons,[93] and Sjoberg,[94] who showed that urban patterning is drastically different in foreign and preindustrial cities; the wealthy, for example, tend to live in the center of preindustrial cities. The concentric ring style of ecology has become passé and has been replaced by two main variants which avoid its problems.

One brand of ecology, though its proponents do not call it that, is the social area analysis of Shevky and Bell.[95] It proceeds from different theoretical considerations but is somewhat reminiscent of early Chicago ecology in its treatment of urban social areas. One might hazard the guess that the main utility of Shevky-Bell analysis will be as a methodological aid in controlling certain social variables—class, family life style, and ethnicity—which cluster in areas within which other variables can then be examined. It is a form of "contextual analysis" with the Census Bureau providing the data to construct the contexts. Analysis of this kind would fit under this paper's rubric of "social life as affected by community settings."

Another variant, which is self-consciously ecological, is the work of Otis Dudley Duncan and his associates and students. This deals with spatial attributes and distributions of social phenomena in the city. It makes use of available census data and modern statistical techniques to examine relationships among variables referring to aggregative community prop-

---

89 Milla A. Alihan, *Social Ecology* (New York: Columbia University Press, 1938); and Walter Firey, *Land Use in Central Boston* (Cambridge, Mass.: Harvard University Press, 1947). An excellent review of classical "Chicago" ecology and of writings criticizing it on theoretical and empirical grounds is given in George A. Theodorson (ed.), *Studies in Human Ecology* (Evanston, Ill.: Row, Peterson and Company, 1961), pp. 3–126.

90 Homer Hoyt, *The Structure and Growth of Residential Neighborhoods in American Cities* (Washington, D. C.: Federal Housing Administration, 1939).

91 Chauncey D. Harris and Edward L. Ullman, "The Nature of Cities," *Annals of the American Academy of Political and Social Science,* CCXLII (November, 1945), 7–17.

92 Noel P. Gist, "The Ecology of Bangalore, India: An East-West Comparison," *Social Forces,* XXXV (May, 1957), 356–365.

93 Floyd Dotson and Lillian Ota Dotson, "Ecological Trends in the City of Guadalajara," *Social Forces,* XXXII (May, 1954), 367–374.

94 Sjoberg, *loc. cit.*

95 See the references in footnote 69. Wendell Bell gives a good brief presentation of the case for social area analysis in "Social Areas: Typology of Neighborhoods," in Marvin B. Sussman (ed.), *Community Structure and Analysis, op. cit.,* pp. 61–92. Discussions of social area analysis, pro and con, are given in the Spring, 1962 issue of *Pacific Sociological Review,* V, 3–16, with articles by Wendell Bell and Scott Greer; Maurice D. Van Arsdol, Jr., Santo F. Camilleri, and Calvin F. Schmid; and Leo F. Schnore.

erties. Exponents of this brand of ecology besides Otis and Beverly Duncan include Leo F. Schnore,[96] Stanley Lieberson,[97] and Hal H. Winsborough.[98]

Duncan and his associates have strong ideas about ecology as an overall approach to sociology, very different from cultural, behavioral, social-psychological, and traditional social organization approaches.[99] They castigate others who use cultural or social-psychological variables such as values or attitudes in their analysis. Fortunately, like many other exponents of special viewpoints, they do not always adhere rigidly to their own rules when they do research. For example, the Duncans report that clerical workers, despite their lower incomes, live in higher status areas than skilled craftsmen, and their explanation of this—though they avoid using the proscribed word—appears to be that clerical workers' values are different.[100] What the Duncan school's ban on cultural or social-psychological variables seems to boil down to, in practice, is that one should infer these variables indirectly from aggregative Census data instead of examining them directly by asking people questions about values or by observing behavior at first hand.

Since these latter-day ecologists do not consistently adhere to their own strictures against the use of behavioral and cultural concepts in analysis, any more than did the early Chicago ecologists, their contributions to community sociology are already extensive, with the promise of more to come. They have focused attention on the importance of aggregative levels of analysis; they have developed, and used, highly efficient statistical techniques to deal with spatial distributions; and they have done pioneering work in comparative urban sociology and in the macro-analysis of national metropolitan structure.[101]

---

[96] The following articles by Schnore are representative: "Satellites and Suburbs," *Social Forces,* XXXVI (December, 1957), 121–127; "The Socio-Economic Status of Cities and Suburbs," *American Sociological Review,* XXVIII (February, 1963), 76–85.

[97] Stanley Lieberson, *Ethnic Patterns in American Cities* (New York: The Free Press, 1963).

[98] Hal H. Winsborough, "An Ecological Approach to the Theory of Suburbanization," *American Journal of Sociology,* LXVIII (March, 1963), 565–570.

[99] Otis Dudley Duncan and Leo F. Schnore, "Cultural, Behavioral, and Ecological Perspectives in the Study of Social Organization," *American Journal of Sociology,* LXV (September, 1959), 132–146; "Comment" by Peter H. Rossi, pp. 146–149; "Rejoinder" by Duncan and Schnore, pp. 149–153.

[100] Otis Dudley Duncan and Beverly Duncan, "Residential Distribution and Occupational Stratification," *American Journal of Sociology,* LX (March, 1955), 493–503.

[101] See especially Otis Dudley Duncan, W. Richard Scott, Stanley Lieberson, Beverly Duncan, and Hal H. Winsborough, *Metropolis and Region* (Baltimore: The Johns Hopkins Press, 1960). Related work without the accompanying ideological statements has also been done by a number of sociologists including Kingsley Davis, Jack P. Gibbs, and Walter T. Martin.

CONCLUDING REMARKS

Even this highly selective discussion of some leading kinds of community research makes it clear that the field is a broad one, and, if the
rate of research activity is any sign, a healthy one. We will conclude with
some evaluative remarks and suggestions.

First, comparative community analysis using variables and relationships among them should receive more emphasis than it has. In this way
we can develop more theoretical propositions and test them and refine
them on the basis of the tests. The logic ideally should be that of survey
analysis, with variables controlled through cross-tabulation. This is less
easily managed when the unit of observation is an entire community
than when it is an individual with his attitudes and simple behavioral
manifestations of them, but it should be kept in view as an ideal. If we
come as close to this as Max Weber did in his comparative analysis of
societies—for example, in his *Protestant Ethic and the Spirit of Capitalism,* in which he roughly matched societies on social structure and
technology and varied religion as an independent variable to explain
economic systems as the dependent variable—then few will be inclined to
criticize us for imperfections in our data.

For variables to examine in these kinds of studies, we can draw inspiration from the traditional typologies. These embody numerous distinct
variables; Wirth mentions dozens in his characterization of urbanism.[102]
Communities can be characterized in numerous ways derived from the
folk-urban typologies and the ways in which these characteristics do and
do not go together can be discovered, as grist for analysis, from available
literature. Future ethnographic studies of single communities can be
enriched if they have as an explicit goal the contribution they might
make to comparative analysis.

Nevertheless, we should not abandon the traditional "community
study" as a type of research. Studies of communities in depth are not only
the raw material for cross-community comparisons; they are valuable in
themselves. Even if we take the construction of abstract theories as the
major goal of sociology, an additional goal is to shed light on how people
live, here and now, in a way that cannot be done without the insights of
sociology. It is significant that a goodly number of community case
studies have made their way into commercial paperback editions; this
seems to indicate that the educated reading public outside the field
accepts community studies as a contribution to social understanding in
which sociologists excel in a distinctive way.

Some subjects which have customarily been investigated within single

---

102 Wirth, "Urbanism as a Way of Life," *op. cit.*

community contexts need not, however, be limited to this kind of research. Besides studying the power structures and class systems of individual communities, we need to classify them and explain them on the basis of other community characteristics. Some people, including Lloyd Warner himself,[103] have already attempted some of this, but the effort has not been carried forward systematically or cumulatively. Like sharpening the typological concepts, this is a task for comparative analysis.

Finally, we have made no mention of one very important and burgeoning activity of community sociologists: research and action programs in community development.[104] We have left this area out of our discussion not because it is unimportant—clearly it is of major importance—but because it is, rather than a separate area of theoretical knowledge, an area in which different areas of knowledge intersect. Almost every one of the subjects of investigation mentioned earlier in this paper has some bearing on community development, though doubtless some more than others. Power structure, stratification, and networks of interpersonal influence would seem especially relevant. Like other practical concerns, community development programs need to derive ideas from basic research; but in addition, they can contribute to basic knowledge if they are conducted and reported, as the best of them are, with this objective.

---

[103] Warner and Low, *The Social System of the Modern Factory, op. cit.*

[104] For a useful overview of the field of community development, see the March, 1958 issue of *Rural Sociology* (Vol. 23), with articles by Irwin T. Sanders, Howard W. Beers, Christopher Sower and Walter Freeman, Robert A. Polson, and Charles R. Hoffer. See also the journal, *International Review of Community Development,* published in Rome, Italy, *passim.*

Part Two

Bases of Community

Organization

CHAPTER II

Familial Bonds, Traditions,
and Ties of Friendship

Before we can begin to measure degree of "community," or select controlled variables of community characteristics as Simpson suggests, we must ascertain what it is that holds a group of people together in a certain pattern that we identify as a community. In their definition of community Arensberg and Kimball referred to this problem: "...Within each community one finds the economic, political, religious, social, even familial activities which create cohesion among its members. . . ." What binds one community together might be completely without meaning in another community that lacks the strong tradition, familial ties, a type of economic system, or religious identification, found in the first community. Thus communities must be typed according to their dominant themes.

The community studies included in this section are placed into one of three broad categories that reflect the dominant theme of the community: A. Familial Bonds, Traditions, and Ties of Friendship; B. Structures of Conflict: Ethnic Relations and Sub-Communities; and C. Political-Economic Structures. The differences, even within categories, are vast, which illustrates the diversity of community types. This diversity brings home the realization that suggesting any "universals" for communities would be risky indeed; for the job of establishing an adequate typology of communities has yet to be done. Without such a typology we are at a loss to place a given community in relation to others.

The categories used here should not be viewed as a developed typology; rather, it is a first step in classifying communities along the lines pioneered by Tönnies. From primary group ties as the dominant theme of community, i.e., family, friendship, to increasingly impersonal elements that are contained in political parties and economic structures, we see a progression from *gemeinschaft* to *gesellschaft*.

Tönnies' typology presents the notions of "natural will vs. rational will." We take license to equate "natural will" with a frame of mind created by strong primary group pressures that seeks to maintain face-to-face relationships, and "rational will" with that frame of mind nutured by, and content with, an atmosphere of impersonal, secondary group pressures. Tönnies' typology suits our purpose better than Redfield's "Folk-Urban" continuum for several reasons. First, because many of the differences we observe are between equally urban communities. Second, folk–urban differences do not go very far toward explaining the nature of sub-communities, or ethnic enclaves which we call "structures of conflict." Although primary-secondary group characteristics are not altogether satisfactory in solving these problems, this typology can place an ethnic enclave in relation to the broader community that has isolated it. The nature of life within the ghetto is much more intensely personal, if only because all members of the group can identify with each other (e.g., "soul brothers") in the face of external pressure. The existence of the urban sub-community cannot be explained as a holdover of "folk" community when it is populated by long-term urbanites; but it might be explained on the basis of the alternative personal patterns of interaction that it provides for the urban dweller who finds himself adrift in a world of secondary relationships in which he feels insignificant or perhaps even forcibly rejected.

FAMILY BONDS, TRADITIONS, AND TIES OF FRIENDSHIP

The common characteristic of the communities in this section is the informal, face-to-face basis of organization found in each. No external pressure, dominant economic institution, nor political charter is needed to draw the members of these communities together. Their common history, or familial ties or shared value orientations, is sufficient to create "community."

The variability within this category is still great. The Italian communities studied by Banfield and Moss and Cappannari have little basis for "community" other than that in the web of suspicion with which the Italian peasant views the world, the fellow villager, although suspect, is preferable to outsiders. Banfield typifies his community as a group of "amoral familists" who share virtually no community sentiment but concern themselves only with the welfare of their immediate family. Thus, although the community is established on the basis of primary relationships, it is anything but the cohesive body that would imply.

The family ties that create the Tennessee Ridge community studied by Matthews do create this close community sentiment to the degree that migrants to a distant urban area seek out community kin and continue to identify with the group even though they are over 500 miles from home. Likewise, the familial ties characteristic of the Irish community not only provide the individual with a sense of belonging, they provide the basis of the economy which links town to countryside. Indeed, without this link of family, the Irish townsman engaged in retail trade lacks a sufficient clientele to survive inasmuch as Irish countrymen buy from townsmen who are kin.

The family is not the only informal basis for community; in Gosforth, the English town studied by Williams, a sense of local identification (or perhaps provincialism) distinguishes "Gosfer folk" from all others and newcomers are accepted or rejected on the basis of how well they fit into the local way of life.

Kin ties may be overruled by ties of "friendship" or patronage such as Pitt-Rivers observed in a Spanish pueblo. A network of patron-client relationships based upon mutual obligations and dependence create "community" in this situation. The dominant theme of the pueblo is the system of egalitarian values based upon reciprocal service; all other considerations are secondary.

Egalitarian values also provide the basis for much of the community feeling in Bremnes, the Norwegian island parish studied by Barnes. Bremnes is a fairly complex community, however, so that although friendship provides the basis for much of life, political decisions and the activities of voluntary organizations are handled formally through committee structure.

The role that tradition and shared value orientation can play in the shaping of a community is illustrated in Vogt and O'Dea's comparison of Rimrock, a Mormon community, with Homestead, a non-Mormon settlement. Several examples illustrate that the shared values of Rimrock enabled it to take effective action while the more individualistic Homesteaders were frozen in inaction.

If any generalization is to be drawn from this section it would have to be that although primary relationships can provide the basis for com-

munity, no common community type need result. As the readings that
follow illustrate, the family may draw a community together tightly as it
does in Ireland or the Tennessee Ridge country, or it may severely strain
the basis for even minimal community sentiment as is the case in the
examples of Southern Italian communities.

5. The Moral Basis of
a Backward Society

EDWARD C. BANFIELD

Americans are used to a buzz of activity having as its purpose, at least in part, the advancement of community welfare. For example, a single issue of the weekly newspaper published in St. George, Utah (population 4,562), reports a variety of public-spirited undertakings. The Red Cross is conducting a membership drive. The Business and Professional Women's Club is raising funds to build an additional dormitory for the local junior college by putting on a circus in which the members will be both clowns and "animals." The Future Farmers of America (whose purpose is "to develop agricultural leadership, cooperation, and citizenship through individual and group leadership") are holding a father-son banquet. A local business firm has given an encyclopedia to the school district. The Chamber of Commerce is discussing the feasibility of building an all-weather road between two nearby towns. "Skywatch" volunteers are being signed up. A local church has collected $1,393.11 in pennies for a children's hospital 350 miles away. The county farm bureau is flying one of its members to Washington, 2,000 miles away, to participate in discussions of farm policy. Meetings of the Parent-Teachers Associations are

SOURCE: Reprinted with permission of the Macmillan Company from *The Moral Basis of a Backward Society* by Edward C. Banfield. Copyright by The Free Press of Glencoe, a Division of the Macmillan Company.

being held in the schools. "As a responsible citizen of our community," the notice says, "you belong in the PTA."

Montegrano, a commune of 3,400 persons, most of them poor farmers and laborers, in the province of Potenza in southern Italy,[1] presents a striking contrast. The commune consists of a town, lying like a white beehive against the top of a mountain, and twenty-seven square miles of surrounding fields and forests. One-third of the Montegranesi live on scattered farms at the base of the mountain and in the valley around it. The others live in the town, but since they are mostly farmers and laborers, their waking hours are spent in the fields below the town or on the footpaths that wind between town and country.

No newspaper is published in Montegrano or in any of the thirteen other towns lying within view on nearby hilltops. Occasional announcements of public interest—"there are fish for sale in the *piazza* at 100 *lire* per *chilo*"—are carried by a town crier wearing an official cap, who toots a brass horn to attract attention. Official notices are posted in the salt and tobacco store, a government monopoly, and on a bulletin board in the town hall. Several copies of three or four newspapers published in Rome, Naples, and Potenza come into town by bus every day or two, but these of course do not deal much with local affairs and they are read by very few.

Twenty-five upper class men constitute a "circle" and maintain a clubroom where members play cards and chat. Theirs is the only association. None of the members has ever suggested that it concern itself with community affairs or that it undertake a "project."[2]

The merchants of Montegrano are well aware of the importance to them of good roads. They would not, however, expect to be listened to by the authorities who decide which roads are to be improved. A Montegrano man might write a letter to the provincial authorities in Potenza or

---

[1] Italy is divided into 92 provinces. The province of Potenza includes 97 communes and covers an area of 414 square miles. Its population was 435,495 in 1951. Potenza and Matera provinces together comprise the region of Lucania, or, as it was formerly called, Basilicata.

For a brief, factual account in English of the physical and social geography of southern Italy, see Robert E. Dickinson, *The Population Problem of Southern Italy,* Syracuse University Press, 1955.

[2] According to J. S. McDonald (in a personal communication), Calabrian towns over 2,000 population generally have a "circle of nobles" or "circle of gentlemen" (*circulo dei civili*) and sometimes a "circle of workingmen," but "they function only as rendezvous. However, back–street drinking dens are important: here the local criminals meet. Otherwise there is no continuous membership of a recreation group (outside nuclear family–clique) for the worker–cultivator class."

to the newspaper there, but it is unlikely that his doing so would make any difference. In fact, the officials would be likely to resent what they would consider interference in their affairs.

There are no organized voluntary charities in Montegrano. An order of nuns struggles to maintain an orphanage for little girls in the remains of an ancient monastery, but this is not a local undertaking. The people of Montegrano contribute nothing to the support of it, although the children come from local families. The monastery is crumbling, but none of the many half-employed stone masons has ever given a day's work to its repair. There is not enough food for the children, but no peasant or landed proprietor has ever given a young pig to the orphanage.

There are two churches in town and two priests, one the son of a Sicilian peasant and the other the son of a prosperous Montegrano merchant. The churches do not carry on charitable or welfare activities, and they play no part at all in the secular life of the community. Even in religious matters their influence is not very extensive. The life of the town goes on very much as usual on Sunday mornings: the artisans are at work on a new building as usual at seven o'clock, the stores are all open, and the country people are on their way down the mountainside with their donkeys. Of the 3,400 people in the commune, not more than 350 hear mass on Sunday. These are mostly women. The few men who go to mass remain standing near the door as if to signify that they are not unduly devout. When the collection plate is passed, many people give nothing and few give more than a half a cent (five or ten *lire*). By tradition the men of Montegrano are anti-clerical. The tradition goes back a century or more to a time when the church had vast holdings in southern Italy and was callous and corrupt. Today it owns only one small farm in Montegrano, and the village priests are both known to be kindly and respectable men. Nevertheless priests in general—so many Montegranesi insist—are money-grubbers, hypocrites, and worse.

When members of the upper class are asked who is known as particularly public-spirited—what private persons are apt to take the initiative in dealing with matters which involve the public welfare—a few mention the Baron di Longo and Colonel Pienso, both of whom live in Rome and are believed to have great influence there. Most people, however, say that no one in Montegrano is particularly public-spirited, and some find the idea of public-spiritedness unintelligible. When an interviewer explained to a young teacher that a "public-spirited" person is one who acts for the welfare of the whole community rather than for himself alone, the teacher said:

No one in town is animated by a desire to do good for all of the population. Even if sometimes there is someone apparently animated by this desire, in reality he is interested in his own welfare and he does his own business.

Even the saints, for all their humility, looked after themselves. And men, after all, are only made of flesh and spirit.

Another teacher said that not only is public-spiritedness lacking, but many people positively want to prevent others from getting ahead.

Truly, I have found no one who interests himself in the general welfare. On the contrary, I know there is tremendous envy of either money or intelligence.

In some southern Italian towns the gentry are said to be indifferent to the misery of the peasants and consumed with hatred for each other. This is not the case in Montegrano. The leading families there get along well together, and many upper class people view the peasant's plight with evident sympathy. These people are not led by their sympathy to try to change things, however.

* * *

The affairs of the commune are conducted by a mayor and elected council and by the provincial civil service which is headed by a prefect in Potenza. The mayor and council propose, but it is the prefect who disposes. Even to buy an ashtray for the city hall requires approval from Potenza; ordinarily, after a certain amount of delay, the decisions of the local elected officials are approved, but this is not always the case and, of course, approval can never be counted upon.

The prefect is represented in Montegrano by the secretary of the commune, a career civil servant assigned from Potenza. With the assistance of two clerks, the secretary transacts all of the routine business of the town. This includes especially the maintenance of tax records, of vital statistics, and the making of disbursements on order of the higher authorities.

The mayor is elected for a four-year term and receives no salary. He represents the commune on all official occasions, supervises the municipal officers, is the legal representative of the commune in dealings with third parties, and has certain powers of certification. In practice, the elected council has little power. In fact, it is seldom possible to get a quorum of its members together at the mayor's call.

The elected officials are office-workers, artisans, and prosperous farmers rather than persons of the highest status. The mayor, for example, is a retired non-commissioned army officer and petty landowner. His council includes as deputy mayor a retired non-commissioned officer in the *carabinieri* police, four artisans or store-keepers, five office-workers, five teachers, two farmers, and a lawyer. The lawyer is the only one who is an "upper-upper," and even he is not of the very highest status.

The officials of the commune have nothing to do with the schools. A director of schools, independently responsible to Potenza, resides in Montegrano and has jurisdiction over the elementary schools of several communes. Public works, another important function, is also administered altogether apart from the elected local government.

The police *(carabinieri)* also are under a separate authority, the Ministry of Justice in Rome. The officer in charge locally (the *"maresciallo"*) cooperates closely with the local authorities, but he is in no sense "their man." As a matter of policy, he is not a native of the town to which he is assigned, and he and his men are under instruction not to fraternize much with the townspeople. The attitude of the *carabinieri* towards all classes is generally good-tempered, businesslike, and aloof.

* * *

What accounts for the absence of organized action in the face of pressing local problems? Why, for example, is nothing done about the schools? To the peasants, many of whom are desperately anxious for their children to get ahead, the lack of educational opportunity is one of the bitterest facts of life. Upper class people are affected too; some of them would like to live in Montegrano and cannot do so because it would cost too much to send their children away to a boarding school. One might think, then, that improvement of the local school would be an important local issue—one on which people would unite in political parties or otherwise. Failing to persuade the government to build a *media* school, upper class volunteers might teach an additional grade or two. Or, if this is too much to expect, the bus schedule might be changed so that the Montegrano children could commute to nearby Basso for the higher grades. However, such possibilities have not been considered.

The nearest hospital is in Potenza, five hours away by automobile. For years Montegrano people have complained that the state has not built a hospital in the village. The doctor and two or three other people have written letters to Rome urging that one be built, but that is as far as the effort to get one has gone. Candidates for local office do not campaign on the hospital "issue," and there has been no organized effort to bring pressure to bear upon the government. Nor has there been any consideration of stopgap measures such as might be taken locally—for example, equipping an ambulance to carry emergency cases from Montegrano and other nearby towns to Potenza.

These, of course, are only two of many possible examples of needs which would give rise to community action in some countries,[3] but about which nothing is done in Montegrano.

The question of why nothing is done raises other questions. Why are the political parties themselves so unconcerned with local issues? Why is there no political "machine" in Montegrano, or even any stable and effective party organization? What explains the marked differences in the appeal of left, center, and right from town to town among towns that on the surface seem so much alike? What explains the erratic behavior of the electorate in a single town from one election to the next? And why do those elected to office at once lose credit with their supporters?

A PREDICTIVE HYPOTHESIS

A very simple hypothesis will make intelligible all of the behavior about which questions have been raised and will enable an observer to predict how the Montegranesi will act in concrete circumstances. The hypothesis is that the Montegranesi act as if they were following this rule:

> Maximize the material, short-run advantage of the nuclear family; assume that all others will do likewise.

One whose behavior is consistent with this rule will be called an "amoral familist." The term is awkward and somewhat imprecise (one who follows the rule is without morality only in relation to persons outside the family—in relation to family members, he applies standards of right and wrong; one who has no family is of course an "amoral individualist"), but no other term seems better.

. . . Some logical implications of the rule are set forth. It will be seen that these describe the facts of behavior in the Montegrano district. The coincidence of facts and theory does not "prove" the theory. However, it does show that the theory will explain (in the sense of making intelligible and predictable) much behavior without being contradicted by any of the facts at hand.

1. *In a society of amoral familists, no one will further the interest of the group or community except as it is to his private advantage to do so.*

In other words, the hope of material gain in the short-run will be the only motive for concern with public affairs.

This principle is of course consistent with the entire absence of civic

---

[3] Cf. for example the handling of the school problem in the southern French village described by Laurence Wylie in *Village in the Vaucluse* (Cambridge, Mass.: Harvard University Press, 1957), pp. 223–227.

improvement associations, organized charities, and leading citizens who take initiative in public service.[4]

2. *In a society of amoral familists only officials will concern themselves with public affairs, for only they are paid to do so. For a private citizen to take a serious interest in a public problem will be regarded as abnormal and even improper.*

Cavalier Rossi, one of the largest landowners of Montegrano, and the mayor of the nearby town of Capa, sees the need for many local public improvements. If he went to the prefect in Potenza as mayor of Capa, they would listen to him, he says. But if he went as a private citizen of Montegrano, they would say, "Who are you?" As a private citizen he might help a worker get a pension, but as for schools, hospitals, and such things, those are for the authorities to dole out. A private citizen can do nothing.

* * *

3. *In a society of amoral familists, organization (i.e., deliberately concerted action) will be very difficult to achieve and maintain. The inducements which lead people to contribute their activity to organizations are to an important degree unselfish (e.g., identification with the purpose of the organization) and they are often non-material (e.g., the intrinsic interest of the activity as a "game"). Moreover, it is a condition of successful organization that members have some trust in each other and some loyalty to the organization. In an organization with high morale it is taken for granted that they will make small sacrifices, and perhaps even large ones, for the sake of the organization.*

The only formal organizations which exist in Montegrano—the church and the state—are of course provided from the outside; if they were not, they could not exist. Inability to create and maintain organization is clearly of the greatest importance in retarding economic development in the region.[5]

* * *

---

4 The importance of voluntary associations in the United States has been explained by their function in facilitating social mobility. This explanation is not incompatible with the one given above.

Those who belong to "do-good" organizations secure gratifications (e.g., status, power, neighborly association, etc.) which have nothing to do with the public-spirited purposes for which the organizations exist. Even so, these public-spirited purposes are not unimportant in the motivations of the participants. Moreover, most of the self-regarded ends which are served do not relate to material gain, or at least not to material gain in the short-run.

5 Max Weber remarked in *The Protestant Ethic and the Rise of Capitalism,* Allen and Unwin ed. (London, 1930) p. 57 that "the universal reign of absolute unscrupulous-

4. *The amoral familist will value gains accruing to the community only insofar as he and his are likely to share them. In fact, he will vote against measures which will help the community without helping him because, even though his position is unchanged in absolute terms, he considers himself worse off if his neighbors' position changes for the better. Thus it may happen that measures which are of decided general benefit will provoke a protest vote from those who feel that they have not shared in them or have not shared in them sufficiently.*

---

ness in the pursuit of selfish interests by the making of money has been a specific characteristic of precisely those countries whose bourgeois-capitalistic development, measured according to Occidental standards, has remained backward. As every employer knows, the lack of *coscienziosita* of the laborers of such countries, for instance Italy as compared with Germany, has been, and to a certain extent still is, one of the principal obstacles to their capitalistic development."

6. Patterns of Kinship, Comparaggio and Community in a South Italian Village

LEONARD M. MOSS
STEPHAN C. CAPPANNARI

In an earlier day, the strategic position of Cortina d'Aglio,[1] astride the confluence of three rivers, served the community by affording a degree of protection against the incursions of brigands and warring barons. For more than ten centuries Cortina remained in relative isolation. In 1875, the post office was established and ten years later, the telegraph line reached the village. By 1892, Cortina was included on the somewhat irregular stagecoach route to the provincial capital. Geographically, Cortina remains relatively isolated to the present day; the nearest secondary State highway is some ten kilometers away.

ACKNOWLEDGMENT: Based on a paper presented to the Ohio Valley Sociological Society, Columbus, Ohio, 27 April, 1957. The authors wish to acknowledge their indebtedness to Duilio Peruzzi and Armand DeGaetano for their aid in assembling materials. The field work by Cappannari was completed in 1954–55 under the auspices of the Fulbright Research Program and the Wenner-Gren Foundation; by Moss in 1955–56 under the Fulbright Research Program.

SOURCE: Reprinted with permission of the authors and publisher from *Anthropological Quarterly*, Vol. XXXIII, No. 1 (January, 1960), published by The Catholic University of America Press.

[1] A pseudonym for a village in the Molisan Appenines.

There is little to differentiate Cortina from hundreds of villages in South Italy. Its history is virtually undistinguished from that of southern Italy generally. Eighty-six per cent of its labor force is engaged in agriculture. Unlike the rest of the South, Cortina exhibits a well-established pattern of individual land-ownership among its peasantry. The basic farming pattern of the Agliese is one of self-sufficiency. Each farmer attempts to supply all of the agricultural needs of his family; he rarely produces a marketable surplus from his small (2 to 3 *hectare* [5 to 7½ acres]) holding. As in most of the South, the farmer generally lives in the village and journeys to his land each day; 81% of the 3532 residents live in the village proper.

The rigors of eking out a meager living from barren soil, the geographic and social isolation of the village, and illiteracy have contributed, over the centuries, to a limited horizon for the peasantry. For the average southern peasant, his world begins and ends with the confines of the village. Even with the advent of the radio, the peasant continues to identify himself with the village. Through bitter experience he has learned to trust, or distrust least, those who live within the sound of the local church bell (*campanilismo*). Government is a meaningless and nebulous concept to the peasant. Rome is distant and epitomizes those who have lived off the labors of the farmer. The land owner, the police, the tax collector, and even the priest have come to symbolize those who are out to milk the peasant.

The traveling merchants who come to the village during the *fiere* (fair) which accompany a *festa* (feast day) are viewed as unscrupulous sharpies. They are wily and full of big city tricks. Even the local merchants are not to be fully trusted. But if one must deal with someone outside the circle of kin, better a *paisano* (fellow-villager) than a stranger. Everyone knows that it is best to "marry women and buy cattle from your fellow villagers."

Most villages in the South exhibit a degree of *campanilismo*. Cortina, however, differs in this respect. There are two church parishes in this village; Santa Maria Assunta surrounds the old castle at the crest of the hill; San Silvestro extends down the hill toward the Valley. The Agliese refer to the parishes as: Upper Land and Lower Land (*Terra di Sopra* and *Terra di Basso*). As we noted, Cortina does not exhibit the usual *campanilismo,* instead it is a case of double-*campanilismo* based on parish lines.

The residents of Cortina claim that the two parishes exhibit such vast differences in pronounciation as to warrant the use of the term "dialect differences." Local conjecture maintains that the two parishes stem from two different "ethnic" groups; the Upper Towners claim that they are of indigenous stock and that the Lower Towners are later arrivals, probably from the region of Naples. These claims are supported by the residents by citing dialect variations. The Upper "dialect" has a "French accent" and the Lower "dialect" is labeled as being more like the Neapolitan pronounciation. A comparison of "dialect" forms does not lend strong support to the claims of "differential" origins. However, what *is* important is the belief on the part of the villagers that the "dialects" differ *and* the fact that they act in accordance with that belief.

From the viewpoint of the Upper Villagers the Lower Town residents are less civil and inferior socially. The Upper Towners regard themselves as possessing a superior "cultured" background; the old castle is located in that part of town and the ducal families of French and Spanish origin lived there.

Should a man from the lower village come to a dance being held in the Upper Town, he would be invited to dance. However, if an upper villager were to go to a dance in the other part of town he might be allowed in but he would not be invited to dance. Of course, he probably would not want to dance with the women anyhow since all Uppers know that the Lower women are whores.

The Lowers are regarded as being too intense in their card playing. A case was cited where lower village men played cards behind locked doors on Christmas Eve; the game went on all through the night and all the next day.

The Upper townspeople regard their hilltop vantage point as more favorable than the depressive atmosphere of the Lower town. The air is fresher, the streets are better, the piazza is nicer, the people are more genteel, in essence, the whole town is a better place to live in. The Lowers, obviously, suffer more, their town is not as nice; because of this the Lowers are not as civil. Even worse, the Lowers are more given to *campanilismo* even though they have no reason to take pride in their town.

From the other side of the parish boundary one receives a different picture. From the viewpoint of the Lowers we learn that the Uppers are not really superior but simply put on false airs. The Lowers claim that they work much harder than the Uppers. The Upper villagers resort to theft and are untrustworthy.

There are more refinements of life in the Lower village according to its residents. The Lower town bars have toilets and the Upper bars do not. The "magnificent" outdoor urinal in the Lower piazza is a great source of local pride. There is even one house with a bidet. The Lower villagers regard their pronounciation as softer and more pleasant than the harsh, French-like accents of the Uppers. On the whole, the Lowers consider themselves as more sincere and less devious than the Uppers.

There are some differences between the two parishes that can be verified by independent observation. Each parish tends toward endogamy. When mixed marriages do occur, it is usually women of the Lower village who marry Upper village men. Upper village women rarely marry Lower village men since they do not wish to live so far out in the country (less than one kilometer from the central piazza).

More artisans and merchants are found in the Upper town. This is probably a hold-over from the service functions performed by the ducal retainers during the feudal period. More farmers live in the Lower village but the Lower village exhibits a higher out-migration rate. In-migrants come from other villages in the Abruzzi and from elsewhere along the eastern coast; they are considered as being of another ethnic group by the Agliese.

Although governed by the same mayor and town council, the citizens of the two parishes share little community feeling in common. Political divisions reflect, to some extent, the split based on *campanilismo*. There are more Communists in the Lower town, more Socialists in the Upper. The majority coalition, a local slate, draws its strength from both parishes. The current coalition, a new alignment of forces since the 1952 election, is right-of-center and includes the neo-Fascists. The political party, as an example of a voluntary association, is, at best, an unstable compromise of highly individualistic attitudes. A cynical Italian joke underlines the problem: A political party composed of five Italians will have six political philosophies.[2]

According to both archpriests in Cortina, religious unity in the village is conspicuously absent. (According to most informants, religion itself is absent). The two parishes have different patron saints and their religious calendars differ somewhat. Despite many attempts on the part of the clergy to weld a bond between the two parishes the division continues. In recent years, the archpriests have exchanged pulpits on varying occasions; this excited little enthusiasm on the part of the parishioners. There are but two *feste* shared in common between the parishes: San Vitale (Patron of the Upper town) and San Antonio Padova (Patron of the Lower town). These *feste* cover two days (20-21 August). Each year a committee is created to collect funds to defray the expenses of the festival (fireworks, a marching and concert band, flowers, etc.). The cost of the

---

[2] For a discussion of the inability of Italian villagers to effect political compromise see Edward C. Banfield, *The Moral Basis of a Backward Community*, New York: The Free Press, 1958.

feste generally exceeds $500; the Agliese now living in Rome and the United States contribute about 60 percent of the funds, and the balance is collected locally. At one time, a joint confraternity composed of members of both parishes arranged the celebrations but, like most voluntary associations, fell apart because of inter-parish and inter-familial rivalries.

In one respect, the parishes seem to be united in that church attendance is, by and large, limited to women. The women take a more active interest in religion than do the men but it should be noted that religious activities involve a minority of the population. The two archpriests united in forming a *Circolo ACLI* (Workers' Catholic Action Circle) and furnished a club house that is used, for the most part, by the two archpriests.

There are few examples, at the community level, of voluntary associations. A war veterans organization exists in Cortina but there is no active membership. The deep-seated *individualismo*, so basic to South Italy, frustrates the creation of common solutions to common problems. There exists a circle of intellectuals, a loosely-knit semi-formalized association, composed of the mayor, pharmacist, attorney, physician, the school teachers, and a minor civil servant (who now lives in Rome but vacations in Cortina each summer). The members pay dues of lire 500 (80 cents) per year and meet, from time to time, at the bar on the Upper town piazza. Aside from the discussions of politics and soccer, this group attempted to create a program of practical education for the school children. They planned to teach the children how to write business letters, use a telephone, make application for jobs, and a host of other matters not covered by the public school curriculum. The program was aborted by a lack of interest on the part of the residents.

One may legitimately wonder about the apparent lack of commonality of feeling in Cortina. It is assumed that village society would tend toward primary group relations within the community. It is assumed, too, that the isolated, relatively homogeneous, peasant community would exhibit a high degree of moral integration and, hence, a strong bond of community feeling.

We have, of course, documented the inter-parish rivalry that exists within the village and this, perhaps, explains, to some degree, why there is little community feeling that cuts across parish boundaries. Yet, it does not explain the lack of community feeling within each parish.

The economic factor cannot be overlooked in this analysis. In the words of one informant: "Life is hell and work is a beast." The economic struggle occupies many of the waking hours of the peasantry. But, this explanation is insufficient in itself to account for the almost complete lack of voluntary associations at the community level.

The families of Cortina, like the South Italian family generally, exhibit a high degree of solidarity. Deeply-rooted traditions plus a pattern of economic self-sufficiency help sustain the monolithic structure of the family.[3]

In Cortina, as elsewhere in the South, the neolocal nuclear family derives its significance from the larger *famiglia*. Marriage is, of course, the union between two *famiglie*; and, the nuclear unit is considered part of the larger consanguineal and affinal family. However, greatest reliance is placed upon the nuclear unit, which becomes a *personal community* for its members.[4] Banfield (1958) identifies the "amoral familism" which stems from this system of support for the nuclear family as one of the major reasons for the near-chaotic political picture of South Italy. In Cortina one normally includes cousins to the third degree as part of the family; although the title *cugino* may be attached to even more remote kin. The term *fratello-cugino* (brother cousin) is limited to first cousins. However, older cousins, regardless of degree, are usually addressed as *zio* (dialect *z'zi*) (uncle). Again, the term *z'zi (z'iutt-e)* or *z'ia (z'iotta)* (aunt) is often used to signify any older member of the kin group.

While separate terms are used to designate father-in-law *(suocero)* and mother-in-law *(suocera)*, the title of address is always *papá* and *mamá* (as is used for one's own parents). As one informant put it: "I couldn't think of calling my father-in-law by his name (Michele) . He has gray hair and little of it, therefore one must use a name of respect." To which the informant's father-in-law replied: "If you called me other than Papá, I would think bad of you."

The family serves not only as a status-giving unit but also tends to provide the individual with most of his psychological satisfactions. While intimate associations may take place outside the family setting, for the most part, the family tends toward self-sufficiency in the socio-psychological realm. Only rarely is a stranger admitted into the home and even then is never admitted into the innercircle of confidence. Family problems remain in the family. To discuss troubles of a personal nature with one outside the circle of kin is to lose face in the village.

Family contacts remain strong even after one has moved from the village. Well-developed lines of communication exist between Agliese families in Rome, Youngstown (Ohio), Fairmount (W. Va.), and Detroit and their kin in the village. Consequently, the average Agliese knows

---

[3] See Leonard W. Moss and Walter H. Thompson, "The South Italian Family; Literature and Observation," *Human Organization*, XVIII (1959), pp. 35–41.

[4] Jules Henry "The Personal Community and Its Invariant Properties," *American Anthropologist*, LX (1958), pp. 827–31.

more about these distant communities than he knows about Naples (which is less than a 100 miles away) .

Beyond the kinship bonds are the ties that exist within the system of *comparaggio* or *comparotto* (godparenthood) . This system stems from the Roman Catholic practice wherein the sponsors guarantee the induction into the faith of the child. The godparents pledge to act as guides for the religious training of the child. The Agliese recognize three degrees of *comparaggio*: godparents at the time of 1) baptism; 2) confirmation and, 3) marriage.[5]

Several informants contended that the godparent at the time of confirmation is more important than the godparent at baptism. It is generally agreed that the godparents at the time of marriage are the least important and, in fact, this godparent role has been replaced by the *testimonie* (witnesses) . However, the witnesses are called *compadre l'anello* (godparent of the ring) .

Godparents are accorded a high degree of respect and are always addressed by the titles: godfather—*compadre* or *padrino* (dialect—*pati'n-o*) (dialect diminutive—*comparil*); godmother *commare* (dialect—*patina*) (dialect diminutive—*commarrella*).

In Cortina, a godmother is never called *Madrina* since this would imply a division of the mother's responsibility and everyone knows that a mother's responsibility may not be shared.

The person chosen for the godparent role may be a relative or a friend. In many cases, it is a person from outside the village. The morality of the godparent is an important factor. A whore or a thief is never chosen. Sometimes the choice is made on the basis of the potential godparent's economic ability to bestow gifts on the child.

When a person is requested to serve as godparent he must accept ("You *cannot* refuse San Giovanni"—patron of godparents) . Likewise, should one wish to be a godparent and make his wish known, the parents are obligated to select that person, even though they wish another to be the sponsor of their child.

For baptism, a person of like sex is usually chosen as godparent for the child. For communion, a person of like sex is always chosen as the godparent of the communicant.

The godparent has a specific role to perform. He is to set a moral example for the child. The godparent is morally responsible for the education and welfare of the child if its parents should die. If the

---

5 Cf. Gallatin Anderson "A Survey of Italian Godparenthood," The Kroeber Anthro. Society Papers, No. 15, 1956; "Il Comparaggio: The Italian Godparenthood Complex," *The Southwestern Journal of Anthropology*, XIII (1957), pp. 32–53.

godparent resides in Rome, or in the United States, and should the child migrate to that place, the godparent is asked to "look after" the child. If the godparent is economically able, he is expected to lend his godchild money at no interest.

One other factor emerges with regard to the bond of *comparaggio*; the godparent is the only one outside the family circle in whom the child may confide. The godparent is the only outsider permitted to share in the problems and joys of the family. In this role, the godparent is cast as intimate and helpmate to the child. They are united in San Giovanni.

In the light of this discussion, it can be seen that the cohesive nature of the family, close kinship ties, and the bonds of *comparaggio* set limits to the social participation of the individual. We have hypothesized elsewhere that the structure of the family is Italy's greatest strength and greatest weakness. Because of familial cohesiveness, Italy has endured through war, depressions, and governmental crises. Yet because of its cohesiveness, the family has limited external contacts for its members and has actually stifled the development of voluntary associations. (Moss and Thomson.)

While identification with community does exist, as we have witnessed in the case of *campanilismo,* it cannot be said that this identification necessarily leads to community participation and community responsibility. Neither have we discovered the close, intimate, primary social relations which, supposedly, encompass the total life of the village. While primary relations do exist outside the family setting, we had best describe these patterns of interaction as *discontinuous circles of intimacy.* Despite its isolated position, relative homogeneity of its population, and smallness of size Cortina exhibits an intricate web of social relations which tends to cast doubt on the legitimacy of those views which maintain the simplicity of peasant society.

7. Neighbor and Kin— Life in a Tennessee Ridge Community

ELMORA MESSER MATTHEWS

BOUNDARY MAINTENANCE: ENDOGAMY AND MIGRATION

External boundaries around the Ridge are not easily penetrated. The practice of valley persons of not marrying "strangers" constitutes the most important means of holding boundaries tight. These are highly stable, intermarrying residential groups that have persisted for five or six generations.

The stability and endogamy of the community are seen in the genealogies themselves and in a comparison of names supplied by couples interviewed with names on the original census forms from the 1850 first individual count through the 1880 release. In the districts involved no family name appears on these census sheets which is not also in the writer's genealogies, and approximately two-thirds of the given names in the 1850-1880 census records are in the genealogies. Residing with the 48 couples of 1880, direct ancestors of the population studied, were the following relatives, who can also be identified genealogically: three of the

Source: Reprinted with permission of the author and publisher from *Neighbor and Kin—Life in a Tennessee Ridge Community* (Nashville, Tenn.: Vanderbilt University Press, 1965).

wives' sisters and two of the husbands' sisters, a husband's brother, a husband's parents, a wife's mother, two uncles, an aunt, two nieces, a nephew, a son-in-law, a daughter-in-law, plus one unidentified school-teacher.

Other support of the community's stability and endogamy lies in the following data. Of the 62 adults questioned in Applecross-Millstone, only two grew up more than ten miles away from their present home, and five have never lived in any other house. Only four of the 62 persons lived more than ten miles away at the time they married. The majority of the couples have known each other "always" and lived less than three miles from one another before marriage. For the 30 Applecross-Millstone couples, the table shows the distances mates lived apart before marriage.

TABLE 1.

Distances Between Residences Before Marriage

Traveling Miles From Each Other	Number of Couples
0–4	19
5–9	8
10–15	3
More than 15	0

There is a significant sex difference in responses to these questions. The man consistently reported he had lived closer to his spouse and had known his spouse longer before marriage. Some of the discrepancy between couples' reports on the length of time they had known each other before marriage lies in the fact that marriage age for men exceeds that for women by six years. The variation in age and memory span does not account for all the difference, however. One husband said he had known his wife "always," and the wife said she had known him "a couple of years" before marriage, but she added, "I had seen him around, of course." Another husband said he lived in "walking distance" of his wife before marriage, and she said they lived "550 miles apart." The matter resolved itself when the couple explained they both had gone to Detroit to work and live with relatives, who were Applecross migrants living in the same Detroit neighborhood.

Migration practices are important in the perpetuation of valley structure. There are two ways in which residents guard against a population threat that would upset their present system of adapting environing conditions to attain their goals. The line is held against outsiders by marriage and property rules, but also the natural increase must be dealt with, since it could give imbalance to the economic structure by decreasing the size of farms. The average completed Applecross-Millstone nuclear family is only 4.7 members. Four of the 13 women past child-bearing age have only one child, and there are just three women who have five or more. Considering the natural increase alone, a minimum amount of emigration is needed to maintain a stationary population.

Allowance, however, must be made for the individuals who do not sufficiently internalize or follow valley norms to remain there. A kind of self-banishment from the area is common after family estrangements or after love loss or property loss. This is what residents mean when they say, "He [or she] ain't been back since." The self-banishment may be permanent, as in suicide cases such as committed by a girl who had separated herself from the deme by her choice of a college education or as committed by a man who shot himself after shooting his former wife. Also, the self-banishment may involve moving completely away or just moving to an acceptable "extension" (see paragraphs to follow), from which one's children might some day return to the valley. There is no problem in making up for population loss below the Ridge, for spouses can always be secured from above the Ridge, where family fertility is higher. One upper-Ridge woman who married a Millstone man and now lives in Millstone, said she was one of thirty-two children, all born of the same parents. Of upper-Ridge families, many of whom are engaged in moonshining, it is said, "They make lots of corn and have a heap of children." It is significant that the population problem is the one world-wide problem that seems to worry these people, and they speak of it often and fearfully.

As the Southern Appalachian study reports, migration involves more than persons moving from one surface of the land to another; migrants feel more secure about leaving an area and are more easily integrated at the receiving end of the migration stream when they are able to join family members who have moved out before them.[1] Three extensions of the Ridge community were located.

One of the extensions is in Brechin, 15 miles northeast of Turnabout Hollow. There Huntlys bought cheap land many years ago and started in the lumbering business. One Brechin resident explained: "This was Miller Holler when we moved in, but there ain't but two Millers left. We call it Huntly Holler now." There have been eight new Huntly houses built in Brechin in the last five years. One ninety-year-old man complained, "If the world stands another hundred years, this'll be as thick as Columbia through here." Then he asked in wonderment: "Did you ever look at the babies in the county hospital? They're as thick as chicks in an electric chicken hatch." Within sight of the man's home, one can count

---

1 Thomas R. Ford (ed.), *The Southern Appalachian Region: A Survey*, p. 76.

seven separate farm houses belonging to his brother, his sister, his sister's
son, two of his sister's sons' daughters, his own daughter, and his daughter's son. Another daughter lives two miles away. A man from Big Rook
recently went bond for a brother's son, who lives several miles away,
when the boy got in legal trouble. Moving from Turnabout Hollow,
these families talk and act like Turnabout people, and they have the
same residence and work patterns. One Turnabout woman said she and
her neighbors were often mistaken for Brechin residents by strangers,
who commented, "You just act like them," or "You talk like them." Even
epidemics, such as the 1957 hepatitis one, have a way of appearing
simultaneously in the two communities.

There is a neighborhood in the county seat of Kinbrace County that is
composed of six or seven families who have moved from the Ridge
community. Two of these moved after they were closely involved in a
triple killing in Turnabout Hollow thirty years ago. A retired Methodist
minister from Applecross is at the center of the county-seat neighborhood. A daughter and a granddaughter of two of the county-seat families
have recently married back into Turnabout Hollow and reside there.

A third extension of these valleys is in Detroit, Michigan, where brothers and cousins since depression years have been going together to find
work. One informant, at 18, and his eight cousins left Applecross and
became employed in a box factory in Detroit. He is back in Applecross
today, but his son has gone to Detroit to work in a brewery; the son was
persuaded by two of his cousins who have jobs selling cigarettes there. A
girl who went to Detroit to visit her sister married her sister's husband's
brother while there. Mention has already been made of the young man
and woman from the valley who went to Detroit to live with relatives,
courted and married in Detroit, and returned to the valley to live.

Moving to join family lines in Brechin or the county seat or in Detroit
550 miles away does not separate a person from valley connections as
cleanly as moving to Nashville or even to some nearby farm communities.
Family lines and attitudes seem to be largely maintained in the county-
seat, Brechin, and Detroit extensions—so much so that these persons are
permitted to move back to their valley homes or to marry back into valley
farms. For a way of life to be continued, a migration stream rather than
individual migrations is required; the streams have been small but they
have been steady. As far as the study reveals, these are the only "acceptable" places for one to move. Moving elsewhere necessitates a break in
marriage alliances and socially alienates persons from the deme.

With such family lines and dominant kinship patterns extended to
rural nonfarm, county seat, and urban areas, one could profitably view
theories of the metropolitan area's exerting dominance from the other

end of the line. Not only does the city exert a wide influence on outlying families and neighborhoods with its occupational structure; it is also affected by the ascriptive emphases of various kinship and ethnic structures. These are rooted in, and maintain connections with, rural farm communities and exert attitudinal and organizational influences into rural nonfarm, town, and metropolitan centers.

8. Shops, Pubs
and Fairs

CONRAD M. ARENSBERG

In many ways the town is an alien world, even a hostile one, to the countryman. He feels its scorn of his rusticity and distrusts its urbane way. Yet the town has an attraction for him no less strong in rural Ireland than elsewhere in the world. It weans away his sons and daughters. It brings him the breath of the outer world. After all, metropolis is a relative term. Metropolitan prestige is an infinite gradation in which the smallest hamlet may have a share with Megalopolis. Metropolitan prejudice is no less capable of minute division, and country towns engender little cockneys as quickly as might London produce a great one. They, too, would feel with Dr. Johnson that the fairest prospect in all Scotland was the road to London Town.

For if Megalopolis is the crossroads of the world, the country town is no less so. The difference is merely one of scale. Broadway, Piccadilly, and the Place de l'Opéra have counterparts in any country town.

In Ireland the parallel is more apt than one might credit at first thought. Irish towns have always been little more than crossroad centres. They are market-towns and administrative seats. Their economics is that of distribution, not production. The industrial revolution has passed

SOURCE: Reprinted by permission of The Macmillan Company from *The Irish Countryman* by Conrad Arensberg. Copyright 1937, 1959 by The Macmillan Company.

southern Ireland by. The shop, the pub, the fair bring the towns their life-blood and link them to their hinterlands and to the outside world. Many of them still collect market tolls on rural produce, as if they still had a ring of stone-wall fortification about them. Many of them have no fair green but throw open all their streets to shouting, bargaining men and milling cattle, on the day of the fair, surrendering themselves entirely to the countryside upon which they live.

One still approaches many of them today as one approached them in the sixteenth century, although now perhaps an automobile road breaks a new entrance into them or the railroad halts a jaunting car's distance away. The roads that radiate inward toward the heart of the town are still lined with labourers' and artisans' thatched cottages long before one reaches the town itself. As one proceeds along them, the cottages give way to shops and public houses which rise higher and more stately as one nears the centre, in the market-place or in the central square. There, quite often, that emporium of the most valuable commodity of all—the local bank—now dominates the scene.

Between the shop-fronts, back lanes lead off to the recesses in which the labourers live; and, off by themselves in a proud segregation, stand the more pretentious houses of a residential area, and the great grey buildings in which local government and justice are housed. But the centre remains the point at which the shop-lined streets that lead from deep within the countryside converge. The life of the country and that of the town meet and mingle along these converging lines.

That mingling represents the latest stage of an age-old struggle in which the countryside has won out at last. It has been a conquest of assimilation, like the victories of Chinese life over the barbarian invader. The town in Irish history was originally, and often long remained, a foreign growth. In the great age of Celtic civilization, the monastery and the royal seat centred Irish life. Later the Celto-Norman castle scorned an urban fortress wall. The town was first a Danish importation; only Galway, of Irish cities, was not a Norseman's settlement. Throughout the long wars and counter-wars with the English foe and the alien English life, the town was many times alternately absorbed by native life and reconquered for the alien. Even Galway still bore its famous inscription above its city gate not three centuries ago. "O Lord," it read, "deliver us from the fury of the O'Flaherties." Law, at first, forbade even the entrance of the 'Irishry' into the towns and then later decreed that no Irishman should trade with another. The towns were to remain English, and later, Protestant, and the merchant-burghers who flourished in them must remain of English blood and habit.

All that, of course, has long since vanished. The Irish have occupied the towns of their own land, their blood and habit hold sway and fashion urban commerce in the towns and cities. The change has been a slow and durable growth, flowing on beneath the surface of political and cultural strife. But like all growth it has been a process of incorporation, too. Today, to a casual eye, the shops, the commerce, the social life of the Irish town is much like that of all modern western Europe.

Such is the history, briefly put, which has provided the scene that interests the social anthropologist. It is in this scene that he can inquire into the bonds this conquest has created. He can appraise through them the factors which make up the countryman's participation in the larger world. Many fields for investigation present themselves in this connection. Townsmen and countrymen are now equally part, each in his own way, of that whole we name Irish society. From his own vantage each acts toward the other and builds up a relationship with him in such a way as to determine in some degree the form of that whole. This relation, an instance of the age-old reciprocity between town and country, invites our examination.

In Ireland today, one can see this relation most definitely and most significantly in the ties between shopkeeper and countryman. In the west and south of the Free State, at least, the landlord is gone and the true big farmer is rare. The town's hinterland is the world of the small farmers. And the town lives by its connection with the social order to which the countryman is attached. One need probe only a little way beneath the surface of conventionalities to learn that the connection is much more than the economics of distribution and exchange.

In the first place, the shop is also the seat of a familistic identification, very like that of land and farm. Ireland is better supplied with shops, at least in number, than any comparable European nation. A very large proportion of her population lives by retail trade. But one must not think of these shops, so numerous in every Irish town, as great department stores, or as units in a country-wide chain. The former, of course, do exist in cities, and the latter, called multiple-shops, are a new invasion. They have little place as yet in the smaller towns. The typical shop is a less imposing affair. It supports, normally, only the family which works it.

Such a shop is most often a small two-story building. The ground floor is evenly divided between the business premises and the household kitchen. In front, a single step in from the street, a single deep room, whose width is that of the building's front, houses counter, shelves, shop-stock and money-till. The business of a lifetime goes forward in this room. In back, a flagstone-floored kitchen with an open hearth duplicates, on a more elaborate scale perhaps, the country farm house kitchen. Like its country counterpart it is the seat of family life.

Upstairs, a front room facing the street is transformed, by family portraits, an ornamental mantle and a piece or two of good mahogany, into a ceremonial parlour. Behind this range the bedrooms of the family. Perhaps, in affluence and refinement there is an upstairs sitting-room as well. For the shop is no mere place of business. It is first of all a household, of which one section and one only is devoted to the world of affairs.

The family which this household houses and supports, in the majority of cases, works the shop in much the same way that the family of the farmer works the land. It conducts its business as a united corporation in which all members may take a hand and each have his place. Husband and wife tend the counter together and between them shopkeeping is divided; sons and daughters work as shop-assistants, as long as they remain at home. Only when affluence lifts the shop to importance and dignifies the shopkeeper with the title and station of merchant, expanding his business to wholesaling, is this arrangement greatly modified.

Yet, self-sufficient as this familistic shop-world is, the countryman has many a connection with it. It lives its own quiet life and plies its own trade so different from the farmer's work upon the farm. Town life breeds its own sentiment and weaves its own bonds, making of the townsmen a community of conduct, feeling and values. But, nevertheless, despite this isolating process which shuts the countryman out, he is not at all remote. The first great tie, and the obvious one, is the economic. The country-dwellers buy the shop goods which move across the townsmen's counters and bring in the moneys realized in fair and market in exchange for retail goods.

But the economic tie is not sufficient, in Irish life, for permanence. Time and assimilation have woven a full social pattern round it. The pattern is really an extension townwards of the countryman's own social order. The market town fills its role as a metropolis of native sentiment in that extension.

There is a saying in the towns of Ireland that summarizes well the movements of town life. "The country-people flock into the towns," they say, "and the townspeople all die out of them." A moment's investigation bears out the fact. Though the town, too, is a familistic world, like the countryside, it differs in that it is a world in slow movement. Generation after generation, a new family sets up shop or public-house, flourishes or fails and then passes on out of the town's life; pressed from behind by the vigour of new country blood or graduated upward economically and socially into the professions. Some families withstand the movement a long time; here and there one can point to a century or more of burgher succession. Others have known a more rapid change of station downward or upward in a single generation. But all of them together can feel the compelling sweep of movement which is part of town life.

Is it really the countryman's vigour that sweeps thus through the Irish towns? I know that is the usual explanation, where such a situation in town and urban life exists. Much has been written in Ireland and in all modern countries about the debilitating effect of urban and near-urban life. It is the fashion to lament the onward sweep which fills the towns and cities with fresh blood, names and faces and pushes out the old. Landmarks change out of recognition; the old families disappear mysteriously, and one can cry out that a new barbarian flood is sweeping away the life's blood of the educated urban classes.

But such a view is very blind. It is astigmatic from a too close looking upon the immediate, instant case. It neglects entirely the organization of human behaviour and sentiment, unreasoned and unplanned though it be, that makes our human societies. It confounds the force of ordered change with weakness and decay.

Nowhere would the view fail worse than in southern Ireland. The countryman who presses in upon the townsman does not drive him out through superior vigour, nor does the townsman fade away in weak decay. Each is caught in a social pattern which fashions many lifetimes and their desires, ambitions, achievements and failures. History and habit have wrought a series of pathways almost as definite as those of a termite's nest; but history and habit care little which termite follows them. Vigour, if it exists, can only be measured in the ease with which the path-follower travels along his course, and the change which his passing makes upon it.

I am sure I shall be accused of a thorough-going, even mystical determinism in human affairs. But let us follow the countryman and the towns-dweller and see wherein my heresy is justifiable and wherein we may temper it.

In the communities my colleagues and I came to know, the country customer who brings his trade into the shop does so in response to the ties of kinship and friendliness. He 'goes with' a shopkeeper or publican, most often, as he 'coors' with his country friends. This is not his only incentive but it is his principal one. The social order of which he is a part embraces the town-dwelling shopkeeper; trade follows friendship. Many indeed are the shops which rely almost entirely upon this 'family trade.' Others know it to be the base upon which they must build.

But, we remember, the relation of kinship and friendship is reciprocal. The shopkeeper is bound in his turn to his 'family trade.' He owes obligation to the 'country cousins' who buy from him. In this way, a durable bond is created which exists over and above the economics of retail trade. It is of the kind that the countryman understands best; it charges the relationship with interest for him; it infuses it with sentiment, habit and reciprocal force. The shopkeeper, too, can rely upon it. Even though he be caught in the demands it makes upon him, he, nevertheless, can rely heavily upon its expectancies.

The ordinary modest retail shop or pub lives upon this tie. In many cases the tie infuses business with a social content which becomes coextensive with the distributive function the shop performs in economic exchange. If the tie is weakened, if it dies, the shop weakens and dies too. And with it dies the family which derives livelihood, status and much of its corporate existence from that shop. For possession of the shop gives status and prestige and marks one's social place for the family, as much as does the 'farm of land' in the countryside. The family's 'name is on the shop' in much the same way as the country family's name is 'on the land.' In fact, almost symbolically, that name is literally on the shop, for in Ireland most often a single word—the family name—rather than any announcement of the type of retail trade carried on—hangs over the door to proclaim the shop's existence to the buying public. And when the 'family trade' dies, that name dies out of the shop world with it.

Business, then, in the market-towns is no frantic search for better qualities at lower prices. It is first of all a technique in social relations. It demands an orientation to a social order, that of the countryman-customer. Customer and retailer are brought together, not primarily through a cheap price nor an eye-compelling package, but through personalities and through blood and marriage bonds.

In this social context, the interests of shopkeeper and farmer coincide. If the shop is to live it must renew its ties with the rural hinterland; if the farm on the land is to grow in status and strength it must ally itself in a higher and wider social sphere, and in so doing, provide well for its dispersed children. This coincidence of interest determines much of the shopkeeper's life; through it the countryman has assimilated the town to his own way of life.

The town represents that higher and wider sphere for the countryman. Its life is that of a higher station in life; it is a centre of metropolitan prestige. So the farmer can come to send his son into a shop, as he sends a daughter 'into the land' in match-making, to provide him with a better place in life, to make a gentleman of him. The shopkeeper may need a young and pliable assistant in his business. He must have one upon whose kindred he can depend for extension of his trade. He takes in the farmer's son.

In this way, the first of the social bonds that unite the shop and the pub to the rural hinterland is created. A pathway is created along which human lives can move and play out their roles in social life. One of the farmer's sons can hope, with luck and affluence, to become a shop-assistant in the market-town. The portion he receives upon the dispersal of the farm family may well take the form of such a start in life. The farmer-father pays the boy's apprentice bond.

Formal apprenticeships still flourish in Irish country towns and nowhere better than in the shop or pub. The country boy is bound in custom and in law to his new employer and learns the alien way of business and social habit under a master's eye. Eventually he may succeed to a shop of his own, but first he 'must serve his time.' In this, rural Ireland has preserved an older form and charged it with its own peculiar content. The town-bred lad is seldom hired; he brings no rural kindred with him. Then, too, he is neither so impressionable nor so easy to control. The country lad, at first, is both. The shopkeeper taps the social order of the countryside in the person of his fledgling 'prentice boy.

But time brings ordered change in social life, in the town no less than in the countryside. The boy grows up; he serves his time. He acquires the experience and the technique which fit him for the role for which his parents paid his apprentice bond. Unless he is to retain a subordinate and unimportant place as shop-assistant for a lifetime, he must move on. He must acquire a shop himself. And so he does, if he humanly can, and to that end his savings go.

So much for the farmer's son. In his person, he represents a rough one-half of the countryside's invasion of the town. Yet he has sisters, too, at home upon the farm. The attraction of metropolis is no less great for them; they, too, must be provided for in the dispersal of the family upon the land. And with them goes the rural social order and the ties of kinship and community.

In this fact one can see another rough half of the rural tide that sweeps into the ranks of business in the towns. The shop-world taps its country hinterland again in the persons of the daughters of the farms. The farmer must, if he can, marry his daughter off well; prestige and alliance go with her and the dowry which she carries as her portion. The shopkeeper must renew his ties with the countryside with each new generation, if the shop is to survive. In this coincidence of interest, again, a great deal of the marriage custom of the town revolves. The world of shops and pubs is caught within the ordered mechanism of change called *match-making*, in the same way as is the 'farm of land.'

Currently in country towns, the 'match' is the accepted type of marriage for publican and shopkeeper as much as it is for the farmer. The more sophisticated and more affluent shopkeepers, those who are close, or would like to be, to the higher status of merchant, would repudiate the rustic word. They would tell you that they make instead 'proper marriage settlements.' But their humbler fellow-tradesmen, whose shops have not such pretensions, are closer to the soil. They would admit what is for both of them the fact.

Consequently, one can find in the town, round the shop and pub, the same reorganization of human relationships that goes forward when the country match transfers land and household command to a marrying son. But there is one great difference. In the town one must bring a country-woman in.

If one analyses the census of marriage, age and occupation in the Free State made in 1926, one can see how general this reorganization is. It lies behind the statistics of a great part of the country. Without it, one cannot explain the striking uniformity that gives a roughly similar grouping of individuals by age, by sex, by marital conditions, in all the towns, except the large cities, of southern Ireland. For instance, shop-assistants everywhere are young unmarried men and women. Entrance into the ownership of shop and public-house takes place at the same age as does entrance into married state. Though the towns show no such marked extremes as do the country districts, marriage is long delayed and bachelorhood and spinsterhood are very frequent by world standards. One need not be a demographer or statistician to be struck with the parallel, and to wonder at such coincidence between the lives of the followers of occupations so dissimilar as agriculture and retail commerce.

For this statistical correspondence overlies the facts of social life. It merely expresses numerically the community of custom between country and town. If one cares to probe deeper, among the lives whose events the census records, one finds the custom at the root of human behaviour and human sentiment. One lays bare the outline of the balance in which the lives of townsmen and countrymen co-mingle in a larger whole.

For setting up a shop means setting up a family; it means marriage and the bringing-in of a country girl. There are exceptions, of course; custom is only a general imperative. Nevertheless, the country match is the generality.

Most often, the shopkeeper-father turns over the shop to the son who is to succeed him when that son marries. The daughter-in-law is the

daughter of a farmer of the countryside. Her people 'walk the shop' as
they would 'walk the land' in a country match. Long negotiation equates
the dowry they give with the shop, its stock, its debts and its prospects.
The two families cast the agreement into proper legal form. The shopkeeper transfers his control and his ownership to the son and the son's
wife. The other shop children are dispersed and are provided for, where
possible. The older generation retires; and a new family is established in
business in the town.

This is a smooth and orderly transition. The shop keeps its identification with human ties unbroken, from parents to children. It renews them
once again, outward into the rural hinterland, in the persons of kindred
the young wife brings 'into the shop.' The shop's life blood is renewed:
literally, in the persons of the new master and mistress; socially, in the
extensions of kinship and alliance; and economically, because trade follows personal ties.

The erstwhile apprentice boy, the farmer's son, who sets up 'on his
own,' follows the same course and makes a comparable transition. His
marriage and his setting up his own shop most often coincide. His savings
and the bride's fortune make possible, together, many a start in the life of
the market-towns. Money buys the shop, credit may stock its shelves, but
it is the social alliance, contracted in a country marriage, which supplies
the trade upon which business rests.

One might ask here if the role of the sexes is not reversible. Might not
the young man marry-in into the shop, and the girl rise 'from assistantship
to full-fledged ownership? Naturally, such a course might well be taken;
a social order allows many channels. It has not the rigidity of formal law.
Or the girl may inherit a shop, or receive one, in the towns, as her
particular portion. For to set up a daughter in a small shop is to provide
well for her and to assure her station for her lifetime; even though little
wealth will come to her through that shop door. But in the scheme of
social emphases, these courses are the exceptions. Practically, for a finally
successful adaptation, the man must rise through an economic apprenticeship. His is the bread-winning role in social life. Only the bride
regularly marries into her new station.

We are dealing here with a social form of nearly universal occurrence
where a society preserves some trace of patriarchal form. It is a structural
necessity where class lines cross-cut a familistic order. In India, for
instance, it is immediately recognizable to the sociologist; for Hindu
society incorporates into religious or formal law much of the social custom which other civilizations allow to flow on unheeded, unrecognized
and unplanned. There, a lower caste often marries its daughters into the

ranks of the next immediately above. The practice is known as hypergamy.

In Western Europe hypergamy is present, in some times and places notably so. The French have recognized it realistically. And here in rural Ireland, the countryman practises it, when he can, though he would be much surprised to hear his efforts on behalf of his daughter so pedantically described. Yet even though the name would mystify him, he would understand the substance of the custom. His daughter is to be married in such a way as to bring credit and alliance to the paternal line upon the farm. That line stands to gain a foothold in the world of shops. For that, the countryman is willing, currently, to pay about twice the usual dowry-price.

And in his willing adherence to custom, stability is achieved. The relationship between class and class, like that in the countryside between kindred and kindred, attains some permanence of form. The bride carries social bonds with her; in this case she carries them upward and townward into the shops and pubs of metropolis.

Her brother, on the other hand, carries with him another social function, in his capacity of male. His place is that of a potential fatherhood in a line of patrilineal descent. He carries on a corporate name upon the land or shop. Where he cannot inherit, in such descent, a sure place among his fellows, he must win it. The man is the bread-winner who carves out a place for his line; round him the family must be grouped. The woman, on the other hand, is the uniting force within the grouping. In this dichotomization of social role between the sexes, the Irish town and the Irish countryside, like the Church to which they both subscribe, are agreed. Hypergamy takes its form in the agreement. Along the lines laid down by the social bonds of apprenticeship and hypergamous marriage, the world of the market-town and the rural hinterland are united; along the same lines the flow of the country-people townward moves.

Once again, then, we see how complete the inclusions of a familistic order are. The shop lives on and renews its strength. Its owner, whether he be townsman bred or migrant country lad, must 'bring a country girl into the shop.' Marriage, the establishment of a clientele, and the attainment of full status in one's class, all converge at a single point.

This order, one must not forget, is nothing esoteric; it is no more mysterious in the towns than it is in the countryside. Habit, sentiment and desire among the constituent human beings, both make it up and are made up by it. It is really the pattern into which all these melt to make a coherency of social life. Nowhere is this fact better illustrated than in the attitudes the Irish townsmen hold about their own positions within this

inclusive pattern. For example, I give you the statement of one townsman, of shopkeeper rank, who could summarize the matrimonial aspirations of his fellows in terms of likes and desires. To us he may seem very
conservative and early Victorian in his standards; but he is none the less
aware of the demands life makes upon his kind:

> When a shopkeeper marries he wants to get a wife who can help him
> in the shop. He doesn't want one who has grand ideas about what a fine
> lady she is, because she is no good in the house and will only drive the
> customers away. That is why he goes to the country to find a wife. The
> country girl has been reared alongside her mother, she knows how to
> cook, sew, keep house, and she hasn't a lot of grand ideas in her head
> that the town girls have. When she comes to town, she feels she's got
> on in the world; while the town girl will only be wanting more than her
> husband can give her, or she won't do her share.

The speaker was a townsman, born and bred, but one can see that he
endorsed the system heartily. He was an older man who had made his
adaptations to social life successfully.

For others, for those whom the life of the town has caught up and who
have acquired 'grand ideas,' as the last speaker called them, adaptation is
more difficult. The town, as I have said, engenders its own near-urban
values. These come to conflict with those which unite the shop world to
its countryside. Thus ambition is born, which means a severance of old
ties. The ties become thwarting chains, and here and there a young man,
caught within the pulls of two incompatible forces, becomes a bitter and
scornful rebel.

One such young man, who found himself swept back into the ways of
the market-towns after a brief flight into larger horizons in Dublin,
fought against the fate that closed him in. He tells his own story:

> This town is very dull. I don't understand what brings you here.
> The trouble with everybody here is that they are all misfits and that
> they are all in jobs they loathe. Successful men give you good counsel:
> they tell you to work hard and forget your troubles. But that is because
> they are in occupations which they like. There is something glamorous
> about being a solicitor, and everybody comes to you. I would like to have
> been one. There will be opportunity here when the older men clear out.
> I went off and studied in Dublin for a long while. Then my father
> died and my mother was stricken with paralysis and I had to come back
> here and work behind the counter, which I loathe. There's no one else
> now but my sister. Most shopkeepers make out through their family
> trade; and the only thing for me to do now is to marry some rich woman
> in from the country and then all her friends will come in. If you want

to get married here there is nothing in it at all but to look out for a
country girl. If you don't want to make a fool of yourself and go in for
politics, you have to depend on your friends and your wife's friends, and
if you can, you've got to marry a girl from the country. Then she'll bring
in all her people for miles round, with all their relatives and their married
families, and they're the ones that will buy your flour and sugar and tea.
You can't get on without them.

In this rebellious young man's lament, another aspect of the life of the
towns appears and takes its proper place. The social order which
demands the maintenance of personal bonds between countryman and
townsman carries with it the seeds of change as well. The young man I
have just quoted is caught within the very wheels of this change. A new
time and place bring new adaptations in human lives and with them new
values which conflict with and destroy the old.

In that fact, simply, lies the explanation of the movement by which the
"country-people flock into the towns and the townspeople all die out of
them."

The rebellious young man shows well in his own history the point at
which change of habit drives the townsman and the countryman apart.
After years of near-urban life the townsman loses touch. He can no
longer meet the rural ways; he is trained in a different habit; he develops
a different turn of mind. He is no longer fitted socially to meet the
countryman on the old terms and to respond to the demands the social
bonds connecting him with the rural hinterland put upon him. If he is
born in the town, a second-generation migrant, he is all the more alien.
Metropolis has won his mind, his heart, his soul. New vistas of advancement and new personal ties grow up which attract him further and
further into the town's life. The bonds with the countryside are broken;
they fall away before a new orientation.

So the shop dies out. The family of which the shopkeeper is a part
moves onward. If it is affluent and ambitious, its members rise into the
professions perhaps, or seek larger worlds to conquer. If it is not, then
oblivion swallows it. It seeks a new place in the ranks of the town in
which the countryside has no part. New blood fills its old place along the
converging lines of shops and pubs which make up the market-town. The
new blood succeeds by virtue of the same ties which originally brought
success to the first immigrants from the countryside. It brings with it new
bonds of friendship and kinship.

This is a continual movement, a flow along definite pathways in which
human lives work out their courses. The country family 'on the land,' as
we know, buds off with each new generation upon the farm. With the

dispersed children go those relationships of a familistic order which unite the human beings in time and space. In this movement ever renewed, yet ever the same, the market-town is caught. Its shops, its pubs, its business life, the whole economic function it performs, flows with this movement.

9. Gosforth and the Outside World

WILLIAM MORGAN WILLIAMS

The people of Gosforth make a sharp distinction between 'Gosfer' folk' and those who live outside the parish. The precise location of the parish boundary is very widely known and a very real difference is recognized between the people who live on either side of it, even where the actual distance is a matter of a few yards. There are several farms situated just inside the parish limits and the families who occupy them make full use of the services and amenities of Gosforth village, despite the fact that all of them could use other centres much more conveniently. In one case the extra distance involved is as much as two miles. On the other hand, there is one farm situated less than ten yards outside the parish boundary: its occupants are rarely seen in Gosforth and seldom mentioned in everyday conversation, although the farmhouse is a mile nearer to Gosforth village than to the hamlet which is the focus of their activities.

This feeling of membership of a social unit with well-defined territorial limits and the accompanying distinctions applied to non-members are very apparent in attitudes towards 'offcomers.' When a stranger comes to live in the parish, his period of 'settling down' is never a very comfort-

SOURCE: Reprinted with permission of the Macmillan Company from *Gosforth: The Sociology of an English Village* by William Morgan Williams. © The Free Press, a Corporation, 1956.

able one. Several families who had recently arrived felt that 'they were not wanted' or that 'people want to know the in's and out's of all your business.' One farmer's wife remarked, 'I don't know anyone in the village yet, and no one speaks to me, but they all know the colour of my wallpaper.'

More often than not the new family's first few months in the parish are marked by a combination of hospitality and hostility, of co-operation and criticism. Interviews with farmers who had recently arrived in the district suggest that the sequence is very much the same in all cases. When a family comes to start farming, their first day is notable for visits from neighbours, who offer to help them in moving in, promise the loan of machinery and make suggestions or supply information about local conditions. The newcomers find in due course that the offers of co-operation are well-meant, and it comes as a severe shock to them to discover that, say, the farmer who had been so obliging about lending a manure drill has consistently been making highly derogatory remarks about them to an appreciative audience in the local public house. One farmer, who thought himself to be on excellent terms with his neighbours, heard that one of them had told several people that the 'offcomer' had ruined many of his hedges because he was unaware of the function of the hydraulic lift on his tractor.

The apparent ambivalence in the attitude of local people is very puzzling to newcomers, many of whom describe it in such terms as 'stabbing you in the back' or 'being two-faced.' Their resentment is frequently increased by the great interest shown in their affairs by their neighbours, particularly if they have come from an urban area where neighbour relationships are poorly developed. Sometimes too the conflict of emotions is heightened when a newcomer confronts a neighbour concerning his behaviour, since the country folk are unable to offer a satisfactory explanation. Not one of the people I questioned about this matter could explain why they behaved so inconsistently, and were very embarrassed when the subject was mentioned.

This seemingly paradoxical behaviour is an expression of the country people's sense of identity and difference. The initial acts of friendship and the offers of co-operation represent, as it were, an invitation to the offcomer to become a member of the community. The derogatory remarks and the stories about the shortcomings of the stranger express the sense of difference from the outside world, of which the stranger is the immediate representative. Thus in offering a newly-arrived neighbour the loan of his machinery a farmer is in effect accepting him as 'one of us'; in criticizing his use of the machinery, the farmer is classifying him as 'someone from elsewhere and therefore different from us.'

As the process of settling down goes on the criticism and hostility usually diminishes. Eventually the newcomer is regarded as having settled down, although—as we have seen already—he will always be to some extent an offcomer.

The length and nature of the period of settling down varies from one person to another according to a complex series of factors. If, for example, the newcomer is a Cumbrian by birth and upbringing who speaks with the local dialect his acceptance takes much less time than that of the 'Southerner.' Among farmers, previous experience of farming considerably reduces the 'settling down' period. Failure to accept certain approved forms of behaviour, albeit unwittingly, is likely to postpone acceptance, while alternatively, relationship by blood or marriage—however remote—with an established member of the community decreases the time taken to settle down very much indeed.

The two extremes in the process of acceptance are illustrated by a comparison of two farmers who came to the parish at about the same time. The first, who had previously farmed a holding some 25 miles away from Gosforth, is a second cousin to two local farmers and more distantly related to several other people in the parish. Although not personally known to the majority of people this farmer appears to have been accepted very rapidly indeed, and the process of settling in seems to have taken place with very little criticism and hostility. The second farmer was born in the South of England, had never farmed before he came to Gosforth, and was not related or known to anyone in the parish. He speaks with what is locally termed a 'la-ti-posh' accent and retains a great many of the urban habits and values he acquired before coming to Cumberland. After nearly seven years this farmer has clearly not 'settled down.' He is the subject of slanderous stories by a large number of people and is still in many ways as much an offcomer as on the day he came.

The variation in the length and nature of the period of acceptance of these two men and their families is directly related to the degree to which they are identified locally as being 'one of us' or 'different from us.' (The recognition of degree of difference is, of course, the underlying factor in the local attitude to 'other people' in general. Applied, *mutatis mutandis,* in varying contexts it explains the differences in attitude towards 'folk in t'district,' 'Cumbrians,' 'Northerners,' 'Southerners,' 'town folk' and so on.) In particular, blood relationship with several parishioners in the case of the first farmer made identification easy, while the second farmer was immediately recognized as 'different.' This 'difference' was emphasized by the fact that the social class of the second farmer was difficult to determine. His wealth, his accent, his general appearance and behaviour, and his ancestry qualified him for membership of the upper-upper class: his occupation and the fact that he sent his children to the village school were characteristics associated with the medial class. (He was, as perhaps might be expected, placed eventually in the lower-upper class.)

In addition to the small number of people who come to live in Gosforth, the inhabitants meet many representatives of the outside world in the numerous officials of county and national agencies who visit (or live in) the parish. In all cases the attitudes and behaviour of the Gosforthians reflect to greater or lesser extent the loyalty of the individual to the community and resentment of external interference in any form. These feelings are often developed to a degree that astonishes officials new to the district.

10. Friendship and Authority

J. A. PITT-RIVERS

The institutions through which the pueblo is governed were discussed
. . . [previously]. Yet in order to make plain how government is carried
out we must examine one further institution, that of friendship, and the
way it interlocks with the structure of authority.

The egalitarian values of the pueblo are one of the themes of this
study. Where all men are equal conceptually, the basis of their co-operation can only be reciprocal service; a voluntary reciprocity dictated by
the mutual agreement of the parties, as opposed to the prescribed
reciprocity of ranks. The spirit of contract, not the spirit of status,
determines their dealings. Such a spirit has already been observed in the
system of co-operation in agriculture. Only one relationship outside kinship is ordained by the values of the pueblo rather than by the free will
of those concerned and that is the neighbour. The supremacy of the
geographical principle of social integration has been mentioned already,
and this evaluation of proximity as a social bond provides the moral basis
of neighbourship. Neighbours are thought to have particular rights and
obligations towards one another. Borrowing and lending, passing
embers,[1] help in situations of emergency, discretion regarding what they

SOURCE: Reprinted with permission from *The People of the Sierra*, published in
Great Britain by Weidenfeld & Nicolson, Ltd., and in the U.S.A. by Criterion Books.
[1] Cooking is all done with charcoal. A charcoal fire is easily lit by placing an ember
from another fire in the bottom of the grate. To light it otherwise involves much
more trouble.

may have chanced to discover, compose the obligations into which neighbours are forced by their proximity, but it must be stressed that the relationship of neighbour is never a formal one.[2] It is a matter of mutual necessity, a relationship into which good people enter willingly. The pueblo rings with accusations, behind the victim's back of course, of being a bad neighbour. "If only one could choose one's neighbours. . . . " To be friendly is the duty of a properly brought-up person towards anyone while he is present, but a neighbour is always present. He might be described, then, as a friend whom circumstances impose upon one.

Friendship, properly, is the free association with a person of one's choice. It implies a mutual liking *(simpatía)*, but, as we shall see, this aspect of it is sometimes put at the beck and call of its other aspect; mutual service. To enter into friendship with someone means putting oneself in a state of obligation. This obligation obliges one to meet his request, even though it involves a sacrifice on one's own part. One must not, if one can help it, say "no" to a friend. On the other hand accepting a service involves him in an obligation, which he must be ready to repay. Hence the necessity for mutual confidence. One must have this as well as *simpatía* for a friend. This much is true of friendship anywhere. What is noticeable in Andalusia is the lack of formality which surrounds it (save in the single instance of the *compadre*). No formal declaration, no ritual initiates it; one enters it through offering or receiving a favour. The instance of the inspector, who refused wine, "who wished friendship with no one" illustrates this point. He would not risk entering into reciprocal obligations which might interfere with his duty. Whether in fact friendship exists or not is frequently in doubt, hence the continual declarations of it, the reproaches for "lack of confidence," the praise acclaiming "a good friend." Hence also the subtle manœuvres intended to test it.

For friendship, to be real, must be disinterested. The language echoes the point continually. People assure one another that the favour they do is done with no afterthought, a pure favour which entails no obligation, an action which is done for the pleasure of doing it, prompted only by the desire to express esteem.[3] On the other hand, the suggestion that

---

[2] As for example in the Spanish Basque village (cf. J. Caro Baroja, *Los Vascos*), where in the funeral procession the coffin is borne by the heads of the four nearest houses, each one having his appointed place. In Alcalá neighbours also bear the coffin, but there is no rule as to which neighbours. It is borne by anyone who offers himself or by a relative. If no one steps forward for this labour then it becomes a service which must be paid. To be borne to one's grave by hired hands is indeed a sign that one has died unloved.

[3] This assurance is also used by all the traffickers in the idiom of friendship who surround the tourist, so that "sin interés ninguno" ("with no thought of interest") comes to mean by inversion "I am not charging you anything, but I expect a tip."

someone's friendship is "interested" is a grave one. Honourable people fight shy of accepting a favour which they will not be able or will not wish to return. The other may wish for one's friendship in order to exploit it. Yet having once accepted friendship one cannot refuse to fulfil the obligations of friendship without appearing oneself the exploiter, for one has entered falsely into a tacit contract. This implication which forfeits a man his shame is used frequently by the exploiters of the principle of friendship.

For the fundamental conception of friendship contains a paradox. A friend is, according to the definition given above, someone whom one likes and admires and wishes to be associated with for that reason. The association is established through a favour which expresses one's *simpatia*. If the favour is accepted, then the bond of friendship is established. Mutual confidence supposedly comes into existence. One is then entitled to expect a return of favour. For favour is at the same time both personal esteem and also service. The word *favor* possesses, like the English word, the meanings of, at the same time, an emotional attitude and also the material gesture which might be thought to derive from this. The former can only be proved by the latter, hence the double meaning of the word. Friendship which is interested is not true friendship since the bond of *simpatia* is missing—in its place is vile calculation. The paradox, then, is this: that while a friend is entitled to expect a return of his feelings and favour he is not entitled to bestow them in that expectation. The criterion which distinguishes true from false friendship flees from the anthropologist into the realms of motive. Yet he may observe that this paradox gives to the institution of friendship the instability which has been noted. The friend who fails one ceases to be a friend. The bond is broken. The way is left clear for a re-alignment of personal relations.

Therefore the element of sympathy is all important. If the friend is deeply attached then he will be true. He will remain with one and sever his friendships with the rival camp. Such a friend is the ideal. He has honour and manliness. But without actually forfeiting his honour he may through skilful evasion manage to maintain his friendships with both sides. These people are famed for the skill with which they dissimulate their feelings. Outsiders who come from other parts of Spain to Alcalá complain of the "indirectness" of the Andalusians. "You never know where you are with them. They will never tell you anything to your face. They will always be charming to you and then behind your back they will betray you." But this histrionic capacity does not mean that they have not strong feelings which they take pleasure in expressing. Hence the importance of gossip. People spend their time discussing how X spoke of Y, how he looked when Z's name was mentioned. Friends inform each other who speaks well and who badly of them behind their back. Every conversation is determined by the relationships of the members of the audience. In this way the process of re-alignment is carried on. Yet there are also true friendships, founded upon affection and esteem, which approximate to the ideal and endure a lifetime. Only they are few. For the struggle for life too easily brings in what one might call the reversed principle of friendship, where considerations of interest dictate the expression of esteem.

The practical utility of such a system is very great. It is a commonplace that you can get nothing done in Andalusia save through friendship. It follows then that the more friends a man can claim the greater his sphere of influence; the more influential his friends are the more influence he has. Friendship is thereby connected with prestige, and boastful characters like to assert how many friends they have, how extensive is the range of their friendships. So while friendship is in the first place a free association between equals, it becomes in a relationship of economic inequality the foundation of the system of patronage. The rich man employs, assists and protects the poor man, and in return the latter works for him, gives him esteem and prestige, and also protects his interests by seeing that he is not robbed, by warning him of the machinations of others and by taking his part in disputes. The relationship of *padrino* and *hombre de confianza* is a kind of lop-sided friendship from which the element of *simpatía* is by no means excluded, though it may happen that owing to the paradox already discussed, the appearance of friendship be used to cloak a purely venal arrangement, a rich man using his money to attain his ends. There appears to have been a change in the evolution of *caciquismo* of which the system of patronage was the core, from the first type of patronage to the second. In the early period *cacique* appears to have meant no more than a person of local prestige, and one finds a young man in a novel of Juan Valera[4] boasting that his father is the *cacique* of the pueblo, yet by the end of its course it has become a term of opprobrium meaning a briber and corrupter, the employer of the *matón* (bully) .[5]

There are many situations in which the *patrono* or *padrino* is of value.[6] He is not only able to favour his protégé within the pueblo. It is,

---

4 J. Valera, *Pepita Jiminez* (Madrid, 1873).

5 Cf. Pío Baroja, *Cesar o Nada,* translated as *Caesar or nothing* (New York. 1922).

6 The power of patronage in former times was certainly greater than it is today. Zugasti (Julián Zugasti, *El Bandolerismo* [Madrid, 1876]) explains the power which it had in relation to the law during his governorship of the province of Cordoba.

The copla of Curro Lopez, a bandit of the first half of the nineteenth century, written while he awaited his execution, speaks of the influence which a powerful patroness once had:

above all, his relationship to the powers outside the pueblo which gives
him value. For example, a *patrono* is required to sign the application for
an old-age pension, testifying that the applicant was once employed by
him. Many such applications are signed by persons who never in fact
employed the applicant. He who can find no one to sign gets no pension.
The *padrino* can give letters of recommendation to people who will do
favours for him, who will protect his protégés.

. . . The lack of mutual rights and obligations outside the elementary
family, the lack even of occasions on which the unity of the extended
family is expressed, for cousins are not bound to be asked and are not
always asked to weddings, makes of kinship a facultative rather than a
firm bond. It is an excellent basis for friendship, but it is not in itself an
important element in the structure of this society. Among the country-
dwellers, marriages are favoured which reinforce this basis, for they need
to cooperate on a more permanent footing than those of the pueblo. One
might say that the nature of the exploitation of the land in small-holdings produces a tendency to extend family ties. Yet in the absence of the
institutions and values which might support such an extension, ties
between kin cannot be regarded as important.

"Ya se murió mi madrina	"Now my madrina has died
La Duquesita de Alba	The dear Duchess of Alba
¡Si ella no se me muriera	Had she not died on me
a mí no me ajusticiaran!"	They would never condemn me to death!"

Quoted by C. Bernaldo de Quiros y L. Ardila, *El Bandolerismo* (Madrid, 1931).

11. Class and Committees
in a Norwegian
Island Parish

J. A. BARNES

I

When we study the social organization of a simple society, we aim at comprehending all the various ways in which the members of the society systematically interact with one another. For purposes of analysis we treat the political system, the pattern of village life, the system of kinship and affinity, and other similar areas of interaction as parts of the same universe of discourse, as though they were of equal analytical status, and we strive to show how the same external factors, principles of organization, and common values influence these different divisions of social life.

SOURCE: Reprinted with permission of the author and publisher from *Human Relations*, VII, No. 1 (February, 1954), published by Plenum Publishing Company, Ltd.

ACKNOWLEDGEMENTS: The first draft of this paper was read at a meeting of the Association of Social Anthropologists at Oxford on 3 October 1953. I am very grateful to those who took part in the discussion, and to Professor Ely Devons, for comments and criticism. I carried out this work during 1952-3 as a Simon Research Fellow of the University of Manchester. I am much indebted to the University for its generous support, and also to St. John's College, Cambridge, who elected me to a Fellowship. My work was made possible only by the whole-hearted cooperation of many men and women in Bremnes, for which I am most grateful.

This task, though always difficult, has been accomplished for a growing number of simple societies, about which we can feel confident that we have an appreciation of what the society *as a whole* is like. When we turn to the enormously complex societies of Western civilization our task becomes much more difficult. Fieldwork in a Western community can lead directly to knowledge of only a very small sector in the social life of a large-scale society. This limited area of detailed knowedge has then to be related, as best we can, to experience and information derived from other parts of the society.

Recently I had the opportunity of studying a parish in Western Norway called Bremnes. During my fieldwork I did not try to gain first-hand knowledge of Norwegian society as a whole. Any such attempt would, I think, have been entirely unsuccessful. Instead I attempted to isolate for study certain aspects of social life in which I was interested, which were relatively unknown, and relatively easy to grapple with. Many writers have discussed the political history of Norway, the development of its economic institutions, the personality of its inhabitants, their forms of religious belief, and similar topics. Some sociological fieldwork has been carried out in the country, but as yet very little is known about the operation of the social class system in a land which prides itself on its affirmation of social equality. Therefore I decided to concentrate my attention on those kinds of face-to-face relationships through which a class system, if there were one, might operate. I was also interested in the way in which collective action is organized in a society of this kind, and was therefore led to consider the working of committees. I chose to study an island parish partly dependent on industry since I believed that there the field data I sought would be easier both to obtain and to understand than in a town.

Bremnes has a domiciled population of some 4600. Of every ten men over fifteen years old, three are engaged mainly in fishing, two in agriculture, another two in industry, and one is a merchant seaman. These occupations account for 84 percent of the adult male population. Another six percent are gainfully employed in other occupations, and the final ten percent are retired. The majority of adult women are housewives. These percentages indicate only the principal occupation, for many men divide their time between different ways of earning a living. All farms are small, very few employ paid labour, and few households can live off their land alone. Therefore most peasants spend at least the time from Christmas to Easter fishing for herring, while others work in the local marine-engine factory. A few men are almost full-time administrators, but the bulk of the work of local government is carried out by part-time officials such as the mayor, the parish treasurer, the tax assessors and collectors, and the chairmen of the various standing committees, most of whom have small-holdings as well as their public work to attend to.

Bremnes is part of Norway, and its inhabitants share much of their culture with their fellow countrymen, as well as belonging with them to a single economic, social, and administrative system. Here it is sufficient to mention that Norway is a democratic monarchy with high taxation and comparatively little extremes of poverty and wealth. Over 95 percent of Norwegians belong to the Lutheran State church. There is no tradition of feudalism, there are no hereditary titles outside the royal family, and virtually all children attend the official elementary schools. An ideal strongly stressed in Norwegian thought is that no man should have more privileges than his fellows.

II

Each person in Bremnes belongs to many social groups. In particular he is a member of a household, of a hamlet, of a ward, and he is a member of the parish of Bremnes. At different times and different places membership of one or other of these groups is definitive for what he does. He goes to the prayer-house with his household, sits at weddings with other members of his hamlet, and pays tax according to his parish. There are other series of groups which to some extent cut across these territor-ially-based ones, although they may themselves be based on territory. Thus for example a man may belong to a hamlet missionary working-party, or to a bull-owning cooperative based on a ward. In formal terms these various groups fit one inside the other, each in its own series. Thus there are three territorially-defined fishermen's associations in the parish. All three belong to the provincial fishermen's association, and this in its turn forms part of the national association. There may be conflicts because of the duties and rights a person has in the various groups in any one series, and there may be conflicts because of his interests in different series. This is true of all societies.

The territorial arrangement of the Bremnes population is fairly stable. The same fields are cultivated year after year, and new land comes into cultivation only slowly. Houses can be moved from site to site, but this is expensive. Land can be bought and sold, but there are several factors tending to discourage frequent sales of land. Thus for the most part the same people go on living in the same houses and cultivating the same land from year to year. This provides, as it were, a stable environment in which social relations are maintained through the decades, and a frame of reference by which individuals can relate themselves to other people. This territorially-based arrangement of persons is, however, only a part of the social system of Bremnes, for men utilize the sea as well as the land.

Herring are not cultivated, they are hunted. They are taken from the sea, where there are no territorially defined rights in property. They are caught by men organized in groups of from five to twenty, whose composition varies from year to year much more than do the household groups who work together on the same holding. The fishing vessel, the temporary home of the fishermen, wears out more quickly than a house or a plot of land, and it can be bought and sold comparatively easily. Even more important, there are no women on board. Wives and children remain behind and stay in one place while the men move from one fishing ground to another, and from one crew to another. Here then we have two distinct kinds of social field, a fluid and a stationary, and we shall presently discuss a third field linking these two. The fluid field is the field of industrial activity, in which men earn money by catching fish; the stable field is the field of domestic, agricultural, and administrative activity ashore, where they, or their wives, spend the money.

The Norwegian fishing industry is efficient; technological change is going on continually, and vessels make use of modern equipment like radio telephones, echo-sounding gear, nylon ropes, radar and asdics. It is a highly competitive industry, each vessel striving against all other vessels. Loyalties to kinsmen, neighbours and friends continue to operate, but only to a limited extent. In their own words, "Herring fishing is war." Any man can try to get himself included in a crew and each owner seeks to engage the crew that will catch most fish. During the herring season, men from Bremnes sail in vessels belonging to other parishes, and vessels registered in Bremnes sometimes have on board fishermen from as much as 600 miles away. In effect, there is something like a free labour market. Men apply for a place in a particular vessel because of contacts they have made, friends or relatives who have already served on board, or the success of the vessel in previous seasons.

An industry of this kind could scarcely operate were the pattern of social relations as fixed and stable as it is in the round of social and economic activities ashore. The greater portion of the herring catch is exported and in order to sell on the world market at a profit the size of the fishing fleet and the amount of capital invested in it have to respond to economic pressures which vary in intensity and point of application. There is a huge marketing organization and various reserve funds which even out part of the differences in earnings between one vessel and another and from year to year. Even so, the amounts earned by the fleet as a whole vary considerably over the seasons, and in any year some crews do very well while others barely earn any money at all. Most of the tasks in fishing can be carried out by any able-bodied man brought up by the sea, so that men can move fairly easily from fishing into other occupations and back again. From the point of view of the individual fisherman, therefore, the herring-fishing industry is intersected by a social field through which he can move fairly freely along lines of friendship and local knowledge, seeking in the main the achievement of economic goals. Every man is in touch, or can put himself in touch, with a large number of other men, differentiated into shipowners, skippers, net bosses, cooks and others, and into good and bad, and to whom he is linked in a variety of ways. The herring-fishing industry also generates its own social field which is influenced by ecological factors, such as the disappearance of the fish, by economic factors affecting alternative opportunities for employment and investment, and by many others. It is a social field only partly made up of an arrangement of lasting social groups.

Thus in terms of this analysis we can isolate three regions or fields in the social system of Bremnes. Firstly there is the territorially-based social field, with a large number of enduring administrative units, arranged hierarchically, one within another. The administration of the parish is carried on through this system, and the same boundaries are used by the voluntary associations. By reason of their physical proximity the smaller territorial units, the hamlets and wards, provide the basis for enduring social relations between neighbours, which find expression in various activities connected with subsistence agriculture, the care of children, religion, entertainment, and the like. The units of the system endure and membership changes only slowly.

The second social field is that generated by the industrial system. Here we have a large number of interdependent, yet formally autonomous units such as fishing vessels, marketing cooperatives, and herring-oil factories, connected with each other functionally rather than hierachically, yet each organized internally in a hierarchy of command. These units, which often are true social groups as well as units of organization, do not necessarily persist through time, nor does their membership remain fixed.

The third social field has no units or boundaries; it has no coordinating organization. It is made up of the ties of friendship and acquaintance which everyone growing up in Bremnes society partly inherits and largely builds up for himself. Some of the ties are between kinsmen. A few of them are between people who are not equals, as between a man and a former employer with whom he has kept in contact. Most of the ties are, however, between persons who accord approximately equal status to one another, and it is these ties which, I think, may be said to constitute the class system of Bremnes. The elements of this social field are not fixed, for new ties are continually being formed and old links are broken or put into indefinite cold storage.

Let us examine more closely the distinctive features of this third social field. As we well know, cognatic kinship does not of itself give rise to enduring social groups. I have my cousins and sometimes we all act together; but they have their own cousins who are not mine and so on indefinitely. Each individual generates his own set of cognatic kin and in general the set he and his siblings generate is not the same as that generated by anyone else. Each person is, as it were, in touch with a number of other people, some of whom are directly in touch with each other and some of whom are not. Similarly each person has a number of friends, and these friends have their own friends; some of any one person's friends know each other, others do not. I find it convenient to talk of a social field of this kind as a *network*.[1] The image I have is of a set of points some of which are joined by lines. The points of the image are people, or sometimes groups, and the lines indicate which people interact with each other. We can of course think of the whole of social life as generating a network of this kind. For our present purposes, however, I want to consider, roughly speaking, that part of the total network that is left behind when we remove the groupings and chains of interaction which belong strictly to the territorial and industrial systems. In Bremnes society, what is left is largely, though not exclusively, a network of ties of kinship, friendship, and neighbourhood. This network runs across the whole of society and does not stop at the parish boundary. It links Bremnes folk with their kinsmen and friends in other parishes as well as knitting them together within the parish. A network of this kind has no external boundary, nor has it any clear-cut internal divisions, for each person sees himself at the centre of a collection of friends. Certainly there are clusters of people who are more closely knit together than others, but in general the limits of these clusters are vague. Indeed, one of the ways in which a cluster of people emphasize their exclusiveness is to form a group, to which one definitely either does or does not belong. The social ties linking the members of the group are then no longer merely those of kinship or friendship.

In parenthesis we may note that one of the principal formal differences between simple, primitive, rural or small-scale societies as against modern, civilized, urban or mass societies is that in the former the mesh

---

[1] Earlier I used the term *web*, taken from the title of M. Fortes' book, *The Web of Kinship*. However, it seems that many people think of a web as something like a spider's web, in two dimensions, whereas I am trying to form an image of a multi-dimensional concept. It is merely a generalization of a pictographic convention which genealogists have used for centuries on their pedigree charts. Recent modifications of this convention include the tribal "sequences" in W. E. Armstrong, *Rossel Island* (1928), p. 37; "psychological geography" in J. L. Moreno, *Who Shall Survive?* (1934), pp. 238–47; and "sets" in E. D. Chapple and C. S. Coon, *Principles of Anthropology* (1942), p. 284.

of the social network is small, in the latter it is large. By mesh I mean simply the distance round a hole in the network. In modern society, I think we may say that in general people do not have as many friends in common as they do in small-scale societies. When two people meet for the first time, it is rare in modern society for them to discover that they have a large number of common friends, and when this does happen it is regarded as something exceptional and memorable. In small-scale societies I think this happens more frequently, and strangers sometimes find that they have kinsmen in common. In terms of our network analogy, in primitive society many of the possible paths leading away from any A lead back again to A after a few links; in modern society a small proportion lead back to A. In other words, suppose that A interacts with B and that B interacts with C. Then in a primitive society the chances are high that C interacts with A, in a modern society the chances are small. This fact is of considerable practical importance for the study of societies by the traditional techniques of social anthropology, when we try to become acquainted with a limited number of persons whom we observe interacting one with another in a variety of roles. In a modern society, each individual tends to have a different audience for each of the roles he plays. Bremnes, in these terms, is an intermediate society.

In some societies close kinsmen and affines are not necessarily social equals, and in that case the network of kinship ties may have a steep social gradient. Similarly, in our own society, in a street with property ranging gradually from mansions at one end to tenements at the other, we can speak of a network of ties between neighbours who do not regard themselves as equal in social status. However, in Bremnes, as in many other societies, kinsmen, by and large, are approximate social equals. Furthermore, at the present time, unlike conditions which prevailed in Bremnes until about a hundred years ago, neighbours are approximately equal in social status. In Norwegian thought, the idea of equality is emphasized, so that even between persons of markedly different economic status there is less recognition of social inequality on either side than would, I think, be the case in Britain. Thus the social network in Bremnes is largely a system of ties between pairs of persons who regard each other as approximate social equals.

III

The organization of the population of Norway into social classes, assuming that there is such an organization, may be said to manifest itself in Bremnes in the social network I have described. The term *social class* is widely used in general conversation, and naturally it has a great variety of meanings. I think that much of the confusion that has grown up around the term is due to our failure to distinguish these different usages. Thus Marx had in mind definite groups into which the population was divided, which were mutually exclusive, collectively exhaustive, endured through at least several decades, and which recruited members by reference to their position in the economic system. The study of class through clique membership, on the other hand, is closer to the idea of class as a network. For instance, in *Deep South*[2] a series of overlapping cliques are used to define the boundaries of class. Most other approaches to class treat it as a kind of social category, of people possessing approximately the same size of house, or paid about the same amount, or standing at about the same level on some commonly-held scale of social esteem. Lastly there is class as a category of thought, a unit of division used when members of a society mentally divide up the population into status categories. It is clear that the question "How many classes are there?" is meaningless when applied to class as a social category, for there are as many or as few as we choose; and there is often no consensus within a society about class as a category of thought. There may be disagreement about the number of social classes when class is treated as a social group, in the same way as there are disagreements about how many genera and how many species there are in zoological taxonomy; but that is a problem that can be solved. When, however, we look at social class as a kind of network, the question of how many social classes there are falls away completely.

I should perhaps emphasize that the concept of a network is only one tool for use in the analysis of the phenomenon of social class. The other approaches I have mentioned above are equally valid, and indeed are necessary to any understanding of this complex social fact. As we are well aware, there is a fair measure of congruence between the different approaches. In general, most of a man's friends have approximately the same income as he has, live in the same sort of house, are classified together by other members of the society, and fight on the same side in those political and industrial struggles in which, if at all, social classes may perhaps be said to function as groups. For the purposes of this paper I shall nevertheless look at social class from merely the one point of view: as a network of relations between pairs of persons according each other approximately equal status.

This choice is not entirely an arbitrary one. It arises from the fact that Bremnes is a fairly small community, with no marked differences of

---

2 A. Davis, B. B. Gardner, and M. R. Gardner, *Deep South* (1941). For a critique of the class concept from a logician's standpoint, see Llewellyn Gross, "The Use of Class Concepts in Sociological Research," *American Journal of Sociology*, LIV (1948–49), 409–21.

culture and, with a few exceptions, minor differences in standards of dress, housing, and the like. In common parlance, there are few class differences in the parish. There are significant differences in income, but these are partly rendered inoperative by the lack of significant differences in patterns of spending. Under these conditions we do not find the emergence of a division of the population into distinct social classes one above the other.

It should be clear that such a division is not ruled out by the idea of class as a network. It is only pairs of persons who are directly in contact with one another in the class network who regard themselves as approximately of equal status; each person does not necessarily regard everyone else in the network as his equal. Suppose that A has a friend B. A regards B as his social equal, perhaps a little higher or a little lower in social status. As we have remarked earlier, not all B's friends are friends of A. Suppose that D is a friend of B, but not a friend of A. Then, if A knows of D at all, he may or may not regard him as his social equal. If, for instance, A regards B as slightly beneath him in social status, but not so far below as to matter; and if B regards D in the same light; then there is the possibility that A will regard D as too far below him to be treated on a basis of equality. Similarly if A is below B and B is below D, A may think that D is too far above him to be treated as an equal. This process is cumulative with every step taken along the network away from any A we chose to start from. Thus for every individual A the whole of the network, or at least that part of it of which he is aware, is divided into three areas or sets of points. One of these sets consists of all those people to whom A is linked by a longer or shorter path, and whom A regards as his social equals. A is similarly linked to each person in the second set, but this set is composed of all the people that A regards as his social superiors. Similarly the people who in A's estimation are his social inferiors form the third set. These sets are like the sets of cousins we mentioned earlier, in that membership of the sets has to be defined afresh for each new individual A that we choose to consider. Thus in the example given above, D belongs to the superior set with reference to A, but to the socially-equal set with reference to B. I think that in some, at least, of the many instances in which people of widely-varying economic position say that they belong to the middle class in a system of three (or more) social classes, they are merely stating that they are aware of the existence of these three sets of persons. It does not of itself imply that society can be divided into three groups with agreed membership.

I do not wish to digress further with the elaboration of this model of a class system. The idea has been developed sufficiently to deal with the comparatively simple conditions prevailing in Bremnes. In the first place,

Bremnes is small, with a great deal of intermarriage. Hence in the network the number of links along the path joining any two members of the parish is small, probably never more than four. Secondly, because Norwegian culture is egalitarian, everyone is ready to treat as an equal others whose income, upbringing, interests, and occupation differ widely from his own. Thirdly, despite the egalitarian dogma, people in Bremnes recognize the existence of differences in social status. They have stereotypes of the upper class who live in big houses in the towns, talk a different language, and have different religious beliefs. Bremnes folk also speak of a lower class, people who wander about unashamed, living on charity and scorning the aspirations of respectable citizens. In between these two classes are "plain ordinary people like ourselves." It is, in fact, the familiar egocentric three-class system, with ego in the middle class. Class is here a category of thought. In Bremnes, conditions are simplified in that, for the most part, everyone appears to think of almost everybody else in the parish as belonging to the same class as himself. Most people in the upper and lower classes, as defined by Bremnes folk, live outside the parish. When they visit the parish, members of these classes are treated by most of the resident population either as social superiors or inferiors, and not as equals.

Within the parish community, the range of variation is just sufficient for a few people, perhaps a dozen or so in number, to be regarded by many others as on the upper fringe of their sets of social equals. Yet others treat these dozen persons as social superiors. Similarly, there are a few people who are, in rather oblique fashion, treated as social inferiors by many in the community. However, this recognition of social inferiority is often masked, since it is impolite for anyone to show openly that he considers himself superior to anyone else.

The range of status variation is likely to increase in the future. In the community, some men are wealthier than others and although they only occasionally use their wealth to buy socially conspicuous goods and services such as cars, large houses, expensive clothes, pleasure yachts, and the like, they do buy more expensive education for their children. Up to the age of fourteen all children receive the same education in the parish schools, but it is the sons and daughters of the wealthier section of the population who, in the main, continue their education for a few years more. For many youngsters, this means leaving the parish and coming into contact with ideas and values different from those they have known at home. They acquire skills which, when they leave school, differentiate them from the majority of the labouring population, and which in a generation or two may well lead to sharper cleavages along class lines, or at least to a recognition of wider differences in social position. Similarly, on evidence from other parts of Norway, I think that the people lowest in the Bremnes social scale, most of whom are itinerant pedlars and beggars, are now more sharply distinguished from the rest of the population than they were a hundred years ago, when many penurious cottars and day labourers lived in the parish; but I cannot document this for Bremnes.

Although there is this tendency towards greater differentiation in social status, it is slowed down by other social processes. Taxation is high, so that it is difficult for a man to amass a fortune, and since capital is taxed as well as income, it is also difficult for him to retain it. As part of the culturally-supported thesis that all should be treated alike, it is universally held that all children should inherit equally. Only a third of a man's wealth can legally be disposed of by will; the remainder must be distributed according to the laws of inheritance or intestacy. In Bremnes few wills are made and in nearly every case all a man's chattels, after provision has been made for his widow, are divided equally among his children. Thus in a society of large families, fortunes are dispersed at death. Even death duties operate differentially on the principle of "he that already hath more shall receive less." Where land is concerned, one child often takes over the whole of his or her father's farm, but even then he (or she) has to buy the land from the father so that the rights of the landless siblings may be protected. In education, inequalities of opportunity are to some extent offset by bursaries and interest-free loans from official sources, and by the custom of allowing adolescents to work for a year or two so that they can save enough to take themselves through the next stage of their education. All these factors hinder the speedy development of wide social differences even though the trend seems to be in that direction.

Thus in general terms we can say that in Bremnes society, apart from the territorial and industrial systems, there is a network of social ties between pairs of persons arising from considerations of kinship, friendship and acquaintance. Most, but not all, of these ties are between persons who regard each other as approximate social equals, and these ties of approximate equality we regard as one manifestation of the social class system, and shall call the class network. Although each link in the class network is one of approximate social equality, not everyone in the network regards everyone else as his equal, and there are a few people in the parish who are regarded by many others, but not by all, as belonging to a higher class. The class network is utilized for carrying out social activities, such as mutual help and home entertaining; class ties and also ties between people of recognized unequal status are used by men for a variety of other purposes, for example, to find places for themselves in the fishing industry.

IV

Cooperative activity requires some degree of leadership and consensus, whether carried out by enduring groups or by ephemeral groupings of persons linked by a network of social ties. Let us now consider some of the mechanisms by which leadership and consensus are obtained in Bremnes social life. Characteristically a network has no head and, as I have here used the term, no centre and no boundaries either. It is not a corporate body, but rather a system of social relations through which many individuals carry on certain activities which are only indirectly coordinated with one another. In Bremnes, as we have seen, there is little class distinction, but the social activities which are typically carried on through the system of social class are there carried on in the same way as in a society with a larger range of class variation. People invite their friends to supper, or to a sewing party for the mission, or for a shooting trip, on the same basis of apparent approximate equality of social status, which is, I think, definitive of class behaviour. The network of friendship and acquaintance, when men seek out industrial opportunities, is used rather differently. Fish are actually caught, and a large number of distinct activities are brought into close coordination with one another. While fishing, men are no longer equals; they are organized in chains of command and differentiated according to function. For as long as the technical process demands, they are organized in fixed groups standing in a definite relationship one to another. At sea the skipper is in charge of his vessel, the coxswain in charge of his boat; they give orders and their subordinates obey. In the same way the marine-engine factory is organized hierarchically for purposes of production, with a board of directors, managers, foremen, and workmen. The groups of men who are thrown together on board fishing vessels or in the sections of the factory develop and perpetutate other modes of interaction which modify the configurations of the class network besides affecting the productive tasks themselves. In Homans' terminology, there is a clear-cut hierarchically organized external system, whereas the internal system is the network of friendship and acquaintance.[3]

Once we leave the field of organized industrial enterprise, the need for quick decisions and for a clear division of responsibility decreases. The achievement of consensus is valued more highly than speed of autocratic command. Decisions have to be made involving collective action: whether the teachers shall have salmon or cod at their banquet; whether the electricity supply cooperative shall take action against a member who has tampered with his meter; whether a boatload of fishermen shall go

---

[3] G. C. Homans, *The Human Group* (1951), pp. 273 ff.

ashore to the cinema or to the prayer-ship. Such decisions are important, but their importance lies more in their consequences for face-to-face relations between members of the society than in their technical merits. Hence it is not surprising that the process of reaching the decision to hold a feast in the prayer-house is more complicated than that by which a command is given to cast a net in the sea. This is true whether the prayer-house is one belonging to a local community or to the hierarchically-organized factory.

Yet, as is usual in the Western world, most of the formal associations in Bremnes concerned with non-industrial activities have what appears on paper to be an hierarchical structure suitable for taking quick decisions in an autocratic way. There is, it is true, no one person in Bremnes who is head of local society, who might be called the chief of the island, but equally Bremnes is not a leaderless society. It is, as we say, a democracy, and there is a common pattern of organization which occurs in nearly every instance of formal social life. Each association has a committee, with powers to act usually for a year but sometimes for longer, elected by an annual general meeting. The committee, if it is big enough, elects a quarter of its members to an executive council to which most of its powers are delegated. The council and the committee each elect one of their members to be treasurer and secretary. The same man is often chairman of committee and council. There is also a deputy chairman and a number of deputy members who function only in the absence of the principal members. This common pattern is followed with only minor variations by sports clubs, missionary societies, producers' cooperatives, and by the local government itself.

All these bodies employ the same procedure for reaching a decision, by simple majority vote of those present and voting, provided there is a quorum. In practice, whenever possible they avoid taking a vote and the great majority of collective decisions are therefore unanimous. This tendency is most marked at the meetings of missionary societies and least at those of the parish council. Even in the parish council, when there is an irreconcilable division of opinion this is sometimes concealed by first taking a trial vote, to decide which view has greatest support; this is followed by a confirming unanimous vote, which alone is recorded in the minutes. Nevertheless there are in fact continual differences of opinion between members of all these different bodies. Why then is the achievement of formally unanimous decisions considered so important? Here I think we are dealing with a principle of fairly wide application. People living and working together inevitably have conflicting interests but in general they have also a common interest in the maintenance of existing social relations. Individual goals must be attained through socially approved processes, and as far as possible the illusion must be maintained that each individual is acting only in the best interests of the community. As far as possible, that is, the group must appear united, not only vis-à-vis other similar groups, but also to itself. Voting is a method of reaching decisions in which divergence of interest is openly recognized, and in which the multiplicities of divergence are forced into the Procrustean categories of *Yes* and *No*. Significantly, voting is rare in simple societies and in small groups of modern society. Membership in a collectivity implies accepting a share in the collective responsibility for the group's actions as well as a share in the decision to act in a certain way. The local associations in Bremnes are in the main face-to-face groups operating in a conservative environment. Even the producers cooperatives, which had been responsible for introducing technological changes, are made up of men who have been neighbours for many years, who are related by kinship and marriage, and who are not trying to alter the existing pattern of social relations on the island, even though they may be trying to alter the position of the islanders as against the rest of the region. In these conditions voting is an inappropriate procedure.

Furthermore, in voting, the worth of one man relative to another is fixed, and in most voting systems all men have equal votes. When decisions are reached unanimously after discussion, each man gives his own weight to the views of his fellows. Individuals present their views as though they had first been stated by someone else; they speak tentatively and cautiously; they try to win the support of divergent colleagues by saying that they agree with them all. The complex process by which a final decision is reached without the cleavages in the group becoming irreconcilable is one that I am not competent to analyse fully. The process is in part a corollary of the emphasis on equality that is noticeable in Norwegian culture. What is significant for our purposes is that it is a recognizable process which goes on in some social contexts and not in others.

There is one context in which voting by secret ballot is almost invariably used. When new committee members and officers have to be elected, pieces of paper are handed round, everyone writes down his choices and folds over his paper before handing it in. Thus the only topic that never comes up for open discussion is the relative worth of members of the community. I think there are two reasons for this. The election of committee members is the one occasion at which an immediate decision is absolutely necessary to prevent the structure of the association collapsing. Secondly it is difficult, though not impossible, to discuss the merits and demerits of one's friends in their presence without committing oneself so much that the appearance of general amity is threatened. As it is, most elections to local committees in Norway consist of re-voting into office the outgoing members, and sometimes a special sub-committee is appointed to draw up in private a list of nominations, so that voting becomes a formality. In this way the rivalries that threaten the unity of the community are hindered from coming into the open. In Bremnes there is, however, often free discussion about who should serve on those committees involving more hard work than honour.

The parish council differs from the other associations on the island in that it is required to act and cannot be merely a mutual admiration society. It is the local government in a society that is changing, even though it is changing fairly slowly. The leaky church roof must be repaired, and as the population increases more classrooms must be built. The council is under constant pressure from the provincial administration to collect taxes and to spend the money collected. Unlike the missionary societies and chess club and women's institutes, the parish council obtains a large part of the revenue for its projects from the State, and higher authorities audit its accounts, approve its budget, and bombard it with correspondence. It may try to move slowly, but it is continually forced to come to a decision one way or the other on issues about which the community has not yet made up its mind, that is to say, about which there are differences of opinion that have not yet been resolved. Hence from time to time a vote must be taken. The usual techniques, or as some would say, tricks, are used by the mayor to gain unanimous approval, such as, for example, making the majority record their vote by remaining seated and the minority by standing up; all those who are in two minds about the issue probably fail to spring to their feet. In the same way, members of council try to avoid having to vote on matters in which they have divided loyalties, claiming that because of ties of kinship and affinity they are likely to be biased and therefore cannot discuss a particular matter fairly. On one occasion I observed, when an unusually controversial matter was up for discussion and three members had, one after the other, spoken briefly to say that they were related to the parties in the case and therefore could not take part in the discussion, the mayor intervened to point out that council members were probably all related in one way or another to the parties concerned, but that nevertheless they must come to a decision. Where associations other than the parish council are concerned, such embarrassing situations can usually be avoided. There is no state administrative machinery behind them to keep them going at all costs, and if serious latent differences are allowed to become apparent, the organizations may split.

Formal associations in Bremnes, despite their hierarchical form of organization, are not authoritarian. The existing structure of social relations in a conservative environment is maintained by seeking for apparent agreement for all decisions. With the parish council, speed of decision is more important and voting is more often employed. In industrial enterprises, both in the marine-engine factory and the fishing industry, where the environment is not conservative and quick decisions are needed, there is an hierarchical structure and this is effective and not merely formal.

V

Although there are many leaders of part of the parish, each of whom operates in certain restricted contexts, there is no overall leadership of the parish valid in a wide range of contexts, such as we are familiar with in the primitive world. We might perhaps call the pattern of public life in Bremnes "government by committee." In formal terms there are no long chains of command on the island. Instead there is a host of small organized groups with overlapping membership, and the whole population is enmeshed in a close web of kinship and friendship which links together all the people on the island, but which also ties them to kinsmen and affines scattered throughout Western Norway, and indeed throughout the whole world. In this system the people formally in positions of leadership are the elected chairmen of the various associations. They hold office for a fixed term but are very often re-elected unless they decide to resign. There are perhaps 50 voluntary associations of one kind or another, as well as about 40 standing committees whose members are appointed or recommended for nomination by the parish council. All these men occupy positions of some public responsibility. Slightly more in the public eye are the mayor, the rector and his curate, and the sheriff. None of these men can be said to represent the parish in its totality to the outside world, and all of them are involved with fractional interests within the parish. The sheriff and the rector are perhaps most removed from internal rivalries, but even they take part in politics, although they are civil servants and directly responsible to higher authorities outside the parish. The holders of both these offices stood as parliamentary candidates in the recent election. They are both elected parish councillors and members of various parish council committees in their own right as well as being ex-officio members of other committees. Even more involved in local politics are the mayor and the chairmen of standing committees.

In fact there are no living symbols of parish unity, or of the relation of the parish to other social groups, in any but a restricted sense. There is no one person in a key position who articulates the parish with a wider social system as happens in many simple societies. The mayor comes nearest to this, for he represents the parish on the provincial council, and is sometimes invited to serve as a director on the boards of public utility companies serving the parish. Yet even so he is not the representative of the parish in ecclesiastical or judicial matters or in the affairs of the missionary societies. This lack of a single leader or symbolic head is perhaps due to the fact that the parish is not a corporate group in the same way that, for instance, a minor lineage is a corporate group among the Tallensi.[4] Bremnes is a parish, a unit of civil and ecclesiastical administration and part of the kingdom of Norway. Yet even in civil and ecclesiastical affairs the parish looks outward in different directions. Ecclesiastically Bremnes is part of Finnås parish union, which is part of Ytre Sunnhordland archdeaconry, which is part of Bjorgvin diocese; in civil matters Bremnes is an immediate subdivision of Hordaland province; while in judicial affairs it forms part of Finnås sheriff's area, which is part of Sunnhordland magistracy. One hundred and fifty years ago Norway was still virtually a Danish colony governed by what we would now call a system of direct bureaucratic rule. The various sections of the bureaucracy were largely separate and the local areas into which the country was divided for different purposes then coincided even less than they do now. During the nineteenth century, as the local population gained a greater share in public affairs, changes were made to bring the ecclesiastical, administrative, fiscal, and judicial divisions into alignment, but the coincidence is still not complete. Indeed the trend is now in the opposite direction, as new systems of organization cut across existing alignments, as for example the Home Guard and the electricity supply grid. The parish is a unit in some of these different organizations, but it is not an exogamous or endogamous unit; it is not an economic unit, and from most points of view it has no culture of its own. Its nearest approach to a social centre is the parish church, and it is here that the largest crowds gather, that common beliefs are affirmed, and changes in social life receive public recognition. Yet the church is not as widely supported an institution as it once was and its sphere of influence has considerably diminished. Although the process of social specialization has not gone as far in Bremnes as it has, say, in a London suburb, Bremnes is definitely not a simple society. The systems of organization within which the people carry on their activities are not congruent with one another. Neighbours, kinsfolk, workmates, fellow members of associations, are all becoming different.

In general, the mesh of the social network is growing larger. Nevertheless, the organization of Bremnes society is still largely an arrangement of

---

[4] M. Fortes, *The Dynamics of Clanship among the Tallensi* (1945), p. 99.

cross-cutting ties and groupings in which not only friends and enemies, but also leaders and followers, are inextricably mixed. No one line of cleavage ever becomes dominant. The territorial system endures and the industrial system commands; but in this society the relationships that are valued most highly are still to be found in the shifting middle ground of social intercourse between approximate equals.

12. A Comparative Study of the Role of Values in Social Action in Two Southwestern Communities

EVON Z. VOGT

THOMAS F. O'DEA

It is one of the central hypotheses of the Values Study Project that value-orientations play an important part in the shaping of social institutions and in influencing the forms of observed social action. By value-orientations are understood those views of the world, often implicitly held, which define the meaning of human life or the "life situation of man" and thereby provide the context in which day-to-day problems are

SOURCE: Reprinted with permission of the authors and publisher from *American Sociological Review*, XVIII, No. 6 (December, 1953), published by the American Sociological Association.

ACKNOWLEDGEMENT: The authors are indebted to the Rockefeller Foundation (Social Science Division) for the financial support of the research reported in this paper as part of the Comparative Study of Values in Five Cultures Project of the Laboratory of Social Relations at Harvard University. We also wish to express our appreciation to Ethel M. Albert, Wilfrid C. Bailey, Clyde Kluckhohn, Anne Parsons, and John M. Roberts for criticisms and suggestions in the preparation of the paper.

solved.[1] The present article is an outgrowth of one phase of the field research carried out in western New Mexico. It presents the record of two communities composed of people with a similar cultural background and living in the same general ecological setting.

The responses of these two communities to similar problems were found to be quite different. Since the physical setting of the two villages is remarkably similar, the explanation for the differences was sought in the manner in which each group viewed the situation and the kind of social relationships and legitimate expectations which each felt appropriate in meeting situational challenges. In this sphere of value-orientations a marked difference was found. Moreover, the differences in response to situation in the two cases were found to be related to the differences between the value-orientations central to these communities.

We do not deny the importance of situational factors. Nor do we intend to disparage the importance of historical convergence of value-orientations with concrete situations in explaining the centrality of some values as against others and in leading to the deep internalization of the values we discuss. But the importance of value-orientations as an element in understanding the situation of action is inescapably clear. All the elements of what Parsons has called the action frame of reference—the actors, the means and conditions which comprise the situation, and the value-orientations of the actors enter into the act.[2] The primacy of any one in any individual case does not permit generalization. Yet the present study testifies to the great importance of the third element—the value-orientations—in shaping the final action which ensues.

FOCUS OF THE INQUIRY

The inquiry is focused upon a comparison of the Mormon community of *Rimrock*[3] with the Texan community of *Homestead,* both having populations of approximately 250 and both located (40 miles apart) on the southern portion of the Colorado Plateau in western New Mexico. The natural environmental setting is virtually the same for the two villages: the prevailing elevations stand at 7000 feet; the landscapes are characterized by mesa and canyon country; the flora and fauna are

---

[1] Clyde Kluckhohn, "Values and Value-Orientations in the Theory of Action: an Exploration in Definition and Classification," *Toward a General Theory of Action,* edited by Talcott Parsons and E. A. Shils (Cambridge: Harvard University Press, 1951), p. 410.

[2] Talcott Parsons, *The Structure of Social Action* (New York: The Free Press, 1949), pp. 43–86; *Essays in Sociological Theory* (New York: The Free Press, 1949), pp. 32–40; *The Social System* (New York: The Free Press, 1951), pp. 3–24.

[3] "Rimrock" and "Homestead" are pseudonyms used to protect the anonymity of our informants.

typical of the Upper Sonoran Life Zone with stands of pinyon, juniper, sagebrush, and blue gramma grass and some intrusions of Ponderosa pine, Douglas fir, Englemann spruce and Gambel oak from a higher life zone; the region has a steppe climate with an average annual precipitation of 14 inches (which varies greatly from year to year) and with killing frosts occurring late in the spring and early in the autumn.[4] The single important environmental difference between the two communities is that Rimrock is located near the base of a mountain range which has elevations rising to 9000 feet, and a storage reservoir (fed by melting snow packs from these higher elevations) has made irrigation agriculture possible in Rimrock, while in Homestead there is only dry-land farming. Today both villages have subsistence patterns based upon combinations of farming (mainly irrigated crops of alfalfa and wheat in Rimrock, and dry-land crops of pinto beans in Homestead) and livestock raising (mainly Hereford beef cattle in both villages) .

Rimrock was settled by Mormon missionaries in the 1870's as part of a larger project to plant settlements in the area of northern Arizona. Rimrock itself, unlike the Arizona sites, was established as a missionary outpost and the intention of the settlers was the conversion of the Indians, a task conceived in terms of the *Book of Mormon,* which defines the American Indian as "a remnant of Israel."

The early settlers were "called" by the Church, that is, they were selected and sent out by the Church authorities. The early years were exceedingly difficult and only the discipline of the Church and the loyalty of the settlers to its gospel kept them at the task. Drought, crop diseases, and the breaking of the earth and rock dam which they had constructed for the storage of irrigation water added to their difficulties, as did the fact that they had merely squatted on the land and were forced to purchase it at an exorbitant price to avoid eviction. The purchase money was given by the Church authorities in Salt Lake City, who also supplied 5000 pounds of seed wheat in another period of dearth. The original settlers were largely from northern Utah although there were also some converts from the southern states who had been involved in unsuccessful Arizona settlements a few years earlier.

As the emphasis shifted from missionary activities to farming, Rimrock developed into a not unusual Mormon village, despite its peripheral position to the rest of Mormondom. Irrigation farming was supplemented

---

4 For additional ecological details on the region see Evon Z. Vogt, *Navaho Veterans: A Study of Changing Values,* Papers, Vol. XLI, No. 1, Peabody Museum of Harvard University, 1951, pp. 11–12; and John Landgraf, *Land-Use in the Ramah Area of New Mexico: An Anthropological Approach to Areal Study,* Papers, Peabody Museum of Harvard University, 1954.

by cattle raising on the open range. In the early 1930's the Mormons began to buy range land, and Rimrock's economy shifted to a focus upon cattle raising. Today villagers own a total of 149 sections of range land and about four sections of irrigated or irrigable land devoted to gardens and some irrigated pastures in the immediate vicinity of the village. The family farm is still the basic economic unit, although partnerships formed upon a kinship basis and devoted to cattle raising have been important in raising the economic level of the village as a whole. In recent years some of the villagers—also on the basis of a kinship partnership—purchased the local trading post which is engaged in trading with the Indians as well as local village business. In addition to 12 family partnerships which own 111 sections of land, there is a village cooperative which owns 38 sections. Privately-owned commercial facilities in the village include two stores, a boarding house, two garages, a saddle and leather shop, and a small restaurant. With this economic variety there is considerable difference in the distribution of wealth.

The Church is the central core of the village and its complex hierarchical structure, including the auxiliary organizations which activate women, youth and young children, involves a large portion of the villagers in active participation. The church structure is backed up and impenetrated by the kinship structure. Moreover, church organization and kinship not only unify Rimrock into a social unit, they also integrate it into the larger structure of the Mormon Church and relate it by affinity and consanguinity to the rest of Mormondom.

Rimrock has been less affected by secularization than most Mormon villages in Utah and is less assimilated into generalized American patterns.[5] Its relative isolation has both kept such pressures from impinging upon it with full force and enhanced its formal and informal ties with the Church, preserving many of the characteristics of a Mormon village of a generation ago.

Homestead was settled by migrants from the South Plains area of western Texas and Oklahoma in the early 1930's. The migration represented a small aspect of that vast movement of people westward to California which was popularized in Steinbeck's *Grapes of Wrath* and which was the subject of investigation by many governmental agencies in the 1930's and 1940's.[6] Instead of going on to California, these homesteaders settled in a number of semi-arid farming areas in northern and western New Mexico

---

[5] Lowry Nelson, *The Mormon Village* (Salt Lake City: University of Utah Press, 1952), pp. 275–85.

[6] See especially the reports of the Tolan Committee, U. S. Congress, "House Committee to Investigate the Interstate Migration of Destitute Citizens," 76th Congress, 3rd Session, Volume 6, Part 6, 1940.

and proceeded to develop an economy centered around the production of pinto beans. The migration coincided with the period of national depression and was due in part to severe economic conditions on the South Plains which forced families to leave their Texas and Oklahoma communities, in part to the attraction of land available for homesteading which held out the promise of family-owned farms for families who had previously owned little or no land or who had lost their land during the depression. The land base controlled by the homesteaders comprises approximately 100 sections. Each farm unit is operated by a nuclear family; there are no partnerships. Farms now average two sections in size and are scattered as far as 20 miles from the crossroads center of the community which contains the two stores, the school, the post office, two garages, a filling station, a small restaurant, a bean warehouse, a small bar, and two church buildings. Through the years, farming technology has shifted almost completely from horse-drawn implements to mechanized equipment.

With the hazardous farming conditions (periodic droughts and early killing frosts) out-migration from Homestead has been relatively high. A few of these families have gone on to California, but more of them have moved to irrigated farms in the middle Rio Grande Valley and entered an agricultural situation which in its physical environmental aspects is similar to the situation in the Mormon community of Rimrock.

THE MORMON CASE

In broad perspective these two villages present local variations of generalized American culture. They share the common American value-orientations which emphasize the importance of achievement and success, progress and optimism, and rational mastery over nature. In the Mormon case, these were taken over from the 19th century American milieu in western New York where the Church was founded, and reinterpreted in terms of an elaborate theological conception of the universe as a dynamic process in which God and men are active collaborators in an eternal progression to greater power through increasing mastery.[7] The present life was and is conceived as a single episode in an infinity of work and mastery. The result was the heightening for the Mormons of convictions shared with most other Americans. Moreover, this conception was closely related to the belief in the reopening of divine revelation through the agency first of Joseph Smith, the original Mormon prophet, and later through the institutionalized channels of the Mormon Church. The

---

[7] The data from Rimrock are based upon seven months' field experience in the community during 1950–51. Additional data on this community will be provided in O'Dea's *The Mormons* (Chicago: University of Chicago Press, 1957).

Mormons conceived of themselves as a covenant people especially chosen for a divine task. This task was the building of the kingdom of God on earth and in this project—attempted four times unsuccessfully before the eventual migration to the west—much of the religious and secular socialism of the early 19th century found a profound reflection. The Mormon prophet proposed the "Law of Consecration" in an attempt to reconcile private initiative with cooperative endeavor. Contention led to its abandonment in 1838 after some five years of unsuccessful experiment. Yet this withdrawal did not limit, but indeed rather enhanced, its future influence in Mormon settlement. The "Law of Consecration" was no longer interpreted as a blueprint prescribing social institutions of a definite sort, but its values lent a strong cooperative bias to much of later Mormon activity.[8] In the context of the notion of peculiarity and reinforced by out-group antagonism and persecution, these values became deeply embedded in Mormon orientations. The preference for agriculture combined with an emphasis upon community and lay participation in church activities resulted in the formation of compact villages rather than isolated family farmsteads as the typical Mormon settlement pattern.[9]

While Rimrock and Homestead share most of the central value-orientations of general American culture, they differ significantly in the values governing social relationships. Rimrock, with a stress upon community cooperation, an ethnocentrism resulting from the notion of their own peculiarity, and a village pattern of settlement, is more like the other Mormon villages of the West than it is like Homestead.

The stress upon *community cooperation* in Rimrock contrasts markedly with the stress upon *individual independence* found in Homestead. This contrast is one of emphasis, for individual initiative is important in Rimrock, especially in family farming and cattle raising, whereas cooperative activity does occur in Homestead. In Rimrock, however, the expectations are such that one must show his fellows or at least convince himself that he has good cause for *not* committing his time and resources to community efforts while in Homestead cooperative action takes place *only* after certainty has been reached that the claims of other individuals upon one's time and resources are legitimate.

Rimrock was a cooperative venture from the start, and very early the irrigation company, a mutual non-profit corporation chartered under

<hr>

[8] The "Law of Consecration" became the basis of the Mormon pattern of cooperative activity known as "The United Order of Enoch." Cf. Joseph A. Geddes, *The United Order Among the Mormons* (Salt Lake City: Desert News Press, 1924); Edward J. Allen, *The Second United Order Among the Mormons* (New York: Columbia University Press, 1936).

[9] Nelson, *op. cit.*, pp. 25–54.

state law, emerged from the early water association informally developed around—and in a sense within—the Church. In all situations which transcend the capacities of individual families or family combinations, Rimrock Mormons have recourse to cooperative techniques. Let us examine four examples.

The "Tight" Land Situation.—Rimrock Mormons, feeling themselves "gathered," dislike having to migrate to non-Mormon areas. However, after World War II the 32 returned veterans faced a choice between poverty and under-employment or leaving the community. This situation became the concern of the Church and was discussed in its upper lay priesthood bodies in the village. It was decided to buy land to enable the veterans to remain. The possibilities of land purchase in the area were almost nonexistent and it appeared that nothing could be done, when unexpectedly the opportunity to buy some 38 sections presented itself. At the time, the village did not have the needed $10,000 for the down payment, so the sum was borrowed from the Cooperative Security Corporation, a Church Welfare Plan agency, and the land was purchased. The patterns revealed here—community concern over a community problem, and appeal to and reception of aid from the general authorities of the Church—are typically Mormon. However, Mormon cooperation did not end here. Instead of breaking up the purchased land into plots to be individually owned and farmed, the parcel was kept as a unit, and a cooperative Rimrock Land and Cattle Company was formed. The company copied and adapted the form of the mutual irrigation company. Shares were sold in the village, each member being limited to two. A quota of cattle per share per year to be run on the land and a quota of bulls relative to cows were established. The cattle are privately owned, but the land is owned and managed cooperatively. The calves are the property of the owners of the cows. The project, which has not been limited to veterans, supplements other earnings sufficiently to keep most of the veterans in the village.

The Graveling of the Village Streets.—The streets of Rimrock were in bad repair in the fall of 1950. That summer a construction company had brought much large equipment into the area to build and gravel a section of a state highway which runs through the village. Before this company left, taking its equipment with it, villagers, again acting through the Church organization, decided that the village should avail itself of the opportunity and have the town's streets graveled. This was discussed in the Sunday priesthood meeting and announced at the Sunday sacrament meeting. A meeting was called for Monday evening, and each household was asked to send a representative. The meeting was well attended, and although not every family had a member present, practically all were represented at least by proxy. There was considerable discussion, and it was finally decided to pay $800 for the job which meant a $20 donation from each family. The local trader paid a larger amount, and, within a few days after the meeting, the total amount was collected. Only one villager raised objections to the proceedings. Although he was a man of importance locally, he was soon silenced by a much poorer man who invoked Mormon values of progress and cooperation and pledged to give $25 which was five dollars above the norm.

The Construction of a High School Gymnasium.—In 1951 a plan for the construction of a high school gymnasium was presented to the Rimrock villagers. Funds for materials and for certain skilled labor would be provided from state school appropriations, providing that the local residents would contribute the labor for construction. The plan was discussed in a Sunday priesthood meeting in the church, and later meetings were held both in the church and in the schoolhouse. Under the leadership of the principal of the school (who is also a member of the higher priesthood), arrangements were made whereby each able-bodied man in the community would either contribute at least 50 hours of labor or $50 (the latter to be used to hire outside laborers) toward the construction. The original blueprint was extended to include a row of classrooms for the high school around the large central gymnasium.

Work on the new building began in late 1951, continued through 1952, and is now (in 1953) nearing completion. The enterprise was not carried through without difficulties. A few families were sympathetic at first but failed to contribute full amounts of either labor or cash, and some were unsympathetic toward the operation from the start. The high school principal had to keep reminding the villagers about their pledges to support the enterprise. But in the end the project was successful, and it represented an important cooperative effort on the part of the majority.

The Community Dances.—The Mormons have always considered dancing to be an important form of recreation—in fact a particularly Mormon form of recreation. Almost every Friday evening a dance is held in the village church house. These dances are family affairs and are opened and closed with prayer. They are part of the general Church recreation program and are paid for by what is called locally "the budget." The budget refers to the plan under which villagers pay $15 per family per year to cover a large number of entertainments, all sponsored by the Church auxiliary organization for youth, the Young Men's Mutual Improvement Association, and the Young Women's Mutual Improvement Association. The budget payment admits all members of the family to such entertainments.

Observation of these dances over a six months period did not reveal any tension or fighting. Smoking and drinking are forbidden to loyal Mormons, and those who smoked did so outside and away from the building. At dances held in the local school there has been evidence of drinking, and at times fighting has resulted from the presence of non-villagers. But on the whole the Rimrock dances are peaceful family affairs.

Rimrock reveals itself responding to group problems *as a group*. The economic ethic set forth by Joseph Smith in the Law of Consecration is seen in the dual commitment to private individual initiative (family farms and family partnerships in business and agriculture) and to cooperative endeavor in larger communal problems (irrigation company, land and cattle company, graveling the streets, and construction of school gymnasium). For the Mormons, cooperation has become second nature. It has become part of the institutionalized structure of expectations, reinforced by religious conviction and social control.

THE HOMESTEADER CASE

The value-stress upon individual independence of action has deep roots in the history of the homesteader group.[10] The homesteaders were part of the westward migration from the hill country of the Southern Appalachians to the Panhandle country of Texas and Oklahoma and from there to the Southwest and California. Throughout their historical experience there has been an emphasis upon a rough and ready self-reliance and individualism, the Jacksonianism of the frontier West. The move to western New Mexico from the South Plains was made predominantly by isolated nuclear families, and Homestead became a community of scattered, individually-owned farmsteads—a geographical situation and a settlement pattern which reinforced the stress upon individualism.

Let us now examine the influence of this individualistic value-orientation upon a series of situations comparable to those that were described for Rimrock.

The "Tight" Land Situation.—In 1934 the Federal Security Administration, working in conjunction with the Land Use Division of the Department of Agriculture, proposed a "unit reorganization plan." This plan would have enabled the homesteaders to acquire additional tracts of

---

10 The data from Homestead are based upon a year's field work in the community during 1949–50. Additional data on this community will be provided in Vogt's monograph on *Modern Homesteaders: The Life of a 20th Century Frontier Community* (Cambridge: Bellknap Press of Harvard University, 1955). See also Vogt, "Water Witching: An Interpretation of a Ritual Pattern in a Rural American Community," *Scientific Monthly,* LXXV (September, 1952).

land and permit them to run more livestock and hence depend less upon the more hazardous economic pursuit of dry-land pinto bean farming. It called for the use of government funds to purchase large ranches near the Homestead area which would be managed cooperatively by a board of directors selected by the community. The scheme collapsed while it was still in the planning stages, because it was clear that each family expected to acquire its own private holdings on the range and that a cooperative would not work in Homestead.

The Graveling of the Village Streets.—During the winter of 1949-50 the construction company which was building the highway through Rimrock was also building a small section of highway north of Homestead. The construction company offered to gravel the streets of Homestead center if the residents who lived in the village would cooperatively contribute enough funds for the purpose. This community plan was rejected by the homesteaders, and an alternative plan was followed. Each of the operators of several of the service institutions—including the two stores, the bar, and the post office—independently hired the construction company truck drivers to haul a few loads of gravel to be placed in front of his own place of business, which still left the rest of the village streets a sea of mud in rainy weather.

The Construction of a High School Gymnasium.—In 1950 the same plan for the construction of a new gymnasium was presented to the homesteaders as was presented to the Mormon village of Rimrock. As noted above, this plan was accepted by the community of Rimrock, and the new building is now nearing completion. But the plan was rejected by the residents of Homestead at a meeting in the summer of 1950, and there were long speeches to the effect that "I've got to look after my own farm and my own family first; I can't be up here in town building a gymnasium." Later in the summer additional funds were provided for labor; and with these funds adobe bricks were made, the foundation was dug, and construction was started—the homesteaders being willing to work on the gymnasium on a purely business basis at a dollar an hour. But as soon as the funds were exhausted, construction stopped. Today a partially completed gymnasium, and stacks of some 10,000 adobe bricks disintegrating slowly with the rains, stand as monuments to the individualism of the homesteaders.

The Community Dances.—As in Rimrock, the village dances in Homestead are important focal points for community activity. These affairs take place several times a year in the schoolhouse and are always well-attended. But while the dances in Rimrock are well-coordinated activities which carry through the evening, the dances in Homestead often end when tensions between rival families result in fist-fights. And there is always the expectation in Homestead that a dance (or other cooperative activity such as a picnic or rodeo) may end at any moment and the level of activity reduced to the component nuclear families which form the only solid core of social organization within the community.

The individualistic value-orientation of the homesteaders also has important functional relationships to the religious organization of the community. With the exception of two men who are professed atheists, all of the homesteaders define themselves as Christians. But denominationalism is rife, there being ten different denominations represented in the village: Baptist, Presbyterian, Methodist, Nazarene, Campbellite, Holiness, Seventh-day Adventists, Mormon, Catholic, and Present Day Disciples.

In the most general terms, this religious differentiation in Homestead can be interpreted as a function of the individualistic and factionalizing tendencies in the social system. In a culture with a value-stress upon independent individual action combined with a "freedom of religion" ideology, adhering to one's own denomination becomes an important means of expressing individualism and of focusing factional disputes around a doctrine and a concrete institutional framework. In turn, the doctrinal differences promote additional factionalizing tendencies, with the result that competing churches become the battleground for a cumulative and circularly reinforcing struggle between rival small factions within the community.[11]

To sum up, we may say that the strong commitment to an individualistic value-orientation has resulted in a social system in which interpersonal relations are strongly colored by a kind of factionalism and in which persons and groups become related to one another in a competitive, feuding relationship. The homesteaders do not live on their widely separated farms and ignore one another, as it might be possible to do. On the other hand, they do not cooperate in community affairs as closely as does a hive of bees. They interact, but a constant feuding tone permeates the economic, social and religious structure of the community.

RELATIONSHIP BETWEEN THE TWO COMMUNITIES

Although there is some trading in livestock, feed, and other crops, the most important contacts between the two communities are not economic

---

11 This relationship between churches and factionalizing tendencies has also been observed by Bailey in his unpublished study of a community in west Texas, in the heart of the ancestral home region of the present residents of Homestead. Cf. Wilfrid C. Bailey, "A Study of a Texas Panhandle Community; A Preliminary Report on Cotton Center, Texas," Values Study Files, Harvard University.

but are social and recreational. The village baseball teams have scheduled games with one another for the past two decades, and there is almost
always joint participation in the community dances and in the summer
rodeos in the two communities. Despite Mormon objections to close
associations with "gentiles," there is also considerable interdating
between the two communities among the teen-age groups, and three
intermarriages have taken place.

In general, the homesteaders envy and admire the Mormons' economic
organization, their irrigated land, and more promising prospects for good
crops each year. On the other hand, they regard the Mormons as cliquish
and unfriendly and fail completely to understand why anyone "wants to
live all bunched up the way the Mormons do." They feel that the
Mormons are inbred and think they should be glad to get "new blood"
from intermarriages with homesteaders. They add, "That Mormon
religion is something we can't understand at all." Finally, the homesteaders say that Mormons "used to have more than one wife, and some
probably still do; they dance in the church, they're against liquor, coffee,
and tobacco, and they always talk about Joseph Smith and the *Book of
Mormon.*"

The Mormons consider their own way of life distinctly superior to that
of the homesteaders in every way. Some will admit that the homesteaders
have the virtue of being more friendly and of "mixing more with others,"
and their efforts in the face of farming hazards are admired, but Homestead is generally regarded as a rough and in some ways immoral community, especially because of the drinking, smoking, and fighting (particularly at dances) that takes place. They also feel that Homestead is
disorganized and that the churches are not doing what they should for
the community. For the past few years they have been making regular
missionary trips to Homestead, but to date they have made no conver-
sions.

COMPARISONS AND CONCLUSIONS

In the case of Rimrock and Homestead, we are dealing with two
communities which are comparable in population, in ecological setting,
and which are variants of the same general culture. The two outstanding
differences are: (a) irrigation versus dry-land farming and associated
differences in settlement pattern, compact village versus isolated farmstead type;[12] (b) a value stress upon cooperative community action
versus a stress upon individual action. The important question here
involves the relationship (if any) between these two sets of variables. Is

---

[12] Cf. Nelson, *op. cit.,* p. 4.

the cooperation in Rimrock directly a function of an irrigation agriculture situation with a compact village settlement pattern, the rugged individualism in Homestead, a function of a dry-land farming situation with a scattered settlement pattern? Or did these value orientations arise out of earlier historical experience in each case, influence the types of communities which were established in western New Mexico, and later persist in the face of changed economic situations? We shall attempt to demonstrate that the second proposition is more in accord with the historical facts as we now know them.

Nelson has recently shown that the general pattern of the Mormon village is neither a direct function (in its beginnings) of the requirements of irrigation agriculture, nor of the need for protection against Indians on the frontier. Rather, the basic pattern was a social invention of the Mormons, motivated by a sense of urgent need to prepare a dwelling place for the "Savior" at "His Second Coming." The "Plat of the City of Zion" was invented by Joseph Smith, Sidney Rigdon, and Frederick G. Williams in 1833 and has formed the basis for the laying out of most Mormon villages, even those established in the Middle West before the Mormons migrated to Utah.[13]

It is very clear that both the compact village pattern and the cooperative social arrangements centered around the church existed before the Mormons engaged in irrigation agriculture and had a strong influence upon the development of community structure not only in Utah but in the Mormon settlements like Rimrock on the periphery of the Mormon culture area. There is no objective reason in the Rimrock ecological and cultural setting (the local Navahos and Zunis did not pose a threat to pioneer settlements in the 1880's) why the Mormons could not have set up a community which conformed more to the isolated farmstead type with a greater stress upon individualistic social relations. Once the Mormon community was established, it is clear that the cooperation required by irrigation agriculture of the Mormon type and the general organization of the church strongly reinforced the value stress upon communal social action.

It is of further significance that as the population expanded and the Rimrock Mormons shifted from irrigation agricultural pursuits to dry-land ranching in the region outside of the Rimrock valley, the earlier cooperative patterns modeled on the mutual irrigation company were applied to the solution of economic problems that are identical to those faced by the Homesteaders. Moreover, in midwestern and eastern

---

13 Nelson, op. cit., pp. 28–38.

cities to which Mormons have recently moved, church wards have purchased and cooperatively worked church welfare plan farms.

In Homestead, on the other hand, our evidence indicates that the first settlers were drawn from a westward-moving population which stressed a frontier-type of self-reliance and individualism. They were searching for a place where each man could "own his own farm and be his own boss." Each family settled on its isolated homestead claim, and there emerged from the beginning an isolated farmstead type of settlement pattern in which the nuclear family was the solidary unit. The service center which was built up later simply occupied lots that were sold to storekeepers, filling station operators, the bartender, and others, by the four families who owned the four sections which joined at a crossroads. Only two of these four family homes were located near the service center at the crossroads. The other two families continued to maintain their homes in other quarters of their sections and lived almost a mile from "town." In 1952 one of the former families built a new home located over a mile from the center of town, and commented that they had always looked forward to "getting out of town."

There is no objective reason in the Homestead ecological setting why there could not be more clustering of houses into a compact village and more community cooperation than actually exists. One would not expect those farmers whose farms are located 15 or 20 miles from the service center to live in "town" and travel out to work each day. But there is no reason why those families living within two or three miles of the village center could not live in town and work their fields from there. In typical Mormon villages a large percentage of the farms are located more than three miles from the farm homes. For example, in Rimrock over 31 percent, in Escalante over 38 percent, and in Ephraim over 30 percent of the farms are located from three to eight or more miles from the center of the villages.[14]

It is clear that the Homesteaders were operating with a set of individualistic property arrangements (drawn, of course, from our generalized American culture) and that their strong stress upon individualism led to a quite different utilization of these property patterns (than was the case with the Mormons) and to the establishment of a highly scattered type of community. Once Homestead was established, the individualism permitted by the scattered dry-land farming pattern, and encouraged by the emphasis upon the small nuclear family unit and upon multi-denominationalism in church affiliation reacted on and strongly reinforced the

---

[14] See Nelson, *op. cit.*, pp. 99 and 144 for data on Escalante and Ephraim.

value stress upon individual independence. It is evident that the homesteaders continue to prefer this way of life, as shown by their remarks
concerning the "bunched up" character of a Mormon village and the fact
that a number of families have recently moved "out of town" when they
built new houses.

Of further interest is the fact that when homesteader families move to
irrigated farms in the middle Rio Grande Valley, the stress upon individual action tends to persist strongly. They do not readily develop
cooperative patterns to deal with this new setting which is similar to the
situation in the irrigated valley of the Mormons at Rimrock. Indeed, one
of the principal innovations they have been promoting in one region
along the Rio Grande where they are replacing Spanish-Americans on
the irrigated farming land is a system of meters on irrigation ditches.
These meters will measure the water flowing into each individual
farmer's ditches, and effectively eliminate the need for more highly
organized cooperative arrangements for distributing the available supply
of water.

In conclusion, we should like to reiterate that we are strongly cognizant of situational factors. If the Rimrock Mormons had not been able to
settle in a valley which was watered by melting snow packs from a nearby
mountain and which provided the possibilities for the construction of
storage reservoir, they certainly could not have developed an irrigation
agricultural system at all. In the case of Rimrock, however, the actual site
of settlement was selected from among several possible sites in a larger
situation. The selection was largely influenced by Mormon preconceptions of the type of village they wished to establish. In fact, Mormons
chose the irrigable valleys throughout the inter-montane west. On the
other hand, the physical environmental features for the development of
irrigation were simply not present in the Homestead setting, and the
people had no alternative to dry-land farming. There is no evidence to
suggest that had they found an irrigable valley, they would have
developed it along Mormon lines. In fact, the homesteaders' activities in
the Rio Grande Valley suggest just the opposite. It is clear that the
situational facts did not *determine* in any simple sense the contrasting
community structures which emerged. Rather, the situations set certain
limits, but within these limits contrasting value-orientations influenced
the development of two quite different community types. It would
appear that solutions to problems of community settlement pattern and
the type of concrete social action which ensues are set within a value
framework which importantly influences the selections made with the
range of possibilities existing within an objective situation.

CHAPTER III

Structures of Conflict:
Ethnic Relations
and Sub-Communities

Sub-communities composed of members of an ethnic or racial minority provide interesting examples for students of the community, and undeniably add color and variety to the urban scene. However, the fact of their existence challenges both the social scientist who must explain why they exist, and the society which must justify creating social conditions that spawn ghettos and minority enclaves.

One can dismiss the existence of an ethnic sub-community on the basis that "Poles want to live together," or "Negroes wouldn't leave the black belt if they could," but this misses the most essential fact about the ethnic community—it is composed of members of a group that has been denied entry into the larger community. Whether or not Negroes like other Negroes as neighbors or value their ghetto style of life is beside the point; the fact that they are forcibly segregated into special areas reflects their subordinate status in society. Thus the ghetto, ethnic community, or sub-cultural enclave is the product not of the sub-group, but rather of the majority that enforces separateness. Ethnic communities are the product of conflict between the majority that jealously guards its superior status, and the minority that is relegated to a subordinate position.

The fact that the conflict between the majority and the sub-community generally remains latent should not be interpreted as evidence that all is well and conflict does not exist after all. Rather, the fact that in the past individuals of ethnic minorities had an avenue of escape into the larger community once they had mastered the trappings of the majority culture probably funneled off much of the antagonism that could have led to rancorous conflict. In a situation in which the individual member of a minority cannot escape, however, but must endure subserviance with no chance of betterment, the probability that his bitterness may grow into open conflict is increased. The stagnated status of the Negro in American society, compared to past European minorities for whom inferior sub-cultural status was a temporary condition, can perhaps best explain the violent turn that community conflict has taken recently. The potential for open conflict is always present when a sub-community exists; in the case of the Negro we are seeing the result of enforced inferiority, of which the ghetto is the most glaring evidence, that has existed for too long and still has no promise of improvement.

Another question we must address ourselves to in order to better understand the ethnic community is what is the nature of "community" within this sub-element. How does it differ from the majority, and why does this difference exist? As Killian points out in the selection included here, the Negro sub-community, and presumably other ethnic communities as well, lacks the formal political structure found in the majority community. In spite of its lack of formal structure, the ethnic sub-community or ghetto tends to have a much more intense, personal base. "Community" based on primary relationships, typical of some of the communities presented in Chapter II, may survive in the ghettos of the urban milieu. Rather than by familial ties, or cultural traditions, the ethnic sub-community is unified by the common fate of its members at the hands of the majority. The solidarity of the sub-community may help the individual to endure the discrimination meted out by the majority, for within his group he can reaffirm his worth by association with equals who share and understand his fate.

Thus, the ethnic sub-community is a holdover of a community type based upon primary group sentiment and behavior in an increasingly formal and impersonal society in which "community" means the focal point of a series of secondary organizations that serve its residents. By the traditional measures of community the ethnic community may be more viable than the larger community that spawned it by rejecting its members. Conflict, therefore, can be a unifying force in a community, not only by unifying the threatened populace, but also as the very basis for the existence of a community. To the majority community the basis for the existence of the ghetto may be of little concern, but for the ethnic community it is the predominant fact of life against which all activities must be reckoned. This central theme of insecurity—fear of "The Man," pogrom, "The Bear," etc.,—creates within the community a solidarity rarely found outside primary groups.

In the excerpt from his book *Germania, U.S.A.*, Iverson makes the distinction between ethnic communities which result when a minority is rejected by the majority society, and status communities which emerge when status equals, capitalizing upon the internal differentiation of their society, close their ranks against outsiders of inferior or superior status. Germania an example of an ethnic is a community which evolved into a sub-community of status elites.

The way of life in an ethnic community can provide the individual with a greater sense of belonging than he finds outside the group so that as the reasons for the existence of the community break down its residents may feel a sense of loss. The end of direct domination by the English landlords in Pentrediwaith, Wales, coupled with economic change that forced its residents to go outside the community for work, resulted in a gradual decline in the viability of the community. The ethnic basis of Pentre that stressed all things Welsh was all that remained to keep it from becoming just a collection of houses. Removal of English discrimination against the Welsh threatened this last vestige of community viability; Frankenberg points out that Pentre is disappearing as its people are absorbed into the dominant English institutions.

The longing of an ethnic group for old cultural ways is illustrated in the brief excerpt from Wood's *Hamtramck*. The Poles that have immigrated to America can pass into the dominant society once they adopt the new culture and abandon their old ways. This too is painful for the minority, for it must give up its culture which is discredited by the majority. For those who are unable or reluctant to abandon their old life style, there are occasional communities like Hamtramck where one can maintain some of his minority culture if he is willing to endure the discrimination that results from living in an ethnic community.

The selection by Jackson spells out the nature of ethnic conflict with illustrations of the relations between the French and English residents of Normanville, an Ontario community. In Normanville, French Catholics are subordinate to the English but the conflict is of low intensity and militancy because relations between the two groups are highly institutionalized in school, church and town hall.

The conflict between the Spanish residents of Taos and the Anglos who have usurped their position of dominance is not institutionalized. Bodine found the numerically superior Spanish could control political affairs but were effectively disenfranchised by the economic dominance of the Anglos who lionized the Indians for their unique culture. Both the Anglos and the Indians were better off economically than the majority of the Spanish, for they could capitalize on tourism, whereas the Spanish were neither wealthy enough to set up businesses in the manner of the Anglos, nor quaint enough to appeal to tourists as did the Indians. The Spanish found themselves in a position of subordination in a community that they dominated numerically and politically.

The two articles dealing with the Negro ethnic community present the best current example of the "structures of conflict." Pfautz documents the social and economic inferiority of the Negro ghettos in three large cities. Both authors demonstrate the dominant position of the racial question in the minds and actions of Negro leaders. Killian introduces Warren's concept of the horizontal-vertical dimensions of community to illustrate that the local, or horizontal, power structure is closed to the Negro leader-agent who must turn to federal, or vertical community, agencies to get any satisfaction.

The spectre of America's unresolved Negro problem hangs heavy over both of these articles. The schism that Pfautz noted between older Negroes who were tolerant of segregation and feared rapid change, and the younger leaders who urged rapid integration, has seemingly come full circle as today young Negroes reject the society that has long rejected them and argue for separate black communities, institutions, and even a separate black nation. Killian's observation of the intensification of conflict as Negroes reject their subservient status, seems like the first flickerings of a dreadful nightmare in the light of America's growing wave of racial violence. The rejection of society and the outbreak of mass violence are desperate actions which have no hope of success but seem destined only to bring further deprivation on the most deprived segment of the community. The point should be made that the Negro ghetto has long been the victim of overt conflict of the type that it now wages on the larger community.

The answer to the problem seems obvious and perhaps impossible to put into action soon enough—the majority society created the ghetto and only it can reform itself to remove the cause of the ghetto. Rebuilding burned-out cities is only part of the answer, for as long as the tradition of inequality that creates ethnic communities persists, so too will group conflict and the potential for violence persist. The ghetto is the product of social conflict and America's dark days will continue until we reform and cleanse this strain of hypocrisy, or until we stifle the outcry and settle down in the false tranquility of a shameful police state.

13. Germania as an Ethnic Community

NOEL IVERSON

THE HISTORICAL PERSPECTIVE

Events in Europe and in North America set the stage for the appearance of a number of well-to-do German communities in the New World during a few years before the American Civil War. In nineteenth-century Germany the middle classes had at last begun to claim their birthright as a central stratum in the German nation, but they were faced with remnants of medieval institutions which blocked their full participation in the national community long after such obstacles had been removed from the path of the middle classes in England and France. The German Turners (some of whom later founded Germania), patriotic spokesmen for the burgeoning middle classes, were in the vexing position of being at the same time members of a powerless class and of a powerful, rising nation. Feeling that their destiny was being unfulfilled because of an obdurate ruling class, this German middle class rose in revolutionary protest against the governing aristocracy in 1830 and, more violently, in 1848. When their radical aspirations were frustrated, they responded with more than the usual readiness to emigrate to the New World.

SOURCE: Reprinted with permission of the author and publisher from Noel Iverson, *Germania, U.S.A.—Social Change in New Ulm, Minnesota,* University of Minnesota Press, Minneapolis. © Copyright 1966 University of Minnesota.

Meanwhile, in the New World the vast expansion into the wilderness had created a vacuum in the American middle classes; this same westward movement, the child of optimism nourished by an enormously rich frontier, had already borne a host of utopian experiments. The more adventuresome settlers of the Atlantic seaboard were eager to found businesses and industries in the territories opening in the West. Those who stayed behind formed a stratum of laborers in the New England factories, where they endured in the congested cities "new misery and new hard masters." Particularly in the Midwest, a shortage of skilled farmers and artisans developed; toward the Midwest numbers of the disillusioned political idealists of 1848 were drawn.

They were imbued with a minority psychology which in France and England during the same period was an inappropriate outlook, not found among the well-to-do middle-class elements who were already defending their gains in property and position with the same determination as the upper classes. The minority psychology made the migrant Germans ripe for utopian experiments—for the formation of withdrawn communities which could serve to bring to reality their dreams of the good life. And so some came close to repeating the experience of those pioneer utopians in America—Charles Fourier, Robert Owen, Albert Brisbane, Josiah Warren, Henry Edger, Étienne Cabet, and John Humphrey Noyes—who had inspired ideal societies intended once and for all to rid their members of the evils of private property.

But the immigrant Germans of the 1850's were spared the inglorious failures of these unflaggingly romantic early American socialists. For if these Germans hoped for a life free of political and religious oppression, by and large they were not inclined to construct models of ideal societies that bore no relation to reality. Furthermore, they did not possess the frontiersman's disposition to break all ties with traditional society and culture; rather, they shared the colonist's desire to preserve the Old World heritage.[1] They dreamed, not of founding a new community in the wilderness wrested from savages and wild beasts, but of working up a settled community more akin to the long-established peasant villages and small towns of nineteenth-century Germany. The migrant Germans therefore chose to settle on improved land rather than on the virgin land of the frontier. Moreover, whenever possible they chose places with climate and vegetation similar to those in the areas they had come from— just as thousands of colonial Germans, for example, had been drawn to the richly wooded land of Pennsylvania. The generation of Germans who had opposed the Metternich system (or had felt the economic disloca-

---

[1] Robert E. Park and Herbert A. Miller, *Old World Traits Transplanted* (New York: Harper & Row, Publishers, 1921), drew this distinction between frontiersmen and colonists.

tions of that period) and fled their homeland sought to realize in the New World their frustrated Old World ambitions.

One semiutopian experiment of the migrant Germans of this generation was Germania, U.S.A.[2] First occupying land only recently delivered from the wilderness by a group of German artisans and workmen from Chicago, the settlement would, in all probability, have failed had it not been that less than three years later a small party of Turners arrived by way of Cincinnati. Acting on behalf of the Turnerbund, they sought a place where they might establish free from outside interference a socialistic community. After a series of misadventures, during which several sites were explored and rejected, they happened upon the present site of Germania. Impressed by the natural beauty of the area, its excellent soil and abundant water, and its heavy forestation, encouraged by the presence of countrymen with similar ideals, the Turners chose this place for their model town. Their utopian venture was soon augmented by the arrival of new settlers from the Cincinnati Turner Society. From less than 150 inhabitants a century or so ago, Germania grew to a population of over 13,000 in 1965.

The Turners of Germania underwent a dramatic social transformation in the space of a few years, changing from talented ethnic leaders to an Americanized status elite. They founded a community of aliens and hence themselves inclined toward ethnic form; but they were well-to-do middle-class and upper middle-class people which disposed them toward organizing as a status community. Though the background of the Germania Turners created these contrary tendencies, history alone provides no general explanation of the processes of change from ethnic to status community, or indeed of the principles of community formation itself. Herein lies the special task of sociological analysis.

THE THEORETICAL PERSPECTIVE

The sociologist shares the historian's interest in the formation and disintegration of communities, an unending process with the appearance of randomness and futility. Sociology emphasizes that human relations tend to stabilize, through the formation of habits, and to systematize into communities—structures that aid the survival of individuals. Though it is obvious that human communities are formed for common survival and develop common goals and values, an infinite variety of styles and meanings of life may theoretically emerge from such formations. And though some communities are more deliberately conceived than others, none has ever succeeded in foreseeing all the consequences of its creation, and none has been free of the onslaught of unforeseen events.

---

2 See Iverson, *op. cit.*, Chapter 3, pp. 53–67, for a more complete discussion of the founding of Germania.

The two notable types of community of special interest here, ethnic and status subcommunities,[3] emerge only within the cultural, social, and territorial dimensions of wider communities. Since they exist as subforms of dominant societies, ethnic communities, and to a lesser extent status communities, are particularly subject to the vicissitudes of change in the wider milieu, however well-conceived and carefully launched they may be. Usually they are neither. And though each has similar purposes—group survival amidst an alien majority or the preservation of a special way of life, for example—the structure and position of each kind of subcommunity with respect to the majority society are quite different. The peculiarities of subcommunity life are to be understood on the basis of the general theory of community underlying this study.

That theory subordinates territoriality to what is sometimes called "social space."[4] By this is meant the common ground, consisting of social relations and cultural patterns, that transforms a plurality of people into a community. Territory alone does not provide this common ground, as most sociologists today recognize.[5] Formerly, the idea of community as a system of institutions occupying a territory—introduced into sociological theory by an English student of jurisprudence, Henry Sumner Maine,[6] and incorporated by Ferdinand Tönnies in his famous *Gemeinschaft-Gesellschaft* dichotomy[7]—emphasized territoriality as fundamental to community. Since the 1920's, however, American sociologists' attention has shifted from the ecological and geographic to the social and cultural aspects of communities, as the "social ecology" of Robert E. Park, Ernest W. Burgess, and Roderick D. McKenzie[8] gave way to a broader concep-

---

[3] Since these are by definition subcommunity forms, this terminology is redundant. To simplify the language, the term subcommunity, which is generic to both ethnic and status variants, will not ordinarily be used in conjunction with "ethnic" or "status."

[4] R. M. MacIver, *Society* (New York: Rinehart, 1937), pp. 150–152; 158–60. MacIver called it "community sentiment" when speaking of its emotive aspect, "social coherence" when stressing the shared purposes of a group occupying a territory and pursuing a way of life somewhat apart from and yet physically within a larger society.

[5] Hannah Arendt, *Eichmann in Jerusalem: A Report on the Banality of Evil* (New York: The Viking Press, Inc., 1963), p. 241. An understanding by no means limited to social scientists, as Hannah Arendt, in thinking about the European Jews' legal relation to the state of Israel, says: " 'Territoriality,' as the law understands it, is a political and legal concept, and not merely a geographical term. It relates not so much, and not primarily, to a piece of land as to the space between individuals in a group whose members are bound to, and at the same time separated and protected from, each other by all kinds of relationships, based on a common language, religion, a common history, customs and laws."

[6] Henry Sumner Maine, *Ancient Law* (New York: Henry Holt, 1906).

[7] *Community and Society*, trans. by Charles P. Loomis (East Lansing: Michigan State University Press, 1957).

[8] *The City* (Chicago: University of Chicago Press, 1925).

tion, initiated by R. M. MacIver and by Eduard C. Lindeman,[9] in which community is seen as a system of common life which need not be restricted to a fixed geographical area[10] (although the territorial community—e.g., the band, tribe, or village—is included as a subtype).[11]

A GENERAL THEORY OF COMMUNITY FORMATION

Communities represent, in addition, human groupings which provide for the basic needs of their members. Communities are total ways of life, forming systems composed of sufficient groups and institutions to enable their members to survive the trials of a normal year and a normal life.[12] Sustaining complete cultures as well as total social systems, communities solve the basic problems of human existence: physical subsistence, the socialization of members, the control of individuals and groups, and defense against outside intervention.[13]

These basic imperatives are met differently by each community, for none evolves precisely the same arrangement of institutions or invests them with quite the same meanings and purposes as any other community. Institutions, and the peculiarities of their reciprocal adjustments, contribute to the uniqueness of each community. In the long run, the "interadjustment of the institutions of one area of social life to influences arising out of another"[14] usually leads to the establishment of a distinct way of life, a process which is illuminated by the general principles of community formation underlying this study: *stabilization, consistency,* and *completeness.*[15]

---

9 MacIver, *Community* (New York: Macmillan, 1917), pp. 22–24; Lindeman, "Community," *Encyclopedia of the Social Sciences* (New York: Macmillan, 1934).

10 One can go too far in this direction also: I do not mean that since MacIver and others conceived this newer idea of community, territory is of little or no importance in the study of human communities, which typically transcend mere physical boundaries. They do, but, again typically, they observe them—at times with awesome ferocity.

11 This discussion follows Don Martindale's *American Social Structure* (New York: Appleton-Century-Crofts, 1960), pp. 132–133, 147–149, and is informed by John Sirjamaki's *Sociology of Cities* (New York: Random House, Inc., 1964), pp. 7–18.

12 Don Martindale, *Social Life and Cultural Change* (Princeton, N.J.: D. Van Nostrand Co., Inc., 1962), p. 44. By "normal" is meant that range of behavior and experience defined as such by a community. See also MacIver, *Society,* p. 9: "The mark of a community is that one's life *may* be lived wholly within it, that all one's social relationships *may* be found within it."

13 Martindale, *American Society* (Princeton, N. J.: D. Van Nostrand Co., Inc., 1960), pp. 254ff.; and *Social Life and Cultural Change,* pp. 39–44. For an earlier and somewhat more involved discussion of the social and cultural implications of these universal human imperatives, see Bronislaw Malinowski's *A Scientific Theory of Culture* (Chapel Hill: University of North Carolina Press, 1944), pp. 125–131.

14 Martindale, *Social Life and Cultural Change,* p. 44.

15 Martindale, *American Social Structure,* pp. 131–132.

All communities, whether subforms such as ethnic and status communities or the most extensive forms, such as nation states,[16] institutionalize behavior and seek to make citizens' activities stable, consistent, and complete. All communities require, as a condition of their existence, that standardized solutions to problems of communal life[17]—institutions—be invented, and that these solutions (which are invested with norms and rules) be made stable. The stabilizing power of institutions is a potent force for community survival. (Tradition marks the organic stability of communities; totalitarianism is the death warrant of tradition.) When, on the other hand, there is but an assemblage of persons, each going his own way, there is no stability in whatever joint efforts may be undertaken and hence no community.

Consistency or pattern must be hit upon if communities are to persist. Behavior and values need to be brought into some general accord (whether formally declared or tacitly understood, the effect—agreement and integration—is the same) if a ruinous competition of redundant institutions is to be avoided.

Finally, the survival of the human community rests upon its ability to provide a total way of life. It is no accident, for example, that societies tend universally to regard chronic bachelorhood as an errant condition, for no society is complete which does not institutionalize (and succeed in upholding) marriage. When a community fails to meet the basic need for institutional completeness sufficient to provide the basic imperatives its existence is imperiled.[18]

ETHNIC AND STATUS COMMUNITIES

I have suggested that human beings exhibit a universal tendency to guide their activities toward community form, that is, to fashion modes of behavior which are stable, consistent, and complete. As a general principle, this tendency operates in all communities—tribes, peasant villages, cities, ethnic communities, or status communities. Ethnic and status communities are special cases of pluralities of aliens or status equals forming

---

16 *Ibid.*, p. 133; Sirjamaki, *op. cit.*, pp. 15–18. Nation states are, of course, societies—national communities. The formal distinction between community and society made here is that a society is man's most extensive system of common life and may contain a number of communities, whereas a community represents the most compact ordering of diverse ways of life in societies.

17 Martindale, *American Social Structure*, p. 306.

18 This is an uncommon occurrence, for man cherishes the communities he forms; they are the source of his comfort, show the dimensions of his hope. He does not carelessly allow rifts between his institutions to grow so deep that his community's existence is threatened. If possible, the necessary adjustments are made long before that threat arises.

inconsonant ways of life within a wider milieu. To account for these particular community types—and thus explain the transformation from ethnic to status community of Germania's Turners—we need to examine the two forms' quite different relations to the majority society and, accordingly, their fundamental social and psychological differences.

The members of every community attempt to monopolize the values created as they worked out a way of life, and to come to the defense of these values whenever forces from outside their community threaten their existence or the distinctiveness of their way of life. The Southern regional community, for example, is currently experiencing the most devastating attack on its cherished beliefs and practices since Emancipation. Under special circumstances, and depending upon its source, this impulse to close against outsiders can contribute to the formation of an ethnic or a status community; but it does not inevitably produce such a community.

Such communities appear, rather, as a result of a combination of forces. The ethnic community is largely the product of contradictory forces of acceptance and rejection which originate in the majority society and are directed toward immigrants. The status community, by contrast, emerges when status equals, capitalizing upon the internal differentiation of their society, close their ranks against outsiders of inferior or superior status.

Though both forms are minority communities existing in complexly structured societies, there is much more of the element of enforced withdrawal in the formation of an ethnic community, which usually happens in response to pressures from the majority (e.g., prejudice or discrimination), than there is in the formation of a status community, which typically appears as a result of internal demands (e.g., snobbery and privilege) to restrict the entrance of aspirants to one's society of status equals.[19]

If American society, for example, resists the introduction of aliens, forcing them to develop their own ethnic communities on American soil, and yet allows American natives to create status communities almost at

---

19 These processes have been described (Martindale, *American Social Structure*, pp. 377ff.) by means of "secondary" principles: "extra-community closure," which means that ethnic aliens are required by majority hostility to find their own defense and succor their own minority needs; "inner–community closure," in which status–seeking natives protect their own style of life from status–threatening outsiders; "extra–community innovation," which means that the majority society seeks the services and products of its ethnic minorities and thus tolerates their presence; and "inner–community differentiation," in which social differentiation within a society leads to a hierarchical structure (of unequal access to power, wealth, and esteem) and hence to the opportunity for some members of society to monopolize access to these values.

will, American society also encourages ethnic communities and has structural conditions which make creating status communities eminently attractive.[20]

THE ETHNIC COMMUNITY

Thus, the wider society reacts to immigrants in its midst—who bring foreign habits, speech, and ideas—in a predictable manner: seeking to protect its monopoly of interests and its total way of life from encroachment and subversion by foreigners, it keeps the aliens semi-isolated, at least socially and psychologically. Specifically, members of certain minority communities are denied a full range of employment opportunities, are kept from settling in some areas, are kept out of native clubs with hallowed traditions. In short, the ethnic community, as a minority or guest element in American society, has been partly closed off from the life of the host community.[21] Full participation in the wider community has been systematically denied the aliens.

Once formed, however, the ethnic community itself tends toward closure, an inner community drive that is reinforced by the prejudice of the majority.[22] Though this development need not be taken up here, it raises the further question as to how the ethnic community can form in the teeth of resistance from the wider community. If this resistance were

---

[20] Theoretically, this statement does not apply in a "classless" society such as the Soviet Union. It finds historical support in the deliberate practice of European monarchs and states of granting special privileges to Jews (at first, mainly to court Jews, international financiers, and other well–to–do individuals; later, to "the whole of Western and Central European Jewry") and of legislating against the assimilation of the Jewish communities into European culture and society (often with the encouragement and sometimes at the insistence of wealthy Jews, whose positions were realistically threatened by the national egalitarian and emancipation movements of nineteenth–century Europe). See Hannah Arendt, *The Origins of Totalitarianism*, 2nd ed. (New York: World, 1958), pp. 11–18.

[21] Martindale, *American Social Structure*, pp. 427ff., 397–398. While not identical with a minority, the ethnic community ordinarily comprises members of a minority. It differs, however, from a minority in its solution to a problem shared by both, namely, the lack of privilege and power in the majority society. The ethnic community is an organized solution to this problem, whereas a minority (e.g., the Negro or the Roman Catholic or the Mexican minority) does not typically form a community. The term *ethnic community* is generic for the guest community in North America.

[22] Thus, for example, the ethnic community places its own restrictions on membership, maintains semisecret associations, and organizes its own social, religious, economic, and (in the case of the Jewish ethnic community) educational institutions. Prevented from full access to the values of the majority, the ethnic minority turns to its own traditions, characteristically arriving at a new point of synthesis in what was its peripheral institution (often the church) and has become its core institution. Assimilation is seen by the founders of the ethnic community as undesirable, for it means the gradual revision and then final elimination of their traditional values.

complete, the ethnic community could not form. Some tolerance of aliens, therefore, is necessary for the emergence of a minority community. The partial reception of the outsiders into the majority community by reason of their possession of valued talents and knowledge is a universal process.[23]

The special circumstances favorable to the establishment of an ethnic community are created when there is both tolerance of and prejudice against pluralities of aliens rather than single individuals. Pluralities of aliens are needed to form an ethnic community within the wider community. This means that the wider community tolerates or perhaps even invites and welcomes numbers of aliens within its ranks. If, however, the wider community shows complete receptivity toward the aliens, there is little incentive for the alien groups to form a withdrawn community within the framework of the whole. A combination of resistance and reception from the wider community is thus requisite for the emergence of the ethnic community.

Though Germania was formed as an ethnic community in response to the forces just described, a full perspective on it requires an understanding of the status community as well.

THE STATUS COMMUNITY

Though in many superficial respects the ethnic and status communities resemble one another, a fact which has led some eminent American sociologists (namely, Warner and his associates) to confuse the two, they have very different origins. Ordinarily, ethnic communities first form at the bottom of society, whereas status communities tend to form at the top. The latter may, it is true, form at the bottom of society—"Hobohemia," for example, was a low-placed status community in American society before the Great Depression.[24] The new middle-class status communities of Park Forest, Illinois, and Drexelbrook, Pennsylvania, further demonstrate that status communities may form at any level of society.[25] American society is interlaced with status communities of great variety,

---

23 Martindale, *American Social Structure*, pp. 381–384. These contradictory tendencies—resistance and receptivity to aliens—in the society at large are resolved by the establishment of institutions intended to serve both the wish to keep the society intact and the desire to seek the values offered by the outsiders. Historically, the latter may be illustrated by silent trade, family clientage, variations on the theme of diplomacy, fictitious adoption, and naturalization.

24 It was brilliantly explored by Nels Anderson, *The Hobo* (Chicago: University of Chicago Press, 1923).

25 For an incisive account of the "packaged suburbs" as status communities, see William H. Whyte, *The Organization Man* (New York: Simon and Schuster, Inc., 1956).

each formed to consolidate and maintain access to general values—for example, the metropolitan Four Hundred or the old Boston elite described by Cleveland Amory.[26]

The differentiation of relations into a hierarchical structure and the closing off of entrance to levels of this structure make possible the formation of the status community; this takes place within the single community.[27] Underlying this process is the shift in the institutional synthesis of the status community. The precise nature of this resynthesis, however, is not the same for both ethnic and status communities. The members of the ethnic community experience the transformation of the peripheral institutions of their homeland into core institutions in the New World, whereas the status community styles itself after institutions of the total society.[28]

A SUMMARY OF CONTRASTS

When the wider community allows a group of foreigners to pursue their own way of life in its midst and yet denies them full access to its opportunities, the immigrants will respond by partial adjustment and partial withdrawal, forming an ethnic community.

The status community forms, on the other hand, when a group of natives develops a sense of honor and a style of life which sets them apart from the majority. It characteristically forms at the upper levels of society, as a monopolistic joining of elitist individuals whose common aim is to consolidate their access to values of prestige, influence, and wealth. It cultivates snobbery and is regarded by outsiders with mixed feelings of resentment and admiration.

It may now be seen why it was necessary to sketch the theory of the status community in order to account for Germania. The theory of the ethnic community supplies the added explanatory power which makes it possible to answer two basic questions: Why did Germania form into an

---

26 *The Proper Bostonians* (New York: E. P. Dutton & Co., Inc., 1947). For further discussion of status communities in the United States see E. Digby Baltzell, *Philadelphia Gentlemen* (New York: The Free Press, 1958) and C. Wright Mills, *The Power Elite* (New York: Oxford University Press, 1956).

27 Martindale, *American Social Structure*, p. 493.

28 It is even possible to create a status community which rests primarily upon the systematic rejection of a society's major institutions—the Beats are a notable recent example (in rootlessness and mobility they compare somewhat to the world's coteries of wealthy international pleasure seekers). Here status is reflected in a style of life which holds up an inverted image to conventional society. The precariousness of this type of status community is dramatized when its real or studied nihilism begins to appeal to a mass audience; most of its members soon disperse under the glare of publicity. One is tempted to conclude that nothing destroys like success.

ethnic community rather than into a status community, as one would superficially expect? What processes emerged as a product of the natural operation of forces which made status community structure congenial to Germania's founders?

THE UNIQUENESS OF GERMANIA

Germania's uniqueness provoked these questions. The presence of aliens from the outside is not in itself sufficient to account for the formation of an ethnic community, even though they may come in great numbers. Large migrations of English and Scotch to the United States occurred without the forming of English and Scotch ethnic communities. Moreover, non-English immigrants did not necessarily form ethnic communities, as revealed by the attitudes of French Huguenots and of educated Italians who fled from political revolutions. One could perhaps formulate a general principle about the failure of an ethnic community to form in such cases: whenever the ethnic alien is of as high or higher class and status derivation as the group within which he is moving, he tends to form status communities rather than ethnic communities.

The uniqueness of Germania can be approached from this standpoint: although its German founders were of a higher class and status than the community they settled in, they nevertheless formed into a true if ephemeral ethnic community, thereby reversing the common pattern of ethnic community formation. No ethnic community so formed, however, can long remain a withdrawn community when the values of the surrounding world are open and accessible to its members. The Turners of Germania very soon realized that greater advantages lay in forming an upper status community which would allow them both to monopolize access to the values of the majority and to preserve their distinctive way of life, than in remaining a withdrawn ethnic community. In the transition from an ethnic to a status community, however, the traditions of the founders of Germania would necessarily be weakened.

HYPOTHESES AND METHOD

Our theoretical and historical understanding of the evolution of the Turners of Germania, from their inception as an ethnic community to their present declining position as an upper status community, may be expressed in the form of two general hypotheses that will guide this study. I. The Germania Turners' marketable talents gave them partial acceptance in America; but in spite of these assets their historical marginality and foreign culture at first forced them into the form of an ethnic community. II. Their superior social and cultural experience, however, when applied to frontier conditions, enabled them to get control of the key positions of influence, prestige, and wealth in Germania. They consequently emerged in their new form as a status elite.

Although in a class and status sense the emigrés who founded Germania were superior to their surroundings, they had cultural and historical peculiarities which provided them an unusually strong inclination to form an ethnic community. For example, as a minority in Germany they had developed a minority psychology. They carried this attitude with them to North America, where they were received with prejudice and hostility. Moreover, they were Germans and aliens, subject therefore to widespread nativist resentment, focused partly in the Know-Nothing movement of the mid-nineteenth century.[29] Many of them were Roman Catholics, a minority religion under attack by the native Americans, who did not always distinguish between Catholic and non-Catholic Germans. And since the Turners spoke German, they felt a temporary practical advantage in associating with other German-speaking immigrants.

The inducements to form an ethnic community were not all negative, however. The Turners shared in the utopian idealism that was prevalent in North America at the time they arrived. Both their own receptivity to utopian experiment and the tolerance by the surrounding community of such ventures contributed to the formation of an idealistic ethnic community. Their sociopolitical institution, the Turnverein, also served as a new point of orientation of their life in the United States, around which they could readily organize a life of their own. Once they had established their own community, the additional motive to preserve their cultural heritage could be felt. Finally, the United States needed skilled artisans and experienced farmers—stable, industrious people to build new communities at the edge of the expanding frontier. The German immigrants from the 1830's to the 1850's were ideally suited to meet this need.

Thus powerful inclinations, positive and negative, were at work in the Turners' withdrawal to ethnic community life. But for the Germania Turners, the very act of ethnic closure raises a question: can an ethnic community endure when formed of people who have superior class and status characteristics? My second major hypothesis suggests that the answer is no, and tells why not.

It was to the advantage of the Turners, as the founding elite, to invite anybody of low status into Germania. Only by becoming a status community could they fully exploit their original superior social and cultural position in Germania. If, on the other hand, the Turners had remained

---

[29] At this stage in the history of German–Americans, there was considerable anti–German sentiment, which later declined, only to revive during and after World War I.

an exclusive German ethnic community, some of them would eventually have had to take menial jobs; as members of an ethnic community, not all could enjoy equally the privileges of high status. By letting in people of lower status, and by forming themselves into a status community, the Turners were able to control Germania's prestigeful and powerful positions.

It can thus be seen that three kinds of immense advantages accrued to the Turners in forming a status community: *economically* the Turners were in a position to assume most of the top positions and the highest paying jobs; in *status,* the Turners benefited by forming a homogeneous, well-known group which gave them high prestige (in addition, the Turnverein represented an unusually high level of intellectual and cultural interests which, if anything, enhanced the pretensions of its members to status) ; with respect to *power,* the Turners were able to monopolize access to the limited political positions of the community. None of these advantages would have been possible to an ethnic community.

RECAPITULATION

Germania, U.S.A., presents an unusual pattern of social and cultural change in the course of the experience of ethnic communities in the United States. Its departure from the normal course is seen in its relative isolation, at the edge of the frontier, from other communities; in the superior class, status, and power situation of its immigrant founders; in their utopian-revolutionary intentions; and, finally, in the transformation of the Germania Turners from a highly placed ethnic minority community to a subcommunity of status elites.

Social change in Germania occurred in two stages: first the founding of the ethnic community, second the shift to status community. Two hypotheses have been set forth to explain these two kinds of change: first, that historical peculiarities gave rise to the ethnic community, and, secondly, that inherent forces led to the re-forming of the original group along status community lines.

14. The Role of the Outsider

RONALD FRANKENBERG

The two groups in Pentrediwaith which I have called "Outsiders" and "Pentre People" are the outcome of developments in Wales similar to the Irish Catholic Peasantry and English Protestant landowner division in Ireland.[1] The Anglican, English-speaking landowners once stood openly opposed in outlook and economic interest to their Welsh Nonconformist tenants and labourers. They may still do so in some parts of Wales. But in Pentrediwaith, as I have tried to show, the situation is more complex. The basic clash of economic interests now occurs outside the village altogether. English gentry as such no longer retain power or importance in the village, but English industrial culture is now regarded as a threat. The criteria of "English-speaking" and "church-membership" no longer divide merely the main economic classes but also form the basis of less fundamental divisions within the village. These attributes, which are associated with class differences in Wales as a whole and which have been so important in Welsh history, play a different role inside the village. For, as I have described, a substantial number of ordinary wage-earning

SOURCE: Reprinted with permission of the author and publisher from *Village on the Border: A Social Study of Religion, Politics and Football in a North Wales Community*, by Ronald Frankenberg, (London: Cohen & West, 1957).

[1] See Arensberg and Kimball, p. 29; J. Pomfret, *The Struggle for Land in Ireland*, 1800–1923, (Princeton, 1930).

villagers do not, in fact, normally speak Welsh or attend chapel. Husband and wife may prefer to speak different languages and profess allegiance to different denominations. Next-door neighbours and friends may be divided in their membership of church and chapel. Only in specific social contexts do these differences become significant.

Remnants of the original class antagonism between English landlord and Welsh tenant persist in modern Pentrediwaith. The influence of economic class is most clearly shown in the membership of local government institutions, and in the official relations of Pentrediwaith councillors and magistrates with similar bodies outside the village and the valley. I have tried to show how economic class divisions are accurately reflected in the election of parish councillors and others, and in their subsequent behaviour. But even in these institutions there is not an uncomplicated opposition of economic interests. The relations between the wage-earners, who form the class from which parish councillors are drawn, and the salaried and self-employed, who make up the county council and the magistrates' bench, are complicated by a factor of "scale." Parish councillors are men with local interests and knowledge. They are deeply and intensively involved in social activities but in a very narrow sphere. They do not concern themselves with, or even show curiosity about, the affairs of even neighbouring villages in the valley. The "magisterial" or "vice-presidential" class participate in the social life of many villages both inside and outside the valley. They are not, however, deeply involved in any single village.

The intensely local preoccupations of the parish councillors have a more general effect on their behaviour, as a body, in relation to other parish councils in the county. As we have seen, the Parish Councils Association of the county meets alternately in the rural west and industrial east. In the minds of the people of the county, Welshness is connected with the west of the county and rural culture, and an English outlook is linked with residence in the industrial east. This is broadly a correct picture, but there are significant exceptions. One is the village of Pentreglo, which we found to be more influenced in its external relations with other parishes by its industrial nature than by its Welshness. In their attitude both to English-speaking industrial areas and to Welsh-speaking Pentreglo, Pentre villagers identified themselves with the rural parts of the county. In their daily life and work the men of Pentrediwaith are becoming more and more involved in the English-speaking industrial economy surrounding Tonmawr.

This uneasy contradiction between Pentrediwaith's past as a small-scale rural community (albeit based on slate mining rather than on farming) and its present integration into industrial Britain also affects social relations within the village. For although most men travel away from the village and work side by side with men from other places, the women still remain in Pentrediwaith for both work and recreation. The men's interests are largely turned towards the problems and amusements of the industrial society outside, while the women remain preoccupied, despite the influence of radio and television, with the affairs of the village. This difference in outlook of men and women pervades all social activity and provides a major division in village social life which cuts across all others.

This state of affairs is, of course, in sharp contrast to the situation in peasant and small-farmer communities where, although men and women have separate tasks and spheres of activity, their roles are complementary.[2] In such circumstances men and women are united by their respective roles in a division of labour advantageous to both. In Pentrediwaith men and women only unite, in this context, to condemn the external circumstances which have forced them apart. Obviously a division between men and women cannot be absolute. Men and women marry and set up households. They co-operate within the home to rear their children, and sometimes they both contribute to a joint family income. Men are related, through their wives, affinally and informally to other groups than their own. Relationships of friendship and hostility in various alliances between single and related households and their neighbours enter into the working of village communal affairs.

Because of Pentrediwaith's place in the wider structure and culture of Britain, external influences lead to the setting up of social activities within the village. Men and women, separately and together, form committees to organize and carry on such activities. Examples are Eisteddfod "parties," Coronation celebrations, carnivals, and football. Loyalties and enmities forged outside these specific activities are carried over into them, until individuals are forced to make decisions which reveal their personal divided loyalties and may also reveal social divisions in the village. It is in order to save Pentre people themselves from making these critical decisions that strangers are forced into positions of leadership in the village. That these leaders are in fact themselves led is shown by the inconsistency of their attitude on village issues. For example, the strangers involved in both the carnival fund dispute and the dispute over the disposal of the coronation football profits reversed their own previous opinions at the second discussion. Between the time that I took the chair at a carnival supporters' committee meeting and the time of the football

---

2 See the works of Rees, West, and Arensberg and Kimball. See also Loomis and Beegle, *Rural Social Systems* (New York, 1950).

supporters' annual general meeting, I also experienced the uncomfortable village pressure that caused them to change their views.

Even the employment of strangers in this role and the use of other devices to avoid conflict were not always successful. Consequently, when the desire to continue an activity was not strong enough to override conflicts, groups of villagers resigned from organizing committees. For this reason, it seemed to me, each kind of recreational activity built up, in the course of its existence, opposition to itself as an activity, independently of the personnel currently engaged in it. This was complicated by interpersonal and intergroup "feuds" amongst its personnel. Some of these "feuds" arose from the carrying out of the activity; others were carried over from other outside relationships. The football club had in 1953 reached a stage when support was so much weaker than opposition that it could no longer carry on. Conversation with villagers led me to suppose that a similar fate had overtaken other activities in the past.

Recreational activities which bring the village into contact and competition with other villages have another function as well. They serve, as the football club did in the years after the war until 1953, as a symbol of village prestige and unity in the face of the outside world. Their exploits are recorded in the local newspapers and noised abroad by villagers. But the internal divisions to which they give rise decrease their efficiency as symbols. The football club won only two games in the 1953-4 season. The quality of performance of the brass band and the choir also decreased as they began to crumble. This external failure in turn still further weakens the internal position of the activity. A poor performance at a football match or play or eisteddfod spoils the village's reputation. I suspect that this hypothesis, of increasing internal and external failure as conflicts surrounding an activity grow, may be more widely applicable.[3]

We have seen that, in Pentrediwaith, activities are started with practical aims and in emulation of similar activities in neighbouring, and even distant, parts of England and Wales. Many Pentre villagers enjoy playing and watching association football, Britain's national game. Other villagers like to sing or play brass band instruments or to listen to those who do. At different times in the past villagers attracted to these and other recreational pursuits have combined with others to take part in them. When they form associations of this kind, there are national organizations in which they can take their place and play their part. But since Pentre people feel themselves to be a community, when they combine with fellow villagers to form a team or "party" their association becomes

---

[3] The rise and fall of social activities in British communities has often been commented on. See for example the works of Kempe and Whiteley.

more than a convenient arrangement based on the "accident" of living together. Combining in recreational activities has social value to the villagers because it emphasizes their relationships one to another in a community. This is true of all communities. But it is especially important when the men no longer work together. In this kind of situation recreational activities provide the only system in which they can "interact" as members of a community.[4]

But these recreational activities often involve competition with other villages and groups. The football team and the brass band take part in contests with those of other villages. The carnival and coronation festivities are judged by the general standards of the surrounding countryside. Therefore, in addition to serving as an internal symbol of the villagers' enduring community of interests, these activities become also a symbol of the village's existence as a community in opposition to other communities and the world at large. Thus activities with their own "practical" ends acquire a symbolic value for the villagers in their external relationships with other villagers. They provide also a medium through which internal village disputes and conflicts find expression. These disputes and conflicts are essentially personal and informal. They arise from the relationships of individual to individual and household to household in a face-to-face society. When an activity is abandoned the conflicts within the village are, temporarily at least, suspended at the same time as the activity they have killed. Thus village unity is emphasized and maintained.

In Pentrediwaith recreational activities are not connected with prosperity or with an institutionalized structure in the village, as they are in some primitive societies.[5] They arise from the meeting of individual interests, where there is no structural arrangement of relations between these individuals, although villagers feel that the village ought to have communal activities. Hence the conflicts which intrude into the activities are between individuals in unformalized relations, and their expression does not end in a return to an ordained pattern of relations. The system is repetitive only in a limited field, and the significant divisions in the society between "Pentre people" and "outsiders" remain unaffected. For these last are reflections of national alignments over which Pentre villagers have no control.

In Pentrediwaith conflicts are carried over from one form of recreational activity to another, as from football to carnival. Furthermore, the

---

[4] See G. Homans, *The Human Group,* for general discussion on the relations of *interaction* and *sentiment.* For particular discussion in a somewhat similar situation to Pentrediwaith, see his discussion of Hilltown in chap. 13.

[5] M. Gluckman, *Rituals of Rebellion in South East Africa,* The Frazer Lecture 1952 (Manchester University Press, 1954).

new conflicts engendered in disputes over football and carnivals may extend back into everyday life and cause further divisions within the village. The degree of success with which villagers continue to co-operate in new activities is a measure of the success with which they are meeting the threat of losing their discrete village identity. But some individuals withdraw in anger or disgust and refuse to take any further part in village activity. When this happens only the sanction of public disapproval can bring them back. It is possible (but I cannot verify this) that the lack of success of Pentrediwaith activities may itself be important in that it concentrates the attention of villagers on to recreational activities. This in turn makes such activities the medium through which villagers express their personal rivalries, conflicts and ambitions.

I have tried to show how Pentre people use "strangers" in this context. This provides one with a point of comparison. In all societies in which opposing groups must continue to live and gain their livelihood side by side there are mechanisms which tend to avoid or diminish conflict between groups. The use of strangers in Pentrediwaith to accept responsibility for decisions which split village opinion is by no means unique. Similar appeals to "external authority" are structural devices which have often been analysed by social anthropologists. The form is the same although the cultural context may be very different in various places and at different times. The leopard-skin chief amongst the Nuer, the Senussi in Cyrenaica,[6] and the monastic settlements in early Wales[7] all provide examples of "stranger" groups which played the same role. These were all protected from the consequences of unpopularity by their relations with the spiritual world. Joking partners amongst the Tonga of Northern Rhodesia are another slightly different instance.[8] The making of decisions by consulting magical oracles or oracles revealing the ancestors' wishes achieves the same result in yet another way.[9]

But in these examples there is a sharp distinction between the practices

---

[6] E. E. Evans-Pritchard, *The Nuer* (Oxford, 1940) and *The Sanusi of Cyrenaica* (Oxford, 1949).

[7] Sir John Lloyd, *History of Wales from the Earliest Times to the Edwardian Conquest*, vol. 1 (London, 1911).

[8] E. Colson, "Clans and the Joking-Relationship among the Plateau Tonga of Northern Rhodesia," *Kroeber Anthropological Society Papers*, Nos. 8 and 9 (California, 1953).

[9] A clear statement of this is made by Professor Fortes, who ends a description of the deciding of a dispute by the elders with this paragraph: "However, to make the decision conclusive and to save it from rankling it was left to an oracle. A fowl was slaughtered with an invocation to the ancestors and the posture in which it died showed which of the disputants was in the right. No one was surprised when Tinta'alem gained the verdict. Thus the ancestors themselves vouched for the legitimate status of Yidaan biis." M. Fortes, *The Dynamics of Clanship among the Tallensi* (1945), p. 70.

of Africa and those of Pentrediwaith. The stranger in Africa, whether human or spirit, acts through mystical sanctions to prevent the divisions inherent in a formal structure from breaking into open conflict. In Pentrediwaith the stranger has no ritual power or licensed freedom to protect him. He is merely removed from the informal conflicts which, with his help, may be resolved without awakening open hostilities. When such a stranger is also an "outsider," his exclusion from informal social contacts is almost complete. For he not only lacks kinship ties with "Pentre people," but is also excluded, both as a participant and as a subject, from the gossip and backbiting of the community. He may not join in criticism of Pentre people, and his own affairs, however scandalous, are of merely passing interest.[10]

Professor Barnes has written of a modern Norwegian community:

> Each person in Bremnes belongs to many social groups. In particular he is a member of a household, of a hamlet, of a ward, and he is a member of the parish of Bremnes. At different times and different places membership of one or other of these groups is definitive for what he does. He goes to the prayer house with his household, sits at weddings with other members of his hamlet, and pays tax according to his parish. There are other series of groups which to some extent cut across these territorially based ones, although they may themselves be based on territory. Thus, for example, a man may belong to a hamlet missionary working party, or to a bull-owning co-operative based on a ward. In formal terms these various groups fit one inside the other, each in its own series. Thus there are three territorially defined fishermen's associations in the parish. All three belong to the provincial fishermen's association, and this in its turn forms part of the national association. There may be conflicts because of the duties and rights a person has in the various groups in any one series, and there may be conflicts because of his interests in different series. This is true of all societies.[11]

I have tried in this book to establish the existence of this principle and to analyse in detail its operation in yet another field of social enquiry. I

---

10 Cf. Colson, *The Makah Indians.*

11 J. A. Barnes, "Class and Committees in a Norwegian Island Parish," *Human Relations,* VII (1954 i), pp. 40–41. For a full exposition of this view see M. Gluckman, "Political Institutions" in E. E. Evans-Pritchard *et al., The Institutions of Primitive Society* (Blackwell, 1954), especially p. 77. See also M. Gluckman, "Social Situation in Modern Zululand," *Bantu Studies,* XIV (1940, 1, 2), p. 27; and Professor Fortes's statement in *Dynamics of Clanship among the Tallensi:* "It is a cardinal principle of Tale social structure that every social grouping defined as a unit in one situation, or according to one principle, dissolves into an association of lesser and differentiated units in another situation or according to another principle. Also E. Colson, "Social Control and Vengeance in Plateau Tonga Society," *Africa* (1953), has a similar statement.

hope that my study emphasizes also one important point which has emerged from other studies. Despite all the cross-cutting divisions, a group such as the Swazi or the Tale people or a Zulu village has symbolic activities which are expressive of its unity. So, too, if a village in Wales is a village it undertakes activities which are village activities. All individuals are expected to join in independently of their relations with one another. If the observations of this study are borne out elsewhere, it seems that we may be able to say that if there are no such activities we have a housing unit and not a village. Perhaps also my study of recreation in Pentrediwaith emphasizes that some form of "ceremonial" in the sense of joint symbolic activities is necessary to maintain group loyalty in an acephalous community. This seems to me especially true when the men of the group no longer work together.

Pentrediwaith, despite its position in England and Wales, still remains in some senses isolated and therefore united. In the past villagers worked together, played together and lived together. Their common history is a factor in their own continued cohesion. They pride themselves on being a group of kin and on being Welsh. Now only the women work together, and each successive failure of a social activity makes the next one more difficult to start. Improvements in public transport, television, radio and the cinema have already diminished the interest of the young people in the village and its affairs. Emigration in search of better economic and leisure opportunities is taking its toll. These developments decrease the number of cross-cutting ties which bind Pentre people into a community. As many of the older villagers fear, the time may come, if these developments continue, when the village ceases to be a village community and becomes merely a collection of dwellings, housing some of the industrial workers of Great Britain.

15. Polish Heritage
and Survivals

ARTHUR EVANS WOOD

. . . Hamtramck is a predominantly Polish community within the De-troit metropolitan area, differing sharply in its demotic composition and in its economic standards from the contiguous and comparable communi-ty of Highland Park. The comparisons we have made will help us to see Hamtramck as a somewhat isolated area dominated by Polish activities, and reflecting vestiges of Polish culture that have come from the old world.

* * *

At the outset we should note that Hamtramck has not been an area of "first settlement;" that is, of the 5174 Polish families (father born in Poland) enumerated in the 1954 school census most of them came to Hamtramck from other areas of the United States, principally New York, Pennsylvania, Ohio, Massachusetts, and from elsewhere in Michigan. Aside from the industrial opportunities afforded in Hamtramck, its communal activities and the fact that it was regarded as their town have

SOURCE: Reprinted with permission of the author's heir and publisher from *Ham-tramck—A Sociological Study of a Polish-American Community* (New Haven: College & University Press, 1955).

made strong appeal to Poles from different parts of the country. They have flocked to it as to a homeland.

* * *

In the process of migration a large part of their traditions and folkways is lost or profoundly altered. This would be especially so in an urban industrial community such as Hamtramck; it would be less so when the migration is to a rural area, such as that in the neighborhood of Cheboygan, Michigan. There the occupations and way of life resemble more those of the homeland.[1] But even in an industrial city like Hamtramck fragments of the old Polish life are clung to, though with ever diminishing strength. Often this means conflict, sometimes overt, as when a Polish father tries to dominate his wife and American-born children, as he would have done in the old country. Perhaps the conflict is more often silent and even unconscious, deep within the soul of the immigrant himself as he yearns for the old ways to the point of nostalgia. It will not be remiss, therefore, to recall a few of the ways by which shreds of the old culture persist in the new setting.

A most obvious survival is that of language. In the Hamtramck school census for 1927 an item was included concerning the language used in the home. It disclosed that in Polish families, with fathers born in Poland, 47.7 percent of them spoke Polish *only* in the home, while 50.9 percent spoke Polish *and* English in the home. The remaining families, 1.3 percent, were reported as speaking *only* English. A new appraisal was made on this point in the school census of 1945, including nearly 8000 Polish families, with the result that 49.3 percent of the Polish families were shown to use *only* Polish in the home, and 50.7 percent both Polish *and* English. Such data reveal a remarkable tenacity in the use of the native language over a period of years.

* * *

It is to be noted that the survival among the Poles of their native language is encouraged in a variety of ways by community agencies. Thus, Polish is an optional subject for students in the Hamtramck high school, though the enrollment for such work has not been large among the young people. Moreover, the Catholic parochial schools play an

---

[1] Survival of the old ways among Polish settlers in this rural area of Michigan is shown in an unpublished thesis by Dr. Peter Ostafin of the University of Michigan.

important role. There are four of these in Hamtramck with an enrollment of approximately 3,000 children in the grades. It is said that nearly all Polish children attend the parochial schools at some time through the grades. In them Polish history and language are taught, though by state law instruction in the common branches must be given in English. The public schools also encourage the reading of Polish by the inclusion of many books in that language in school libraries. Such books are not widely read by the children, but are taken home for use by their parents. In this way the school system is commended to the parents and the community at large. The city library, as well, cultivates the reading of Polish by the inclusion of over a thousand Polish books which have an extensive circulation. Above all, the Polish language is preserved through the church services, through the Polish newspapers in Hamtramck and Detroit, and through numerous community gatherings and societies where Polish is spoken. This situation may alter in a generation or two; but there is no present indication of much change with respect to language habits. So long as Hamtramck maintains its character as a kind of cultural island, we may expect the language bond to be conserved.

Besides language another means of furthering a lively interest in traditional Polish ways is through activities that pertain to ancient customs. The most deep-seated of these are associated with religious rites that find expression at weddings and funerals, or on other occasions. The great religious festivals were commemorated in the old village life with symbolic or playful activities that assuaged the monotonous routine of life with joyous expectancy. They may seem strangely out of place in a sordid, industrial American community, yet their persistence bears evidence to the strong hold they have upon the people.

16. A Study of French–English Relations in an Ontario Community: Towards a Conflict Model for the Analysis of Ethnic Relations

JOHN JACKSON

In any analysis of ethnic relations we can usually assume the existence of conflict. In this article we hope to construct a set of hypotheses concerning variations in conflict states which, in principle, may be tested. The conflict model was developed from data now being collected in an Ontario community composed of French- and English-speaking residents. The materials will be used merely to illustrate, not, at this stage, to support any stated hypotheses. The following four questions summarize the complete project:

(1) Park's ethnic relations cycle suggests an inevitable sequence of the processes of contact, competition, conflict, accommodation and assimi-

SOURCE: Reprinted with permission of the author and publisher from *Canadian Review of Sociology and Anthropology*, III, No. 3 (August, 1966).

ACKNOWLEDGEMENT: This paper was read at the Eastern Canadian Sociologists' Meeting, Windsor, Ontario, February 24, 1966. Portions of the paper first appeared in John D. Jackson, "Ethnic Relations and a Community School System: A Sociological Perspective on Community Conflict," [mimeograph] (East Lansing, Michigan: Institute for Community Development, 1965).

The author wishes to acknowledge a grant received from The Canada Council enabling him to be free to conduct the research upon which this paper is based.

lation. Is this an adequate explanation of ethnic relations, or are conflict and assimilation more usefully viewed as interdependent processes?

(2) What aspects of a conflict situation vary in relation to each other and in relation to conditions external to a conflict system? Is it possible to identify such aspects of social conflict as intensity, militancy or violence, and the degree of regulation, and to specify their interrelations?

(3) To what extent would these aspects or variables influence the assimilation of ethnic groups? For example, does the regulation of ethnic conflict act to deter or to stimulate assimilation?

(4) To what extent might a proposition relating conflict regulation and assimilation be conditioned by variations in local community structures? For example, it is well-known that decisions regarding many important spheres of community life such as education are made by extra-local agencies. If education were a focus of a local ethnic conflict, would the influence of extra-local agencies in this sphere affect the mode of regulation and thus the assimilation process?

This article deals with the second of these four questions. We see social conflict as a normal and natural outcome of structural processes—of the interplay of power and position, and of boundary-maintenance activity—not as pathological. Moreover consensus does not entail an absence of conflict. Either state may be functional or dysfunctional to a system, depending on the level of analysis assumed by the investigator. Hence van den Berghe in a recent article suggests that "consensus within groups is, in part, a function of dissension between groups . . . in-group unity is reinforced by inter-group conflict."[1] Herein lies the paradox. Social conflict is an interactional state: that is, the conflicting parties must be in contact and there must be a certain amount of interaction before a state of conflict may be said to exist. Without community there is no conflict and without conflict there is no community.[2]

It is frequently easier to state what something is not than what it is. *Social* conflict is not a result of individual hostilities or aggressive impulses, nor a result of misunderstandings or poor communication. An illustration used by Coser in his *The Functions of Social Conflict* is relevant here: "A worker engaged in strike activity in order to increase his wages, his status or the power of his union, and one who releases aggression against the boss because he perceives him as an oedipal figure, are dissimilar social types. Displaced father hatred may attach itself to

---

1 Pierre L. van den Berghe, "Dialectic and Functionalism," *American Sociological Review*, XXVIII, 703 (October, 1963).

2 Ralf Dahrendorf, *Class and Class Conflict in Industrial Society* (Stanford: California, 1959), p. 225.

any suitable object—boss, policeman or staff sergeant. The economic fight of workers against the boss, on the other hand, is based on their *particular positions and roles in the economic and political system.*"[3] Similarly, the struggle of *les Franco-Ontariens,* the French-Canadians of Ontario, to extend the use of French as the language of instruction in certain local schools is not a result of the actions of disgruntled malcontents, but, rather, the result of a struggle for status and identification emerging from their *particular positions and roles in the social system.* Social conflict is a structural, not an individual, property.

A word concerning the substantive area: without doubt, sociological studies of French-English relations have suffered from a geographically narrow perspective. In a review of the literature published a decade ago by Philippe Garigue,[4] 170 out of 2949 entries were directly concerned with French-Canadians outside the Province of Quebec; only fourteen of these referred specifically to the French-Canadians of Ontario. True enough, more than three-quarters of those Canadians of French origin live within the borders of Quebec. However, the influence that the French minorities outside of that province have had and will have on the totality of French-English relations in Canada far exceeds their numerical strength. In spite of the lack of systematic studies of the problem outside Quebec, there has been a tendency to generalize from the Quebec situation to "French Canada" as a whole. The dangers inherent in this type of generalization are apparent in an observation made in the preliminary report of the Royal Commission on Bilingualism and Biculturalism: "The divergent preoccupations of French Quebec and the 'French Minorities' of the other provinces were very evident . . . regional differences seemed, during this first sampling of opinion, to be almost as marked in French Canada as they were in English Canada."[5] Thus it is important to study the various configurations assumed by French-English relations in different regions of the country.

The community selected for this study, which we will, for the time being, call Normanville, Ontario, has a population of around 5,000. Approximately 56 percent of the citizens are of French origin; about one-third are of British origin, the balance being composed of members of various other ethnic groups. In no way was this community selected as being representative of some larger region. At best, it is representative of a

---

[3] Lewis A. Coser, *The Functions of Social Conflict* (New York, 1956), p. 50. Emphasis added.

[4] Philippe Garigue, *A Bibliographic Introduction to the Study of French Canada* (Montreal, 1956).

[5] The Royal Commission on Bilingualism and Biculturalism, *Preliminary Report* (Ottawa, 1965).

small portion of southwestern Ontario. The project consists of three phases, the first two of which are now complete. From April 1964 to May 1965, frequent trips were made to the community to ascertain its utility as a research site. During this period, 25 interviews of "key" citizens were conducted. An eight-month period of intensive observation commenced in May 1965, during which some 45 interviews were conducted, 55 meetings of various local associations were attended, and considerable time was spent observing the life of the community in its churches, homes, taverns, and on its street corners. The final stage will involve a more formalized collection of data bearing on the hypotheses emerging from these initial phases.

CONFLICT DEFINED

Prior to specifying variables and hypotheses, a statement concerning precisely what is meant by social conflict is in order. Following Dahrendorf, social conflict is defined as consisting of "all relations between sets of individuals that involve an incompatible difference of objectives [with regard to positions, resources or values]."[6] This definition is similar to those proposed by Bernard,[7] Boulding,[8] and Coser.[9] The definition suggests at least three empirical conditions which must be met if a relationship between two or more sets of individuals is to be designated as conflictive. There must be *parties,* that is, sets of individuals exhibiting some level of organization. There must be some level of *interaction* between these parties; without contact there can be no conflict. Finally, a condition of *position* and *resource scarcity* must exist; each party cannot occupy the same positions at the same time and each cannot have all it desires of available resources.[10]

CONFLICT PARTIES

As obvious as these conditions may be, they are basic to a description of a conflict system. First, with reference to *parties*—a statistical category cannot be a party to a conflict situation. A minimum level of organization is required. The category of *quasi-group,* as advanced by Ginsberg

---

6 Dahrendorf, *op cit.,* p. 135.

7 Jessie Bernard, "Parties and Issues in Conflict," *The Journal of Conflict Resolution,* I, p. 112 (June, 1957).

8 Kenneth E. Boulding, *Conflict and Defense* (New York, 1962), p. 5.

9 Coser, *op. cit.,* p. 8.

10 Though not as elaborate, these conditions follow closely those listed by Mack and Snyder in a recent synthesis of materials on social conflict. Raymond W. Mack and Richard C. Snyder, "The Analysis of Social Conflict—Toward an Overview and Synthesis," *The Journal of Conflict Resolution,* I, (June, 1957), pp. 212–48.

and used by Dahrendorf,[11] would appear to meet the minimum requirement. Ginsberg defines quasi-groups as: "aggregates or portions of the community which have no recognizable structure, but whose members have certain interests or modes or behaviour in common, which may at any time lead them to form themselves into definite groups. To this category of quasi-groups belong such entities as social classes [and, I would add ethnic groups] which, without being groups, are recruiting fields for groups."[12] The degree of organization beyond this minimum requirement is an empirical problem.

In the community under study, census materials suggested the possibility of three such groups—French-speaking Catholics, English-speaking Catholics, and English-speaking Protestants. Given this possibility, an observer can direct several questions to the data to arrive at an initial impression of the degree of organization exhibited by these groups. To what extent do persons identified as members of these groups tend to interact more with each other than with out-group members—in cliques, friendship groups, and through visiting patterns? Observations to date, which are yet to be confirmed, point to basic cleavages along linguistic and religious lines.

First, there is a deep religious cleavage with little informal association between Catholics and Protestants. Second, there is a linguistic cleavage among Catholics, with French speakers associating more with each other than with English speakers. This second split is less intense than the first, French- and English-speaking Catholics being interlaced through a network of intermarriages. This informal separation is further intensified by residential segregation, the French-speaking Catholics generally residing in that portion of Normanville locally referred to as "the village" or "the town." English-speaking citizens, particularly Protestants, reside in the newer suburban areas of the town and represent a relatively new addition to the community, most having moved in during the 1950's.

A second general question concerns the extent to which the more formal institutional and associational life of the community corresponds to basic ethnic and religious groupings. Again, there is a division along religious lines with the life of the Protestant sub-community revolving around two churches, a public school, and their related associations. Within the Catholic sub-community, church-related associations and the school system (the separate school system) split along linguistic lines. English-speaking Catholic associations, such as Knights of Columbus and

---

[11] Dahrendorf, op. cit., p. 180.
[12] Morris Ginsberg, Sociology (London, 1953), p. 40.

the Catholic Parent Teachers Association, tend to involve both French-and English-speaking Catholics. French speaking associations, *La Société Saint-Jean-Baptiste,* the related *Caisse Populaire,* and *l'Association de Parents et d'Instituteurs de Langue Française d'Ontario* are exclusively French in membership. French-speaking members of the Catholic sub-community are also, individually and through the above mentioned local associations, affiliated with various provincial associations such as *l'Association Canadienne-Française d'Education d'Ontario, l'Association des Commissions des Ecoles Bilingues,* and *l'Association des Enseignants Franco-Ontariens.*

PARTY CONTACT AND INTERACTION

Thus, at the interpersonal and the institutional level there is sufficient evidence to conclude the existence of three parties, ethnic-religious group-ings, to a potential conflict situation. Having established identifiable parties, there remains the condition of *interaction* between these parties. What kinds of contact are observable? In what manner do the parties articulate their conflicting interests? Given identifiable quasi-groups, a mass and direct involvement of all members, short of war, revolution, or riot, is a rare phenomenon. Generally, conflict relations are carried on by representative associations and individuals—by *conflict agents.* The category of conflict agents is actually an aspect of the more generic cate-gory of parties, but it is an identification of agents and the type of contact between them that provides the material necessary for specifying the forms of interaction existing between the conflicting parties.

In Normanville, two levels of agent interaction are observable. First, there is the level of individual representatives or agents where, in such settings as the school system and on local political bodies, persons desig-nated as representatives of quasi-group interests meet to articulate these interests. Second, at the associational level some associations or organiza-tions specifically act to articulate the interests of their respective groups.

Publicly, local political life at the municipal level proceeds in much the same way as in any other small town, without recognition of ethnic-religious divisions. Informally, however, these divisions are perceived and acted upon as significant dimensions of local political life. Candidates for municipal offices view their campaigns in ethnic-religious terms, calculat-ing the number of votes they may expect from each of the three group-ings according to their position in the scheme. A known Catholic with an "English" name directs his campaign toward the French-speaking sub-community, feeling sure that he will receive sufficient votes from the English-speaking sub-community. Members of the English-speaking Prot-estant sub-community will put up a candidate to represent their interests, selecting an English-speaking Catholic. There is a belief that an English-speaking Protestant does not have a chance.[13] Once elected, such persons act unofficially as individual agents representing the interests of their supporting quasi-groups. Appointments to such political bodies as the library board, parks board, and board of adjustment are made with the three quasi-groups in mind. Considerable argument and discussion outside of public sessions of political bodies revolve around the merits of this man or that man because of whom he represents or because of his knowledge and talents.

It is in the local separate school system where conflict agents are more formally recognized. Because of the religious division of schools, the interaction between agents at the local level takes place within the Catholic sub-community. The English-speaking Protestant sub-community is completely removed from school issues. In most cases, members of this group are quite unaware of the presence of French- (officially termed "bilingual") and English-language classrooms and the accompanying complex administrative structure.

The Normanville separate school system consists of three schools, each having bilingual and English classrooms.[14] Although there is no legal, that is legislative, recognition of the bilingual system, custom dictates that teachers of bilingual classes will be of French origin with a command of both languages. Teachers of English classes are native English speakers, with or without a command of French (usually without). In any one school, then, there will be a group of teachers who to one degree or another are committed to French education and the continued existence of the bilingual system. That is, there will be a number of individuals in any one school who act as conflict agents for their respective ethnic groups.

The presence and actions of conflict agents are even more clearly revealed in the dual inspectorate common in school districts of this type. Under usual Ontario conditions, that is, in a unilingual school district, there is but one inspector.[15] Inspectors are appointed by the Department of Education to oversee the curricula and administrative aspects of the Education Act. In a district with a bilingual system, however, two inspectors are appointed, one for the bilingual schools and classrooms, one for the English schools and classrooms. In Normanville, both inspectors are

---

[13] See also Aileen D. Ross, "The Cultural Effects of Population Changes in the Eastern Townships," Bernard R. Blishen *et al.*, eds. *Canadian Society* (New York, 1961), pp. 109–10.

[14] The information used here was taken from data collected in 1964; certain minor changes have occurred which I will not incorporate at this time.

[15] I am referring to separate school districts; there is also a public school district, but these have little contact with each other since the domains do not overlap.

Roman Catholic. The bilingual inspector is Franco-Ontarian. They have equal status and are responsible directly to the Department of Education.

Based on a majority formula determined by precedence, one inspector assumes responsibility for the administration of the district and the curricula problems of his ethnic group, the other limiting himself to the curricula problems of the other ethnic group. In Normanville, where approximately 70 percent of the enrolment is in the English system, the administrative responsibilities fall to the English inspector. Some eight or nine years ago, when the proportions were reversed, the administration was under the office of the bilingual inspector. In a much more formal way, then, the dual inspectorate builds party representation into the system.

There is a second level of contact and interaction between the parties. Associations, too, operate as conflict agents. But here the contact moves toward the provincial level, particularly in the sphere of education. The large, active, and influential *l'Association Canadienne-Française d'Education d'Ontario* acts to stimulate and aggregate local interests and to articulate these at the provincial level. Activity is directed toward the minister's office and the department rather than toward the legislature. It is at this level where government agencies act as conflict agents for majority interests, working out compromises and accommodations with minority agents.

POSITION AND RESOURCE SCARCITY

The final category of required empirical conditions is that of *position* and *resource scarcity*. A condition of position scarcity arises when, for example, desirable positions in the social structure are assigned by ascription based on ethnicity, and consequently, members of subordinate ethnic groups are blocked from attaining these positions. It is very difficult, in Canada, for a person to be both a French-Canadian and a corporation executive. The low representation of French-speaking Canadians in higher status occupations is well demonstrated by John Porter in *The Vertical Mosaic*.[16] Using 1961 census materials, in Ontario those of French origin were under-represented in the managerial, professional and technical, and clerical and sales occupational categories, and over-represented in the craftsmen, labourers, and agriculture categories.[17] I have yet to gather data of this type in the community under study. However, in local industries the lack of Franco-Ontarians in executive offices

[16] John Porter, *The Vertical Mosaic* (Toronto, 1965), pp. 91–98.
[17] Dominion Bureau of Statistics, *1961 Census of Canada*, Vol. III—Part I, Labour Force: Canada and Provinces, Table 22 (Ottawa, 1964).

compared to their overwhelming presence in the plants is easily observable.[18]

Resource scarcity is a question of supply and demand; both parties cannot have all they want. Power is a resource. The ability to influence or to exercise power as a means of gaining control over desirable ends, in reference to the school system for example, is a crucial element in the playing out of a conflict situation.

THE VARIABLES OF CONFLICT

Thus, the empirical conditions or prerequisites for a conflict situation are these: if two or more ethnic quasi-groups (that is *parties*) *are in contact and interacting* in a superordinate-subordinate relationship (that is, under conditions of *position* and *resource scarcity*), then a state of conflict exists among them. Social conflict is thus defined as a structural state rather than as a variable. This point of departure demands that the variables of conflict be identified and their interrelations specified. Inventories of variables appear in Coser,[19] Dahrendorf,[20] Mack and Snyder,[21] and Williams.[22] The selection of the variables for this paper was based partly on their importance in the literature and partly on their applicability to the situation under study.

The five variables selected are members of what may well develop into four classes of variables as empirical studies dealing with social conflict increase. The first class has to do with the strength of a conflict and involves the variables of *intensity* and *militancy*. The second class, involving the degree to which a conflict is *institutionalized,* is concerned with variations in the regulation and formalization of the conflict relationship. The third class refers to issues: the question whether a conflict is *over a basic consensus* or takes place *within a basic consensus* belongs to this class. The fourth class refers to the broader social context within which a particular conflict is located, as for instance the degree to which several potential conflict fronts (such as class, ethnicity, religion, and rural-urban residence) are *superimposed.*

INTENSITY AND MILITANCY

The strength of a conflict situation seems to vary along at least two dimensions which exhibit some degree of independence. On one hand,

---

[18] See also Everett C. Hughes, *French Canada in Transition* (Chicago, 1943), pp. 46–65.

[19] Coser, *op. cit.*

[20] Dahrendorf, *op. cit.*

[21] Mack and Snyder, *op. cit.*

[22] Robin M. Williams, Jr., *Strangers Next Door: Ethnic Relations in American Communities* (Englewood Cliffs, N. J., 1964).

there is the importance of the conflict itself to the parties and the resulting degree to which they and their members are involved. On the other
hand, there is the extent to which the parties utilize coercive weapons to
attain their ends. Several hours have been spent in Normanville attending meetings and conferences of associations devoted to the articulation
of local Franco-Ontarian interests. The numbers of people involved and
the frequency of meetings indicate a level of involvement, at least, beyond
what might be termed "low." At the same time, the sessions are exceedingly calm; there is an absence of threatening or intimidating statements
directed toward the opponents; few press releases are made, and there
have been no efforts at circulating petitions or organizing demonstrations.
In other words, involvement appears to be fairly extensive, but there is
an extremely low level of militancy.

The intensity of a conflict, according to Dahrendorf,[23] is defined as
the degree of involvement of the parties, that is, as the amount of energy
expended and the significance of the cause. The presence of organized
groups operating as conflict agents, the extent to which members of
related quasi-groups or parties participate in these associations, and the
extent to which the activities of these groups are directed toward the
articulation of party interests, would seem to be likely indicators of
intensity.

Militancy refers to technique or strategy, the weapons chosen as it
were. It is the use of coercive measure in pursuing party interests. The
use of petitions, non-violent demonstrations, and strikes would indicate a
medium to low level of militancy; the use of violence would constitute a
high level of militancy. Most discussions of conflict, both in the literature
and by the public, define conflict *per se* in terms of this one variable.[24]
Thus, an observable level of militancy is designated as conflict; if the
level of militancy is considerably reduced, most would say that conflict
has disappeared. But such is not the case; conflict is a structural state.[25]

---

[23] Dahrendorf, *op. cit.*, p. 211.

[24] See, for example, Tamotsu Shibutani and Kian M. Kwan, *Ethnic Stratification*
(New York, 1965), p. 401.

[25] Admittedly, the distinction between intensity and militancy requires further refinement, especially with regard to empirical referents. This distinction was initially
based on Dahrendorf's notions of intensity and violence (note: Dahrendorf, *op. cit.*,
pp. 212–13) which appeared unsatisfactory in relation to the data in question. With
respect to intensity, involvement of quasi-group members in conflict agencies and as
conflict agents seems to be a key referent. The *Petit Larousse* definition of the word
intensité is a closer approximation to the meaning intended than the general meaning
of "intensity" in English. *Intensité* is defined as "Expression de la valeur numerique
d'une grandeur." This suggests the concept of size or, in this case, the extent of
involvement. In contrast, militancy refers to specific acts directed against the opponent
rather than the extent to which quasi-group members are involved in these acts.
Although a certain degree of intensity would appear to be a prerequisite for militancy,
it also seems that there can be considerable involvement without militancy.

THE INSTITUTIONALIZATION OF CONFLICT

The second class of variables involves the regulation of conflict. Some students of conflict have suggested that conflicts tend to be "programmed for continuation."[26] The process of programming a conflict for continuation is a process of institutionalizing the relationship between the conflicting parties. A set of regulations and a set of positions and roles emerge to define and stabilize a conflictive relationship, permitting each party to operate in relation to its opponent with some degree of order and predictability. Labour-management relations represent a typical example of institutionalized conflict.[27]

The position of the bilingual school system in Ontario is also a form of institutionalized conflict. The presence of public and separate schools and the division of the latter into French and English language systems is a recognition of the three parties involved. Furthermore, the development of the dual inspectorate has provided a formal means through which the interests of both parties within the separate system may be articulated. This process regulates, but does not solve or resolve, conflict. Indeed, I would agree with Dahrendorf that conflicts of a structural type, social conflict, are not resolvable except through the elimination of one of the parties.[28] Certainly, issues are resolvable, but a state of conflict will remain as long as a power differential between two or more parties remains intact. And it is difficult to conceive of groups involved in boundary-maintenance activity without a resulting power differential.

LEVEL OF CONSENSUS

With regard to the third class of variables, that of issues, Coser distinguishes between "conflicts arising within the same consensual framework . . . and . . . those which put the basic consensus in question."[29] Whether a particular conflict is of one or the other type would seem to have ramifications for the degree of intensity, and perhaps the degree of militancy. A basic consensus as such is no more than a preexisting agreement or accommodation between the parties involved. Empirically, then, the requirement is one of locating and describing the nature of such agreements. Given this information, it is possible to determine whether a conflict is primarily over or within a basic consensus.

The current Franco-Ontarian school issue takes place within a basic consensus, a consensus emerging from the modification of Regulation 17

---

26 Irving L. Horowitz, "Consensus, Conflict and Cooperation: A Sociological Inventory," *Social Forces*, XLI (1963), 182.

27 Robert Dubin, "Industrial Conflict and Social Welfare," *The Journal of Conflict Resolution*, I (June, 1957), 187–92.

28 Dahrendorf, *op. cit.*, pp. 223–25.

29 Coser, *op. cit.*, p. 73.

in 1927. Regulation 17, passed by the province of Ontario in 1912, destroyed all previous accommodations which had evolved since the creation of Upper Canada, accommodations or, if you wish, a basic consensus concerning the operation of French language schools. The use of French in schools attended by Franco-Ontarians was limited to the first year and decisions regarding its use in new schools and its use as a means of communication between teacher and pupil were placed in the hands of the chief inspector of the province.[30] By 1915, 190 school districts were excluded from provincial grants for refusing to adhere to the regulation.[31]

Following 15 years of intense conflict, the regulation was modified and a new accommodation was reached between the contending parties. This new accommodation provided the basic consensus within which the conflict has proceeded over the last three decades. Should this accommodation be called into question, and there is some indication that it may be,[32] then we might well expect a renewal of intensity similar to that exhibited in 1912.

SUPERIMPOSITION OF CONFLICT FRONTS

The final class of variables refers to the social context within which a particular conflict takes place, a particular community or region, for example. Several theoretical works on social conflict[33] have noted the coincidence of significant social categories as a highly influential variable. That is, to what extent are such potential conflict fronts as class, religion, ethnicity, and political affiliation superimposed, creating a single, dominant cleavage? If in Normanville, for example, all and only French-speaking Canadians were Catholic, lower class, and voted Socialist, and were confronted with an English-speaking population, all members of which were Protestant, upper class, and voted Conservative, then there would be a high degree of superimposition.

A complete superimposition of conflict fronts is perhaps empirically rare in industrial societies. In Normanville, the very presence of a significant body of English-speaking Catholics prevents a complete superimposition of linguistic, religious, and ethnic fronts. Perhaps the fact that not all Franco-Ontarians are in lower income groups and not all English-

---

30 L. Tremblay, *Entre Deux Livraisons* (Ottawa, 1963).

31 C. Hopkins, *The Canadian Annual Review* (Toronto, 1915), p. 506.

32 L'Association Canadienne-Française d'Education d'Ontario, *et. al.*, "Brief Submitted to the Provincial Committee on Aims and Objectives of Education in the Schools of Ontario," mimeograph (Ottawa, 1965); and *Memoire à la Commission Royale D'Enquete sur le Bilinguisme et la Biculturalisme* (Ottawa, 1964).

33 James S. Coleman, *Community Conflict* (New York, 1957), p. 22; also Coser, *op. cit.*, p. 76; Williams, *op. cit.*; and Dahrendorf, *op. cit.*, p. 213.

speaking residents are in higher income groups is of more importance. In any case, it is not difficult to accept the proposition that the degree of superimposition will influence the intensity of a conflict situation.

HYPOTHESES

The five variables proposed suggest many useful hypotheses both within the suggested classes (that is, between militancy and intensity) and between these classes. I will deal, for the present, with hypotheses only of the latter type. *Institutionalization, the level of consensus,* and *superimposition* are taken as determinants. The degrees of *intensity* and *militancy* are taken as resultants.

A conflict which is institutionalized to one degree or another implies that the parties and their claims are recognized as legitimate and that the means are provided for the articulation of their claims or interests. Since militant behaviour is generally undertaken as a means of demonstrating power and demanding recognition, it would seem to follow that conflicts once institutionalized will exhibit less militancy. Militant tactics have been used by American Negro organizations at the local community level as a means of attaining recognition. Once negotiations between representatives of these organizations and "the white power structure" are achieved, the militant behaviour is usually reduced. This is not to say that militant tactics completely disappear from the scene, but there is a reduction especially of violent forms.[34] Lieberson and Silverman in a recent article on racial riots note that "a more responsible government [that is, city government] makes riots less likely because it provides *regular institutional channels* for expressing grievances."[35] Thus, the following hypothesis:

Theoretical Hypothesis I.—The institutionalization of the relations between conflicting parties reduces the level of militancy exhibited by both parties.

The passing of Regulation 17 did lower the level of institutionalization. French-speaking inspectors were divested of their authority and were no longer recognized as conflict agents for the minority party, thus cutting off one previously existing channel of communication. In turn, the degree of militancy expressed by both parties increased considerably. This was perhaps more so with the minority party; mass demonstrations ensued locally and in the Ottawa region; petitions were circulated

---

34 Dahrendorf, *ibid.,* 228. Also, L. Killian and C. Grigg, *Racial Crisis in America* (Englewood Cliffs, N. J., 1964), p. 136.
35 Stanley Lieberson and A. R. Silverman, "The Precipitants and Underlying Conditions of Race Riots," *American Sociological Review,* XXX (December, 1965), 896. Emphasis added.

locally.[36] The 1927 modifications again recognized the legitimacy of the minority's claims and re-established the Franco-Ontarian inspectors. The degree of militancy dropped considerably following these alterations.

The problem of possible relationships between institutionalization and intensity is left open. The level of consensus in question would seem to have more effect on intensity than the degree of institutionalization. Involvement may be just as high in an institutionalized as in a non-institutionalized conflict. But if a basic consensus is the focus of conflict, it would be expected that the issues are more important to the parties and that a higher level of involvement or intensity would follow. It might also follow that if the fundamental agreements between conflicting parties are in question, the level of militancy will increase. However, the degree of institutionalization perhaps has a stronger effect on militancy. Therefore, if issues involving a basic consensus can be approached in a regulated manner, militancy may still remain at a low level even though intensity has increased. The following hypotheses express these relations:

Theoretical Hypotheses II.—Conflicts within a basic consensual framework tend to exhibit a lower level of intensity than conflicts over a basic consensus.

Theoretical Hypothesis III.—If the institutionalization of the relations between conflicting parties is reduced, the level of militancy will increase in both types of conflict—those over and those within a basic consensual framework.

Theoretical Hypothesis IV.—If conflicts over a basic consensual framework take place in a situation where the relations between the parties remain at a relatively high level of institutionalization, the degree of intensity will tend to increase while the degree of militancy will tend to remain at a low level.

Regulation 17 focused directly on a basic consensual framework regarding the operation and status of Franco-Ontarian schools in Ontario. As such, the level of intensity was extremely high. Members of local Franco-Ontarian communities were thoroughly involved in associations representing their interests. Before its conclusion in 1927, the issue had involved (in addition to the Ontario legislature) the federal parliament, the British privy council, the legislature of Quebec, and the Vatican. Certainly, the militancy, although its level was high, was prevented from erupting into an extremely violent conflict by the very fact that through the involvement of these bodies a certain level of institutionalization was maintained.

---

36 *Mémoire au sujet de Paroisses Canadiennes-Françaises à Windsor* (Windsor, 1914).

The final variable, posited as a member of a class of variables dealing with the context in which a conflict takes place, is that of superimposition. If the membership of major conflict fronts do not coincide, the members of any single front will be subject to a multitude of cross pressures. The extent of involvement in and the importance of any single issue would, therefore, be lower than if the reverse were the case. Certainly, the energies involved or expended by conflict groups with overlapping memberships would reduce the potential for a highly intense confrontation between any two. Thus, the following hypothesis:

Theoretical Hypothesis V.—Given an ethnic conflict, the degree to which ethnicity is superimposed on other potential conflict fronts varies directly with the degree of intensity exhibited by that conflict.

CONCLUSION

The aforementioned variables and their interrelations were developed *a posteriori*. The resulting model, yet to be refined and tested, suggests the utility of a conflict perspective in contrast to an assimilation model in the analysis of French-English relations in particular and ethnic relations in general. However, in order to demonstrate this utility, specific indicators must be delineated for each of the variables and a set of testable hypotheses constructed.

Certainly, there are other variables. One wonders to what extent the relations posited between the above determinants and resultants may be affected by local variations in community structure. For example, if local decision-making machinery is not involved in crucial issues whatever they may be, the interest-articulating activity of conflict agents will take place beyond the local community. What effects might this have on the intensity and militancy of a conflict at the local level? The presence of one or more ethnic groups in a community, such as Normanville, though providing a major prerequisite for conflict, also tends to establish a set of communal issues exclusive of ethnic interests. Roads must be built, sewers provided, recreational facilities made available, taxes kept at a minimum, and so on. If members of a given community are strongly identified with these kinds of communal interests, there may be a tendency to avoid issues which might damage this level of co-operation. This, in turn, may have more effect locally on militancy than the degree to which an ethnic conflict is institutionalized.

There are also the problems of cultural and structural assimilation and the manner in which these may be related to the variables of conflict. A conflict model permits one to specify certain variables which differentially effect these two dimensions of assimilation. It allows one to view conflict and assimilation as interdependent rather than as components of a sequential process destined to conclude in complete assimilation. For example, the institutionalization of ethnic conflict, though contributing to cultural assimilation through the establishment of lines of communication, contributes to the maintenance of structural separation, the opposite of assimilation, insofar as it serves to recognize conflicting parties and provide a means for their continued existence. Furthermore, if the intensity of a conflict increases, the degree of structural separation will increase. Thus, conflicts over a basic consensus, the breakdown of prior accommodations, will tend to reverse the assimilation processes. It is in this sense that the proposed model is offered as one alternative to Park's race relations cycle and its assumption of "eventual assimilation."[37]

A final word on Normanville: today it appears as a placid, friendly town. And indeed it is. But the intensity and militancy of the Franco-Ontarian-English conflict is currently at a low level because the relations between the groups are highly institutionalized—in school, church, and town hall; because the current issues take place within a basic consensual framework; and because the degree to which major conflict fronts are superimposed is low. This does not, however, suggest that the conflict itself has disappeared—that "we have no problems here."

---

[37] Robert E. Park, *Race and Culture* (paperback edition, New York, 1964), p. 283. See also Amitai Etzioni, "The Ghetto—A Re-Evaluation," *Social Forces*, XXXVII (March, 1959), pp. 225–226. The author suggests that competition, conflict, accommodation, and assimilation might be viewed as alternatives rather than as stages in a fixed sequence. Criticisms of the inevitability of assimilation also appear in Nathan Glazer and Daniel P. Moynihan, *Beyond the Melting Pot* (paperback edition, Cambridge, 1964), pp. 12–23, and in Milton M. Gordon, *Assimilation in American Life* (New York, 1964), Chap. I. The distinction between cultural and structural assimilation is made, among others, by Gordon, *ibid.*, Chap. III, and by S. N. Eisenstadt, *The Absorption of Immigrants* (London, 1954), pp. 12–15.

17. A Tri-Ethnic Trap:
The Spanish Americans in Taos

JOHN J. BODINE

This paper will examine certain of the factors of acculturation that define the relationships established between three ethnically separable populations in the New Mexico community of Taos. Crucially important is the documentation of the value of ethnocentrism. For each group this has required the adherence to certain attitudes that are apparent in the interactions that occur.

There is ample demonstration in the literature of acculturation that bi-ethnic communities are complex subjects for study, and the variability they display has frustrated many anthropologists who have attempted to construct a meaningful typology of acculturational models.[1] The examination of a tri-ethnic situation poses even more difficulties. However, I feel that such investigation can provide very fruitful insights into the nature of culture contact.

With the appearance of summary studies of the history of relations, like Edward Spicer's *Cycles of Conquest,* we are in a much better position to investigate the realities of interaction that occur in the many tri-ethnic communities of the Southwest. One such community that can be consid-

SOURCE: This paper was originally presented at the 1968 annual spring meeting of the American Ethnological Society, permission to print granted by the author.

[1] Nancy O. Lurie, "Culture Change," *Introduction to Cultural Anthropology* (Boston: Houghton Mifflin Company, 1967).

ered archtypical in terms of the intensity of tri-ethnic contact is Taos, New Mexico. For the purposes of this paper, the spotlight will be turned on the Spanish-Americans of this mountain valley town to illuminate their special position in the complex web of acculturational forces that bear heavily on them in 1968.

Taos is home for the Taos Pueblo Indians, a sizable colony of Anglo-American artists and tourist entrepreneurs, and a numerically dominant group of Spanish-Americans. First it is important to summarize briefly certain historical facts that laid the groundwork for the present set of relationships. We know that effective Anglo-American control of this region began with the usurpation of political domination in the late 1840's. Until then Taos and her sister communities along the upper Rio Grande were governed, if tenuously, by Spain and briefly by Mexico. The people of Hispanic culture were politically and economically the dictators of their fate. They shared the resources of the region with the indigenous Indian populations and had established, more or less successfully, a working set of relationships between themselves and the Indians. There never seems to have been a serious question in the Spanish mind that their cultural system was superior to that of the persistently pagan Pueblos. Until the arrival of members of the special Anglo-American colony around the turn of the 20th century there was comparatively little reason for them to doubt their superiority.

In 1898 the first Taos artists took up residence in this small "Mexican" town and soon afterward ethnicity-seekers, led by a former empress of Greenwich Village and the salons of Florence, Mabel Dodge, arrived in Taos. When Taos was "discovered" the Spanish, tucked away in their small and relatively isolated mountain communities, were perpetuating a life-way akin to peasant settlements elsewhere in the Southwest and in Mexico. They were people of the land for whom life was difficult and inevitably so. Stoicism made its harsh reality a bit more bearable. Of course this is a value they share with their cultural peers elsewhere in the Hispanic world. I feel it is probably an important factor limiting their frustration and possible rebellion against the injustices they received from Anglo society.

The reasons for the attraction of Taos for artists and ethnicity-seekers alike are vitally important in determining the present position of the Spanish. These Anglos were drawn to this valley by the presence of the Taos Indians and what they conceived to be their immutably mysterious culture. They came as well because Taos offered a remarkably beautiful environment and a rather effective degree of isolation wherein they could develop their artistic and intellectual talents. Finally, in order of importance, they could savor certain elements of Hispanic culture so markedly imprinted on New Mexico. All of these factors convinced them that they were residents of an area that was different and quite foreign by comparison with most other U.S. communities. Therefore they emphasized and attempted to preserve those elements of ethnic difference which fed their special mental appetites. They did not consciously attempt to disturb the tenor of relationships established between the Indians and the Spanish.

On a formal and quite vocal level the Anglos expressed, and still do, an attitude of tolerance and acceptance of both individual as well as cultural idiosyncrasy. While they sought from the two other ethnic groups proof of cultural difference which they found quaint, charming, mysterious and psychically satisfying, they never relinquished their claim to their own cultural superiority. As bearers of the civilization of the now dominant society, they made it crystally clear to both the Indians and the Spanish that they were the representatives of the new order that inevitably would be established. This points up again that the value of ethnocentrism is the base on which interaction can so often be interpreted. If other values and attitudes had not developed Taos would be more similar to other bi- or tri-ethnic communities.

One would expect, as elsewhere, that the members of the two European-derived groups would jockey for first place in the status structure, but there would be little question that the Indians occupied the position at the bottom. However, the Taos Anglos in weighing the elements of ethnic attraction have consistently placed the Spanish-Americans on the lowest rung of the ladder. The reasons are clear. The Anglo of Taos tenaciously holds the belief that this community is a kind of Utopia. It is transformed into a never-never land by the rather constant employment of a kind of mental gymnastic in which imagination reigns supreme. From the Anglo point of view one can legitimately speak of the "mystique" of Taos. In its creation the Anglos glorified Taos Indian culture and relegated the Spanish-American to the bottom of the prestige structure.

With these facts in mind we can proceed to examine in a more concrete manner the realities of interaction. We are faced with a cultural triangulation which demands daily and face-to-face contact by members of each ethnic group. Today the Anglos firmly control the one important commodity that Taos sells: ethnicity. Tourism is the only industry that matters and no one is unaffected by its operation. The Spanish have been able to improve their economic lot by finding employment in the many Anglo-owned tourist businesses. They provide the Anglos with a pool of cheap labor from which waitresses, service station attendants, store clerks, domestics and all manner of menials can be drawn. Some Indians also serve in these capacities, but Anglos have frequently found them to be less dependable in terms of faithfully reporting for work. The Spanish are more attuned than the Indians to the Anglo-American attitudes toward work (Bodine, 1964). By and large the Spanish need steady employment more than many Indians. They often do not have the extended family to fall back on if they lose a job. This has greatly increased their reliability as employees, but it has created a certain amount of resentment toward Anglos as well. The Spanish have learned that if they do not closely follow Anglo orders they can be quite quickly and easily replaced. The Anglos demand and receive faithful service due to this usually subtle form of coercion. Many Taos domestics, for example, are willing to work for 75¢ an hour. Of course there are only so many positions available. The significant decrease in agricultural production in the valley and the general increase in the Spanish-American population have thrown great numbers of Spanish into the unskilled labor market. Taos cannot support them all, so many are forced to leave each year to seek either permanent or seasonal work elsewhere. Many are absorbed into the produce centers of the West and follow the harvests from Colorado sugar beets to Washington apples.

However, it should be noted that in spite of the substandard wages for many jobs, there has been a gradual increase in affluence among the Spanish-Americans who remain in the area. Never as protected by the government as the Indians, the Spanish have nevertheless managed slowly to raise their standard of living. The great amount of truly desperate poverty that was certainly characteristic before World War II has diminished. An increase in various kinds of welfare programs has been important in helping many, particularly the physically unfit and the aged. These aids are relieving the younger generations of the responsibility for total support. However, the Spanish are far from having achieved an economically comfortable status by national standards, as all recent government surveys have demonstrated.

The change which led to this slow road toward economic betterment began during the Second World War in which great numbers of Spanish-Americans served. Men in the armed forces sent home more cash than many of their families had ever seen and in their absence this money usually went into the purses of the women. Spanish-American women had rarely been in such a position. Cultural patterns decreed that the husband was the acknowledged head of the household and controlled all strategic income. There had been little opportunity for the women to rise above their position of economic subservience. Suddenly they were in control. At first many were totally irresponsible in handling this money, but gradually most learned to direct the financial affairs of their families and they came to enjoy their new position of responsibility.

Many men returned from the War to find their wives were not only capable of handling their own affairs but determined to preserve their new-found independence. In many cases the traditional structure of husband-wife status and role playing was broken. The women refused to remain at home as long-suffering "servants" of the men. If the men proved to be poor providers, the women left the home to find work. Such a move would have been improper under the traditional system. The Spanish-American male came back from service to face the problems of adjustment that hit many veterans and frequently to find that the family he left was not the same. Alcoholism increased as did the divorce rate. A major factor preventing even more widespread chaos was the maintenance of the traditional family relations by the older generation—the parents of the veterans and their wives. Their conservatism tended to hold in check the rebellious nature of the younger women and the confusion of their sons.

To a much greater extent than with the Indians, the War succeeded in implanting new needs and desires in the minds of the Spanish. They are now significantly directed toward attaining the economic standing of the Anglo-American and many have dedicated themselves to that aim with an almost fanatic zeal. However, in Taos they are consistently frustrated in their attempts to achieve their goals. The Anglos still consider them lower-class citizens. The Spanish represent the poverty-ridden masses who lost control of their town as Anglo settlers and businessmen poured in and took over the reins of economic exploitation. Naturally the Anglos have no intention of relinquishing their hold on these operations, which they often worked very hard to develop. Therefore the Spanish find themselves victims of a system which demands attitudes of accommodation in decided contrast to their personal goals of achievement, but which has so far offered them no real avenue of escape. They are trapped.

The economic structure is not the only aspect of life in Taos through which the Spanish have suffered prestige and status deprivation. Religion constitutes another if somewhat different force. The majority of the Spanish-Americans of Taos are practitioners of the brand of Hispanic folk Catholicism found elsewhere in the United States and in Mexico. The details need not be repeated here since they have been admirably reported by others, e.g., Madsen, 1964. One special aspect of their religious system does need mentioning.

Due partly to the rather effective isolation from their cultural peers, the Spanish-Americans of this region kept alive a religious cult that largely disappeared elsewhere. This is the *penitente* movement, which is still operative although considerably slowed down. Excessive self-flagellation and crucifixion are not as characteristic as in the past. The official wrath of the Church was felt by these people in a blanket decree of excommunication imposed by the archbishop of Santa Fe. It resulted in the *penitentes* surrounding their devotion with utmost secrecy so that now, although the decree is lifted, it is very difficult to obtain accurate information on this practice. However, the attitudes held by most Anglos can be easily summarized.

One would suppose that the mysterious nature of *penitente* activity would have been a factor to intrigue and inflame the imaginations of the ethnic-seeking Anglos. Indeed, Anglo-Americans were fascinated by the macabre processions and crucifixions that took place each year in the valley. But their fascination was not accompanied by respect for these customs. Catholicism generally and the *penitente* cult in particular engendered more prejudice than admiration. The majority of Anglos were either Protestants or non-practitioners of religion. Settling themselves in a sea of papists only tended to reify their anti-Catholic feelings. Even Anglo-Catholics found the excesses of *penitente* custom incomprehensible. So this spectacular ethnic difference figured rather unimportantly in the attractions of the area. On the other hand, Indian religion was lauded by most Anglos as being beautiful in its symbolism and majestic in its performance.

This has been a very hard thing for the Spanish to swallow. Regardless of whether as individuals they were loyal members of the Church, certainly Catholicism or at least Christianity was the only road to salvation. For generations the priests had worked to convert the pagan Indians to the True Faith. Their reluctance to accept this core aspect of civilization was taken as proof of their inferiority. Most Spanish are still very derogatory in their remarks about the nominal adherence to the Church of most Indians. To discover that the Anglos heaped praise on the Indian religion, while either ignoring or belittling their own, increased not only their resentment toward Anglos but toward the Indians as well. Yet the Spanish are forced to pay lip service to the importance and beauty of Indian culture since they are painfully aware that most tourists come to Taos not to see them but to see the Indians and their famed four- and five-storied pueblos. Again they are forced into the background and have been unable to convince anyone that their cultural system is more advanced, more respectable and far more worthy of emulation than that of the Taos Indians. I strongly suspect, but have no means of measuring it, that a certain amount of Spanish resistence to acculturation is prompted by their need to demonstrate cultural superiority. Any number display definite signs of social paranoia.

One rather small victory the bearers of Hispanic culture have achieved is to insist on the term "Spanish-American." They point out rather vehemently that they are the pure and direct descendants of the Spanish *conquistadores*. They are Spanish, not Mexican. Use of the term "Mexican" is definitely derogatory in Taos. Significantly the Indians insist on calling them just that, although not too openly anymore.

It is true that certain families of Taos can trace their genealogies back to the time of the de Vargas reconquest in 1692. At least there were Bacas, Lujans and so forth on the expedition, some of whom settled in Taos Valley. But today there are very few, if any, "pure" line families left. The majority possess a very mixed background. Intermixture with persons of Indian ancestry has produced a population that can hardly be categorized as Spanish, let alone Castilian as a few insist they are. In fact if you establish sufficient rapport, most Spanish-Americans at Taos will tell you of the Indians they know in their ancestry.

Anglos willingly employ the term Spanish. Their motives again seem to be linked with their desire to consider all aspects of Taos as being different and special. By acceding that their darker neighbors are indeed Spanish effectively separates them from the vast sea of lower-class Mexican-Americans found elsewhere in the southwestern United States. Actually the Spanish-Americans of Taos have never been totally successful in this mild effort to distort reality, although certainly there are not the very real ties with Mexico that one finds farther south. And as a small element of the Taos "mystique" the term Spanish-American, which does not mean simply Spanish-speaking, is appropriately accepted.

There is an area of Taos life in which the Spanish have succeeded in maintaining control. They rather effectively dominate the local political scene and become deeply involved in small town politics. They can elect to office Spanish-American candidates because their superior numbers permit them to control the vote. Until recently no Anglo-American had any interest in being an elected official in Taos town or county. Anglos relished their enclaved minority status in this "foreign" community and were quite willing to allow the local inhabitants to run the petty affairs of government. Salaries are substandard anyway, so few Anglos were tempted.

The Spanish-American mayors and their councils have frequently used their positions of authority to try and thwart attempts by the Indians to gain any more prestige within the Taos social milieu. They can always be counted on to oppose the claims of the Indians to grazing, water, a right of way or even a cash settlement for past land grabs by either the Spanish or the Anglos. The Spanish-Americans are easily aroused over such issues and become the staunchest supporters of the cause against the Indians. I feel there is little question that the Spanish suffer most from the injustices of the past. Naturally their ire is raised when they see the Indians, who have received so many benefits from the federal government, attempt to obtain even more. However, I believe that a good part of their resentment is the result of the discrimination emanating from Anglo-American society. They try to retaliate by any means available and they certainly cannot accept further blessings bestowed on the Taos Indians regardless of whether those blessings will affect them directly or not.

Among the many other factors that could be employed to document the position of Spanish Taoseños, one stands out as crucial in helping to formulate Anglo attitudes. Whenever anything happens in Taos of a criminal nature the finger is pointed first at the Spanish-American community. Vandalism, theft and physical violence are frequent. Anglo women have been raped on occasion. Such behavior, including rather rampant juvenile delinquency, is readily understandable and for many of the same reasons that such problems occur in similar populations in other communities. Since most of the Spanish are economically lower-class, they bear many of the problems that such a predicament so frequently creates. High unemployment and consequent idleness often leads to frustration. Moreover there still exists the value of *machismo* in the Spanish community, even though it has declined since the Second World War. But fighting was long an established mechanism through which *machismo* was expressed. The weekly brawls at "Old Martinez Hall" in Ranchos de Taos became almost legendary. The lower-class Spanish still have their own *cantinas* where physical violence often occurs. The Anglos have little patience with such behavior. They imperfectly understand the stresses and strains facing many of the Spanish and most have never heard of the term *machismo*. This issue, however, greatly increases their distrust of the Spanish-Americans and is partly responsible for the very real degree of social separation that exists in Taos.

Only in the past few years has there been any significant invasion by Spanish-Americans into the clubs, restaurants and bars patronized by the Anglos. Even today few Spanish venture into these places and those who do must be the more affluent since the prices are pitched to snare the tourist dollar. Moreover most Spanish-Americans still feel out of place and Anglos do little to help them overcome their self-consciousness. Indeed, many Anglos would prefer that large numbers did not invade their places of enjoyment. There are Anglos who resent the fact that some of the Spanish are now in an economic position to measure up to them.

Token acceptance is often reflected in hearing an Anglo refer to a particular Spanish-American or family by saying, "He is a *nice* Spanish boy" or "I have always liked María and José. They are quite different from most of the others."

It is obvious that many of the well-known signs of prejudice and discrimination are characteristic of Taos. They are perhaps more subtly expressed there due to the special set of attitudes that has created the Taos "mystique." Significantly both the Indians and the Spanish have been affected by the creation of this somewhat imaginary environment. Indeed as I have shown in another study, Indian culture has been decidedly influenced by the special breed of Anglo who settled Taos.[2] Everything should be so beautiful and serene. It is not, of course, but the idea is sufficiently attractive that nearly everyone is infected with it. A member of any of the three ethnic groups is apt to make the plea at a time of community crisis, "Let's not allow this issue to destroy the marvelous harmony that we three peoples of Taos have achieved." Verbalization of the possibility of such destruction rather pointedly demonstrates that harmony in Taos is rather superficial. If harmony is destroyed I am confident that the push will come from the Spanish-Americans, as perhaps other papers in this symposium will support. After all, it is they who find themselves firmly held by the tri-ethnic trap of Taos, New Mexico.

REFERENCES

ALTUS, WILLIAM D. "American Mexican: The Survival of a Culture." *Journal of Social Psychology,* 29 (1949), 211-220.

BODINE, JOHN J. "Symbiosis at Taos: The Impact of Tourism on the Pueblo." Paper presented at the Central States Anthropological Society Meetings, Milwaukee, 1964.

————. "Attitudes and Institutions of Taos, New Mexico: Indices for Value System Expression." Unpublished Ph.D. dissertation, Tulane University, 1967.

COKE, VAN DEREN. *Taos and Santa Fe: The Artists' Environment 1882-1942.* Albuquerque: University of New Mexico Press, 1963.

DOZIER, EDWARD P. "Rio Grande Pueblos." in *Perspectives in American Indian Culture Change.* Chicago: University of Chicago Press, 1961.

EDMONSON, MUNRO S. *Los Manitos.* New Orleans: Middle American Research Institute, 1957.

FECHIN, ALEXANDRA. "European Aspects of Cosmopolitan Taos," *New Mexico Quarterly,* 21 (1951), 158-161.

GILLIN, JOHN. "Acquired Drives in Culture Contact," *American Anthropologist,* 44 (1942), 545-554.

---

2 John J. Bodine, "Attitudes and Institutions of Taos, New Mexico: Indices for Value System Expression," (unpublished Ph.D. dissertation, Tulane University, New Orleans, 1967).

LUHAN, MABEL DODGE. *Edge of the Taos Desert.* New York: Harcourt, Brace & World, Inc., 1937.

LURIE, NANCY O. "Culture Change," in *Introduction to Cultural Anthropology.* Boston: Houghton Mifflin Company, 1967.

MADSEN, WILLIAM. *The Mexican-Americans of South Texas.* New York: Holt, Rinehart & Winston, Inc., 1964.

McWILLIAMS, CAREY. *North From Mexico: The Spanish-Speaking People of the United States.* Philadelphia: J. B. Lippincott Co., 1948.

PARSONS, ELSIE CLEWS. "Taos Pueblo." *General Series in Anthropology No. 2.* Menasha, Wis.: George Banta Publishing Co., 1936.

SANCHEZ, GEORGE I. *The Forgotten People.* Albuquerque: University of New Mexico Press, 1940.

SENTER, DONOVAN. "Acculturation among New Mexican Villagers in Comparison to Adjustment Patterns of other Spanish-Speaking Americans," *Rural Sociology,* 10 (1945), 31-47.

SIEGEL, BERNARD J. "Suggested Factors of Culture Change at Taos Pueblo," *International Congress of Americanists,* 29 (1952), 133-140.

SPICER, EDWARD. "Spanish-Indian Acculturation in the Southwest," *American Anthropologist,* 56 (1954), 663-678.

————. *Cycles of Conquest.* Tucson: University of Arizona Press, 1962.

18. The Power Structure of the Negro Sub-Community: A Case Study and a Comparative View

HAROLD W. PFAUTZ

In the contemporary setting of rapid change, clear-cut issues, and sometimes overt conflict in race relations in many American cities, studies of the power structure of the Negro sub-community come to have strategic value on both theoretical and practical grounds. In contrast to a traditional lack of solidarity and powerless leadership, recent events and studies demonstrate a growing ability to act together and to develop a leadership which can make effective demands on the dominant group.[1] This situation provides an unparalleled opportunity to observe the formation, modes of operation, and functional significance of community power structures. In addition, reliable knowledge concerning the nature and functioning of Negro sub-community leadership on all levels—com-

---

SOURCE: Reprinted with permission of the author and the publisher from *Phylon*, XXIII, No. 2 (Summer, 1962).

[1] Cf., e.g., Lewis M. Killian and Charles U. Smith, "Negro Protest Leaders in a Southern Community," *Social Forces*, XXXVIII (March, 1960), 253–57 and Martin Luther King, *Stride Toward Freedom* (New York, 1958).

munity, region, and nation—is one *sine qua non* of a responsible and successful expedition of the desegregation process.

The present study of the power structure of a Negro sub-community furthers the comparative note struck by Barth and Abu-Luban.[2] To "Regional City"[3] and to "Pacific City,"[4] it adds empirical data on Providence, Rhode Island, a New England community of moderate size with a long history of race relations, a formally liberal tradition, a significant degree of sub-community identity, a clear-cut sub-community power structure, yet an economically depressed Negro population and a recent past of accommodating leadership. After a brief consideration of the history of the Negro sub-community in Providence, its power structure will be described and compared with those of Regional City and Pacific City. Finally, some practical and theoretical implications of the findings will be discussed.

THE NEGRO IN PROVIDENCE

The history of the Negro in Providence and in the state of which it is the capital goes back to the seventeenth century.[5] Its merchants not only played a prominent role in the early slave trade but also, motivated by their religious convictions, were largely responsible for the abolition of slavery in the latter part of the eighteenth century. Although an effective and viable anti-slavery tradition had an early development in Providence, the general body of its citizens were highly discriminatory in their acts and hostile in their attitudes toward the city's 1500 "free people of colour." Negroes were legally declared ineligible to vote in 1822 and received the franchise only after a bitter struggle, two decades later.[6] Moreover, there were anti-Negro riots in 1824 and 1831, each of which involved the razing of the city's already segregated Negro settlements. Nevertheless, by the time of the Civil War, despite (and largely because of) the generally prejudiced environment, Providence Negroes had

---

2 Ernest A. T. Barth and Baha Abu-Luban, "Power Structure and the Negro Community," *American Sociological Review*, XXIV (February, 1959), 69–76.

3 Cf. Floyd Hunter, *Community Power Structure* (Chapel Hill, 1943), pp. 114–50. Regional City involved a long-established, relatively static and traditional Deep South urban situation with a clearly identifiable sub-community power structure.

4 Cf. Barth and Abu-Luban, *op. cit.* Pacific City involved a relatively new and dynamic Northwest coast urban situation which, according to the researchers, lacked sub-community identity and clear-cut organization for power.

5 The account of the early history of the Negro in Providence leans heavily on Irving H. Bartlett, *From Slave to Citizen* (Providence, R. I.: The Urban League of Greater Providence, 1954).

6 This was the occasion of "Door's Rebellion," a suffragist movement which attained the proportions of a local civil war. Ironically, the working class Suffragists refused to include Negroes in their program, and the latter attained the franchise ultimately through the efforts of the "aristocratic" Legal Party. Cf., Bartlett, *op. cit.*, pp. 39–43.

developed thriving community organizations of their own—churches, mutual aid societies, schools, and the like. Some among them amassed considerable property and began to provide community leadership, winning a long and drawn-out battle for non-segregated public education in 1886.

Between 1865 and 1910 the state's Negro population almost doubled (from 4087 to 7529), largely through migration from the upper South. And, by the turn of the century, Rhode Island Negroes could look back on a period of solid accomplishment in the area of civil rights. From 1900 until the beginning of World War II, however, almost no real progress was made. The dynamic struggle for equal citizenship which had characterized the city's race relations in the nineteenth century was succeeded by a period of stagnation in the first four decades of the twentieth century. To be sure, a local branch of the National Association for the Advancement of Colored People was established in 1914, but it was able to make little headway against the conservatism of the local community and internal struggles for power within the organization.[7] During this era the sub-community leadership seemed primarily oriented to Negro society. It was vested in a small group of men who were content, for the most part, to play the role of accommodating leaders.

The Negro population of Providence continued traditionally unskilled, ill-housed, and poorly paid to such an extent that the "old" leadership was completely by-passed in a revolt of the younger elements just before World War II. In 1939 the "young Turks" went directly to leading white citizens and succeeded in securing the cooperation of the latter in establishing a local branch of the Urban League with a full-time, paid, professional director. The cleavages in the Negro community in general and in its leadership in particular that resulted from this development are still evident. Nevertheless, the League, in its two decades of operation, has come to be accepted as the official spokesman for Providence Negroes.[8] It has extended its activities throughout the state, has been moderately successful in opening up new skilled and white-collar occupations, and has been the informal organizing force behind movements to bolster the civil rights of local Negroes. A State Commis-

---

[7] Leadership disputes within the branch continued through the Forties. In 1945 one election was voided through the action of the national office of the NAACP. Cf., Barbara Elizabeth Chandler, "The Position of the Negro in Providence" (unpublished B.A. thesis, Department of Sociology, Bates College, April, 1947).

[8] The community has (quite unconsciously) sought to turn the League into a social casework agency. Whenever difficulties involving a "racial" factor develop in the schools, public housing, neighborhoods, etc., community officials immediately get in touch with the League on the unstated assumption that the League can "solve" the problem on an informal basis.

sion Against Discrimination was established in 1951; the Commission's directive was broadened to include the policies and practices of the city's Public Housing Authority in 1956; and, currently, there are lively grass-roots movements to secure fair housing legislation for the state as well as a human relations commission for the city.

By 1950 Providence Negroes numbered 8304 (see Table 1), and comprised 3.3 percent of a total population of 248,674. While the city lost population with a percentage decline of 1.9 during the decade 1940-1950, the Negro sub-community experienced a moderate increase of 30 percent.[9] As might be expected, the Negro population is residentially segregated: more than one-half of the Negro residents are concentrated in only two of the city's 37 census tracts. In 1950 the "index of dissimilarity" between the Negro and white residential patterns was 65.[10]

Perhaps the most signal indicators of the minority status of Providence's Negro population are data on their occupational and income status which are reported in Table 1, together with comparative data on Regional City and Pacific City.[11] The relatively depressed and static situation of Negroes in Providence is suggested by its closer similarity to the Southern than to the Northwestern case. Whereas only approximately 10 percent of Providence and Regional City Negroes were in white-collar occupations, more than 15 percent of the Negro labor force in Pacific City were so employed. Moreover, approximately one-fifth of the Negro labor forces in the New England and Southern cities were still in traditional private household service occupations in contrast to only one-tenth of Pacific City's Negroes.[12]

---

9 According to the 1960 census, these trends have continued. Providence experienced a 17 percent decline in total population between 1950 and 1960; its Negro population increased 34.3 percent; and the latter now number 11,153 and constitute 5.4 percent of the total population. The population of Regional City increased 47.1 percent and that of Pacific City increased 19.1 percent during this same period. The percentage increases of the Negro populations for these two cities were 53.7 and 71.7 respectively. In 1960 the proportion of Negroes in Regional City increased to 38.3 and the correlative figure for Pacific City was 4.8 percent. Cf., U. S. Bureau of the Census, *U. S. Census of Population: 1960. General Population Characteristics.* Final Report PC(1)-12B, 41B, and 49B, Table 21 (Washington, D. C., 1961).

10 The "index of dissimilarity" is defined as the sum of the positive (or negative) differences between two percentage distributions. It indicates the percentage of one group which would have to move to a different area to match that of the other on a proportional basis. The larger the value of the index, the greater the spatial separation. Cf., Otis Dudley Duncan and Beverly Duncan, "A Methodological Analysis of Segregation Indexes," *American Sociological Review*, XX (April, 1955), 210–17. Parenthetically, despite much civil rights activity in Providence during the past decade, the value of the index based on census data for 1960 has remained practically constant and now stands at 64.

11 Data on the socio-economic characteristics of the population for cities, by race, has yet to be made available by the Bureau of the Census.

12 Significantly, a comparative study of the process of school desegregation in a number

Turning to the data on income distribution, the median income of Negroes in Regional City in 1949 was lowest ($1046), followed by Provi-

TABLE 1.

Selected Demographic and Socio-Economic Characteristics of Providence, R. I., Regional City, and Pacific City and Their Negro Populations, 1950

Characteristic	Providence	Regional City	Pacific City
Total population (1950)	248,674	331,314	457,591
Percentage change (1940-1950)........	—1.9	9.6	27.0
Total Negro population (1950).........	8,304	121,285	15,666
Percentage change (1940-1950)........	30.0	16.1	313.5
Percent Negro	3.3	33.6	3.4
Median income white (1949)	$1824	$2218	$2356
Median income Negro (1949)	$1150	$1045	$1709
Percent white collar (Negro)	9.7	9.4	15.2
Percent private household service (Negro)	18.4	22.2	10.5

SOURCE: U. S. Bureau of the Census, *U. S. Census of Population: 1950. Characteristics of the Population* (Washington, D.C., 1952).

dence ($1150), while Pacific City Negroes had the highest median income ($1709). Whites in Regional City earned, on the average, twice as much as Negroes; in Providence they earned 1.6 times as much; and in Pacific City they earned only 1.4 times as much.[13] Indeed, the picture presented by both the Southern and New England cases is that of a very small number and proportion of middle and upper-income recipients, complemented by a large mass in the low-income brackets.[14] On the other hand, the form of the income distribution among Pacific City Negroes involves significant numbers and proportion in the middle-income categories. Thus, whereas approximately two-thirds of all employed Negroes over 14 years of age earned less than $1500 a year in Providence and Regional City (64.2 percent and 68.48 percent, respectively), less than half (44.5 percent) of Pacific City Negroes were in this class.

On the basis of these data, Providence Negroes clearly continue to be economically depressed and the object of considerable discrimination and prejudice. In part this is due to the small size and proportion of the Negro population in comparison to the dominant white group, a fact

of communities discovered that the proportion of Negro females employed in domestic service was highly and significantly inversely correlated with non-compliance. Cf. Harry V. Ball and George E. Simpson, "A Comparative Study of Compulsory School Desegregation in Fifty-two Selected Communities" (paper read at the 56th Annual Meeting of the American Sociological Association, St. Louis, Missouri, August 29-September 2, 1961).

13 Studies suggest that it is the relative difference rather than the absolute difference in income that is a valid indicator of the state of race relations in a communiy. Cf., *ibid.*

14 As late as 1947, Chandler concluded that while there were distinctions between "old- and new-comers" and "East Side and West Side," among Providence Negroes, because of the small size and lack of economic development of the Negro sub-community, no social classes existed. Cf. Chandler, *op. cit.,* p. 113.

which inevitably minimizes the former as a political threat. Another factor is the generally depressed economic situation of the city and state which, in the nature of the case, bears hardest on the minority members of the community.[15] Finally, the previously mentioned schisms within the Negro sub-community and its leadership have necessarily weakened its ability to present a solid front and successfully to make collective demands on the dominant group.

Presently, a series of already accomplished as well as proposed urban renewal and redevelopment programs will ultimately involve the relocation of approximately 80 percent of all Providence Negroes. The issues brought to the surface by this massive dislocation, plus the current pressures and climate of opinion connected with the desegregation process on the national level, will bring about, for better or for worse, a new era in local race relations. In this context the sub-community leadership is already engaged in an internal competition for power and status as well as in an external power struggle with the dominant whites.

THE NEGRO SUB-COMMUNITY POWER STRUCTURE

Data for reconstructing the power structure of the Negro sub-community in Providence were gathered by a modified version of the methods employed by Hunter and Barth and Abu-Luban. A list of potential influentials was compiled from a variety of sources including local clergymen, business and professional men, as well as a newspaper clipping scrapbook maintained by the local Urban League. In view of the small size of the Negro sub-community and the correlative assumption that all of the leaders were well known and known to one another, interviews were begun immediately with those on the list who were mentioned by at least three different sources—e.g., two individuals and the newspaper.[16] In addition to questions concerning his own social and economic characteristics, each interviewee was asked the following:

> If you were requested to choose a committee of ten Negro leaders in Providence (either men or women) who together would formulate a general policy affecting the Negro community as a whole, and you wanted to choose those individuals who, if they were to express their approval of a particular policy, would influence the greatest number of Negroes in the community to support it—whom would you choose?[17]

---

[15] Cf. Kurt B. Mayer and Sidney Goldstein, *Migration and Economic Development in Rhode Island* (Providence, 1958).

[16] The writer is indebted to Miss Marjorie Gaysunas for an extremely skillful and tactful series of interviews.

[17] Because of the small size of the community, not every informant was able to name ten different leaders.

The first ten interviews provided a list of 38 different individuals, and six additional interviews added no new names. Since this suggested that the complement of perceived leaders had been exhausted, interviewing was stopped at this point. The Negro sub-community leaders with whom we will be concerned were arbitrarily defined as those among the 38 mentioned who received at least four votes.[18] The final result was a list of 16 top leaders, each of whom had been interviewed.[19] And, in Table 2, these leaders, ranked by the number of votes each received from his 15 peers in the interviews, are presented. Data on the number of mutual choices, age, occupation, and "social orientation"[20] are also included.

TABLE 2.

Selected Characteristics of Negro Sub-Community Leaders in Providence, R. I., Ranked by Number of Votes Received in Leadership Poll

Leader	Number of Votes	Number of Mutual Choices	Occupation	Age	Social Orientation
Young	15	10	Agency director	56	Integration
Stephens	15	7	Mortician	51	Integration
Masters	15	9	Maintenance superintendent	47	Middle-road
Stewart	8	3	Management analyst	44	Integration
Spear	8	5	Agency director	46	Middle-road
Roberts	8	5	Real estate	79	Middle-road
Moore	8	5	Lawyer	72	Segregation
Miller	7	4	Union official	40	Integration
Dunham	7	5	Post office clerk (ret.)	62	Middle-road
Hardy	7	3	Physician	71	Segregation
Dunham, Jr.	5	3	Lawyer	30	Integration
Stone	5	2	Minister	63	Segregation
Sullivan	4	2	Bank manager	39	Integration
Worth	4	1	Trucker	71	Segregation
Gold	4	4	Mortician	72	Segregation
Gold (Mrs.)	4	0	Housewife	72	Segregation

Needless to say, the most striking characteristic of the list is the complete unanimity regarding the top three leaders, which is indicative of the clarity with which the power structure of the Negro sub-community is perceived. Parenthetically, these three men (Young, Stephens, and Mas-

---

18 Of the remaining 22 potential influentials, two received two votes and 20 received one vote in the course of the 16 interviews.

19 Both Hunter and Barth and Abu-Luban developed selected lists of influentials from which ten were to be nominated by the interview panels. Hunter obtained interviews from 23 sub-community leaders who voted for ten among a list of 34 potentials. Cf. Hunter, *op. cit.*, pp. 114–18. Barth and Abu-Luban interviewed 36 potentials who voted for ten among themselves. Cf. Barth and Abu-Luban, *op. cit.*, pp. 71–72.

20 See below for a discussion of "social orientation."

ters) were not only mutual choices but also meet one another in a variety of contexts, both formal and informal, which allows for constant and efficient intercommunication. For example, all three serve on the boards of the local branches of the Urban League and the NAACP; they belong to and have served as officers and board members of the two oldest formally organized Negro men's social clubs in Providence; and they also engage in mutual home visiting and entertaining.

In Table 3 some selected characteristics of the power structures of the Negro sub-communities in the three cities are presented. In view of the already demonstrated similarity between the Southern and New England situations in regard to the socio-economic status of their respective Negro populations, it is not surprising to find a degree of similarity in certain dimensions of their sub-community power structures. In contrast to Pacific City, the Negro leaders of Providence and Regional City are older and more provincial. The age difference is approximately ten years; and, whereas almost 90 percent of the Pacific City leaders were born outside of the state, the percentages for Providence and Regional City are 58 and 69, respectively. On the other hand, the occupational status of the Negro leaders is quite similar in all three cities—essentially a matter of professionals, minor managers and officials, and small businessmen.

TABLE 3.

Selected Demographic and Socio-Economic Characteristics of Negro Leaders in Providence, R. I., Regional City and Pacific City

Characteristic	Providence	Regional City*	Pacific City†
Size of leadership group.............	16	34	36
Average age in years................	57.5	54.3	44.8
Range in years......................	30–85	40–73	—‡
Average length of residence in years..	45.5	—‡	16.5
Percent born outside of the state.....	68.7	57.9	88.9
Percent born in the city.............	22.2	15.7	—‡
Occupational Distribution			
Professional	37.5%	55.9%	50.0%
Managers and officials..............	31.2	5.9	—
Small business	25.0	32.3	22.2
Clerical and sales	—	—	11.1
Other	6.3	5.9	16.7
Total	100.0%	100.0%	100.0%

* Cf. Hunter, *op. cit.*, pp. 114–150.
† Cf. Barth and Abu-Luban, *op. cit.*, pp. 69–76.
‡ Data not available.

The functional significance of the observed demographic differences in the makeup of the sub-community power structures inheres in their social psychological implications. The greater age and provincialism of the Negro leaders in Providence and Regional City might involve an

entirely different "political generation" from that represented by the
Pacific City leadership.[21] This, in turn, suggests the risk of a "trained
incapacity" to deal with the rapidly changing form and content of race
relations in the former two situations. In addition, the lack of leaders in
large-scale commercial and financial operations in all three cases makes
not only for a relative lack of power, given the institutional concept of
"men of power" employed by most students, but also a serious gap in
available perspectives for formulating strategy and tactics in community
power struggles.[22]

As previously noted, the Negro power structure in Providence was split
in 1939 in connection with the establishment of a branch of the Urban
League. This schism continues in effect today along generational, organizational and orientation lines, tempered by the presence of a few "middle-roaders."

The executive director of the local Urban League, who has served in
this capacity for more than two decades and who, perforce, has constant
dealings with all sub-community leaders, was asked to rate each one
according to the following types of "social orientation":[23] (1) integration: activities and concerns anchored in and identified with the total
community; participates actively in integrated organizations; (2) segregation: activities and concerns anchored in and identified with the local
Negro sub-community; participates actively in segregated organizations;
 (3) middle-road: active in both integrated and segregated organizations;
identification vacillates between the total community and the Negro sub-
community.

The clarity of the generational split between the "old" and the "new"
leader is suggested by the data in Table 4 where the leaders have been
arranged by "social orientation," age, and votes in the leadership poll.
Six of the 16 leaders were categorized as "integration" oriented; their
average age was 43.3 years; and they received an average of 6.3 votes. In
contrast, six others were categorized as "segregation" oriented; their average age was 70.2 years; and they received an average of 5.3 votes. There
were four "middle-roaders" with an average age of 58.5, who received an
average of 8.8 votes. In general, the younger, integration-oriented leaders
are more active in and identified with the Urban League, whereas the

---

21 Cf. Heberle's discussion of "The Problem of Political Generations" in Rudolf
Heberle, *Social Movements* (New York, 1951), pp. 120–27.

22 Barth and Abu-Luban, for example, conclude that "no genuine power structure had
developed" in Pacific City due to the lack of large scale business and industrial organizations. *Op. cit.*, pp. 69 and 76.

23 The writer is indebted to James M. Williams, executive director of the Urban
League of Rhode Island, for his many kindnesses and active participation in this study.

older leaders tend to be more active in and identified with the local branch of the NAACP. Significantly, the two older "middle-road" leaders (Roberts and Dunham, Sr.) are the only members of their generation to play active roles in the "new" Urban League, suggestive of their "broker" role and function.

On the basis of these data, the sub-community power sturcture of Providence would seem to be more oriented to "integration" than to "segregation." The differences, however, are often accommodated by the presence of the middle-roaders. And the strength of the latter is suggested by the fact that their average number of mutual choices in the leadership

TABLE 4.

Number of Votes in Leadership Poll and Age of "New" and "Old" Leaders of the Negro Sub-Community in Providence, R. I., by Social Orientation

| Type of Leader | Social Orientation | | | | | | | | |
| | Integration Number of | | | Middle-Road Number of | | | Segregation Number of | | |
	Name	Votes	Age	Name	Votes	Age	Name	Votes	Age
Old	...	...	...	Roberts	8	79	Moore	8	72
				Dunham	7	62	Hardy	7	71
							Stone	5	63
							Worth	4	71
							Gold	4	72
							Gold (Mrs.)	4	72
New	Young	15	56	Masters	15	47	...	...	...
	Stephens	15	51	Spear	8	46			
	Stewart	8	44						
	Miller	7	40						
	Dunham, Jr.	5	30						
	Sullivan	4	39						

poll was 6.0 in comparison to 4.8 among the "integration-oriented" and 2.5 among the "segregation-oriented" leaders. Indeed, while the local sub-community leadership in Providence is currently more militant than it has been in the past, it is typically a matter of "protest within the status quo."[24]

DISCUSSION AND CONCLUSIONS

A brief account has been presented of the history of the Negro and of race relations in a moderate-sized urban New England community, together with a picture of the power structure of the Negro sub-community. The latter, in turn, has been compared with studies made in

24 Cf. Hunter, op. cit., p. 128 and Oliver Cox, "Leadership Among Negroes," in Alvin W. Gouldner, ed., Studies in Leadership (New York, 1950), p. 270.

Southern and Northwestern urban situations. A number of theoretical and practical inferences can be drawn from the data involved.

In the first place, it is worth noting that many of the recent criticisms which have been made of the so-called reputational approach to the study of community power structures have considerably less validity when applied to the Negro sub-community.[25] This tends to be true of the Negro sub-community in general and of places which involve relatively small numbers and proportions of Negroes in particular.

The high degree of consensus in regard to the top three leaders of the Providence Negro power structure suggests that there may be less of a gap between "reputation" and "behavior" in the case of Negro sub-community leaders. This, of course, is related to the "form" of the Negro sub-community social structure which is likely to be monolithic in character, involving a small, articulate leadership at the top and an undifferentiated and inarticulate mass at the bottom.[26] Further, despite tendencies toward differentiation of leadership types according to issues which have been observed in metropolitan centers with large Negro populations,[27] there is only one issue in the final analysis: the ubiquitous race question. Thus, in Providence, despite the intense competition between generations and organizations for sub-community power and status, one of the most "segregation-oriented" and competitive "old" leaders voluntarily substituted himself for one of the "new" and younger leaders who failed to appear in court on time in connection with an injunction suit the latter had filed in protest against an urban renewal plan which would force the relocation of a large number of Negro families.

We would also point out that the institutional formulation of "men of power" espoused by Hunter and others is not without its ideological implications when it comes to social action.[28] Being "counted in" in community decision-making necessarily involves "protest within the

---

25 Cf., e.g., Robert A. Dahl, "A Critique of the Ruling Elite Model," *American Political Science Review*, LII (June, 1958), 463–69; Nelson Polsby, "The Sociology of Community Power: A Reassessment," *Social Forces*, XXXVII (March, 1959), 232–36 and "Three Problems in the Analysis of Community Power," *American Sociological Review*, XXIV (December, 1959), 796–803; Peter H. Rossi, "Theory and Method in the Study of Power in the Local Community" (paper presented at the Conference on Metropolitan Leadership, Northwestern University, April, 1960; mimeographed); and Raymond E. Wolfinger, "The Study of Community Power," *American Sociological Review*, XXV (October, 1960), 636–44.

26 Cf. Rossi, *op. cit.*, pp. 37–38.

27 James Q. Wilson, *Negro Politics* (Glencoe, Illinois, 1960).

28 James B. McKee, "Community Power and Strategies in Race Relations: Some Critical Observations," *Social Problems*, VI (Winter, 1958–59), 195–203.

status quo." Direct action outside of the institutionalized distribution of power (the social movement), however, is an increasingly obvious alternative for Negro leaders. To date, vested interests in segregated economic, political, and social markets, the saliency of "respectability" for the Negro middle class, as well as the lack of formal and visible barriers to equality in Northern urban centers (which minimize opportunities for dramatic protest), all conspire to favor being "counted in." In Providence, for example, the Urban League has become such an efficient "minority group" casework agency and locus of control and communication in local race relations that it is always consulted by white community leaders in connection with policy decisions affecting the community. On the other hand, it often finds itself unable to press its demands on the dominant group power structure lest it risk its hard-won formal respectability and social work "trouble-shooting" effectiveness. To the extent that Negro leaders become aware that the status gains which result from being formally counted in often involve the risk of being informally and effectively "counted out" or neutralized in the power struggle, militant protest outside of the institutional distribution of power is a greater probability.

The power structures of Negro sub-communities in American cities are in a process of schism and realignment under the impact of desegregation movements and activities. On the practical side, lack of knowledge of the dramatic changes taking place with regard both to the personnel and the tactics of the sub-community leadership on the part of the dominant group power structure invites communication breakdowns which can lead to mutual miscalculations and, ultimately, to civic violence. Within the Negro community, the lack of experience and of a full complement of perspectives to bring to bear on community problems as well as the often wasteful competition among leaders and agencies for power and status (all of which are the heritage of the vicious circle of discrimination and prejudice) further complicate the problem. The challenge this situation presents to social scientists of theoretical as well as of social action persuasion is as pressing as it is obvious.

19. Community Structure
and the Role of the
Negro Leader–Agent

LEWIS M. KILLIAN

Amidst the tension and turmoil of the struggle over civil rights, that peculiar form of the American community known as "the Negro community" stands unchanged in many of its essential aspects. Wherever Negroes from a sizable proportion of the population of a city or town, the territorial shape of their "community within a community" can be delineated, even though the boundaries be vague and unstable. The segregated institutions—economic, religious, educational and social—persist despite token integration. In numerous small, Southern towns where the mood of protest has not yet been manifest in action, the Negro community still remains a peaceful "service community" accommodating to the needs and demands of the dominant white populace. But in many cities throughout the nation the Negro community has taken on a new significance. Though retaining its old form, the "new Negro community" has come to life as the Negro revolt has swept the nation.

SOURCE: Reprinted with permission of the author and publisher, originally published in *Sociological Inquiry*, XXXV, No. 1 (Winter, 1965).

ACKNOWLEDGEMENT: The author is indebted to Charles M. Grigg, Director, Institute for Social Research, Florida State University, for his criticism of the propositions advanced in this paper.

It can no longer be taken for granted that the biracial community is divided into two segments, one of which rules while the other serves. Instead, more and more American communities reveal themselves as two sub-communities confronting each other with challenge, on the one hand, and resistance, on the other. The significance of the novel behavior of what appears on the surface to be the "old Negro community" is painfully impressed on white community leaders. But the sudden shift of the historic Negro community from accommodation to protest, from subservience to challenge, may have an even broader significance for the study of social change. The differences in the structure of the white and Negro sub-communities may constitute a variable which, apart from the superior power of the white sub-community, affects the progress of desegregation. But, as E. Franklin Frazier observed in 1962, ". . . scarcely any studies have been concerned primarily with the manner in which the organization and social life of the Negro community influence the nature and extent of desegregation."[1]

THE NEGRO SUB-COMMUNITY

Because of segregation, ecological, social and psychological, the Negro community is a true community in the sociological sense. It has the essential characteristics of *locality* and *community sentiment*. But as we go beyond these minimal characteristics, we readily see that the Negro community differs in some important respects from the "wider American community" in the modern United States.

First, it is a "sub-community" except in those rare cases of all-Negro communities. It represents a separate growth within the framework of a larger community which is historically, culturally and self-consciously white. This is not to ignore the fact that there have been and still are other sub-communities in American cities. But the rigid barriers to escape even for the upwardly mobile Negro, and the continued augmentation of the population by internal migration, have given the Negro community a tenacity not shared by immigrant communities.

Second, the Negro community is a natural, but not a formal, community. As a sub-community it lacks the formal political organization which is a typical, even though non-essential, feature of the wider community. While its individual members may in some instances participate in the government of the wider community, the Negro community as such has no government.

---

[1] E. Franklin Frazier, "Desegregation as an Object of Sociological Study," in Arnold M. Rose, ed., *Human Behavior and Social Process* (Boston: Houghton Mifflin Company, 1962), p. 609.

Finally, as Myrdal implied in calling it "a pathological form of an American community," the Negro community represents in its institutional structure a weak and inferior imitation of the wider, essentially white, community.[2] Its associations constitute special interest groups, organized not for participation in the activities of the wider community, but because of exclusion from these activities. The Negro church, historically the oldest and strongest of Negro institutions, has not served as a link with the religious life of the larger community. Instead, as Frazier observed, it "has provided a refuge in which Negroes could find protection against a hostile world."[3]

Negro education, while officially part of the community educational system, has been a separate and unequal subsidiary of this system. This has been particularly true in the South, where the Negro school system is tied to the community system only at the top, at the level of the superintendent, while below is an autonomous but powerless structure of supervisors, administrators and faculty. Negro businesses, in spite of the long history and success of some of them, have constituted a marginal and insignificant segment of the larger economy. It is doubtful that it is just race prejudice and fear of embarrassment during collateral social activities that causes chambers of commerce to continue to ignore Negro businessmen as potential members. In most cases, the Negro entrepreneur is simply not important enough in the economy of the community for business leaders to consider him. Moreover, there is no indication that white business leaders have been inclined to take seriously the duplicate organizations of the Negro community, such as Negro chambers of commerce, civic leagues, business leagues and even the National Negro Business League. Myrdal characterized the National Negro Business League and the Negro business and professional associations as "substitutes for the ordinary professional organizations which to a large extent—and in the South, regularly—exclude Negroes."[4] He quotes Ralph Bunche as saying, "In terms of its influence on economic betterment of the Negro the National Negro Business League has been inconsequential . . . it has pursued the narrowest type of racial chauvinism, for it has organized, not business, but Negro business, and has employed the racial situation as its main stock in trade in bidding for the support of Negro patronage."[5] As for the many voluntary associations which have been an outstanding feature of the Negro community, Myrdal concluded, "It is only as a

---

[2] Gunnar Myrdal, *An American Dilemma* (New York: Harper and Row, Publishers, 1944), pp. 927f.

[3] Frazier, *op. cit.*, p. 618.

[4] Myrdal, *op. cit.*, p. 816.

[5] *Ibid.*, pp. 815–816.

means of recreation that (they) can be given a high evaluation."[6] It may be said in general that, although Negroes have organized business, professional and civic associations in imitation of similar associations in the white community, in these associations they have only "played at" being business, professional or civic leaders.

While the Negro community does not have a formal, official political structure, it has had an informal political organization in Northern cities. More recently, such organizations have emerged in Southern cities where the Negro vote has been worthy of the consideration of white office seekers. But the storm of the Negro protest broke before Negro political organization achieved the power and the autonomy which once characterized Irish and Italian political machines. The onset of the Negro revolt found the Negro political leader, with a few notable exceptions, still largely dependent upon white political leaders for his influence. While he could bargain with white politicians and play one against the other, he could not challenge any of them. It has only been in the past decade that some Negro leaders have gained sufficient strength to bargain for status gains for the Negro community, such as commitments to token integration or improved job opportunities, rather than for long overdue physical repairs to the still segregated and still inferior Negro community. But except in a few cases such as that of Adam Clayton Powell, the Negro political leader still remains a "straw boss" in a white-dominated political organization.

The two types of associations in the Negro community which have come closest to exerting real power in the institutions of the white community have been labor unions and protest organizations. Even their power has been largely limited to Northern communities, however.

The first Negro labor leader of national importance, A. Philip Randolph, developed in a field of segregated labor, that of sleeping car porters. Moreover, his leadership has been much more significant on the national level than as an influence in local communities. But the rise of industrial unionism permitted a broadening of the scope of Negro leadership in the ranks of labor. In spite of the fact that Negroes occupy a subordinate position even in the most thoroughly integrated unions, they have still participated more fully in the later stages of the American labor movement than in any other phase of American life, except perhaps the Armed Forces. The high status of Randolph in the structure of the A.F.L.-C.I.O. and the real power which he exerts in its councils reflect the fact that participation of Negroes in at least a segment of organized labor has been genuine, not make-believe. On the other hand, the

---

6 *Ibid.*, p. 955.

attempt of the industrial unions to extend this integration of Negro labor into locals in Southern communities has fallen far short of its goal. Hence, Frazier's statement, "as a result of the urbanization of the Negro population, the entrance of the Negro worker into industry and changes in American society there have emerged leaders of Negro labor whose voices carry more weight than that of the Negro intelligentsia and oftentimes more than that of Negro political leaders," applies only rarely to Negro communities in the South.[7] In many Southern communities, Negroes, even when they belong to unions, exert no real power and hold no positions of leadership other than token ones.

The leading protest organization during most of the history of the Negro community, the National Association for the Advancement of Colored People, has occupied a unique position. It is one association which cannot be characterized as an attempt to duplicate the institutions of the white community. It is, instead, a peculiar product of the minority community. If it must be compared to any institution of the white community, it has corresponded most closely to government. With its legalistic emphasis, it has served the function of defending the Negro community against laws which were enacted and enforced by local and state governments for the benefit of the white community. It has been comprehensive, rather than segmental, in its scope, in that it has been concerned with the legal aspects of many phases of life in the Negro community. Furthermore, its national organization and the resources which it could concentrate in a single community have given the local branches a potential for influence not found in other organizations of the local Negro community. But, again, in most Southern communities this power remained latent until the 1954 school desegregation decisions acted as a stimulus for the development of a new mood of protest.

THE NEGRO REVOLT:
FROM SELECTIVE ATTACK TO CONFRONTATION

It was this highly developed, selectively applied, legalistic approach of the N.A.A.C.P. which led to the overthrow in 1954 of the legal support for segregation. But in the opinion of most observers, it was this same approach which resulted in tokenism and led to the Negro revolt. Even after 1954, the legal offensive conducted by the N.A.A.C.P. continued to be strategically selective in its objectives. The targets were primarily segregated school and public recreational facilities. In many cases the involvement of the Negro community was extremely limited even though

---

[7] Frazier, *The Negro in the United States* (New York: Crowell, Collier and Macmillan, Inc., 1949), pp. 553–554.

the test cases were class actions. Extensive support in the local community was not even needed, since one or a few plaintiffs were sufficient to enable the N.A.A.C.P. lawyers to launch their legal attack and to pursue their strategy until at least a token victory was gained. In many communities the great majority of Negroes were merely spectators during the legal battle.

The Montgomery bus boycott marked a turning point in the Negro protest movement, for here the narrowly circumscribed boundaries of legalistic tactics were overrun, and large numbers of Negroes in the local community became active participants in the struggle. Furthermore, the objective was not carefully selected as in the usual test case. The Montgomery movement constituted a spontaneous confrontation of the white community by an aggrieved and aroused Negro community.

The sit-ins of 1960 demonstrated even more clearly the spontaneity of the Negro revolt and the reluctance of large numbers of Negroes to follow the cautious strategy of the N.A.A.C.P. Since the sit-ins there has been a rapid broadening of both the objectives of the Negro protest and the extent of involvement of local Negro communities. Instead of demands for desegregation of a school system or a golf course, there have been demands for desegregation of lunch counters, restaurants, swimming pools, libraries, city buses, churches, privately operated amusement parks and, in some communities, "all public facilities." To demands for desegregation have been added demands for increased opportunities on all levels of employment, and there has been an intensification of the drive for voter registration. In military parlance, it might be said that Negroes are now "attacking all along the front." Although Negro youth and the leaders of the many new protest organizations seem to be disproportionately involved, there is much more extensive involvement of the Negro community as a whole in the protest movement than there was before 1960. In situations such as those in Birmingham, Alabama, Albany, Georgia, and Cambridge, Maryland, there have been massive confrontations of the Negro and white sub-communities. These constitute extreme cases of a type of confrontation which has occurred in many other communities.

THE WHITE SUB-COMMUNITY

In such confrontations, the structure of the white sub-community is markedly different from that of the Negro sub-community which challenges it. The structure of the white sub-community is in actuality the structure of "the community" as it is described in standard sociological works. As such, it is distinguished first of all by its formal, political structure. But the concept of "community power" today implies another, informal power structure. Without debating whether this power structure ever acts as a monolithic structure, it is important to recognize that there is a division of labor in the social system and thereby a distribution of power. Roland Warren describes the community as a "system of systems" and views the power structure not as one pyramid but as a multiplicity of power pyramids.[8] He defines the community as a "combination of systems and units which perform the major functions having locality relevance."[9] These systems fit into both horizontal patterns (roughly equivalent to Homans' "internal system") and vertical (hierarchical and external) patterns. An example highly relevant to the present analysis is a single company as a typical community unit serving the "major locality relevant function" of production-distribution-consumption. A typical unit of the horizontal pattern in this sub-system is the chamber of commerce, while the typical superior unit of the vertical pattern is a national corporation. City commissions, county commissions, boards of education, ministerial associations, central labor organizations, united funds, councils of social agencies, boards of realtors, and county medical associations readily come to mind as units of horizontal patterns which give the essentially white community a complex organization without parallel in the Negro community. Nor are these sub-systems "make-believe." They make very real decisions for the community about those areas in which they are presumed to have special competence. As Warren states it:

> More and more, the community depends for its integration on formal structures, such as the community press, the municipal government, the council of social agencies, the city planning commission, to achieve at least the minimum of integration, so that the parts of the system can function in systematic relation to one another and so that the locality relevant tasks can be performed.[10]

This integration of the formal structures implies not only a division of labor but also mutual support. It is here that the work of Hunter in describing the informal power structures becomes relevant.[11] The articulation of the various sub-systems is strengthened by overlapping memberships and, more significantly, by the informal social relations between important members of the various power pyramids. In this respect segregation has one of its most important effects, for the Negro leader is almost totally excluded from the "luncheon circuit" and the private clubs

---

[8] Roland Leslie Warren, *The Community in America* (Chicago: Rand-McNally, 1963), pp. 44–48.

[9] *Ibid.*, p. 9.

[10] *Ibid.*, p. 142.

[11] Floyd Hunter, *Community Power Structure* (Chapel Hill: University of North Carolina Press, 1953).

which Hunter found so significant as mechanisms for producing and maintaining like-mindedness among community leaders.

THE ROLE OF THE NEGRO LEADER-AGENT

From this consideration of the structures of the two sub-communities and from observation of some cases of confrontation, propositions concerning the position of the Negro leader as spokesman for his sub-community are derived. These propositions are offered as hypotheses relating to what may be called "the role of the Negro leader-agent." They become most relevant and may be tested best when community race relations are at a stage of negotiation between white and Negro leaders.

The Negro leader-agent speaks as a charismatic leader in a loosely structured social movement to white agents who are "experts" in a bureaucratized community structure. The Negro protest leader is likely to have achieved his status largely through his eloquence or his display of courage. In specific instances, the spokesman for Negro communities have been ministers, teachers, housewives, doctors or even students. Often the demands which they voice have as much the character of slogans as of well-reasoned proposals. But in their character as proposals, these demands call for adjustments in specific sub-systems of the articulated white community structure. Hence a demand may be referred to specialists in a specific sub-system. Immediately this places the Negro leader-agent at a disadvantage in three respects.

First, he speaks as a "non-expert" to experts in the area of activity at issue. Thus, a Negro minister finds himself discussing discrimination in housing with a licensed realtor with years of experience in the housing market. A Negro doctor argues for employment opportunities with a personnel manager who talks in terms of job specifications, aptitude tests and seniority. Overwhelmed, the Negro leader-agent may find himself quickly forced into the position of dogmatically reiterating his demands without reference to the arguments of his opponent. While these arguments may be delaying tactics, such is the essence of negotiation, be it in race relations, union-management relations, or international diplomacy. In some cases, of course, the white spokesman may not be negotiating in good faith at all. But if the white agent is prepared to bargain, the Negro may, by his reactions, lead the interaction into what Blake and Mouton have called the "psychodynamic fallacy." This occurs when an "incorrect personality-based ascription of motivation for warfare" is given.[12] Thus

---

12 Robert R. Blake and Jane S. Mouton, "The Intergroup Dynamics of Win-Lose Conflict and Problem-Solving Collaboration in Union-Management Relations," in Muzafer Sherif, ed., *Intergroup Relations and Leadership* (New York: John Wiley & Sons, Inc., 1962), p. 113.

the Negro leader-agent takes the white agent's arguments as the rationalizations of a prejudiced person rather than as the tactics of a bargaining agent. When he reiterates his demands, almost as slogans, rather than countering the tactics, he appears either unintelligent or unreasonable. This leads the white agent, in turn, into the psychodynamic fallacy, and he breaks off the negotiations on the ground that the Negro is simply an agitator who makes impossible demands for the sake of "stirring up trouble."

Situational pressures which follow the agents into the conference room reinforce this tendency for each to break off negotiations rather than to persist until a compromise is achieved. The Negro leader is haunted by the prevailing mood of the Negro protest movement symbolized by the slogan "Freedom Now!" Hence, he tends to approach the negotiation as a zero-sum game and easily falls into an "all-or-nothing" attitude. The constantly repeated question of Negroes, "How much longer must we wait?", gives the Negro leader the feeling that time is running out, not only for the white man but for him, and that there is no room for compromise.

The white leader is moved to impatience with negotiations by the fact that his potential losses seem so much more tangible than his potential gains. The gains from compromising are either moral ones—"advancing the American Dream"—or the nebulous prospect of preventing disorders that might not occur anyway. The persistent conviction of many members of the white power structure that they can, by vigorous police action, suppress Negro demonstrations militates against their regarding racial peace as a superordinate goal which constitutes a reward for compromise. The white businessman, for example, can more easily visualize a loss of trade because of desegregation than he can a gain, and he tends to regard the approval which he might get from liberals as inadequate compensation for a loss of profits. Hence, the white leader tends to regard a "standpat" position as the safest bet.

Second, even if there is only a small differential in the technical knowledge of the two negotiators, the Negro agent finds himself frustrated by the stabilizing, yet conservatizing, influence of the complex, bureaucratic community structure. Such a structure, with its horizontal and vertical patterns, both reduces the freedom of the individual spokesman and protects him from the necessity of making on-the-spot decisions. Pushed to the brink of making a concession, the white agent can take evasive action by appealing to the sub-system which he represents—the employer to his board of directors, the store manager to his national office or to other merchants in the chamber of commerce, the minister to his board of deacons. Ironically, the Negro leader may enjoy more autonomy in relationship to his own sub-community than does the white leader. The social movement which he leads may be more flexible than the bureaucratic structure which the white agent represents. But, as Dubin has pointed out in discussing union-management negotiations, "In continuous relations, the autonomy of leadership in one organization is decreased by the need to take into account limitations on leadership decisions in the other."[13]

Third, the support provided each sub-system by other elements of the articulated community social system makes negotiation appear even more like a "shell-game" to the Negro agent. The agent for any one sub-system can evade a decision by pleading that the concurrence of other sub-systems is necessary. For example, in one community a prolonged stalemate over the desegregation of lunch-counters developed. The variety store managers took the position that they would open the counters if the city commission would first ask them to do so and promise police protection during the transition. The city commission refused to make such a request. They argued that the decision was up to the store managers and that a governmental agency should not take the first step and thus appear to encourage desegregation.

Confronted with such a diffuse decision-making structure, the Negro leader or agent is sooner or later likely to oversimplify the community system and approach it at only one point—that of government. As has already been suggested, government can and does "pass the buck" as does any other sub-system. Nevertheless, there is strong pressure on the Negro leader to act as if the community power structure was a monolithic pyramid with government at the apex. Theodore H. White observes:

> Of these elements of the "power structure," Negroes have leverage only in one, government. . . . Exploiting this strength, Negro leaders insist that government use *its* leverage on all other elements of the "power structure" private and public. They propose that government press itself into every area of decision, that it penetrate and dominate everywhere that discrimination in any form is practiced.[14]

While this strategy offers some prospects of success at the national level, it promises to be self-defeating in the local community. It forces the local government more and more into the position of defender of the *status quo* in all sub-systems of the community. Its ability to act as a neutral agency of social control, as a referee in the struggles between the

---

[13] Robert Dubin, "Leadership in Union-Management Relations as an Intergroup System," in Muzafer Sherif, *op. cit.*, p. 74.

[14] Theodore H. White, "Power Structure, Integration, Militancy, Freedom Now!" *Life*, LV (November 29, 1963), p. 82.

Negro community and other sub-systems, is lessened as it becomes the "universal antagonist" of the Negro community or, conceivably, of the white community. As government is forced into this role and, at the same time, other sub-systems find themselves challenged more intensely by Negro demands, the election of city officials will depend more and more on their stand on racial issues.

But no matter what the sub-system through which the Negro leader-agent challenges the white community, he is handicapped by the fact that he is not a part of the horizontal pattern of that sub-system. A notable exception is the Negro attorney who, in litigation, has the status of an officer of the court. Otherwise the Negro leader-agent is constantly challenged to establish the legitimacy of his role. The role of the white agent is defined by his position in the formal structure of the sub-system for which he speaks. But the Negro agent usually purports to speak for the entire Negro community, a community which has no formal structure. It is no easy task for him to establish his legitimacy, since an essential source of validation in any negotiation is acceptance by the opponent as a legitimate agent. Furthermore, the Negro leader-agent often lacks competence in his role; for, in a society in which "the schematic solution to race conflict has removed Negroes from the community," this is an emergent role.[15] Unless he is an experienced lawyer or a labor leader he is likely to have had little or no experience in the role of negotiator: he needs to be socialized into the role.

But paradoxically, the only people who can socialize him for the role are his white antagonists. Roy Wilkins has said, "Wherever there is reasonable acceptance by the white leadership, you will find responsible response on the the part of the Negro leadership."[16] Realistically, "reasonable acceptance" on the part of white leadership cannot mean an attitude of readiness to accede to Negro demands, any more than willingness to negotiate with a labor union implies readiness to surrender on the part of management. It can, however, mean acceptance of the Negro leader as a legitimate bargaining agent by those white leaders who must be in his role-set if he is to have a role as agent. Only they can extend the various social systems of the community to encompass the Negro community.

It may be that efforts on the part of Negro leaders themselves to learn more about the techniques of bargaining will increase their effectiveness as leader-agents. But the reasons why they are inexperienced in bargaining with white people are largely beyond their control. No amount of

---

15 Jessie Bernard, *American Community Behavior* (New York: Holt, Rinehart & Winston, Inc., 1962), p. 225.

16 White, *op. cit.*, p. 93.

rehearsal for the role or study of its requirements will make the Negro leader-agent effective unless he is allowed to actually play it by white leaders.

It may be postulated that until this is done Negro leaders will be responsive almost exclusively to the strident demands of the Negro protest movement and scarcely at all to the complexity of the problems of changing a social system. They will, moreover, continue to appear to be irresponsible.

In communities in which white leaders refuse to negotiate at all, the significance of these structural obstacles to effective negotiation is masked by the obdurate resistance to change by the white community. But this analysis suggests that the abandonment of "last-ditch resistance" to change in racial patterns will reveal the fact that Negro-white relations display the generic characteristics of intergroup systems despite their distinctive racial overtones.

CHAPTER IV

Political–Economic

Structures

The communities portrayed in this section have formal bases of organization unlike the previous examples which had informal, personal bases. Rather than being held together by kin ties, or by a common fate with the other members of a sub-community, the residents of these communities are linked by an incorporated community area, a political structure, and agencies and social institutions. Secondary group ties, bureaucratized procedures and institutionalized role relationships dominate community activity that in "folk" or "ethnic" communities were settled on the basis of family influence, friendship, and "understandings" between informally powerful figures.

Although formal organization differentiates the following communities from previous examples, informal, personalistic ties persist in them as well. Applying Warren's vertical and horizontal dimensions of community, we see that horizontal dimensions of community organization are much more prone to influence on an informal basis. Another way of stating this is that the horizontal axis reflects personalistic, primary group ties, whereas the vertical axis reflects that rationalization of attitude that compartmentalizes functions of community into distinct agencies and roles. Within our category of formally organized communities, we can mark the degree of progression along the continuum of our primary vs. secondary bases for community organization typology by the relative importance to community life of horizontal vs. vertical dimensions. By this measure, we could conceptualize ideal type urbanism as that stage at which personal factors would cease to influence community life that is based on a completely rational, bureaucratized structure.

The small community studied by Agger and Ostrom is a good example of how a formally organized community can be influenced by strong personalistic factors. The types of leaders that comprise the horizontal political sub-structure have personal traits that determine the role they play in the informal contacts which determine community affairs. This community evidences few "urban" traits on our continuum of community types.

Dahl described five possible patterns of horizontal community leadership that have existed in New Haven, Connecticut, at various stages in time. The importance of the formal community structure in determining community action is illustrated by the fact that economic notables or "bosses" encounter increasing difficulty in exercising "backstage" control with each successive stage. This suggests that one effect of the shift from informal to formal community structure might be increasing pluralism of community leadership. Thus urbanism could bring about increased "democracy" in community life.

A common theme in American community studies is that the community is dominated by businessmen and business ethics. To test this, Miller compared two American cities with an English city. He found that businessmen do in fact dominate the power structure of the American communities, whereas, for a variety of reasons, representatives of other sectors of society are much more likely to be represented in "English city."

D'Antonio, Form, Loomis and Erickson tested Miller's hypothesis that "businessmen exert predominant influence in community decision-making" in several Southwestern U.S. and Mexican cities. They found that businessmen dominate community affairs in both societies, but the government challenges this dominance much more in Mexican communities.

In a study of another Mexican community, Tijuana, Klapp and Padgett report similar findings but report a much stronger governmental role than did D'Antonio, *et al.* In Tijuana, the local, or horizontal, government is weak, and the real source of power is the national, or vertical, government. The horizontal structure does not disappear, it merely signifies less and less as forces outside the community begin to exert control through local institutions that are organized and directed by the vertical structure.

20. The Political Structure of a Small Community

ROBERT E. AGGER
VINCENT OSTROM

A central problem in the study of political behavior is the ordering of the roles and positions that constitute the political structure of a community. A series of studies on that problem has been conducted in a small rural community of 3,000, about equally divided between town and country areas. A survey was made of a randomly selected sample of 260 persons. In addition, specialized studies were made with more intensive interviewing and more extensive observations.[1]

A political organization or structure involves a network of communication channels through which messages flow in transmitting, receiving and acting upon demands. The major modes of communicating demands involve discussion and participation in different types of public activities and meetings. In this study a political role was conceived as the patterns

SOURCE: Reprinted with permission of the authors and publisher from *Public Opinion Quarterly*, XX (1956).

ACKNOWLEDGEMENT: The Social Science Research Council, the Center for Advanced Study in the Behavioral Sciences and the Northwest Regional Project of the W. K. Kellogg Foundation's Cooperative Program in Educational Administration for research support.

[1] Agger, Robert E., *The Dynamics of Local Political Participation: Empirical Research and Theoretical Inquiry* (Ph.D. Thesis, University of Oregon, 1954). Keith Goldhammer, *The Roles of School District Officials in Policy-Determination in an Oregon Community* (Ph.D. Thesis, University of Oregon, 1954).

of behavior which characterize political activity in this communication process.

Data about the top leadership group and their political roles were secured largely by participant observation and informal interviews. Below this level, the data on the general interview schedule were used. Roles were defined in terms of replies about behavioral practices including: (1) giving advice, (2) discussing public affairs with officials, community leaders, associates or friends, (3) taking an active part on particular policy issues, and (4) attending meetings involving questions about public affairs. These behavioral practices were then used to define role aggregates. These were: advisors, talkers, listeners, workers, and nonparticipants.

The *Advisors* were people to whom others had come for advice on policy matters relating to the local community. The *Talkers* report that they discussed one or more of these policy matters "frequently" with friends or others. (Some of the Talkers engaged in other political activities, but none reported serving as Advisors.) *Listeners* were those who reported attending meetings at which community policy questions were a major subject of discussion but not engaging in frequent policy discussion nor in advising. *Workers* took "an active part on public issues" but neither discussed policy matters frequently outside their family nor advised others. *Non-Participants* engaged in none of these activities. Of the 260 respondents, 20 were Advisors;[2] 37 were Talkers; 33 were Listeners; 24 were Workers; and 132 were Non-Participants.

THE TOP LEADERSHIP

Three individuals, two residents of the city and one resident in the rural area, were the most influential persons in the community. Associated with these three were a few other men who comprised the membership of the top leadership group. This group was informally organized as a card-playing club. One particular civic association was the instrument for much of their community activities. In addition, there were a variety of face-to-face associations in business relationships, formal organizations, informal social relationships and kinship groupings.

The three key leaders each held public offices and a high proportion of the top leadership group had held some public office in the past. All of the members of the group occupied relatively high socio-economic positions in the community. They were all most active in community politics.

---

2 A small group classified as Passive Advisors have been dropped from consideration in this article. They were fourteen persons, thirteen of whom were women, who reported serving in an advisory capacity but had an extremely low range of political activity in other regards and shared many of the characteristics of the Non-Participants.

The top trio of leaders shared a belief that the "good" community was a relatively small, semi-rural community of Jeffersonian virtues. They were not dedicated to freezing the status quo, but were almost scientific in their assessment of long-range, indirect consequences of policies with an interest in making as sure as possible that a policy change was either necessary to bridge an existing "cultural lag" or to take care of some "unanticipated consequences." They were aware of changes in the state and nation; they had better communication channels with the "outside world" than anyone else in the community. They accepted, even if they did not sympathize with, "inevitable" social forces.

Social harmony, absence of rigid social class distinctions and practices, and political stability were integral parts of their vision of the good community. Thus their interest in retaining power was assumed to be in the interest of all, rather than in the interest of any particular group or aggregate. The group whom they felt they represented was the whole community rather than any of its parts. Any threat to their position of leadership was felt to be a threat to the entire community.

As a consequence of their community orientation in political leadership, the members of the top leadership group held more moderate and tentative attitudes about current political questions than other politically active businessmen who did not hold responsible roles in political leadership. Since these individuals were themselves influential in shaping policies in the community, their more tentative and moderate attitudes unquestionably facilitated their capacity to accommodate to a wide variety of demands and to safeguard their positions. Their power positions in turn reinforced their flexibility. There was no necessity for them to make extreme, inflexible demands, since they had what they wanted. In contrast, those who were moderately active in community affairs tended to be much more extreme in their political opinions.

A few businessmen interested in expanding business opportunities in the community recognized the necessity of overcoming the opposition of the top leadership group if their efforts were to succeed. They wanted to establish a chamber of commerce to help expand the existing volume of business and to attract new enterprises. They urged a municipal program of factory site acquisitions and the annexation of new areas in order to extend municipal services. They wanted the city government to oppose the relocation of a major state highway now intersecting the town in order to maintain the transport and tourist business.

As these "boomers" began to shift from making isolated demands toward organized efforts to take concerted action, they were invited to join some of the associations controlled by the top leadership group. These "invitations" were frequently accompanied by explicit promises of indulgences or implicit threats of deprivations. Every evidence points in the direction of the "boomers" taking a place in the power structure of the top leadership group with an appropriate accommodation in policies but without any shift in leadership position on the part of the key leaders. The other alternative for them is to establish a competing political alignment and attempt to gain control of the appropriate political agencies in the community.

ATTRIBUTION OF INFLUENCE

Data were secured in the general interview schedules on the identification of the "generally most influential" person in the community. 32 different persons were nominated 161 times as "generally most influential" in the town sample, and 69 different persons were nominated 170 times in the country sample. Eleven persons, about one-third of those nominated, accounted for 75 percent of all nominations in the town sample and 24 persons, again one-third of the nominees, accounted for 76 percent of all nominations in the country sample. Two individuals account for 34 percent of all the nominations in the town sample, whereas three individuals account for 36 percent of all the nominations in the country sample.[3]

Of the three individuals we described above as most influential, two are among the most often named trio, and if the responses from the country sample were included, the third member of that clique would be the fourth ranked generally influential. There were some apparent inaccuracies in the popular perception of the power structure, however. Mr. C is a city councilman from a ward with the most depressed socioeconomic conditions in the community. While his position in the power structure is an intermediate one of seeking the amelioration of specific conditions in his constituency, his constituents perceive him as being at the apex of the power structure. They apparently fail to comprehend the full dimensions of the power structure in the community as a whole. Mr. D's general influence also appears to be exaggerated for a similar reason. He had been greatly concerned about welfare policies in the community, but had withdrawn from active participation in these affairs after failure to make adequate progress.

Approximately 27 percent of the combined town and country samples nominated one of the top leadership trio as one of the generally most influential policy-makers in the community. Thirty-one percent of the re-

---

3 Cf. George Belknap and Ralph Smuckler, "Political Power Relations in a Mid-West City," in *Public Opinion Quarterly*, XX (1956). In a study of a mid-west community, Belknap and Smuckler found that 35 percent of those nominated accounted for 66 percent of all nominations from a list of 60 persons nominated by two panels of nominators totaling 159 persons.

spondents were unable or refused to respond to the question. The bulk of the other respondents nominated one or another of the top leadership group as most influential. Of the respondents reporting that someone else came to them for advice during the past year, some 55 percent nominated one of the top leadership trio as one of the generally most influential policy-makers, and only ten percent of this aggregate failed to name any-one. Thus, a body of secondary leaders are available to link other elements of the population into the influence processes of the power structure in dealing with demands as they arise.

THE POLITICAL SUB-STRUCTURE

Altogether the top leadership group comprised less than one percent of the population. By using the five role categories of Advisors, Talkers, Listeners, Workers, and Non-Participants defined by selected sets of behavioral practices, some general characterizations can be made of the political substructure of the community.

The Advisors.—The Advisors were the more highly educated, had higher incomes and in other ways resemble the sort of people one might expect to articulate policy demands. Their similarity to and inter-actions with the top leaders suggest a similarity in policy interests, views and values. The Advisors were more frequently men than women. Almost two-thirds of them reported reading two out-of-town newspapers regu-larly, an indication of their relatively cosmopolitan orientation. They infrequently read the local newspaper, but were not disposed to leave the community. They associated with school and governmental officials more frequently than any other aggregate, and they were the most frequent voters in both school and city elections. All of them belonged to at least two organizations in the community, most of them belonging to at least six organizations. They were the most Republican of any aggregate in the sample.

They were the most aware of the influential positions of the top trio and the top leadership group in general. Almost half of this aggregate held public office at one time or another. When education, number of organizational memberships and associations with school and city offi-cials were controlled, the Advisors were still significantly more aware of the degree of general influence of the top trio than others who were at the top educational levels, who have high organizational memberships and who frequently associate with officials. Their articulateness, their high status, their general activity level, and their sophisticated concerns with community politics make them a relevant and important political aggregate in shaping community policies.

The Talkers.—The Talkers resembled the Advisors more closely than any other role aggregate in terms of their education and income levels. They were significantly greater consumers of the local newspaper but somewhat more disposed than the Advisors to leave the community. There was a high ratio of females among the Talkers. They associated with school and city officials and employees less than Advisors, but they associated more frequently with city officials than did any other aggregate. They reported a relatively high level of voting in school and local elections. They belonged to organizations, although less extensively than the Advisors. They were also more Democratic in party affiliation than the Advisors.

The Talkers were less aware of the power structure and particularly the roles of the top trio than the Advisors, and less aware in these respects than even the Workers. However, more than one in four of them did nominate one of the top trio as most influential in the community. The Talkers constituted the largest single aggregate of political participants and, as with the Advisors, could be expected to articulate demands in relation to the top leadership.

The Listeners.—The Listeners had somewhat higher educational and income levels than the Talkers. They read the local newspaper much less than the Talkers, but were somewhat less disposed to leave the community. The Listeners were almost equally men and women. They associated more frequently with school people than did any other aggregate except the Advisors, and more frequently with city officials and employees than any except Advisors and Talkers. Fewer of them voted in school elections, but their local government voting rates were about the same as those of the Talkers. Fewer Listeners than Talkers were members of organizations; almost one-fourth of the Listeners reported no organization membership. They were the most Democratic in their party preferences.

The Listeners were more aware of the influence of the top trio than any other aggregate except the Advisors. Almost 40 percent of them indicated their willingness to go to one of the top trio for advice in one of the three policy-making areas. This factor supports the general pattern of characteristics that emerges, leading to the inference that these people were neither active supporters of the *status quo* nor articulate propounders of policy change. They were not actively community-oriented in general. Their political passivity as represented by their meeting-going rather than more active participation was supplemented by their failure to read the local paper and their failure to become joiners.

The Workers.—The educational levels of Workers and Listeners were almost identical, but the Workers had substantially lower incomes. They read the local paper somewhat more than did the Listeners, but less than did the Talkers. They were the least disposed of any aggregate to leave the community. There were somewhat more females than males in their ranks. They associated only slightly less than Listeners with teachers, school officials, and employees, but none of them reported frequent associations with city, county, state and federal officials. Fewer of the Workers than the Listeners voted frequently in school elections, but fewer Workers were non-voters. They were somewhat more active in local elections than Listeners. Fewer Workers belonged to any organization as compared with Listeners. The Workers were somewhat more Republican than the Listeners, although a majority was Democratic.

TABLE 1

Distributions of Socio-Political Characteristics Among The Political Role Aggregates

Characteristic	Advisors (N = 20)	Talkers (N = 37)	Listeners (N = 33)	Workers (N = 24)	Non-participants (N = 132)
Sex					
Male	55%	28%	49%	42%	48%
Female	45	72	51	58	52
Education					
Some college or more......	60	27	18	17	6
Less than college..........	40	73	82	83	94
Occupation of Self or Husband					
Professional, managerial					
and officials	80	54	39	50	34
Clerical and skilled labor..	20	35	36	33	30
Unskilled and farm labor..	0	11	25	17	36
Annual Income					
$5000 or more.............	55	32	30	26	21
$3000 to $4999............	35	41	49	30	45
Less than $3000............	10	27	21	44	34
Formal Organization					
Memberships					
Belong to six or more......	90	43	30	33	8
Belong to one to five......	10	49	46	38	49
Belong to none............	0	8	24	29	43
Local Newspaper Consumption					
Read regularly	35	67	37	42	28
Do not read regularly.....	65	33	63	58	72
Out-of-town Newspaper					
Consumption					
Read two regularly........	65	49	31	29	37
Fail to read two regularly..	35	51	69	71	63
Length of Residence in					
Community					
Sixteen years or more......	50	30	24	35	40
Three to sixteen years.....	30	54	61	52	39
Less than three years......	20	16	15	13	21
Disposition to Move Away					
Yes	40	49	39	26	55
No	60	51	61	74	45

TABLE I—continued

Distributions of Socio-Political Characteristics Among The Political Role Aggregates

Characteristic	Advisors (N = 20)	Talkers (N = 37)	Listeners (N = 33)	Workers (N = 24)	Non-par- ticipants (N = 132)
Associations with Government Officials and Employees					
Frequently	50	33	24	0	11
Infrequently or not at all..	50	67	76	100	89
Associations with School Officials and Employees					
Frequently	75	41	46	42	17
Infrequently or not at all...	25	59	54	58	83
Voting in School Elections					
Always	55	42	41	17	14
Nearly always or sometimes.	25	36	25	58	28
Do not vote	20	22	34	25	58
Voting in City Government Elections					
Always	80	53	53	63	28
Nearly always or sometimes.	15	25	25	21	32
Do not vote	5	22	22	16	40
Party Affiliation					
Republican	68	44	37	46	49
Democrat	32	56	63	54	51
Nominations of Most Gener- ally Influential					
One of the top trio	55	32	39	22	20
Someone else	35	41	43	61	38
No one	10	27	18	17	42

Only one out of five Workers nominated one of the top trio as the most generally influential, in contrast to almost two out of five Listeners. In this respect they most closely resemble the Non-Participants of all the aggregates. The very low income Workers tended to be constituents of Mr. C (Table I), the aforementioned councilman from the poorer part of town. Their political activity appeared to be of a negative or defensive character supporting Councilman C's opposition to anything involving increased local taxes, rather than their making positive demands and working for extended public services.

The Non-Participants.—The Non-Participants play no active political roles, but it is illuminating to compare their characteristics to those of the several aggregates of participants. They constituted some 51 percent of the population. They had the lowest educational level and the smallest number of higher incomes of any aggregate. They had somewhat fewer people with extremely low incomes than the Workers. Fewer of them read the local newspaper and they were more disposed to leave the community than any other aggregate. There were slightly more women than men in their ranks. They associated less with the school or governmental officialdom, and they voted less than did any other aggregate in both school and local elections. They were the non-joiners, *par excellence*. They were about equally Democratic and Republican. They were the least able or willing to name one of the top trio or for that matter, anyone, as being generally influential. Yet one out of five did name one of the top trio, and more than half named someone as most generally influential in the community.

Without being able to measure the demand flows by a sample survey, it is still fairly safe to say that the political system involves a large degree of independent decision-making by people at all levels in the power structure for many policy matters. The various role-playing aggregates not only differ from each other in terms of the characteristics discussed above, but they were viewed and treated differently by both the top leadership and the businessmen who were dissatisfied with the current community policies. The top leadership group devoted particular attention to the Advisors, whereas the power-aspirants were especially solicitous of the Talkers. The Talkers constituted an appealing aggregate to the power-aspirants, who hoped that they could stimulate the Talkers into more active roles to rival the organization of secondary leaders associated with the top leadership.

The analysis of the characteristics of the several aggregates of role-players, as well as their interactional and psychological relationships to the top leadership group, may result in a better understanding of the structure and dynamics of power when a number of communities have been comparatively studied in this way.

21. Five Patterns of Leadership

ROBERT A. DAHL

The number of theoretically possible patterns of integration is almost infinite. However, because of their familiarity and generality, five possibilities were considered in our study of New Haven. These were:

1. Covert integration by economic notables.
2. An executive-centered "grand coalition of coalitions."
3. A coalition of chieftains.
4. Independent sovereignties with spheres of influence.
5. Rival sovereignties fighting it out.

The first of these, covert integration by the economic notables, is a common answer suggested by studies of a number of other cities. In this pattern the top leaders consist of a unified group of private citizens who arrive at agreements about policies by covert negotiations and discussions carried on in the privacy of their clubs, homes, business firms, and other private meeting places. Leaders gain their influence from their wealth, high social standing, and economic dominance. Usually the leaders are wealthy executives in important business firms; if this pattern

SOURCE: Reprinted with permission of the author and publisher from *Who Governs? Democracy and Power In An American City*, Copyright © 1961 by Yale University Press.

fitted New Haven, presumably the top officers of Yale would be included because the university is one of the largest property owners and employers in the city.

A revealing aspect of this hypothesis is its insistence on the essentially clandestine or covert exercise of influence by the "real" leaders. Why? Because in most cities today the overt, public incumbents in the highest official positions—the mayors and other elected politicians, city officials, party chairmen, and so on—are rarely drawn from the ranks of wealth, social standing, and corporate office. By contrast, the patricians of New Haven were an *overt* political elite. They made no bones about their dominance. They not only openly occupied key positions in the religious, educational, and economic institutions of New Haven, but they also held a visible monopoly of all the important public offices. This, as we have seen, is indisputably not so today. If individuals of wealth, status, and corporate position dominate politics, evidently they *must* do so covertly.

The hypothesis of covert control by the economic notables is both widely popular and strongly supported by many scholarly studies, from the Lynds' monumental examination of Muncie, Indiana in the twenties and thirties to Floyd Hunter's more recent analysis of the "power structure" of Atlanta.[1] Indeed the term "power structure" has so much passed into the vocabulary of the informed man that it has become a current bit of jargon among educated inside-dopesters. Although careful analysis has shown that the conclusions about influence contained in the academic studies often rest upon dubious evidence and even that some of the data found in the works themselves actually run counter to the conclusions,[2] some communities do seem to have conformed to this pattern in the past and some may today. Certainly some citizens of New Haven believe firmly in the existence of a covert elite and offer plausible evidence to support their view.

I believe the evidence advanced in this study is sufficient to warrant the rejection of the hypothesis that this pattern applies to New Haven. In every city where economic notables are alleged to rule covertly, it is important to note, evidently they do so by means sufficiently open to permit scholars and newspapermen to penetrate the veil; indeed, an inspection of the information contained in descriptions of these cities indicates that the job of probing into the clandestine structure of power has presented few barriers to the assiduous researcher. It is all the more

---

[1] Robert S. Lynd and Helen M. Lynd, *Middletown* and *Middletown in Transition* (New York: Harcourt, Brace and World, 1929 and 1937); Hunter, *Community Power Structure* and *Top Leadership, U.S.A.*

[2] For a detailed analysis of this point, see the forthcoming companion volume by Nelson W. Polsby, *Community Power and Political Theory*.

improbable, then, that a secret cabal of notables dominates the public life of New Haven through means so clandestine that not one of the 50 prominent citizens interviewed in the course of this study—citizens who had participated extensively in various decisions—hinted at the existence of such a cabal; so clandestine, indeed, that no clues turned up in several years of investigation led to the door of such a group.

To abandon the hypothesis of covert integration by economic notables does not mean that the economic notables in New Haven are without influence on certain important decisions.

* * *

What the evidence seems to establish rather conclusively is this: if one wants to find out how policies of different leaders are coordinated in New Haven, one must consider some pattern other than covert integration by economic notables.

A second pattern is envisioned in an alternative hypothesis: that today the top leaders are more likely to comprise a coalition of public officials and private individuals who reflect the interests and concerns of different segments of the community. In this view, a coalition is generally formed and the policies of the coalition are coordinated largely by elected leaders who draw on special skills and resources of influence that leaders without public office are not likely to have. This pattern of integration is usually associated with vigorous, even charismatic elected chief executives; presumably it was characteristic of the presidencies of FDR and Truman.[3]

In its implications the hypothesis of an executive-centered coalition is radically different from the first possible pattern. Where covert domination by economic notables reflects relatively stable social and economic factors, the executive-centered coalition may be more ephemeral; the coalition may fluctuate greatly in strength and even dissolve altogether when the coalition's leaders can no longer reconcile their strategies and goals. Moreover, in the pattern of covert domination, influence derived from public office and popularity with the electorate is completely subordinate to influence derived from wealth, social standing, and corporate position; in the executive-centered coalition, the prerogatives of public office, legality, legitimacy, and electoral followings are independent sources of influence with a weight of their own. Finally, the hypothesis of a covert elite logically leads to a certain pessimism about popular government. If government officials and elected politicians are merely

---

3 See Arthur M. Schlesinger, Jr., *The Coming of the New Deal* (Boston: Houghton Mifflin Company, 1959), Part VIII; James M. Burns, *Roosevelt: The Lion and the Fox* (New York: Harcourt, Brace & World, Inc., 1956); Richard Neustadt, *Presidential Power* (New York: John Wiley & Sons, Inc., 1960).

handmaidens of the upper classes, one cannot expect much in the way of peaceful reform via politics. Change must come about either through the gradual action of outside factors, like changes in industrial organization or technique, or else through a revolutionary seizure and transformation of the state by leaders of social segments who for some reason cannot win elections and attain public office. The hypothesis of integration by an executive-centered coalition, by contrast, allows for the possibility that reformist or radical coalitions (as well as conservative ones) may, by peacefully winning elections, obtain control of the powers of government and introduce durable changes in the distribution of access to influence, wealth, education, and social standing.

The third pattern is seen as integration of policies in different sectors by a coalition of chieftains. Something like it fits the various party and nonparty coalitions that control policy-making in Congress and particularly in the Senate.[4] The difference between the second pattern and this one is of course only one of degree; in marginal cases it would be impossible to say whether a particular pattern of integration should be called executive-centered or a coalition of chieftains.

A coalition of chieftains, like the executive-centered coalition, is consistent with the hypothesis that nowadays top leaders are likely to be public officials and private individuals who reflect the varying and even conflicting interests and concerns of different segments of the community. In the executive-centered coalition, integration of policy is achieved largely by means of the skills and resources of an elected leader; in a coalition of chieftains, integration takes place mainly by negotiations among the chieftains that produce exchanges of information and eventuate in agreement. The executive-centered pattern contains a sizable degree of hierarchy in the distribution of influence among the leaders. The chief executive is at the center of a "grand coalition of coalitions"; in the extreme case he is the only leader with great influence in *all* the allied coalitions, perhaps the only leader who even *participates* in all of them. Moreover, his special resources mean that every other leader in the grand coalition is more dependent on the executive for perpetuation of his influence than the executive is dependent on him. In a coalition of chieftains, on the other hand, if hierarchy appears, it is weak and may rest almost exclusively on a central position in the network of communi-

---

4 Recent observers describe Congress in terms that would fit the pattern here, although each offers highly important differences of emphasis and interpretation. Cf. David B. Truman, *The Congressional Party* (New York: John Wiley & Sons, Inc., 1959), Ch. 4; William S. White, *Citadel, The Story of the U.S. Senate* (New York: Harper & Row, Publishers, 1956), Chs. 8 and 14; Roland Young, *The American Congress* (New York: Harper & Row, Publishers, 1958), Ch. 3.

cations occupied by a particular leader or set of leaders. Thus, although a few chiefs may be somewhat more influential than others, they are all highly dependent on one another for the successful attainment of their policies. There is some specialization of influence by issue-areas; a chieftain in one area may be deferred to on matters lying in his domain, and he in turn defers to other chieftains in matters lying in theirs. But the chiefs actively coordinate their policies through extensive interchange of information and reciprocal favors. An awareness that their most important policy goals do not conflict and a predisposition for similar strategies provide a basis for agreement on strategies.

Since a coalition of chieftains depends almost entirely on likemindedness, reinforced by the arts of negotiation and compromise, the life of a coalition may be short or long depending on the state of agreement and the negotiating capacities of the chiefs. A coalition may reflect persistent goals held among durable social and economic segments of the ephemeral goals of social elements in flux.

With some reservations as to historical accuracy, the fourth and fifth patterns might be regarded as analogous to a system of independent city-states or petty sovereignties. This is the pattern of congressional action dominated by virtually autonomous committees that was described by Woodrow Wilson in his classic *Congressional Government*. It is approached in some ways by what two recent observers find to be the pattern of decision-making in New York City.[5] In this system of petty sovereignties each issue-area is controlled by a different set of top leaders whose goals and strategies are adapted to the particular segments of the community that happen to be interested in that specific area. As long as the policies of the various petty sovereignties do not conflict with one another, the sovereigns go about their business without much communication or negotiation. When policies do conflict, the issue has to be settled by fighting it out; but since the sovereigns live within a common system of legal norms, constitutional practices, and political habits, "Fighting it out" means an appeal to whatever processes are prescribed, whether voting in a legislative or administrative body, decision by judges, executive approval, or elections. The practice of fighting it out increases the likelihood of appeals to the populace for support, and hence the extent to which leaders shape their policies to what they think are the predominant preferences of the populace. However, since fighting it out is mutually costly and the results are highly uncertain, strong spheres of influence may develop with a relatively clear understanding as to the limits of each sphere; in this case, fighting it out is avoided, appeals to

---

[5] Herbert Kaufman and Wallace Sayre, *Governing New York City, Politics in the Metropolis* (New York: Russell Sage Foundation, 1960), Ch. 19.

the populace are less likely, and policies are shaped more to meet the goals of leaders, subleaders, and special followings.

Thus the way in which petty sovereignties integrate their policies tends to assume one of two patterns, depending on the extent to which the policies of the one sovereign are consistent with those of the other. If the petty sovereigns perceive their policies to be strictly inconsistent, in the sense that a gain for one means an equivalent loss to the other, then conflict is unavoidable and fighting it out is likely to be the method of settlement. This is the case, for example, if the sovereignties are two highly competitive parties, both intent on winning office for their candidates.

However, if the petty sovereigns perceive their policies to be consistent or even complimentary, in the sense that a gain for one entails no loss for the other and may even produce a benefit, then fighting it out is likely to be avoided. Possibility of conflict is minimized by mutually accepted spheres of influence, combined with a strong presumption that the status quo must be adhered to; it is also understood that if disagreements arise they are to be resolved by implicit, or occasionally explicit, bargaining among the petty sovereigns without an appeal to the populace or other external authorities.

These five patterns of coordination seemed to us most likely to cover the range of possibilities in New Haven, though the likelihood of finding still other patterns could not be excluded a priori. During our investigation of New Haven two possible variations on the five patterns became obvious. First the prevailing pattern might vary with different combinations of issue-areas. For example, the pattern of integration applying to nominations and elections might not be the same as the pattern applying to education and redevelopment. Second, patterns of integration might vary over time. The variations might be long-run changes, such as the decline of the patrician oligarchy; they might be short-run changes; conceivably, one might even encounter more or less regular fluctuations in integrative patterns associated with, say, periodic elections. Except for the first pattern (covert integration by economic notables), which it now seems safe to reject, all of these possibilities appear to be entirely consistent with the evidence so far. All of the remaining four patterns have actually existed in New Haven in recent years. Before 1953 there existed a pattern of independent sovereignties with spheres of influence, which I shall call Pattern A. This gave way briefly to a coalition of chieftains and then, under Mayor Lee, to an executive-centered "grand coalition of coalitions," which I shall call Pattern B. Standing quite apart, the pattern of integration with respect to the political parties has been that of rival sovereignties fighting it out, which I shall call Pattern C.

22. Industry and Community Power Structure: A Comparative Study of an American and an English City

DELBERT C. MILLER

The role of business leaders[1] within a local community poses some challenging questions about the on-going processes of community

SOURCE: Reprinted with permission of author and publisher from *American Sociological Review*, XXIII (February, 1958), published by the American Sociological Association. This research has been incorporated in the author's forthcoming *International Community Power Structures: Comparative Studies of Four World Cities, Seattle, Washington; Bristol, England; Cordoba, Argentina; and Lima, Peru* (Bloomington: Indiana University Press, 1969).

ACKNOWLEDGMENT: I am indebted for research assistance to Stuart D. Johnson, William Wilkinson, Esther Hirabayashi, and Anthony Baker, all of the University of Washington. Financial support by the Graduate School of the University of Washington is gratefully acknowledged. This report is one of a series describing tests of 12 hypotheses of community power structure in Pacific City (studied 1952–54; 1956–57) and English City (studied 1954–55). Other published work includes Delbert C. Miller, "The Seattle Business Leader," *Pacific North West Business*, XV (February, 1956), pp. 5–12; and "The Prediction of Issue Outcome in Community Decision Making," Proceedings of the Pacific Sociological Society, *Research Studies of the State College of Washington*, XXV (June, 1957), pp. 137–147.

[1] Cf. Howard R. Bowen, *Social Responsibilities of the Businessman* (New York: Harper & Row, Publishers, 1953), esp. Chapters 8 and 9; William H. Whyte, Jr., *Is Anybody Listening?* (New York: Simon and Schuster, Inc., 1952), Chapter 1.

decision making. Why do business leaders take an active interest in community affairs? What is the extent of their influence in the community? How do they exercise this influence?

These questions have been asked by sociologists who have sought answers by conducting research on both the community[2] and the national level.[3] However, community power structure as a field of knowledge still has wide areas in which research data are lacking.[4]

The purpose of this paper is to describe and analyze the characteristics of decision makers in an American and an English city. It has been repeatedly asserted that businessmen (manufacturers, bankers, merchants, investment brokers, and large real estate holders) exert predominant influence in community decision making. This is the central hypothesis under test. Hunter has recently demonstrated this hypothesis in his study of a large regional city of southern United States.[5] This paper applies Hunter's basic methods to two cities of similar size and economic structure. The research design has been altered only to refine the conceptual framework and provide for more extensive data to test the hypothesis.

RESEARCH DESIGN

Two cities with similar economic, demographic, and educational characteristics were selected. "Pacific City" is located in the Pacific Northwest, U.S.A., "English City" in Southwestern England. Both are comparable in many features with Hunter's Southern City. All of the cities qualify under the Harris classification as "diversified types."[6] The following summary shows the close similarity of the three cities.

---

[2] Robert S. Lynd and Helen M. Lynd, *Middletown in Transition* (New York: Harcourt, Brace & World, Inc., 1937); Floyd Hunter, *Community Power Structure* (Chapel Hill: University of North Carolina, 1954); James B. McKee, "Status and Power in the Industrial Community: A Comment on Drucker's Thesis," *American Journal of Sociology*, LVIII (January, 1953), 364–370; Roland J. Pellegrin and Charles H. Coates, "Absentee-owned Corporations and Community Power Structure," *American Journal of Sociology*, LX (March, 1956), 413–417; Donald W. Olmsted, "Organizational Leadership and Social Structure in a Small City," *American Sociological Review*, XIX (June, 1954), 273–281; Peter R. Rossi, J. L. Freeman, and James M. Shiften, *Politics and Education in Bay City* (forthcoming); Floyd Hunter, Ruth C. Schaffer, and Cecil G. Sheps, *Community Organization* (Chapel Hill: University of North Carolina Press, 1956).

[3] Robert S. Brady, *Business as a System of Power* (New York: Columbia University Press, 1939); C. Wright Mills, *White Collar, The American Middle Classes* (New York: Oxford University Press, 1951); C. W. Mills, *The Power Elite* (New York: Oxford University Press, 1956); Karl Mannheim, *Freedom, Power, and Democratic Planning* (New York: Oxford University Press, 1950).

[4] Ralph B. Spence, "Some Needed Research on Industry Within the Community," *The Journal of Educational Sociology*, XXVII (December, 1953), 147.

[5] Hunter, *op. cit.*, p. 113.

[6] Employment in manufacturing, wholesaling, and retailing is less than 60 percent, 20 percent, and 50 percent respectively, of total employment in these activities. See

Southern Regional City in 1950 had a population of 331,000. It serves as the commercial, financial, and distributive center for the Southeastern section of the United States. It manufactures aircraft, textiles, and cotton waste products; is a transportation center of rail, air, bus, and truck lines; and is a center of education possessing a large university and many small colleges.

Pacific City had a population of 468,000 in 1950. It is the commercial, financial, and distribution center for the Pacific Northwest. Major transportation lines are centered in the city and it has a fine port. The city is the largest educational center of the region with a state university and many small colleges.

English City, also a regional city, serves as the commercial, financial, and distributive center of the West of England. Its population in 1950 was 444,000. The major manufactures are airplanes, ships, beer, cigarettes, chocolate, machinery, and paper. It possesses an ocean port. The city houses a provincial (state) university and many private grammar schools.

The community power structure[7] is composed of key influentials, top influentials, the community power complex, and those parts of the institutionalized power structure of the community that have come into play when activated by a community issue. When not active, the community power structure remains in a latent state. In this paper attention is centered upon the role of the top influentials and the key influentials as representative of a significant part of the community power structure.

The Top Influentials (T.I.) are persons from whom particular members are drawn into various systems of power relations according to the issue at stake.

The Key Influentials (K.I.) are the sociometric leaders among the top influentials.

Lists of leaders were secured from organizations and informants in nine institutional sectors: business and finance, education, religion, society and wealth, political and governmental organization, labor, independent professions, cultural (aesthetic) institutions, and social service. The initial lists included a total of 312 names in Pacific City and 278 in English City.

Chauncey D. Harris, "A Functional Classification of Cities of the United States," *Geographical Review* XXII (January, 1943), 86–89.

[7] Cf. Albert J. Reiss, Jr., "Some Logical and Methodological Problems in Community Research," *Social Forces*, XXXIII (October, 1954), 51–57; Gordon W. Blackwell, "A Theoretical Framework for Sociological Research in Community Organization," *Social Forces*, XXXIII (October, 1954), 57–64; Conrad W. Arensberg, "The Community Study Method," *American Journal of Sociology*, LX (September, 1954), 109–124. The theory and concepts used in this paper were developed jointly with William H. Form of Michigan State University.

Ten expert panel raters were selected on the basis of the following qualifications: (1) knowledge of the leaders in one institutional sector with special thoroughness, (2) broad knowledge of the community, (3) many contacts with T.I. but not themselves K.I. Raters meeting these qualifications are commonly found among public relations officals, newspaper reporters, and some government officials. Raters were asked to designate each person as *most influential, influential,* or *less influential* on the specific criterion: "Person participates actively either in supporting or initiating policy decisions which have the most effect on the community." Those nominated most frequently as most influential were selected for interviewing.[8]

Personal interviews were held with a 50 percent stratified random sample of 44 T.I. in Pacific City and 32 T.I. in English City. The sample had been stratified according to the nine institutional sectors enumerated above, and corresponding proportions of leaders from each sector were interviewed. During the interview each top influential was asked the following question: "If you were responsible for a major project which was before the community that required decision by a group of leaders—leaders that nearly everyone would accept—which ten on this list would you choose, regardless of whether they are known personally to you or not? Add other names if you wish."

Each respondent was asked to check a social acquaintance scale for each T.I. by don't know, heard of, know slightly, know well, know socially (exchange home visits). He was also asked to check each T.I. with whom he had worked on committees during the past two years.

The interview included questions on current issues, role played by respondent, persons and organizations that worked for and against issues. Ratings were also secured of influential organizations and associations in the community. The interview concluded with the question: "There are several crowds in (Pacific City) that work together and pretty much make the big decisions. Is this true or false?" The responses were probed.

A questionnaire was left with each respondent at the time of interview. The questionnaire called for background data, career history, business participation (other than own business), social, civic, and professional participation. These questionnaires were later collected through the mail or by a personal visit.

Newspaper accounts during the period of the study were used to record activities of T.I., committee appointments of T.I., activities of their

---

[8] A valuable test of this technique has been conducted by Foskett and Hohle. See John M. Foskett and Raymond Hohle, "The Measurement of Influence in Community Affairs," *Research Studies of the State College of Washington,* XXV (June, 1957), 148–154.

wives, community issues, and interactions between institutions of the community.

Informants were interviewed to validate findings on clique behavior, and to describe activities of top influentials and the community power complex in the resolution of current issues.

TEST OF THE HYPOTHESIS

Evidence for a test of the hypothesis that business men exert a predominant influence in community decision making was secured from three major sources: from interviews (1) Degree of sector representation based on panel selection of T.I., (2) Sociometric rank of each T.I., (3) Committee participation score of T.I.; from questionnaires: (1) Participation scores in business, social, civic, and professional organizations of T.I.; from newspapers: (1) Participation mentions (acts and opinions) of T.I., (2) Current committee appointments of T.I. for community activities.

In each of the three cities a panel of representative judges from various institutional sectors designated the most influential leaders in the community. Table 1 shows the institutional affiliation of the T.I. selected by the panels in the three cities. Business has the largest representation among the T.I. but there is a considerable spread over the other institutional sectors. A chi square test applied to the frequency distribution in the three cities failed to reveal any significant variation in the panel

TABLE 1

Top Influentials by Institutional Affiliation as Selected by Expert Citizen Panels

Institutional Affiliation	Pacific City (N = 44)	English City (N = 32)	Southern City (N = 40)
	Percent	Percent	Percent
Business	33	34	58
Labor	14	19	5
Education	10	9	5
Government	17	9	5
Independent professions*	12	13	15
Religion	7	9	0
Society and wealth	0	7	12
Social welfare and cultural leaders (combined)	7	0	0
Total	100	100	100

* Hunter says that both of the lawyers in Southern City are corporation lawyers. I have been inclined to classify them as part of the business representation, but I have not because they are lawyers of independent law firms. Lawyers are classified under independent professions unless they were reported as salaried employees in a business firm.

selections. However, a different pattern emerged when the K.I. were selected by the T.I. themselves.

The K.I. are a significant feature of any community power structure for they are the sociometric leaders. The initiation and sanction of policy tends to be centered about them so that they may greatly influence the values which dominate in decision making. The K.I. are those persons who were most often chosen by the T.I. as the ten leaders they would want if they were responsible for a major project before the community and they were seeking leaders nearly everyone would accept.

The 12 influentials with the highest sociometric choice status are shown in Table 2 for the three cities. In Pacific City and Southern City of the United States business representation predominates among the K.I. A comparison of the proportions of business representation within the T.I. (Table 1) and the business representation within the K.I. (Table 2) reveals that the T.I. chose business men more frequently as K.I., in the two American cities.[9] In contrast, English City retains a representation of

TABLE 2

Key Influentials as Selected by Top Influentials
and Ranked by Status as Influential Policy Makers

Pacific City	English City	Southern City
1. Manufacturing executive	1. Labor party leader	1. Utilities executive
2. Wholesale owner and investor	2. University president	2. Transport executive
3. Mercantile executive	3. Manufacturing executive	3. Lawyer
4. Real estate owner—executive	4. Bishop, Church of England	4. Mayor
5. Business executive (woman)	5. Manufacturing executive	5. Manufacturing executive
6. College president	6. Citizen party leader	6. Utilities executive
7. Investment executive	7. University official	7. Manufacturer owner
8. Investment executive	8. Manufacturer owner	8. Mercantile executive
9. Bank executive—investor	9. Labor leader	9. Investment executive
10. Episcopalian bishop	10. Civic leader (woman)	10. Lawyer
11. Mayor (lawyer)	11. Lawyer	11. Mercantile executive
12. Lawyer	12. Society leader	12. Mercantile owner
Business representation: 67 percent	Business representation: 25 percent	Business representation: 75 percent

business among its K.I. (25 percent) that corresponds closely to the business representation among its T.I. (34 percent). Moreover, English City reveals a more even representation from the various institutional sectors of the community among its K.I.

This marked difference between the American cities and English City raises questions about community organization. Why should two labor

---

[9] A test of the significance of the difference between the proportions of business representation in Pacific City showed that the difference was significant at the .02 level. No statistically significant difference was found for Southern City, although the direction toward increased business representation among its key influentials is indicated. If the two corporation lawyers were classified as business, the business representation would be 92 percent, and a significant upward difference.

leaders be among the outstanding leaders in English City while not one labor leader appears among the key influentials of the two American cities? These and other questions will be explored later when the findings of further analysis have been presented.

TABLE 3

Spearman Rank Order Correlations Derived From Policy Committee Choice Rankings of Top Influentials and Ranking on Various Measures of Community Behavior

Policy Committee Choice Rank Compared With:	Pacific City (N = 44)	English City (N = 32)
Committee appointments accepted during past two years, as shown by newspaper reports...................	.51	.43
Committee participation for two year period, as designated by T.I. on the interview schedule............	.84	.67
Newspaper mentions of community activities and statements	.15	−.31
Participation in other businesses as owner or director.....	.53	.33
Participation in social clubs.............................	.51	.47
Participation in civic organizations.......................	.58	.43
Participation in professional organizations................	.45	.34
Total social participation in business, social, civic, and professional organizations........................	.59	.48

Evidence for the influence of the K.I. was sought by establishing measures of actual behavior for all the T.I. These measures included the activity of T.I. in committee work as reported in the newspapers over a two year period, and by their own statements of committee participation. Likewise, we sought evidence of their activity as spokesmen in community life as reported by the newspapers. Participation scores were derived from adapted Chapin Social Participation scales for social, civic, professional, and other business affiliations.

Table 3 shows the Spearman rank-order correlations of the top influentials for these various forms of community behavior in Pacific City and English City. These correlations indicate that there is a definite correspondence between the policy committee choices designating K.I. and actual behavior patterns in both Pacific City and English City. The highest correlation is shown to be that between policy committee choice rank and the committee participation for a two year period as designated by the T.I. on the interview schedule. K.I. are very active in community affairs. However, this activity may not be reflected in newspaper accounts. There is no significant correlation in Pacific City between committee choice status and newspaper mentions of community activities; in English City there is a low negative correlation indicating that K.I. have received less newspaper publicity than T.I. This lack of publicity is in keeping with two features of civic activity as engaged in by K.I.:

(1) much of their activity is policy making and is carried on quietly, and (2) there is a social convention that "key" leaders do not seek publicity. In England, a deliberate effort is made by some K.I. to keep their names from the newspaper as a role requirement of their social class. The similarities exhibited by K.I. in the two cities suggest that there are many common role patterns. The influentials participate widely in social, civic, and professional organizations. Based on his research contacts, the writer believes that key community leaders develop skills and influence that enable them to originate action for others. It would appear that such leaders could exchange positions with comparable influentials in other American or English cities and soon come to function effectively as K.I. in another community. However, marked differences may be discerned between Pacific City and English City. In general, there is more participation of all kinds by Pacific City K.I., and especially in other businesses. This is because the K.I. in Pacific City have a much higher business composition and because they rely more heavily on voluntary organizations for influence in community decision making.

CONCLUSION

Validity of the K.I. as identified is now assumed to be demonstrated with sufficient confidence to validate the hypothesis for Pacific City. Businessmen do exert a predominant influence in community decision making in Pacific City and Southern City. However, in English City the hypothesis is rejected. The K.I. come from a broad representation of the institutional sectors of community life. Why should this difference exist between the two American cities and the English city? Two major factors seem to explain much of this difference. The first is the difference in occupational prestige values between the United States and England. In contrast to the United States "the social status of industry in England, and so of its captains, is low by comparison with the law, medicine, and the universities."[10] Top business managers are recruited from the universities (and upper-class families) where the tradition of a liberal education predominates, and this kind of education emphasizes humanistic values and minimizes the business orientation that characterizes the social climate of the typical American university campus. Many top business leaders, educated at Oxford and Cambridge, reported during interviews that they regarded business life as a very useful activity but did not view it as occupying the whole man. They expressed a respect for scholarly pursuits. Indeed, specialized courses in business administration

---

10 Bosworth Monck, "How to Make a Captain of Industry," *The Listener* (January 13, 1955), p. 57. Cf. C. J. Adcock and L. B. Brown, "Social Class and the Ranking of Occupations," *British Journal of Sociology*, VIII (March, 1957), 26–32.

in the university are very few, and the tradition continues that business management is learned by experience within the firm. This value system plays a role in the selection of community leaders in English City just as the larger emphasis and prestige of business leadership influences the selection of community leaders in the two American cities.

A second major factor is the structure of city government. In Pacific City the city council is composed of nine members elected at large on a non-partisan ballot. These nine members have the following occupational affiliations:

Newspaper owner-editor	Business
Merchant	Business
Merchant	Business
Newspaper owner-editor	Business
Merchant	Business
Merchant	Business
Housewife (formerly teacher)	Professional
Jeweler (and labor officer)	Skilled worker
Bus operator	Semi-skilled worker

A background of small business predominates. None of the council members was chosen as a top influential by our panel raters or by top influentials. There is every indication that the top community leaders do not regard the council as a strong center of community power. The council tends to make decisions on community issues after a relatively long period of debate and after power mobilization has taken place in the community. During this period such groups as the Chamber of Commerce, the Labor Council, Municipal League, Parent-Teachers Association, and Council of Churches take stands. Council members may be approached and appeals made to them. Newspaper editors write articles. K.I. may make open declarations for or against the current issues and use their influence with the "right persons or groups." The mayor as administrative head and an elective official is both relatively powerful as patronage dispenser, and, at the same time, exposed to pressure from citizens to whom he may be indebted for his position either in the past or in the future.

In contrast to this pattern, English City has a city council composed of 112 members drawn from 28 wards. Each ward elects four members. When the council is organized, members are appointed to committees that meet once or twice a week. Issues that arise in any part of the community are quickly brought to the council's attention. The city clerk is the administrative head of the city government. He is a civil servant appointed by the council on the basis of his administrative ability and serves under a requirement of impartiality as elections come and political parties change in power. The members of the council are released by their employees from work at the time of meetings. They are paid a stipend by the local government for time lost from work and for any personal expenses incurred in attending meetings within or outside the city. Table 4 shows the occupational composition of 110 members (2 vacant seats) of English City Council in 1955.

TABLE 4
Occupational Composition of English City Council in 1955

32 Percent Trade Union Members N = 37	30 Percent Business Group Members N = 33	37 Percent Other Community Sectors N = 40
2 Foremen	4 Manufacturers	2 Solicitors
16 Skilled workers	7 Wholesale and	1 Doctor
5 Semi-skilled workers	retail owners	1 Dentist
8 Clerical workers	1 Cinema owner	1 Engineer
4 Trade union officials	4 Contractors	1 Accountant
2 Unskilled workers	8 Company directors	1 Auctioneer
	and secretaries	1 Teacher
	1 Bank official	2 Ministers
	8 Insurance officials	3 Political party organizing secretaries
		3 National government officials
		12 Housewives
		12 Retired workers

The council is composed of three major groups, trade union members (32 percent), business members (30 percent), and other community members (37 percent). Five of the twelve K.I. of the community are members and play major roles in their respective parties. The council is the major arena of community decision. Issues reach it directly, are investigated by council committees, and are decided upon by a vote taken in the full council. Community organizations play important roles in debating the issues, but these are definitely secondary or supplementary activities. The community value system condemns any pressure tactics on the council as "bad taste." However, in the council a caucus of elected party leaders is held before any important vote and a position is taken by the leaders for the party. The "whip" is applied and members are expected to vote as instructed. Such action is rationalized as necessary for responsible party government.

Two factors, a different occupational prestige system and a different council-community power complex, seem to explain the variation in the composition of key influentials who come to power in Pacific City and English City.

23. Institutional and Occupational Representations in Eleven Community Influence Systems

WILLIAM V. D'ANTONIO

WILLIAM H. FORM

CHARLES P. LOOMIS

EUGENE C. ERICKSON

In a recent study, Delbert C. Miller demonstrated the necessity of using the comparative method of community study to test even the simple proposition that "businessmen exert predominant influence in

SOURCE: Reprinted with permission of the authors and publisher from *American Sociological Review*, Vol. XXVI, No. 3 (June, 1961), published by the American Sociological Association.

ACKNOWLEDGMENT: We should like to express our appreciation for support by funds made available by the Division of Hospital and Medical Facilities of the United States Public Health Service for project W-108, "Anglo-Latino Relations in Hospitals and Communities," and the Carnegie Corporation for a project dealing with the United States-Mexican Border. Both projects are under the general direction of Charles P. Loomis. We should also like to acknowledge the work of the following persons for

260

community decision-making."[1] For his test he selected an American and an English city with similar economic structures. The characteristics of the decision-makers in these two cities were compared with those found by Hunter in Southern City.[2] Miller concluded that the hypothesis that businessmen predominate in community decision-making could be accepted for the two American cities but had to be rejected for the English City.[3] The crucial and differentiating community variables seemed to be differences in occupational prestige systems and differences in articulation between local government and other elements in the community power complex.

RESEARCH DESIGN

The aim of this research note is to extend the search for crucial community variables in community influence systems by comparing the findings from recent research in six Southwestern American communities and two Mexican communities with the communities studied by Miller. This comparison will be concerned primarily with the relative "contribution" of different institutional and occupational sectors to the group of "top decision-makers" in the community. Since the method of identifying these persons was primarily by reputation rather than by direct observation, it may be more accurate to refer to them as "influentials."[4]

Following the suggestion by W. H. Form and D. C. Miller, the influentials are considered in two categories: top and key influentials. Top influentials (TI) are persons from whom particular members are drawn into various systems of power relations according to the issue at stake; the key influentials (KI) are sociometric leaders among the top influentials. As in the case of Miller and Hunter, the TI in this study were 30 to 50

---

data collection: William V. D'Antonio and James Officer, Juarez; R. Clyde McCone and Eugene C. Erickson, El Paso; Sigurd Johansen and Laiten L. Camien, Las Cruces; Orrin E. Klapp and L. Vincent Padgett, Tijuana; Aubrey Wendling, San Diego; Robert C. Hanson, Denver; Edward H. Spicer and James Officer, Tucson; and Frank and Elizabeth Nall, McAllen. D'Antonio was also the field director of the entire project.

[1] Delbert C. Miller, "Industry and Community Power Structure: A Comparative Study of an American and an English City," *American Sociological Review*, XXIII (February, 1958), 9–15.

[2] Floyd Hunter, *Community Power Structure* (Chapel Hill: University of North Carolina, 1954).

[3] See Miller, *op. cit.*, pp. 10–11 for a description of his technique to identify top decision-makers. Both Miller and Hunter utilized a reputational approach to identify community decision-makers.

[4] See Peter W. Rossi, "Community Decision Making," *Administrative Science Quarterly*, I (March, 1957), 415–443. A central focus of the broader research is to test whether the influentials in these eight cities are indeed the key decision-makers in hospital issues which develop in the communities. Every effort was made in interviews with panel members to obtain nominations of persons who were key decision-makers in a range of concrete issues.

consensual nominations obtained from panels of knowledgeables who represented the main institutional sectors in the city and the KI were the ten most influential persons selected by the TI in personal interviews.

RESEARCH SITES

The communities selected for study represent a wide range in size, industrial structure, and ethnic composition, the three most important variables for the purposes of the wider study. This range enabled us to probe the question whether such community variables affect the social composition of local influentials.[5]

Table 1 displays for each city data on the main industries, estimates of their populations, and the percentage of persons with Spanish surnames. The task of making the data on industrial composition comparable for cities in the three countries was difficult. Nelson's service classification of American cities was used,[6] and an effort was made to apply his method to arrive at a comparable classification for the Mexican cities.[7]

Brief descriptions follow for the six American and two Mexican cities which were selected for the broader study. The two Mexican cities chosen for study are the two largest Mexican cities on the border.

> *Ciudad Juarez, Chihuahua,* is a commercial and distributive center of north central Mexico. It is also a minor manufacturing center. As a transportation center, it probably reflects the extensive tourist trade which comes to Mexico through El Paso and Juarez. In addition, it is the largest of the Mexican border cities.
>
> *Tijuana, Baja California,* is also a commercial and distributive center for the northwestern-most corner of Mexico. It is a minor manufacturing

---

[5] The variables of size and, more indirectly, industrial structure will be considered in this paper. The variable of ethnic composition will be reported separately.

[6] The Nelson classification considers the proportion of the labor force engaged in performing a service for the 897 urban concentrations of 10,000 or more persons in the United States. The mean proportion of persons engaged in a particular service in all 897 cities is calculated for each service group and standard deviations in excess of the mean are calculated. The classification of a city in one group arbitrarily reflects an excess of at least one standard deviation of the labor force employed in that service group. The service data are taken from the *1950 U.S. Census of Population Classification of Industry Groups* (Vol. 2, Table 35, "Economic Characteristics of the Population . . ."). See Howard J. Nelson, "A Service Classification of American Cities," *Economic Geography,* XXXI (July, 1955), 189–210.

[7] The classification of Mexican cities was based on a service classification of municipios of over 10,000 population which includes a city of over 10,000. There were 37 municipios which fell within our criteria from the six border states. The Mexican and U.S. Census have non-comparable categories for "trade" and "service." For this reason two different categories were made for the Mexican cities. The commercial (C) includes Nelson's retail and wholesale trade, finance, insurance, and real estate. The service (S) includes Nelson's professional and personal service, and public administration.

center. It is also a transportation center and attracts tourist trade from the western states, particularly from the San Diego environs.

Denver is a commercial, financial, and distributing center for most of the mountain states. It is the center of vast mining activities. It manufactures tires, rubber accessories, porcelain, serums, fishing equipment, saddlery, and other products. Sugar refining, meat packing, and flour milling are major industries. It is a transportation center for rail, air, bus, and truck lines. Six colleges and universities are located in the city.

San Diego is a commercial and financial center of southern California

TABLE 1

Service Classification, Estimated Population, and Percentage of Persons with Spanish Surname of Eleven Cities

City	Service Classification[a]	Estimated Population of Central City at Time of Study[b]	Percentage of Spanish Surname Population in 1950
		N	*Percent*
Pacific City	F2	552,200[d]	N/A[c]
English City	e	444,200[f]	N/A
Southern City	F2	331,300[g]	N/A
Denver, Colorado	WF	527,500	6.0
San Diego, California.	Pb2PsF	522,600	4.6
El Paso, Texas.......	T	263,000	49.0
Tucson, Arizona	Ps2PfF	110,000	21.1
McAllen, Texas	RWF	32,000	57.1
Las Cruces, New Mexico	Pb2R	22,500	48.7
Ciudad Juarez	CS[h]	250,000[i]	96.0[j]
Tijuana	CS[h]	160,000[k]	97.0[j]

[a] Taken from Howard J. Nelson, "A Service Classification of American Cities," *Economic Geography*, XXXI (July, 1955), 189–210. Key: Mf, Manufacturing; R, Retail Trade; Pf, Professional Service; T, Transportation and Communication; Ps, Personal Service; Pb, Public Administration; W, Wholesale Trade; F, Finance, Insurance, and Real Estate. A "2" after the symbol signifies the city fell two standard deviations from the mean.

[b] Except where noted differently, these estimates are taken from "Survey of Buying Power," *Sales Management* LXXXII (May 10, 1959), and are the estimates as of January 1, 1959, pp. 201–780.

[c] Non-ascertainable.

[d] Estimate as of January 1, 1955, taken from *Sales Management, op. cit.*, LXXIV (May 10, 1955), p. 732.

[e] The city is described as "commercial, financial, and distribution center of the West of England. . . ."

[f] Estimate as of June, 1953, as noted in *Whitaker's Almanac*, (1955), p. 663.

[g] Estimate as of January 1, 1951, taken from *Sales Management, op. cit.*, LXVI (May 10, 1951), p. 212.

[h] See footnote 7, *supra*. Key: C, Commercial; S, Service.

[i] Estimate based on census taken by municipio government, January, 1959.

[j] The percentage of Mexican persons in the population in 1950; from *Septimo Censo General de Poblacion, 6 de Junio de 1950*.

[k] Estimate obtained by researchers in the area.

with especially large proportions of its population employed in public administration and personal service. Its industries include fishing, fish packing, and aircraft. It is an important transportation center with an ocean port. One major college is located there.

   El Paso is a transportation and communication center and a major tourist port of the southwestern United States. Its industries include clothing manufacturing, metal and oil refining, and meat packing. It houses two major military installations and a small college.

   Tucson is a financial and commercial center of southern Arizona. A high proportion of its population is employed in personal and professional service. Its favorable climate attracts considerable tourist trade and a number of state, federal, and private hospitals. It has a major state university.

   Las Cruces serves as a commercial center of a district rich in cotton, corn, fruit, alfalfa, truck and dairy products. A high proportion of its population is employed in public administration. It houses a state university.

   McAllen is a financial and commercial center for its area. It is an important gateway to Mexico and popular winter resort. It distributes the vegetables and citrus production from the lower valley of the Rio Grande. It has a small college.

FINDINGS

   Table 2 provides data on the institutional affiliation of the top influentials of ten cities.[8] As in the cases of the Miller and Hunter studies, the sector which provided the largest number of top influentials was business. This was true not only for the seven American cities, but also for the two Mexican cities. In fact, with the exception of San Diego, Tijuana had the largest proportion of businessmen among the top influentials of the ten cities studied. Apparently size of city is not related to the proportion of businessmen found among the top influentials of the community.

   Along with business only government and the independent professions were the sectors which had representation in all of the cities. San Diego had the least broad representation of institutions among the top influentials, with only five sectors represented, and Denver, the broadest, with all sectors represented. Six to ten institutions were represented in the other cities, a situation quite similar to Miller's findings. Yet none of the southwestern or Mexican cities had as high a percentage of representation from non-business sectors as Pacific and English cities.

   The two Mexican cities give the strongest evidence of a challenge to business by another sector of the community, namely government. This

---

[8] Data for McAllen are not included here because only information on key influentials is available.

TABLE 2.
Institutional Identification of Top Influentials in Ten Cities

Institutional Affiliation	Pacific City† (N=44)	English City† (N=32)	Southern City† (N=40)	Denver (N=50)	San Diego (N=30)	El Paso (N=62)	Tucson (N=45)	Las Cruces (N=43)	Ciudad Juarez (N=50)	Tijuana (N=30)	Total (N=426)
	Percent	Percent	Percent	Percent	Percent	Percent	Percent	Percent	Percent	Percent	Percent
Business	33	34	58	50	80	57	58	44	46	67	52
Government	17	9	5	8	3	10	4	9	40	20	13
Independent professions	12	13	15	8	3	15	11	12	4	3	10
Education	10	9	5	8	0	0	7	7	2	3	5
Communications*	...	...	...	6	9	8	11	7	0	3	5
Labor	14	19	5	2	3	0	0	0	2	3	4
Religion	7	9	0	6	0	8	2	2	2	0	4
Welfare and cultural (Civic leaders)	7	0	0	8	0	2	2	9	4	0	4
Society and wealth	0	7	12	2	2	2	4	0	0	0	3
Agricultural*	...	...	...	2	0	0	0	9	0	0	1
Total	100	100	100	100	98	102	99	99	100	99	101

* Two institutions, "Communications" and "Agriculture," are not mentioned by Miller in "Industry and Community Power Structure," *American Sociological Review*, XXIII (February, 1958), 9–15, or in "Decision-Making Cliques in Community Power Structures: A Comparative Study of An American and An English City," *American Journal of Sociology*, LXIV (November, 1958), 299–310. However, in Miller, "Industry and Community . . . ," *op. cit.*, p. 14, the members of the Pacific City Council are classified according to their institutional affiliation. Therefore, his "top influential" category *may* include some representatives from communications since newspaper owner-editors were classified as "Business." Agriculture has been added as a separate category.

† Miller, "Industry and Community . . . ," *op. cit.*, Table 1, p. 11.

should be expected because of the different institutional arrangements that arose out of the Mexican Revolution. The latter, which began in 1910, was "one of the most significant and far-reaching Latin American social movements the twentieth century has seen."[9] As a result, a single political party, the *Partido Revolucionario Institucional* (PRI) came into power and has dominated the institutional life of Mexico ever since. Only recently have business and religion begun to reassert their independence or autonomy. In fact, the predominance of business over government representatives among influentials in Cd. Juarez and Tijuana may be a reflection of the proximity of these cities to the American border, and with this location a more rapid rate of social change compared to other Mexican cities.[10]

Let us now shift our attention from the top influentials to the key influentials in the 11 cities. A comparison of institutional representation among the key influentials is found in Table 3. As in Pacific and Southern City, business representation is dominant in all the American cities as well as in Tijuana. Cd. Juarez presents the only exception, namely that, like English City, it contains a sector (government) which has a greater or equal representation with business. The fact that this is not true of the other Mexican city calls for an explanation.

The states of Chihauhua and Baja California, in which Cd. Juarez and Tijuana are respectively located, have been among the main centers of the growing minority party, *Partido Accion Nacional* (PAN), the Party of National Action. Much of the strength of PAN in the presidential elections of 1958 came from these two border regions. In fact, the PAN presidential candidate is a citizen of Cd. Juarez and a key influential. Three other PAN leaders were also chosen as KI. All four became politically active in the last six years and ran for public office, with one of them winning a surprise victory in 1955. In an earlier study of business and politics in Cd. Juarez during 1954-55,[11] three of these men were listed as key business influentials. In view of their newly acquired political identity it is not surprising that they remained key influentials. The PAN leaders in Tijuana, however, were not among the top influentials in that city.[12]

[9] George I. Blacksten, "Revolutions," in Harold E. Davis, ed., *Government and Politics in Latin America* (New York: The Ronald Press Company, 1958), pp. 131–132.

[10] See William H. Form and William V. D'Antonio, "Integration and Cleavage Among Community Influentials in Two Border Cities: A Comparative Study of Social Relations and Institutional Perspectives," *American Sociological Review*, XXIV (December, 1959) 804–814.

[11] William V. D'Antonio, "National Images of Business and Political Elites in Two Border Cities," unpublished Ph.D. dissertation, Michigan State University, 1958.

[12] This type of analysis has been urged by Robert A. Dahl, "Business and Politics: A Critical Appraisal of Political Science," *The American Political Science Review*, LIII (March, 1959), 1–34.

TABLE 3.
Occupational-Industrial Identity of Key Influentials in Eleven Cities

Occupational Categories	Pacific City*	English City*	Southern City*	Denver	San Diego	El Paso	Tucson	McAllen	Las Cruces	Juarez	Tijuana	Total
Business												(83)
Finance	4	...	1	5	4	3	3	7	...	2	1	30
Merchant	3	...	3	2	3	...	5	4	3	1 (1)†	5	29
Manufacture ...	1	3	2	1	2	2	...	1	1	2 (3)†	4	19
Transportation and utilities ...	...	...	3	1	...	...	...	...	1	...	...	5
Government												(14)
Political	2	...	...	...	...	...	...	...	...	4	...	6
Mayor	1	...	1	...	...	1	...	...	...	1	1	5
Other government ...	...	...	...	...	...	1	...	...	...	1	1	3
Professional												(20)
Independent												
Lawyer	1	1	2	...	1	...	...	1	1	...	...	8
Physician	...	...	...	...	...	...	...	...	1	...	...	1
Dependent												
Education	1	2	...	1	...	...	1	...	2	...	...	7
Religion	1	1	...	...	...	...	1	...	...	1	...	4
Communications ...	...	...	...	1	2	3	2	...	1	...	...	9
Agriculture	...	...	...	...	...	...	...	...	3	...	...	3
Welfare and culture ...	...	2	...	...	...	...	...	...	...	...	...	2
Labor	...	1	...	...	...	...	...	...	...	...	...	1
Total	14	10	12	11	12	11	12	13	13	12	12	132

* Delbert C. Miller, "Industry and Community Power Structure," *American Sociological Review*, XXIII (February, 1958), Table 2, p. 12.

† Alternate classification of politicos.

It may be necessary to include in this kind of analysis the sector of mass communications that was omitted by Miller and Hunter. Newspaper editors or owners were found among both the top and key influentials in four of the five southwestern U.S. cities studied. In the study of issues it appeared that understanding the local decision-making process may not be possible without giving adequate attention to the strategic position of the newspaper editor. Evidence from our present study demonstrates that major issues have been successfully resolved or blocked by the position taken by the newspaper editor. On the other hand, Miller's data suggest a relative absence of access to top influential circles by representatives of other communications media, such as radio and television. The fact that newspaper editors were not listed as top influentials in either Mexican city deserves comment. The major papers in these cities are owned by a chain whose chief is a strong supporter of the PRI (ruling) party. While local editors in Mexico may have some independence, their residence in a particular city is often relatively short, preventing their developing stable relationships. Since they are generally not perceived to be free and independent spokesmen, long tenure in the city may be necessary before they become community influentials.

It is noteworthy that though publishers or editors are in the list of key influentials in El Paso, Tucson, San Diego, and Las Cruces, they are completely absent in Pacific, English, and Southern cities. Could it be that short tenure in these communities also explains their absence from influential circles? Long-tenured editors often establish themselves as spokesmen for the public; indeed, they often develop public opinion. Whether the editors' positions are their own or whether they reflect those of other "influentials" is, of course, problematic.[13] Since community projects are always of concern to editors but not always the concern of other influentials, it is not surprising that newspapermen are often considered to be top influentials in American cities.[14]

The dominance by financiers, merchants, and manufacturers of the key influential positions in the southwestern cities is amply demonstrated. Nine out of the eleven cities reported at least one financier among the KI;

[13] In a private communication, Delbert C. Miller indicated that in his studies newspaper editors were considered by the KI to be captive rather than independent. For this reason he placed them in the business sector. While Floyd Hunter tends to agree, publishers were found among the first, second, and third raters in *Top Leadership, U.S.A.* (Chapel Hill: University of North Carolina Press, 1959), pp. 177–179.

[14] Though his focus is the relation of mass media to mass society, C. Wright Mills has made similar observations in *The Power Elite* (New York: Oxford University Press, 1956), p. 315. He notes, "They [the mass media] are also among the most important of those increased means of power now at the disposal of elites of wealth and power; moreover, some of the higher agents of these media are themselves either among the elites or very important among their servants."

these financiers constituted almost one-quarter of all the KI. Only English City and Las Cruces failed to list a financier. Merchants and manufacturers were represented in nine of the eleven cities. The merchants (both wholesale and retail) constituted almost one-quarter and the manufacturers constituted one-seventh of all the KI. Only English City and El Paso failed to list a merchant and only Tucson listed no manufacturers among the key influentials. While the peculiar industrial structure of the city may account for the latter, the absence of a financier in English City or Las Cruces cannot be explained in terms of absence of that function.

The most frequently found occupations next to business where those in communications and law. Lawyers were represented eight times in seven cities. It may well be that the lawyer is becoming or has been an effective link between business and other sectors, if he is not in fact a businessman himself.

Mayors were chosen as KI in five of the eleven cities, as were other governmental officials and political leaders. While it may be argued that the central role of government in resolving local issues should result in the mayor being among the key influentials, mayors were not represented in six cities and they were outnumbered by other governmental officials and politicians. This situation points to the need for extensive exploration of the relations between the governmental and other power structure variables in the city.[15] Labor union officials lacked representation in the key influence structure of all cities except English City. In like manner, agriculture was represented only in Las Cruces. Religion, education, welfare and "society" had scattered representation. Only one medical doctor was found among the KI, namely, in Las Cruces, the smallest of the cities in the study.[16] With lawyers excluded, educators, clergymen, and physicians are represented in six of the eleven cities, with educators having the largest numbers. There appeared to be no relationship between the number and distribution of professions among the KI and city size and industrial composition.

CONCLUSION

This note compares data on top influence structures of several southwestern and Mexican border cities with those presented by Miller. Our data lend additional weight to his hypothesis that businessmen tend to be most highly represented among top and key influentials. Moreover, the

---

15 Dahl, *op. cit.*

16 The place of physicians in the general influence structure and in the decision—making process revolving around hospital issues is a central theme of the broader study. These findings will be reported elsewhere.

data from the two Mexican cities further support his contention that differences in the articulation of government to other elements of the community power complex results in rejecting the model of general business dominance. We tentatively suggest more information is needed on the place that newspaper editors and publishers occupy in the community influence structure. The explanation we suggested calls for further testing.

Further, although the cities studied were not drawn with the explicit view of determining the effect of size on representation of particular sectors of the community, there seems to be no consistent difference as one moves across this variable. Only in extreme cases did we find that the economic base of the community seemed to supply (and therefore effect) the composition of the top influence structures. We were unable, at this stage, to check other variables which might explain variations found in the representations of certain professions.

24. Power Structure and Decision-Making in a Mexican Border City

ORRIN E. KLAPP
L. VINCENT PADGETT

Of the Mexican cities on our southern border, Tijuana, Baja California, is perhaps the most famous, the fastest growing, and one of the least known either sociologically or practically.[1] This study is an effort to explore its power structure: the local elite, sectors of greatest influence, the social integration of the elite, patterns of community problem-solving, and roles played by influential persons.

Tijuana is ecologically a part of greater San Diego. Historically, it grew up since 1920 as a playground and tourist attraction for the sister

SOURCE: Reprinted with permission of the authors and publisher from *The American Journal of Sociology*, LXV, (January, 1960), published by The University of Chicago Press.

[1] Tijuana was selected as a site for investigation because it belongs to a pair of border cities (San Diego–Tijuana) that can ultimately be compared with other pairs, for example, El Paso, Texas, and Juarez, Mexico (William D'Antonio, National Images of Business and Political Elites in Two Border Cities" [Ph.D. dissertation, Michigan State University, 1958]), in the series of which this study is part, namely, a project, "Relations of Anglo-Latino Groups with Hospitals and Communities," carried out under the auspices of the United States Department of Health, Education, and Welfare through Michigan State University and directed by Dr. Charles P. Loomis.

city. It has an inadequate economic base, if judged in terms of stable
sources of employment, and basic food supplies, which must be brought
in from the United States. Its population, which has grown from 27,000
in 1940 to 59,000 in 1950 and to about 160,000 in 1959, is largely
dependent on American tourist trade and employment on the United
States side. Many of the new arrivals are "trapped" migrants who came
from the interior of Mexico with the hope of becoming United States
citizens. The municipal facilities have proved inadequate in view of the
growth of population as shown by pressing problems of water, sewage,
schooling, and social welfare. Some of Tijuana's most persistent problems
are due to its ambivalent relationship with San Diego, involving United
States tariff restrictions and numerous misunderstandings, political
dependence upon Mexicali, the state capital, and a kind of orphan
relationship with Mexico City. Acculturation is much in evidence; English
is frequently spoken and the dollar is freely used.

Despite acculturation and the closeness of Tijuana to San Diego, there
is a minimum of interaction between the two except for shopping and
relatively little consistent and effective co-operation between their
leaders. Thus we have an ecological area without a unified and effective
power structure; rather, more or less autonomous and unclearly identified local elites work with varying degrees of power, publicity, and
responsibility. It is the problem of this paper to delineate the Tijuana
elite.

We used a method similar to that used by others, namely, compiling
the opinions of well-informed people in the community as to who are the
leaders, using the opinions to establish a rank order, and then interviewing leaders so identified.[2] While it is not our intention to depart from
customary meanings of words like "power," "elite," and "leadership,"
certain definitions are in order: by "elite" we mean people who are
generally recognized to be near the top of a social rank system; those
among the elite who are reputed by knowledgeable persons to exercise
the most power or influence in the entire community or one of its major
sectors we designate as influentials,[3] by "knowledgeables" we mean those

---

[2] Our method follows that developed by our colleagues at Michigan State University,
Charles P. Loomis, William H. Form, and William D'Antonio, with advice from Floyd
H. Hunter.

[3] Power is used here as defined by Hunter: "the ability of persons to move goods and
services toward defined goals" (*Community Power Structure* [Chapel Hill: University of
North Carolina Press, 1953], pp. 80–81), without distinguishing it from influence as is
done by Robert Bierstedt; "Influence is persuasive while power is coercive" ("An Analysis of Social Power," *American Sociological Review*, XV [December, 1950], 730–38).
Hunter makes a distinction, however, between wealth and society prestige and actual
community power. Our concern here is, primarily, with reputed power or influence,
although our interview data and other observations suggested aspects of the objective
power structure.

who because of their position can reasonably be presumed to have wide contact with the community and close knowledge of how and by whom important decisions are made.

We arrived at a list of the top 30 influentials[4] of Tijuana, as shown in Table 1. To the extent that this rank order gives a true picture[5] of the

TABLE 1.

Top Thirty Influentials

No.	Major Designation	Other Major Sectors of Activity	Votes
1.	Businessman (commerce)	...	21
2.	Businessman (commerce)	"High society"	20
3.	Business (industry)	...	19
4.	Government official	...	14
5.	Businessman (commerce)	"High society"	10
6.	Professional	Government official	11
7.	Businessman (commerce)	"High society"	10
8.	Business (commerce)	Politics, government, education	10
9.	Businessman (industry)	Commerce, politics	10
10.	Businessman (commerce)	"High society"	9
11.	Businessman (industry)	Politics	8
12.	Businessman (industry)	Commerce	7
13.	Businessman (commerce)	...	7
14.	Businessman (industry)	...	7
15.	Businessman (commerce)	...	6
16.	Businessman (commerce)	...	6
17.	Businessman (communication)	...	7
18.	Businessman (commerce)	...	6
19.	Professional	...	5
20.	Labor leader	Politics	5
21.	Government official	Professional	5
22.	"Society" leader	Retired businessman	5
23.	Government official	Professional	4
24.	Businessman (commerce)	...	4
25.	Government official	Politics, professional	4
26.	Businessman (commerce)	...	4
27.	Businessman (commerce)	...	4
28.	"Society" leader	Commerce	3
29.	Government official	Professional	3
30.	Government official	Professional	3

distribution of local influence in Tijuana, we would say that the majority of Tijuana's "TI's" (Top Influentials) are businessmen; that busi-

---

4 Based on ratings by thirty knowledgeables of the "ten most influential" in the entire community, all listed who received three or more votes.

5 For critical discussion of the reputational method and its place among other methods of community power study see Peter H. Rossi, "Community Decision Making," *Administrative Science Quarterly*, I (March, 1957), 415–41; and Robert O. Schulze and Leonard U. Blumberg, "The Determination of Local Power Elites," *American Journal of Sociology*, LXIII (November, 1957), 290–96. We have used the positional criteria recommended by Schulze and Blumberg to the extent that our initial list was made up of incumbents of the principal political, business, and other important statuses of the

nessmen have a higher average rank order than government officials, labor leaders, professionals, and "society" leaders; and, that, while TI's are often active in education, religion, health and welfare, and "society" (as shown by our interview data), they do not come from these sectors. The main TI sources are business (commerce and industry), government communication (newspapers, radio, and television), political parties, and labor. Two main types of TI's are represented in this picture; one is a businessman who works through service clubs and *ad hoc* committees to deal with civic problems; the other is a politician who works through government position and connections, is likely to belong to the Masons, and frequently is actively connected with labor organizations.

Although the majority are businessmen, we are not able to say that businessmen "run the town," for those in political positions, which are seldom held by them, have connections with outside sources of power, such as the national high command of the PRI (Portido Revolucionario Institucional, the dominant political party of Mexico). Because of our focus on local power relations, these outside sources are not covered here. To many of our questions about centers of influence the answer was that they were located outside Tijuana, especially in Mexicali and the Federal District. It is common knowledge, for example, that groups outside Tijuana have considerable voice in selection of the mayor; also the state police has jurisdiction in the enforcement of laws controlling vice and gambling. Again, all the banks in Tijuana are branches of national firms with headquarters in Mexico City, and—while the managers are not mentioned among Tijuana influentials—doubtless the policies of the banks have major influence.

Several possibilities can be visualized regarding the kinds of relationships that exist among the TI's. Do they work together on major problems or fall into separate camps, crowds, or cliques? Is there a pyramid with established "kingmakers," such as that described by Hunter, or a less-well-integrated structure such as two camps, more or less opposed, a congeries of well-knit cliques and crowds, fluid coalitions, or individualistic competition without much co-operation?

---

community. Studies of stratification such as W. Lloyd Warner, Marcha Meeker, and Kenneth Eeels, *Social Class in America* (Chicago: Science Research Associates, 1949), show considerable agreement between reputational and objective methods of ranking. Allison Davis, B. B. Gardner, and M. R. Gardner found that upper-class persons have the most accurate view of the gradations in the status system and that people tend to visualize class groups below them more clearly than those above them (*Deep South* [Chicago: University of Chicago Press, 1941]). The high position of our informants added to the validity of the picture they gave, but this was undone to some degree by the relatively poor integration of the community. Another source of bias is the fact the majority of our interviewees and raters were businessmen and were comparatively ready to inform us, whereas people in the political and labor camps were aloof, even reticent.

To the question, "Is there a crowd who make most of the big decisions?" the response was uniformly negative. One TI described the situation as "all checks and balances." The No. 1 TI is generally characterized as a lone wolf or one-man show, even an outsider, who does not work with others. Also Nos. 10 and 11 are characterized as aloof and individualistic, as a statement by one of them illustrates: "I run my business; I make jobs; I re-invest; that is the way I help Tijuana." Some TI's have "blind spots" or at least lack of awareness of what others are doing; this applies notably to businessmen in relation to labor and vice versa; it is also shown in the businessman's distrust of politicians. On the other hand, we do not find evidence of polarizing feuds. Nor is there lack of civic spirit. Most TI's expressed a strong affection for the community, though few grew up there; they defend Tijuana, distinguish outsiders, and blame external forces for community problems. We did find an important clique of businessmen (Nos. 2, 3, 5, 12, and 26), referred to locally as "Los Caballeros de Batalle," who have strong *esprit de corps,* work hard to raise money for civic needs, and have been involved in many key issues. At the time of this study, they had a good working relationship with the mayor in spite of the gap between businessmen and politicians. It plays the role of spearhead but is not always able to obtain enough support from other TI's to achieve its goals. It comes closer than any in Tijuana, outside of government itself, to providing over-all leadership for the general community. The one conspicuous handicap for sustained rational action is lack of staff.

Each TI, it developed, has at least one strong personal tie with some other TI in Tijuana, indicated by terms like *muy amigo mio* and *compadre;* family liaisons are also important. Our impression is that such connections are more important in the power structure there than in most American cities and provide a reliable working relationship in business and politics which is a key part of the informal structure, frequently strong enough to override formal procedures and norms. The closest parallel in the United States might be called "cronyism" or "buddyism."

An element in the integration of the elite of Tijuana is "high society." In Tijuana there is no "old" aristocracy; indeed, TI's smile at the suggestion of one. Only two of thirty TI's were born in Tijuana, and no set is recognized as an arbiter of taste and protocol. There is, indeed, a loosely knit and poorly defined—though identifiable—group of social leaders who have recently become wealthy, drawn largely from business and the professions. Their social activities center around Rotary, Lions, and the country club, the latter being the most exclusive. Their membership is comparatively open, and rising persons can hope to find access to the best circles. These associations integrate the business set but seldom draw from labor and politics.

Summarizing the integration of the Tijuana power elite, we would say: (1) business TI's feel apart from those in government, politics, and labor; (2) TI's in government, politics, and labor tend to hang together as co-operating crowds; (3) relationships between the business and political-labor camps vary in effectiveness, depending upon who achieve power in the latter group; (4) within business there are a dominant clique, several independent TI's, and a number of other cliques, friendships, and coalitions; (5) "high society" is drawn mostly from business and mainly integrates it; and (6) churches do not seem to be important in the power structure or to have much function in integrating the elite. In general, the power elite of Tijuana is fragmented, and the term "structure" should be applied to it only with the above qualifications.

How does an elite thus fragmented deal with pressing community issues? Can further elements of structure be seen in its patterns of problem-solving and leadership roles? Of course, top influentials are not concerned with all levels and kinds of community decisions, nor do they speak with freedom of all decisions they make. The issues explicitly discussed by the leaders we talked to were either acute situations resulting from rapid population growth or the long-standing problems of a border city.

Comparing the course and outcome of civic actions during the period of our study enabled us to identify some typical patterns. (For purposes of this study we are excluding those decisions which are normally made and implemented by the municipal government.) The scope of these decisions is more limited than one would find in an American city of similar size because of the inadequate municipal tax base,[6] rudimentary development of bureaucracy,[7] and legal subordination of city to state government.[8] As a consequence, voluntary action by individuals and citizen groups plays a comparatively more important part.

The simplest type of community action might be aptly termed the "one-man show": a top influential perceives a need, decides what to do, and acts without consulting others; it may be in such matters as organizing a golf tournament to attract tourists, raising funds for the needy, or building schools. He provides all or most of the funds himself, distributes

---

[6] The state pre-empts many tax sources, the city is overpopulated with people unable to pay taxes, and the methods of taxing are not so effective as they might be.

[7] Inadequate funds have not permitted the establishment of many public services, and the principle of the merit system has not been widely applied.

[8] See *Constitución del Estado de Baja California del Norte* (Mexicali, 1953), and *Ley orgánica municipal del estado* (Mexicali, 1953).

the benefits, and takes the credit. A second common pattern is spontaneous fund-raising and planning by *ad hoc* committees, service clubs, and labor unions, from their own membership and from the general community; for example, the Lions raised funds for a school for under-

As a "New" City	As a Border City
Schools	Tourism
Elementary and secondary	Vice and gambling control
University of Baja, California	United States tariffs
Health	Maintenance of the "free zone"[9]
Red Cross facilities	Trapped migrants
Inadequate hospital	
Lack of over-all organization	
Water	
Sewage	
Streets	
Social welfare	
Poverty	
Dependency	
Juveniles	

privileged children, the Alba Roja labor union built a school, and a TI formed a committee to raise funds for a Red Cross hospital.

A more complex process develops when there is need to get consensus among divergent groups. In the cases we observed, the typical sequence was more or less as follows:

1. A TI defines a goal or a need.
2. He talks to his friends.
3. They inform the mayor of their intentions and seek his co-operation: active help, indorsement, or a promise to be neutral.
4. They form a *junta* or committee to direct the effort.
5. They hold a banquet or civic meeting to which TI's from all important sectors are invited, seeking support for their proposal; the meeting is widely publicized in the press.
6. Opposition may be manifested by
   a) Failure to attend the meeting
   b) Objections stated at the meeting
   c) Counterpressures on the mayor
   d) A statement in the press, or
   e) Pressures at the state and/or federal levels.
7. If there is concerted opposition from the TI's of one of the sectors, a

---

[9] Since 1934 the Mexican government has allowed goods to come into Baja California from all parts of the world duty-free. There was a definite move in Mexico City, at the time this study was made, to revoke the privilege.

stalemate typically develops. The effects of the fragmented power structure are plainly evident here.
8. Efforts to break the stalemate typically involve appeals to prominent
persons, organizations, or government officials outside the community.
9. On the other hand, consensus enables leaders to develop maximum
community resources (whether or not sufficient to achieve the goal) or
to present a unified appeal to higher authorities for aid.

A fourth possibility is united community action against an outside
force. For example, a clique of TI's organized a *Tijuanense* boycott
against certain San Diego merchants who had consistently opposed easing
California-United States tariff restrictions. In another case, the governor
of Baja California, in evicting some squatters from the Tijuana River
Valley, precipitated community-wide demonstrations and a petition by
TI's of all sectors to the president of Mexico to suspend the governor's
powers.

Certain roles played by TI's became evident in the way they spoke of
each other and of themselves in interviews.[10] Without presuming to
exhaust the system of power relationships, roles played by business TI's
include the following:

> The one-man show, who undertakes civic projects on his own and takes
> all the credit
> The lone wolf, who works without publicity or connection with teams or
> organizations
> The team player, who works readily with others for civic betterment
> The sheer economic dominant, who sticks to business and has influence
> solely through money, property, and the people he employs
> The social lion, whose prestige may or may not be associated with eco-
> nomic dominance or work on community projects
> The senior citizen, once active in civic associations or politics and still
> influential through advice and connections
> The initiator who identifies a need and proposes the solution.

And among TI's in politics, prominent roles were:

> The incorruptible who is elevated to public post because he conspicuously
> avoids appearance of self-gain
> The "do-gooder" politician, who actively attacks evils and pursues the
> community good

---

10 Mexicans who spoke English well readily characterized themselves and other TI's
by American labels (O. E. Klapp, "Social Types: Process and Structure," *American
Sociological Review*, XXXIII [December, 1958], 674–78).

The negotiator who works through personal contacts to bring parties together and put over deals and compromises favorable to his side

The perennial office-holder who influences community decisions through his many connections in addition to office and technical competence.

Some of these roles, of course, could be played by the same person; and none covers the totality of any influential's civic behavior.

Much of the leadership of this community is outside governmental institutions, operating through civic associations, labor organizations, and *ad hoc juntas* or committees. Much is informal, working through cliques, friendship, and personal connections. Much is not public, except in stages where community support is desired to resolve a conflict or provide funds; generally speaking, the citizens at large do not make major decisions.

This does not mean that power is monolithic or hierarchic, in that a single group runs things. Hunter's model of a pyramid of power or a "kingmaker's" clique does not apply to Tijuana, not only because many of the key decisions are made outside, but because, even where local decisions could be made, the elite is not well integrated. Some TI's act independently, impasses frequently develop, and the solution of local problems has been slow. Political office-holders are connected with the leading national party, the PRI, which dominates local elections and appointments;[11] but, in spite of party connections, persons in city government have quite limited local power, as shown by the difficulty in supplying public services and by the independent power and action of business TI's. In relation to outside powers, too, Tijuana is far from mistress of its own affairs; indeed, the city might be said to be caught in a vise between decisions made in Mexico City or Mexicali and in the United States. Thus the Tijuana "power elite," as we have identified it, is not very powerful.

Seeking for a model which better fits Tijuana than Hunter's, from among those developed in the study of American community power structures, we reject Miller's institutional ring or cone model[12] as rather too complex for the Tijuana situation. Although Tijuana has some of the features which Miller ascribes to his model, namely, lack of solidarity among top influentials and of hierarchical dominance by one institu-

---

11 Generally speaking, Mexico has a one-party system though without totalitarian power and unity. See L. Vincent Padgett, "Mexico's One-Party System: A Re-evaluation," *American Political Science Review*, LI (December, 1957), 995–1008.

12 Delbert C. Miller, "Decision-making Cliques in Community Power Structures: A Comparative Study of an American and an English City," *American Journal of Sociology*, LXIV (November, 1958), 299–310.

tional sector and fluidity of coalitions, this city does not have the size,[13] complexity, and heterogeneity of interests in various sectors to have different crowds of TI's coming in to dominate as issues change. In spite of the absence of a kingmaking group, the faces are pretty much the same in various issues.

Long's picture of the local community as an ecology of games[14] strikes us as applicable to the lack of integration of the Tijuana power structure. There seems to be a series of intersecting games with comparatively little unified leadership responsible for the entire community and its welfare. Games played locally, games played from Mexicali, Mexico City, and even the United States, determine what goes on in Tijuana. In Long's terms, Tijuana has no government. Yet counterbalancing this somewhat is almost a small-town *esprit de corps,* paradoxical in a city with such growth, mobility of population, and emphasis on exploitative games. Were the economic and political situation more favorable, this civic spirit might be translated by the truly excellent local leaders into more effective community action.

---

[13] The population of Tijuana is about 160,000; of Southern Regional City, 331,000 (Hunter); of Pacific City, 468,000; and of English City, 444,000 (Miller).

[14] Norton E. Long, "The Local Community as an Ecology of Games," *American Journal of Sociology,* LXIV (November, 1958), 251–61.

Part Three

The Community and the

Larger World

The common trait among the communities portrayed in this volume is not organization or life style, for that has been demonstrated to be highly variable, but rather, the fate that all face. Even the most remote hamlet cannot escape the influence of the larger society which we have called the vertical community. This influence takes many dimensions, from cultural imports that replace native handicrafts with mass-produced goods and regional peculiarities with a common culture, to domination of the local economy and political life as nationally organized corporations and political institutions overwhelm local structures.

A good deal of sociological literature has been concerned with the breakdown of local institutions and the "loss of community." Often this "breakdown" represents a loss of primary relationships as the basis for community organization or economic control, with formal organizations appearing in their stead; but it can also mean disappearance of a life style or actual death of the local community. The changing nature of community removes certain elements from the individual's life for which there may be no replacement. The sense of belonging to a certain place is lost in a geographically mobile population. A local perspective that shapes one's world view becomes meaningless when every villager, as a result of improved travel and communications, is first a citizen of his nation and only incidentally a member of the local community. In short, the vertical community is replacing the horizontal as the important dimension, and those elements that typify the horizontal are passing out of the picture. As the world view of the individual expands, the inner circles of community, as presented by Redfield, cease to dominate the thinking of men, and the attractions of the broader world break down that provincialism which typifies the viable small community. One might decry this trend, or conversely, he might praise it, for just as breakdown of the extended family releases the individual from kin ties, so too does the disappearance of the local community free him from personalistic community pressures. We prefer to take neither position, but rather, view community change in perspective of the changing nature of social life. With increasing size of society and improved means of establishing and maintaining hierarchical controls, locality and personalistic factors have less relevance than they once did. The modern corporation with its vast network of operations that are directed by a central office has similarly transformed industry, and governmental vastness has made virtually all people victims of each other's fate.

The effect of bigness in all facets of society can be most readily observed in the community setting, for many if not all societal institutions are represented, yet our subject of study is limited enough that we can conceptualize the transformation as a whole rather than simply observing change of an isolated institution. Community study provides the golden opportunity for the study of social change in that we can observe the process *in vivo*.

CHAPTER V

Expanded Horizons—World
Views in Changing Communities

What is the effect of the local community becoming less an independent entity as it is exposed to the influences of the larger world? All of the excerpts reprinted in this section deal, in some way, with this question. As the local populace becomes aware of the outside world, and eventually comes to identify with and participate in it, we observe the transition from provincial attitudes to increasing cosmopolitanism. The importance of this transition is universally recognized, but whether it is beneficial or detrimental to community life is a matter of some conjecture.

Critics of the small town point to its narrow provincialism as a stumbling block to social progress, while its champions hearken back nostalgically to the viable local community as a bulwark against the dread "mass society." As the following selections indicate, both views are probably distortions of reality. Provincials are not so narrow that they are unaware of the outside world, as Halpern noted of the Serbian peasants he studied, nor do they reject social progress when it can better their lives, as the changes in St. Denis and Dragor illustrate. The member of the urban milieu is not nearly so malleable by mass society as he may seem from afar; suburban Levittowners were so locally oriented that they seemed almost unaware of the larger community. Nor has the vertical community overwhelmed local culture and traditions over the protests of the local citizenry; for as the brief excerpt from Littlejohn's *Westrigg— The Sociology of a Cheviot Parish* illustrates, the local citizenry more likely than not aided the breakdown of the horizontal community by discarding their old ways for the new.

Halpern has provided an illustrative definition of provincialism and Miner has demonstrated how economic dependence of the local community on the vertical sphere leads to cultural dependence which effectively destroys provincial ways and attitudes. That this loss of provinciality need not be disruptive is shown in the example of Dragor, Denmark. Dragor changed from a maritime village to an urban annex in a few decades virtually without socio-cultural conflict.

In their study of Wissous, a Paris suburb, the Andersons conceptualize the transition of Wissous in much the same terms that we used in defining the typology of communities presented in Part Two. As a result of improved transportation and communications between the village and Paris, Wissous has lost its personalistic village way of life and has become an extension of the city with its impersonal aura.

The personalistic vs. impersonalistic attitude is representative of the two types of community leaders discussed by Merton. The informally oriented, personalistic locals differ greatly from the more formalistic cosmopolitans of Rovere. The example of Rovere illustrates that a community is not either provincial or cosmopolitan, but rather has elements and representative leaders, that reflect both qualities in the community.

Gans challenges the notion that we "lose" community because we live in urban, or suburban, settlements. His study suggests that change in the community need not imply dire predictions about the future, and that much of our concern is misplaced nostalgia.

25. The Orašac Villager
and the World Outside

JOEL MARTIN HALPERN

The universe of the Orašac peasant centers on his household, his neighborhood, his clan, and his village. The world outside the village is of secondary importance, although he is very much aware of it and interested in it. Toward each larger and more distant sphere of influence and association, from the relation of Orašac to its surrounding village and market town, to Šumadija and Serbia, to the rest of Yugoslavia, and to the vast world beyond, his feelings become less intense.

NEIGHBORING VILLAGES AND THE MARKET TOWN

Part of the peasant's fervent attachment to his own plot of land is projected to his immediate surroundings. Not only does he invariably say that his village is the best in the area, but he also feels that he personally would not be happy living elsewhere. People are inherently proud of what is theirs, an attitude brought out in conversations on almost any subject. Despite constant instruction on the values of industrialization, and professed desires to leave the village in order to better serve their country, this attitude is even reflected in the essays of many of the school

SOURCE: Reprinted with permission of the author and publisher from *A Serbian Village* (New York: Columbia University Press, 1958).

children, who speak of their birthplace with the greatest attachment and affection.

It is not uncommon to hear a man from Orašac declare emphatically that he could never live in neighboring Kopljare village "because it is too flat there," and for the Kopljare man to reply that he could not possibly settle in Orašac "because of the hills," although a casual traveler finds it hard to see any great difference in the topography of the two villages.

* * *

A new settler is not quickly accepted by the traditional villagers. Some smaller clans have been in Orašac almost 25 years but are considered newcomers. There are also two families who moved to Orašac 30 years ago, from a Serbian village near the Bulgarian border. They are still referred to as "The Bulgarians." The ethnic German miners and the few Slovenes are thought of as temporary residents and have limited contact with the villagers. For the most part they do not venture away from the kolonija into the village proper. The village priest is known as *Crnogorac,* Montenegrin, since he recently came to Orašac from there, and a schoolboy whose parents were born in Bosnia is called *Bosanac* and ridiculed by his classmates because he speaks a slightly different dialect.

The Orašac peasant is parochial but in no sense isolated. His greatest degree of contact with the world outside the village, other than via the national institutions present in the village, is through Arandjelovac.[1] At least one and often two members of most households go to the market town every Friday. Some villagers have special customers to whom they bring a specified amount of kajmak, wine, or brandy each week, but most bring their produce to trade on the open market. Peasants buy and sell to one another as well as to the townsfolk. This is especially true in the sale of livestock. Continuing the theme of inter-village rivalry, a peasant will sooner trust a fellow villager than one from another hamlet. Before a livestock transaction occurs, the first question is not on the qualities of the animal under consideration but, "Which village are you from?"

The long, narrow row of shops lining the town's main street is occupied by various private craftsmen and several state-controlled stores. The peasants' purchasing of staples and certain consumer goods has already been discussed, but much of their town business is at the sandal-maker's, potter's or tanner's. The town has always supported a much greater variety of craftsmen than has the village. The variety of crafts still

---

[1] Orašac County is similar to most others in Šumadija in that it consists of a group of 20 or so villages oriented toward one small town which acts as both market and administrative center.

operating today reveals the extent to which the peasants depend on them. Other reasons for a trip to town are errands at the county seat, the court, the health clinic, or a visit to a relative.

The most important events attracting villagers into town are the *vašari*, the county fairs and livestock markets which occur several times a year. The fairs are arranged in a patterned fashion, with specified spots for the various activities. The Friday marketplace functions as usual, but the vacant lots and hills beyond are filled with the overflow of carts piled high with bulk produce, with a turbulent mass of squealing pigs, placid cows, and animated villagers, clinching bargains, amidst shouting and hand-slapping. Temporary stands are set up to sell household goods, such as tin and wooden utensils, made and sold by craftsmen from the South. The main feature of the fair is the amusement section, complete with games of chance and gypsy musicians. Afterwards there is traditionally a dance for the young people, around the town churchyard on another hill overlooking the market scene.

ŠUMADIJA AND SERBIA

Beyond the scope of the surrounding villages and market town, the peasant thinks in terms of Šumadija and Serbia. Within this sphere the Orašac peasant will insist that the region of the Jasenica basin is the best part of Šumadija.[2]

Šumadija in general has been a very homogeneous area during the last century and a half, although the composition of the population has altered slightly since the war. Most of the non-Serb population is concentrated in the towns. They include factory workers from other areas, a few Tsintsar merchants and a small group of Jewish professional and business people. Before the war the number of Jews was considerably higher, and many refugees were hidden in peasant cottages during the German occupation. In contrast to the traditions of distrust and anti-Semitism which exists in other parts of Eastern Europe, the Serbs in the towns and the peasants who came in contact with the Jews thought of them as clever, rich, and with "good souls." Two peasant households in Orašac still correspond with Jews whom they had sheltered in their homes and who later went to Israel.

There is one group of people counted in the official census as of Serb nationality and Orthodox religion whom the peasants nevertheless consider outsiders. It is the *Cigani*, the gypsies. In Šumadija there are

---

[2] The peasants of the Jasenica region regard those to the north, in the Kosmaj area, as not being true Šumadijans, calling them *šijaci*. They consider themselves to be *Eroji*, true descendants of the Dinaric herdsmen, while they, in turn, are regarded as Šijaci by people further south.

actually two kinds of gypsies, the kind the Orašani refer to as "our gypsies" and the type that live in more southern parts of Šumadija and other areas of Serbia who are wandering smiths and entertainers.

The gypsies of the first type are sedentary. There are none in Orašac village, but there is a settlement of them in Ranilović, a small group in Kopljare, and a *Ciganska Mala,* or gypsy quarter, in Arandjelovac. They live much as the Serb peasantry does, speaking Serbian, observing slavas, and practicing both agriculture and herding to some extent. They are easily distinguished by their darker skin and other physical features. Despite their seeming adaptation to peasant life, they are rarely successful farmers and usually occupy the most marginal land. Their homes are shabby even when compared to the poorest peasant house. They supplement their income in other ways. The men make and repair various types of metal cooking utensils, and fashion such items as wool combers, wooden mixing troughs, spoons, spindles, and cheese boxes. In so doing they fulfill a distinct economic need and yet do not compete with any of the village or town craftsmen. This is also true of their other major occupation, that of serving as musicians, entertainers, and fortunetellers. Whatever else the peasant may say about gypsies, he is full of admiration for their ability as musicians, and the larger weddings in the village are frequently classified according to the number of gypsy musicians hired for the event.

The other type of gypsies, the nomadic ones, are also craftsmen and entertainers. Once or twice a year a caravan of several gypsy families passes through Orašac to sell kettles and frying pans and to tell fortunes by reading the future in a ball of fuzz plucked from the "client's" clothing. There is one group that brings a chained toothless dancing bear to the villages each year, making the animal perform in return for flour, bacon, beans, and dried meat. Money is rarely given. In the scattered villages of Šumadija, where entertainment is limited, the coming of these wandering gypsies is eagerly anticipated.

Despite the fact that the peasants consider the first type as their gypsies, all gypsies in general are regarded with condescension and suspicion. They are thought to be lazy, unreliable, and thieves. Villagers explain that they rarely leave their cottages unoccupied "because of the gypsies," and children are told, "If you're not good we'll give you to the gypsies" or "The gypsies will come and take you away."

To the Orašac villager Serbia is the logical extension of Šumadija, and he speaks with pride of Šumadija as the heart of Serbia. Although geographically this is so, the peasants have a somewhat different explanation, based on cultural traits. In the first place, "Šumadija is the most desirable part of Serbia, the richest, most attractive area, and the home of the most *kulturni* people."

Being a Šumadinac, the Orašac peasant feels himself to be something of a privileged character, but basically he considers himself a Serb. He is passionately proud of his Serbia and will fight to defend it against all enemies, as has been amply demonstrated in the past 150 years. This great pride in nationality is no doubt due in part to the origin of Serbia as a peasant state.

Although the Orašani conceive of Šumadija as an integral part of Serbia it does not follow that they similarly conceive of Serbia as a part of Yugoslavia. Yugoslavia is a political creation of the First World War, compounded of two small independent states, Serbia and Montenegro, and parts of the defunct Turkish and Austro-Hungarian Empires. The common bonds in all Yugoslavia are much less obvious than in the case of Serbia alone, or even Serbia and Montenegro, where the great majority of the people share a religion and historical tradition. Since the Serbs are by far the largest national unit in Yugoslavia, and also because they were an independent state for almost a hundred years before the creation of Yugoslavia, it has been rather difficult for them to think of Yugoslavia as a federal or multinational state. This led to severe tensions in the inter-war years. Although the present government is a federal state with individual constituent republics and although open conflict has been eliminated, the problem has by no means been completely solved.

* * *

THE REST OF YUGOSLAVIA

The inhabitants of Orašac are aware that they are formally citizens of Yugoslavia, but only the village intellectuals would speak of themselves as Yugoslavs or of their language as Serbo-Croatian. It is possible that this attitude will gradually change, for the idea of a united Yugoslavia and "the brotherhood of our peoples" is very strongly emphasized by the school and government organizations.

ORAŠAC AND THE WORLD BEYOND YUGOSLAVIA

Less than six copies of the two main Belgrade newspapers are received in the village each day, and there are only about 20 radios or crystal sets, so it is not surprising that the villagers' news of world developments is rather sketchy. At the same time, despite the fact that they are most preoccupied with earning a living and with local affairs, they have a very definite interest in other parts of the world. To fail to mention this interest and indicate some of their feelings and attitudes on the subject would be to neglect a limited but significant aspect of their culture.

One of the primary stimuli for this interest has been the considerable periods spent by many village men abroad, as a result of military service. In the First World War they participated in campaigns in Albania and Greece, and by their imprisonment in Czechoslovakia they saw something of a different way of life. In the Second World War 70 Orašac men spent the war in German prison camps with British, French, and American soldiers, while others fought with the partisans when they cooperated with the Russians. This, added to the fact that Orašac itself has twice in this century been occupied by German armies, could not very well help but affect the outlook of the whole village. In the last century there were, of course, the wars against the Bulgarians and Turks.

* * *

Many of the younger villagers have been to the movies in Arandjelovac, where they have seen foreign films, including American ones. Their contacts are much more limited than those of the town children, however, for the latter were familiar with the term *kauboj* (cowboy) while village children had no idea what it meant. It is possible that with film showings at the village Cooperative Home there will be more consciousness of foreign countries in general. The films have the greatest effect on the younger generation. Many of the older people have never seen a motion picture and have no desire to do so, particularly since they must pay for the privilege.

26. Old and New

HORACE MINER

In every phase of life in St. Denis one finds cultural changes which have come about in the last one or two generations. Every society becomes altered through the years, but rural French-Canadian culture has changed more in the last forty years than it did in the preceding century. An intimate analysis of the parish social structure showed the direction of these changes and also indicated the reasons for these altered folkways. Here we shall devote our attention explicitly to the problems associated with this breakdown of old traditions and the diffusion of urban traits into the country.

The social organization of the rural French in Canada is losing its folk character. Folk songs have lost their place in the life, and folk tales no longer have their old appeal. Folk medicine is giving way more slowly, but the doctor and public heath nurse are making inroads. Many of the old culture traits are so closely allied to the thrifty, close-family economy that they have resisted change to a remarkable degree. Thus, flax is flailed, wool is spun and woven, and clothes are made from this local *étoffe*. The family bread is baked in outdoor ovens. The soap is made in great caldrons. Some of the traits have resisted change, but for each of these there is some complementary alteration of custom. Every farm has its threshing machine. All wool is carded at a mill. Some clothing is

SOURCE: Reprinted from *St. Denis—A French–Canadian Parish,* by Horace Miner, by permission of the University of Chicago Press.

bought from the store and by catalogue; city fashions have local social value. A baker passes through the parish twice a week. Soap is bought in some quantity from the local store, and the lye for home soap production is no longer made. These trends are toward industrialization and urbanization, toward the acquisition of city manners. The reason for the change is not simply the proximity of the urban culture to the rural; nor is the change to be understood simply in terms of improved standards of living, for the standards of day-laboring families have declined.

Fundamentally the culture shift is toward increasing dependence of the local society upon the great industrial civilization of which it is becoming a part. The old social structure, its sanctions, and its mores were based on an independent, self-sufficient farming economy. With the exception of a very few items obtainable in trade, all an individual's needs were satisfied through locally practiced techniques and locally produced materials. As long as this local independence was maintained, there was no concern about social or economic conditions in the rest of the world. This self-sufficient economy was made possible by a family system which provided adequate *mains d'œuvre* to feed and clothe the *habitants* without the use of farm machinery. Such tools and simple equipment as were necessary were made locally. This economy and family system were structurally dependent upon a continual supply of new land upon which surplus children could be established. New France provided these conditions for over two centuries.

During the settlement and expansion period the rural parishes were not dependent upon a money economy. The money which was used consisted of the currency of half a dozen different countries.[1] If a man wanted to buy a *cariole,* he could use either crop capital or the money into which it might have been converted. Transportation difficulties favored money exchange in preference to barter in kind over any any distance. But the large cities were easily accessible only to a few parishes. The remote parishes had less use for money, as their inhabitants never got to the city. Even commerce with the itinerant peddler was often in kind.

In the latter half of the nineteenth century young men were forced to go farther and farther afield to find land on which to settle. In those times rural sons were rarely given advanced education, as there was not the capital with which to train boys for professions. New settlements, such as that around Lac St. Jean, absorbed some of the new generations.

---

[1] Words used in referring to the present standardized currency reflect the variation existing well past the conquest. *Piastre* and *sou* are used for "dollar" and "cent"; and *trente sous* carries the connotation of its old equivalent, "twenty-five cents." The term *louis* has died out in the last fifty years.

The movement was toward more and more marginal land. The shift from a self-sufficient to a dependent economy is best understood in terms of this increasing land pressure. In other words, the basic human geographic conditions upon which the social structure was built were being altered through the operation of the social system itself. The changed land conditions in turn created problems in the society, which was based upon specific geographic requirements, and the society changed to meet the problems.

It is a commonplace that social systems change to meet their structural problems. When the traditional ways cease to solve the problems of life, social behavior varies from the old ways until a solution is found. If the new ways are successful, they in turn will become traditional. Thus, when the English suppressed female infanticide among the Toda, traditional polyandrous marriage could not take care of the increasing percentage of females. A type of adelphic "group marriage" grew up to meet this new structural situation.[2] The social changes in French Canada are to be understood in the same light. In this case, however, structural problems in the society are due to the operation of the traditional system itself.

This suggests another consideration in the study of cultural integration. Not only must the degree of integration within the society be considered but also the degree to which the culture is adjusted to its habitat.[3] If this adaptation of the society to the environment is bad in terms of the immediate economy, the integration of purely social elements based on the economy will be weak. If the adjustment is poor from a long-term view, the integration of the purely social elements may be of a high degree for centuries.[4] A consideration of cultural integration should not be content with only the investigation of the interadjustment of institutions and mores but also with the integration of these with the habitat. The extent to which a society is internally well integrated expresses the probability of conflict and change. In the same way the degree to which the integration between the society and its habitat is satisfactory, even from a long-term point of view, is expressive of probable conflict and change.

Those cultures which have been long isolated from outside factors, which might change the basic conditions upon which the culture is based, are usually highly integrated both in the purely social sense and in terms of a long-term economic adjustment. Plains Indian tribes restricted their

2 W. H. R. Rivers, *The Todas* (London: Macmillan & Co., Ltd., 1906).

3 The former has been designated as "internal integration"; the latter, as "external integration."

4 Such cases would involve some exhaustion of the local habitat.

bison kill so that the faunal feature of the habitat upon which they depended was not exhausted until after white contact. A highly socially integrated tribe might have existed for centuries with economic traditions demanding wasteful kills. In terms of the complete cultural adjustment, the degree of integration would have been low.

French-Canadian culture was one which had a high degree of internal social integration based on a short-term adjustment to the environment. It took two centuries for the weakness of the territorial adjustment to appear. The problem having arisen, the society has tried to adjust itself, to integrate itself more adequately to its environment. In so doing, it has seized upon elements of American social environment, in contrast to the purely physical environment on which French-Canadian culture was once founded. The growing dependence on this new and unstable environment has made the culture subject to the vicissitudes of an industrial society whose own integration is very weak.

Land pressure alone created the structural problem in the society and accounts for the necessity for change and some of the actual cultural changes, but an even greater amount of change is only indirectly related to the basic structural problem. The growing lack of land forced parents to seek other outlets for their children. The society was experiencing trial-and-error behavior in an attempt to find a solution to its problem. The conflict between the old patterns of establishment and the lack of land was a gradually growing one. There was no sudden disruption of the traditional ways, only an increasing attempt to find other ways. All the new ways involved dependence upon the industrial civilization surrounding the old culture. The diffusion of elements of material and non-material culture from the cities to the country has been a feature of this growing dependence of the latter on the former.[5] Good unsettled lands being rare, one way of placing children was to educate them or to buy farms from farmers willing to move to more marginal land. These two simple possibilities implied basic social changes. Each necessitated capital in money. The only way to secure such capital was to sell produce to the cities. Traditional modes of agriculture did not even furnish a surplus of produce. Agricultural methods were changed in order to develop a surplus. These changes were aided and abetted by representatives of the urban industrial society which was to absorb the surplus. Primary among the changes was the adoption of simple farm machinery: harrows, mowers, binders, and small threshing machines. Crop rotation was also introduced. These innovations made possible the development

---

[5] A unique feature of diffusion from industrial society is the concerted effort of this type of culture to inject its material culture into the borrowing society—the attempt to "create a market."

of a crop surplus. The raising of animals for market was less dependent upon outside factors other than the market, but the crop
surplus made the feeding of more animals possible. The crop and animal
surplus did give the farmer money with which to establish his children,
but he had lost his old independent economy and had become dependent
upon items of material culture which he could not produce but had to
buy with part of his surplus. Even more vital, the placement of children
now became increasingly dependent upon the fluctuating market from
which the farmer got his money. He is now doubly dependent upon the
cities—not for the support of his family, for the old economy did that,
but for the placing of his children.

About the same time that these changes in agricultural method were
being effected, another outlet was found for unestablished children. This
was in industrial and urban employment. The need for workers in these
places caused the great emigration of farmers' available children from the
country to cities in the United States and Canada. This new form of
economic establishment completed the solution of the structural situation
produced by the exhaustion of available land. It will be noted that this
solution, like the others, was based on a new type of environment—a
social, rather than a physical, environment. That this new environment
was unstable, as the old one had not been, was discovered with the
economic depression. Farmers might occasionally lose a crop from adverse
weather; but never was their whole economic basis destroyed, as was the
case with farmers' sons in the city. This outlet for children did not
diminish gradually as the land had done, but closed almost at one blow.
The markets for crop surplus also fell; and investments, another feature
of the new economy, were lost. Still, the *habitant* suffered less than
almost anyone else in North America, for he had clung to a great deal of
his independent economy. Inbred conservatism had kept him from one-
crop farming. Households could still be fed and clothed no matter what
industry did, but the *habitant* was faced anew with his old problem of
providing for the establishment of his children. The society's adjustment
had failed. Rural French Canada is in this structural conflict position
now.

Before discussing the recent social responses to the problem, let us
consider what the change from an independent to a dependent community is doing to the culture. The loss of stability resulting from the
shift in economy has already been noted. An alteration of social values
has resulted from this change. In the old culture pattern, a young man
aspired to have a farm like his father and therefore modeled his behavior
after that of the farmers with whom he would eventually identify. Now a
large part of the youth knows it can never farm and that it must find

work in the city. The values of this group are increasingly influenced from the city. Urban ways have definite value to these young men, for the closer they can identify with the city, the better is their chance of success there. The old culture patterns are sufficiently strong to keep young women from going to the cities in search of work as the men do. The old patterns are not strong enough, however, to keep a girl from desiring such work, finding it through relatives and friends, instead of personal search, and going to the cities to fill positions. The movement of women into urban employment is less than that of men. In order to compete for the men with city-turned eyes, rural girls are adopting city fashions and customs. Thus, urban values are becoming important for the girls also. If the young people oriented toward the city came from a different group of families from those oriented toward the country, one might find the development of two groups differing in styles and customs. Members of both of these groups actually belong to the same families. There is then, because of family solidarity, a diffusion of city ways among even the rurally inclined youth. Still, those young men whose dress and behavior are most strikingly of city origin are men interested in getting to the city. There is a separation into two groups of families whose interests are different, as suggested above: the landed and nonlanded or day-laboring families. The very limited economy of this latter group tends to repress the tendency to adopt urban modes.

In addition to these factors influencing change of values it must be remembered that a number of adult farmers and *rentiers* spent several years in cities in the United States. This breaking of the isolation in which the old culture was maintained has had its effect. Even a short time spent in the industrial centers resulted in altered values, in spite of the fact that much of the old life was continued in these cities. The change in mourning customs is best understood in terms of this return movement from the cities. The diffusion of urban ways received its start through these various channels. The growth of literacy and the introduction of the newspaper, radio, and advertising have maintained and developed the consciousness of the value of the city manner of doing things. The diffusion of these patterns has but started, having been restricted by the close family economy. The loss of isolation through increased social mobility of all sorts has set up the conditions of social contact through which cultural diffusion is possible. The forced change to a dependent economy has motivated the acceptance of new culture patterns.

The adoption of the urban elements makes the local society dependent upon the urban centers to maintain its new mixed culture. The new traits are altered to fit into the old culture pattern. This alteration in the process of diffusion is the usual thing between any two cultures. When the difference between the cultures is great, the two contexts into which a single trait is put vary considerably. Even when the difference is as slight as this between two Western cultures, there is alteration of borrowed traits in adoption. The fact that the English play croquet gives the game class significance when borrowed by the French. A knowledge of bridge is likewise a mark of sophistication. Borrowed food ideas get social significance from their origin and become "company" dishes in many cases. The new association of the culture trait does not always depend upon the larger English-French or urban-rural context. An electric motor may be mounted on a spinning wheel frame, giving a novel, yet natural, combination of new and old culture elements. A harmonica player adopts the foot-patting technique and the repertoire of the fiddler. The harmonica slips into the culture pattern of the violin. New combinations of new elements are made and become established as proper. Spats worn over rubbers are practical in keeping melting snow from running down into the shoes. This combination is generally accepted by the young men as the proper way of wearing these articles.

The old culture background is capable of reacting to these new borrowed elements. Cultural needs are now usually met by borrowing. Before this was possible, the local culture was capable of producing its own answers to its needs. Naturally these answers were new traits—but local ones based on the local culture. Necessity gave the *platée* accepted meaning as a unit of measure on a par with any other. Curved roofs developed naturally from straight ones; galleries from raised porches. New weaving designs and *boutonné* bed covers grew from older, simpler manners of weaving. The new traits, however, which are entering from without, are based on a foreign background and are, therefore, dependent upon the outside culture for development. The threshing machine was first run by windmills, then by horse treadmills, now by gasoline engines; and there is talk of electric ones. Each of these steps was originated outside the parish. The farmer adopted the changes in time, although the lag in adoption of traits often lasted long enough to bridge one of the steps. With each step he became more dependent. At first he needed only elements with which he was familiar: wind and horses. Then he had to buy gas, and soon he will be paying for electricity. He is becoming more and more dependent on the products of the outside world. To accomplish this he had to sell an equal value of local produce, thus putting himself in relation to the consumer market over which he has no control. When he was independent, he had control of all the economic factors which affected his life.

27. The Parish and the Town

JAMES LITTLEJOHN

. . . Working class countrymen have accepted the town working class's low estimation of 'isolation,' and that isolation means being restricted in one's association with others. Isolation has no absolute meaning but is contingent upon the possibilities of association with others. The contingencies limiting association are both physical and social—geographical location and occupation. However, the vast majority of countrymen are obviously more limited than townsmen.

The space of the isolation so far considered is a purely physical space—people are prevented by their position in physical space from meeting others. Social space is of a different nature and has to be described in terms of participation. It is difficult to separate the two types of space in analysis of rural-urban attitudes, but there is some evidence to suggest that in this situation limitations on social space are as important as those on physical.[1]

Despite the fact that everyday commercial ties between parishioners

SOURCE: Reprinted with permission from *Westrigg—The Sociology of a Cheviot Parish*, published in Great Britain by Routledge & Kegan Paul and in the U.S.A. by Humanities Press.

[1] Cf. R. Firth, *Two Studies of Kinship in London* (London: 1956). Some of the effects of isolation of the individual on his health are discussed in W. Watson and M. Susser, *Sociology in Medicine*, Oxford University Press, forthcoming.

and Broadfield are more numerous than with Craigton, parishioners prefer to visit the latter. Now the difference between the two towns is simply that the latter is more 'townlike' than Broadfield. To say this is hardly illuminating but I shall try and isolate the difference between the two, which difference will indicate what I mean by 'townlike.'

It is sometimes said that country people migrate to towns because of the greater opportunities for entertainment in them. Yet there is no form of entertainment in Craigton which cannot be found in Broadfield. There is a cinema in both places, a dance hall in both, public houses and cafés in both. But there is this difference—that the area of choice is greater in Craigton, and this town has a more modern façade and copes with a greater number of people. Craigton is, in ecological terms, a 'centre of dominance' for a large area, whereas Broadfield to quote a parishioner is a 'dead wee hole.' It has far fewer shops and pubs and cafés. Each town has one dance hall and one cinema. The Broadfield cinema building is a converted church hall, whereas the Craigton one was built as a cinema and except in size looks like any modern cinema. Similarly, several of the Craigton pubs have the glitter and shine of modern metropolitan pubs, but only one of the Broadfield ones has. The Craigton dance hall manages far more often to engage nationally celebrated country dance bands. In short, the difference between the two towns is not that one provides entertainment and the other does not, but that Craigton offers mingling with larger crowds of people, a greater range of choice, and an opportunity to participate in cultural forms, the styles of which are nearer to those found in large towns.

In short, by spending one's time in Craigton rather than in Broadfield one is affirming one's participation in a culture freer of local peculiarities of style than that of Broadfield, and one's capacity to enter into associations (however ephemeral) not determined by a narrow locality. A 'local community' it seems is not a group that anyone particularly wants to belong to.

My first chapters showed how the population of the local rural community was drawn into a wider, more extended network of relationships. This means that this population, brought into contact with a much wider range of persons than formerly, have been forced to compare their status and circumstances with that of others in the wider network, particularly townsfolk. It seems from the evidence presented that the parishioners have to a large extent accepted the evaluation of their status and circumstances which the others hold. This view I think is what a farmer was expressing when he said: 'In the old days you couldn't get anywhere, you just stayed here and you never knew anything else. So everyone was content. Now everywhere and everything's within reach, but because they (i.e., parishioners) know other people can get anything there's nobody contented now.'

The countrymen who actually do migrate to the town would in this view simply be those who have wholly accepted this evaluation. This seems consistent with the findings of the social survey that: 'It was fairly clear that potential migrants tended to regard their environment more critically than those who did not wish to move,' and 'what is strongly suggested by the anomalous and apparently inconsistent nature of some of the evidence is that rural migration in many cases has sprung basically from a general dissatisfaction with rural life rather than with one or other aspect of it.[2]

Studies of rural communities in Britain tend to emphasize 'these aspects of culture which distinguish (the community) from large urban centres'[3] or to analyse mainly those interpersonal relationships based on bonds of kinship and neighbourhood which make up the local social network.[4] In this study the emphasis has been rather on the similarity between Westrigg and urban centres and on those relationships through which parishioners participate in a more extended network of social relations. It seemed to me to be necessary to treat the parish in this way, partly because the farms there are enterprises in the 'agricultural industry' and not family farms, and partly because the most significant social process in the recent history of the parish has been its induction into the wider network.[5] Where this process has advanced to the degree it has in Westrigg the local community becomes less 'an area of common life,' than an area within which the individual chooses his associations subject to such barriers as are imposed by social class or physical distance. The people round him are no longer all actual neighbours but only possible neighbours. The locale itself ceases to be the actual place where he lives and has his being and becomes one possible place amongst others, to be compared and evaluated with others.

---

[2] Bertram Hutchinson, *Depopulation and Rural Life in Scotland* (H.M.S.O.: 1950), pp. 17–18.

[3] W. M. Williams, *The Sociology of an English Village* (London: Routledge & Kegan Paul, 1956), p. 200.

[4] As is so excellently done in R. Frankenberg, *Village on the Border* (London: Cohen & West, 1957).

[5] The writers on rural sociology in Britain already mentioned, Arensberg, Rees, Williams and Frankenberg, all note that this process is under way in the communities they have studied.

28. Change and Conflict
in the Vanishing Village

ROBERT T. ANDERSON
BARBARA GALLATIN ANDERSON

In the 1890's Dragor, Denmark, was, as it had been for two centuries, a harbor community, its existence so bound up with the sea that the union of its culture and its maritime fishing economy seemed inextricable. Despite its geographic proximity to the capital and a history of centuries of exposure to potential innovations from sea traffic, Dragor's inhabitants were isolated and conservative. The life of the city dweller was remote from them.

Yet change came, swiftly in consideration of the cultural tenacity of the past, and so pervasively that few aspects of the village's cultural inventory emerged without profound alteration. And what is yet more striking, the adjustment from maritime village to urban annex has been accomplished in a few decades and has been embraced by an entire population *virtually without sociological conflict*. How was it achieved?

The early heralds of change were not auspicious. Technological progress affected every local industry. The final decay of the once great sailing fleet took place shortly after the turn of the century. Sound

SOURCE: Reprinted with permission of the authors and publisher from *The Vanishing Village: A Danish Maritime Community* (Seattle: University of Washington Press, 1964).

fishermen had increasing difficulty competing for local and world markets as developments in transportation made distant, richer fishing
grounds profitable. The ancient home occupations of weaving and open-
air linen bleaching could not compete with new factories. Shipwrecks,
long a source of salvage bounty, became less frequent and required
expensive specialized equipment.

Yet little by little the technological progress that brought economic
crisis to the village also brought its solution. In the course of two decades
Dragor found itself a suburb of Copenhagen with its economic base in
the capital city.

Immigrants from Copenhagen accounted for the growth of the community. At the turn of the century the first Copenhageners came as
summer residents. They built small villas in the northern end of town
which they left uninhabited during the greater part of the year. In 1907 a
railroad was built between the capital and Dragor, significantly augment-
ing the suburban exodus. Although railroad travel was not cheap, it was
reasonable enough for people in the professional classes and it was fast.
Thus it became feasible for the villa people to remodel their houses and
live all year round in this beautiful little harbor town. The real expansion, however, waited until after World War II. By that time the need for
housing was acute in the capital and it was practical to meet this need by
the construction of suburban communities, particularly in view of the
developments that had taken place in the areas of communication and
transportation.

The train, buses, bicycles, and private motorized vehicles which permitted the arrival of Copenhageners also permitted Dragorians to commute, an opportunity that was quickly grasped as the old forms of local
occupation became unprofitable and forced the villagers to look to the
city for a means of earning a living. The local people became part of this
great urban labor force. Many commuted daily to the capital and others
found new types of employment within Dragor's limits as a result of the
increased needs of the growing community for goods and services.

Through seven hundred years of recorded history Dragor had habit-
ually increased its population by the immigration of outsiders. Throughout the Hansa period until approximately 1500 the population had been
almost completely transient—summer residents coming from all over
Denmark, from Germany, Holland, Sweden, and elsewhere. Subsequent
centuries witnessed Dragor's growth as a permanent settlement, including
individuals from Sweden, Norway, other parts of Denmark and from the
neighboring Dutch-settled town of Store Magleby. These earlier immi-
grations, however, were of an essentially different kind. With one major

exception, these immigrants contributed little new to the culture content but tended, rather, to be absorbed rapidly and to become indistinguishable from older Dragorians. This was possible because the migrants came in small numbers relative to the size of the community, and because they made a break with their former homes.[1] The exception is the Dutch immigrants, who came in relatively large numbers in the seventeenth and eighteenth centuries and retained their contacts with their fellow Dutch Amagerians. As a result Dragor acquired Dutch characteristics. The twentieth-century immigration was, on the other hand, one of vital, everyday intercourse—of massive social interaction. This provided the demographic base for extensive sociocultural change.

The year 1907, at which time Dragor and Copenhagen were joined by the railroad, may be taken as the date marking the end of the old era and the beginning of the new. The subsequent change constituted a social and cultural revolution, for it occurred rapidly and pervasively within the time span of a single generation. That it occurred with a general lack of cultural conflict appears to be due first of all to the fact that, in almost every citable instance, change did not involve the replacement of long-established culture patterns by radically new ones. Instead, new patterns were developed out of the old or grafted on to them. This merging of the old and the new cushioned Dragorians particularly during the early phases of urban contact and permitted a relatively easy adjustment of the people to concomitant change. Old patterns offered Dragorians a firm foothold while they grappled with the new.

This may be illustrated, both as regards their exposure to new technological exigencies as well as to changes of a strictly social order. In terms of the former adjustment, for example, eventual addition of motors was to only slightly modified versions of the old boats, and fishing traps and nets remained largely the same with only the manner of their employment changed. For all the differences that steamships implied, the old hierarchy of command and the experience of voyaging at sea remains similar in maritime employment. The job of piloting, despite advances, is essentially still to keep the craft in navigable waters. The work of Dragor's few farmers is simplified by the use of tractors and the absence of cattle, but the seasons of plowing, sowing, and harvesting were not altered. The great development of wage labor, and the disappearance of a semisubsistence economy represent primarily the increased participa-

---

[1] This process seems similar to that defined as cultural crystallization by George M. Foster in *Culture and Conquest: America's Spanish Heritage*, Viking Fund Publications in Anthropology No. 27 (New York: Wenner-Gren Foundation for Anthropological Research, 1960), 227–34.

tion of the population in what was originally only a variant of local economic life. The few who participated in a purely money-wage economy at the turn of the century paved the way for the masses.

Technological and economic changes aside, developments in other aspects of culture were also rooted in the retention and modification of older cultural patterns. While much of the elaboration which contributed a local stamp to the annual cycle of fêtes in Dragor has been leveled out of existence with urban contact, there was always a nationally common core to their celebration and it was to this "heart" of their festivities that Dragorians could cling as an honored tradition. Much of the rites of passage, similarly derived from a common religious base, has not altered. Social organization has retained the old prestige-ordering system in new forms of hierarchical evaluation. Even sexual practices and the patterning of relations between the sexes is still founded on old principles more leniently interpreted and broadened in application.

A second and largely derived circumstance conducive to change without cultural conflict may be attributed to the harmonious system adjustments during the transitional period of the different aspects of the old Dragorian and the new urban cultures. In general, neither localized culture lag nor precocity was ever extensive enough to precipitate severe or long-felt friction.

Thus, in old Dragor with the decline in maritime employment and related businesses, the need for a shift in economic orientation was concomitant with the opening up of Copenhagen as a source of wage employment. This was a development possible only because of advances in the fields of transportation and communication—the same advances that had contributed so decisively to the economic decline of Dragor as an isolated village. Similarly, the former elaboration of the midwinter holidays, so well adjusted to a maritime economic cycle with winter inactivity, changed with urbanization to a cycle of fêtes characterized by a fairly even spacing of work-free days throughout the year and was coordinated with the growth of year-round wage labor. The addition of retirement fêtes to the rites of passage developed as old age ceased to be an almost imperceptible change in the life of an individual but became marked instead by an abrupt termination of adult economic activities.

Changes in social organization also represent harmonious adjustments to changes in economic life. The isolation of the nuclear family vis-à-vis the larger kinship groups and the disintegration of neighborhood solidarity are congruous with the increased economic independence and hence social identity of the individual and of the family unit. With techno-economic change the old prestige and class systems became modified, to the extinction of a functioning class organization, as a type of occupation, its most significant criterion, was altered. The breakdown of the church community and of the integrity of communal village government are relatable to the centrifugal tendencies of Dragor's economic ties with Copenhagen.

The cultural change within social organization had wide ramifications within other aspects of culture. With the breakdown of larger kinship groups, annual fêtes and individual celebrations have become the occasion for smaller, domestic family get-togethers or for the meeting of a few friends. Similarly the baptism rite has lost much in ceremonial magnitude and display as a result of the lack of neighborhood participation. The disappearance of the classes led to the loss of class-delineated balls and hence much of the grandeur of holiday celebrations. This relaxation of local allegiance is equally consistent with the loss of communal solidarity as evidenced here again by the declining concern with church activities and local government.

Sex life both in and outside of marriage was shown to have, within the culture of old Dragor, a functional interrelationship with coexistent patterns for defining male and female roles, the meeting of the sexes, religious attitudes, kinship behavior, and class. That is, the village's sexual practices were in support of the total cultural equilibrium of the community. While change was achieved through the familiar device of reinterpreting old patterns, sexual behavior nevertheless provides the single area in which culture conflict was discovered in conjunction with transition from village to urban status.

A third explanation of Dragor's cultural pliancy must be related to the concomitant lack of internally or externally engendered social conflict. Its only documentation was in short-lived hostility of the youth groups to summer visitors during a few years at the turn of the century. There was no opposition of antagonistic social *groups* to encourage the exclusive adoption of either the old or the new cultural forms as symbols of a superior evaluation of culture choice. Developments were allowed to proceed solely in response to the desire of Dragorians for improved economic well-being and a higher standard of living, defined in terms comprehensible to villagers and city dwellers alike.

This lack of social conflict relates to Dragor's resolution of her techno-economic predicament at the end of the last century without serious friction with Copenhageners. While the migration of city dwellers to Dragor was associated for some villagers with the community's loss of social and cultural integrity, the newcomers brought increased economic opportunities to that part of the population supplying goods and services locally. Further, these urban immigrants did not represent an alien group in competition with Dragorians for jobs, nor were they in a

position of economic sovereignty. At that crucial period, the shift by
Dragorians to an urban-oriented way of life came as a welcome palliative
to an economically depressed village.

That the change to urban modes was prestigeful constitutes a fourth
and last factor favoring smooth transition. A high evaluation of the city
way of life was partially an adjustment to the inevitable, a product of the
contemporary successful competition of Dragorians within the urban
economy through conformance to urban culture patterns. But it is also
strongly relatable to the ease with which one can identify with a group
regarded as economically and socially privileged. This high evaluation
resides additionally in Copenhagen's historical supremacy in so many
areas of activity. It was the center of government, home of the king as
well as the parliament, of commerce and industry, of cultural activities,
of the church hierarchy, and so on. The spread of urban values was
swiftest and most thorough, however, with the younger generation and is
here perhaps attributable to the attendance of all Dragorian children at
a single, nationally supervised school. The urban values of textbooks, of
the teachers, who have almost unanimously been of nonlocal origin, as
well as of children of immigrant urban families influenced the values of
all Dragorian children during their formative years. This uniform motivation toward acceptance of urban culture was decisive during the early
years of the century, and the adults of today who were children then
reinforce these convictions in their children.

This shift in values goes far to explain those many changes which strike
the eye, and yet seem avoidable. Here change appears significant for its
symbolic function in the adaptive situation. On the whole, we find
that village-centered diversions and local variations of nationally observed
holidays and rites were abandoned. For example, children no longer set
out wooden shoes for *askefis* on New Year's Eve. *Kis* is not played on
Christmas Eve. Wedding celebrants do not serpentine through the village. The society balls are gone and with them a constellation of related
custom. The local black confirmation costumes have been done away
with to adopt the white dress of the city. These changes, negligible in
terms of culture content, were exceedingly significant socially for they
represent the negation of group symbols, traits that branded Dragorians
as villagers, different from city people. In their place, urban symbols,
such as the decorative Christmas trolls, the small group party, and public
entertainment were substituted.

In sum, the urban assimilation of Dragor was a massive process. It
involved major changes in the social and cultural entity. It took place in
a relatively short period of time. Dragor stands, however, a witness to the

fact that abrupt, major change can take place with a minimum of social disorganization and of cultural conflict.[2]

---

[2] This chapter was written before the authors had seen Margaret Mead's analysis of rapid, massive, and relatively frictionless cultural change among the Manus. Dragor is similar to her Melanesian case insofar as it too suggests that short-term, all-inclusive change can be a smoother process than change of lesser scope. Cf. Margaret Mead, *New Lives For Old: Cultural Transformation—Manus*, 1928–1953 (New York: New American Library, 1961), pp. 372–77.

29. The Village and the City

ROBERT T. ANDERSON
BARBARA GALLATIN ANDERSON

URBAN REVOLUTION

* * *

Urban influences, then, increasingly affected Wissous from the eleventh century on. Especially after the seventeenth century we can outline developments deriving above all from urban growth affecting Wissous, its region, and France at large. The impact on the village was indirect, however. Urban and rural patterns of life continue localized, each in its own arena, and the village responded with essentially crescive adaptations, developing a commercialized agriculture different from older agrarian practice, yet still appropriately rural. City and village met at the market place, but each remained distinct.

Urbanism may be described as a life style characterized by social impersonality rather then intimacy. It is characteristic of a society that is too large and complex for pervasive face-to-face interaction. The introduction of urbanism is a primary process in which city ways intrude into

SOURCE: From *Bus Stop For Paris: The Transformation of a French Village* by Robert T. Anderson and Barbara Gallatin Anderson. Copyright © 1965 by Robert T. Anderson and Barbara Gallatin Anderson. Reprinted by permission of Doubleday & Company, Inc.

the domain of village ways. In Wissous, urbanism came when city people and city customs were transplanted into the very bosom of the community. Urbanization in this sense is a thing of only the last few decades in Wissous, and is still incomplete.

Wissous is located approximately ten miles south of Paris on the plain of Longboyau. But the meaning of ten miles distance from Paris depends upon local ecology. Wissous, it happens, lies to this day in the rural countryside. Throughout most of its history the village was effectively remote from Paris. During the Revolution and the Empire it was necessary to have a passport from the mayor to make the trip to the city. Until recent times, roads were deplorable—even hazardous—and effectively hindered easy communication. By the nineteenth century the situation had improved so that the Wissousian could take a daily stagecoach to Paris, leaving in the morning and returning in the evening. A major step forward took place in 1893 when a railroad service was inaugurated from the capital to the nearby village of Antony and beyond. A regular horse coach carried the villagers to and from the train station. Even so, it was not a trip to be taken lightly. (A little earlier another railroad line cut through Wissous, but it did not connect directly into Paris.) In 1899, one of the Wissous schoolteachers wrote that "Wissous is truly favored by its lines of communication," but actually, in modern terms, communication with the city was restricted. At times farmers drove their produce into market. Others made the trip but rarely. A few urbanized individuals had lived in the village since the sixteenth century, when a distinctively urban way of life was still incipient in Paris itself. But otherwise, life in the village was essentially remote until well into the twentieth century. In this small society, villagers lived mainly unto themselves. Twentieth-century communities located more than twice as far from Paris, but east or west of Wissous, became sociologically much closer to the metropolis by virtue of direct connections with the city communication network (see map)[1].

The change in Wissous did not take place until the 1920's and 1930's. By the 1920's, industry in the Seine-et-Oise area had grown out from Paris enough to make commuting from Wissous to its outer edge possible, and in a relatively short period of time a number of commuters were added to the community. The major turning point, however, came in 1936 when the Paris-Antony railroad was replaced by bus service, with a shuttle bus to Wissous. Although it ran only a few times a day at wide intervals, it was the precursor of regular, cheap transportation to the city. Not only did the number of urbanized individuals in the community increase

---

[1] Philippe Varaigne, *Wissous et son eglise* (Tours, Gibert-Clarey, 1955), pp. 108-9.

enormously, but Wissousians themselves began to regard to trip into Paris as an ordinary, if necessary a daily, event. With this sociological incorporation of the community into the city came a change from a village way of life toward a city way of life. Informants' descriptions of life in the Wissous of 1900 to 1920 are descriptions of small community behavior, of an intimate face-to-face group. While still recognizable, the pattern now is losing its dominance. Many residents are strangers to one another, and take no more note of one another in their village encounters than they would if they lived in Paris. Witness, for example, the biography of Mme. E. Within her quarter she continues an intimate neighborliness. Some of the women in her courtyard keep an eye on the old lady's window, largely out of idle curiosity no doubt. Yet as a result they know her comings and goings, and their assistance or company is always nearby if she wants it. Down the street the farmer still treats her as befits an old villager—he would rather not take money for the breakfast milk he provides. After all, she has sewn for several generations of his womenfolk. On the other hand, the old priest who understood her so well is gone, and the new priest is rather urbane. He seems very remote from Mme. E. even as he ministers to her, and, in her eyes, his television set and small car symbolize loyalty to another world. In fact, he does live in another world, a world of urban thoughts and cosmopolitan interests. But it is a world that has recently become a major part of Wissous. And so, as the little old lady walks the streets of the old village, she moves in space as she moves in time, out of her rustic environs. And the small children playing in the streets take no notice of her as she wends her way. Once upon a time they would have.

30. Types of Influentials:
The Local and the
Cosmopolitan

ROBERT K. MERTON

The terms "local" and "cosmopolitan"[1] do not refer, of course, to the regions in which interpersonal influence is exercised. Both types of influentials are effective almost exclusively within the local community.

SOURCE: "Types of Influentials: The Local and the Cosmopolitan" and "Spheres of Influence: Monomorphic and Polymorphic" by Robert K. Merton from *Communications Research, 1948-1949*, edited by Paul F. Lazarsfeld and Frank N. Stanton. Copyright 1949 by Harper & Brothers. Reprinted by permission of Harper & Row, Publishers.

1 Upon identification of the two types of influentials, these terms were adopted from Carle C. Zimmerman, who uses them as translations of Toennies' well-known distinction between *Gemeinschaft* (localistic) and *Gesellschaft* (cosmopolitan). The sociologically informed reader will recognize essentially the same distinction, though with different terminologies, in the writings of Simmel, Cooley, Weber, Durkheim, among many others. Although these terms have commonly been used to refer to types of social organization and of social relationships, they are here applied to empirical materials on types of influential persons. *Cf.* Ferdinand Toennies, *Fundamental Concepts of Sociology* (New York: 1940), a translation by C. P. Loomis of his classic book, *Gemeinschaft und Gesellschaft,* and more importantly, a later article bearing the same title. See also Carle C. Zimmerman, *The Changing Community* (New York and London: Harper & Brothers, Publishers, 1938), especially pp. 80 ff. For a compact summary of similar concepts in the sociological literature, see Leopold von Wiese and Howard Becker, *Systematic Sociology* (New York: John Wiley & Sons, Inc., 1932), especially pp. 223–226n.

Rovere has few residents who command a following outside that community.

The chief criterion for distinguishing the two is found in their *orientation* toward Rovere. The localite largely confines his interests to this community. Rovere is essentially his world. Devoting little thought or energy to the Great Society, he is preoccupied with local problems, to the virtual exclusion of the national and international scene. He is, strictly speaking, parochial.

Contrariwise with the cosmopolitan type. He has some interest in Rovere and must of course maintain a minimum of relations within the community since he, too, exerts influence there. But he is also oriented significantly to the world outside Rovere, and regards himself as an integral part of that world. He resides in Rovere but lives in the Great Society. If the local type is parochial, the cosmopolitan is ecumenical.

Of the thirty influentials interviewed at length, fourteen were independently assessed by three analysts[2] as "cosmopolitan" on the basis of case materials exhibiting their orientation toward the Rovere community, and sixteen, as "local."

These orientations found characteristic expression in a variety of contexts. For example, influentials were launched upon a statement of their outlook by the quasi-projective question: "Do you worry much about the news?" (This was the autumn of 1943, when "the news" was, for most, equivalent to news about the war.) The responses, typically quite lengthy, readily lent themselves to classification in terms of the chief foci of interest of the influentials. One set of comments was focused on problems of a national and international order. They expressed concern with the difficulties which would attend the emergence of a stable postwar world; they talked at length about the problems of building an international organization to secure the peace; and the like. The second set of comments referred to the war news almost wholly in terms of what it implied for interviewees personally or for their associates in Rovere. They seized upon a question about "the news" as an occasion for reviewing the immediate flow of problems which the war had introduced into the town.

Classifying influentials into these two categories, we find that twelve of the fourteen[3] cosmopolitans typically replied within the framework of

---

2 This complete coincidence of assessments is scarcely to be expected in a larger sample. But the cosmopolitan and local syndromes were so clearly defined for this handful of cases, that there was little doubt concerning the "diagnoses." A full-fledged investigation would evolve more formal criteria, along the lines implied in the following discussion, and would, accordingly, evolve an intermediate type which approaches neither the local nor the cosmopolitan pole.

3 It should be repeated that the figures cited at this point, as throughout the study, should not be taken as representative of a parent population. They are cited only to

international and national problems, whereas only four of the 16 locals spoke in this vein. Each type of influential singled out distinctively different elements from the flow of events. A vaguely formulated question enabled each to project their basic orientations into their replies.

All other differences between the local and cosmopolitan influentials seem to stem from their difference in basic orientation.[4] There is a tendency of local influentials to be devoted to localism: they are more likely to have lived in Rovere for a long period, are profoundly interested in meeting many townspeople, do not wish to move from the town, are more likely to be interested in local politics, etc. Such items, which suggest great disparity between the two types of influentials, are our main concern in the following sections. There we will find that the difference in basic orientation is bound up with a variety of other differences: (1) in the structures of social relations in which each type is implicated; (2) in the roads they have traveled to their present positions in the influence-structure; (3) in the utilization of their present status for the exercise of interpersonal influence; and (4) in their communications behavior.

STRUCTURES OF SOCIAL RELATIONS

ROOTS IN ROVERE

Local and cosmopolitan influentials differ rather markedly in their attachment to Rovere. The local influentials are great local patriots and the thought of leaving Rovere seems seldom to come to mind. As one of them gropingly expressed it:

> Rovere is the greatest town in the world. It has something that is nowhere else in the world, though I can't quite say what it is.

When asked directly if they had "ever thought of leaving Rovere," thirteen of the sixteen local influentials replied emphatically that they would never consider it, and the other three expressed a strong preference to remain, although they believed they would leave under certain conditions. None felt that they would be equally satisfied with life in any other community. Not so with the cosmopolitans. Only three of these claim to be wedded to Rovere for life. Four express their present willing-

---

illustrate the heuristic purpose they served in suggesting clues to the operation of diverse patterns of interpersonal influence. As is so often the fact with quantitative summaries of case studies, these figures do not confirm interpretations, but merely suggest interpretations. The tentative interpretations in turn provide a point of departure for designing quantitative studies based upon adequate samples.

[4] Nothing is said here of the objective determinants of these differences in orientation. To ascertain these determinants is an additional and distinctly important task, not essayed in the present study.

ness to live elsewhere and the remaining seven would be willing to leave under certain conditions. Cosmopolitans' responses such as these do not turn up at all among the locals:

> I've been on the verge of leaving for other jobs several times.

> I am only waiting for my son to take over my practice, before I go out to California.

These basic differences in attitude toward Rovere are linked with the different runs of experience of local and cosmopolitan influentials. The cosmopolitans have been more mobile. The locals were typically born in Rovere or in its immediate vicinity. Whereas 14 of the locals have lived in Rovere for over 25 years, this is true for fewer than half of the cosmopolitans. The cosmopolitans are typically recent arrivals who have lived in a succession of communities in different parts of the country.

Nor does this appear to be a result of differences in the age composition of the local and cosmopolitan groups. The cosmopolitans are more likely to be younger than the local influentials. But for those over 45, the cosmopolitans seem to be comparative newcomers and the locals Rovere-born-and-bred.

From the case materials, we can infer the bases of the marked attachment to Rovere characteristic of the local influentials. In the process of making their mark, these influentials have become thoroughly adapted to the community and dubious of the possibility of doing as well elsewhere. From the vantage point of his seventy years, a local judge reports his sense of full incorporation in the community:

> I wouldn't think of leaving Rovere. The people here are very good, very responsive. They like me and I'm grateful to God for the feeling that the people in Rovere trust me and look up to me as their guide and leader.

Thus, the strong sense of identification with Rovere among local influentials is linked with their typically local origins and career patterns in this community. Economically and sentimentally, they are deeply rooted in Rovere.

So far as attachment to Rovere is concerned, the cosmopolitans differ from the locals in virtually every respect. Not only are they relative newcomers; they do not feel themselves rooted in the town. Having characteristically lived elsewhere, they feel that Rovere, "a pleasant enough town," is only one of many. They are also aware, through actual experience, that they can advance their careers in other communities.

They do not, consequently, look upon Rovere as comprising the outer-most limits of a secure and satisfactory existence. Their wider range of experience has modified their orientation toward their present community.

Sociability: Networks Of Personal Relations

In the course of the interview, influentials were given an occasion to voice their attitudes toward "knowing many people" in the community. Attitudes differed sharply between the two types. Thirteen of the sixteen local influentials in contrast to four of the fourteen cosmopolitans expressed marked interest in establishing frequent contacts with many people.

This difference becomes more instructive when examined in qualitative terms. The local influential is typically concerned with knowing as many people as possible. He is a "quantitativist" in the sphere of social contacts. Numbers count. In the words of an influential police officer (who thus echoes the sentiments of another "local," the mayor):

> I have lots of friends in Rovere, if I do say so myself. I like to know everybody. If I stand on a corner, I can speak to 500 people in two hours. Knowing people helps when a promotion comes up, for instance. Everybody mentions you for the job. Influential people who know you talk to other people. Jack Flye [the mayor] said to me one day, "Bill," he said, "you have more friends in town than I do. I wish I had all the friends you have that you don't even know of." It made me feel good . . .

This typical attitude fits into what we know of the local type of influential. What is more, it suggests that the career function of personal contacts and personal relations is recognized by the local influentials themselves. Nor is this concern with personal contact merely a consequence of the occupations of local influentials. Businessmen, professionals, and local government officials among them all join in the same paeans on the desirability of many and varied contacts. A bank president recapitulates the same story in terms of his experience and outlook:

> I have always been glad to meet people. . . . It really started when I became a teller. The teller is the most important position in a bank as far as meeting people goes. As teller, you must meet everyone. You learn to know everybody by his first name. You don't have the same opportunity again to meet people. Right now we have a teller who is very capable but two or three people have come to me complaining about him. He is unfriendly with them. I told him, you've got to have a kind word for everyone. It's a personal and a business matter.

This keynote brings out the decisive interest of local influentials in all manner of personal contacts which enable them to establish themselves when they need political, business, or other support. Influentials in this group act on the explicit assumption that they can be locally prominent and influential by lining up enough people who know them and are hence willing to help them as well as be helped by them.

The cosmopolitan influentials, on the other hand, have notably little interest in meeting as *many* people as possible.[5] They are more selective in their choice of friends and acquaintances. They typically stress the importance of confining themselves to friends with whom "they can really talk," with whom they can "exchange ideas." If the local influentials are quantitativists, the cosmopolitans are "qualitativists" in this regard. It is not *how many* people they know but the *kind of people* they know that counts.[6]

The contrast with the prevailing attitudes of local influentials is brought out in these remarks by cosmopolitan influentials:

> I don't care to know people unless there is something to the person. I am not interested in quantity. I like to know about other people; it broadens your own education. I enjoy meeting people with knowledge and standing. Masses of humanity I don't go into. I like to meet people of equal mentality, learning and experience.

Just as with the local influentials, so here the basic attitude cuts across occupational and educational lines. Professional men among the cosmopolitans, for example, do not emphasize the importance of a wide and extensive acquaintanceship, if one is to build up a practice. In contrast to a "local" attorney who speaks of the "advantage to me to know as many people as possible," a "cosmopolitan" attorney waxes poetic and exclusive all in one, saying:

> I have never gone out and sought people. I have no pleasure in just going around and calling. As Polonius advised Laertes,
> "Those friends thou hast, and their adoption tried,
> Grapple them to thy soul with hoops of steel,
> But do not dull the palm with entertainment
> Of each new-hatch'd unfledged comrade . . ."

---

[5] This was interestingly confirmed in the following fashion. Our informants were confronted with a random list of names of Rovere residents and were asked to identify each. Local influentials recognized more names than any other group of informants, and cosmopolitans, in turn, knew more persons than the non-influential informants.

[6] In this pilot study, we have confined ourselves to the expression of attitudes toward personal contacts and relations. A detailed inquiry would examine the quantum and quality of *actual* personal relations characteristic of the local and cosmopolitan influentials.

In a later section of this study, we shall see that these diverse orientations of locals and cosmopolitans toward personal relations can be interpreted as a function of their distinctive modes of achieving influence. At the moment, it is sufficient to note that locals seek to enter into manifold networks of personal relations, whereas the cosmopolitans, *on the same status level,* explicitly limit the range of these relations.

PARTICIPATION IN VOLUNTARY ORGANIZATIONS

In considering the "sociability" of locals and cosmopolitans, we examined their attitudes toward informal, personal relationships. But what of their roles in the more formal agencies for social contact: the voluntary organizations?

As might be anticipated, both types of influentials are affiliated with more organizations than rank-and-file members of the population. Cosmopolitan influentials belong to an average of eight organizations per individual, and the local influentials, to an average of six. There is the possibility that cosmopolitans make greater use of organizational channels to influence than of personal contacts, whereas locals, on the whole, operate contrariwise.

But as with sociability, so with organizations: the more instructive facts are qualitative rather than quantitative. It is not so much that the cosmopolitans belong to more organizations than the locals. Should a rigorous inquiry bear out this impression, it would still not locate the strategic organizational differences between the two. It is, rather, that they belong to different types of organizations. And once again, these differences reinforce what we have learned about the two kinds of influentials.

The local influentials evidently crowd into those organizations which are largely designed for "making contacts," for establishing personal ties. Thus, they are found largely in the secret societies (Masons), fraternal organizations (Elks) , and local service clubs—the Rotary, Lions, and the Kiwanis, the most powerful organization of this type in Rovere. Their participation appears to be less a matter of furthering the nominal objectives of these organizations than of using them as *contact centers.* In the forthright words of one local influential, a businessman:

> I get to know people through the service clubs; Kiwanis, Rotary, Lions. I now belong only to the Kiwanis. Kiwanis is different from any other service club. You have to be asked to join. They pick you out first, check you first. Quite a few influential people are there and I get to meet them at lunch every week.

The cosmopolitans, on the other hand, tend to belong to those organizations in which they can exercise their special skills and knowledge. They are found in professional societies and in hobby groups. At the time of the inquiry, in 1943, they were more often involved in civilian defense organizations where again they were presumably more concerned with furthering the objectives of the organization than with establishing personal ties.

Much the same contrast appears in the array of public offices held by the two types of influentials. Seven of each type hold some public office, although the locals have an average somewhat under one office per official. The primary difference is in the *type* of office held. The locals tend to hold political posts—street commissioner, mayor, township board, etc.—ordinarily obtained through political and personal relationships. The cosmopolitans, on the other hand, more often appear in public positions which involve not merely political operations but the utilization of special skills and knowledge (e.g., board of health, housing committee, board of education) .

From all this we can set out the hypothesis that participation in voluntary associations has somewhat different functions for cosmopolitan and local influentials. Cosmopolitans are concerned with associations primarily because of the activities of these organizations. They are means for extending or exhibiting their skills and knowledge. Locals are interested in associations not for their activities, but because these provide a means for extending personal relationships. The basic orientations of locals and cosmopolitan influentials are thus diversely expressed in organizational behavior as in other respects.

AVENUES TO INTERPERSONAL INFLUENCE

The foregoing differences in attachment to Rovere, sociability, and organizational behavior help direct us to the different avenues to influence traveled by the locals and the cosmopolitans. And in mapping these avenues we shall fill in the background needed to interpret the differences in communications behavior characteristic of the two types of influentials.

The locals have largely grown up in and with the town. For the most part, they have gone to school there, leaving only temporarily for their college and professional studies. They held their first jobs in Rovere and earned their first dollars from Rovere people. When they came to work out their career pattern, Rovere was obviously the place in which to do so. It was the only town with which they were thoroughly familiar, in which they knew the ins and outs of politics, business, and social life. It was the only community which they knew and, equally important, which knew them. Here they had developed numerous personal relationships.

And this leads to the decisive attribute of the local influentials' path to success: far more than with the cosmopolitans, *their influence rests on an elaborate network of personal relationships.* In a formula which at once simplifies and highlights the essential fact, we can say: *the influence of local influentials rests not so much on what they know but on whom they know.*

Thus, the concern of the local influential with personal relations is in part the product and in part the instrument of his particular type of influence. The "local boy who makes good," it seems, is likely to make it through good personal relations. Since he is involved in personal relations long before he has entered seriously upon his career, it is the path of less resistance for him to continue to rely upon these relations as far as possible in his later career.

With the cosmopolitan influential, all this changes. Typically a newcomer to the community, he does not and cannot utilize personal ties as his chief claim to attention. He usually comes into the town fully equipped with the prestige and skills associated with his business or profession and his "worldly" experience. He begins his climb in the prestige structure at a relatively high level. It is the prestige of his previous achievements and previously acquired skills which make him eligible for a place in the local influence-structure. Personal relations are much more the product than the instrumentality of his influence.

These differences in the location of career patterns have some interesting consequences for the problems confronting the two types of influentials. First of all, there is some evidence, though far from conclusive, that the rise of the locals to influentiality is slow compared with that of the cosmopolitans. Dr. A, a minister, cosmopolitan, and reader of newsmagazines, remarked upon the ease with which he had made his mark locally:

> The advantage of being a minister is that *you don't have to* prove yourself.
> You are immediately accepted and received in all homes, including the
> best ones. [italics inserted]

However sanguine this observation may be, it reflects the essential point that the newcomer who has "arrived" in the outside world, sooner takes his place among those with some measure of influence in the local community. In contrast, the local influentials *do* "have to prove" themselves. Thus, the local bank president who required some forty years to rise from his job as messenger boy, speaks feelingly of the slow, long road on which "I worked my way up."

The age composition of the local and cosmopolitan influentials is also a straw in the wind with regard to the rate of rise to influence. All but two of the 16 locals are over 45 years of age, whereas fewer than two-thirds of the cosmopolitans are in this older age group.

Not only may the rate of ascent to influence be slower for the local than for the cosmopolitan, but the ascent involves some special difficulties centered about the local's personal relations. It appears that these relations may hinder as well as help the local boy to "make good." He must overcome the obstacle of being intimately known to the community when he was "just a kid." He must somehow enable others to recognize his consistent change in status. Most importantly, people to whom he was once subordinate must be brought to the point of now recognizing him as, in some sense, superordinate. Recognition of this problem is not new. Kipling follows Matthew:13 in observing that "prophets have honour all over the Earth, except in the village where they were born." The problem of ascent in the influence-structure for the home-town individual may be precisely located in sociological terms: change of status within a group, particularly if it is fairly rapid, calls for the revamping of attitudes toward and the remaking of relations with the mobile individual. The pre-existent structure of personal relations for a time thus restrains the ascent of the local influential. Only when he has broken through these established conceptions of him, will others accept the reversal of roles entailed in the rise of the local man to influence. A Rovere attorney, numbered among the local influentials, describes the pattern concisely:

> When I first opened up, people knew me so well in town that they treated me as if I still were a kid. It was hard to overcome. But after I took interest in various public and civic affairs, and became chairman of the Democratic organization and ran for the state legislature—knowing full well I wouldn't be elected—they started to take me seriously.

The cosmopolitan does not face the necessity for breaking down local preconceptions of himself before it is possible to have his status as an influential "taken seriously." As we have seen, his credentials are found in the prestige and authority of his attainments elsewhere. He thus manifests less interest in a wide range of personal contacts for two reasons. First, his influence stems from prestige rather than from reciprocities with others in the community. Secondly, the problem of disengaging himself from obsolete images of him as "a boy" does not exist for him, and consequently does not focus his attention upon personal relations as it does for the local influential.

The separate roads to influence traveled by the locals and cosmopolitans thus help account for their diverging orientations toward the local community, with all that these orientations entail.

SOCIAL STATUS IN ACTION: INTERPERSONAL INFLUENCE

At this point, it may occur to the reader that the distinction between the local and cosmopolitan influentials is merely a reflection of differences in education or occupation. This does not appear to be the case.

It is true that the cosmopolitans among our interviewees have received more formal education than the locals. All but one of the cosmopolitans as compared with half of the locals are at least graduates of high school. It is also true that half of the locals are in "big business," as gauged by Rovere standards, whereas only two of the 14 cosmopolitans fall in this group; and furthermore, that half of the cosmopolitan influentials are professional people as compared with fewer than a third of the locals.

But these differences in occupational or educational status do not appear to determine the diverse types of influentials. When we compare the behavior and orientations of professionals among the locals and cosmopolitans, their characteristic differences persist, even though they have the same types of occupation and have received the same type of education. Educational and occupational differences may *contribute* to the differences between the two types of influentials but they are not the *source* of these differences. Even as a professional, the local influential is more of a businessman and politician in his behavior and outlook than is the cosmopolitan. He utilizes personal relationships as an avenue to influence conspicuously more than does his cosmopolitan counterpart. In short, *it is the pattern of utilizing social status and not the formal contours of the status itself which is decisive.*[7]

While occupational status may be a major support for the cosmopolitan's rise to influence, it is merely an adjunct for the local. Whereas all five of the local professionals actively pursue local politics, the cosmopolitan professionals practically ignore organized political activity in Rovere. (Their offices tend to be honorary appointments.) Far from occupation serving to explain the differences between them, it appears that the same occupation has a different role in interpersonal influence according to whether it is pursued by a local or a cosmopolitan. This bears out our earlier impression that "objective attributes" (education, occupation, etc.) do not suffice as indices of people exercising interpersonal influence.

The influential businessman, who among our small number of inter-

---

[7] The importance of actively seeking influence is evident from an analysis of "the upward mobile type," set forth in the monograph upon which this report is based. See also Granville Hicks, *Small Town* (New York: Crowell Collier and Macmillan, Inc., 1946), p. 154, who describes a local influential in these terms: "He is a typical politician, a born manipulator, a man who worships influence, *works hard to acquire it,* and does his best to convince other people that he has it." (Italics supplied)

viewees is found almost exclusively among the locals, typically utilizes his personal relations to enhance his influence. It is altogether likely that a larger sample would include businessmen who are cosmopolitan influentials and whose behavior differs significantly in this respect. Thus, Mr. H., regarded as exerting great influence in Rovere, illustrates the cosmopolitan big-business type. He arrived in Rovere as a top executive in a local manufacturing plant. He has established few personal ties. But he is sought out for advice precisely because he has "been around" and has the aura of a man familiar with the outside world of affairs. His influence rests upon an imputed expertness rather than upon sympathetic understanding of others.

This adds another dimension to the distinction between the two types of influential. It appears that the cosmopolitan influential has a following because *he knows;* the local influential, because *he understands.* The one is sought out for his specialized skills and experience; the other, for his intimate appreciation of intangible but affectively significant details. The two patterns are reflected in prevalent conceptions of the difference between "the extremely competent but impersonal medical specialist" and the "old family doctor." Or again, it is not unlike the difference between the "impersonal social welfare worker" and the "friendly precinct captain." It is not merely that the local political captain provides food-baskets and jobs, legal and extra-legal advice, that he sets to rights minor scrapes with the law, helps the bright poor boy to a political scholarship in a local college, looks after the bereaved—that he helps in a whole series of crises when a fellow needs a friend, and, above all, a friend who "knows the score" and can do something about it. It is not merely that he provides aid which gives him interpersonal influence. It is *the manner in which the aid is provided.* After all, specialized agencies do exist for dispensing this assistance. Welfare agencies, settlement houses, legal aid clinics, hospital clinics, public relief departments—these and many other organizations are available. But in contrast to the professional techniques of the welfare worker which often represent in the mind of the recipient the cold, bureaucratic dispensation of limited aid following upon detailed investigation are the unprofessional techniques of the precinct captain who asks no questions, exacts no compliance with legal rules of eligibility and does not "snoop" into private affairs. The precinct captain is a prototype of the "local" influential.

Interpersonal influence stemming from specialized expertness typically involves some social distance between the advice-giver and the advice-seeker, whereas influence stemming from sympathetic understanding typically entails close personal relations. The first is the pattern of the cosmopolitan influential; the second, of the local influential. Thus, the operation of these patterns of influence gives a clue to the distinctive orientations of the two types of influential.

* * *

SPHERES OF INFLUENCE: MONOMORPHIC AND POLYMORPHIC

In Rovere, influentials differ widely with respect to the *number of spheres* of activity in which they exert interpersonal influence. Some influentials, and these may be termed *monomorphic,* are repeatedly cited as exerting influence, but only in one rather narrowly defined area—e.g., the area of politics, *or* of canons of good taste, *or* of fashion. The monomorphic influentials are the "experts" in a limited field, and their influence does not diffuse into other spheres of decision. Others, and this includes a good number of the top influentials, are *polymorphic,* exerting interpersonal influence in a variety of (sometimes seemingly unrelated) spheres. Although the types were readily identifiable in the Rovere study, much remains to be learned about them. Above all, the dynamics of these types needs to be established. Under which conditions does the influential remain monomorphic? Is this a stable type—or, is it rather a *stage* in the development of influence, such that the monomorphic in due course tends to become polymorphic through the operation of the transfer of prestige from one sphere to others (the "halo effect")? Perhaps monomorphic influence occurs only in certain spheres involving high specialization of skill and little public recognition. Under such conditions, a monomorphic influential—the biophysicist, for example—may be asked for advice only on matters touching upon his special sphere of competence—"what should we do about a National Science Foundation?"—and his influence may be such that monomorphic influence soon gives way to the polymorphic exercise of interpersonal influence in diverse respects: "authority" may be generalized and transferred.

We may go on to inquire into the comparative number of spheres in which the local and the cosmopolitan influentials are effective. One gains the impression from the Rovere materials that locals and cosmopolitans not only exert influence in different spheres, but also that the locals are the more likely to be polymorphic and the cosmopolitans, monomorphic. Apparently, the influence of the locals, based largely on their personal "connections," ramifies into many and diverse spheres; influence of the cosmopolitans, more often stemming from certain types of seeming expertness, tends to be more narrowly circumscribed.

So, too, it will be instructive to learn whether the *same* individuals exert monomorphic influence upon some persons and polymorphic influences upon others. It may turn out, for example, that influentials advising people of their own social statum characteristically do so in a variety of fields whereas they are influential for a more limited range of decisions for followers of a lower social stratum. However this may be, it should not be assumed that *individuals* "are" monomorphic or polymorphic, but rather that they *operate* as the one type or the other, according to the structure of the situation.

All this highlights the need to clarify such terms as "men of influence" or "opinion-leaders." An individual may be regarded as influential when he has a large following in one sphere of activity just as another may be so regarded because he has several small followings in diverse spheres. Further inquiry into interpersonal influence must seek to identify the monomorphic and polymorphic influentials, locate these within the local social structure and establish the dynamics of change from one type to the other.

A final suggestion is needed for future studies into the interpersonal influence-structure of a community. This preliminary inquiry strongly suggests (and this is borne out by the Southtown study) that formal criteria such as education, income, participation in voluntary organizations, number of references in the local newspaper and the like,[8] do not provide adequate indicators of those individuals who exert a significant measure of interpersonal influence. Systematic interviewing supplemented by direct observation are required. Otherwise put, location within various social hierarchies of wealth, power, and "class" does not predetermine location within a local structure of interpersonal influence.

---

[8] Influence through mass media is patently not the same as interpersonal influence. It is suggestive, for example, that neither in Rovere nor in Frank Stewart's Southtown was the editor of the local newspaper included among those exerting appreciable interpersonal influence.

31. The Vitality of
Community Culture

HERBERT J. GANS

Leading with their assumption of homogeneity and conformity, many critics see the culture of communities like Levittown—those features transcending social life—as marked by sameness, dullness, and blandness. The image of sameness derives from the mass-produced housing, and also from the prevalence of a national and equally mass-produced culture of consumer goods which is extended to characterize the consumers themselves. Part of the critique is tinged with political fear that the national culture and the deleterious effects of conformity may sap the strength of local organizations, which will in turn break down the community social structures that act as barriers between the individual and the state. According to theorists of the mass society, the individual then becomes submissive and subject to demagoguery that can incite mass hysteria and mob action, destroying the checks and balances of a democratic society. This hypothesis, developed originally by Ortega y Gasset, the Spanish conservative philosopher who feared popular democracy, gained prominence during the 1930s when Hitler and Stalin systematically eliminated local organizations to forestall opposition to their plans. In America, this

SOURCE: Reprinted with permission of the author and publisher from *The Levittowners—Ways of Life and Politics in a New Suburban Community* (New York: Random House, Inc., 1967).

analysis has flowered with the increasing centralization of the federal government, but suburbia is considered particularly susceptible to the dangers of mass society because of the rootlessness and absence of community strength supposedly induced by the large number of transients.[1] Other observers, less fearful of mass society, stress the blandness of suburban life, which, they fear, is producing dull and apathetic individuals.[2]

These charges are serious and, if accurate, would suggest that suburbia is a danger to American democracy and culture. Most of them, however, are either inaccurate or, when accurate, without the negative consequences attributed to them. Levittown is very much a local community; if anything, it neglects its ties to the larger society more than it should. It is not rootless, even with its transients, and it is not dull, except to its teenagers. The critics' conclusions stem in part from the previously mentioned class and cultural differences between them and the suburbanites. What they see as blandness and apathy is really a result of the invisibility and home-centeredness of lower middle class culture, and what they consider dullness derives from their cosmopolitan standard for judging communities, which condemns those lacking urban facilities—ranging from museums to ethnic districts—that are favored by the upper middle class.

They also look at suburbia as outsiders, who approach the community with a "tourist" perspective. The tourist wants visual interest, cultural diversity, entertainment, esthetic pleasure, variety (preferably exotic), and emotional stimulation. The resident, on the other hand, wants a comfortable, convenient, and socially satisfying place to live—esthetically pleasing, to be sure, but first and foremost functional for his daily needs. Much of the critique of suburbs as community reflects the critics' disappointment that the new suburbs do not satisfy their particular tourist requirements; that they are not places for wandering, that they lack the charm of a medieval village, the excitement of a metropolis, or the architectural variety of an upper-income suburb. Even so, tourism cuts across all classes. A neighbor, returning from a trip to Niagara Falls, complained bitterly about commercialization, using much the same language as the critics do about suburbia. What he felt about the Falls, however, he did not feel about Levittown.

---

[1] See, e.g., Erich Fromm, *The Sane Society* (New York: Holt, Rinehart and Winston, 1955), pp. 154–163; and Maurice Stein, *The Eclipse of Community* (Princeton: Princeton University Press, 1960), Chaps. 9 & 12.

[2] This charge is made by John Keats, *The Crack in the Picture Window* (Boston: Houghton Mifflin, 1956) and, in more qualified and muted tones, by David Riesman, "The Suburban Dislocation," *The Annals*, CCCXIV, Fall 1957, 123–146.

We are all tourists at one time or another, but most communities can serve both tourist and residential functions only with difficulty. For example, the crowding and nightlife that attract the tourist to Greenwich Village make it uncomfortable for the resident. Although the tourist perspective is understandable, and even justifiable, it is not by itself a proper criterion for evaluating a community, especially a purely residential one like Levittown. It must be judged first by the quality of community life and culture it offers its residents; the needs of the tourist are secondary.

THE NATIONAL CULTURE AND THE COMMUNITY

To the outside observer, Levittown appears to be a community on which the national American culture has been imprinted so totally as to leave little room for local individuality. The houses express the current national residential style: pseudo-Colonial fronts borrowed from the eighteenth century glued on a variety of single-family house styles developed between the eighteenth and twentieth centuries, and hiding twentieth century interiors. Schools are contemporary, modular, one-story buildings that look like all other new schools. The shopping center is typical too, although the interior is more tastefully designed than most. It consists mainly of branches of large national chains, whose inventory is dominated by prepackaged national brands, and the small centers are no different. The old "Mom and Pop" grocery has been replaced by the "7 to 11" chain, which, as its name indicates, opens early and closes late, but sells only prepackaged goods so that each store can be serviced by a single cashier-clerk. Even the Jewish and Italian foods sold at the "delis" are cut from the loaf of a "pan-ethnic" culture that is now nationally distributed.

A large, partially preplanned residential development must almost inevitably depend on national organizations, since these are the only ones that can afford the initial capital investment and the unprofitable hiatus before the community is large enough to support them properly. This is as true of stores in a new shopping center—which sometimes wait years before they show a profit—as it is of churches and voluntary organizations. In addition, Levittown itself is in some ways a national brand, for the size of Levitt's operation in an industry of small entrepreneurs has made his communities a national symbol of low-price suburbia. This has helped to attract national organizations, as well as transients who work for large national corporations. When they move into a new metropolitan area, they usually do not know where to find housing, and having heard of Levittown, are likely to look there first. The brand name "Levittown" makes the housing more trustworthy than a small subdivision constructed by an unknown local builder.

Although Levittown would thus seem to be, as much as any community in America, an example of Big Culture, this is only superficially true, for the quality of life in Levittown retains a strictly local and often anti-national flavor, exploiting national bodies and resources for strictly local purposes whenever possible. To the visitor, the Levittown houses may look like all other pseudo-Colonial ones in South Jersey, but Levittowners can catalog the features that distinguish their houses from those in nearby subdivisions. The stores may be chains selling brand-name goods, but the managers become involved in local activities and enable local groups to hold bazaars and other fund-raising affairs, including bake sales which compete with store merchandise. The same patterns obtain in voluntary associations and churches. For example, the Boy Scouts are run by an intricate national bureaucracy which sets detailed rules for the activities of local troops. Since the organization must attract children, however, what actually goes on at troop meetings bears little resemblance to the rules, and the less the national office knows, the better for it and the troop leader.

The priority of local concerns is even more emphatic in government, for federal agencies and national party headquarters are viewed mainly as sources of funds and power to be used for local needs. A civil defense agency was set up in Levittown, not to satisfy national regulations, but because the county civil defense director was running for political office. The national program provided him an opportunity to distribute some funds to local communities, which in turn enhanced his political fortunes. Federal funds which came to Levittown for civil defense were used for local police and fire needs as much as possible within the limits of the law. Similarly, when the township committee in 1960 invited both Nixon and Kennedy to campaign in Levittown, its purpose was not to support the national candidates of the two parties but to gain publicity for Levittown.

Many Levittowners work in branch offices or factories of national corporations, and their reports about their work and their employers suggest that national directives are often viewed as outlandish and unreasonable, to be sabotaged in favor of local priorities. However much a national corporation may give the appearance of a well-run and thoroughly centralized monolith, in actual fact it is often a shaky aggregate of local baronies. The result is considerable skepticism among Levittowners about the effectiveness and power of national corporations, a skepticism easily extended to all national agencies.

Generally speaking, Levittowners do not take much interest in the national society, and rarely even see its influence on their lives. As long as they are employed, healthy, and able to achieve a reasonable proportion of their personal goals, they have no need for the federal government or any other national agency, and being locals, they do not concern themselves with the world outside their community. Indeed, they might better be described as *sublocals*, for they are home-oriented rather than community-oriented. Although the lower middle class is somethimes said to reject bigness, the Levittowners do not share this feeling. They do not scorn big supermarkets and national brands as do the critics, and although they do not see the big society very clearly, it appears to them as an inept octopus which can only cope with the community through force or bribery. It is opposed not because of its size, but because it is an outsider. When a national service club organized a branch in Levittown, one of the Levittowners said, "They are big and they can help us, but we don't have to follow national policy. . . . National headquarters is only a racket that takes your money." The cultural orientation toward localism is supported by more pressing sociological factors; if a local branch of a national association is to succeed, it must adapt itself to local priorities in order to attract members, and national headquarters must be opposed if it refuses to go along. The most disliked outsider is not the national society, however, but the cosmopolitan with his "Brookline values."

All this does not, of course, imply that the national society and culture are powerless in Levittown. When industrial giants set administered prices for consumer goods sold in the local shopping center, or when Detroit engineers the annual style change in its automobiles, the individual purchaser can only express his discontent by refusal to buy, and when it comes to necessities, he lacks even that choice. In Levittown, however, the discontent and the lack of choice are minimized, for most people have enough money to pay administered prices and enough freedom to choose among products. In fact, they find themselves well served by the corporations who sell them their housing, food, furnishings, and transportation. However, Levittowners are less concerned with "consumption" than the critics. They care less about the things they buy and are less interested in asserting individuality through consumer behavior, for they do not use consumption to express class values as much as the upper middle class does. They may not like mass-produced bread as well as the local bakery product they perhaps ate in childhood, but they do not make an issue of it, and do not feel themselves to be mass men simply because they buy a mass-produced item. Goods are just not important enough. Only when they become tourists are they "materialistic"—and traditional. One of my neighbors who was once stationed in Japan was not at all concerned about the national prepackaged brands sold in Levittown, but talked frequently about the commercialization of Japanese culture and the unattractive goods he found in the souvenir shops.

THE MASS MEDIA

For Levittowners, probably the most enduring—and certainly the most frequent—tie to the national culture is through the mass media. Yet even this is filtered through a variety of personal predispositions so that not many messages reach the receiver intact. Few people are dominated by the mass media; they provide escape from boredom, fill up brief intervals, and (perhaps most important) occupy the children while the adults go about their business.

The most frequently used mass medium is television, with newspapers, magazines, and paperback novels following in that order. In working class homes in Levittown as elsewhere, the TV set is likely to be on all the time, even when company comes, for as one Levittowner explained, "If conversation lags, people can watch or it gives you something to talk about." This statement suggests more the fears that working class people have about their social skills than their practice, for conversation does not often lag, at least among friends.

Middle class people, surer of their social skills, use television more selectively. The children watch when they have come in from play; after they are put to bed the adults may turn on the set, for television fills the hours between 9 P.M. and bedtime, when there is not enough of a block of time for other activities. A few favorite programs may get rapt attention, but I doubt that television supplanted conversation among either middle or working class Levittowners. There is no indication that television viewing increased after people moved to Levittown, for no one mentioned it when interviewed about changes in spare-time activities. I suspect that viewing had actually decreased somewhat, at least during the time of my study, when gardening was still a time-consuming novelty for many people.

Television viewing is also a much less passive activity than the critics of the mass media suspect.[3] Routine serials and situation comedies evoke little response, although Levittowners are sensitive to anachronisms in the plots and skeptical of advertising claims.[4] Dramatic programs may provoke spirited—and quite personal—reactions. For example, one eve-

---

[3] This cannot be surmised either from inferences about media content or from sociological surveys, but becomes quite evident when one watches TV with other people, as I did with my neighbors.

[4] I had observed the same reactions among the working class Bostonians I studied previously, although they were more interested in the performers than the Levittowners. Herbert J. Gans, *The Urban Villagers: Group and Class in the Life of Italian-Americans* (New York: The Free Press, 1962).

ning my neighbors and I watched an hour-long drama which depicted the tragic career of an introverted girl who wanted desperately to become a serious actress but was forced to work as a rock-and-roll dancer, and finally decided to give up show business. One neighbor missed the tragedy altogether, and thought the girl should have kept on trying to become an actress. The other neighbor fastened on—and approved of— the ending (in which the actress returned to her husband and to the family restaurant in which she had been "discovered") and wondered, rightly, whether it was possible to go back to a mundane life after the glamor of the entertainment world.

People do not necessarily know what they want from the media, but they know what they do not want and trust their ability to choose correctly. A discussion of television critics one night revealed that Levittowners read their judgments, but do not necessarily accept them. "The critics see so much that they cannot give us much advice," said one. "They are too different in their interests from the audience, and cannot be reviewers for it," said another.

Forty percent of the people interviewed said they were reading new magazines since moving to Levittown; general-interest periodicals—*Life, Look, Reader's Digest, Time,* and the *Saturday Evening Post*—led the list. Only 9 of the 52 magazines were house-and-garden types such as *American Home* and *Better Homes and Gardens,* but then 88 percent of the people were already reading these, at least in the year they moved to Levittown. Although not a single person said these magazines had helped in the decision to buy a home in Levittown, 57 percent reported that they had gotten ideas from the magazines to try out in their houses, primarily on the use of space, furniture, and shrubbery arrangements, what to do about pictures and drapes, and how to build shelves and patios. The magazines provided help on functional rather than esthetic problems of fixing up the new house. People rarely copied something directly from the magazines, however. Most often, their reading gave them ideas which they then altered for their own use, sometimes after talking them over with the neighbors. Similarly, people who adopted new furniture styles after moving to Levittown got their inspiration from their neighbors rather than from magazines, although all who changed styles (but only 53 percent who did not) said they had obtained some hints for the house from the home and garden magazines.

The media also provide "ideas" for community activities, but these are altered by local considerations and priorities. For example, a few days after the Nixon-Kennedy television debates in 1960, candidates for township offices were asked to participate in a similar debate in Levittown. Everyone liked the idea, but after a few innocuous questions by out-of-town reporters, the debate turned into the traditional candidates night, in which politicians from both parties baited their opponents from the audience with prepared questions. Sometimes, local organizations put on versions of TV quiz games, and honored retiring officers with a "This Is Your Life" presentation. A few clubs, especially Jewish ones, held "beatnik" parties, but since most Levittowners had never seen a beatnik, the inspiration for their costumes came from the mass media.

The impact of the media is most apparent among children; they are easily impressed by television commercials, and mothers must often fight off their demands on shopping trips. But the adults are seldom touched deeply; media content is always secondary to more personal experience. For example, people talked about articles on child-rearing they had seen in popular magazines, but treated them as topics of conversation rather than as possible guides for their own behavior. A neighbor who had read that "permissive" child-rearing was going out of style after thirty years had never even heard of it before, even though she had gone to college. I remember discussing Cuba with another neighbor, an air force officer, shortly after Castro confiscated American property there. Although he had been telling me endless and angry stories about being exploited by his superiors and about corruption among high-ranking officers, he could not see the similarity between his position and that of the Cuban peasant under Batista, and argued strenuously that Castro should be overthrown. His opinions reflected those of the media, but their content did not interest him enough to relate it to his own experiences. He did, however, feel that Castro had insulted the United States—and him personally—and the media helped him belong to the national society in this way. Indeed, the media are a message from that society, which, like all others, remains separate from the more immediate realities of self, family, home, and friends. These messages really touch only the people who feel isolated from local groups or who, like the cosmopolitans, pay close attention to the printed word and the screen image.

LEVITTOWN AND THE MASS SOCIETY

The Levittowners' local orientation will not prevent them from becoming submissive tools of totalitarian demagogues if, according to the critics of mass society, the community is too weak to defy the power of the state. Social scientists concerned about the danger of dictatorship have often claimed, with De Toqueville, that the voluntary association is the prime bulwark against it. For example, Wilensky writes: "In the absence of effective mediating ties, of meaningful participation in voluntary associations, the population becomes vulnerable to mass behavior, more susceptible to personality appeals in politics, more ready for the demagogues who exploit fanatical faiths of nation and race."[5]

If Wilensky is correct, Levittowners should be invulnerable to mass behavior, for they have started about a hundred voluntary associations and 73 percent of the two interview samples belong to at least one. Levittown should also be more immune than other communities, for about half of both interview samples reported more organizational participation than in the former residence.[6] The way they participate, however, has little consequence for their relation to the national society. The handful of leaders and really active people become familiar with the mechanics of organizational and municipal politics, but the rank-and-file members, coming to meetings mainly for social and service reasons, are rarely involved in these matters. Yet not even the active participants are exposed to national issues and questions, and they learn little about the ways of coping with the manipulatory techniques feared by the critics of mass society.

Nor does participation necessarily provide democratic experience. Organizations with active membership are likely to have democratic politics, but when the membership is passive, they are often run by an individual or a clique and there is little demand for democratic procedure. Nothing in the nature of the voluntary association would, however, preclude mob behavior and mass hysteria when the members demand it. The ad hoc groups that arose during the school budget fight and in the controversies over liquor, nonresident doctors, and fluoridation, often acted in near-hysterical ways. Admittedly, these were temporary organizations; permanent ones, conscious of their image, are more likely to refrain from such behavior and, like political parties, often avoid taking stands on controversial issues. They do inhibit mob action—or, rather, they refuse to be associated with it, forcing it into temporary organizations. Yet if the majority of a permanent group's membership is angry about an issue, it can act out that anger and even put its organizational strength behind hysteria. At the time of racial integration, a sizable faction in one of the men's groups was contemplating quasi-violent protest, and was restrained as much by pressure from the

---

[5] Harold L. Wilensky, "Life Cycle, Work Situation and Participation in Formal Associations," in Robert W. Kleemeier, ed., *Aging and Leisure* (New York: Oxford University Press, 1961), p. 237. See also William Kornhauser, *Politics of Mass Society* (New York: The Free Press, 1959), Chap. 3; and S. M. Lipset, *Political Man* (Garden City: Doubleday & Co., Inc., 1960), pp. 66–67.

[6] Fifty-six percent of the random sample and 44 percent of the city sample reported more participation than previously.

churches, the builder, and some government officials as by cooler heads within the group.

Mob action and mass hysteria are usually produced by intense clashes of interest between citizens and government agencies, especially if government is not responsive to citizens' demands. If an issue is especially threatening and other avenues for coping with it are blocked, irrational action is often the only solution. Under such conditions, voluntary associations can do little to quell it, partly because they have no direct role in the government, but mainly because their impact on their membership is, in Wilensky's terms, not meaningful enough to divert members from affiliating with violent protest groups. Even national officers of voluntary associations can rarely control irrational actions by local branches, especially since these rarely come to "national's" attention.

The other relationships of the individual Levittowner vis-à-vis the national society are so indirect that it would be hard to pinpoint where and how the two confront each other. It would be harder still to convince the average Levittowner, locally oriented as he is, to change his stance. Unlike the aristocrat or the intellectual, who was once able as an individual to influence the national society and still attempts to do so, the Levittowners come from a tradition—and from ancestors—too poor or too European even to conceive the possibility that they could affect their nation. And unlike the cosmopolitans of today, they have not yet learned that they ought to try. As a result, the Levittowner is not likely to act unless and until national issues impinge directly on his life. When this does happen, he is as frustrated as the cosmopolitan about how to be effective. All he can really do is voice his opinion at the ballot box, write letters to his congressman, or join protest groups. In times of crisis, none of these can change the situation quickly enough, and this of course exacerbates threat, hysteria, and the urge toward mob action or scapegoating.

The national society and the state have not impinged negatively on the average Levittowner, however; indeed, they have served him well, making him generally content with the status quo. The Congress is dominated by the localistic and other values of the white lower middle and working class population, and since the goods and services provided by the influential national corporations are designed largely for people like the Levittowners, they have little reason to question corporate behavior. The considerable similarity of interests between Levittowners and the nationally powerful agencies, private and public, makes it unnecessary for the Levittowners to concern themselves with the national society or to delude themselves about the sovereignty of the local community.[7]

---

[7] In this respect, the Levittowners differed significantly from the residents of Spring-

What appears as apathy to the critics of suburban life is satisfaction with the way things are going, and what is interpreted as a "retreat" into localism and familism is just ahistorical thinking. Most lower middle and working class people have always been localistic and familistic; even during the Depression they joined unions only when personal economic difficulties gave them no other alternative, becoming inactive once these were resolved or when it was clear that political activity was fruitless.[8] Indeed, the alleged retreat is actually an advance, for the present generation, especially among working class people, is less isolated from the larger society than its parents, less suspicious, and more willing to believe that it can participate in the community and the larger society. The belief is fragile and rarely exercised, but people like the Levittowners confront the national society more rationally than their ancestors did, and if the signs of progress are few, progress has nevertheless taken place. Whether there has been enough progress to prevent the emergence of dictatorship in a severe national crisis is hard to tell, but certainly the Levittowners and their community fit few of the prerequisites that would make them willing tools of totalitarian leaders today.

---

dale, a rural community in New York State, who developed a set of illusions to hide their dependence on state and national political and economic forces. See Arthur J. Vidich and Joseph Bensman, *Small Town in Mass Society* (Princeton: Princeton University Press, 1958).

[8] Part of the difficulty is that critics compare the present generation to the previous generation, that of the Depression, which was an unusual period in American history and no baseline for historical comparisons of any kind.

CHAPTER VI

Economic Pressures
from the
Vertical Community

Economic pressure from the vertical community is generally the first influence which the local community experiences as it loses its isolation and gets involved in the larger world. This pressure may take the form of the locally-owned and run industry being bought out, or perhaps forced out of business, by a large corporation; or it may appear as chain stores and absentee-owned shopping centers that threaten local merchants. New managers with "big city notions" begin to replace local bosses who operated in a personalistic manner, and the whole tenor of community economic matters changes from the familiar, low pressure ways of the small town, to those of bureaucratic organizations that stress efficiency. As the readings that follow demonstrate, changes in the economic sphere of community life have ramifications for the social-political sphere as well.

In their study of Springdale, Vidich and Bensman were concerned with the impact of "mass society" on the local community. Springdale found itself dependent on outside forces that it was helpless to influence. Those members of the community most favorably linked to the mass society were socially, economically, and politically ascendant, whereas the true "locals" found themselves losing ground through no apparent fault of their own. The result was that the local community resented those very forces to which it had become dependent, a condition that Vidich and Bensman called "rural ambivalence." Inasmuch as this ambivalent state was also observed in several other communities, including Yankee City and Cornucopia which are not rural, we feel that a more general term—"vertical ambivalence"—would be appropriate to describe the frustration that the horizontal community experiences in its dealings with the vertical community.

The controls on the local community exercised by extra-community, or vertical influences, may be formal or informal as Warren demonstrates in a brief article on "Dairyville." Along with his discussion of how extra-community controls affected Dairyville, Warren presents a useful typology of community affiliations.

The portion of the Yankee City study that is included here deals with the effect on the community of the local shoe industry changing hands. From locally owned firms run by men who were locally oriented and highly involved in community affairs, Yankee City experienced a transition to absentee-owned plants which were but a rung in a nationally-based corporate ladder, run by impersonal managers who were not concerned with local affairs. This transition dealt a severe blow to the local way of life that led to rancorous conflict.

Cibola, the community studied by Schulze, experienced a similar change in its economy. Although rancorous conflict did not occur, mainly because the transition was much more gradual than occurred in Yankee City, the effect on Cibola's social-political structure was equally dramatic. A bifurcation of power occurred in which the economic dominants—absentee managers who did not get involved in local affairs, and social-political leaders who were "locals"—operated in separate spheres. Although the local social-political sphere was actually dependent on the actions of the economic dominants, little influence was wielded by the absentee-managers who virtually ignored local affairs.

Cibola is compared to Wheelsburg by Clelland and Form with similar findings reported for both communities. As in Cibola, the power structure of Wheelsburg bifurcated with the managers of absentee-owned corporations dominating economic matters, while social-political affairs remained in the hands of local figures. However, the bifurcation of Wheelsburg was not nearly so complete as what occurred in Cibola. The authors suggest that other community variables, such as the fact that whereas Cibola was a satellite of a large metropolis, Wheelsburg was an independent community, might explain the differences found.

The influence of the community's economic structure in shaping social-political affairs is shown in the editor's study of Cornucopia. By studying the community at three stages in time, we find that different power structures emerge depending on the industrial structure that existed at that time. Local ownership of the town's major industry produced a pyramidal power structure in which both spheres were dominated by the factory owner. With the closing of the dominant industry a condition of uncertain dominance resulted and a factional power structure emerged. It was not until a large absentee-owned corporation located in Cornucopia that the pattern of bifurcation along the lines observed in both Cibola and Wheelsburg became apparent. We suggest that the reason why this bifurcation occurs can be ascertained by looking at the absentee-manager's role. Unlike local figures whose lives are linked to the community, the absentee-manager is linked to the corporation and thus to the vertical community. They must be "cosmopolitans," using Merton's criteria, because of the nature of their professional role.

32. Springdale and the Mass Society

ARTHUR J. VIDICH
JOSEPH BENSMAN

Springdale is connected with the mass society in a variety of different forms. The cumulative effect of these various connections makes possible the continuous transmission of outside policies, programs and trends into the community, even though the effects of the transmission and the transmitting agents themselves are not always seen. Outside influences can be transmitted directly by a socially visible agent such as the extension specialist who lives in the community for the purpose of acting upon it. Outside interests and influences can also be expressed indirectly through members of the community: policies and programs of relatively invisible outside interests are transmitted by heads of local branches of state and national organizations, by heads of local businesses dependent on outside resources and by heads of churches attached to larger organizations. In some instances the community is affected by the consequences of decisions made by business and government which are made with specific reference to the community, i.e., the decision to build a state road through the community or the decision to close down a factory. Plans and decisions that refer directly to the community are made from a distance

SOURCE: *Small Town in Mass Society* (Princeton, N. J.: Princeton University Press, 1958). Reprinted by permission of Princeton University Press.

by invisible agents and institutions. Perhaps most important are the mass decisions of business and government which are transmitted to the rural scene by the consequences of changes in prices, costs and communications. These affect the town even though they are not explicitly directed at it, and they comprise the invisible social chain reactions of decisions that are made in centers of power in government, business and industry. The invisible social chain reactions emanating from the outside no doubt alter the life of the community more seriously than the action of visible agents such as the extension specialist.

These types of transmission do not represent mutually exclusive channels, but rather exist in complex interrelationship with each other. They merely suggest the major ways in which the community is influenced by dynamics which occur in the institutions of mass society. How these combined dynamics in their various combinations affect the fabric of life in Springdale can be seen by examining the way in which cultural importations and economic and political connections shape the character of community life. In their net effect they influence the psychological dimensions of the community.

CULTURAL IMPORTATIONS FROM MASS SOCIETY

The external agents of cultural diffusion range from specific observable individuals placed in the local community by outside institutions to the impact of mass media of communications and successive waves of migration. The consequence of these modes of diffusion lies in the effect which they have on local styles of living.

FORMAL IMPORTING ORGANIZATIONS

The adult extension program of the land grant college is mediated at the local level by the county agent and the home demonstration agent who respectively are concerned with farming methods and production, and patterns of homemaking and family life. These agents carry out their program through the Farm and Home Bureau organizations. In Springdale township these agencies have a membership of 300-400 adults. The county agent is primarily concerned with introducing modern methods of farm production and operation and with fostering political consciousness among the farmers. As a type of executive secretary to the local Farm Bureau whose officers are local farmers, the agent acts as an advisor in planning the organization's program, which includes such items as production and marketing problems, parity price problems and taxation problems.

The organizational structure of the Home Bureau parallels the Farm Bureau. From skills and techniques and personnel available at the extension center, local programs consist, for example, of furniture refinishing or aluminum working as well as discussions on such topics as child-rearing, nutrition, penal institutions and interior design. The Home Bureau extension specialist trains a local woman in information and techniques which are reported back to the local club. This program, geared as it is to modern homemaking, child-rearing and the feminine role, has the effect of introducing new styles and standards of taste and consumption for the membership.

Other institutional connectors similar to the above in organizational structure account for the introduction of still other social values and social definitions. The 4-H Club, the Future Farmers of America and the Boy and Girl Scouts, as well as the Masons, Odd Fellows, American Legion, Grange and other local branches of national organizations and their auxiliaries, relate the Springdaler to the larger society through the social meanings and styles of activity defined in the programs, procedures and rituals of the national headquarters. State and national conventions, but not office holding, of these as well as church organizations directly link individuals to the outside. In effect these arrangements regularize and institutionalize the communication and organizational nexus between the small town and the point of origin of new ideas and values.

New cultural standards are also imported by agents who are not permanent residents of the town or who have only a transient relationship with it. These include the teachers at the central school, many of whom view their jobs as a temporary interlude in a progression of experience which will lead to a position in a city system. The other agents of contact are a wide variety of salesmen and "experts" who have a regular or irregular contact with business, government and private organizations. From the surrounding urban centers and the regional sales offices of farm implement and automobile manufacturers and nationally branded products, modern methods of merchandising and business practice are introduced. Experts in civil defense, evangelism, fire-fighting, gardening, charity drives, traffic control and youth recreation introduce new techniques and programs to the local community. This great variety and diversity of semi-permanent and changing contacts in their cumulative effect act as a perpetual blood transfusion to local society. The net effect that these agents have as transmitters of life styles depends in a measure on their position and prestige in the community. The differential effect of these cultural contacts is treated below.

THE UBIQUITY OF MASS MEDIA

Social diffusion through the symbols and pictorial images of the mass media of communications has permeated the community, reducing the local paper to reporting of social items and local news already known by everyone. Few individuals read only the local weekly paper; the majority subscribe to dailies published in surrounding cities and in the large metropolitan areas. This press, itself part of larger newspaper combines, presents an image of the passing scene in its news and national syndicated features to which the population of an entire region is exposed.

The mass culture and mass advertising of television and radio reach Springdale in all their variety. Television, particularly, is significant in its impact because for the first time the higher art forms such as ballet, opera and plays are visible to a broad rural audience. National events such as party conventions, inaugurations and investigative hearings are visible now to an audience which was previously far removed from the national centers of action and drama. Because of the relative geographic isolation of Springdale, television has made available entirely new areas of entertainment, information and education. It has created new leisure-time interests, has introduced new modes of leisure-time consumption and has led to the acceptance of standardized entertainment models. Wrestling, Arthur Godfrey and Howdy Doody are common symbols of entertainment. Equally available and pervasive among the classes and individuals to whom they appeal are pocket books, comic books, and horror and sex stories. Micky Spillane, Willie Mays, Davy Crockett and other nationally prominent personages as well as nationally branded products are as well known and available to the small town as they are to the big city. The intrusion of the mass media is so overwhelming that little scope is left for the expression of local cultural and artistic forms.

However, the diffusion of the printed word is not limited to the mass media; it is present also in the realm of education, both religious and secular. The state department of education syllabus defines minimum standards and content for subject matter instruction. Courses of Sunday school instruction are available for all age levels, and each faith secures its material from its own national religious press. In each of these major institutional areas the standards and content of instruction are defined in sources available only in standardized form.

THE IMMIGRANT AS CULTURAL CARRIER

Specific individuals are carriers of cultural diffusion, and the volume and extent of migration in and out of the community suggests the degree and intimacy of its contact with the mass society. In a community which is regarded as stable and relatively unchanging by its own inhabitants, only 25 percent of its population was born locally. Another 25 percent has moved into the community since 1946 and 55 percent are new to the community since 1920. Moreover, of the 45 percent who have moved to the community since 1932, more than 30 percent have lived for a year or longer in cities with populations in excess of 25,000; 7 percent in cities with populations in excess of one-half million.

Each decade and each generation introduces a new layer of immigrants to the community. The agricultural and business prosperity of the 1940's and early 1950's has brought city dwellers to farms and to businesses on Main Street, and the housing shortage has led workers to reclaim long-abandoned farm dwellings. The 12 percent of new people who moved into Springdale in the thirties came in response to the effects of the depression. From 1918 to 1928 the Poles moved onto farms abandoned by descendants of original settlers. Indeed, the ebb and flow of migration extends back to such eras of political and economic upheaval as the depression of the 1890's, the Civil War, the depression of the 1830's and the mass movement of people during the Indian Wars and the opening of the territory in the early 1800's. Each new wave of migrants, bringing with it the fashions and thought styles of other places, influences the cultural development of the community.

The cumulative consequences of these channels of diffusion and the quantity and quality of the "material" diffused denies the existence of a culture indigenous to the small town. In almost all aspects of culture, even to speech forms, and including technology, literature, fashions and fads, as well as patterns of consumption, to mention a few, the small town tends to reflect the contemporary mass society.

Basically, an historically indigenous local culture does not seem to exist. The cultural imports of each decade and generation and the successive waves of migration associated with each combine to produce a local culture consisting of layers or segments of the mass culture of successive historical eras. In the small town the remaining elements of the gay-ninety culture are juxtaposed against the modern central school. The newer cultural importations frequently come in conflict with the older importations of other eras. The conflict between "spurious" and "genuine" culture appears to be a conflict between two different ages of "spurious" culture.

BUSINESSMEN

For storekeepers, filling station operators, appliance dealers, automobile and farm equipment dealers and feed mill operators, the external world is a source of supply for the goods and commodities which they sell on the local market. Their position in relation to their source of supply and the overall condition of the national economy determines the level of their business activity, ceilings on their potential income, and hence indirectly their style of life. To analyze this group we must consider separately the position of the independent shopkeeper, the businessman who operates on a franchise and the feed mill and farm implement dealer.

The shopkeepers who make up the bulk of the business community have experienced a slow and gradual decline in their class position relative to other groups in the community. This is mainly due to the breakdown of their monopolistic position with respect to the local market, but it is also related to the rise of other groups. The development of the automobile, the appearance of the chain stores in surrounding areas and the expansion of mail order sales have placed them in a competitively disadvantageous position. Moreover, the nationally branded and advertised product, with its fixed profit margin determined by the producer, has tended in a general way to determine his volume/profit ratio in a way increasingly disadvantageous to him. His decrease in profits in relation to volume has driven him to a greater competition with other local shopkeepers—a competition which takes place in the form of despecialization, greater reliance on credit trade and keeping his shop open for long hours. The first two of these responses to his dilemma have further depressed his profit/volume ratio: in the one case by reducing his return on his investment and in the other case by increased losses due to bad debts. He keeps his business open in an effort to improve his investment/profit ratio and this he can do only by staying in the store himself.

The economic position of the small shopkeeper prevents him from reinvesting earnings in his own business. He sees little to be gained by modernizing and expanding his store in an effort to increase profits. Hence, the very bases on which the business group could achieve a class ascendancy are not open to it. Moreover, the long hours which he keeps in his store prevent him from holding a secondary occupation and limit his activities in community affairs. As a result he lives in an atmosphere of social and economic scarcity relative to his position 30 years ago and relative to other segments of the community. This accounts for the dominant psychology of scarcity-mindedness which is characteristic of this most numerous segment of the business class.

The position of the businessman who operates on a franchise is more obviously linked to the mass society. Usually he not only has a single source of supply, but also his source of supply (a petroleum company, for example) specifies the business practices and standards which must be maintained in order to retain the franchise. If the retail outlet is owned by the supplier (as with some filling stations) rents may be charged on a sliding scale according to volume of business—less volume, less rent—with the consequence that the profit margin of the local operator is not fixed.

More important, however, are the combined effects of the distribution policies of the petroleum products companies and appliance producers. Most of the big producers of these products maintain a local outlet; in some cases a single product may be retailed in two or three small-scale local outlets. In at least one line, household appliances, price cutting has become a standard form of competition. The effect of this proliferation of outlets is to depress the business chances of any single operator retailing a given branded product.

This group responds to its economic situation by increasing business hours, by carrying secondary lines and by intensive competition for "service" trade. Business is conducted at almost any hour of the day or night. Since these are one-man businesses, other members of the family are soon incorporated in the work process; children are helpers, wives act as secretaries and clerks. In the extreme case, the family life of the filling station operator orients itself almost completely to "keeping the business open"; the husband and wife are on duty together or the husband is absent from home except to sleep. This group is known to the community primarily through its occupational circumstances and its relationships are based upon being entrepreneur and having a clientele. As individuals they are relatively unimportant to the community since there is a high rate of turnover of franchises.

There are three individuals in the business class who are exceptions. These are the feed mill operators and the farm implement dealers who in Springdale consist of one feed mill operator located on the periphery of the township, one implement dealer located in the village, and one large-scale combined feed mill, housing supply and farm implement partnership. Because they service an agricultural industry which since the early forties has been prosperous, they are favorably situated in the local economy.

In terms of their customer relationships they are most intimately tied to the farmers, especially to the prosperous farmers who do most of the buying. Because of their market position their economic fate is intimately related to that of the farmers. In the period of farm ascendancy at the time of the study, they too were prosperous and exhibited all of the same aspects of expansion, investment and opportunity-consciousness already described for the farmer. In addition, however, because they are businessmen and the most successful businessmen, they have achieved the respect, admiration and enmity of the business community as well as of the town at large.

They are the most heavily capitalized group of individuals in the community and play an important credit function in the local agricultural economy. Because of the farmer's economic dependence on them and the interlocking character of their mutual fate, the feed mill and implement dealers identify themselves with the farmer's interests. In local politics they are in a position to provide the leadership in organizing the farmer's interests and frequently act as spokesman for the farm community. This is particularly true of the feed mill and implement partnership since it is the community's dominant enterprise; the other feed dealer is less important because his business is small and is located on the periphery of the town, and the other implement dealer is unimportant politically because being an Italian he is ethnically peripheral.

Thus two sub-groups of the business community, shopkeepers and franchise operators, experience a social and economic decline relative to a third, the feed and implement dealers.

These shifts in relative success are linked to accessibility to economic opportunity which is largely defined by external forces.

FARMERS

As noted earlier, there are two classes of farmers, the rational and the traditional. A major difference between them is the way they organize their production in relation to the mass market and government regulations.

Those who gear themselves to the mass market address themselves to favorably pegged prices, subsidies and quotas. As a consequence when prices and regulations are favorable they accept the favorable environment as a condition for their operations. They invest and expand, work hard and are successful. Their success stimulates confidence and buoyancy and produces an expansionist psychology.

In a peculiar way the traditional farmers who as a group do not gear themselves to the mass market do this specifically because of their relations with the mass market. As older farmers they have learned from the depression that they can be economically vulnerable, and they have learned that they can survive in the community by being immune to the market. The depression experience was so bitter for them that they have learned nothing since. Thus it happens that at the time of the study they were still living in the market of the early thirties.

To show how the internal status position of the farmer is related to the institutional structure of the larger society account must be taken of the fluctuations in the agricultural economy over the past 30 years. The agricultural depression beginning after World War I and extending to the beginning of World War II placed the farmer in a depressed (indebted) economic position. The decline of the farmer in Springdale was more extreme than in the nation at large during this period because Springdale is a marginal agricultural area with relatively poor land and a high rate of feed purchases. Farmers were either dispossessed, displaced or they retrenched to a heavily indebted minimum standard of consumption and operation. In this period the farmer verged on being declassed or actually was declassed.

Today the farmer is an important and ascendant segment of the rural middle class. From a position of near bankruptcy in 1933 he had risen (at the time of the field work for this study) to a position of heavy capitalization and social prominence. His rise coincided with the rationalization of marketing procedures (the Federal Milk Price Order in the New York Milk Shed), federal agricultural policies, and the rise in the market value of his products since the early 1940's. Specific agricultural policies which have contributed to his rise include the price support program, farm credit programs, and fertilizer and other land improvement give-aways. A little recognized source of preferential treatment given him by an outside agency lies in the structure of United States income tax laws, which allow for rapid depreciation of plant and equipment, little accountability on cash sales and a broad base of allowable operating expenses.

Although the status of all farmers is equally linked to decisions and policies of these larger institutional structures (the price structure and federal agricultural legislation), all farmers do not equally orient their operations to legislation and regulations oriented to them. At this point the rate of status ascendancy of the individual farmer is probably directly related to the extent to which he accepts the preferential treatment accorded him in these larger policy decisions. Those who have been most swift and efficient in adjusting to the changing conditions of the agricultural economy over the past 20 years constitute the most rapidly ascending segment of farmers.

As a consequence of the character of the institutional connectors which link the farmer to the great society, the status of the farmer relative to other local groups is relatively independent of local community forces. By the same token, his status is directly related to price structures and mass decisions and policies. Alterations in these external forces, such as a tumbling in farm prices, can cause an upheaval in the status structure of the local community.

This analysis does not exhaust the class groups. Other groups are occupationally less directly connected with the mass society and its markets. The aristocrats are oriented to the market only by fixed interest rates established in previous economic periods; their income from annuities, insurance payments and fixed inheritances declines in an inflationary period. The shack people, with the exception of their consumption function, are separated from the market by their unwillingness to direct their attention to it for any sustained period of time, even though their consumption standards are inflated at those times when they do address themselves to the market. The marginal middle class groups economically are not in a position to be directly and importantly related to the market except through the general price level. Their relationship to the market is mediated through their imitation of more prestigeful and successful groups which are located in the community.

OCCUPATION, CLASS AND COMMUNITY

Those groups which are favorably linked to the mass society are in a position to be socially, economically and politically ascendant in the community; in Springdale these are the rational farmers. Those groups which are unfavorably linked—segments of the marginal middle class— find it difficult to achieve the wherewithal to practice the preferred styles of life. Moreover, a favorable position with respect to certain aspects of mass society can and does in the long run produce optimism, buoyancy, aggressiveness and high self-esteem among members of a given class. Thus the psychological foundation of the class of rational farmers has changed over time. On the other hand, a negative position *vis à vis* mass society produces feelings of penury, scarcity, defensiveness and defensive social snobbery. Each of these sets of attitudes becomes a basis for further social and economic orientations for the affected classes.

THE POLITICAL SURRENDER TO MASS SOCIETY

Local political institutions consist of a village board, a town board and local committees of the Republican and Democratic parties. The jurisdiction of the village board includes powers of control and regulation over a variety of community facilities and services—street lighting, water supply, fire protection, village roads, street signs and parks. To carry out the functions empowered to it, it possesses the power of taxation. The town board is concerned chiefly with fire protection, the construction and maintenance of roads; through its participation on the county board of supervisors, it participates in programs connected with welfare, penal and other county services.

However, at almost every point in this seemingly broad base of political domain the village and town boards adjust their action to either the regulations and laws defined by state and federal agencies which claim parallel functions on a statewide or nationwide basis or to the fact that outside agencies have the power to withhold subsidies to local political institutions.

Local assessment scales and tax rates are oriented to state equalization formulas which partially provide the standardized basis on which subsidies are dispersed by the state. State highway construction and development programs largely present local political agencies with the alternative of either accepting or rejecting proposed road plans and programs formulated by the state highway department.

The village board, more than the town board, is dependent on its own taxable resources (taxes account for almost half its revenues) and best illustrates the major dimensions of local political action. The village board in Springdale accepts few of the powers given to it. Instead, it orients its action to the facilities and subsidies controlled and dispensed by other agencies and, by virtue of this, forfeits its own political power. Solutions to the problem of fire protection are found in agreements with regionally organized fire districts. In matters pertaining to road signs and street signs action typically takes the form of petitioning state agencies to fulfill desired goals "without cost to the taxpayer." On roads built and maintained by the state there is no recourse but to accept the state traffic bureau's standards of safety. A problem such as snow removal is solved by dealing directly with the foreman of the state highway maintenance crew through personal contacts: "If you treat him right, you can get him to come in and clear the village roads." In other areas of power where there are no parallel state agencies, such as for garbage collection or parks, the village board abdicates its responsibility.

As a consequence of this pattern of dependence, many important decisions are made for Springdale by outside agencies. Decisions which are made locally tend to consist of approving the requirements of administrative or state laws. In short the program and policies of local political bodies are determined largely by acceptance of grants-in-aid offered them —i.e., in order to get the subsidy specific types of decisions must be made—and by facilities and services made available to them by outside sources.

Psychologically this dependence leads to an habituation to outside control to the point where the town and village governments find it hard to act even where they have the power. Legal jurisdictions have been supplanted by psychological jurisdictions to such an extent that local political action is almost exclusively oriented to and predicated on seeking favors, subsidies and special treatment from outside agencies. The narrowing of legal jurisdictions by psychologically imposed limits leads to an inability to cope with local problems if outside resources are not available.

Power in local political affairs, then, tends to be based on accessibility to sources of decision in larger institutions. Frequently this accessibility consists merely of the knowledge of the source, or it may mean a personal contact, or an ability to correspond to get necessary information. Under these circumstances, power in the political arena is delegated to those with contacts in and knowledge of the outer world and to those who are experts in formal communication with impersonal bureaucratic offices. These are, on the individual level, the lawyer and, on an institutional level, the political party. The lawyer gains his paramountcy through technical knowledge and personalized non-party contacts up the political hierarchy with other lawyers. He is the mediator between the local party and the party hierarchy, and transforms his personalized contacts into political indispensability in the local community. His access to outside sources of power determines his power and predominance in the local community.

THE SOCIAL PSYCHOLOGICAL CONSEQUENCES OF THE RURAL SURRENDER

A central fact of rural life then, is its dependence on the institutions and dynamics of urban and mass society. The recognition of this dependence and the powerlessness associated with it give to the agents and institutions of the great society a degree of respect and admiration which, however, does not always connote approval. Rather, there is a high degree of ambivalence with respect to these agents and institutions. They have respect because of their power and wealth, and because their norms have the legitimacy of acceptance in wide areas.of the society at large. On the other hand, the very dominance of the mass institutions causes resentments, since, in the light of this dominance rural life in its immediacy is devalued. Hence, for example, although the standards of the land grant college are accepted, the institution and its agents may be resented for the role they play in innovation.

The phenomenon of psychological ambivalence to the mass society is particularly reinforced by the fact that slight changes in the policies and dynamics of the mass institutions can have profound effects on the rural way of life and on its major social and economic classes—i.e., parity policies, industrial relocations, new state roads and state subsidization formulas. In response to these conditions, the members of the rural community and their political spokesman resent their dependency and powerlessness and channelize it into anti-urban politics and policies. In relation to the outer world, there exist two types of political victory; when rural rather than urban areas get a disproportionately large share of the benefits of the state budget and when the city can be made the object of investigation on grounds of corruption or vice by politicians surrounded by a halo of rural images. At the same time a personal identification with important urban political officials lends an individual prestige in the rural community.

33. Toward a Typology of Extra-Community Controls Limiting Local Community Autonomy

ROLAND L. WARREN

Many aspects of community living are determined in whole or in part by decisions made outside the community by policies and procedures of state or national organizations, by state and federal law, and by developments in the national economy. It is extremely difficult to separate these aspects from more locally determined institutional functions without cutting some of the live connective tissue which most sociologists agree is essential to community structure and process. Perhaps for this reason, community studies are often conducted as though communities were independent islands, cut off from interaction with their geographical regions and with the larger culture. "There are few studies which attempt to show how the larger society affects the community under investigation; and there are no studies which undertake to conceptualize fully and in detail the relationship between the community and the larger whole."[1]

SOURCE: Reprinted with permission of the author and publisher from *Social Forces,* XXXIV, No. 4 (May, 1956).

[1] Julian H. Steward, *Area Research: Theory and Practice* (Bulletin 63, New York: Social Science Research Council, 1950), pp. 22–23.

To a great extent, American communities are simply points of geographical contact of criss-crossing networks of different organizations like the Presbyterian Church, the Grange, Rotary International, Standard Oil Company of New Jersey, Atlantic & Pacific, and so forth. Reiss has observed that "The query seldom is made whether there is some sense in which an institution, e.g., a church, is not a community institution. . . . The criteria of whether a phenomenon is or is not communal or possesses communal properties must be answered in terms of communal criteria and not by 'location' of the phenomenon in a community or 'allocation to residents of a community.' "[2]

A measure of the reality and effectiveness of the local community as a significant sociological group lies in the extent to which the fact of locality influences the behavior of the inhabitants with respect to each other and with respect to the institutional functions of the community. Presumably, communities vary in the extent to which they are merely "junctions" for regional and national networks of goods, services, and institutional behavior patterns and control, with little locally initiated and locally determined action, on the one hand; or, on the other hand, the extent to which they are strong locality groups with the bulk of their activities, though following regional and national culture patterns in varying degrees, nevertheless initiated, determined, and directed from within the community itself.

Not only would communities differ on such a scale, but the various commercial establishments, community facilities, and associational activities within the same community would range themselves along a scale from local initiation, determination, and execution of policy, on the one hand, to locally based operation but initiation and determination of policy and program from outside the community.

The present paper will report on some conceptual and typological considerations which arose out of an attempt to delineate and describe some of the formal extra-community controls which both affect local processes and limit local action. It was conducted in a small, incorporated western New York village of some 1351 residents (referred to as "Dairyville" in this report) as part of the Alfred University Area Study program.[3]

---

[2] Albert J. Reiss, Jr., *A Review and Evaluation of Research on Community*. A Working Memorandum Prepared for the Committee on Social Behavior of the Social Science Research Council (Nashville, Tenn.: Vanderbilt University, 1954), p. 79.

[3] The project, which lasted a college year, involved preliminary definition of the problem, examining basic laws and charters, development of schedules, interviewing, gathering statistical data, and analysis of data. The following participated in this project: Willard Humphrey, Sara Jacob, Gale Stickler, Mary Jane Villareale, Sheldon Zwickel.

SOME DIMENSIONS OF COMMUNITY AUTONOMY

Community autonomy is perhaps a useful term for conceptualizing the determination by local people of the goals, policies, and operations of local community units. In the exploration of the relationship of the larger society to local community organizations, such community autonomy can be considered in several different dimensions. Among these are the following:

1. The extent of actual measurable difference in important variables, which are largely within the control of the local community, between one community and others of similar size. One community may have a local bandstand or civic auditorium or baseball team, another not, thus indicating considerable local autonomy in such matters.

2. The extent to which people *feel* that they exert much or little local control over their institutions. This would be exemplified by their responses to polls or interviews regarding the extent to which they feel they are dominated by regional offices, state regulations, national associations, and so on.

3. The proportion of community activities which are "absentee-owned." This concept would have to be broad enough to include the U.S., Post Office as well as chain stores, newspapers, theaters, and other types of activity.

4. The locus of decisions which affect the behavior of local associations or governmental units. Which decisions are made in the county seat, or the state capital, or Washington? Which are made by state and national voluntary associations, trade associations, or wholesale houses; which are made by denominational boards, and so on?

5. The number and type of institutional services which are organized on a regional, state, or other extra-community basis but which serve local people, such as state employment services, branch offices of the Social Security Administration, regional hospitals, particularly the specialized ones, and so on.

6. When grievances or dissatisfaction arise, the question of whether lines of redress lie within the community or require decisions which must be made outside the community. For example, if a person feels he has received spoiled food at the grocery store, or unfair treatment at the railroad station, post office, gas company, or public school, what is the organizational channel in each case through which such grievances are handled?

7. The extent and type of extra-community affiliation or absence thereof of the various local functioning units: stores, industries, schools, churches, clubs, governmental units, and so on.

FORMAL AND INFORMAL EXTRA-COMMUNAL CONTROLS

The distinction between formal and informal social controls is a useful one in tracing the various types of relationship existing between the community and the larger society. In the pilot study of Dairyville, three types of informal control were distinguished as operating to limit local autonomy:

1. Control through *cultural patterns* which prevail in the larger culture. An example is the pattern of predominantly individual ownership of small economic enterprises like stores, farms, etc. There is no formal law which prescribes this type of ownership exclusively, and there are several other possibilities equally permissible under the formal controls of the law, yet individual ownership of such enterprises prevails in Dairyville as it does in the larger region and nation around it. Similarly, other aspects of behavior and social structure reflect the larger culture not so much through formal controls as through folkways, mores, fashions, fads, and so forth.

2. Pressures through the *informal group structure*. Controls operating through the informal social structure were much in evidence in Dairyville. An example would be the decision of a local grocer to patronize one wholesale establishment rather than another for purely personal reasons of family, friendship, or politics.

3. *Competition* or the concept of *the market*. Several store owners maintained that they set their prices according to their own policies and were not influenced by the price level or price policy of similar stores in other communities, or by the retail price list suggested by wholesalers. Yet without further study it was the unanimous observation of the study group that competition of local stores with those in surrounding communities actually played an important role in setting retail prices, and that, if Dairyville prices get too high, local people will increase their trade in surrounding communities to the detriment of the local stores.

Turning now to the more formal types of control limiting local community autonomy, the following typology emerged from the study as a useful set of distinctions:

  a) Extra-communal governmental controls limiting autonomy of local community units.
    1. Regulations by the governmental unit's own basic law and administrative promulgations (state education law and decisions governing local schools).
    2. Regulation by other laws which apply to local units, governmental or nongovernmental (general laws governing sanitation, working

conditions, wage deductions, and so on, at county, state, or national level).

b) Extra-communal non-governmental controls limiting autonomy of local community units (chartering requirements maintained by state or national organizations which have chartered "branches" in the community).

Both (a) and (b) can be further divided topically into the relevant spheres of activity: control over membership, policies, finances, etc.

TYPES OF AFFILIATION

One readily available avenue for tracing relationships between the community and the larger social system is through a description of the types of affiliation of local units with county, state, national, or regional groups. To be useful for comparative purposes within the community, a typology of such affiliational relationships should be applicable not only to churches and voluntary associations, but also to stores, industries, governmental units, public school system, and so on through the institutional structure.[4] The following typology was found to be useful, though not perfect.

1. *The independent unit.*—It is not affiliated. It may have loose ties with other organizations (an independent grocer with a wholesaler), but these involve only a minimum of outside control, if any at all.

2. *The affiliate.*—

a) The autonomous unit which is loosely affiliated for purposes such as sharing information or certain types of service, but which is otherwise largely independent.

b) The unit with a large measure of autonomy whose existence nevertheless presupposes affiliation, for example, the local Home Bureau unit.

---

[4] This is perhaps a relevant place to introduce a useful typology devised by Reiss, *op. cit.,* pp. 90–91; as "a basis for distinguishing the communal properties of institutions:

(a) Institutions derive from the communal system when the arena of interaction primarily is local, the goals of action are local and the generic characteristics of the institution are patterned through interaction in a residence-sustenance context. . . . [Examples: a rooming house or restaurant]

(b) Institutions which are not specific to a communal system may develop a specific communal form of the institution when both the means and the ends are derived primarily from the local system. . . . [Example: a local improvement association]

(c) An institution may utilize the means of a community system to facilitate the implementation of non-communal institutional goals. . . . [Examples: A.M.A. schools, churches]

(d) An institution may be localized in a community, but it is only symbiotically related to the local system. [Examples: offices of governmental units, universities, military establishments]."

3. *The branch.*—Its existence depends on its being "chartered" by a larger organization, whose programs and policies it follows with relatively little local community control (Red Cross, American Legion, Catholic Church).

TABLE 1.
Typology of Dairyville Local Community Units

| | | Affiliate | | |
Area of Activity	Independent	a. Part of independent federation	b. Association of affiliated units	Branch
Industries	5			
Stores	9	4		2
Service trades	8	3		2
Governmental units				2
Churches		1	1	4
Schools				1
Voluntary associations	3	5	2	15

Applying this typology to community units investigated in the study of Dairyville yielded the pattern shown in Table 1.

The purpose of the present paper is to report on the typological aspect of the Dairyville study, as a slight but perhaps useful contribution to the relatively unexplored task of studying the various types of interrelation of local community and larger society. The concepts and distinctions outlined are somewhat rudimentary. Yet they suggest possibilities for delineating and conceptualizing possible relationships in a way which is amenable to further research.

CONCLUSION

A few observations regarding the substantive findings in Dairyville may be of interest. The ordering of types of affiliation by different kinds of community-based unit was facilitated by the use of the suggested typology in Table 1. Village and town governments were by definition affiliated, as was the central school. But is is interesting that all of the churches were affiliated, taking more or less stringent regulation from outside the community, while local industries were completely independent of outside affiliation, were locally owned, and represented in this respect high community autonomy. Similarly, the stores and service trades were preponderantly non-affiliated, while the voluntary associations were almost completely affiliated.

It should be noted that affiliation is only one of the dimensions of community autonomy, as mentioned earlier in this paper. Nevertheless, the data from this study do not in themselves lend support to the widely held assumption that churches and voluntary associations represent democratic grass roots control, while businesses represent autocratic control by "absentee owners." Of course, Dairyville may not be typical in this respect.

A finding which helps interpret the above observation is the extent of awareness of the verbal versus the actual controls over local units. Many interviewees remarked that while the larger organization had nominal formal control over this or that aspect of the local unit, actually the local would often simply disregard this and go ahead with its own program, if there should be a difference in point of view. Putting it another way, this study investigated the formal controls operating from outside the community of Dairyville, but considerable modification of these controls in informal practice was observed.

An interesting finding of the study was the extent to which Dairyville people lacked interest in or knowledge of avenues of redress, should they feel they had a complaint or grievance with respect to organizations controlled from outside the community. Presumably, we had hypothesized, local branches or affiliates would occasionally have matters on which they would want to protest or appeal the decision of a larger unit which would govern their local operation. Hence, we expected to get meaningful answers as to means of redress and instances in which redress had been sought. Either we were not able to make ourselves clear in interpreting this matter, or the interviewees had poor recollection of such instances as had occurred, or they resisted giving the information, or else there is little local occasion in Dairyville to protest decisions made by extra-community groups.

34. The Factory in the Community

W. LLOYD WARNER
J. O. LOW

Two other important causes of the strike must now be dealt with. The first is the expansion of the hierarchy upward, out of Yankee City, through the expansion of individual enterprises and the establishment by them of central offices in distant large cities. The second is the expansion of the structure outward from Yankee City through the growth of manufacturers' associations and labor unions, also with headquarters outside Yankee City and with units in many other shoemaking communities in New England and elsewhere. Both of these developments have gone on concurrently, each reacting upon the other. And both decrease Yankee City's control over its shoe factories by subjecting the factories, or segments of them, to more and more control exerted from outside Yankee City.

In the early days of the shoe industry, the owners and managerial staffs of the factories, as well as the operatives, were residents of Yankee City; there was no extension of the factory social structures outside the local community. The factories were then entirely under the control of the

SOURCE: From *Industry and Society*, William Foote Whyte, ed., copyright by McGraw-Hill Book Company, 1946. Used by permission of McGraw-Hill Book Company, New York.

community; not only the formal control of city ordinances and laws, but also the more pervasive informal controls of community traditions and attitudes. There were feelings of neighborliness and friendship between manager and worker and of mutual responsibilities to each other and to the community that went beyond the formal employer-employee agreement.

In the days of local capitalism, the shoe manufacturers were accepted by all social strata as leaders of the total community. Shortly after the death of the most powerful of these business leaders, a number of prominent Yankee City men published a memorial volume that contained the usual words of high praise for great men. Since these same words, unlike those of many memorial volumes, were said about him by ordinary men of the street and were used during the strike, it is important to examine them. A member of one of the oldest families of Yankee City wrote:

> He (the manufacturer) was one of the most remarkable men ever connected with Yankee City; a businessman of liberal culture, of fine literary taste, gifted as an orator, in music and theatricals. . . . He was an acquisition to any society. He honored any public station, however high. . . . He achieved more in his 50 years of life than most men can point to after marking a very old age. . . .
>
> He was identified with the public health of this city and was a conspicuous figure in all its great social functions as long as his health permitted it. He was a leading financier and a man who at once took and ever afterwards occupied a prominent position in this community. For years, by common consent, he was the leading man of the city. . . . Forcefulness of character made him the commanding spirit in every undertaking in which he shared and in every circle in which he moved.

Our analysis of the manufacturer's participation in the community provides the crucial evidence to show why he became the powerful collective symbol that was used against the contemporary managers during the strike.

> In the business and financial sphere he was:
> 1. Owner and head of his million-dollar shoe company.
> 2. President of one of the most powerful banks in the city.
> 3. Member of the board of trustees of the Financial Institute, a firm of the utmost prestige and power in the community.
> 4. Director of the Security Trust Company, another powerful financial institution.
> 5. Director of the Yankee City Gas and Electric Company.
>
> He was involved in a large number of civic enterprises and was a member of many civic institutions. He was:

    6. Director and one of the founders of the city's most important hospital.

      7. Director of the public library.

      8. Member of the school committee.

      9. Trustee of the Revere Free School.

    10. President of the City Improvement Society.

He also took an important part in politics. He was:

    11. Chairman of the Republican City Committee.

    12. Member of the city council.

    13. Delegate to the National Republican Convention.

    14. Mayor of the city.

He was also prominent in church and religious affairs. He was:

    15. President of the Yankee County Unitarian Club.

    16. President of the Yankee County Unitarian Conference.

He was a leader in fraternal affairs and was:

    17. Past Master of St. John's Lodge.

    18. Member of several important fraternal orders.

He was an active member of some of the most exclusive clubs of the city including:

    19. The Drama Club.

    20. The Thursday Night Club.

    21. The Friday Evening Club.

    22. The February Club.

    23. The Revere Club.

    24. The Country Club.

The evidence demonstrates that in all these organizations he was active and powerful. This brief survey of some of his participation in the community demonstrates that his activities ramified throughout the city and that much of the life of the city was centered in him. It also demonstrates that he accepted responsibility for the larger affairs of the community and helped integrate its activities, for he provided responsible leadership for the whole life of the community. "He was a man you could depend on."

Very much the same could be said about his two successors. They, too, were responsible elders of the city. They not only provided jobs and wages through their factories, but they were citizens of the town and men who felt obligated to it. Their membership in local institutions compares very favorably with that of their predecessor.

In the days before big-city capitalism took control, the local enterpriser was financed by Yankee City banks. These banks and other investment houses possessed more autonomy and prestige then than they do now. In the development of the local shoe industry, local financiers played important and necessary roles and, at least part of the time, were silent partners in the business. Much of the wealth they derived from their investments was reinvested in Yankee City. The money was put into new enterprises, their own living, or civic activities. Their white Georgian houses on Hill Street, whose gardens bordered those of the manufacturers, were majestic symbols of their power and prestige and forever reminded and often reassured everyone of the visible presence of these powerful and protecting men in Yankee City.

The Yankee City financiers, too, were men of responsibility, dominated by sentiments of local pride. They did well for themselves, but they also did well for the city. Perhaps the price was high, but the product bought by the rest of the community was substantial and of high quality. Their philanthropies, combined with their power and leadership, contributed enormously to the city's development and provided a firm foundation for the larger civic life of the community. Parks, libraries, hospitals, societies to help the unfortunate and aged, foundations to send young men to college, endowments of schools, churches, and many other worthy civic enterprises were granted and maintained by the money and leadership of the local financiers and manager owners.

The essential point to remember for these leaders of industry and finance is that they were subject to local control (1) because they were dominated by local sentiments which motivated them "to take care of their own people," and (2) they were under the powerful influence of the numerous organizations to which they belonged and of their personal contacts with local citizens, which directly related them to influence from every part of the city.

The advent of big-city capitalism shattered this closely woven network of personal relations, loyalties, and obligations. Yankee City shoe factories are no longer owned exclusively by local citizens. More and more of them have been absorbed by larger enterprises whose executive offices are in New York City. At the time of our study, the largest shoe factory in Yankee City was owned by a company which operated several other factories in New England and which also owned the nationwide *ABC* chain of retail shoe stores, all of which were controlled from a central office in New York. Even some of the smaller Yankee City shoe factories, although still locally owned and managed, sold most of their shoes to chain-store organizations.

Yankee City has become but a pin point upon the map of industrial empire for these large investment houses. The flow of wealth from Yankee City's banks and factories, once a great local arterial system giving life and strength to the town, now has shrunk to an infinitesimal part of big-city, world-wide capitalism and is of no vital significance in the life of this great system.

The extent of this change may be seen from the following account of the finances of the *ABC* company, which appeared in a June, 1945, issue of a large New York newspaper:

> A group headed by Oppenheimer and Co. and Brandeis and Son, and including the Stultz Co., has concluded an agreement for purchase of the majority of Lion Shoe Corp. stock, it was announced today.
>
> Lion Shoe will be merged into its wholly owned retail subsidiary, the *ABC* Shoe Corp., with subsequent public issue of securities of the latter company.
>
> Abraham Cohen, associated with the companies in an executive capacity for more than 20 years, will be elected president and general manager. Frederick Stultz, president of the Stultz Co., will be made chairman of the board.
>
> The *ABC* Shoe Corp. owns a number of factories equipped to manufacture 20,000 pairs of shoes daily and operates a chain of 110 stores in 56 cities.

Decisions on these high levels of national and international finance are being made without regard for the needs and vital interests of Yankee City. The old ties between top management and the community have completely broken down.

As the vertical hierarchy of the factory system extended to executive offices in New York, even the local factory managers came to be, for the most part, "outsiders" and members of ethnic minorities. They had their factories in the town and some of them drove down to work in the morning and left at night. The workers knew or felt that the forces that controlled local men would not control these outsiders. The vast network of relations and memberships that made the former owners local leaders, as well as local manufacturers, had been reduced to a purely economic one of employer and employee. It was that and nothing more. It is small wonder that the workers during this strike "gave the horse laugh to the managers when they talked about being good fellows."

At the time of the strike the few local men who were managers, although born and reared in Yankee City, were little more than the factory managers for big-city capitalists, for they occupied inferior positions in this vastly extended vertical structure. They were not in a position to take leadership. They were not in a position of great power where they were free to make the decisions that always characterized the lives of the owners of the previous period.

Each of these local men felt what had happened very deeply and some of them were explicit enough about it to say so. We knew some of them well. They were not the weak or unscrupulous men that their opponents made them out to be. Personally, they were men of good reputations in the business world. Some of them had been trained by their own fathers to be community leaders but their place in the new socioeconomic structure of Yankee City prevented them from playing this role and each in his own way contributed directly to the defeat of the managerial group. Part of their ineptness was due to their inability to measure up in their own minds to the great men of the past. This was a dead past, glorious and safe, when men knew themselves to be free men and Yankee City was "the hub of the universe." This whole period was symbolized in the memories of the workers and management by the names and reputations of the former owners. The lives of these men epitomized the period for all those who remembered. They symbolized the longing of everyone to return to those days when it was possible for one of them, with all his power and prestige, to stop and gently chide Sam Taylor, the cutter, for not calling him by his first name, and he and Sam could talk about "the trouble in the cutting room." Power was under control and security was present then; manager and worker were part of a self-contained system in which each knew his part in the total system.

In these days of big-city capitalism, when Yankee City had lost control of its own destinies, few workers would go up to the "big boss" to tell him "what's wrong in the cutting room," and those who did were not considered the respected friends of the workers but "stool pigeons who were getting theirs from management."

During the strike the local men cut poor figures as fighters for management's side. Two of them openly lined up with the strikers. Local sentiment and the feeling against "the foreigners" was too much for them. They materially contributed to the workers' victory.

One of them damaged the cause of management when he tried to fight the head of the union during a peace conference. Everyone said he blustered and acted badly when he used such tactics. He was under the control of higher management and occupied an inferior managerial position where he had little freedom to assume command and take leadership. Yet he had learned from "one of the grand old men" of the last period, when he worked for him, how his kind of man should act and he knew that an owner and manager should assume control. It seems a reasonable hypothesis that the conflict between his beliefs on how a manager should act and what he was permitted to do by his status greatly contributed to causing his unfortunate act, an act which materially aided the union. He tried to take command in a situation where it was impossible to do so, and instead of commanding he could only "bluster."

His antagonist, on the other hand, was "top manager" of the union. He did have power and he could make decisions. His beliefs about what should be done and his status were commensurate and he used them to the greatest effect for the cause of the union.

All these local men knew somehow they were not the men their "fathers" were and these dead men, symbolizing the glorious past, over-awed and helped defeat them. While the men of yesterday are dead, "their souls go marching on" in the memories of the living. They have become collective symbols of that lost age when the prestige and power of local financiers and local producers "took care of our own people." These symbols were powerful influences upon the sentiments of workers as well as managers during the strike crisis. Sapping the confidence of the local managers, they gave strength to the strikers who dramatized their cause in terms of a struggle of Yankee City against big-city capitalism.

From this analysis of today's and yesterday's owners several important propositions can be offered that contribute to our understanding of the strike. The vertical extension of the corporate structure of the shoe manufacturing enterprises had pushed the top of the hierarchy into the great metropolises and, in so doing, had brought in outsiders who were foreigners in culture, had no local prestige, and were lacking in under-standing and feeling for the local workers and the town itself. This extension of the industrial hierarchy reduced the local men to inferior positions in the hierarchy, where they were incapable of making decisions and could not initiate actions that would give them the power of leadership for the workers and for the rest of the town.

The local managers, reduced to inferior statuses in the industrial hierarchy also occupied lower social class ranking in the community than their predecessors. This greatly reduced their strength as leaders who could form community opinion in times of crisis when the position of management was threatened. They could no longer lead the worker or the community. Because of this inferior position of the managers, those men in the community who would once have been their natural allies and who enjoyed top social class position were now above them and shared none of their interests, were hostile to them and friendly to the workers.

In "the good old days," the people of Yankee City felt that they all shared in a common way of life, in which business and industry was closely integrated into the community. This way of life had its frictions and conflicts, but it provided all the people with a set of common symbols to guide their behavior, and it also provided effective leadership from the top of the social order. Furthermore, these personal ties made it possible for workers to redress their grievances through going right up to members of management.

When New York financiers assumed control of the industrial hierarchy, the social and civic leaders of Yankee City were no longer active in local management. The management of industry was no longer directly tied in with the wider life of the community. This split between management and the community made it possible to mobilize the workers into an organization to fight management.

35. The Role of Economic Dominants in Community Power Structure

ROBERT O. SCHULZE

That persons occupying positions of economic importance are among the key wielders of local influence and control has long been one of the most commonplace assumptions of American sociologists and one of the most consistent findings of research concerned with American communities and community power structures.[1] With very few exceptions,

SOURCE: Reprinted with permission of the author and publisher from *American Sociological Review*, XXIII (February, 1958), published by the American Sociological Association.

ACKNOWLEDGMENT: Expanded version of paper read at the annual meeting of the American Sociological Society, August, 1957. I wish to thank Morris Janowitz and Melvin Reichler, both of the University of Michigan, for their helpful comments on this paper.

[1] In addition to the well-known works of the Lynds, Warner, Hollingshead, Mills, and Hunter, see: Roland J. Pellegrin and Charles H. Coates, "Absentee-Owned Corporations and Community Power Structure," *American Journal of Sociology*, LXI, No. 5 (March, 1956), 413–419; George Belknap and Ralph Smuckler, "Political Power Relations in a Mid-West City," *Public Opinion Quarterly*, XX, No. 1 (Spring, 1956), 73–81; A. Alexander Fanelli, "A Typology of Community Leadership Based on Influence and Interaction Within the Leader Subsystem," *Social Forces*, XXXIV, No. 4 (May, 1956), 332–338; Robert E. Agger, "Power Attributions in the Local Community," *ibid.*, 322–331;

however, most studies relevant to the role of economic dominants in community control structures have focused on current power configurations. Relatively little research attention has yet been devoted to historical shifts in local power structures associated with the metropolitan and bureaucratic drift of American life.[2] Likewise, while most relevant studies have indicated that a considerable number of persons of significant local influence are men of economic substance, they have not revealed the pattern of community involvement (nor changes in that pattern) of the economically most-powerful considered as a category. Thus, we have heard a good deal about the activities and influence of the "X" family and its equivalents in American communities, but rather less about the "Y" families, and almost nothing at all about the ratio of "Xs" to "Ys" either currently or over time.

This paper reports some findings of an investigation of the power structure of a middle-sized American community—findings concerned primarily with the historical role of the economic dominants in that community's power structure.[3] Although the study has among its numerous limitations those inevitable in any piece of single-community research, it is hoped that it might be theoretically and methodologically suggestive for research in other communities, especially those which—like the subject of this study—have become satellites in a society increasingly dominated by giant metropolitan centers and large national corporations.

The rudimentary theory underlying this research may be briefly summarized. The basic assumption was that as the functional relationship of the community to the larger society changes, so does the nature and form of its control structure, and so, too, does the role of its economic dominants in that structure.

It was hypothesized that in the community *relatively* self-contained and uninvolved in the larger social and economic system, the community with few and scattered commitments beyond its borders, local power would tend to be structured as a pyramid and heavily concentrated at the apex. More specifically, it was surmised that those persons who exercised major control over the community's economic system would tend to be the same persons who exercised preponderant control over its socio-political system, and that this latter control would be reflected, at least in

Peter Rossi, "Historical Trends in the Politics of an Industrial Community," paper presented at the 51st annual meeting of the American Sociological Society, September, 1956.

[2] Rossi's study is a notable exception.

[3] Robert O. Schulze, *Economic Dominance and Public Leadership: A Study of the Structure and Process of Power in an Urban Community,* microfilmed Ph.D. dissertation, University of Michigan, 1956. (University Microfilms, Publication No. 21,359.)

part, by their active leadership and participation in the political and civic life of the community.

With increasing urbanization and as the community passed beyond what Lloyd Warner has called "the period of local capitalism,"[4] however, it was suggested that the economic dominants would begin to withdraw their interest and active attention from the local socio-political system. Although the major economic units would have grown in size and potential influence, it was hypothesized that several factors would militate against the effective exercise, the actual "cashing-in" of their power in the community. The most significant of these would be the fact that the local community would have become ever less important to the survival and prosperity of its dominant economic units. As the activities of these units became increasingly directed toward—and by—populations and groups other than the local ones, the relevance of local community organizations and the impact of local political influences on the major economic units would accordingly diminish. As this occurred, the local power structure would in effect, bifurcate—with those who exercised primary direction over its socio-political system no longer being essentially the same set of persons who exercised primary control over its economic system.[5]

An effort was made to test this general theory in Cibola, a Midwestern industrial community of some 20,000 inhabitants, located approximately 30 miles from Metro City, one of the nation's largest metropolitan cen-

---

4 W. Lloyd Warner and J. O. Low, "The Factory in the Community," in William Foote Whyte (ed.), *Industry and Society* (New York: McGraw-Hill Book Company, 1946), p. 35.

5 It is not suggested that the decline in the economic dominants' leadership and participation in community decision-making processes stems wholly from their diminishing concern with local affairs. With their attenuation of local involvement, it is obvious that effective contact and meaningful communication between economic dominants and diverse elements of the community population are likewise reduced, contributing to what has been referred to as the loss of "multi-class leadership" by the top business groups in American communities. In such a situation, economic dominants—when they occasionally may want to influence community decisions—may find that their local leadership base has so shrunken that their effectiveness is impaired. Somewhat illustrative of this was the case of Cal Lamkin, the general manager of a large industrial plant in the community studied. Long inactive in local political and voluntary associational affairs, Lamkin was eventually prevailed upon to stand for election to the board of directors of the local Chamber of Commerce. To the considerable embarrassment of the Chamber's officials, however, Lamkin failed to muster sufficient votes to win a seat on the board. Cf. Wilbert E. Moore, *Industrial Relations and the Social Order* (New York: Crowell, Collier and Macmillan, Inc., 1951) , pp. 547–553. Although presented in casual terms somewhat different from those suggested in this paper, the best known and perhaps most sanguine statement of the American business elites' loss of multi-group leadership is contained in Kenneth Galbraith, *American Capitalism and the Concept of Countervailing Power* (Boston: Houghton Mifflin Company, 1952).

ters. Founded in 1823, Cibola grew rather slowly until World War II. Between 1940 and 1950, however, its population increased over 50 percent, a shift symptomatic of countless other changes to which the community has lately been subject. One of the principal changes has been the gradual absorption of its major industrial plants by large, absentee-owned corporations, a trend sharply accelerated during the World War II period.

In our research, we attempted to reconstruct Cibola's economic dominants from the time of its founding in 1823 until 1955, and to determine the general nature and extent of their overt involvement in the political and civic life of the community.

The economic dominants for the various historical periods were operationally defined as those persons who: (a) occupied the top formal roles in the largest industries and banks in the community; or (b) were members of the boards of directors of two or more of these industries and banks, thus serving formally to "interlock" the dominant economic units; or (c) were the largest property owners in the community.[6]

Insofar as local involvement was reflected by occupancy of formal offices in the political and civic organizations in the community, the research tended clearly to support the basic hypothesis. *The historical drift has been characterized by the withdrawal of the economic dominants from active and overt participation in the public life of Cibola.* Tables 1, 3, and 4 are presented to illustrate this withdrawal.

TABLE 1.

Number and Percent of Economic Dominants in Public Office, 1823–1954 Periods

Period	Number of Economic Dominants	Number of Economic Dominants in Public Office	Percent of Economic Dominants in Public Office
1823–1860	12	10	83
1860–1900	21	17	81
1900–1940	43	12	28
1940–1954	31	7	23

Table 1 indicates that prior to the turn of the century, fully four-fifths of Cibola's economic dominants held public office in the community,

---

6 Specific criteria for classification as an economic dominant in each historical period were based on such measures as number of employees (industries), capital worth (banks), and assessed valuation of holdings (property owners). Various source data were utilized in the determination of these measures, including county tax records, city directories and histories, newspapers, records of individual companies and of the Chamber of Commerce and the State Historical Collections, plus such standard references as *Poor's Register of Directors and Executives* and *Polk's Bank Directory*.

while since 1900, the proportion has declined to approximately one-quarter.[7] Likewise, as shown in Table 3, the proportion of economic

TABLE 2.

Changes in Number of Economic Dominants and Number of Available Offices, 1823–1954 Periods

Period	Percentage Change in Number of Economic Dominants	Percentage Change in Number of Public Offices in City Government
From 1823–1860 to 1860–1900 periods ..	plus 75	plus 80
From 1860–1900 to 1900–1940 periods ..	plus 105	plus 183
From 1900–1940 to 1940–1954 periods ..	minus 28	minus 30

dominants who have held the top political office in Cibola has sharply diminished. Not indicated in either of these two tables is the fact that *none* of the most recent type of economic dominant—the managers of the absentee-owned corporations—has held any public office (elective or appointive) in the community.

There was some evidence that in the early decades of this century the arena of active local involvement of Cibola's economic dominants shifted

TABLE 3.

Number and Percent of Economic Dominants in Office of Village President or Mayor, 1823–1954 Periods

Period	Number of Dominants in Office of Village President or Mayor	Percent of Dominants in Office of Village President or Mayor	Percent of "Politically-Active" Dominants in Office of Village President or Mayor*
1823–1860	5	42	50
1860–1900	7	33	41
1900–1940	2	5	17
1940–1954	1	3	14

* "Politically-Active": All those economic dominants who had held *any* public office.

from politics to the important voluntary associations. Even in this area, however, an appreciable subsequent diminution of active participation has been apparent—perhaps best reflected by the declining number of dominants holding responsible office in the community's most influential association, the local Chamber of Commerce.

---

[7] It might be suggested that the declining proportion of economic dominants in public office was a function of the fact that the number of dominants increased at a greater rate than the number of available offices, and therefore, that the declining proportions are spurious. This was not the case. Changes in the number of economic dominants throughout the four periods were very closely paralleled by proportionately similar changes in the number of available public offices. (See Table 2.)

It is suggested that the withdrawal of the economic dominants was primarily a consequence of the changing relationship of the community's economic system to that of the larger society. Prior to about 1900, three

TABLE 4.

Number of Economic Dominants in Offices of the Chamber of Commerce, 1920–1955*

Period	Median Number of Memberships per Year on Board of Directors	Number Serving as President
1920–1927	6	3
1927–1934	3	2
1934–1941	3	0
1941–1948	2	1
1948–1955	1	0

* The Cibola Chamber of Commerce was founded in 1920. From that date until 1953, the number of directors was 15; in the latter year, the number was increased to 18. Directors serve two-year terms and are eligible for reelection.

aspects of Cibola's economic life were especially notable: (a) all of its economic dominants were local residents; (b) all of its dominant economic units were locally-owned; and (c) the majority of its dominants were associated in extensive economic networks *within* the community.

Our research established that in the pre-1900 period, almost 70 percent of the economic dominants had known business or financial ties—as partners, co-officers or co-directors—with other dominants in the community. Thus, throughout most of Cibola's history, its "average" economic dominant was not only a local resident, or merely the head of a single major economic unit; he was also directly and indirectly linked with a considerable number of other major economic units and dominants within the community.

Combined, these factors provided most economic dominants with deep, branching roots in Cibola. The business and financial links, in particular, afforded many of them a basis for shared concern in the local community. The economic networks served to weld together blocs of dominants, giving them frequent and specific occasion for interpersonal contact. By the same token, the very diversity of the "average" dominant's local economic commitments meant that there was always a variety of areas and methods in which local political considerations could impinge upon his pecuniary and related interests. The evidence suggests that these considerations were closely associated with the high incidence of involvement by economic dominants in the socio-political system of the community.

The period since 1900, and more particularly, since 1930, has been marked by the increasing absorption of the local economic system into the larger industrial complex, especially that of Metro City. While several complex social factors were patently involved, the following three seem most closely related to the eventual withdrawal of the economic dominants from active participation in the political-civic life of Cibola:

(a) the establishment by a growing number of locally-owned industrial units of direct supplier relationships with a small number of large non-local manufacturing plants; (b) the subsequent introduction into the local economic system of an increasing number of branch plants of large, absentee-owned corporations; and (c) the concomitant dissolution of the extensive networks of interlocking director and officerships which had formerly served to link significant numbers of local economic dominants within the community.

Consequently, the overt direction of the political and civic life of Cibola has passed almost wholly into the hands of a group of middle-class business and professional men, almost none of whom occupies a position of economic dominance in the community. That this has in fact been the case was suggested in another aspect of our research by the finding that only two of Cibola's 17 current economic dominants were perceived by the local voluntary association heads to have been among the 18 most influential leaders in the community.[8] And both of these two, by the way, were heads of relatively small, locally-owned economic units.

. Patently, these data reveal changes only in the level of overt and manifest involvement of the economic dominants in the local power structure. It may be suggested, of course, that covertly—"behind-the-scenes"—the economic dominants continue to exercise considerable direction and control of community affairs. However, the findings of another part of our research strongly suggest that things may, in fact, be what they seem.

In an effort to view the community power structure "in action," we endeavored to determine the patterns and processes of local decision-making in a series of recent community episodes (including a successful campaign to change the structure of municipal government from a mayor-alderman to a city manager form, and an ambitious but unsuccessful annexation effort).[9] Our findings in this aspect of the research forced us to conclude that the recent economic dominants—and especially those

---

[8] The heads of 143 voluntary associations in Cibola were asked a series of five questions intended to elicit their perceptions of the most influential leaders in the community. On the basis of their total "nominations," the eighteen most frequently cited persons were designated as the "public leaders" of Cibola. See Robert O. Schulze and Leonard U. Blumberg, "The Determination of Local Power Elites," *American Journal of Sociology*, LXIII, No. 3 (November, 1957), 290-296.

[9] In these reconstructions, a variety of source materials was utilized, including intensive interviews with the seventeen current economic dominants, the eighteen persons perceived by the 143 local voluntary association heads as the community's most influential leaders, and a selected number of informants. In addition, relevant newspaper files, Chamber of Commerce records and reports, and city council minutes were reviewed.

representing the growing number of large, absentee-owned corporations —appear indeed to have dissociated themselves from active involvement in Cibola's power structure.

These episodes reflected a growing adherence on the part of the absentee-owned corporations in Cibola to a "hands-off" position with regard to local political decision-making. And while it cannot be conclusively documented within the limits of the present paper, this evolving policy is graphically suggested by presenting excerpts from interviews with several executives in the larger economic units.

The general manager of the second largest manufacturing plant in the community, commenting on our findings that but two of the top ten officials in his plant actually resided in Cibola, stated:

> That's a sore spot with me. I've always felt that if I'm going to work in a town, I ought to live there. But there's no consensus on that by a long ways. It's been discussed at the highest levels in our corporation—I know because I've been on the company's community relations committee ever since it was set up. The company has decided that it won't encourage its executives to live in the communities where they work if they don't already or if they don't want to. . . . The company doesn't feel its people—at least its executives—have to live in a town in order to have good community relations. Just about the opposite, as a matter of fact. You're always subject to a hell of a lot of local pressures if you're there. If they know where you are, you're always a target. So maybe it's better not to be in a position to be asked to do something than to have to say, "No."

In discussing the paucity of both formal and informal contacts between corporation officials and local leaders, the assistant general manager of the largest industrial plant in Cibola said:

> No, I've almost never gone downtown for lunch "with the boys." I sometimes get my hair cut in [Cibola], but outside of that I don't show my face any more than I feel I absolutely have to. . . . The people at the Chamber of Commerce seem to fall all over themselves trying to do anything we want—but the point is, we don't really *want* anything there except for the people to have a good opinion of us. But mostly due to this placating attitude of the town's leaders, I'm afraid to say much or be around much.

The corporations were interested, to be sure (as the title of one company's "kit for divisional executives" indicated) in "Making Friends for [U.S. Motors] in the Local Community," but a growing number of them were coming to regard "making friends" and "getting involved" as inconsonant. The general manager of another large plant summed up his attitude:

> One sure way to give [our firm] a black eye would be for me to get myself into things so deeply in town that no matter what I did, I'd end up alienating a lot of people.

And another:

> You've got to remember that what I do doesn't affect us just here. The guy who represents our company in this area could affect our reputation a lot of other places as well. . . . Why, if I went out and got myself [involved] in local politics, you'd see a new boy in these shoes so damned fast it'd make your head swim.

Meaningful participation in the decision-making processes of a community such as Cibola was mainly regarded by these corporations as entailing risks to their operations and to their positions in the larger social system—risks which could not be offset by any palpable advantages which might accrue to them through playing significant roles in the local power structure. They were clearly cognizant, for example, of the possibility that involvement by their executives in local affairs might induce conflicting loyalties. Likewise, their executives recognized that decisive involvement in critical community decisions posed the threat of alienating significant superiors and publics at the extra-community level, thus endangering their larger occupational and public relations objectives. It seems tenable that it was the very sensitivity of the large corporations to socio-political determinations at the regional and national levels which militated against their involvement in these matters at the level of the local community.

The central finding of the Cibola study—the bifurcation of the community's power structure, stemming from the withdrawal of the economic dominants from active direction of the political and civic life of the community—appears quite generally to corroborate the investigation of Peter Rossi and his associates of the changing patterns of political participation in a middle-sized industrial community in New England.[10] Likewise, our findings seem to be consistent with C. Wright Mills' observations regarding the altered position of large economic units in the power structures of local communities.[11] On the other hand, the Cibola findings do not appear consistent with Hunter's research in Regional City, nor, especially, with that of Pellegrin and Coates in Bigtown.[12]

In addition to the obvious and perhaps significant differences in the

---

[10] Rossi, *op. cit.*

[11] C. Wright Mills, *The Power Elite* (New York: Oxford University Press, 1956).

[12] Floyd Hunter, *Community Power Structure* (Chapel Hill: University of North Carolina Press, 1953); Pellegrin and Coates, *op. cit.*

sizes of the several communities involved, it will be noted that Hunter and Pellegrin and Coates studied the structures and dynamics of community power in Southern cities, while Rossi's and the present research concern New England and Midwestern communities, respectively. In correspondence with the writer, Pellegrin has suggested that the disparate findings may be largely the function of regional differences: the historical tradition of paternalism being perhaps stronger in the South than in the North. It has also been suggested that economic dominants may become involved in community power structures independent of the desires of their economic units to guide or influence local decision-making. Thus, for example, to the extent that economic dominants represent the wealthier interests in the community and are a major source of voluntary donations to local charities and similar activities, they may be coopted into decision structures by those actively "in charge" in order to reinforce the latter's control positions and to guarantee a continued source of contributions. Likewise, to the extent that the economic dominants represent the upper prestige levels in a community, they may be drawn into the control structure by the active community leaders in an effort by the latter to legitimize their own prestige positions.

It should be noted, however, that both of the foregoing hypothetical instances cast the economic dominants in the role of rather reluctant participants in local power structures. In such situations, it would be *other* members of the community, not the economic dominants nor the dominant economic units themselves, who would have most stake in the latters' local involvement. And this, in turn, would have, perhaps, significant ramifications for the kinds of roles which the economic dominants played in community power structures and for the degree of interest and local concern with which they acted out these roles.

Whatever the reasons for the apparent differences in the nature and extent of economic dominant involvement in local power structures—and the delineation of these reasons should certainly be one objective of future research—the Cibola study appears to document the absence of any neat, constant, and direct relationship between *power as a potential for determinative action,* and *power as determinative action, itself.* It suggests, likewise the need to re-examine the role of economic dominance in community power structures in view of the continued drift of American society, on the one hand, toward the concentration of population in suburban and satellite communities, and, on the other, toward the continuing expansion of huge economic bureaucracies.

36. Economic Dominants
and Community Power:
A Comparative Analysis

DONALD A. CLELLAND
WILLIAM H. FORM

INTRODUCTION

Three avenues to the study of American community power structure have received widest attention during the last decade. The earliest approach studied a single set of community influentials who allegedly made the major community decisions.[1] Adherents of this method have generally concluded that business leaders are the "ruling elite" or at least *primi inter pares* in the community power structure. The second method discerned the power structure by examining how specific persons and

SOURCE: Reprinted with permission of the authors and publisher from *The American Journal of Sociology*, LXIX, No. 5 (March, 1964), published by the University of Chicago Press.

ACKNOWLEDGMENT: We are grateful to Professor James B. McKee for a critical reading of the manuscript.

[1] The tradition of Robert S. Lynd and Helen Merrill Lynd, *Middletown in Transition* (New York: Harcourt, Brace & World, Inc., 1937); C. Wright Mills, *The Power Elite* (New York: Oxford University Press, 1956); Floyd Hunter, *Community Power Structure* (Chapel Hill: University of North Carolina Press, 1953), and many others.

groups behaved in specific community issues and decisions.[2] Those using this technique have generally found a pluralistic system of decision-making. The third avenue has investigated the forces changing the character of persons holding positions of potential power.[3] Irrespective of approach, an ideological question has been persistent—whether the community is governed informally by an economic elite or whether the dominant pattern is political pluralism, a situation where decision-makers represent groups with differing interests.

One instructive way of posing this controversy is to ask what types of relationships characterize the stratification orders in American communities in the past and in the present.[4] More specifically, the sociological question is: To what extent has private economic power been translated directly into community or public power? Although R. O. Schulze did not formally place his research within the Weberian framework, operationally he did study the question we have posed by tracing historically the place of economically powerful figures in the public life of Cibola.[5] The study reported here attempts to replicate his investigation in a different type of community, which we shall call "Wheelsburg."

Schulze's findings upheld his hypothesis that as a city grows from an isolated, self-contained entity to an urbanized community "increasingly involved and interrelated in the large social complex," its sociopolitical power structure changes from a monolithic one dominated by persons possessing great economic power to a bifurcated structure comprising "two crucial and relatively discrete power sets, the economic dominants and the public leaders."[6] Economic dominants were defined as "those

---

2 E.g., Robert A. Dahl, "Equality and Power in American Society," in *Power and Democracy in America,* ed. William V. D'Antonio and Howard J. Ehrlich (Notre Dame, Ind.: University of Notre Dame Press, 1961); Nelson W. Polsby, "The Sociology of Community Power: A Reassessment," *Social Forces,* XXXVII (March, 1959), 232–36; Linton C. Freeman *et al.,* "Local Community Leadership," Syracuse College Paper No. 15 (Syracuse, N.Y.: Syracuse University, 1960); Edward C. Banfield, *Political Influence* (New York: The Free Press, 1961); and many others.

3 Robert A. Dahl, *Who Governs?* (New Haven, Conn.: Yale University Press, 1961); Constance Green, *Holyoke, Massachusetts* (New Haven, Conn.: Yale University Press, 1939); Thorstein Veblen, *Absentee Ownership* (New York: The Viking Press, Inc., 1939); and the works of R. O. Schulze cited in n. 5.

4 In the framework of Max Weber as explicated in "Class, Status and Power," in *From Max Weber: Essays in Sociology,* ed. and trans. Hans H. Gerth and C. Wright Mills (New York: Oxford University Press, 1946).

5 Robert O. Schulze, "Economic Dominance and Public Leadership: A Study of the Structure and Process of Power in an Urban Community" (microfilmed Ph.D. dissertation, University of Michigan, 1956); "The Role of Economic Dominants in Community Power Structure," *American Sociological Review,* XXIII (February, 1958), 3–9; "The Bifurcation of Power in a Satellite City," in *Community Political Systems,* ed. Morris Janowitz (New York: The Free Press 1961), pp. 19–80.

6 "The Bifurcation of Power . . . ," *op. cit.,* pp. 21–22.

persons who occupy the top formal statuses in the major economic units
within the community area,"[7] and public leaders (or top influentials) as
those who, in the opinion of community "knowledgeables," exercise
major influence and leadership in community affairs.[8]

Schulze tentatively explained the dissociation of economic dominants
from local political-civic affairs by the following three trends:

> (a) the establishment by a growing number of locally-owned industrial
> units of direct supplier relationships with a small number of large, non-
> local manufacturing plants; (b) the subsequent introduction into the local
> economic system of an increasing number of branch plants of large, absen-
> tee-owned corporations; and (c) the concomitant dissolution of the exten-
> sive networks of interlocking directorates and officerships which had
> formerly served to link significant numbers of local economic dominants
> within the community.[9]

These trends have also occurred in Wheelsburg, but to a more limited
degree. The greatest variation between Cibola and Wheelsburg is in the
first factor, because in Wheelsburg many local supply plants were established to serve the local automobile firms.

COMPARISON OF THE COMMUNITIES

The two communities differ significantly in a number of ways. For
most of its history Cibola was a small independent town. It is now a
satellite city of approximately 20,000 inhabitants located just beyond the
standard metropolitan area of a large midwest industrial center containing more than 3,000,000 people. The five largest of its eight major

---

[7] *Ibid.*, p. 21. For Schulze's operational criteria for determining economic dominants
and public leaders see *ibid.*, Appendixes A and B, pp. 73–75. Essentially the same criteria
were utilized to identify the dominant economic units (and consequently economic
dominants themselves) in the two cities. Number of employees, capital worth, and
assessed valuation were used as measures. However, since Wheelsburg is a much larger
city than Cibola, the minimum figures for cutoff points were necessarily larger. In Cibola
the only dominant economic units were manufacturing plants, banks, and savings and
loan companies. In Wheelsburg a wider variety of economic units was included in the
dominant group, e.g., department stores, utilities, and insurance companies. In addition
to the heads of the major economic units, all who were on the board of directors of two
or more of the major economic units were also identified as economic dominants.

[8] As suggested by Hunter, *op. cit.* The "knowledgeables" who were interviewed in the
two studies differed somewhat. Schulze's knowledgeables were the heads of local voluntary associations. This research relied on the nominations of fourteen high-ranking
officials from seven institutional sectors of the community (mass communication, business, union, welfare, education, government, religion). David A. Booth and Charles A.
Adrian compared the results of the method used by Schulze with the simpler method we
employed, and found almost identical results (see their "Simplifying the Discovery of
Elites," *American Behavioral Scientist,* V [October, 1961], 14–16).

[9] Schulze, "The Role of Economic Dominants . . . ," *op cit.,* p. 6.

industrial plants were absentee-controlled. Cibola is an extreme example of a city that "has felt the full impact of the metropolitan drift of American life."[10] A period of rapid expansion began during World War II with the establishment just outside the city's boundaries of a gigantic war production plant which employed over 40,000 workers at its peak. After the war the economic instability of absentee-owned companies occupying this plant caused wide and rapid fluctuations in the local labor force. Consequently, during the 1940's the community experienced rapid fluctuation and high turnover in population. At the time of Schulze's study employment at the main plant had leveled off at 9500 as it became tied securely to the motor vehicle industry.

Wheelsburg is located about 60 miles west of Cibola. It is an independent city of over 100,000 dominating a metropolitan area with a population of approximately 180,000. Like Cibola, its economy is based primarily on motor vehicle production. In fact, the same motor vehicle company is the largest single employer in both communities. In Wheelsburg the company employs nearly 15,000 workers. However, significant sections of Wheelsburg's labor force are employed in state government and in a nearby state university. Wheelsburg's period of most rapid industrial and population growth occurred earlier than Cibola's, between 1900 and 1920. This growth largely reflected the success of locally owned automobile and supplier plants. Since 1920 Wheelsburg's growth has been moderate and steady even with the large invasion of absentee-owned companies. Such companies came earlier to Wheelsburg, but entered and grew more gradually than in Cibola.

Currently, 13 of the 20 non-financial dominant economic units are absentee controlled.[11] Unlike Cibola, (a) Wheelsburg's major firms have been fairly stable operations, (b) the vast majority of its labor force has always been employed within the city limits, (c) very few of its economic dominants have lived beyond the city's contiguous suburbs, and (d) the city is removed from the influence of a large competing metropolis. Wheelsburg, then, is a much more stable and "normal" type of community setting in which to test Schulze's hypothesis.

Following Schulze's method closely, we tested his main hypothesis by (1) reconstructing the formal participation patterns of economic dominants over the past century in the political and civic activities of the

---

10 Schulze, "The Bifurcation of Power . . . ," *op. cit.*, p. 24.

11 An absentee-controlled company is defined as one having a majority of its board of directors living outside of the local community. In both Cibola and Wheelsburg, slightly less than 50 percent of the dominant economic units were absentee-controlled—five of eleven units in Cibola and thirteen of twenty-seven units in Wheelsburg. In both cities, all of the financial units (three and seven, respectively) were locally owned.

community: (2) ascertaining the representation of current economic dominants among public leaders, that is, in the "reputational" power structure; and (3) analyzing the role of current economic dominants in specific community issues and programs.

ECONOMIC DOMINANTS AS POLITICAL AND CIVIC LEADERS

In Wheelsburg, as in Cibola, the proportion of economic dominants who occupied high local governmental offices declined dramatically over the century. Data in Tables 1 and 2 reveal that in both communities prior to 1900 the economic dominants were highly represented in local government. The comparable percentages in each table are virtually identical. Although the twentieth century ushered in a sharp decline in the proportion of economic dominants holding public office in both communities, this decline was sharper in Wheelsburg than in Cibola. Moreover, in both cities, but especially in Wheelsburg, the offices held by economic dominants have been increasingly appointive rather than elective. Indeed, no economic dominant has served as mayor since 1899, or as councilman since 1932.

The trend of these developments in Wheelsburg may be seen more clearly by examining the data in terms of twenty-year periods. A precipitous decline in public officeholding by economic dominants occurred in the 1900–1920 period, with relatively little change thereafter. However, there has been a continuing change in the type of office held. In each succeeding twenty-year period, fewer of the economic dominants who held office were elected. Increasingly, they have come to hold advisory

TABLE 1.

Economic Dominants Serving in Public Office in Wheelsburg and Cibola

Period	No. of Economic Dominants	Percent			
		In Public Office	In Elective Office	On Governing Body	In Highest Public Office
1823–60:					
Wheelsburg	*	...	...	...	...
Cibola	12	83	83	75	50
1860–1900:					
Wheelsburg	44	73	64	57	30
Cibola	21	81	67	57	33
1900–1940:					
Wheelsburg	80	25	11	4	0
Cibola	43	26	16	12	5
1940–59:					
Wheelsburg	71	14	0	0	0
Cibola	31	23	13	10	3

SOURCE: Cibola data, see Schulze, "The Bifurcation of Power . . . ," *op. cit.*, pp. 37–38.
* Wheelsburg was not incorporated until 1859.

and honorary positions in local government. Since it is probably fair to assume that the power potential of appointive offices is less than that of

TABLE 2.

Offices Held by Politically Active Economic Dominants in Wheelsburg and Cibola*

| Period | No. of Politically Active Economic Dominants | Percent | | |
		In Elective Office	On Governing Body	In Highest Public Office
1823–1860:				
Wheelsburg	...	...	...	...
Cibola	10	100	90	60
1860–1900:				
Wheelsburg	32	88	78	41
Cibola	17	88	71	41
1900–1940:				
Wheelsburg	20	45	15	0
Cibola	12	64	45	18
1940–1959:				
Wheelsburg	10	0	0	0
Cibola	7	57	43	14

SOURCE: Cibola data, see Schulze, "The Bifurcation of Power . . . ," *op. cit.*, pp. 37–38.
  * "Politically active" refers to economic dominants holding any appointive or elective office.

elective offices, the shift of economic dominants from the latter may be taken as evidence of continuing loss of formal political power.

Schulze suggests that after 1900 the arena of local involvement of the economic dominants shifted from politics to voluntary associations. The Wheelsburg data confirm his observation. Thus data in Table 3 show

TABLE 3.

Economic Dominants as Board Members of Chamber of Commerce

| Period | Median No. of Memberships per Year on Board of Directors* | | No. Serving as President | |
	Wheelsburg	Cibola	Wheelsburg	Cibola
1901–6	8	...	3	...
1906–13	9	...	4	...
1913–20	9	...	4	...
1920–27	10	6	3	3
1927–34	9	3	2	2
1934–41	9	3	2	0
1941–48	4	2	0	1
1948–55	3	1	3	0
1955–59	5	...	0	...

SOURCE: Cibola data, Schulze, "The Bifurcation of Power . . . ," *op. cit.*, p. 49. Since the Cibola Chamber was founded in 1920, there are no data for earlier periods.
  * The number of directors varied from 15 to 18 in Cibola and from 15 to 21 in Wheelsburg.

that at the beginning the economic dominants were highly represented among the members and officers of the Chamber of Commerce, and that their representation declined at a later era. Apparently the Wheelsburg economic dominants were even more powerful in the Chamber than their Cibola counterparts, for one of their number was president during 19 of the first 20 years of the organization's existence. During the past two decades their representation in the Chamber has declined, but not so sharply as in Cibola. An historical analysis of the proportion of officer-ships held by Wheelsburg economic dominants in other civic organizations (major service clubs, community chest, and the board of trustees of the leading local hospital) reveals patterns of withdrawal similar to that evident in Table 3. While it is difficult to estimate the power potential of these officerships, current public leaders or top influentials regard the Chamber of Commerce as the single most influential organization in the city. Yet, as indicated above, direct control of this organization by economic dominants has probably declined over the years.

In both Wheelsburg and Cibola economic dominants reduced their incumbency in public offices at the turn of the century. A similar withdrawal from civic leadership positions began about 1940.[12] A comparative analysis of the economic development of the two communities corroborates some of Schulze's explanations and contradicts others. The evidence fails to support Schulze's position that the growth of absentee ownership and the dissolution of local business ties (interlocking directorates) among the economic dominants account for their withdrawal from public office. In both communities these phenomena occurred *after* the withdrawal; in Cibola, the first absentee-controlled plant was established in 1932, and in Wheelsburg as late as 1940 two-thirds of the major economic units were locally owned. Moreover, 80 percent of the Wheelsburg economic dominants maintained local business ties with other economic dominants as late as 1940. A third factor which Schulze associated with withdrawal, namely, the growth of direct supplier relationships to non-local industries by locally owned plants, must also be discarded, for in Wheelsburg no such growth took place and yet the pattern of withdrawal was similar to that of Cibola. Moreover, in Wheelsburg this withdrawal does not seem to have been forced by the growing political power of ethnic groups as was the case in many American cities.[13] There

---

12 "Withdrawal" is probably an apt phrase, because no evidence is available to suggest that there was community pressure on the economic dominants to reduce their community involvement. However, individual economic dominants were constantly changing. Their withdrawal consisted not so much in dropping civic leadership positions as in the failure of new economic dominants to seek such positions.

13 E.g., in New Haven, from the late nineteenth century until recently, local politics were controlled primarily by "ex-plebes," individuals on the rise from the ethnic

has never been a large ethnic proletariat in Wheelsburg, nor have local politics ever been heavily based on ethnic lines or class conflict.

What factors, then, are associated with the sharp decline in political participation by economic dominants (i.e., the bifurcation of political and economic power structure) since the turn of the century? At the broadest level of explanation, the increased involvement of the community and its economic units in state and nationwide social economic systems was, no doubt, an important factor. More specifically, in Wheelsburg, the end of the period in which political and economic power tended to coincide was marked by the rise of a new breed of economic elite, namely, managers and owners of the new automobile and supply plants. Younger, wealthier, operating larger businesses, more directly involved in the day-to-day operation of their businesses, introducing a wide variety of new products, these men did not participate in local politics probably largely because they lacked the time and because they probably found that business was much more exciting. A growing separation of wealth and social honor may have been a second factor, but the new economic elite was partly based on old local wealth and the majority were entrepreneurs rather than simply managers of companies financed by non-local capital. However, in the absence of ethnic and class cleavage in the community, it is doubtful that the new economic dominants, many of whom were classed Horatio Alger success models, lacked the popularity needed for election. They probably did not choose to run.

On the other hand, later withdrawal from civic leadership positions seems to be associated with the introduction of absentee-owned plants and the related decrease in common local business ties (interlocking directorates) among the economic dominants. The importance of the latter factor is underscored in Wheelsburg where economic dominants not only have more local economic linkages but also comprise a larger proportion of the local civic leaders.[14]

The so-called pattern of withdrawal needs to be interpreted within a broad context of the local participation. In Wheelsburg, the historical pattern has been for the economic dominants to become officers of new organizations as they emerged in the community, then to retain membership, and later to withdraw from active participation. Thus when the

---

proletariat, who gained office through "the skills of ethnic politics." From 1842 to 1898, New Haven politics were dominated by the leading entrepreneurs. It may be significant that the period of dominance by economic dominants is almost identical in New Haven, Wheelsburg, and Cibola (see Dahl, *Who Governs?*, chap. iii and iv).

[14] Sixty-five percent of the economic dominants in the 1940–59 period were associated as officers, partners, or directors in at least one other business with other economic dominants.

Chamber of Commerce was created, dominants were its earliest officers; when the service clubs arose they again became officers; when the Community Chest arrived they became its sponsors and officers; and they sponsored the largest hospital and dominated its board. This pattern of domination and later "withdrawal" is subject to various interpretations. We are inclined to believe that it demonstrates two related phenomena: (a) assumption of officerships in new organizations validated not only their importance to the community but the power and status of the original officers, namely, the economic dominants, and (b) the policies, direction, and administration of the new organizations were set and institutionalized by the original officers. After this initial period the organizations needed only informal and non-official guidance from the dominants and not their active officeholding. In other words, a change in officers did not necessarily mean a change in policy or loss of power and control by dominants.[15]

COMMUNITY INFLUENCE OF
ECONOMIC DOMINANTS

In order to assess the community influence of current economic dominants in Wheelsburg, two procedures were used. First, their reputational influence was investigated by assessing their representation in the list of public leaders (community influentials as determined by the method outlined in n. 8). Second, their "actual" influence was probed by examining their role in a number of community issues or projects.

In 1958-59, 39 individuals were found to be economic dominants, and coincidentally, 39 people were designated as public leaders. The names of 12 persons (31 percent) appeared on both lists. This overlap is considerably higher than that found in Cibola where only two of 17 economic dominants were among the community's 18 public leaders. Moreover, eight of the top 15 public leaders in Wheelsburg, including the top four, as rated by the public leaders themselves, were economic dominants. Although major absentee-owned corporations were "underrepresented" among the economic dominants who were also public leaders, "U.S. Motors" (the absentee-owned industrial giant in the community) was represented by three executives (two of whom were not defined as economic dominants). From these observations we cannot conclude that two discrete power sets are found in Wheelsburg.

In order to substantiate the basic dissimilarities between the economic dominants and public leaders in Cibola, Schulze examined their patterns

---

[15] Lest the concentration on "withdrawal" be overwhelming, it should be noted that almost half the economic dominants in the 1940–59 period held civic leadership positions in Wheelsburg and that their participation in the Chamber of Commerce was increasing.

of political and civic participation. He found that the economic dominants had held only about half as many governmental offices as the
public leaders. The same was true in Wheelsburg, although both groups
were less active. Somewhat surprisingly, economic dominants were as well
represented as the public leaders in the five most influential associations.
Table 4 reveals a similar situation of high participation by both economic dominants and public leaders in Wheelsburg's most influential
associations. However, the Cibola situation of wide differences between
public leaders and economic dominants in the number of officerships
held in these associations was not in evidence. Table 5 reveals that a
higher proportion of economic dominants in Wheelsburg (from both
locally and absentee-owned companies) have in the past held office in the
five most influential organizations. Differences are small between the two
communities in the proportions currently holding such offices. In short,
both Tables 4 and 5 document no deep bifurcation in associational
participation between Wheelsburg's economic dominants and public
leaders. The relatively high rate of participation by absentee-owned
corporation executives is especially notable.[16]

One of the reasons for the failure of economic dominants to participate
in the civic life of Cibola was that they regarded the city mainly as the
locus of their work life and not their community life.[17] Moreover, their
private economic interests were primarily non-local. This may not be
surprising since the city's largest economic units were absentee-owned
and oriented toward a national market. However, Table 6 indicates that
a much more extensive network of economic ties exists in Wheelsburg
than in Cibola.[18] Despite a high degree of absentee ownership in
Wheelsburg, a fairly extensive network of economic ties unites the interests of the economic dominants and the public leaders. These ties may
explain the higher rate of civic participation by its economic dominants
and their closer social integration to public leaders.

As a final demonstration of the bifurcation of Cibola economic dominants and public leaders, Schulze analyzed the decision-making process

---

[16] Although managers of the largest absentee-owned corporation did not dominate the
local scene as extensively as in the case of Bigtown, they did have representatives on
most of the local bodies to co-ordinate knowledge of what was going on in the city. For
data on Bigtown see Roland J. Pellegrin and Charles H. Coates, "Absentee-owned Corporations and Community Power Structure," *American Journal of Sociology*, LXI
(March, 1956), 413–19.

[17] A large proportion lived in other communities in the metropolitan area and may
have participated in the associational life of these other communities.

[18] "Economic ties" are instances in which a pair of individuals serve as officers or
directors of the same firm. Each pair is counted as one economic tie. For example, if
four public leaders serve on the board of directors of a bank, there are six economic ties
(pairs).

TABLE 4.

Membership of Current Public Leaders and Economic Dominants in the Most
Influential Associations*

Association	Public Leaders	Percent Belonging to Association Economic Dominants		
		Local	Absentee	Total
Chamber of Commerce:				
Wheelsburg	87	96	100	97
Cibola	78	100	87	94
Rotary:				
Wheelsburg	49	38	40	38
Cibola	50	70	14	47
Kiwanis:				
Wheelsburg	18	13	7	10
Cibola	44	30	0	18
Lions:				
Wheelsburg	5	8	0	5
Cibola	11	0	0	0

SOURCE for Cibola data: Schulze, "The Bifurcation . . . ," op. cit., p. 47.

* In Cibola the five most influential associations were determined by polling the voluntary association heads, public leaders, and economic dominants. The four associations listed above and the Junior Chamber of Commerce were named by all of the groupings questioned. These organizations were also designated by Wheelsburg public leaders as highly influential. Since few public leaders or economic dominants were young enough to be eligible for membership in the Junior Chamber of Commerce in either city, and none were members, this association was omitted from the table.

TABLE 5.

Officerships of Public Leaders and Economic Dominants in
Five Most Influential Community Associations

	Public Leaders		Economic Dominants					
			Local		Absentee		Total	
	Wheelsburg	Cibola	Wheelsburg	Cibola	Wheelsburg	Cibola	Wheelsburg	Cibola
Percent having served as president of at least one of the five associations....	31	61	25	20	20	0	23	12
No. of presidencies occupied in the five associations....	17	14	8	2	3	0	11	2
Percent currently serving as officer or board member in at least one of the five associations*...	18	44	4	10	27	30	13	18
No. of officerships or board memberships currently held in the five associations....	7	12	1	1	4	2	5	3

SOURCE: Cibola data, Schulze, "The Bifurcation of Power . . . ," op. cit., p. 48.

* "Currently" refers to the year of research: 1954 for Cibola, 1958–59 for Wheelsburg.

on two important community issues. The economic dominants refused to become involved in resolving either of them, leaving the public leaders autonomous but perhaps without a solid power basis for community action.

In Wheelsburg, an analysis of eleven community issues[19] revealed that

TABLE 6.

Number of Known Local Economic Ties
Among Public Leaders and Economic Dominants

| | | Economic Dominants | |
	Public Leaders	Local Firm	Absentee Firm
Public leaders:			
Wheelsburg	23	31	8
Cibola	4	3	2
Local-firm dominants:			
Wheelsburg	...	47	11
Cibola	...	15	0
Absentee-firm dominants: *			
Wheelsburg	...	...	2
Cibola	...	...	2

SOURCE: Cibola data supplied by Robert O. Schulze in an unpublished manuscript.
* In neither Wheelsburg nor Cibola were there any economic ties between absentee-firm dominants from *different* corporations. In the case of two absentee firms in Wheelsburg, a second person in addition to the general manager was defined as an economic dominant because he held a directorship in a local bank as well as an officership in an absentee-owned firm.

eight of the economic dominants who were also public leaders were among those mentioned as influential in initiating and resolving these issues. Economic dominants, including some representing absentee-owned corporations, either initiated or co-initiated programs of action for six of the eight issues in which they were involved. Although this evidence suggests that economic dominants have not withdrawn from community decision-making and that they are not just ceremonial leaders, apparently they do not form a monolithic power elite. Different indivduals

---

19 These issues were selected and recapitulated by the public leaders in interviews. They included hospital expansion drive, downtown development, establishment of a metropolitan planning agency, improvement of airport terminal facilities, establishment of a tricounty planning agency, annexation of a school district to the city, widening of a city street, ban on Sunday shopping, proposed shift of location of city hall, proposed sale of bonds by the city to finance construction of parking facilities, and proposed annexation of a suburban shopping center. Our inspection of newspapers and other documents reveals that these indeed represent nearly the full range of community issues during the last five or six years. One or two others might be added by other local interests such as organized labor (see William H. Form and Warren L. Sauer, "Community and Labor Influentials: A Comparative Study of Participation and Imagery," *Industrial and Labor Relation Review*, XVII [October, 1963], 3–19).

became involved in different issues, doing so in the process of playing their own "games."[20]

Not all of the broad community issues in which economic dominants were involved were controversial. Some of them may more properly be called "projects." The major issues in Cibola seemed to involve a higher degree of conflict in the political arena. Perhaps this conflict reflected the inertia of partisan party politics which existed in the community as late as 1947. In addition, both of the major issues in Cibola—adoption of a new city charter and annexation—were the direct results of rapid urbanization and industrialization, processes which had occurred at a more gradual rate in Wheelsburg. There, political life seemed less marked by conflict, for local government not only was non-partisan but it traditionally and customarily responded to the needs of business.[21] It is highly probable that the lack of political conflict and the tendency for community decision-making to be channeled to the private rather than public sphere are interdependent. In Wheelsburg there was little evidence of basic differences in values among the economic dominants, the public leaders, and the elected officials. If representation of conflicting interests or values is chosen as the indicator of pluralism in the power structure, Wheelsburg (and most American communities) will be judged less pluralistic than if a weaker test of pluralism, such as the participation of separate individuals in different issues, is used.[22]

Thus, the social climate of the decision-making roles of the economic dominants in the two cities is not identical. Whether Wheelsburg dominants would become involved in highly conflictful issues should they arise is not known. Certainly they hesitated to publize their involvement in controversial issues.[23] One large firm, for example, refused to become overtly involved in an annexation issue despite the fact that its economic interests were involved. However, it made its position known. What covert influence this might have had cannot be accurately appraised. Yet, since executives of the absentee-owned corporations were less likely to become involved in community decision-making than economic dominants from

---

[20] Norton E. Long, "The Urban Community as an Ecology of Games," *American Journal of Sociology*, LXIV (November, 1958), 251–61.

[21] Form and Sauer, *op. cit.*

[22] For a fuller discussion of this problem see Marshall N. Goldstein, "Absentee Ownership and Monolithic Power Structures: Two Questions for Community Studies," in *Current Trends in Comparative Community Studies*, ed. Bert E. Swanson (Kansas City, Mo.: Community Studies, Inc., 1962), pp. 49–59.

[23] The same attitudes were revealed in interviews conducted by Rossi in Mediana. This does not mean that economic dominants had withdrawn from local influence systems because, as Rossi points out, "this is the age of community projects" (Peter H. Rossi, "The Organizational Structure of an American Community," in *Complex Organizations*, ed. Amitai Etzioni [New York: Holt, Rinehart & Winston, Inc., 1961], p. 301).

locally owned enterprises, possibly Wheelsburg's pattern of influence is evolving toward the type found in Cibola. On the other hand, both economic dominants and public leaders work hard to solve issues without conflict, and controversial issues probably arise less often in gradually expanding cities such as Wheelsburg than in cities which have grown very rapidly and have experienced extreme economic fluctuations, such as Cibola. Further research is required to determine the power roles of economic dominants in cities differing in size, social composition, economic composition, and economic history.

CONCLUSIONS

Comparative analysis of the roles of economic dominants in power structures of a satellite and an independent city reveals that in both communities the formal political and economic power structures which were once melded have tended to become bifurcated over time. This process seems to have paralleled the integration of local economic units into national markets and the process of governmental centralization. The economic dominants, once highly active leaders in civic associations, have tended to reduce their participation in this area, especially in the satellite community. This withdrawal coincided roughly with the rapid extension of absentee ownership in both cities. Currently, the nearly complete bifurcation of economic dominants and public leaders (top influentials) found in the satellite city was not as evident in the independent city, where an extensive network of economic ties bound the two groups together. Moreover, unlike the economic dominants in the satellite city, those in the independent city have not abandoned their decision-making role in community issues.

While the evidence cited in this research is not conclusive, it points to variable patterns of relations between economic dominants and public leaders in different types of communities. Apparently the absence of local party politics, a history of local industries becoming absentee-owned rather than the introduction of branch plants from outside the community, the institutionalization of local political controls, and the absence of ethnic, class, or other cleavages which contribute to partisan politics reduce the withdrawal rate of economic dominants from participation in community associations and local power arrangements. The time is ripe for many rapid comparative studies of a wide range of communities to determine more precisely the factors responsible for the bifurcation of persistence of ties between economic dominants, civic leaders, and community influentials.

37. Change Comes to Cornucopia—Industry and the Community

ROBERT MILLS FRENCH

A community's economic structure plays an important role in determining its social-political characteristics. This was illustrated in Williams and Adrian's study of four Michigan communities. They found that Alpha differed from the other three cities primarily because its economy was dominated by locally-owned and managed industry, whereas Beta, Delta and Gamma were typified by more absentee-owned industry influence.[1] In this characteristic Alpha was closer to early Yankee City or Middletown which also had locally-dominated economies.

The key element in the transformation of Yankee City was the absentee-owned shoe manufacturers that replaced local firms.[2] Schulze also found that the shift in domination of the local economy from local hands to absentee-interest was the key element of change.[3] Cibola's leadership

---

[1] Oliver P. Williams and Charles R. Adrian, *Four Cities—A Study in Comparative Policy Making* (Philadelphia: University of Pennsylvania Press, 1963), especially Chapter II.

[2] W. Lloyd Warner and J. O. Low, "The Factory In The Community," in William Foote Whyte, ed., *Industry and Society* (New York: McGraw-Hill Book Company, 1946), pp. 21–45.

[3] Robert O. Schulze, "The Role of Economic Dominants In Community Power Structure," *American Sociological Review*, XXIII (February, 1958), 3–9.

bifurcated with absentee-interests controlling the community's economy; local figures continued to dominate the social-political scene. Schulze documented the breakdown of the old pyramidal power structure in which a small group of local economic dominants controlled all the aspects of community life, political and social affairs as well as the economic scene. A more pluralistic political and social order ensued with middle-class business and professional men assuming the leadership that had been the domain of the economic dominants.

The new economic dominants of Cibola, the representatives of large, absentee-owned corporations, maintained a "hands-off" policy concerning local affairs. In Cibola, as in other communities where outside economic control has been observed, the corporate executives took an interest in local affairs only when the interests of the firm were involved.[4]

Thus the impact of national corporations on the community appears to result in a dual process of increasing pluralism in local social-political affairs while the community's economic determination passes into the hands of outsiders who remain aloof from local affairs. As Schulze observed, a bifurcation of community power takes place.

SETTING OF THE STUDY

Although bifurcation and lack of corporate manager participation in local affairs has been observed in several communities, how this transformation is accomplished is not well known. What is needed is documentation of the process as it occurs. The study of Cornucopia was made with this end in mind.

In the spring of 1964 Cornucopia, Illinois, was a small town (about 11,000 population) with an uncertain future. It had just become widely known that the Chromeboat Auto Company had selected Cornucopia as the site of a large assembly plant that was scheduled to open the following year and would eventually employ 5,000 workers. Just what this meant to the community was not certain, but it seemed sure that Cornucopia would never again be the typical Midwestern town that it had

---

4 *Ibid.;* Williams and Adrian, *op. cit.;* Donald A. Clelland and William H. Form, "Economic Dominants and Community Power, A Comparative Analysis," *American Journal of Sociology,* LXIX, No. 5 (March, 1964), 511–521; Ted C. Smith, "The Structuring of Power in a Suburban Community," *Pacific Sociological Review,* III (Fall, 1960), 83–88; Arnold M. Rose, "Communication and Participation in a Small City as Viewed by its Leaders," *International Journal of Opinions and Attitude Research,* V (Fall, 1951), 367–390; M. Kent Jennings, *Community Influentials,* (New York: The Free Press, 1964); Jackson M. McClain and Robert B. Highsaw, *Dixie City Acts: A Study in Decision-Making* (University, Ala.: University of Alabama, Bureau of Public Administration, 1962); Roland A. Pellegrin and Charles H. Coates, "Absentee-Owned Corporations and Community Power Structure," *American Journal of Sociology,* LXI (March, 1956), 413–419.

always pictured itself to be. Along with the note of optimism that the business community had in anticipation of the coming growth, was a feeling of apprehension that Chromeboat would bring in "undesirables" and would attempt to run the town. The study of Cornucopia commenced at this point.

The plan of study was to ascertain the nature of Cornucopia's social life and political structure immediately preceeding the impact of Chromeboat, to provide a comparative base against which change could be measured. It quickly became apparent, however, that an additional dimension—Cornucopia's past—would have to be considered to fully understand what was occurring in the community. The study that resulted considers Cornucopia at three stages in its life: first, its early days when a single locally-owned firm dominated the social and economic affairs of Cornucopia; second, the period just before the coming of Chromeboat (1964) and shortly after the collapse of the dominant local industry; and third, three years later (1967) when the community was experiencing the immediate impact of Chromeboat. Stages two and three were studied by direct observation; stage one was reconstructed through records, old newspapers and interviews with survivors of this early era.

The reputational, positional and decision-making techniques of assessing community power were all employed in the 1964 and 1967 studies to avoid getting a distorted picture of community influence.

EARLY CORNUCOPIA AND THE AMERICAN SEWING MACHINE COMPANY

Like Middletown or the early Yankee City, Cornucopia's major industry from the 1890's through the 1940's, the American Sewing Machine Company, was a locally-run concern. Although the original owners were outsiders who came to Cornucopia for the purpose of founding the factory, they settled in the community and became permanent residents. The company was owned and managed by the Bainbridge family and their relatives by marriage from the founding of the plant in 1886 to 1948 when they sold out to an absentee firm. How successful the American was during its period of local ownership is debatable. There were periods of "boom and bust" but according to the last local manager, Bernard Tally, the firm never failed to make a profit.

After the local owners left, the firm fell on hard times. Foreign competition apparently made it difficult for domestic manufacturers to show a profit, and in 1952 the American was sold to an absentee-owned holding company that closed the factory and liquidated its assets.

The resultant situation, which continued until the coming of Chromeboat, left Cornucopia with a number of smaller firms, both locally and absentee-owned, none of which dominated or controlled the community.

The esteem with which the owner-managers of the American plant have been held throughout Cornucopia's history is reminiscent of Warner's portrayal of the local barons of Yankee City, e.g., the managers of men were gods whose authority and wisdom was recognized and referred to long after they were dead.[5] The American's founder, Bainbridge, was held in awe and his isolationist, high-tariff national policy was highly thought of. Even today his wisdom may be evoked in a discussion of world affairs.

Implicit in the remembrances of past "giants" is the assumption that they had the interests of the community at heart. Participation in civic duties, perhaps by holding political office as did the early leaders of Cibola,[6] is seen as part of their community function that was more than merely an economic role.

Unlike Cibola's early leaders, the managers of American did not take part in politics, and until Bernard Tally became president in 1928, they avoided involvement in community affairs. No president or officer of the American Co. was ever elected to a public office. Tally deviated somewhat and participated in several community organizations, but he did not enter local politics or become intensely involved in any community issue. The mayor's office was seen as an honorarium and local politics as a housekeeping function. So long as the American wasn't threatened by increased taxes or new legislation the plant managers avoided taking a role in the political organization.

Lack of participation by the factory managers did not mean lack of control, for our informants pointed out that what the American Company wanted in local matters, it got. The firm's taxes were quite low and in the event that the plant manager did take a stand, his view was dominant. A single example will suffice to show how the American owners exercised their influence in community affairs. Perhaps the key issue in assessing the influence of the American plant in Cornucopia occurred in the late 1930's. There was a local campaign to have a municipal light and power company in Cornucopia. The American opposed the idea because it sold many washing and sewing machines to private power companies and none to municipal power plants. Tally stated the company position in a letter that appeared in the local newspaper, and in addition talked against the proposal to individuals in the factory and the community. The campaign soon lost support and nothing more was heard about municipally-owned utilities.

Company policy was not to become formally involved in community issues, but rather to approach workers and other community members on

5 W. Lloyd Warner, ed., *Yankee City* (New Haven: Yale University Press, 1963), pp. 325–331.

6 Schulze, *op. cit.*

a man to man basis. Tally considered the American a "community plant" that had the interests of the town at heart and in turn could count on staunch loyalty from the workmen and townspeople.

Although none of the managers or plant executives ever held the mayor's office, the mayor was usually an American employee. Working for American was apparently important in whether or not a candidate got elected. The plant manager would urge the workers to vote for the "factory candidate." Inasmuch as American employed the majority of household heads in the community, management support was not to be taken lightly. Many of Cornucopia's mayors were factory workers and, in fact, Wes Cornow, the mayor at the time of the 1964 study, got his start in city politics as an American candidate.

Certainly having economic influence over community leaders gave the American owners great control over community decisions. Although Tally denied ever coercing a mayor to do American's bidding, he commented: "I thought possibly it was wise to have someone there (in the mayor's office) that might listen to any objections we had if something occurred that was going to be detrimental to us. . . .Having mayors in our employ made it easier to talk to them."

That the power structure of early Cornucopia was pyramidal seems certain. A few wealthy industrialists, bankers and businessmen controlled the community for over half a century; all were subordinate to the will of the town's economic mainstay—The American Sewing Machine Company. One man, the head of American, was the final authority in many issues. If he did not "run the town" it was primarily because it was not advantageous to do so. When the plant manager chose to exert his influence in an issue he got his way, for he was the apex of a pyramidal power structure based on economic control.

THE INTERIM COMMUNITY—CORNUCOPIA BEFORE THE COMING OF CHROMEBOAT

The closing of the American Sewing Machine Company brought about a drastic change in the power structure and general life of Cornucopia. Although the closing meant the removal of the town's economic mainstay, it also meant freedom from pyramidal control of community affairs. What power structure arose in the vacuum left by American's withdrawal from local affairs was established in a study employing several research techniques. Positional figures were located; a reputational power structure was constructed by use of Schulze and Blumberg's battery of five questions;[7] decisional leaders were sought along the lines

---

[7] Robert O. Schulze and Leonard U. Blumberg, "The Determination of Local Power Elites," *American Journal of Sociology,* LXIII (November, 1957) , 290-296.

suggested by Polsby.[8] Regardless of technique used, the same small group of influentials appeared. With one exception high ranking on reputational indices implied overt participation in community decision-making. The exception, R. Fengler, was one of the two most powerful figures in the community; his views on a community issue were often expressed by an underling in his employ. Although he eschewed personal participation, community leaders were well aware of his influence on most issues: his participation was in the form of behind-the-scenes manipulation.

The casual observer of Cornucopia in 1964 might have concluded that the pyramidal power wielded by the American Sewing Machine Company had been assumed by an influential local figure, Fred Husk. As the publisher of the town's only newspaper, head of several businesses, key man in the Republican party, and member of a bank board, Husk appeared invincible. Indeed, a cursory examination of community decision-making would show that whereas issue specialization characterized the participation of most community leaders, Husk was involved in virtually all issues and was chairman of several important committees. City-county politics was dominated by Husk for he held the reins on the only viable political party; what he said went, candidates that he favored were nominated.

If one assumes that public opinion and domination of formal avenues of decision-making do in fact determine community power, then Husk would obviously be a pyramidal power. Greater familiarity with Cornucopia demonstrated, however, that another leader wielded substantial power outside the formal structure. R. Fengler, a banker-landowner and the wealthiest man around, participated little but nonetheless had great influence. To the community at large Fengler was virtually unknown. He had only recently returned to continue his deceased father's business, and did not live in Cornucopia. His community role was not portrayed in Husk's newspaper, the main source of local information for most Cornucopians. Fengler's influence was well known to the small group of citizens who involved themselves in politics and important issues, however. Not only did Cornucopia not have a pluralistic power structure; the majority of its citizens were ignorant of the power structure that affected their lives.

FACTIONAL POWER STRUCTURE

The true nature of Cornucopia's power structure in 1964 was succinctly put by Fengler during an interview: "If it's a question of politics or

---

[8] Nelson W. Polsby, "How To Study Community Power: The Pluralist Alternative," *Journal of Politics,* XXII (1960) , 474-484.

public opinion, then he's (Husk) the one. If it's a question of money, it's me." Time and again the dominance of the two men in different spheres of community life was demonstrated. In matters of acquiring land or raising large sums of money, whether it was for the purpose of building a school or YMCA or planning the path of a highway, Fengler was the key man. With his cooperation the issue had a good chance of success, without it failure was likely. It was common knowledge among lower-ranking leaders that before beginning a project that would require land acquisition or fund raising, it was wise to see Fengler. For example, the local YMCA committee decided that a new building was needed. Suitable land was located that belonged to a local merchant who saw the opportunity to make a larger profit by putting an exorbitant price on the land. He soon had a change of heart, however, when Fengler, who had been approached by the YMCA board for help, let it be known that some land he owned, needed by the merchant for expansion of his business, was increasing in value. A land swap was made between the merchant and Fengler, and the YMCA got its land at a low price from Fengler. Similar evidence of Fengler's ability to realize his will through subtle pressure appeared repeatedly. A fund drive was assured success in the business community if Fengler favored it. Unlike Husk, who would publicly broadcast his views, Fengler's tactics were personal and behind the scenes. A phone call to a reluctant merchant, or a delay in granting a contribution to the favorite project of an opposing leader would generally be sufficient warning to get full cooperation.

In contrast to Fengler's little-known manipulation, Husk gained influence in the community by dint of much effort. His attitude was paternalistic, and his every action was couched in the rhetoric of "what would be best for Cornucopia." He used the newspaper as a personal sounding board on issues, often stepping out of his publisher's role to personally write editorials. He made his presence felt by participating actively in many issues, often taking the chairmanship of a committee. His techniques of getting cooperation were heavy-handed, often running to threats and intimidation at public meetings or through the newspaper. That he had great success in his efforts is undeniable; he controlled local politics, and shaped much of the public opinion of Cornucopia.

The realm in which Husk was dominant was of little importance to Fengler who avoided direct participation in local politics and did not court public favor. This lack of interest was not true of Fengler's father, however, who in the last years of his life fought Husk bitterly for control of the newspaper. The battle ended in the state supreme court and although Husk won control he maintained a good deal of bitterness against the Fenglers. Even though his opponent died, Husk refused to let the feud die and continued to occasionally attack the junior Fengler's interests through the newspaper. By and large, however, the two leaders do not intrude into each other's realm and what we observed in 1964 was a factional power structure, with Husk dominating political and organizational activities, Fengler, the major financial dealings in the town. Each had his loyal followers, but for most of the lower-ranking community leaders learning to deal with both leaders was a necessity of life.

UNREALIZED BIFURCATION

In spite of the fact that they did not have the economic control that the American Sewing Machine Company abdicated, Husk and Fengler successfully moved into the power vacuum left by Tally. A look at Cornucopia's economy in 1964 helps to explain how they were able to dominate the community.

After a brief period of economic decline brought on by American's closing, new industry was attracted to Cornucopia and the economic life of the community was soon dependent upon many smaller corporations ranging in 1964 from an absentee-owned firm with 677 employees to local firms with under ten workers. The majority of jobs in Cornucopia were with absentee-owned firms. In effect, social and economic bifurcation had already been accomplished by 1964. How far bifurcation had already advanced is illustrated by a profile of Cornucopia's economy made in December, 1964. At that time there were 36 firms in Cornucopia of which 19 (53 percent) were locally-owned, 17 (47 percent) were absentee-owned. The absentee-owned firms were much larger on the average than the local companies so that of Cornucopia's 2362 employees, local firms employed 454 (19 percent), whereas the absentee-owned firms employed 1908 or 81 percent of the total work force.

In spite of the dominant role that absentee-owned industry played, no single corporation dominated the town's economy with its payroll or taxes as did the American Co., so the true situation of community dependence on outside forces was not realized. The local heads of absentee-owned industry did little to change this, for they were uninterested in local affairs. We observed that the absentee-managers were hardly known in the community and interacted little on either the social or organizational level. Social-organizational bifurcation had also occurred with locals dominating community affairs and the outsiders making little effort to break out of their isolation. Power bifurcation, however, had not occurred, for although the economic fate of the community was primarily in the hands of the absentee economic dominants, they remained uninvolved and lacked the unity and desire to challenge the local leadership for control.

Local leaders had assumed positions of dominance that were in fact without an economic base. The very real economic sanctions that the old pyramidal power had had to back up its demands were lacking for the factional leaders but they acted in a manner that suggested that they had inherited that control. The lack of interest shown by the true economic powers—the absentee-managers—meant that community power observed in 1964 was wielded without access to the ultimate economic sanction of denying dissenters their livelihood. Bifurcation had occurred but the economic power lay dormant, and the social-organizational-financial figures were free to rule. The power structure was like that of a village without an industrial base, e.g., Springdale, the small community studied by Vidich and Bensman,[9] when in fact, Cornucopia was, and had been for all of its life, an industrial town.

It is puzzling why members of the community accepted the dominance of Husk, and to a much lesser extent Fengler. Fengler's financial power gave him an element of suasion over the businessmen of Cornucopia but it was seldom exercised save in matters of public welfare from which Fengler would not directly benefit. Husk lacked even this, for although he was wealthy and personally influential, he never had control over the town's economy or even an important segment of it. Perhaps the community was slow to realize that the situation had changed and Husk was not in the same position as were the directors of American. Or perhaps the people of Cornucopia were used to being dominated and accepted Husk simply because he was the local figure most prepared to seize the dominant paternalistic role that they were too lackadaisical to attempt to shake off.

CORNUCOPIA 1967—CHROMEBOAT MAKES ITS IMPACT

From the very start of the 1967 replication research it was obvious that leadership had changed in Cornucopia since 1964. Respondents were often confused about how to answer questions that had not troubled them in the earlier interview. One of the leaders summed up his difficulty in answering: "Your questions are tougher to answer now than they were three years ago. There are more people involved, but it's hard to say who's really running things." Another was more direct: "Leadership in town has diversified—Husk no longer can tell the town how to run things."

These impressions were borne out by both the reputational and decision-making indices. The top position reputationally, occupied by Husk in 1964, had been assumed by Fengler, and two other leaders were rated equal to Husk in the second position. In addition, more individuals

---

9 Arthur J. Vidich and Joseph Bensman, *Small Town in Mass Society* (New York: Doubleday & Co., Inc., 1958).

were perceived as wielding a good deal of influence in community affairs than in 1964.

When community decisions were assessed the dispersal of power is readily seen. Whereas Husk had dominated most community decisions observed in the 1964 study, he was the key figure in only one new issue along with an ongoing project begun before 1964. Other leaders dominated the remaining issues, and their participation appeared to be determined by personal interest rather than by general influence in the community. Husk's support for two major projects was not even sought, and local figures had dared to openly oppose Husk in those issues in which he participated. Increasing pluralism in decision-making is illustrated by the fact that although only half as many issues were observed in 1967 as in 1964, more individuals participated in some important capacity in 1967 than in 1964.

Husk's major decline is in being perceived as an acceptable participant in a community project. His inflexibility and outspokenness have made him many enemies, and he is no longer seen as a good man to get a job done in most issues. Partly this is a function of the increasing pluralism we observed; as more people get involved in an issue, it becomes more important to have participants who can compromise and not attempt to force their own point of view. Husk attempts to dominate every meeting he attends, every individual he encounters. To avoid being made subservient to Husk, other leaders circumvent him.

The change in the nature of community projects is perhaps even more significant in explaining Husk's decline. In 1964 whether an issue would succeed or fail was dependent on mobilizing local resources, or in some cases on getting sufficient state funds to carry out the building of a road or bridge. Husk, as the local opinion shaper, could do a great deal to mobilize local resources and, as an influential Republican and bridge builder (his major business is an engineering firm), he could land state projects for the area.

In 1967 local resources were no longer the main source of funds for local projects; Chromeboat now became the primary source of community funds. In both major fund drives observed, Chromeboat's contribution outweighed all others combined, and taxes on the factory would similarly dominate the tax coffers. Effectiveness of community leaders is increasingly measured by how successful they are in getting a contribution from Chromeboat. In 1964 Husk supposedly had influence with Chromeboat because he served as local contact man when Chromeboat was making arrangements to come to Cornucopia. This "influence" was negated when Husk opposed the corporation over how much tax money it should pay. The tax battle is viewed in Cornucopia as Husk's attempt to control Chromeboat, a forlorn hope since in all factory-community relationships to date the influence has been one way—the factory with its unlimited resources influencing the community. Husk's falling-out with the Chromeboat management appeared to be an important element in his declining power.

Lack of influence in state government has also decreased Husk's influence in Cornucopia. With the current Democratic administration of Illinois Husk's outspoken Republicanism could hardly win favors from the governor. Husk's previous prestige has been assumed by Henry, a local industrialist who is a personal friend of the governor. In truth, there is little evidence of effective influence at the state level by any local figure. For example, the Rt. X bypass issue failed repeatedly in spite of all local efforts, until Chromeboat made it known to state officials that the bypass was essential to the corporation's operations.

Local leadership's role is increasingly becoming one of appealing to the proper outside authority for necessary funds. The type of pressure activity practiced effectively in the local community by Husk is simply out of place in this new situation. The decline of Husk as the dominant figure in Cornucopia has been hastened, if not brought about, by the impact of Chromeboat. In a very brief period the factory has had an effect on community leadership and decisions made so that we can state with some certainty that community power is becoming increasingly pluralistic. Has it had a similar impact on the economy that would support the bifurcation hypothesis?

CHROMEBOAT AND THE LOCAL ECONOMY

The one effect of the coming of Chromeboat that was reiterated many times was the rising wage scale and difficulty of getting help. Local plant managers assured us that applicants for jobs that in the past would never have gotten beyond the front door were being hired at higher wages than the best workers formerly made. Typical comments were: "The only help left on the old $1.50 wages are illiterates or housewives," or "We used to pay $1.35 for floor-sweepers, now they won't come in for less than $2.25, it's not Cornucopia anymore!" How much wages had increased was not agreed upon by local industrialists. Estimates ranged from 15 to 30 percent overall, with increases up to 50 percent for skilled help in crucial areas.

Some informants maintained that the wage increase was not Chromeboat's doing; rather, the entire area was growing so rapidly that labor was tight. This avoids the fact that the wage spiral began when Chromeboat began its operations, and that Chromeboat is the largest employer in the area.

Chromeboat introduced a higher wage scale than any other firm in the area largely because its wages are determined by a nationwide contract with the United Auto Workers. Chromeboat could not take advantage of a lower local wage scale for as part of a national corporation it has vertical[10] ties that transcend local considerations. That the local Chromeboat factory is as dependent on, and as helpless to control, the vertical structure as are other facets of the community, was emphasized by a threatened shutdown of the Cornucopia operation because a feeder plant on the East Coast had experienced a strike. Under the economic influence of Chromeboat, Cornucopia can expect to be increasingly affected by fluctuations of the vertical community, not only by a nationally negotiated wage scale, but also by labor unrest, government policies, international affairs, etc.

That economic matters in Cornucopia are increasingly being dictated by Chromeboat is readily demonstrated. Increased investments in land, home building, and expansion of businesses are made with an eye on Chromeboat. The local lack of available housing has meant that most of Chromeboat's workers live outside Cornucopia in subdivisions that have grown in response to demands made by new workers. Shopping centers in these new housing areas have drawn off much of the retail trade that might have come to Cornucopia merchants. Although economic growth in Cornucopia has not been as great as might have been expected, mainly due to a lack of action on the part of local investors, it is not an exaggeration to say that the coming of Chromeboat rescued the community from a long-stagnated economy.

Industry already in Cornucopia, which was primarily of the low overhead, limited expansion type, has been adversely affected not only by rising wages and labor shortages but also by inability to compete with Chromeboat for use of railroad facilities. It seems likely that some of the smaller firms in Cornucopia will not survive the impact of Chromeboat.

Does this mean that Cornucopia is experiencing bifurcation? That Chromeboat operates as though the local community did not exist and still is the most dominant factor in the life of the community, would argue that bifurcation has already occurred. What bifurcation means to the local community is that its economic life is determined by forces outside of its realm, beyond its control. This accurately describes what is happening to Cornucopia.

THE ABSENTEE MANAGERS AND THE COMMUNITY

Have the executives of Chromeboat taken an active role in local affairs? The answer is an emphatic "no," they took no greater role in community affairs than we had observed for executives of smaller firms

---

[10] The concept "vertical and horizontal community" as used in this discussion was developed by Roland L. Warren, *The Community in America*, (Chicago: Rand McNally and Co., 1963). See especially Chapters 3, 8 and 9.

in 1964. The plant manager, Herder, held a membership in the Chamber of Commerce and several other organizations, but his participation was limited to an occasional appearance, and he viewed his token memberships as necessary for good community relations. Several other Chromeboat executives held memberships in the Chamber of Commerce but made it clear that they attended only when Herder could not in order that Chromeboat should be represented.

In addition to their almost complete lack of interest in community organizations, the Chromeboat executives chose not to live in Cornucopia. Of all the higher ranking executives, only Herder lived in Cornucopia, and he did so because it was imperative to his community relations role. The other executives lived in a nearby metropolitan area and commuted.

Why did the absentee-managers of Cornucopia's factories avoid involvement in community activities? The experience of John Watt, head of a foundry that in 1967 was the third largest employer in Cornucopia, illustrates the dilemma of the absentee-manager if he does take an active role in local affairs. Watt had become involved in Rotary, served as president of the Chamber of Commerce, and sat on the city council. Shortly before we talked to him in 1967 he withdrew from Rotary and the city council and refused to accept the renomination as Chamber president. When asked about his withdrawal from public life Watt replied: "If something affects this company I can yell as a citizen; as a councilman I was in a bind. As a plant manager I needed one thing, as a councilman I knew another would be best . . ." He also pointed out that community activities did not serve to advance his career and might actually have harmed him because they took time that might have been used in corporate affairs.

To appreciate the behavior of the absentee-managers in Cornucopia and other communities we must assess the role of the corporate executive. The role of the absentee-manager can be divided into three sub-roles; 1) his personal life as a member of the community, 2) his professional role as plant manager in relation to local government, welfare agencies, employees, etc., and 3) his professional role as a member of a large corporation that operates in the national marketplace. The first two roles are concerned with the horizontal dimension of the community, whereas the third deals with the vertical dimension.[11]

Already we have an indication of why absentee managers remain uninvolved locally, for as the example of John Watt illustrated, becoming

---

11 *Ibid.*

involved in local issues may place contradictory demands on the individual manager. If, as in the case of Watt, the manager takes a personal interest in the community he might confound his local professional role. Does he work for the benefit of the community even though it might prove detrimental to his factory? If so he would undoubtedly encounter difficulty in his vertical role should profits fall as a result of his personal community role.

The nature of the absentee-manager's life tends to minimize the importance of his personal role. The community he finds himself in is not his home in the sense that he grew up there and has local family ties and long-term friendships. Nor is he permanent, for intra-corporate transfers are frequent and the manager knows he will leave the community at some not-too-distant time. In other words, the corporate manager's ties are to the firm, not to the community.

The local professional role of the absentee-manager is also relatively unimportant. Profit and loss are computed on performance in the national market, local trade is not a factor. Other than labor recruitment and taxes the corporation has little to do with the local community. Even wages are determined in the national sphere and in the event of a tax dispute such as Chromeboat found itself in in Cornucopia, specialists provided by the central office move in to handle the affair. In short, like the personal role, the absentee manager's local-professional role is of little importance compared to his vertical professional role.

This emphasis on extra-local role stands in sharp contrast to the local merchant or professional man who probably has no important vertical ties and relies primarily on personal relationships to hold clientele. To this person the local community is the center for all aspects of life, from family ties and friendships to his livelihood.

The local industrialist also differs from the absentee-manager in the importance he attaches to the various roles. The vertical professional role of the local industrialist, such as the owner-managers of the American Sewing Machine Company, would probably be limited to distributing the firm's product in the larger market. Unlike absentee-managers, the local industrialist would not have to answer to higher management, and his location in the community would be permanent. Although personal affairs in the local community are held to be important for the local industrialist, as we observed in the case of Bernard Tally, his professional role in the community is actually the dominant one. Although Tally spoke of the man-to-man basis of his relationships in Cornucopia, it is quite clear that this meant boss to worker, dominant to subordinate, whether the issue was politics, wages, or a current project. His goal was

to hold the status quo on taxes and cost of utilities and forestall unioni-
zation and wage increases to create a favorable local environment for his
factory.

A typology of role emphasis is suggested by the preceeding discussion:

TYPOLOGY OF ROLE EMPHASIS

Absentee Managers	Local Industrialist	Local Merchants and Professional Men
Vertical (National) Professional Role	Horizontal (Local) Professional Role	Personal (Local) Role

The absentee-managers of the bifurcated community have not withdrawn from participation in community affairs. This implies that they
originally moved into and then surrendered the positions abdicated by
local industrialists who did take an active role in the local community.
Instead, the absentee-managers never assumed the local role of the pyramidal power-wielding local industrialists. Because the crucial vertical
role of the absentee-manager would be hampered by local activism, the
local role of the corporation representatives is minimized, thus allowing
local figures to assume control of local issues.

The important point is that bifurcation occurs because the economy
and social-political sphere are in the hands of men who differ in the focus
of their lives and the roles they play. The corporate manager's world is
the vertical community; the local activists', the horizontal community.
The modern corporation has created a new type of figure in the local
community—the vertically-involved corporate manager who perhaps
determines the fate of a community in which he has no personal stake.

SUMMARY AND CONCLUSIONS

In the transition of Cornucopia's power structure from pyramidal to
factional to bifurcated-pluralism, control of the economy has been the
key element. In the early period of the community the dominant locally-
owned and managed industry was able to wield pyramidal power. When
the firm closed down, local factions moved in to claim the power the
industrialists had long held. The faction heads found it impossible to
hold absolute power inasmuch as control of the economy was not in their
grasp but was spread over several absentee-owned firms that had recently
moved into the community. The economic power was too diffuse to be
realized and the local factional heads dominated Cornucopia. The basis
for bifurcation of power existed at this time but it remained unrealized
until after the coming of Chromeboat. In a brief period of time the
absentee-owned Chromeboat corporation dominated the local economy

and the first signs of pluralism within the social-political sphere were noted.

Briefly summarized: bifurcation occurs as nationally-linked corporations with interests and managers that range beyond the local community replace local industry. As the bifurcation of social-political and economic power progresses, community projects concerned with welfare, civic improvement, etc., become the dominant concerns of local leaders. Economic dealings, which previously would have been dominated by local industrialists, are now completely removed from the local community, and the new economic dominants remain uninvolved in local affairs. When the community realizes its dependence on the absentee-owned corporation and its freedom from local figures, the local social-political sphere becomes more pluralistic because the control of local "giants" over all spheres of life no longer exists. With its autonomy lost and its authority restricted to a limited sphere of activity, the local dominant group appears assailable. As a consequence, community affairs pass out of their private domain.

CHAPTER VII

Population Movements
and the Fate of the
Local Community

Many of the preceding readings have dealt with the threat to the local community from vertical or extra-local factors. In the concluding selections we look at several ways in which the fate of the local community may be resolved.

Hawley, in an excerpt from his classic *Human Ecology,* discusses migration. The horizontally based local community is the "dependent community" by Hawley's measures—the urban center and the vertical dimension of the community form the "independent" community. Population and investment flow in a constant direction toward the independent community. A discussion of the selectivity process that determines who migrates is also included in this excerpt.

As an illustration of the process of migration, we have included a brief section of Arensberg and Kimball's study of Ireland. Ireland provides perhaps the best example of migration, inasmuch as the Irish have been forsaking their homeland in large numbers for over one hundred years. The role that the family plays in preparing the child for migration, launching the move, and maintaining ties with him although he is far away is presented.

The pattern of migration need not take the individual far from his original community as the study by Wylie demonstrates. He focuses on Roussillon, a small community in southern France, and shows how population movement is from Roussillon to other nearby villages, or to the dominant city of the area, but seldom extends beyond the local region. Within the community itself there is a small core of permanent residents that on cursory observation lends an aura of great stability. Beyond this small core, however, the population of Roussillon is in a state of constant flux as residents move throughout the region.

Ross deals with a special problem of population movement—invasion of a community, or an area, by another, culturally distinct, group. In the example she studied, the conflict was between the original settlers—English-Canadians, and the invading French-Canadians. Although this study was made many years ago, it is quite timely, for the process of conflict and the psychological ramifications of that conflict are quite similar to the strain that occurs in today's urban areas as Negroes attempt to break out of the ghetto. The analogy between the English-Canadians and white suburbanites threatened by French-Canadians and Negroes respectively seems especially appropriate when we observe that just as the English had lost much of their sense of community and thus were poorly equipped to fight off the well-organized French, today's member of a rather amorphous suburb faces a group with great solidarity as a result of long ethnic-community status.

Adams looks at another psychological factor involved in the fate of the community. Whether one perceives his community as a dying or a viable entity may be determined by the success or failure of his own economic aspirations. If we relate this observation to Vidich and Bensman's observation that the most successful members of a community are those linked to the mass society, we can see the reciprocal relationship of social and psychological factors. One's success in business is affected by whether or not he has made a successful accommodation to mass society; this in turn leads to a psychological state that affects one's outlook, which in turn can affect the role one takes in the community, and thus can cause one to fight to preserve the community, or give up because failure seems certain.

The last two articles deal with the death of the community. Cottrell's Caliente died rapidly as the result of technological change removing its economic base. He observed that the "most moral" citizens of Caliente, i.e., those with the most invested in the community, the most stable and involved members, paid the price of social change.

Simon and Gagnon compare three southern Illinois communities that face similar fates unless their failing economies, based on coal mining, can be revitalized. The task before the local community is to attract new businesses and industry, but the inherent conservatism of the small town makes this a formidable job.

The very solidarity of the small community may prohibit it from making a successful adjustment to a type of community that is dominated by vertical factors. If it does make a successful adjustment and manages to attract absentee-owned industry, the community survives as a place, but the basis of life that made it what it was changes, and small-town life disappears just as surely as if the town had died. If small-town attitudes are maintained intact, few opportunities are provided for the youth of the community, which migrates to urban centers, and the community ceases to exist as its aging population dwindles and it becomes just another collection of old homes and boarded-up business establishments devoid of that element we call "community."

38. Mobility and Change

AMOS H. HAWLEY

CAUSES OF MIGRATION

A circumstance which seems to attend all occasions of migration is what may be called overpopulation. The term overpopulation is used advisedly, for it describes a relative condition; it is a matter of the ratio of number to the opportunities for life. A surplus number of people may come about through excessive natural increase such as occurs in each generation in many old agrarian areas. Excess population, however, is often produced by an abrupt reduction in the food supply. Famines are usually a consequence of crop failures or other cataclysms rather than of slowly accumulated deficiencies of food supplies. A similar effect resulted from the destruction of cotton crops by the boll weevil in southern United States during the first quarter of the present century. It was pointed out in an earlier chapter that overpopulation also may be a function of the ratio of numbers to jobs available as well as to the supply of food or raw materials. Thus an area with more wage workers than opportunities for employment is overpopulated in the same sense as an agricultural area in which famine conditions prevail. This kind of situation, since it is a product of market conditions, is far more dynamic than one harnessed to seasonal changes. It may give way very quickly to a

SOURCE: Reprinted with permission of the author and publisher from *Human Ecology*, published by The Ronald Press Co., New York, 1950.

condition of underpopulation with a revival of production or a realignment of market relations.

Migration involves, however, a destination as well as a starting point.
Overpopulation is the stimulus; it describes the conditions in the home
area which make migration advisable. For the stimulus to become effective there must be a destination, a place or area in which circumstances
are favorable to the absorption of additional settlers. The cause of migration, in other words, appears to be twofold: it consists in an excess of
numbers in the area of origin, and underpopulation in the area of
destination. These correspond to the "push" and the "pull" factors set
forth by A. C. Haddon[1] and others.

In other words migration seems invariably to be a matter of the
comparative desirability of areas. Contrary to the older view of historians
and anthropologists, it is likely that there have been few if any instances
of blind wandering or spontaneous desertion of areas. The abrupt and
violent invasions of Europe by Asiatic hordes so often cited as evidence of
sheer expulsion appear to have been inadequately described. Penetrating
study such as that of Gilbert Murray[2] reveals that the early Barbarian
invasion of Hellas was preceded by a long period of small-scale movements to and from the area by families singly and in small groups. In this
way the peninsula was explored and knowledge of the superior opportunities it afforded became available to the band which subsequently over-
ran and occupied the land. Virtually all extended movements are similarly prefaced by periods of discovery. Incidental contacts, bold pioneering, sallies by venturesome individuals, trading relationships, or even
chance departures from a beaten track may be the initial source of
information about a neighboring area. Not infrequently the appraisal of
opportunities to be found in a possible place of destination may be
inadequate or misleading. But whether correct or incorrect, based on
facts or hearsay, information or misinformation, as the case may be, these
reports are a decisive element in releasing and directing the flow of
migration.

The outpouring of Europeans to colonial frontiers, though at first
organized and supervised by business enterprises in the form of the
plantation, was initiated and continuously stimulated by the knowledge
of unused resources at the various destinations. That the "free land"
slogan was at odds with the land requirements of the modes of life of
native peoples did not modify the force of the "pull" felt in Europe. To
the European farmer and raw-material producer lands serving as breed-

1 A. C. Haddon, *The Wandering of Peoples* (Cambridge, 1919), Chap. i.
2 Gilbert Murray, *The Rise of the Greek Epic* (Oxford, 1911), p. 67.

ing grounds for game animals or for periodic pasturage were unused lands and therefore available for their occupancy.[3] The superior opportunities in overseas areas provided a release to the pent-up pressures in the homeland and surplus population drained into a stream of migration.

The operation of "push" and "pull" influences is very nicely illustrated by the ebb and flow of European migration to the United States. Harry Jerome observed a close correlation between immigration and the business cycle as measured by pig iron production.[4] He found that changes in the flow of overseas migration lagged approximately six months behind business cycle alternations. Jerome's findings were confirmed in a later study of Swedish migrations to this country by Dorothy S. Thomas.[5] The movement of the Swedish population to the overseas destination, she pointed out, occurred chiefly when economic conditions in Sweden were depressed and opportunities in the United States were abundant. No other combination of circumstances in the two areas produced an appreciable volume of migration from the one to the other.

Stated differently, it appears that migration flows from areas of low rates of capital investment to areas of high rates of capital investment. Thus may be understood the failures of attempts of modern nations to induce emigration of their citizens to agricultural dominions. The unwillingness to move, despite the promise of subsidies, reflects a lack of suitable opportunity as defined in the industrial economy of the present era. Agriculture is a depressed industry, subordinated economically and politically to mechanical industry.[6] It attracts relatively little capital and yields a low level of living. Hence the trend of settlement is away from rather than toward agricultural settlement.

The effect of knowledge is displayed indirectly in the distance covered by migration. Ravenstein, in his studies of rural migration to European cities, observed a predominance of short-distance moves.[7] Evidently the knowledge of alternative opportunities varies with distance. The northward movement of Negroes in the United States, prior to 1916 especially, also followed the short-distance pattern, proceeding as a state-to-state

---

[3] See the discussion of "open" and "closed" resources in H. J. Nieboer, *Slavery as an Industrial System* (The Hague, 1910) , p. 418.

[4] Harry Jerome, *Migration and Business Cycles*.

[5] Dorothy S. Thomas, *Social and Economic Aspects of Swedish Population Movements, 1750–1933* (New York, 1941) , pp. 166–69.

[6] Cf. Owen Lattimore, "The Mainsprings of Asiatic Migration," in Isaiah Bowman (ed.) , *The Limits of Land Settlement* (New York, 1937) , Chap. v.

[7] E. G. Ravenstein, "The Laws of Migration," *Journal of the Royal Statistical Association*, XLVIII (1885) , 167-235; LII (1889) , 241-305; see also S. Stouffer, "Intervening Opportunities: A Theory Relating Mobility and Distance," *American Sociological Review*, V (December, 1940) , 845-68.

displacement.[8] In the more recent migrations to war-industry centers workers who moved the shortest distances found better jobs and found them more quickly than workers who moved long distances.[9] In general, long-distance migrants are solicited or recruited. Agents of employers and others interested in adding to the population of a locality are sent out to propagandize, offer inducements, and provide assistance to potential imigrants. Without such carriers of information the flow from distant places would be slow. A large part of European migration to North America was solicited as is also much of the interregional movement of labor in the United States.

That the information which guides migrants is frequently inadequate or erroneous is evident in the large backflow that has attended modern migrations. In earlier periods the price of error was a heavy mortality rather than a return movement. Of the 60 million Europeans estimated to have moved overseas in the 19th century, approximately 20 million returned to Europe. In other words, a minimum of 80 million moves was needed to produce a net migration of about 40 million.[10] Likewise, to establish a net migration from farms to cities in the United States of 6.3 million, in 1920-30, and of 2.2 million in 1930-40, required 31 and 22 million moves, respectively. The lost motion and wastage of resources resulting from misguided migrations are tremendous.[11] It is for this reason that modern governments have sought to regularize and facilitate migration through systems of employment exchanges.

As a simplified statement of causation, therefore, it may be concluded that migration presupposes a condition of disequilibrium in the form of an excess number of people in one locality, and either incompletely used resources or disequilibrium in the form of too few people in an alternative place of settlement. The effect of migration is to permit a restoration of equilibrium at both the point of origin and the point of destination.

---

[8] National Resources Committee, *The Problems of a Changing Population* (Washington, D. C., 1938), 99.

[9] *National Defense Migration,* Hearings before the Select Committee Investigating National Defense Migration, House of Representatives, Part 27, Washington Hearings, Feb. 1942, (Washington, 1942), 10322.

[10] A. M. Carr-Saunders, *World Population,* 49-50.

[11] In a study of intrastate migration to Flint and Grand Rapids, Michigan, during the depression years 1930 to 1935, it was found that while the unemployment rate prior to migration was significantly higher for migrants than for nonmigrants, the differential was much greater in the post-migration period. That may have been due to unequal access to sources of information concerning available jobs. Whether the high unemployment rates of migrants at destinations resulted in a return movement is not known. (Ronald Freedman and Amos H. Hawley, "Unemployment and Migration in the Depression, 1930 to 1935," *Jorunal of the American Statistical Association,* XLIV [June, 1949], 260-72.)

Like every other simple theoretical formulation this one assumes all related conditions to be constant. That related conditions are not constant in practice is evident in the vast differences in the responsiveness of peoples to migratory stimuli. Apparently there is a more complex causation than that contained in complementing conditions of overpopulation and underpopulation. If so, we should expect to find the complicating factors as elements of different types of community structure. As already observed, the existence of destinations for movement is contingent upon available knowledge which is in itself incidental to the structure and functioning of the community. But the organization of the community conditions the migratory tendency in other ways as well.

MIGRATION AND THE INDEPENDENT COMMUNITY

The independent community, by virtue of its self-sufficiency and insularity, imposes numerous restraints on migration. Self-sufficiency necessitates a steadfast adherence to proved techniques and arrangements, and stability, in turn, preserves the independent existence. This is both cause and effect of the nature of the community's relation to the land. The population, in producing its own sustenance directly from local resources, is bound to the land by a routine of long-run processes, such as the maturation of plants and the breeding cycles of food animals. It is thus immobilized. Nomadic peoples are only somewhat less restricted than sedentary. Although the former are mobile in the sense that they circulate over relatively large areas in the course of the seasonal round, nomadic life is stabilized on the basis of movement. The pastoral economy involves a commitment to seasonally governed processes from which the population is seldom able to extricate itself.

The attachment to place which arises in the isolation of self-sufficient existence is in itself a powerful deterrent to movement and resettlement elsewhere. Behavior becomes intimately and almost inextricably bound up with the objects and characteristics of the universe of daily life. This association is reinforced by the interlocking of habit systems in which each behavior pattern is contingent upon every other, the whole constituting an effective mode of life. Habit and habitat are in fact inseparable abstractions; the habitat is simply that segment of the physical world to which the habits of the group apply. Thus where the objects of the habitat are stable over long periods of time there is a strong disinclination to move, not only because of the profound implication in a familiar context but also because habits are probably not applicable elsewhere. It is not surprising, therefore, to find in the members of the independent community a pronounced identification with the place of abode. Rather than the lands belonging to them, many preliterate peoples regard themselves as belonging to the land.[12] Similarly among peasant peoples the family is often identified with the land it occupies. A family bereft of its land holdings is without status and by the same token is excluded from active group membership.

Not only is there a fixity as to place, but the very cohesiveness of the community enables it to withstand many migration stimuli. The interdependences among its individuals are overlaid by sentiments of right and duty and cemented by common loyalties. Thus the shock of adverse climatic fluctuations or of depredations by enemies, which produce temporary shortages, are absorbed by the systems of mutual aid and sharing. Adjustments are made in the rate of consumption of the entire population which, though they may not prevent increased mortality, nevertheless make it possible for the community to survive the crisis. The resiliency of the independent community is the principal source of its strength, without which it probably could not retain its foothold in a hostile environment. So vital an element is group cohesion, in fact, that migration must be a mass movement, if it is to occur at all. An individual or even three or four individuals together cannot subsist apart from the larger whole. There are no facilities for life outside the community of which one is a member.

The lack of preparation for movement becomes acutely apparent when migration offers the only hope for survival. In the absence of very efficient transportation facilities, movement requires large amounts of per capita wealth in the form of food reserves to sustain the migrants through the time of transit, and transport for the carriage of necessary tools and possessions. Even after a destination is reached the need for food stores continues, since the migrants must be tided over the long period of waiting for crops to mature. But these requirements may seldom be fulfilled, especially in view of the expediency of migration of people adapted to a self-sufficient mode of life. Hence an extraordinary mortality usually attends their attempts to move and take up residence in a new area. Mortality risks are aggravated further by an indefinite prolongation of the period of adaptation at the destination resulting from the inappropriateness of the migrants' techniques for working the land and the trial and error search for new techniques which ensues.

Migration from the independent community, therefore, tends to be a last resort to which recourse is had only after all other solutions to

---

12 M. Mead, *Cooperation and Competition among Primitive Peoples* (New York, 1937), p. 21; and W. I. Thomas, *Primitive Behavior*, p. 32.

overpopulation have failed. In most instances a major catastrophe seems required to set a migration in motion. Minor and recurrent occasions of disequilibrium find their remedies not in movement but in higher than normal mortality rates.

MIGRATION AND THE DEPENDENT COMMUNITY

Population living under conditions of dependent community organization is unhampered by the resistance which besets the independent community, though it is confronted by a different set of restraints peculiar to its more complex mode of life. The primary orientation of the dependent community is not to the land but to a network of intercommunity relations. And that network of relations or market situation, since it constitutes a highly flexible and changeable sustenance base, presupposes maximum mobility. In consequence, population in general, if not individuals in particular, is prepared for and habituated to readjustment through migration. Nor are migrants deterred, assuming employment opportunities to be available at the selected destination, by the prospect of a long period of waiting for the income flow to begin. The wage job with its weekly or monthly payment simplifies the problem of establishment in a new context of relationships. It should be noted, however, that a great part of the mobility required by market fluctuations does not issue in migration. It occurs as a movement of capital, materials, and products to people, as a flow of communications, and as extensive daily journeys to and from places of work and service. Nevertheless, migration is a commonplace response to changes in opportunity and is relatively uninhibited by deep involvement in the seasonal round.

Nor do the community units possess the resiliency and thus the restraining power observed in the independent community. It was noted earlier[13] that associational units, through which are carried on most of the activities of the dependent community, are based on a market and when the market is reduced below a minimum the units cease to operate. The associational unit cannot retain its personnel through periods of severe adversity. There is thus an element of insecurity of position in the organization of such a unit which supplies, if not an incentive, at least a low resistance to migration. And when curtailment or loss of function occurs, migration may become a necessity. It is of more than passing interest in this connection to note that the progressive transfer of manual skills to machinery, which has given rise to large numbers of semiskilled workers, has further enhanced the readiness to move in that portion of the labor force. On the one hand, the loss of skill means for the worker

---

[13] Amos H. Hawley, *Human Ecology* (New York: Ronald Press Co., 1950).

less security of job tenure, and, on the other hand, it gives him a much greater industrial versatility. He can acquire proficiency in any of a wide assortment of machine-tending jobs in a few hours or a few days.

Migration is facilitated also by the existence of a highly developed transportation and communication system. Instead of having to provide their own vehicles and sources of power, migrants to and from the dependent community, even though they possess but little wealth, may secure passage to distant points. The risks as well as the costs of movement are small. Furthermore, the relatively free flow of communications gives wide dissemination to news and information about opportunities available elsewhere.

All aspects of the relation of the individual to the large and intricately organized community seem to make for a readiness to move. The standardization of techniques and forms of communications provides a broad universe of familiarity within which individuals may circulate relatively unrestricted by traditional resistances. Local loyalties and the rule of sentiment are irrelevant in such a context. Dependences involve strangers for the most part rather than kinsman, and strangers may be replaced by other strangers without seriously disturbing the rhythm of functions. Rights to possessions and land, which are an important basis of the attachment to place in the independent community, are rendered convertible by the aid of money. With money the individual many carry his rights abstractly in his pocket and convert them to specific rights of one kind or another as the occasion may warrant. Through this means he may delegate his rights and their complementary responsibilities, as he has in regard to political, charitable, and even religious participation. These activities are carried on by professional representatives while the individual is left free to move.

The very circumstances in the dependent community that encourage migration operate also as controls upon movement. Although, for example, the dynamic market nexus is more or less continuously provoking movement and redistribution, it at the same time sets limits on the range of migration. Settlement is held within the scope of the market, to use Adam Smith's phrase; that is, interdependent individuals and community units cannot scatter so widely as to lose access to one another.[14] It is for this reason that large expanses of relatively unused though productive lands are to be found on the peripheries of highly

---

[14] According to F. J. Turner, at one time in the colonial period of North America settlers were held within the coastal area wherein was located the only known deposits of salt. The inland spread of settlement was limited to the distance that could be traveled periodically to obtain salt. (*The Frontier in American History* [New York, 1921], pp. 17–18).

developed areas, as in the western sections of Canada and the United States and in the interior of Australia.[15] Transportation costs from such zones to market centers are too great to permit an economic use of the lands.

Interestingly enough, motor vehicle transportation seems to have introduced a new resistance to migration. The lengthening commuting radius afforded by the automobile has reduced the amount of migration necessary, at least within local areas. Instead of having to live within walking distance of the job or of a public transportation facility, the worker may locate his residence ten or more miles away. Thus he has acquired a wider area in which he may seek employment without having to move his residence. Investigation would probably show a declining ratio of residence changes to job changes since 1900.[16] It has been observed that new mining operations may be started without the necessity of providing housing facilities at the mine site. Workers show an increasing disposition to live in permanent towns and cities and to travel 20 to 40 miles daily to the mine shaft.[17] One result of this has been to bring into use many small raw material deposits that were neglected formerly because of the transportation and overhead costs of working them. The full effect of the increasing commuting radius on the amount of migration, however, has yet to be felt.

The limitation of market scope is an index of a more diffuse resistance to migration which has developed with the rise of the dependent community. The progressive subdivision and subsequent rationalization of tasks has produced an intensive organization of virtually all elements of life. There remain few interstices into which movement may occur unhampered by institutional restraints. All lands and resources are blocked out and owned. Enterprises are secured and protected by franchises and other monopoly controls. They offer a job structure into which a migrant may be fitted only if there is a vacancy and if he meets stated specifications. Additional controls are imposed by labor unions and professional groups which strive to maintain a scarcity of their skills by limiting the numbers admitted to membership. So compact is the organization of the dependent community that the potential migrant

---

15 See, for example, T. C. Feldman, *The Federal Colonization Project in the Matanuska Valley, Alaska* (Seattle, Wash., 1942–43).

16 A Detroit traffic survey brought to light the fact that of all industrial workers who changed jobs in 1936, only 10 percent changed residences. Unfortunately, similar data for earlier years are not available. (Reported in *National Defense Migration,* Part 18, Detroit Hearings [Sept., 1941], p. 7102.)

17 Carter Goodrich, *et al., Migration and Economic Opportunity* (Philadelphia, 1936), pp. 311–15.

must wait for a relaxation of controls before he may move. And even then he must be guided by a fund of detailed information.

Finally, there is the phenomenon of attachment to place which often operates as an effective restraint. Nostalgia, the acute form of homesickness which seems to render the afflicted temporarily incapable of sustained activity, is generally recognized as a disease requiring treatment.[18] No doubt much of the backflow from migration is due to that ailment. Carefully conceived resettlement projects have attempted to anticipate disruptions arising from nostalgia by moving entire communities rather than selected individuals or families.[19] The reluctance of many of the skilled workers to accompany the movement of industries from Hartford and New Haven, Connecticut, in 1929, despite the inducements that were offered them, was based on a preference to remain in a familiar environment. In many instances the decision to stay behind meant employment in jobs requiring less skill and paying lower wages.[20] The fluidity of contemporary life notwithstanding, there seems to be a pronounced tendency to become involved in a local complex of relationships from which it is difficult to extricate one's self.

SELECTIVITY OF MIGRATION

Young adults, who comprise the more vigorous, self-reliant, and adaptable segment of population, are more migratory than are other age groups. Tables 1 and 2 show the marked preponderance of this age group in foreign immigration and in internal migration.

The sex distribution of migrants also reveals a selectivity. The sex selection, however, is not so simple as that observed for age. Table 3 indicates that while males were predominant in the migration to the United States in 1907, their number had declined to or below the expected proportions by 1930. Evidently in long-distance migrations, especially those involving a radical readjustment at the destinations, males are the first to move. The females follow after the males have succeeded in establishing themselves in the new community. This seems to be what is indicated in the last two columns of Table 3. That is, the relatively high ratios of married women to married men, in 1930, suggest that immigration in that year was bringing family members who had been left behind until the principal hazards of resettlement were overcome.

But in short-distance migrations, rural to urban movements in particu-

18 "Nostalgia," *Encyclopaedia Britannica* (11th ed., 1924), XX, p. 457.

19 See Carter Goodrich, *et al., op. cit.,* pp. 548–50.

20 Ewan Clague and Walter J. Couper, *After the Shutdown* (New Haven, 1934), pp. 50–51.

lar, females tend to be numerically dominant. In Table 4 it may be observed that 52 percent of the migrants to cities within states are females, and that this proportion drops to 51 percent in urbanward

TABLE 1.
Age Composition of Immigrants at Ten-Year Intervals,
United States, 1820–1930

Year of Immigration	Total	Under 15	15–40	Over 40
1820	100.0	14.8	68.1	17.1
1830	100.0	27.5	62.2	10.3
1840	100.0	23.7	68.0	8.3
1850	100.0	21.9	67.3	10.8
1860	100.0	16.0	74.6	9.4
1870	100.0	23.0	64.8	12.2
1880	100.0	19.1	71.6	9.3
1890	100.0	19.0	69.2	11.8
1900	100.0	15.5	73.8	10.7
1910	100.0	14.9	74.7	10.4
1920	100.0	18.4	66.8	14.8
1930	100.0	16.3	68.2	15.5

Source: W. F. Willcox (ed.), *International Migrations*, Vol. II, (New York, 1931), p. 114.

TABLE 2.
Percent Age Distribution of Total Population, Nonmigrants and Migrants,
United States, 1935–40 *

Age†	Total Population	Nonmigrants	Migrants
Total	100.0	100.0	100.0
Under 5	8.0	9.2	.....
5–13	15.2	15.2	15.8
14–17	7.3	7.5	6.4
18–19	3.9	3.7	4.3
20–24	8.8	8.1	13.4
25–29	8.4	7.6	14.0
30–34	7.8	7.2	11.6
35–44	13.9	13.7	15.7
45–54	11.8	12.2	9.6
55–64	8.0	8.4	5.3
65 and over...................	6.9	7.2	3.9

* Source: U. S. Bureau of the Census; *Population, Internal Magration 1935 to 1940; Age of Migrants* (Washington, D. C., 1946).

† Age is reported as of 1940, though the migrations occurred during the 5-year period 1935 to 1940.

movements which cross state lines and to less than 50 percent in movements between noncontiguous states. Females begin their migration from rural areas at an earlier age than do males, concentrating much of their movement between the ages of 18 and 30 years. After age 30 and until age 55 males move in larger proportions than females. The latter return to predominance in the years following age 55. This age-sex pattern is

TABLE 3.

Percent Male of All Immigrants, 1907 and 1930, and Married Females Per 100 Married Males, 1910 and 1930, by Selected Nationality Groups, United States.

Nationality of Immigrant	Percent Male		Married Females per 100 Married Males	
	1907	1930	1910	1930
Bulgarian	97.3	31.7	5	1063
Dutch and Flemish	67.1	59.5	69	98
English	64.8	49.6	77	104
French	57.8	55.3	86	107
German	60.5	50.5	65	146
Greek	96.5	41.3	8	656
Irish	56.5	48.8	70	97
Lithuanian	72.3	29.8	38	643
Mexican	81.3	53.0	62	121
Polish	73.0	46.7	23	171
Romanian	92.6	28.7	10	611

SOURCE: W. F. Willcox, op. cit., pp. 112–113.

undoubtedly a result of the scarcity of economic opportunities for unattached females in rural areas.

In fact, the differential movements of age and sex groups are almost entirely expressive of an occupational selection at work in migration. Disequilibrium, of course, is felt first and most forcefully as unemployment or labor shortage. Furthermore, it may concern any number from one to all the occupations represented in the communities in question. Migration is a means of redistributing that part of a population most directly affected by conditions of disequilibrium in closer conformity with the distribution of opportunities. Unfortunately we lack systematic studies of the operation of occupational selection. But its workings are abundantly illustrated in labor recruiting practices, such as indenture, slavery, contracting, and direct solicitation. The entire rural to urban migration, moreover, has been and still is a movement of occupationally dispossessed agriculturists to unskilled and semiskilled jobs in mechanical and service industries.

Differentials in migration, however, may also indicate variations in ability. It would appear that the task of moving and beginning life anew in a strange situation entails risks which many individuals are biologically and perhaps psychologically unable to assume. This may, for example, partially account for the age variations just noted. If true, such differences should be observable within as well as between age groups. Here

TABLE 4.

Percent Age and Sex Distribution of All Migrants to Urban Places by Distance of Migration, United States, 1935-40.

Age	Within States			Between Contiguous States			Between Noncontiguous States		
	Total	Male	Female	Total	Male	Female	Total	Male	Female
Total	100.0	47.7	52.3	100.0	48.6	51.4	100.0	50.4	49.6
Under 5	—	—	—	—	—	—	—	—	—
5–13	13.6	6.9	6.7	12.9	6.5	6.4	11.2	5.6	5.6
14–17	5.7	2.7	3.0	5.3	2.5	2.8	4.6	2.2	2.4
18–19	4.3	1.6	2.7	4.3	1.7	2.6	3.7	1.8	1.9
20–24	14.3	5.6	8.7	15.0	6.2	8.8	14.7	7.2	7.5
25–29	14.7	6.9	7.8	15.9	7.5	8.4	16.6	8.4	8.2
30–34	12.4	6.2	6.2	12.9	6.6	6.3	13.0	6.7	6.3
35–44	16.1	8.5	7.6	16.9	9.1	7.8	17.0	9.1	7.9
45–54	9.5	5.0	4.5	9.3	5.1	4.2	9.8	5.2	4.6
55–64	5.2	2.5	2.7	4.5	2.2	2.3	5.4	2.5	2.9
64 and over	4.2	1.8	2.4	3.0	1.2	1.8	4.0	1.7	2.3

SOURCE: U. S. Bureau of the Census, *Population, Internal Migration 1935 to 1940; Age of Migrants* (Washington, D. C. 1946).

again the existing knowledge is inconclusive. There is some evidence to support the conclusion that the biologically fit or the healthy move more readily than the unhealthy.[21] A recent study by Ronald Freedman, however, indicates that in the United States rural migrants to cities experience more days of disabling illness than do nonmigrants in the cities of destination. Furthermore, this differential is consistent in all income classes.[22] Information on selectivity with reference to mental health is no more satisfactory. Data on commitments to mental institutions in New York state show higher frequencies of mental disorder among migrants than among other native residents of the state.[23] It is not possible to determine from these data, however, whether the higher rates are due to selectivity or to difficulties of adjustment to the circumstances of life in the state of New York.

There is even greater confusion over the selectivity of migration in respect to intelligence, possibly because of the larger amount of research that has been done. Since migration may be assumed to require initiative and aggressiveness, it is reasonable to expect that the more intelligent individuals are most likely to move. The immediate difficulty encountered in testing this hypothesis lies in securing an adequate measure of intelligence. A few studies using school achievement as a gauge of intelligence have indicated a better than chance migration of the more advanced individuals.[24] But uncertainty is injected into these findings by another study using grade performance data which revealed that children of migrants are no better than average,[25] though whether the

21 A. B. Hill, *Internal Migration and the Effects on the Death Rate, with Special Reference to the County of Essex* (London: Medical Research Council Report Series, No. 95, 1925), cited in *Research Memorandum on Migration Differentials* (New York: Social Science Research Council, Bull. 43, 1938), 92-97, and E. P. Hutchinson, "Internal Migration and Tuberculosis Mortality in Sweden," *American Sociological Review,* I (April, 1936), 273-85.

22 Ronald Freedman, "Health Differentials for Rural-Urban Migration," *American Sociological Review,* XII (October, 1947), 536-41.

23 Benjamin Malzberg, "Rates of Mental Disease among Certain Population Groups in New York State," *Journal of the American Statistical Association,* XXXI (September, 1936), 545-48. A more recent study dealing with a section of Baltimore indicates that mental and personality disorders are more closely associated with intracity mobility than with urban-rural and intercity movements. (See Christopher Tietze, Paul Liemkau, and Marcia Cooper, "Personality Disorder and Spatial Mobility," *American Journal of Sociology,* XLVIII (July, 1942), 29-39.

24 Wilson Gee and Dewees Runk, "Qualitative Selection in Cityward Migration," *American Journal of Sociology,* XXXVII (September, 1931), 254-65; and T. C. McCormick, "Urban Migration and Educational Selection—Arkansas Data." *Ibid.,* XXXIX (November, 1933), 355-59.

25 Otto Klineberg, "The Intelligence of Migrants," *American Sociological Review,* III (April, 1938), 218-24.

children of migrants are the proper subjects for study is open to question.

A more recent study reveals that the level of educational achievement of migrants does not differ significantly from that of nonmigrants at either the source or the destination when age, sex, marital status, occupation, previous occupational mobility, and employment status are held constant.[26] Still another research based upon intelligence test scores of rural youth in Kansas found that the more intelligent by that measure not only moved in larger numbers but also moved farther and to the larger cities.[27] It is probable, of course, that selectivity in Kansas may differ from that operating in other places.

Thus while the weight of evidence seems to support the hypothesis of intelligence selection, considerably more research is necessary. The control of two factors should produce more stable results than have been attained heretofore. First, a distinction should be observed between primary and secondary migrants, or those who are responsible for the migration and those who merely accompany the primary migrant.[28] Albert H. Hobbs noted rather important differences between these two groups both in respect to educational achievement and gradepoint scores in school.[29] Secondly, the characteristics of the community from which migration proceeds should be controlled. It is entirely likely that a community in which opportunities are permanently depleted may produce a type of migrant different from one in which opportunities are but temporarily restricted.[30] Obviously more detailed information than has yet been available is required to ascertain the effects on migration of differentially distributed intrinsic factors.

---

[26] Ronald Freedman and Amos H. Hawley, "Educational and Occupational Selectivity of Migration in the Depression, 1930-35." (Unpublished manuscript.)

[27] Noel P. Gist and Carroll D. Clark, "Intelligence as a Selective Factor in Rural-Urban Migrations," *American Journal of Sociology*, XLIV (July, 1938), 36-58.

[28] Suggested by Otto Klineberg, *op. cit.*

[29] Albert H. Hobbs, *Differentials in Internal Migration* (Philadelphia, 1942), pp. 66-78.

[30] Jane Moore, *Cityward Migration: Swedish Data* (Chicago, 1937), pp. 28-42.

39. Demography and Familism

CONRAD M. ARENSBERG
SOLON T. KIMBALL

Of the demographic phenomena the small farmers [of Ireland] present, the decline of population is most easily isolated. The facts are as follows: there has been a continuous and characteristic decline since the great famine of 1845. Numbers have fallen from 6,548,000 in 1841 to 2,963,000 in 1926. With the exception of Dublin, the whole of the country has suffered in this decline. On the whole, however, the country districts have suffered at a greater rate than have the towns. In 1841, 80 percent of the population was rural; today only 63 percent. In other words, since 1841 there has been an almost continuous increase in the town population at the expense of the rural, though the two have shared a common decline. Put in terms of percentages: since 1841, the country districts have lost 64 percent of their population, towns from 200 to 500, 49 percent, towns from 5000 to 10,000, 25 percent, and towns other than Dublin over 10,000, 13 percent. Dublin, on the other hand, has gained 47 percent. That the enormous emigration associated with this decline is a matter of the

Source: Reprinted with permission of the authors and publisher from Conrad M. Arensberg and Solon T. Kimball, *Family and Community in Ireland*, Cambridge, Mass.: Harvard University Press, Copyright 1940, 1968, by the President and Fellows of Harvard College.

contemporary generation is evident when it is recognized that 30 percent of the native-born Irish were living in other countries in 1926.

The closest approach among European countries is the case of Norway, where fifteen percent live outside. Italy, which has provided so many citizens for the United States and the Argentine, has only four percent of its natives residing in foreign countries. Since 1911 there has, however, been a check in the decrease; only five percent of the population was lost between 1911 and 1926. The region of our investigation, County Clare, shares in this general loss, falling in population from 250,000 in 1841 to 95,000 in 1926. Since 1911 it has lost only eight percent.

As the statistics show, this loss of population is in the main a problem of the country districts. The towns have gained proportionately to the countryside; though in a lesser degree, they have, of course, shared the common loss. Many causes for this decline have been operative and, as the excellent work by Dr. William Forbes Adams, *Ireland and Irish Emigration to the New World*,[1] shows, emigration is no new factor in Irish life. The great impetus for an enormous exodus of population was the famine of 1845, but since then emigration has flowed on continuously, coming to an end only in 1932 when for the first time for at least a century more Irishmen returned than left the country.

But far from the famine's having started the emigration from the present Free State, "the growth of emigration between 1815 and 1845," concludes Dr. Adams, "not only made possible the flight after the famine, it caused that flight. The thirty years before 1845 spread the emigrating spirit through all but the highest class until it became the favorite remedy for hard times. The tremendous rush of the next fifteen years could not have taken place without aid from the earlier emigrants." Since then, the land agitation, dissatisfaction with British rule, and periodic hard times have taken their toll, coupled with what Adams calls the greatest single cause of human migration, the work of powerful interests developed first in the early days of Irish emigration, "organizing and developing (immigrant) traffic for their own profit." The movement began long before the great burst of the fifties and has been continuous ever since.

Many attempts have been made to find causes for this emigration. Perhaps the most successful have been those dealing with economic factors. Among the most frequently suggested is the change in agriculture since the famine. The assumption advanced is that the change from tillage to livestock production has cut down the rural employment, which in turn has driven the rural population to emigrate. Undoubtedly, there

---

[1] Dr. William Forbes Adams, *Ireland and Irish Emigration to the New World* (New Haven: Yale University Press, 1932).

has been a correlation, particularly in the earliest years and at the time of the land clearances after the famine. In fact, from 1847 to 1852 (the famine years) there was a huge decrease in the area under small holdings of 1–30 acres, a decrease of 1,395,000 acres, but since then, in the years from 1852 to 1909 (after which holdings began generally to be increased), the corresponding decrease was only 155,000 acres.

The Report on Agricultural Statistics, 1847–1926, published by the Free State Department of Agriculture and Commerce, from which the figures are derived, comments that "this comparatively small transference of land from small holdings with high densities to larger holdings with low densities had but little effect upon reducing tillage or increasing livestock,"[2] the agricultural changes which are supposed to have affected emigration. The report demonstrates that between 1854 and 1912 the smaller the holding, the larger the increases in densities of all livestock, except dry cattle two years old and over, and the larger the decrease in density of ploughed land.

In other words, the change in agriculture, whatever may have been its effect upon employment prospects for the small farmer outside his own farm, proceeded more rapidly on the small farms. The tables of the report show that large farmers decreased their tillage at a more rapid rate than small farmers only in the periods of 1917 to 1926 and 1854 to 1874, while continuously over the whole period 1874 to 1926 small farmers "got out of tillage more rapidly than large farmers." Too close appeal accordingly cannot be made to changes in agriculture for an understanding of Irish emigration.

In fact local densities of population do not now and never have shown a great deal of correspondence with densities of tillage. The highest percentage of agricultural land ploughed (29 percent) was reached in 1851. Since then it has fallen steadily, to 13 percent in 1926. Sweden comes nearest to this low percentage of tillage, with 52 percent of her arable land tilled. Consequently, the Irish population was at no time solely dependent upon tillage crops.

Before 1881 a correlation could be drawn with some accuracy between the decrease in tillage and the decrease in rural population. Thus in poor law unions (administrative areas) in which ploughed land decreased population also decreased as shown in Table 1.[3]

But since 1881 similar tables show that there is no correspondence between the decreases, and that even those poor law unions in which tillage has increased show an ordinary loss of population. Consequently, decline in tillage had little effect upon the emigration after 1881. This

---

[2] *Agricultural Statistics, 1847–1926*, p. xliii.
[3] *Agricultural Statistics, 1847–1926*, p. lxi.

becomes even more evident when it is understood that in both 1854 and 1912 the thirteen counties densest in rural population included only six of the counties densest in ploughed land. "Dense tillage was in the east, dense rural population in the west,"[4] as it still is.

In the same search for economic causes, a better case has been made for

TABLE 1.

Relation between Decrease in Ploughed Land and Decrease in Population

Decrease in Ploughed Land (percent)	Decrease in Population (percent)
0–20	13
20–30	26
30–40	28
50 and over	34

the change from milch cattle to beef cattle production. As we have seen, milch cows are characteristically associated with the small farmers. During the period of emigration, the number of dry cattle has risen in proportion to the number of milch cattle almost steadily; the range is from 2372 total cattle to the 1000 milch cows in 1854, to 3334 to the 1000 in 1926; fluctuations have been very slight. It is true that the number of milch cattle has also risen steadily, if slowly. Such a change in actual numbers of cattle and in proportions of dry to milch cattle, the latter capable of yielding the greater amounts of food for farm consumption, may have had some effect upon the displacement of human beings by cattle, but certainly not a great enough one to determine the emigration. The lack of correspondence between these changes is evident when it is remembered that the change has taken place principally in the former tillage areas, and also that in 1926 the areas of greatest milch cow density were substantially the same as in 1854. The very little direct correspondence there can be is well exemplified in the contrast between County Clare, which fell from a population of 336 to the 1000 acres of crop and pasture to 129, while milch cows remained practically the same in number (100 to 110 to the 1000 acres), and County Mayo (a poorer region), where population fell only from 375 to 245 and milch cows also remained practically the same (90 to 100).

From these figures it is evident that the decline in rural population is not directly correlated with decline in tillage or change in cattle production. The failure of employment coincident upon that change cannot be assigned as the sole cause of emigration.

DISPERSAL AND EMIGRATION

The internal reorganization of the family consequent on the marriage

[4] *Agricultural Statistics, 1847–1926,* p. lvi.

of one of their number produces a marked change in the situation of the as yet unprovided-for brothers and sisters. The other members of the family broken up by the marriage of one of their number on the home farm must be provided for elsewhere. They feel themselves entitled to portions, either in the form of dowries to marry into another farm or of some other means of establishing themselves. The sons and daughters who are not to be portioned at home, in the words of the Luogh residents, "must travel." To that end both the savings of the family, created through their united efforts under the headship of father and mother, and the incoming dowry, are devoted. In Luogh there had been only four marriages in ten years; two of them were the usual farm-transferring matches, one a returned emigrant who married a boyhood sweetheart and bought a farm, and one a widower who took a second wife and a second fortune. An old woman described the situation: "There aren't any matches nowadays. Nobody has a fortune to give his daughter and the young men must travel." Yet the woman who lamented this state of affairs was carefully husbanding half crowns for her baby granddaughter's fortune.

Nevertheless this necessary dispersal of the members of the family at its reorganization does not ordinarily destroy the family ties. The bonds of affection and family obligation still hold. If they have emigrated, the family members send back remittances and passage money for nephews and nieces and brothers and sisters left at home. A great many farms, especially in West and North Clare, are partially supported by Christmas gifts sent from children living abroad. It is unfortunate that the authors have not statements of the amount of these annual remittances for local districts. The total for Ireland, however, is enormous. There is a marked tendency for emigration from a local region to perpetuate itself, sons and daughters of each generation going out to join the members of the last. One district round Cross to the west of Carrigaholt, a little settlement on the Loop Head peninsula which juts out from Clare into the Atlantic at the Shannon's mouth, is said locally to be supported by sons in the Shanghai police force. The first to go became chief of police in the International Settlement there, and many places in the force have gone to men of Cross.

The authors had the opportunity of examining some of the family setting in which emigrant remittances operate in Luogh. There the greatest number of emigrants had gone out to Boston. In one family, there was a succession of nephews and nieces following uncles and aunts from the same farmhouse for four generations. In four recent cases Luogh boys and girls had married one another in Boston. In two more they had married in Ireland and emigrated together.

Remittances from sons and daughters arrive around Christmas. In one family the farmer's wife had written to children in America saying that the family were trying to acquire an addition to their holding from the Land Commission. The children sent them the purchase price. In this case the daughter sent her regular Christmas remittance as well. When she was admonished by her parents for such generosity, she wrote: "I would think it wasn't Christmas and I hadn't any father and mother if I didn't send them something."

Her mention of the festival in the same breath with her parents is understandable when it is realized that Christmas is the family festival *par excellence* in Ireland.

The role played by emigrated relatives in providing for the children upon the home farm and the role of the dispersed children in helping the old couple and the brother or sister at home is part of the general "friendliness" by which the Irish countryman sums up the family obligations. The two roles are felt to be the same, and they are described in the same terms, as the obligations of actual charity between country families, agricultural cooperation, and ceremonial assistance at marriages, wakes, and funerals. Brother and sister send back gifts to the home farm, especially when the old couple are still alive. Gifts of money, clothing, and presents of all descriptions are sent back. Geese, farm delicacies, and such mementos as shamrocks go from the farm to those relatives that keep in touch.

At family crises, such as death, marriage, and birth, the new bonds come strongly into play and, where possible, the dispersed relatives come back to the farm at that time. The emigrant returns, if he does so at all, to the very townland of his birth, either to buy the old place or to settle near-by. In fact, there are many instances of countrymen, returned Americans, Australians, South Africans, and British soldiers, who have roamed over the world but have never seen more of Ireland than their route to and from their port of embarkation and the nearest market towns.

40. Demographic Change in Roussillon

LAURENCE WYLIE

In the *Dictionnaire des Communes* a village in southern France is described in cryptic detail:

Roussillon (Vaucluse), ar. Apt. c. Gordes, 713 h., PTT; SNCF V Cavaillon, 20 k., M. Bonnieux, 8 k., ou Apt, 10 k.

Once deciphered, this reference pinpoints the village of Roussillon and relates it to the rest of the world for us, but the image it evokes is stark. We are not told of the dramatic red and orange cliffs on which the village is built or of the luscious melons and succulent asparagus grown in the surrounding fields or of the children kicking their soccer ball in the school yard. These are my impressions of Roussillon where I lived in 1950–51 and visited in 1958 and 1959. Lying behind both the dictionary definition and my memories is the many-faceted object itself—the rural commune of Roussillon where about seven hundred people live and face the problems posed by their own society and by the world which lies

SOURCE: Reprinted with permission of the author and publisher from *Mediterranean Countrymen*, Julian Pitt-Rivers, ed., published by Mouton & Co., Paris, 1963.

ACKNOWLEDGMENT: I am grateful to Nicholas Hopkins for helping prepare the statistics used in this study and to Anne Stiles Wylie for helping to give them meaning.

433

around them. The Roussillonnais seem to form a group apart, a clearly defined unit within the borders of their commune.

Each year, of course, this apparently monolithic population suffers from erosion. Like almost all the villages of France—and I had chosen Roussillon to study because it was a representative commune, a *commune-témoin*—Roussillon grew rapidly during the nineteenth century, reached a peak in the late 1860's and then gradually declined in size:

1801 — 1100		1936 — 841	
1861 — 1568		1946 — 779	
1901 — 1123		1951 — 730	
1921 — 936		1954 — 713	
1931 — 930		1959 — 680	

'Ah, yes,' one concludes on seeing these figures, 'Roussillon is suffering the fate of most villages. This is only another example of the *exode rural* which is draining the countryside. Some of the young people move away every year, leaving a community of old people behind. The old ones die, and no one new comes to take their places.'

Recently I have been studying in detail the problem of the *exode rural* in order to learn what, specifically, happens to the people who emigrate from Roussillon. In the summers of 1951 and 1959 I analyzed the census lists of 1946 and 1954 with the *secrétaire de mairie* of the commune, who told me what had happened to each person. In order to compare the demographic movement of the two five-year periods, I had a card made for each inhabitant of the commune whose name appeared in the censuses. The results of this simple operation were so surprising that my conception of the demography of Roussillon was changed. The image I had had of the population of the commune was basically inaccurate, but it is a misconception underlying most of what has been written about rural demography. The difficulty lies in the fact that in studying demographic problems we rely too exclusively on global census figures which obscure the reality of population movements. For clarification, one must delve below this level and study the case of each individual.

The startling fact disclosed by my accumulation of individual census cards was that Roussillon does *not* have a relatively stable though slowly diminishing population of about seven hundred. The total number of individuals listed in the 1946 and 1954 censuses is not some seven hundred but 1150! Still there were never over seven or eight hundred individuals in the commune at any one time during this 13 year period. Obviously the turnover was large.

The 1150 individuals listed in 1946 and 1954 are only those who happened to be in the commune at the two points in time when the censuses were made. There is no way of knowing how many other individuals moved into the village during the period from 1946 to 1959 and moved away without being counted because they were not there when a census was made. It seems likely, however, that during the 13 year period there were at least 2000 people who lived in Roussillon long enough to call themselves inhabitants of the commune. If there were 1150 in the eight years 1946–1954, and if the same proportions held for the 13 year period, then the figure 2000 would be only a safe minimum. When I think of the number of individuals I knew in Roussillon during the year 1950–51, who had moved there after the census of 1946 and who moved away before the census of 1954, my own belief is that the total may well be nearer 2500. Only research in the municipal archives could give us a definite answer. Since we do not know positively the number of individuals who lived in Roussillon between the years 1946 and 1959, let us for the present accept the minimum number, the 1150 people listed in the censuses of 1946 and 1954.

Of these 1150 people, how many remained in the commune for the entire 13 year period? By checking all the cards, I found that only 275 individuals were present at the four points in time for which we have information, 1946, 1951, 1954 and 1959. Of these 275 persons, 137 were born in Roussillon. Only 137 native Roussillonnais among 1150 residents —and possibly as many as 2500—in a 13 year period!

What has happened to our image of the population of Roussillon as a stable, well-delineated unit? It must be discarded in favor of a more accurate picture of this population as a small core surrounded by a constantly shifting mass moving in and out of the community.

This phenomenon seemed sufficiently interesting to warrant further study. Who were the people moving away from Roussillon? Who were those moving in to replace them? Who were the individuals forming the small, relatively stable core of the population? These were questions I wanted to answer. Unfortunately, I was 3000 miles from the communal archives of Roussillon and from the statistical treasures of INSEE (Institut National de la Statistique et des Etudes Economiques) in Marseille. I had at my disposal only the census listing of 1946 (containing the birthdate, birthplace and profession of each individual), the census of 1954 (without birthdates, birthplaces and professions, but including population statistics from a questionnaire completed by the census takers), my personal check lists made in 1951 and 1959 of what had become of individuals listed in the censuses of 1946 and 1954, and finally an anonymous file of registered voters born in Roussillon but living elsewhere in France in 1959.

This information is far from being as complete as I would like. However, it still enables me to answer certain basic questions which come to mind when we discover the demographic turmoil of this community. Who are the people that have left the community? Are they young people going off to the city to work? Are they farmers' children or are they from the families of the village artisans, shopkeepers and *fonctionnaires?* Or are the emigrants rather family units—parents and small children? Where do these people go? To Paris? To the big regional centers, Marseilles and Avignon? Or to nearby towns and farms? Are the emigrants natives of Roussillon or not?

The same sort of questions may be raised about the hundreds of people who have come into Roussillon to take the places of most of the people who have gone. Who are they? Where do they come from? How old are they? Are they farmers or villagers? Where were they born? Are they really new arrivals or are they former inhabitants who are returning home?

Finally, one wonders about the population core of the community. Of the 275 people who remained in Roussillon from 1946 to 1959, how many were farmers and how many villagers? Are certain age groups stay-at-homes? Do certain family clans form the nucleus of the community? To what degree does this core population dominate Roussillon?

To understand the large demographic turnover in Roussillon we must consider two essentially different aspects of the problem. The natural causes of demographic movement—birth and death—must be studied apart from the problem of migration. Of the hundreds of people who entered and left Roussillon from 1946 to 1959, there were obviously some who entered by birth and others who departed through death.

By adding the number of births to the number of deaths that took place in our 13 year period:

	1946–59
Births	85
Deaths	126
Total	211

we find that a relatively small percentage of the turnover took place through natural causes. When we compare the birth rate of Roussillon with that of France as a whole, however, a question arises. Since the war, the French birth rate has been high. Why should it be so low in Roussillon?

	Births per 1000	
	Roussillon	*France*
1946–51	7.9	21.0
1954–59	9.6	18.4

One answer is that it is not quite so low as it looks, because until 1957 the birth of a child in France was recorded only in the town hall of the place of birth. This meant that the birth of a child to Roussillon parents in the hospital of Apt was recorded in Apt, not in Roussillon. Until this procedure was changed, it obviously distorted the birthrates of both Roussillon and Apt, or whatever city in which the child was born. There is no complete record of how many children were born to Roussillon parents during our thirteen year period. I would estimate that the two or three Roussillon babies born every year in city hospitals must be added to the official total of births for the commune. Even with this increased figure the birth rate is not so high as the rate for France as a whole.

Unlike the statistics on births, the statistics on deaths are accurate: every death of a Roussillon inhabitant is recorded in the town hall, whether the death occurs in the commune or not.

	Deaths per 1000	
	Roussillon	France
1946–51	10.2	13.1
1954–59	15.7	11.9

These global death rates for the commune conceal an important aspect of rural life that is rarely mentioned in studies on rural demography—the essential differences between village and farm.

For official statistical purposes, a rural community, as opposed to an urban community, is defined as any commune whose *agglomération* or *bourg* has no more than 2000 inhabitants. The people of the farms and the people of the villages are lumped together. The fact is, however, that life in the *bourg* and life in the *campagne* are very different. One aspect of the difference is reflected in the death rate:

Rousillon:	Death Rate per 1000	
	Bourg	Campagne
1946–51	13.6	8.0
1954–59	21.6	12.6

Why should so many more people die in the *bourg* than in the *campagne?* Villages attract elderly people. There are always a few country people who, when they retire from active work on the farm, move to the *bourg* because village life is somewhat more comfortable. Moreover, it is frequently the ambition of city people to move to the country when they retire. By 'country,' however, they do not mean 'farm,' but the 'village.' Roussillon, like most villages, has its share of elderly people from Marseille, Nice and other urban centers, who came to Roussillon to find a quieter and cheaper place to live. Often they run a little business to help make ends meet—a café, a grocery, a variety store—but still they have time to work in the garden, hunt and putter around. Sometimes they become lonely and move back to the city, but usually they live on in Roussillon. It is natural, therefore, that the *bourg* should have a higher death rate than the *campagne*.

Why the death rate has risen in the last five years when it has fallen nationally requires explanation. Fifty of the fifty-six people who died in Roussillon between 1954 and 1959 were over sixty years old, and most of them were over seventy. The oldest was the dean of the community, Madame Carbonnel, who died in 1956 at the age of 102. These people were the remnant of the Roussillon of the nineteenth century when the population was twice the size it is now. The deaths among this numerous older generation make the death rate unnaturally high.

Deaths in Roussillon account for some of the large population turnover, but by no means the most substantial part. The birth rate, even when we augment it to include unrecorded births, is modest. Natural demographic movement, therefore, can account for no more than 250 entries and departures in Roussillon. If we add this figure of 250 to the 275 people who stayed in Roussillon for the whole thirteen year period with which we are concerned, we are still far from the total of 1150 who were recorded in the censuses of 1946 and 1954 and from the 2000 or 2500 people who at some time during the thirteen years were officially residents of Roussillon. The great turnover in the population must be explained by migration.

How many people moved away from Roussillon? In order to find out I took the *listes nominatives* of the censuses of 1946 and 1951 and checked them with the *secrétaire de mairie* of the commune to learn what had happened to each individual listed in the census. We checked the 1946 census in 1951 and the 1954 census in 1959, giving me two five-year periods which furnish comparable statistics. The results are as follows:

1946–51:   222 emigrants   (29 percent of the population of the commune in 1946, 779)

1954–59:   148 emigrants   (21 percent of the population of the commune in 1954, 713)

The figures for the first period are undoubtedly larger than they might normally have been because of the movement of refugees after the war. There was, for example, a social worker from the Côtes du Nord with her own three children and six others from her region who had been living in Roussillon during the war. The figures for 1954–59 are apparently more normal. It would seem that 20 to 25 percent of the inhabitants listed in a given census leave sometime during the following five years, or about five percent a year. Because there are people moving away every year who arrived in the commune after the census was made, five percent is a minimum figure. The actual rate would probably be a good deal larger.

Most people in talking about the *exode rural* assume that the loss of rural population is a loss of farm population. However, as I have said earlier, statistics for every rural commune include the commercial, artisan and even manufacturing population of the *bourg* as well as the farming population of the *campagne*. To determine whether the *exode rural* is primarily an agricultural phenomenon, one must distinguish between the two elements of the population.

Emigrants from Roussillon

| | Numbers | | Percentages of population | |
	Bourg	Campagne	Bourg	Campagne
1946–51	117	105	38	22
1954–59	40	108	17	23

Here again we see that the departure of refugees abnormally increased the number of emigrants from the *bourg* for the five-year period, 1946–51. The emigration from the *campagne* seems to be rather stable, however. Four to five percent of the farming population listed in a given census leaves Roussillon every year.

It is commonly assumed that emigrants from the rural areas are young people who are leaving the farms to live and work in the city. This popular image of the *exode rural* is false as far as Roussillon is concerned.

| | Numbers | | Percentage of the emigrants | |
	1946–51	1954–59	1946–51	1954–59
Single emigrants	48	42	22	28
Individuals emigrating in *ménages*	174	106	78	72

Most of the people leaving the commune are not single individuals forced off the farm for lack of work. Three-quarters of the emigrants leave in family units. For a fuller understanding an analysis of the difference between the *bourg* and *campagne* must be made:

Numbers of Emigrants

| | Bourg | | Campagne | |
	1946–51	1954–59	1946–51	1954–59
Alone	33	19	15	23
In *ménages*	84	21	90	85

Percentage of Emigrants

	Bourg		Campagne	
	1946–51	1954–59	1946–51	1954–59
Alone	28	47	14	21
In *ménages*	72	53	86	79

There is a notable difference in the patterns: In the *campagne,* the emigrants leave primarily in family groups; in the *bourg* (except for the period directly after the war) the division is more nearly equal. More single people leave the *bourg* than the *campagne.*

It is impossible to know exactly how old emigrants are when they leave Roussillon since we do not know at what moment during the two five-year periods they left. We can, however, learn something by taking the ages of the emigrants at the end of the five-year period and grouping them as children, adolescents or adults.

Age Group	Numbers		Percentage of the emigrants	
	1946–51	1954–59	1946–51	1954–59
5–15	60	34	27	24
16–21	26	18	12	12
22 or over	136	95	61	64

It is obvious from these statistics that most of the people leaving Roussillon are not adolescents seeking work in the city. Most of the emigrants are adults accompanied by their children. Our previous information concerning emigrating *ménages* is confirmed.

As far as broad age groups are concerned, relatively few of the emigrants from either the *bourg* or *campagne* are adolescents.

Age in 1951	Number of Emigrants, 1946–51		Percentage, 1946–51	
	Bourg	Campagne	Bourg	Campagne
5–15	33	27	28	26
16–21	9	17	8	16
22 or older	75	61	64	58
Age in 1959	Number of Emigrants, 1954–59		Percentage, 1954–59	
5–15	6	28	15	26
16–21	6	12	15	11
22 or older	27	68	68	63
Unknown	1	. . .	2	. . .

If instead of dividing the emigrants into three groups, children-adolescent-adults, we use the finer division of five-year groups, we can then construct population pyramids which bring out more subtle patterns of emigration. Disregarding for a moment the traditional arrangement of such pyramids with men on one side and women on the other, we shall construct them with the *bourg* emigrants to the left and *campagne* emigrants to the right.

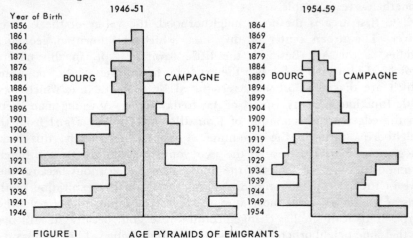

FIGURE 1   AGE PYRAMIDS OF EMIGRANTS

Several conclusions may be made on the basis of these pyramids. First, it is obvious that the wartime migrations affected the *bourg* rather than the *campagne*. Most of the refugees from other parts of France who spent the war years in Roussillon lived in the village. These refugees were, as one would expect, mostly young children and adults. During the 1954-59 period, on the contrary, a larger percentage of the emigrants from the *bourg* were adolescents and young adults. The *bourg* emigration is more subject to fluctuation.

The emigration from the *campagne* on the other hand, shows a relatively stable pattern. The largest group of emigrants consists of young parents with their children. Indeed, the *campagne* half of the pyramids looks very much like a half of the population pyramid for the total population of Roussillon. The people who move away from the country are, generally speaking, typical of the population of the community as a whole.

There seems to be no significant difference in the figures on men and women:

Age Group	1946–51				1954–59			
	Bourg		Campagne		Bourg		Campagne	
	M	F	M	F	M	F	M	F
5–15	16	17	6	21	3	3	14	14
16–21	2	7	8	9	0	6	6	6
22 or older	36	39	30	31	14	13	40	28

Instead of making a simple list of all the communes to which people went on leaving Roussillon, it is more revealing to group the destinations. Generally speaking, there are six areas beyond the limits of Roussillon to which people may be expected to move. Some are ill-defined, but they are nonetheless recognizable.

The first area is the home neighborhood, the valley of the Calavon River. The urban center of this area, which is known in geological studies as the Apt Basin, is the little town of Apt. In this natural ecological unit man has drawn the artificial boundaries of the communes which are of course officially recognized by everyone but which have little function in many aspects of day-to-day living. A young man living on the edge of the commune of Roussillon may marry a girl from the neighboring farm in the commune of Goult. Statistically, this is an exogamous marriage because the two young people are from different communities, but ecologically the marriage is endogamous because they live in the same neighborhood. A farmer may on the expiration of the lease of a rented farm move into the next commune to lease another farm. Statistically he has changed communities, but because he still lives in the same neighborhood, he feels no essential change. The Apt Basin is the region where an inhabitant of Roussillon may move and still feel at home.

The second area is the *département* of the Vaucluse. It includes the Apt Basin but extends beyond it. This is the administrative, cultural and historical unit of which the Roussillonnais feels himself a part. It includes the principal commercial center of Cavaillon, the administrative center of Avignon, the fertile truck farms of the Rhône Valley and the barren uplands culminating in Mont Ventoux. A Roussillonnais recognizes this unit more consciously than he recognizes the Apt Basin. He would never say that he is 'from the Apt Basin' but always 'from the Vaucluse.' He considers the Vaucluse as his *pays*. Each year in Paris there is a banquet of Vauclusiens which reflects this feeling of cultural solidarity. A Roussillonnais could move to another part of the Vaucluse without leaving his *pays*.

The third area to which a Roussillonnais may move is Marseille and the region around Marseille, including the educational center of Aix-en-Provence and the industrial center of Berre. When a Roussillonnais goes to the city to continue his education or to work in a factory or a shop, it is to this area that he most naturally turns.

The fourth area is the part of the Midi that borders the Mediterranean, faces the Vaucluse across the Rhône, or adjoins the Vaucluse to the north and east. It includes all of provence, much of Languedoc and the Mediterranean part of Savoy. It is a linguistic unit, and like the Apt

Basin, it is an ecological unit but on a larger scale.

The fifth and sixth areas are simpler to define: metropolitan Paris and the rest of France. Theoretically there might be a seventh area—the countries beyond the national border to which a Roussillonnais could move, but in practice this emigration does not take place. There must, however, be a seventh rubric to cover the cases of emigrants whose destination is unknown.

In the following tables, I have not included the figures for the smaller geographical units in the totals for the larger units of which they are a part. For example, the number of Roussillonnais emigrating to the Vaucluse does not include the number emigrating to the Apt Basin, and the number going to the Midi does not include the number going to the Marseille area.

	Destination of Emigrants			
	Number		Percentage	
	1946–51	1954–59	1946–51	1954–59
Apt Basin	65	40	29	27
Vaucluse	24	24	11	16
Marseille	77	33	35	22
Midi	12	17	5	12
Paris	2	12	1	8
France	0	8	0	5.5
?	34	8	15	5.5

The most important conclusion to be drawn from these statistics is that more than a quarter of the emigration from Roussillon is to nearby communes. It is also interesting to note that Marseille draws so many emigrants, although it should be pointed out that the figure for 1946-51 is abnormally high because it includes those people from Marseille who took refuge in Roussillon during the war and had not returned home by 1946. The other places are scattered through the Vaucluse and elsewhere in the Midi. The nearest commercial center, Cavaillon, attracts a large number of emigrants, but there is no other discernable focus of migration.

Regardless of the reputation of Paris for attracting people from all over France, it apparently has little attraction for the people of Roussillon. The eight people who went to Paris between 1954 and 1959 were a Parisian and his two children (who have a summer place in Roussillon) and five Algerians (who worked briefly in Roussillon's moribund ochre mine before moving on to the metropolis).

There is an important distinction between the *bourg* and *campagne* emigrants: More *bourg* people are attracted by city life, while country people more often move to another rural commune in the neighborhood.

| | Destination by Numbers of Emigrants | | | |
| | Bourg | | Campagne | |
	1946–51	1954–59	1946–51	1954–59
Apt Basin	31	7	34	33
Vaucluse	15	6	9	18
Marseille area	77	33	27	17
Midi	5	4	7	13
Paris	1	6	1	6
Elsewhere	0	0	0	8
?	8	1	26	7

| | Destination by Percentage of Emigrants | | | |
| | Bourg | | Campagne | |
	1946–51	1954–59	1946–51	1954–59
Apt Basin	26	17	29	27
Vaucluse	13	14	8	17
Marseille Area	42	38	26	16
Midi	4	10	7	12
Paris	1	14	1	6
Elsewhere	0	0	0	7
?	7	2	25	7

Another source of information concerning the destination of people who move away from the commune of Roussillon is the INSEE file in which registered voters are classified by place of birth. This offers a less immediate check on the destination of emigrants than I have used above, but it is still interesting to compare these figures with the others.

| Registered voters born in Roussillon but living elsewhere in France | | |
	Numbers	Percentage
Apt Basin	154	36
Vaucluse	128	30
Marseille area	88	21
Midi	30	7
Paris	5	1
Elsewhere	22	5

Some of these figures may be usefully broken down into still smaller categories. Of the 154 people who live in the Apt Basin, 133 live in communes actually bordering on the commune of Roussillon. These people have then not really left home. They have merely moved to another part of the neighborhood. I also note on my individual record cards that of the 128 people who live elsewhere in the Vaucluse, only 16 live in Avignon while 39 live in Cavaillon: it is the commercial capital, not the administrative capital, of the region that attracts immigrants. A parallel situation exists in the Marseille area: there are only 22 native Roussillonnais in the city of Marseille itself, but 28 in the oil refinery area of Berre.

There is less information available on immigrants than on emigrants. I do not have a list of the individuals who have moved into the commune since 1954, and there was no census in 1959 on the basis of which such a list could be made. The names of all the immigrants could be dug from the archives of the town hall in Roussillon, but for present purposes we must rely on the information that is immediately at hand. The principal sources remain the *listes nominatives* of the censuses of 1946 and 1954 (especially the former, since it gives the birthplaces and professions of inhabitants) and the anonymous information in the questionnaire which formed part of the 1954 census. From these sources we learn something about the people who lived in Roussillon in 1946 and 1954 but were not born there, and who therefore present a sample of the sort of immigrants Roussillon attracts. On the basis of this information and of some of the conclusions I have drawn concerning emigration, we can formulate a few generalizations concerning immigration.

By a simple calculation we can determine the net population gain through immigration for our two five-year periods, 1946-51 and 1954-59:

		Net Population Gain through Immigration		
Population of the commune	in 1946	779	in 1954	713
Net loss by death and emigration	1946–51	–262	1954–59	–204
Remainder of population	in 1951	517	in 1959	509
Actual population total	in 1951	730	in 1959	680
Less remainder		–517		–509
Population gain	1946–51	213	1954–59	171
Less gain by birth		– 31		– 34
Gain by immigration	1946–51	182	1954–59	137

Although a few of those recorded as immigrants are undoubtedly infants born in a city hospital to parents living in Roussillon, by far the largest number are people moving into the commune and taking the places of people who have departed. The old cliché of rural demographic change, a relatively stable though slowly decreasing population, is obviously without basis. In truth, there is a large and constant turnover. The net loss in the total population figures may be simply explained by the fact that not quite as many people move to the commune as move away from it:

	1946–51	1954–59
Emigrants	222	148
Immigrants	182	137
Net loss of population through migration	40	11

According to the census of 1954 there were 413 people who were living in Roussillon but were not born there. Of these, there were 208 males and 203 females, figures that are noteworthy only because they are so close. On the basis of available information, all we can do is place in general age groups the people who were living in Roussillon in 1954 but who were not born there:

Age group	Numbers	Percentage of Total
0–14 years old	51	12
15 to 24 years old	45	11
25 to 44 years old	104	25
45 years old or older	213	52
Total	413	100

By far the largest group of Roussillonnais born elsewhere are adults. This does not mean that the immigrants are older people. Many of them have lived in Roussillon since they were children. For a more subtle understanding we must ask when the Roussillonnais born elsewhere moved to Roussillon.

	0–14 years old	15–24	25–44	45 or more	Total
1953–54	17	18	14	14	63
1950–52	20	10	30	21	81
1945–49	8	7	23	32	70
1940–44	6	4	11	15	36
1930–39	—	6	18	41	65
1920–29	—	—	6	25	31
Before 1920	—	—	2	65	67

From this table, based on figures from the 1954 census, we may conclude that there has been no single period of heavy immigration. Rather, the movement has been steady over a long period of years. This fact is confirmed if we see at what period the adults over 25 came to Roussillon:

Period of arrival	Numbers	Percentage
1950–54	79	25
1940–49	81	25
1920–39	90	28
Before 1920	67	22
Total	317	100

At first glance it may appear that recent immigration was heavier, but if we take into account the attrition through death and emigration we see that in Roussillon there has been a steady flow of immigrants for many years.

Where do the immigrants come from? The *liste nominative* of the 1946 census, which lists the place of birth, gives an answer to this question, even though it is indirect because a person may have lived in a half-dozen communities between the day of his birth and his arrival in Roussillon. However, it is an answer worth having if we can assume that a person's birthplace and the general area from which he moves to Roussillon are not usually too far apart.

The 1946 census has one further disadvantage. The two men who took it in Roussillon neglected to record the birthplaces of 265 individuals! Fortunately, through correspondence, I have been able to learn the birthplaces of 117 of these people, and it seems that the lacunae were left almost at random. I have assumed that we may, by studying only the 630 Roussillonnais whose birthplaces we know, still give a fair picture of the origins of the people.

This assumption is justified by information from another source. In the 1954 census, one of the questions asked of all inhabitants was: 'In what commune did you live before you came to Roussillon?' By comparing the information given in answer to this question with the birthplaces of the 384 Roussillonnais not born in Roussillon, we find that the results are amazingly close.

About half of the immigrant Roussillonnais come from neighboring communes of the Apt Basin. About 15 percent come from elsewhere in the Vaucluse and the other come in fairly equal proportions from the Marseille area, from elsewhere in the Midi, and from other parts of France. However, contrary to the impression given by the statistics, there were not fewer foreign-born in Roussillon in 1954 than in 1946. The apparent difference arises from the difference in the questions asked on the two censuses. Most of the foreign-born (37 Italians, 3 Belgians and 3 Swiss) did not come directly to Roussillon, but lived for a while in

Birthplace (1946) and	Numbers		Percentage	
Previous Residence (1954)	1946	1954	1946	1954
Apt Basin	172	229	45	55
Vaucluse	64	52	17	13
Marseille	30	38	8	9
Midi	46	42	12	10
France	29	35	7	9
Foreign	43	17	11	4
	384	413		

another French community. With this difference in mind, we can see that our two tables are closely parallel.

Information available from the 1954 census does not distinguish between the *bourg* and the *campagne* populations, but by analyzing the data in the census of 1946, we can see an essential difference between the origins of the two groups of immigrants:

Census of 1946: Birthplace of Roussillonnais not Born in the Commune

Birthplace	Numbers		Percentage	
	Bourg	Campagne	Bourg	Campagne
Apt Basin	52	120	35	51
Vaucluse	24	40	16	17
Marseille	22	8	15	3
Midi	18	28	12	21
France	15	14	10	6
Foreign	17	26	12	11
	148	236		

The difference is that the *campagne* draws a higher percentage of people from neighboring rural communes, while the *bourg* attracts more people from the Marseille area. This parallels our information concerning the destination of emigrants: country people are more likely to move to rural communes; *bourg* people more frequently move to the city.

Up to this point I have considered the elements in the demographic situation in Roussillon which make for change. Let us turn the question about and see what generalizations can be made about the more stable

part of the population, the 275 people who lived there during the entire
period from 1946 to 1959.

Birthplace	Numbers	Percentage
Roussillon	137	50
Elsewhere	138	50

Only half of the core are really born-and-bred Roussillonnais!

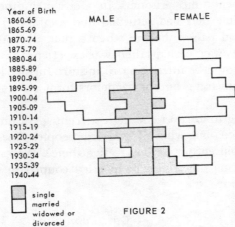

FIGURE 2

single
married
widowed or
divorced

Other characteristics of the core become apparent if we examine the
pyramid of this segment of the population:

The core is dominated by older people. One hundred and eighty individuals in the core were born before the First World War, only 95 since
1914. This larger number of older people is the remainder of the nineteenth century Roussillon whose population was twice as large as today's.
Another feature of the core, also reflecting the general French demographic pattern, is the excess of older women over older men.

An unusual characteristic of the core population in Roussillon, however, is the large proportion of unmarried men. There are only seven
women over thirty who are unmarried, but there are 38 men! It is
certainly not a generally accepted idea that single men form a stable part
of the population, but in Roussillon a large number of old bachelors
form an essential part of the core. This is not a phenomenon of the *bourg*
alone. The proportion of farmer to bourgeois bachelors is about the
same.

The explanation for this high proportion of unmarried men is not
clear, although I can suggest several possible explanations. In the first
place, a good many of the bachelors were born between 1900 and 1914.
According to the marriage pattern, these men would have married

women born in the following ten-year period. However, the marked decrease in the birthrate during the First World War substantially limited the number of women in this age group. The post-war increase in the birthrate did not make up the deficit.

The next large group of unmarried men was born in the 1920's. The general decrease in the French birthrate in the 1930's reduced the supply of postwar wives. Furthermore, these men were precisely the individuals whose normal period of courtship was interrupted by the Second World War. Some of them were prisoners in Germany; others were in the *maquis*. By the time they had returned and established themselves economically, they had passed the age when a man normally married. Yet they did not move away; perhaps their war experience gave them their fill of adventure. It would be interesting to inquire further into this surprising situation in which a group of bachelors form a conservative element in the community.

It was surprising to discover the high percentage of unmarried men in the core population, but what of married people? Does marriage to a native of Roussillon encourage one to live there? We can give a partial answer by comparing the origins of married couples in the core and in the total population.

	Core Population 1946–59	Total Population 1946
Total married couples	78	144
Married couples, birthplace unknown	7	39
Married couples, birthplace known	71	105

Number of married couples, birthplace known:	Core Population 1946–59	Total Population 1946
Both born in Roussillon	14	12
Husband born in Roussillon	14	14
Wife born in Roussillon	12	27
Both born elsewhere	31	52
	71	105

Percentage of married couples, birthplace known:		
Both born in Roussillon	19	11
Husband born in Roussillon	19	13
Wife born in Roussillon	16	26
Both born elsewhere	46	50

We see from this table that there is a tendency for young people, both of whom were born in the commune, to remain there after they are married. On checking the individual census cards, I find that there is no lag in this custom. Some of the twelve couples listed in the census of 1946 have died, but other young people born in Roussillon and living there in 1946 have since married other natives, so that in 1959 there were 14 couples of which both members were born in Roussillon, two more than in 1946.

However, almost half the couples of the core population were born outside the commune—almost exactly the same proportion as in the general population. It is interesting to note on the individual census cards, incidentally, that seven of the core married couples—the Boscherinis, the Castellis, the Gillis, the Gnettis, the Gulinis, the Ughettos and the Zanganis—were born in Italy but have lived in Roussillon for many years. They represent the long-standing tradition of population movement from Italy to Southern France. In Rousillon these couples and their children are so firmly rooted that they form an integral part of the core of the population.

In some parts of the world it is the custom for women to go to their husbands' community to live. In other parts of the world men live in the home of their wives. In Roussillon there seems to be no clear pattern in this respect.

The question of the rôle which family clans play in the population is an obvious and an important one, but to give a satisfactory answer we need complete genealogical and marriage data which unfortunately I do not have. The best I can do with the limited information immediately available is to list the family names which are represented in the core by at least two *ménages* or by five individuals.

Name	Number of Individuals	Number of Ménages	Individuals born In Roussillon
Agnel	5	1	5
Bernard	5	1	2
Blanc	8	3	2
Bonnelly	4	2	1
Bourgues	9	2	7
Cartoux	6	2	2
Chauvet	6	3	2
Dauphin	4	3	2
Doucende	7	1	3
Gauffridy	7	1	3
Grégoire	4	2	3
Gulini	5	2	1

Name	Number of Individuals	Number of Ménages	Individuals born In Roussillon
Icard	22	6	17
Jouval	5	3	5
Langarel	5	1	3
Malbec	6	2	6
Mariani	5	1	3
Mathieu	11	3	7
Melon	5	3	4
Sautel	4	2	2
Tamisier	8	3	8

It is surprising that the only large family within the core of the population is the Icard tribe. There are 33 for whom I have census cards, and there must be five or ten more who were not there when either census was taken. If we add to this group the Audes, the Dauphins, the Cartouxes and other families related to the Icards by marriage, the clan becomes even larger.

At this point, any of the Icards would be quick to point out that they are not all related! My suspicion is, however, that if we had sufficient genealogical information, we would find that the Icards are in fact all related but not closely enough for them to care or even know about the relationship. Generally speaking, the people of Roussillon are not interested in genealogy or in relationships beyond the more immediate ones, unless other factors such as business or friendship make it interesting to remain aware of family connections. The size of the real Icard clan, therefore, cannot be measured accurately without further information. In reply to our question, however, it would seem that family clans are not essential in determining membership in the core.

The distribution in the core population between *bourg* and *campagne* may usefully be compared to that of the total population of Roussillon in the census years, 1946 and 1954.

	Numbers		Percentage	
	Bourg	Campagne	Bourg	Campagne
1946	307	472	39	61
1954	238	475	34	66
Core, 1946–59	94	181	34	66

The core is divided between *bourg* and *campagne* in approximately the same proportion as the whole population.

Figures show that the core is represented normally in all economic activities too. A list was made of the men from the core born before 1926 and who were living in Roussillon from 1946 through 1959. By the end of this period of thirteen years, most of these men would have chosen a profession and have settled in it more or less permanently.

Cultivateur	65
Artisan	14
Journalier	9
Facteur	3
Retraité	3
Négociant	2
Notaire	1
Voyageur de Commerce	1
Transports publics	1
Chauffeur	1
Cantonnier	1
Radio	1
No profession	4
Profession unknown	5

We may compare this distribution with that of the whole active population of 1954 by condensing our information into the categories used by the census and comparing our results with the figures of 1954.

Source of Livelihood	'Core' Males Born before 1926	Total Active Population Census of 1954
	Numbers	
Agriculture	65	218
Commerce	17	74
Public Employees	6	17
Mining	10	12
Liberal Professions	1	1
	99	322

Source of Livelihood	'Core' Males Born before 1926	Total Active Population Census of 1954
	Percentages	
Agriculture	66	68
Commerce	17	23
Public Employees	6	5
Mining	10	4
Liberal Professions	1	0.3

It is clear that the professional pattern of the core is essentially the same as that of the general population.

We have seen that in many respects the core seems not to differ from the rest of the population. There is an essential difference, however, in the rôle this group plays in the political life of the community. In the election of 1959, nineteen of the twenty-six candidates for the municipal council were members of the core population. Of the seven others, five had lived in Roussillon for at least ten years. There were only two who had lived in the community for a very short time. One was André Lagier, a Parisian man of letters and administrator, who had a summer home in Roussillon. The other was Pierre Geoffroy, the husband of the new school teacher, the nephew of a senator from the Vaucluse, and a well-known businessman in the Apt Basin. With these striking but easily understood exceptions, the core population dominated the election. Ten of the thirteen winning candidates were members of the core.

It is interesting to note, however, that there was not one of the candidates with the name Icard, the name of the most numerous clan in the commune. Apparently, it is easier to gain a position of political power if one is part of the core, but all its members do not rank high in the power structure.

The relationship of the demographic mobility to land tenure is a factor which should be studied but it could be fully understood only through a detailed analysis of the *cadastre* in the archives of the town hall of Roussillon. I do know that all but three of the core families own property in the commune, a fact which suggests that land tenure may be a basic factor in the demographic movement of the Roussillonnais. Future research on the problem should start at this point.

The present study was undertaken in order to learn more precisely how the *exode rural* takes place. Is it true that Roussillon, like many other rural communities in France, is slowly dying because of the departure of young farm people for the city? As evidence from my census cards accumulated, a completely new picture of the demography of Roussillon came into focus. It became apparent that this supposedly stable community had an astonishing mobile population. Far more people leave Roussillon each year than I had ever imagined, and almost as many people move into the community from the outside. Furthermore, the turnover in the population is a venerable phenomenon: it has been going on for decades. Technological change and the upheaval of war have intensified the movement, but they have not caused it.

To understand the demography of a rural community the movements of farm people must be considered apart from those of village people.

Bourg and *campagne,* we have seen, are more distinct entities than city people imagine them to be. When we speak of the rural population moving to the city we assume that we are speaking of farmers, but in Roussillon it is the *bourg* people who are more likely to move to other towns or to a big city. Demographic movement in the *campagne* characteristically involves tenant farmers whose lease has expired and who move with their families to another farm in the *pays.* They are no more fixed to specific plots of land than city people are to specific jobs. Furthermore, Paris offers little attraction to any of the Roussillon emigrants; their movements are largely confined to the Midi.

The illusion of demographic stability is created primarily by two factors. The first is that the people who move into Roussillon are very much like the people who leave. It is not so much that the young are replaced by the old, but whole families move away and are replaced by families of about the same composition and professions. Even more important in creating the illusion is the existence of a surprisingly small group of people, the core population, which remains in the commune. In most respects they are similar to the migrants, but it appears that a large proportion are property owners. The political power is largely in their hands. Some of them, like the Icard families, own little land and are not elected to office, but I know from living in the town that they have social power. They set the tone of life and maintain it as migrant families come and go. They are the culture bearers.

When one returns to Roussillon after a long absence and sees Madame Icard, 'La Léoncie,' sitting in the same chair in the town square surrounded by women of her gossip circle, one has the impression that nothing has changed. When one goes into the Café des Sports and finds Aimé Icard standing at the bar where one said goodby to him ten years ago, one feels the continuity of life. The fact is, though, that the members of Madame Icard's group have changed, and the owner of the café and the men standing at the bar with Aimé are not the same people we left ten years ago. On seeing our old friends, we have a sense of stability. We know, now, however, that outside of the small hard core, all is flux.

41. The Cultural Effects
of Population Changes
in the Eastern Townships

AILEEN D. ROSS

This paper presents the first or exploratory phase of research in a study of the effect of invasion on the morale of a community. Although many studies have been made of spacial succession, and some of changes in social attitudes, there has been little attempt to investigate the relationship between these two phenomena, in other words, to show whether, or how, the solidarity of a group is affected by an ecological succession.[1] The process of invasion has been described in connection with different areas of a city. The invasion of one section of a city by an outside ethnic group is a common phenomenon. The general pattern is that, with its first indication, the morale of the resident group strengthens, but eventually one point breaks, that is, someone sells out to one of the invaders. Then another gains a foothold—a house or a shop—and, once the area is well penetrated, both the invasion and exodus gather momentum.

This is a study of a large rural area in which the invasion has taken

Source: Reprinted with permission of the author and publisher from *Canadian Journal of Economics and Political Science*, IX (November, 1943).

[1] Cf. Professor Dawson's discussion on ecological tension-making factors (C. A. Dawson and W. E. Gettys, *An Introduction to Sociology* (New York, 1937), pp. 325 ff.

place over so long a period of time, and over such an extensive region, that the invaded population as a whole has taken longer to realize its significance. In this situation it is much easier to trace and observe the psychological effect of invasion on the invaded group.[2]

The field of research chosen for this study was made up of the four counties of Compton, Richmond, Sherbrooke, and Stanstead in the eastern townships of the province of Quebec. Interviews, practically all indirect, were obtained from the different sections—industrial towns, county towns, summer resorts, villages, and rural areas. The village of Sawyerville in Compton County was studied especially intensively. The French-Canadian invasion of the eastern townships has taken place at an uneven rate, and one can therefore observe the whole cycle of its effect going on at the same time in the many different communities. This cycle begins with attempts of organized resistance on the part of the English to the first French-Canadians that come in, passes through the stages of discouragement as the pressure increases, and ends with the complete apathy of the English when they realize that the invasion is beyond their control.

The eastern townships were first opened up as an English settlement in 1792.[3] The English system of land division, as opposed to the French seigneurial system, was adopted, and efforts were made to encourage colonization.[4] English-speaking settlers—American, Scotch, Irish, and English immigrants—began to come in around 1800. It was not long after, however, that French-Canadians also began to settle in the area, for a law, passed in 1774, authorizing priests only to "tithe those who held lands under the seigneurial tenure" was changed in 1849 to allow the church to set up parishes outside the seigneurial boundaries.[5] After this, the movement of French population gathered momentum as it was aided and often organized by the Roman Catholic Church.[6] The French moved in from several points. In the northeast they came from the county of

---

2 This problem has been studied in Cincinnati with reference to the Negro invasion. Cf. J. A. Quinn, "Community Studies in Cincinnati," *Publications of the American Sociological Society*, XXV, 143.

3 Jean Hunter, "The French Canadian Invasion of the Eastern Townships" (unpublished M.A. Dissertation, Department of Sociology, McGill University, Aug., 1939), p. 1.

4 There is some dispute as to the actual boundary of the area originally included in the townships, but it is usually supposed to include twelve counties which are divided into 91 townships. *Ibid.*, p. 4.

5 M. Q. Innis, *An Economic History of Canada* (Toronto, 1935), p. 138.

6 Raoul Blanchard, "Les Cantons de l'est." *Revue de géographie alpine*, XXV, 1937, 194: "Il n'y a aucun doute que des prêtres canadiens aient prêche l'invasion des Cantons, suscité et aidé quelques compagnies de colonisation; mais la faim de terres, la nécessité de trouver un exitoire à une population en accroissement rapide ont été plus éfficaces que leurs exhortations. Le succés de l'invasion français dans les Cantons de l'est s'apparente au jeu de grandes forces naturelles."

Beauce, down through Frontenac, into the county of Compton; from the north they came in through the counties of Megantic and Atharbasca; and from the west through Bagot, Shefford and Missiquoi counties. Thus the townships were penetrated on three sides, and the first-comers gradually spread through the remaining area.[7] At first the French moved in rapidly to the unsettled parts of the townships. Later, separate families or individuals gradually filtered into communities which had been previously settled by the English.[8]

TABLE 1.

French-Canadian Population in the Eastern Townships, 1861–1931*
(French-Canadian population as a percentage of the total numbers)

Counties	1861	1871	1881	1901	1911	1921	1931
Compton	14	24	38	48	56	64	67
Richmond	15	33	43	61	70	76	79
Sherbrooke	24	42	48	58	60	68	72
Stanstead	8	24	31	46	51	61	66

NOTE: The year 1891 is omitted as figures on racial origin were not included in the census of that year.
* Hunter, "French-Canadian Invasion," appendix B, XXXVI, Table 13.

This movement into the townships has continued at a steady and fairly even rate, and shows no signs of abating. The proportionate increase of French-Canadians from 1861 to 1931 (figures for 1941 are not yet available), in the four counties under observation, appear in Table I. The proportionate increase between the two years, 1861 and 1931, is shown on the adjoining maps.

The year 1861 is the first for which detailed statistics can be obtained of the proportionate increase of French-Canadians in the townships. This year marks approximately the beginning of the period of urbanization of the region, and also that of the cessation of British and American immigration. A number of other significant developments set in about this time. The birth-rate of the English population began to show symptoms of decline, and the first English settlers commenced to leave for the West, the United States, and the cities. These factors all had an important bearing on the movement of French population into the region. It was, however, the coming of industry which was perhaps the determining factor in bringing in such large numbers of French-Canadians that the former English residents felt forced to migrate.

As the English-Canadians were the industrial leaders in other parts of Canada it was natural that they should lead in the industrialization of

---

[7] Hunter, "French Canadian Invasion," p. 37.
[8] *Ibid.*, p. 38.

this region.[9] In his study of Drummondville, in the eastern townships, Dr. E. C. Hughes shows, that in that town, out of eleven industries, employing 4400, only two—with a total employment of 70—are owned and operated by French-Canadians; the other nine were founded by companies operating outside the eastern townships.[10] The greater proportion of their managers and technical staff come from outside Canada, and many of the foremen, skilled operators, and clerical workers are English-speaking, while the semi-skilled and unskilled labour are French-Canadian.[11] This is only one example of a movement that is taking place all over the province of Quebec.[12] It is very seldom that the former English-Canadian residents of the eastern townships become prominent or are absorbed in these large industrial undertakings. They bitterly resent the invasion, but seem unaware that it is this precise increase in English- and American-controlled and managed industry that has been the most important factor in drawing in the French-Canadians. This is because the coming of industry coincided with the need for further outlets for the surplus French-Canadian rural population. They had outgrown the resources of their own expanding social system, and, while some of them left for New England or the West, the majority have been gradually moving into the industrial towns and cities of Quebec.[13] This is indicated by population figures which show that the greatest absolute increase in total *and* in French-Canadian population in the eastern townships has been precisely in those areas where there has been urban development.[14]

In this question of industrial labour it is important to see why English-

---

9 *Ibid.,* p. 141.

10 E. C. Hughes, "Position and Status in a Quebec Industrial Town" *American Sociological Review,* III (October, 1938), 710.

11 *Ibid.,* p. 713.

12 E. C. Hughes, "Industry and the Rural System in Quebec," *Canadian Journal of Economics and Political Science,* IV (August, 1938), 349: "But in all [the industrial towns of Quebec] the same general pattern prevails. Labour is largely native; the management is alien to the native culture. The source of the industrial population is to be found in the rural situation. . . ."

13 Hunter, "French Canadian Invasion," p. 176. See also Hughes, "Industry and the Rural System in Quebec," p. 347, for a description of the effect of industrialization on a town in the eastern townships. Between 1911 and 1937 the population increased from 2,605 to 19,424, or about 750 percent. Analysis of this increased population showed that it was native to the vicinity and of country and village birth.

14 *Ibid.,* p. 346. Also in his article, "Position and Status in a Quebec Industrial Town," p. 709. Also, Hunter, "French Canadian Invasion," p. 96: "On the whole, then, the numerical growth of both the total and the French population, over the period 1861–1931, has been determined by the degree of urban development in each township. . . . Most of this growth has apparently consisted of French population. In other words, the surplus French population which was being produced not only in the old French parishes . . . but in the eastern townships itself . . . was being absorbed, in part at least, by the growing towns in the eastern townships."

Canadians were not held in the townships by the coming in of industry, and why they did not respond to the demand for cheap labour. The English were ahead of the French in acquiring the education and skills necessary to fit them for jobs which would give them a higher standard of living. Improvement in agricultural techniques, too, came earlier to the English, largely because their dwindling families forced them into the mechanization of their farms, but also because their agricultural products entered the wider provincial markets before those of the French. The French-Canadians to a large extent still run their farms on the family basis. So the English, in spite of the isolation of some of the rural population, have been more under the influence of the outside world than have the French-Canadians.[15] This influence has had the effect of indoctrinating them with an urban pattern of expectations. Their ambitions have been oriented toward an ever-higher standard of living and an increasing desire for social prestige.[16] This means that they will seek to give their children the type of education which will make them successful in the city, and so further encourage them to leave the farms and the townships.[17] On the other hand, the expectations built up in the French-Canadian parish, by education and attitude, are that at least some of the children shall remain on the land, and those that do not are not imbued with the ambitions that bring success in an urban industrial environment.[18] Therefore, from the point of view of the English, the French-Canadian invasion was possible because of the great amount of sparsely settled land, the rural-urban trend which drained many of the English farms and villages of their younger population, the declining birth-rate, the movement of English population from the townships to the West—when it began to open up at the end of the nineteenth century—and, perhaps the chief factor of all, the industrial development which began in the 1870's after the building of railways. From the point of view of the French-Canadians, the invasion was due to the natural expansion of a

---

15 *Ibid.,* p. 142: "The French-Canadians entered a competitive system without the skills and attitudes necessary for competition on an equal footing."

16 Personal interview: "The English are graduating to a higher standard of living and so leaving the townships. The French are coming in at the standard of living which the English are at here."

17 Hunter, "French Canadian Invasion," p. 141.

18 *Ibid.,* p. 142. Also, E. C. Hughes, "Position and Status in a Quebec Industrial Town," p. 173: ". . . the higher ambitions . . . are pointed toward the church, liberal professions and politics. Hence, technical and managerial success has no symbolic value." Many interviews, such as the following, showed this lack of ambition, on the part of the French: "The French don't seem to have any ambition, they don't want to get on, they seem quite content to get just enough to exist on." "The French will work for anything, and so they keep the wages down."

population which had outgrown the resources of its own land, and had had no reduction in birth-rate.[19]

Economic factors alone have often been responsible for the migration of population. At other times psychological factors enter to complicate the causes of migration. The purpose of this study is to enquire into those psychological factors which have generally been ignored. Other rural parts of Canada have been deeply affected by the rural-urban trend, by the falling birth-rate, by the coming of industry, and yet not all the people have migrated. Some still remain on the land and in the small towns and villages. What have been the additional factors present in the eastern townships which have caused the English to abandon that area completely? Here I am referring to the rural and village population, as there is some indication that a nucleus of English will remain in the larger industrial towns.[20] The answer is that although the English have had increased contact with each other because of the automobile, telephone, and other means of communication, they have become increasingly conscious of their growing isolation in the midst of a foreign culture.

The solidarity of the invaded group is a determining factor in the rate of invasion. It is at this point that the concept of morale becomes important. Morale has come to be seen as a crucial concept in the waging of war; it is an equally important concept in any group situation. Recently a good deal of attention has been directed to this problem, but the actual factors that go to make up the morale of a group have not yet been specifically stated.[21] Morale has been defined as "the basic set of group ideas and attitudes emotionally toned toward some common end."[22] Morale is therefore thought of in terms of groups and goals. The morale of the individual can partly be explained by the nature of the social situation in which he finds himself, and partly by how he feels this

---

[19] Horace Miner, *St. Denis* (Chicago, 1939), p. 86: "The whole social system and the family system upon which it is dependent are based upon large families and the eventual establishment of all the children, save one, outside the paternal home. To function properly there must be a continual outlet for this surplus. . . . During the first two centuries after the French came to Canada, there was always unopened land on which the noninheriting sons could establish themselves. When these lands in Quebec were taken up, there were industrial opportunities in Quebec and New England to absorb the surplus."

[20] Hunter, "French Canadian Invasion," p. 176.

[21] A. U. Pope, "The Importance of Morale," *Journal of Educational Sociology* (December, 1941): "The factors that make for high morale or destroy it are numerous and of varying degrees of efficacy highly complicated in their relations. Many of these factors are not clearly known and their relations especially need to be investigated."

[22] Kimball Young, *Social Psychology* (New York, 1938), p. 655.

situation is affecting some purpose or value of his own.[23] Therefore morale is largely due to the attitude of the individual to the situation— what he believes to be the case—although what he believes may not have any connection with the actual facts. Ideas and beliefs are thus important not in terms of their truth or falsity but in terms of the way they influence the people who believe them.[24] As the English-Canadians believe that the coming of the French is inevitable, this belief colours all their behaviour. The French obviously cannot come into the townships which still have a large English population, to any great extent, unless the English first leave. But only one interviewee of all those interviewed expressed this idea: "The English left the farms first—or the French couldn't have come in." To the great majority of the English population still remaining in the townships, the coming of the French is so inevitable that they feel it is better to get out now while the "going is good."[25] This inevitableness was expressed in such remarks as: "They're swamping us—it's just a question of time!" "They're walking right over us." "I don't see anything that will stop the French coming in." "All the villages back of here are French now—it's just like the tide coming in, one after the other has fallen to the French." Even when only a few French-Canadians come into a village, or buy farms in its vicinity, the discouragement of the English is so great that they express this in such phrases as: "The French are coming in steadily." "This summer they swarmed in." "The French are pouring into Sawyerville." "The French are gaining ground."

A crucial indication that the invasion has begun in an English village is when the French first buy property. As long as they come in merely as casual labour there is the hope that if or when the industry leaves—as it often does when it depends on the extractive resources of the area—the French labourers will leave too. But the buying of property means that

---

23 Cf. D. C. Miller, "Economic Factors in the Morale of College Trained Adults," *American Journal of Sociology* (September, 1941); G. Bateson and Margaret Mead, "Principles of Morale Building," *Journal of Educational Sociology* (December, 1941), 206; Louis Wirth, "Morale and Minority Groups," *American Journal of Sociology* (November, 1941), 415.

24 Kimball Young, *Social Psychology*, p. 461: "We cannot understand any social behaviour without taking into account two factors—individual capacity, attitudes and ideas on the one hand, and cultural, historical forces on the other. . . ."

25 Personal interview: "You know there's something psychological about their attitude to the coming of the French. It isn't purely a question of economics, it's a question of attitude. The English are discouraged, they're giving up. They all feel that they're going to have to sell out eventually, and so they think that they might as well sell now, when they can get a good price. I tell you it's not the French who have taken the country around here, it's the English who have given it up because of their indifference and ignorance. They're just handing the country over to the French."

they have come to stay. Therefore such remarks as "the French are buying right in the village" are pregnant with meaning, because in the minds of the English population it is the beginning of the end. Generally, the next crucial sign of the invasion is the building of a Roman Catholic Church and a schoolhouse. Then a general store is bought or built by a Frenchman, and the English believe that pressure is put on the local French residents to patronize it. Finally, the small village industries gradually get into the hands of the French. The English attitude to this is expressed in such stories as:

"Just the other day an Englishman's butter factory burnt down near here, and first thing we found the French were putting up a $12,000 plant. About $6,000 was a subsidy from the government—they did it so that the Englishman wouldn't build again. They pushed him out. Now he has to go somewhere else. I've seen that kind of thing happen several times. They want to get the English out."

The helpless feeling of the English is partly due to their firm belief that the invasion is strongly organized. The French-Canadians are always referred to as "they," that is, as a unit, and to the English this unit is synonymous with the Roman Catholic Church. It is true that the French still have a strong rallying centre in their church,[26] and it is the policy of the church to take leadership especially in the new parishes that are gradually set up as the invasion progresses. The French-Canadians, too, have a strong rallying centre in the desire of a minority group to survive *as* a separate group. Furthermore, their community solidarity has not yet been as much affected by urban influences as has that of the English.[27] The feeling of the strength of this organization finds expression in such phrases as: "There is a definitely organized French group in our community to buy up the land, they do it in a scientific fashion." "The French are working strategically to plant their people in different parts of the country." "Some say they have a syndicate formed to supply money to these people to buy the English places." This organized "push" against the English is largely ascribed to the Roman Catholic Church; "The priest finds out about farms for sale and furnishes the money to the

---

26 E. C. Hughes, "French-Canadian Communities," *Publications of the Society for Social Research* (University of Chicago Press, June, 1936), 1. Also, S. M. Jamieson, "French and English in the Institutional Structure of Montreal" (unpublished M.A. dissertation, Department of Sociology, McGill University, 1938), p. 8: "The Roman Catholic Church has come to be the most important institution in French Canada, as its clergy has steadily extended and consolidated its supervision and control over social activity." Also *ibid.*, p. 22.

27 Henry Durant, "Morale and Its Measurement," *American Journal of Sociology* (November, 1941), 406: "The greater the homogeneity of the group and the closer the identity of the leader with the led, the fewer will be the problems encountered in maintaining high morale."

people." "This priest boasts that by the time he leaves, this will be a completely French village."

The English themselves make sporadic attempts to counterorganize against the invasion: "The village of C. is keeping the French out." "The English are anxious to keep the land from the French—they parcel it out so as to get more English on it." "There's a valley on one side of D.—the French are on the hill beyond—that's as far as they can get—yet!" But the English have no rallying centre. Their religious institutions, instead of being a strong binding factor—as they probably were in the days when the English population was increasing—are now thrown more and more into competition because of their dwindling congregations.[28] In the village of Sawyerville three large Protestant churches struggle to survive with an average congregation of 35 at the Anglican Church, fifteen at the United, and four or five at the Baptist.[29] The relative importance of the priest and the Protestant minister in the community can be seen in such remarks as the following, made by a Protestant minister: "The priest doesn't preach a sermon, he gets up there and lays down the law. I take hours to make up a sermon, and then they don't believe me!" In former days the Protestant church was one organization where all members of the family could find some common interest. Now with the waning of its influence and the coming of associational life to the rural community— another contribution from the city—the former unified rural family is being divided into age groups according to some specific interest. The mother may be in the Women's Institute or the Eastern Stars, the father a member of the Orange Lodge or a farmers' club, and the children may belong to the Young People's Association or the Boy Scouts.

Contrary to expectation, a study of the associational life of the English population of the eastern townships would seem to indicate extreme over-organization. This may be due to any one of three factors: either an attempt to hold the remnants of their community life, that is, an attempt to organize themselves against the invasion; or to the fact that the dwindling English group are trying to maintain all the associations begun while there was still a large enough English population to support

---

28 D. Sanderson, *Rural Sociology and Rural Social Organization* (New York, 1942), pp. 321 ff., shows that in a study of 140 rural village communities chosen from different parts of the United States, that between 1924 and 1936 church attendance declined by 20 percent. He also describes the competition that comes to a community when it is "over-churched." This also showed in interviews; "G is riddled with religious dissension." They have no loyalty or attachment for the Church here." "It's terrible the way the churches here refuse to work together."

29 J. H. Kolb and E. deS. Brunner, *A Study of Rural Society* (Boston, 1940), pp. 56–59, point out that the solidarity of the neighborhood is maintained longer when it is inhabited by a homogeneous religious group.

them; or to the same restlessness seen in urban centres where new organizations are being constantly organized. This latter factor would seem to be the real cause because of the willingness with which community leaders in the townships seem to promote new associations, although already overburdened by their leadership in others. A week's programme of some of these community leaders would intimidate even the most ardent city "joiner." Over-organization means a strain on the leadership resources of the community. When this takes place it is inevitable that a certain amount of competition and even of conflict will come in.[30] It often means, too, that the same people belong to most of the associations, which causes further competition for their time and energy. An indication that the associational life of the townships is not satisfying, although heavy, was evident in the way the people welcomed a new adult educational project because there was "nothing in the townships for the people." Therefore, although associational life may enrich a community, it can also have a detrimental effect. The associational life of the younger people seems to be markedly on the decline. This is partly due to a lack of leadership, but also to lack of young people to support the existing organizations. In one county town there is no one left between the ages of 21 and 35, and in many other centres there are too few to permit stimulating associational life.

The English-Canadian rural communities are also losing the neighbourhood as an integrating factor. A generation ago the common activities and common life of the rural population were strong bonds holding them to their neighbourhood group. This made for a homogeneity of experience which brought a feeling of solidarity. Increased communication is slowly dissolving the neighbourhood, for now not only can the former isolated rural person get into town, but the influences of the town can get out to him. This has meant that the primary group life, typical of rural communities in the past, has given way to the more impersonal character of urban society. When an individual participates in secondary groups he becomes more self-sufficient, as he is no longer able to identify himself closely with the group. Also, as the primary group weakens, he no longer holds such a strong sense of obligation to his neighbour, or loyalty to the group traditions. This change to secondary relationships has caused extensive changes in rural social institutions and the rural way of life. It has also caused far-reaching changes in the psychological and social structure of the neighbourhood.[31]

So the English population of the eastern townships as a whole has no

---

30 D. Sanderson and R. A. Polson, *Rural Community Organization* (New York, 1939), p. vi.

31 P. H. Landis, *Rural Life in Process* (New York, 1940), chaps. XI, XII.

rallying centre. The morale is low, and although this lack of morale would seem typical of many rural communities today,[32] it is ascribed by the English to the French. Many studies have shown that when two ethnic groups live in close competition, any little incident that occurs will be attributed to the aggressive intention of the other group. In the eastern townships conditions which are prevalent in other parts of the country are attributed by the English to the French, and by the French to the English. In other words, racial prejudice against another group tends to make the group blind to underlying trends. When an incident of any magnitude occurs, the other group will be used as a scapegoat.[33]

There are still, however, a few remaining communities where the proportion of English is so great, and the community itself has been so relatively isolated from outside contacts, that the community morale is still high. Such a community is the village of Sawyerville, in Compton County. Here, of a population of 470, 122 are French. Sawyerville is used as a service village for the surrounding farms and hamlets which are still largely English, and the English leadership is still strong enough to produce good community solidarity. The majority of the French in the village are a shifting population of unskilled labour drawn there by a stave factory and several sawmills. It is a population which comes and goes, and therefore the comparatively small group of stable French have not yet acquired enough power to make themselves felt. Only one municipal councillor out of six is French, and out of four general stores only one is owned by a Frenchman. But the shadow of the invasion is heavy over Sawyerville. As amongst all the remaining English of the townships, the French are an ever-present reality. This is shown in the municipal council: "The French will have to have another councillor soon, they're getting uneasy." It is shown in the commercial world when an English storekeeper needed a new clerk: "I'll have to get a French girl now, that's sure. Even an English girl who speaks French won't do." It is shown by the remarks of one of the three Protestant ministers: "There *is* going to be only one church in Sawyerville, and that's the Roman Catholic one!"

When two ethnic groups live in close spatial proximity, they must find some basis for accommodation. The economic accommodation of the two ethnic groups has already been referred to. On the "social" level they must first accommodate as neighbours. The first French-Canadians to come in to many of the older settled English communities often came in for skilled jobs, such as barbers or station agents. They were generally well educated and could mix socially with the English. However, when the

---

[32] In this discussion of the morale of the English communities, cf. *Rural Life Studies* (United States Department of Agriculture, April, 1942).

[33] John Dollard, *Caste and Class in a Southern Town* (London, 1938), p. 287.

invasion got under way, the French-Canadians came in largely as unskilled labour and farmers. They could seldom speak English, and were not on the same cultural or educational level. The result was that they had no basis for contact or friendship with the English inhabitants.

The two groups will also have to accommodate as members of a community. The symbol of the community is the municipal council. Here accommodation is usually accomplished by an attempt at proportionate representation. Generally too, as the French come into a community, there is an implicit "understanding" that one year there will be an English mayor, the next year a French. Various remarks show that this question of municipal power is another crucial point at which the English attempt to make a stand—how consciously organized this stand is, is difficult to determine. Two ethnic groups must also accommodate on the level of communication. During the first stages of the invasion it was the French who learned and spoke English. It is now still noticeable, that even with the invasion in its last stages, the only English who are learning, or who speak French, are those who are forced to do so because of business. Therefore, the English have made no attempt to accommodate to the French on the level of communication. Perhaps this is an indication that they have given up the fight; on the other hand, it might be another symptom of underlying resistance.[34]

The absence of any overt conflict between two ethnic groups, living in close proximity, is not necessarily an indication of complete accommodation. It may merely be a temporary lull while underneath forces of suspicion and hatred are ready to break out in time of crisis. The war has been a crisis in the relationships of the French and English population of the eastern townships. It has given an opportunity for more overt expression of the underlying aggression of the two groups. Economically it has meant that the labour supply of many of the English farms has been seriously cut down. The older people struggle to keep up the farms, and even to produce the extra commodities demanded by the government, with a great shortage of labour and machinery. Many have become so discouraged with these conditions that they are selling out. A study of the farm auctions in the past three years would give some indication of their rate of discouragement. They also remember that when the last war was over many farmers' sons did not want to return to the farms. So they wonder if it is worth struggling on when they may have no inheriting sons. In the small local industries the Englishmen who have enlisted, or gone into war industries, are being rapidly replaced by Frenchmen. A

---

34 H. A. Miller, *Races, Nations, Classes* (Philadelphia, 1924), p. 37, shows that language is one of the compensatory forms of defence against aggression.

stave factory in Sawyerville, where "70 percent of my men were English before the war, now 70 percent are French" would not be untypical. The war has also given the French-Canadians an opportunity to gain in professional fields. In several villages the English doctors have been replaced by French. Entry into the professional fields is one of the last crucial steps in the invasion. The English remember, too, that the last war accelerated the invasion: "The French are coming in all around, it started in the last war." "The French bought up the farms in the last war." To many of the English living in parts of the townships where the invasion came only at a late date, it began with, and in fact was due to, the last war. So this war means that their very farms and homes are in danger. The war, therefore, is a crisis which brings out the underlying antagonisms of the two groups. It has increased the hostile feelings between them: "You see a growing antagonism between the French and the English." "There usen't to be any feeling between the French and English before the war—but it's getting pretty hot now!" The discouragement of the English in the general conditions of the times has been intensified by war conditions. And this discouragement is translated into bitterness which imputes all their troubles to the coming of the French. It is another case of attributing aggressive intention to the other group.

There are several conclusions which can be drawn from the exploratory phase of this study. It is evident that a group which is threatened by invasion tends, at first, to draw closely together. The sense of a common danger strengthens the in-group feeling. There may be efforts to organize to resist the invaders. However, the invaders will eventually find a weak spot, someone, for instance, who is willing to sell for a good price. Even after they have acquired this first foothold, the invaded group may attempt continued organized resistance. This falls off as the invasion gathers momentum. A general feeling of discouragement begins to spread. This may or may not be overtly expressed. In the townships there are many communities which are still attempting to find some means of cooperation with the French. This was evident when adult community schools were set up in some of the larger English centres. The committees tried to plan the curriculum to interest and attract the French. Experience has shown that music is the one basis on which the two groups can meet with any degree of success. But on the whole the English have given up trying to meet the French on a social level. Both groups see that their children have little contact. It is all right for them to play together when they are small, but when they get older there must not be any chance of their intermarrying.

Each English person or family that leaves the townships is a significant reminder of what is in store for the remaining English. This feeling is intensified when one of the leading figures, a doctor or a storekeeper, leaves. As the English population gradually dwindles, the English lose more and more control of the community. Problems are there, but they now have no power to deal with them, especially when the majority of the municipal council becomes French. This loss of control over their own lives is one of the strongest factors in lowering morale. Finally, when only a few English are left, their discouragement gives way to apathy. Only a handful of English farmers remain around the village of Leeds, which once was a thriving English community. Their attitude is shown by the following remark made by one of their sons: "My family's waiting for the French to buy their farm, the other farmers are too."

The morale of the group depends on the morale of the individual. It is a question of individual as well as group security. The interviews showed clearly that the attitude expressed by the individual to the invasion correlated with the actual effect it was having on his social and economic status and personal interests. It is also probable that other factors such as cultural background, education, age, sex, religion, and degree of contact, would correlate closely with the intensity of the attitude.

A determining factor of the strength of the morale of an invaded group is the proportionate number of invaders present in the community. As has been suggested, a shifting population is not so alarming to the English as one which comes in and prepares to stay by buying property. This is a "visible" sign of their arrival—as is the building of a church, school, or store. Secondly, the morale will depend on the amount of leadership remaining in the invaded group. It will also depend on the amount of economic competition between the two groups. The English managerial groups who have come in to the industrial towns, and are a small group surrounded by French, are not as concerned about the invasion as are the older English settlers. Their economic position is secure. They will be needed no matter how far the invasion sweeps in around them. And finally, the strength of the morale will be partly determined by the amount of foreign language which is heard in the community. In any racial situation language is an important differentiating mark. This is because it is a symbol of unity to a sense organ in the same way that physical traits are to the eye. When these physical traits are associated with the other group they become important symbols which intensify prejudice.[35] Although there are no visible signs, such as colour or facial characteristics, to differentiate the French and English, their different languages are a constant reminder of their division. Many of the English people remarked on the increase in French heard in the

---

[35] *Ibid.*, pp. 59 ff.

last few years: "I can't get over the change in Sawyerville, you hear French spoken everywhere now. In the post office you used only to hear English—but now you don't hear a word—only French. On the streets it's the same." "Twenty years ago you never heard French spoken—now you hear it everywhere." The final step in the invasion, to the English, is when the name of their community is "translated" into French; when, for example, the old English name of Abbotsford becomes St. Paul d'Abbotsford.

One hypothesis that emerges from this preliminary stage of study is that, although the underlying causation of invasion is largely economic, certain psychological factors enter, such as beliefs and fears, which determine the rate at which the process will proceed. The object of the ensuing study will be to discover the bearing these factors have in relation to the morale of a community.

42. The Small Trade Center: Processes and Perceptions of Growth or Decline

BERT N. ADAMS

The fate of the small town in modern industrial society has for several decades been a subject of nostalgia, of pictorial representation, of literature, and of scattered research efforts. Most observers admit that the small town is in trouble, and the smaller and more isolated the town the greater are its difficulties. Causes of difficulty are correctly perceived to be to a great extent external to the small town, with much having been written about urban appeal to young people and the influence of economic-technological changes in the larger society upon the hinterlands. Considerably less attention has been paid to the *internal* conditions contributing to individual or community stability, to the stages in the loss of services in the declining village, or to people's perceptions of small town economic conditions. These are the issues with which this paper seeks to deal.

Many studies of towns, even those noting the problems of population loss and economic problems, have focused upon large communities where

SOURCE: This research was supported by funds from The Institute for Research on Poverty, and from the Graduate School, University of Wisconsin, Madison, Wisconsin.

decline is in fact atypical.[1] The towns in the greatest difficulty are those of 2500 persons or less and which are too far from any urban center to be incorporated into its commuter zone; these are our concern.[2] The six villages selected for intensive investigation—two in Missouri and four in Wisconsin—are all farm trade centers. The four Wisconsin communities were chosen because of their wide range with respect to population gain or loss, and the two Missouri communities because of the author's familiarity with their region. The six ranged in population, according to the 1950 census, from just over 500 to about 950, and in distance from the nearest SMSA from 45 to 90 highway miles. Between 1950 and 1960 one of these towns lost over fifteen percent of its population, two others lost between five and ten percent, one remained virtually stable, another gained between five and ten percent, and the last increased by more than 25 percent. The population of the state of Missouri grew by 9.2 percent during this period, and Wisconsin increased by 15.1 percent. Thus, only one of the six increased in population as fast or faster than its state as a whole.

Within these communities positional leaders and businessmen, a few housewives and retired persons, were interviewed first, usually numbering about a dozen individuals. Subsequently, the "snowballing" technique was used to incorporate those persons whom the earlier respondents indicated we "should definitely talk to." The common method was to follow up on a comment such as: "Well, if you really want to find out about the Headstart Program here, talk to Mrs. Findlay," or "I can't say for sure why we never really tried to get a new industry to come here, but Mr. Backus, our retired bank president, should certainly know." In all, interviews were held with 108 persons, ranging from 14 in one community to 21 in another. In addition, census records, business records, and personal recall by the respondents were used to piece together the picture of economic and other changes over the past three decades. The composite picture emerging from the interviews and records forms the substance of our discussion.[3]

---

[1] William Simon and John H. Gagnon, "Decline and Fall of the Small Town," *Trans-action*, IV, No. 5 (April, 1967), pp. 42–51. This article, reprinted in this volume, discusses towns of 3,000, 7,000 and 9,000 inhabitants. A recent study by Lois Dean includes towns ranging in population from 9,000 to 80,000. Lois R. Dean, *Five Towns*. (New York: Random House, Inc., 1967).

[2] On population change in Wisconsin villages, see Glenn V. Fuguitt, *Growing and Declining Villages in Wisconsin: 1950–1960*. (Madison: University of Wisconsin, Department of Rural Sociology, Population Series #8, 1964).

[3] It should be kept in mind throughout that while the findings correctly represent the six villages, the small size of the sample means that the processes and perceptions reported are of course in need of further verification in other communities.

FACTORS IN TRADE CENTER AVOIDANCE OF DECLINE

It is easy to combine the findings on urban migration of young people, the greater distances which people will travel for goods and services, and difficulties confronted by the mining or railroad town when the economy or technology changes,[4] and conclude that decline and eventual death are the inevitable lot of the small town in modern society. Such has not yet, however, become the case with the small trade centers of the United States since mid-twentieth century. Rather, a good number have declined, another substantial portion have been relatively stable in population, and a few have grown. The situation, in other words, is not yet such that "nothing can be done" in the face of competition and urban appeal.

Some of the factors studied in their effect upon small town growth or decline include size, centralization of services, and the presence of specialized institutions, such as county government.[5] The positive association between such factors and population change has been weak enough to lead the authors to state that other variables are needed to explain small town growth or decline.[6] Therefore, besides minimizing the likelihood of large numbers of urban commuters, we have omitted county seats, college communities, and have kept the size range fairly narrow. This has made possible the isolating of certain variables which appear to be necessary conditions for population and economic stability in the small trade center.

The two factors which were isolated early in the study and reinforced as we entered each of the six communities might be called *extra-local orientation* and *risk-taking willingness*. The former is, very simply, a direct confrontation of the issue of increased consumer travel distance in search of goods and services. The latter indicates whether or not key community personnel are willing to take economic chances in order to lure new industry or to develop natural resources. Industry is thus not considered to be an independent variable in its own right, but is dependent upon risk-taking for its importance. The status of the six communities on extra-locality, risk-taking, and industry may be seen in Table I.

---

[4] See Simon and Gagnon, *op. cit.;* and W. F. Cottrell, "Death by Dieselization: A Case Study in the Reaction to Technological Change," *American Sociological Review*, Volume 16, No. 3 (June, 1951), 358–365. Both are reprinted in this volume.

[5] Glenn V. Fuguitt, "County Seat Status as a Factor in Small Town Growth and Decline," *Social Forces*, XLIV, No. 2 (December, 1965), pp. 245–251; Glenn V. Fuguitt and Nora Ann Deeley, "Retail Service Patterns and Small Town Population Change: A Replication of Hassinger's Study," *Rural Sociology*, XXXI, No. 1 (March, 1966), pp. 53–63.

[6] Fuguitt and Deeley, *op. cit.,* 63.

TABLE 1.

Extra-Locality, Risk-Taking, and Industry in Six Villages, According to Population and Distance from SMSA

Village	Approx. 1950 Population	Pct. Change, 1950–1960	Road Miles from SMSA	Extra-Locality	Risk-Taking	Natural Resource or Industry	Industry from 1950–1960		
							Industry Lost	Current Industry	New Industry
I	700+	25+	65	High	Moderate	Lake	...	Dairy	...
II	750	5–10	45	Moderate	High	...	Railroad	Dairy, Paper Mill	Furniture Company
III	800	0–5	60	Moderate	Fairly High	...	Railroad	...	Flour Mill
IV	600+	−5–10	45	Moderate	Moderate	...	...	Canning Plant	...
V	950	−5–10	55	Fairly Low	Low	...	...	Feed Mill, Garment Fac.	...
VI	500+	−15–20	90	Low	Low	State Park	Lumber Mill	...	...

Neither the presence of a natural resource or industry, the loss of an industry, nor the number of current industries bears much relationship to population change between 1950 and 1960. Furthermore, the development of a natural industry and the luring of new industry are both predicated more than anything else upon the willingness of economic influentials to invest money and "take a chance." Thus, the several dimensions of extra-locality and risk-taking should be delineated before their importance can be illustrated.

EXTRA-LOCALITY AND RISK-TAKING DESCRIBED

The distinction between local and cosmopolitan orientations to life has been drawn in such social settings as suburbia and complex organizations, and among such persons as professional scientists and modernizing farmers.[7] Lerner, for example, states that "local" farmers "show no interest in affairs outside their immediate community."[8] However, more than "showing interest" is signified by our term "extra-local." Extra-local outlook and appeal are based on the admission that the small community (or the individual businessman or professional) is unlikely to prosper strictly on locally-determined standards or on the patronage of local residents or those from the immediate hinterland. The businessman manifests an extra-local outlook by keeping apprised of the current prices for his goods elsewhere, by being alert to new products as they appear, by comparing wholesalers, and by watching a large area for bargains in order to minimize his own overhead. The locally-oriented businessman may overprice his merchandise or have an inadequate or outdated inventory. For a small town professional to manifest an extra-local outlook means primarily that he keeps informed of the latest developments in his profession. The dentist without a high-speed drill, or the doctor or lawyer not aware of the latest research or cases, respectively, is in a poor bargaining position for the patronage of a modern clientele.

Outlook, however, is but one portion of extra-local orientation. Virtually all of the successful businessmen, professionals, and industrialists—and stable or growing communities corporately—enter openly the regional competition for patronage. A key to extra-local appeal is adver-

---

7 William M. Dobriner, "Local and Cosmopolitan as Contemporary Suburban Character Types," in William M. Dobriner, ed., *The Suburban Community*. (New York: G. P. Putnam's Sons, 1958), pp. 132–143; Alvin Gouldner, "Cosmopolitans and Locals: Toward an Analysis of Latent Social Roles, I," *Administrative Science Quarterly*, II, No. 3, (December, 1957), pp. 281–306; Barney G. Glaser, "The Local-Cosmopolitan Scientist," *American Journal of Sociology*, LXIX, No. 3, (November, 1963), pp. 249–259; Daniel Lerner, *The Passing of Traditional Society*. (New York: The Free Press, 1958), pp. 331–335.

8 Lerner, *op. cit.*, p. 331.

tising not just in the local paper but in those of surrounding communities as well.

The risk factor appears in the form of willingness to reinvest profits, to take out loans, to extend credit, and to finance building and/or advertising campaigns. Without corporate risk-taking, it is virtually impossible to gain new industry or to develop such resources as may be at hand.[9] The importance of extra-local orientation and risk-taking in stabilizing the population and/or economy of the small town can best be illustrated by a detailed reference to several of the sample communities.

Extra-Locality and Risk-Taking Illustrated

A most instructive extra-local vs. local comparison can be drawn between villages I and VI. Each has a natural resource or industry at its disposal, the former being located on a large and beautiful lake and the latter less than three miles from a state park. Village I leaders, in the early 1950's, became aware both of their increasing plight in the regional competition for consumers and of their advantageous recreational location. The campaign which they hammered out had three parts: (1) they advertised in the urban newspapers of the region "choice lakeshore sites" for retirement or summer homes; (2) four venturesome businessmen sold their businesses and built boat rental agencies and docks—one of the men on his own and the other three as partners; and (3) they pooled a moderate amount of money to build a city park and the first units of an assembly where groups could come for conferences, retreats, and recreation. The key element in their success was an extra-local orientation based upon the realization that without drawing residents and patronage from a wide area they were in trouble. The risk factor was secondary, involving only the initial cost of developing the assembly ground, the continuing expense of advertising, and the conviction on the part of a few men that an investment in boating would pay off. The success of this extra-local venture came rapidly and has not abated.

The contrast in village VI is striking if not poignant. The establishment of a state park nearby was greeted locally with neither interest nor enthusiasm. Locals liked their privacy and conceived of themselves as related almost exclusively to the surrounding farms as a trading center. The marginal nature of many of these dairy farms meant inevitable consolidation and loss of consumers from the hinterland. Reaction on the

---

9 On lack of willingness to take risks, see Arthur J. Vidich and Joseph Bensman, *Small Town in Mass Society*. (Princeton, N.J.: Princeton University Press, 1958), 53, 78; on risk-taking as a proposed solution to small town problems, see Glenn V. Fuguitt, "The Small Town in Rural America," *Journal of Cooperative Extension*, (Spring, 1965), 25.

part of community leaders to incipient decline was almost uniformly localistic and fatalistic. "We can't compete with the city." "All our young people are leaving, but what can you do?" These comments, made to the interviewer, were not a recent but a long-term characteristic of the residents. The lack of both extra-local orientation and of risk-willingness resulted in a continuing loss of young people and in the town being unable to realize the possible advantages of the state park. One of the remaining businessmen discussed the park thus: "Well, the state officials came around five years ago talking about building a dam in the park and developing a lake. I think this might help our town, but we're not counting on it being built." A probing attempt to find out if he or any businessman had tried to exert pressure or to raise matching funds in order to get the dam built came up with a consistently negative result. No one, it appears, had even thought of it. "They'll do what they want," was the general consensus regarding the state. Several businessmen and women indicated that the demise of their business was only a matter of time; two had set their date of closing. The three most successful pointed out the inability of the community to effect a corporate economic risk for the sake of new industry or business. One put it this way: "A few years ago we had a development corporation, but only five of us joined, and we didn't do anything. We didn't really want new businesses because they would just take away consumers from us. We couldn't seem to get any money together to interest new industries. One problem is that the banker and the retired folk control most of the money. Mr. Clayton (the banker) won't invest because he's not convinced this town can ever recuperate, and the retired folk won't invest in this town 'cause their children have all left. They would rather sit on their money 'til they die so their kids—wherever they are—can inherit it." Here, then, is a community which missed any earlier opportunity it might have had for rejuvenation and currently is characterized by businessmen who don't want more businesses, by a banker who won't take risks, by some retired persons who are "sitting on" their profits, and by a corporate leadership which can see little opportunity in a nearby state park.[10] This community is now in the latter stages of decline, as evidenced by the fact that in 1965 persons 65 years of age and older accounted for 64 percent of its population.

Why, in the early stages of decline, did the influentials in village I see the future in lake front homes, boating, and assemblies, while those in village VI could not envision an equal potential in the state park? The

---

[10] The issue of community leadership patterns or power structures is being considered more fully in a separate paper.

respondents were simply unable, in retrospect, to explain why, except that, to them, this was the normal way to react. Perhaps a part of the explanation lies in the marginal nature of the farm land surrounding village VI and the good dairy land surrounding village I. It seems possible that the subsistence problem may have resulted in a generally more pessimistic or defeatist approach to life among the residents of the region around village VI. Another possible explanation may lie in the different power or leadership structures of the two communities, but this is the subject of another paper. Regardless of how the difference is explained, it was most apparent in the course of the interviews that the major influence upon both the economy and the population of villages I and VI had been the extra-local or local orientation of the residents.

Illustrations of the importance of extra-locality can also be found in other villages, and the necessity of risk-taking becomes even more apparent. Village II was one of two villages affected by the change to diesel railroad service and a lessening of passenger service on the railroads. Formerly a service point and junction, this town was in danger of rapid decline when no longer valuable to the railroads.[11] However, soon after the rail yards closed down a lawyer, grocer, furniture store owner, the local banker, a hardware store owner, and four other businessmen organized under the title "Community Redevelopment Committee." They each contributed several thousand dollars of their profits and purchased a large, empty building from the railroads. The most immediate result was the luring of a furniture company from a larger town by providing a building and a small amount of new cash for equipment. Several of the "Committee" members are convinced that they have already made back in business what their original risk cost them. Others are satisfied that the individual "pay off" is only a matter of time. All are optimistic about the future of their community and about their ability to bring other industries to town. Interestingly enough, the success of the first venture has persuaded others to join the Committee, thus lessening the individual risk and increasing the resource pool. An important point is that for village II to stabilize its economy and population it was not necessary for *all* the community members with money to join the Committee; it was only necessary that several key leaders be willing to risk their profits —to do more than talk—in order to revitalize the community.

Villages IV and V look quite similar according to the 1950-1960 population change figures. However, by 1965 village IV had begun to show signs of stabilization, while V was continuing to lose inhabitants at a slow but constant rate. The major influence upon IV's restabilization has

---

11 See Cottrell, *op. cit.*, for an illustration of this problem.

been one man from Minnesota. This man bought the bank in 1958 when its resources amounted to $2,000,000 and has since quadrupled them. His expansion campaign involved several steps, all of which involved either individual risk-taking or extra-local orientation, or both. First, he determined to loosen (rather than tighten as his predecessor had) credit terms, and to give more loans for new housing. Second, he publicized a dinner and evening of square dancing and entertainment at the bank's expense, actually taking over the center of town for the event. This gave him an opportunity to inform those attending of his new policies. Third, he not only advertised these policies in the newspapers of surrounding communities, but kept his eye on the want ads of city newspapers for the equipment he needed to modernize the bank. A vault, draperies, a counter to refinish, large supplies of ball point pens, plate glass—these and other supplies he found at bargain prices and brought them to his bank. The first two years of his ownership saw a sharp decline in cash reserves. This dip was a result of his investment in equipment, his new credit terms, and the fact that certain residents did not yet accept him into the town—he was not yet "one of them." However, the effect of his policies and campaign soon became apparent to other businessmen in town. New houses were going up. People from surrounding communities came to village IV to do their banking, and stayed to shop. The outflow of business to other communities changed to a more balanced in-out pattern. Not yet has this village solved the problem of young people leaving, for this is based on industrial or other opportunity and not just business flow; and factionalism has prevented the establishment of a viable redevelopment organization. However, involvement in the regional competition for consumers has been substantially changed for the better by the extra-local orientation of one influential man.

Much less effective in altering the course of either economic or population decline has been the extra-local campaign of a 5-and-10¢ store owner in village V. Having grown up in this community, he had worked for several years as a sales manager for Sears in a nearby metropolis. Some five years before the interview he bought the store and returned to his hometown to enjoy the advantages of small town and rural life.[12] He immediately noticed the weekend exodus of shoppers particularly to a town of 1700 people located 18 miles away and one with 9000 inhabitants 25 miles away. He went through the basic extra-local process of comparing prices, increasing and diversifying inventory, placing advertisements, and using gimmicks such as prize nights in order to bring patrons from

---

12 See Simon and Gagnon, *op. cit.*, for some of the typical advantages of rural and small town life most often mentioned. See also Joseph P. Lyford, *The Talk in Vandalia*, (Fund for the Republic, Inc., 1962).

other communities to his store on Friday nights. The result has been individual financial success, but this has not "rubbed off" on the community in general, and he readily admits the need for recreational facilities and other services to increase his Friday night appeal. Few businessmen in village V have joined in the regional competition, and the corporate trend in the community is still economic and population decline.

Acquaintance with these villages leads to several conclusions regarding individual success and population or economic stability in the community. First, extra-local orientation is a necessary condition for *individual* success. The businessman or professional whose interest stops with local news and whose appeal is to "the old bunch" of patrons faces long-term difficulties. Second, the extra-local orientation of one or more businessmen may be sufficient to stabilize the economy, but may or may not greatly affect the decline in population. Third, key leaders must band together in corporate risk-taking as well as extra-locality in order to meet the necessary conditions for population stability or growth. Extra-locality and effective corporate risk-taking appear to account for much of the stability and growth of small towns not accounted for by the presence of specialized institutions or by external forces. Put antithetically, lack of extra-locality, of risk-taking, of specialized institutions, of size, and of commuter incorporation appears to be virtually a sufficient condition for economic and population decline.

THE EFFECT OF DECLINE ON SERVICES OFFERED

There is, we have argued, a method by which the small trade center may better its chances for survival. This includes broadening its consumer base beyond its immediate hinterland and luring or developing industry which will hold or bring new population. Yet the fact is most small communities are unable or unwilling to effect these conditions or to avoid the general trend toward decline.

Why cannot most small trade centers avoid decline? The external factors such as urban opportunity and competition are, of course, a part of the reason. Internally, it is related to the positions and outlooks of small town professionals, businessmen, and industrialists. Professionals, who according to Vidich and Bensman generally have the ability to mediate between the small town and the larger society, may be in a poor position to effect extra-locality as the dominant character of communities the size of ours.[13] Either they are absent from the village or else, as in the case of many lawyers and school officials, if they try to bring an extra-

---

[13] Vidich and Bensman, *op. cit.*, 89.

local orientation into the community they may be treated as outsiders. Industrialists, even when the company is locally owned, are geared to a wide marketing area and are neither active in community politics nor interested in luring other industries. Of the eight industries in our six villages, only the owner of the dairy in village II is a contributing member of a redevelopment group. This man is a long-term resident of the community and his involvement is predicated upon other considerations than personal economic motives. Businessmen, who comprise the financial backbone of community redevelopment attempts, are simply less and less willing to take risks. They save rather than invest. Most are locally oriented, seeking to develop a clientele whose loyalty is personal rather than being based upon economic advantage to the consumer.[14] Small trade centers such as I and II are exceptional in their growth.

The rule or trend is decline, and it is possible to piece together the steps by which services are lost to the declining community. Assuming that a community is large enough to provide specialized professional services, large dry goods such as appliances and automobiles, and the day-to-day necessities for people in their hinterlands, such as groceries, drugs, feed, and gasoline, the process of departure is generally as follows. First to leave are the specialized professionals, especially dentists, then doctors and lawyers. They move to larger places or centralized clinics on the correct assumption that a regional clientele will seek them out. Second, large dry goods establishments close down, leaving the sale of new cars to garages, with the cars on order rather than in stock, and the sale of appliances to the general dry goods or hardware store. People will travel several miles to buy items such as cars, refrigerators, and couches, and the regional competition drives out the small town outlet early. Simultaneously, specialized services such as beauty parlors, laundries, paint stores, and TV repair shops fold. Third, duplicate businesses are driven out by competition for a contracting clientele. If there are two hardware stores one may go under; if there are three groceries one or two may close. The same is true for filling stations, feed stores, and other retail establishments.

Village IV, at the time of writing, is in the second phase, village V in phase three, and village VI in the phase of losing duplicates. In 1965, for example, village VI had the following services to offer: a post office, a bank, two taverns, a barber shop, three filling stations, two restaurants, three grocery stores, a recreation (pool) hall, a hardware store, a fire station, and four churches. One restaurant and one grocery had already set the date for closing, and one filling station was strictly marginal. The

---

[14] *Ibid.*, 53.

only businesses doing well economically are the hardware store, the recreation hall, and a restaurant—all of which are owned by "localities" and hold a virtual monopoly on business from the village and hinterland. The penultimate phase of decline leaves a trade center offering primarily those day-to-day services needed by the immediate hinterland: groceries, filling stations, feed stores, and general dry goods, and usually but one establishment of each type. Three exceptions to this phase should be noted. If a community is located at an important highway junction more than one filling station may survive. This, however, defines the community as more than a farm trade center. Also, a specialized service, such as the barber shop in village VI, may survive if the owner does not have to make his whole living that way. The owner keeps his barber shop open but a few hours a week and the remainder of the time he is town constable or sheriff; he simply does not have to live on what he makes barbering. The third exception is that taverns and churches appear to be the last to lose their duplicates. (Perhaps this is because at the tavern the resident of a dying community can drown his troubles and at the church he can forget them.) Not entirely facetiously, however, these are two institutions which aid the individual in coping with his and his community's plight. Another way in which he copes is by the process of projection, but that is the subject of our next section.

PROJECTION OF PERSONAL SUCCESS OR FAILURE

Within the six communities visited there are individual successes and failures, some whose economic position is improving and others who are marginal or going under economically. By and large, these persons are able to realistically perceive their own condition and to admit it. The exceptions are a few successes who talk like failures and a few failures who talk like successes. In one instance of the former exception the reason for the image of poverty is that the aging couple, who own a hardware store, want to keep their profits. They neither want to reinvest in business overhead or inventory, nor do they want to be asked to support local causes or campaigns. However, several informants individually and confidentially let the interviewer know that Mr. and Mrs. Cameron are "loaded;" that they also own a filling station out on the highway. The other exception is illustrated by a small number of businessmen in financial difficulty, particularly some in village V, who claim that both they and the community are doing just fine and that a brighter day is just around the corner. The Chamber of Commerce line was not always convincing to the interviewer, nor did it agree with other informants' conceptions of who is doing well in the community.

By and large, however, people evaluate themselves realistically or in keeping with the facts. The successes are only too willing to admit and explain their success, while the failures and marginals are sometimes embittered but most often resigned to or fatalistic about their plight. How does one's personal situation affect his perception of how the community is doing? In one of the most interesting sections of *Small Town in Mass Society*, Vidich and Bensman indicate the modes of psychological adjustment which residents of Springdale use in the face of their community's vulnerability and lack of autonomy.[15] A key mode is particularization, or recognizing specific situations of community dependence but not viewing the community as a whole. Springdalers simply do not generalize the specific, and are thus "not explicitly aware of the total amount of the dependence." In our communities, however, the tendency appeared to be just the opposite: the individual tended to *project* or generalize his own experience—whether success or failure—rather than particularizing it. For example, in village V, Mrs. Dunbar, owner of a dry goods store who is planning to sell and return to the farm, admitted that the town was in trouble. "Yes, we're losing people around here all the time. Just look up and down the street and you'll find plenty of vacant buildings. We just can't compete." When asked about the success of the feed mill and of Mr. Taylor's 5-and-10¢ store, she explained that the mill serves a wide area and Mr. Taylor "worked at Sears in the city where he learned a lot more than most of us know about how to run a business." Well, you might say, this isn't projection it is realism. However, interviews with Mr. Taylor and other scattered successes in village V produce precisely the opposite result. That is, they project or generalize their success to the community and particularize the persons who have failed. According to Mr. Taylor: "Our town is doing OK. We've had a little bad luck lately. Mr. Charles, who with his wife ran the laundromat, was an alcoholic and when he and his wife broke up they sold the business. Mrs. Dunbar just doesn't try; her heart isn't in the business and she'll be better off on the farm." One by one he explains away the business failures. "But what," the interviewer asks, "about the empty buildings in town?" "If you had come two years ago you would have seen all the buildings in use, and if you come back next year they'll probably be full again."

Thus, the majority of business and professional persons in these six villages have worked out a most ingenious method for making sense of their worlds. Whether you call it projection or the reduction of cognitive dissonance, the dominant practice is to generalize one's own condition to the community and to particularize the situations of those who diverge. This holds as true for the successful members of village V, who are optimistic about their town, and for the unsuccessful members of village

---

15 *Ibid.*, 299 and following.

II, who are pessimistic despite obvious signs of vigor, as it does for those who correctly perceive their community's growth or decline.

SUMMARY AND CONCLUSIONS

The obverse side of the coin of urbanization in modern industrial society is the trend toward small town decline. This decline is not at present, however, a uniform occurrence in all small towns. Rather, they may be stabilized by centralization or the presence of specialized functions and, according to the present study, by extra-local orientation and risk-taking in the part of key leaders. Many of the instances of small trade center stability or growth can be accounted for by these factors.

Yet the major trend is still one of decline. Internally, the loss of services ordinarily follows this pattern: first professionals, then large dry goods and specialized retail services, then duplicate businesses, and finally the most frequent day-to-day services demanded by the community and hinterland. The further a community goes along the path toward death, the more difficult it appears to be to reverse the process without outside intervention.

People's perceptions of their own economic conditions are usually quite accurate. But if this differs from the community's general condition, the tendency is to project one's own situation upon the community. This, of course, aids the individual in coping, since failure is not taken personally and success, while viewed as an individual achievement, is perceived as reflected in the community as a whole, for the successful man cannot seem to face the reality of being part of an unsuccessful town.

Are extra-locality and willingness to take risks sufficient conditions for community stability? No, they are not. If all small towns suddenly became extra-locally oriented and willing to invest in new industry, only some would be successful. It is, thus, because only a minority of trade centers have this corporate orientation that it is effective. Are extra-locality and risk-taking merely stop-gap measures on the road to eventual decline? Is small town decline a universal process of the small getting smaller and the large getting larger, which we happen to have caught in mid-stream? It is frankly too early to answer this unequivocally. Nevertheless, evidence appears to point to the great majority of U.S. towns the size of ours going the way of village VI by the year 2000. The 1960's and 1970's are, in fact, very likely the crucial period during which the successes are becoming more clearly distinguished from the declining communities. Involved in this distinguishing process are extra-local orientation and willingness to take economic risks; most small trade centers will effect neither.

43. Death by Dieselization:
A Case Study in
the Reaction to
Technological Change

W. F. COTTRELL

In the following instance it is proposed that we examine a community confronted with radical change in its basic economic institution and to trace the effects of this change throughout the social structure. From these facts it may be possible in some degree to anticipate the resultant changing attitudes and values of the people in the community, particularly as they reveal whether or not there is a demand for modification of the social structure or a shift in function from one institution to another. Some of the implications of the facts discovered may be valuable in anticipating future social change.

The community chosen for examination has been disrupted by the dieselization of the railroads. Since the railroad is among the oldest of those industries organized around steam, and since therefore the social structure of railroad communities is a product of long-continued pro-

SOURCE: Reprinted with permission of the author and publisher from *The American Sociological Review*, XVI (June, 1951), published by the American Sociological Association.

cesses of adaptation to the technology of steam, the sharp contrast between the technological requirements of the steam engine and those of the diesel should clearly reveal the changes in social structure required. Any one of a great many railroad towns might have been chosen for examination. However, many railroad towns are only partly dependent upon the railroad for their existence. In them many of the effects which take place are blurred and not easily distinguishable by the observer. Thus, the "normal" railroad town may not be the best place to see the consequences of dieselization. For this reason a one-industry town was chosen for examination.

In a sense it is an "ideal type" railroad town, and hence not complicated by other extraneous economic factors. It lies in the desert and is here given the name "Caliente" which is the Spanish adjective for "hot." Caliente was built in a break in an 80 mile canyon traversing the desert. Its reason for existence was to service the steam locomotive. There are few resources in the area to support it on any other basis, and such as they are they would contribute more to the growth and maintenance of other little settlements in the vicinity than to that of Caliente. So long as the steam locomotive was in use, Caliente was a necessity. With the adoption of the diesel it became obsolescent.

This stark fact was not, however, part of the expectations of the residents of Caliente. Based upon the "certainty" of the railroad's need for Caliente, men built their homes there, frequently of concrete and brick, at the cost, in many cases, of their life savings. The water system was laid in cast iron which will last for centuries. Businessmen erected substantial buildings which could be paid for only by profits gained through many years of business. Four churches evidence the faith of Caliente people in the future of their community. A 27-bed hospital serves the town. Those who built it thought that their investment was as well warranted as the fact of birth, sickness, accident and death. They believed in education. Their school buildings represent the investment of savings guaranteed by bonds and future taxes. There is a combined park and play field which, together with a recently modernized theatre, has been serving recreational needs. All these physical structures are material evidence of the expectations, morally and legally sanctioned and financially funded, of the people of Caliente. This is a normal and rational aspect of the culture of all "solid" and "sound" communities.

Similarly normal are the social organizations. These include Rotary, Chamber of Commerce, Masons, Odd Fellows, American Legion and the Veterans of Foreign Wars. There are the usual unions, churches, and myriad little clubs to which the women belong. In short, here is the average American community with normal social life, subscribing to normal American codes. Nothing its members had been taught would indicate that the whole pattern of this normal existence depended completely upon a few elements of technology which were themselves in flux. For them the continued use of the steam engine was as "natural" a phenomenon as any other element in their physical environment. Yet suddenly their life pattern was destroyed by the announcement that the railroad was moving its division point, and with it destroying the economic basis of Caliente's existence.

Turning from this specific community for a moment, let us examine the technical changes which took place and the reasons for the change. Division points on a railroad are established by the frequency with which the rolling stock must be serviced and the operating crews changed. At the turn of the century when this particular road was built, the engines produced wet steam at low temperatures. The steel in the boilers was of comparatively low tensile strength and could not withstand the high temperatures and pressures required for the efficient use of coal and water. At intervals of roughly a hundred miles the engine had to be disconnected from the train for service. At these points the cars also were inspected and if they were found to be defective they were either removed from the train or repaired while it was standing and the new engine being coupled on. Thus the location of Caliente, as far as the railroad was concerned, was a function of boiler temperature and pressure and the resultant service requirements of the locomotive.

Following World War II, the high tensile steels developed to create superior artillery and armor were used for locomotives. As a consequence it was possible to utilize steam at higher temperatures and pressure. Speed, power, and efficiency were increased and the distance between service intervals was increased.

The "ideal distance" between freight divisions became approximately 150 to 200 miles whereas it had formerly been 100 to 150. Wherever possible, freight divisions were increased in length to that formerly used by passenger trains, and passenger divisions were lengthened from two old freight divisions to three. Thus towns located at 100 miles from a terminal became obsolescent, those at 200 became freight points only, and those at 300 miles became passenger division points.

The increase in speed permitted the train crews to make the greater distance in the time previously required for the lesser trip, and roughly a third of the train and engine crews, car inspectors, boilermakers and machinists and other service men were dropped. The towns thus abandoned were crossed off the social record of the nation in the adjustment to these technological changes in the use of the steam locomotive. Caliente, located midway between terminals about 600 miles apart, survived. In fact it gained, since the less frequent stops caused an increase in the service required of the maintenance crews at those points where it took place. However, the introduction of the change to diesel engines projected a very different future.

In its demands for service the diesel engine differs almost completely from a steam locomotive. It requires infrequent, highly skilled service, carried on within very close limits, in contrast to the frequent, crude adjustments required by the steam locomotive. Diesels operate at about 35 percent efficiency, in contrast to the approximately 4 percent efficiency of the steam locomotives in use after World War II in the United States. Hence diesels require much less frequent stops for fuel and water. These facts reduce their operating costs sufficiently to compensate for their much higher initial cost.

In spite of these reductions in operating costs the introduction of diesels ordinarily would have taken a good deal of time. The change-over would have been slowed by the high capital costs of retooling the locomotive works, the long period required to recapture the costs of existing steam locomotives, and the effective resistance of the workers. World War II altered each of these factors. The locomotive works were required to make the change in order to provide marine engines, and the costs of the change were assumed by the government. Steam engines were used up by the tremendous demand placed upon the railroads by war traffic. The costs were recaptured by shipping charges. Labor shortages were such that labor resistance was less formidable and much less acceptable to the public than it would have been in peace time. Hence the shift to diesels was greatly facilitated by the war. In consequence, every third and sometimes every second division point suddenly became technologically obsolescent.

Caliente, like all other towns in similar plight, is supposed to accept its fate in the name of "progress." The general public, as shippers and consumers of shipped goods, reaps the harvest in better, faster service and eventually perhaps in lower charges. A few of the workers in Caliente will also share the gains, as they move to other division points, through higher wages. They will share in the higher pay, though whether this will be adequate to compensate for the costs of moving no one can say. Certain it is that their pay will not be adjusted to compensate for their specific losses. They will gain only as their seniority gives them the opportunity to work. These are those who gain. What are the losses, and who bears them?

The railroad company can figure its losses at Caliente fairly accurately. It owns 39 private dwellings, a modern clubhouse with 116 single rooms, and a 12-room hotel with dining room and lunch counter facilities. These now become useless, as does much of the fixed physical equipment used for servicing trains. Some of the machinery can be used elsewhere. Some part of the roundhouse can be used to store unused locomotives and standby equipment. The rest will be torn down to save taxes. All of these costs can be entered as capital losses on the statement which the company draws up for its stockholders and for the government. Presumably they will be recovered by the use of the more efficient engines.

What are the losses that may not be entered on the company books? The total tax assessment in Caliente was $9946.80 for the year 1948, of which $6103.39 represented taxes assessed on the railroad. Thus the railroad valuation was about three-fifths that of the town. This does not take into account tax-free property belonging to the churches, the schools, the hospital, or the municipality itself which included all the public utilities. Some ideas of the losses sustained by the railroad in comparison with the losses of others can be surmised by reflecting on these figures for real estate alone. The story is an old one and often repeated in the economic history of America. It represents the "loss" side of a profit and loss system of adjusting to technological change. Perhaps for sociological purposes we need an answer to the question "just who pays?"

Probably the greatest losses are suffered by the older "non-operating" employees. Seniority among these men extends only within the local shop and craft. A man with 25 years' seniority at Caliente has no claim on the job of a similar craftsman at another point who has only 25 days' seniority. Moreover, some of the skills formerly valuable are no longer needed. The boilermaker, for example, knows that jobs for his kind are disappearing and he must enter the ranks of the unskilled. The protection and status offered by the union while he was employed have become meaningless now that he is no longer needed. The cost of this is high both in loss of income and in personal demoralization.

Operating employees also pay. Their seniority extends over a division, which in this case includes three division points. The older members can move from Caliente and claim another job at another point, but in many cases they move leaving a good portion of their life savings behind. The younger men must abandon their stake in railroad employment. The loss may mean a new apprenticeship in another occupation, at a time in life when apprenticeship wages are not adequate to meet the obligations of mature men with families. A steam engine hauled 2000 tons up the hill out of Caliente with the aid of two helpers. The four-unit diesel in command of one crew handles a train of 5000 tons alone. Thus, to handle the same amount of tonnage required only about a fourth the manpower it formerly took. Three out of four men must start out anew at something else.

The local merchants pay. The boarded windows, half-empty shelves, and abandoned store buildings bear mute evidence of these costs. The older merchants stay, and pay; the younger ones, and those with no stake in the community will move; but the value of their property will in both cases largely be gone.

The bondholders will pay. They can't foreclose on a dead town. If the town were wiped out altogether, that which would remain for salvage would be too little to satisfy their claims. Should the town continue there is little hope that taxes adequate to carry the overhead of bonds and day-to-day expenses could be secured by taxing the diminished number of property owners or employed persons.

The church will pay. The smaller congregations cannot support services as in the past. As the church men leave, the buildings will be abandoned.

Homeowners will pay. A hundred and thirty-five men owned homes in Caliente. They must accept the available means of support or rent to those who do. In either case the income available will be far less than that on which the houses were built. The least desirable homes will stand unoccupied, their value completely lost. The others must be revalued at a figure far below that at which they were formerly held.

In a word, those pay who are, by traditional American standards, *most moral*. Those who have raised children see friendships broken and neighborhoods disintegrated. The childless more freely shake the dust of Caliente from their feet. Those who built their personalities into the structure of the community watch their work destroyed. Those too wise or too selfish to have entangled themselves in community affairs suffer no such qualms. The chain store can pull down its sign, move its equipment and charge the costs off against more profitable and better located units, and against taxes. The local owner has no such alternatives. In short, "good citizens" who assumed family and community responsibility are the greatest losers. Nomads suffer least.

The people of Caliente are asked to accept as "normal" this strange inversion of their expectations. It is assumed that they will, without protest or change in sentiment, accept the dictum of the "law of supply and demand." Certainly they must comply in part with this dictum. While their behavior in part reflects this compliance, there are also other changes perhaps equally important in their attitudes and values.

The first reaction took the form of an effort at community self-preservation. Caliente became visible to its inhabitants as a real entity, as meaningful as the individual personalities which they had hitherto been taught to see as atomistic or nomadic elements. Community survival was seen as prerequisite to many of the individual values that had been given precedence in the past. The organized community made a search for new industry, citing elements of community organization themselves as reasons why industry should move to Caliente. But the conditions that led the railroad to abandon the point made the place even less attractive to new industry than it had hitherto been. Yet the effort to keep the community a going concern persisted.

There was also a change in sentiment. In the past the glib assertion that progress spelled sacrifice could be offered when some distant group was a victim of technological change. There was no such reaction when the event struck home. The change can probably be as well revealed as in any other way by quoting from the Caliente *Herald:*

> ... (over the) years ... (this) ... railroad and its affiliates ... became to this writer his ideal of a railroad empire. The (company) ... appeared to take much more than the ordinary interest of big railroads in the development of areas adjacent to its lines, all the while doing a great deal for the communities large and small through which the lines passed.
>
> Those were the days creative of (its) enviable reputation as one of the finest, most progressive—and most human—of American railroads, enjoying the confidence and respect of employees, investors, and communities alike!
>
> One of the factors bringing about this confidence and respect was the consideration shown communities which otherwise would have suffered serious blows when division and other changes were effected. A notable example was . . . (a town) . . . where the shock of division change was made almost unnoticed by installation of a rolling stock reclamation point, which gave (that town) an opportunity to hold its community intact until tourist traffic and other industries could get better established—with the result that . . . (it) . . . is now on a firm foundation. And through this display of consideration for a community, the railroad gained friends—not only among the people of . . . (that town) . . . who were perhaps more vocal than others, but also among thousands of others throughout the country on whom this action made an indelible impression.
>
> But things seem to have changed materially during the last few years, the . . . (company) . . . seems to this writer to have gone all out for glamor and the dollars which glamorous people have to spend, sadly neglecting one of the principal factors which helped to make . . . (it) . . . great: that fine consideration of communities and individuals, as well as employees, who have been happy in cooperating steadfastly with the railroad in times of stress as well as prosperity. The loyalty of these people and communities seems to count for little with the . . . (company) . . . of this day, though other "Big Business" corporations do not hesitate to expend huge sums to encourage the loyalty of community and people which old friends of . . . (the company) . . . have been happy to give voluntarily.
>
> Ever since the . . . railroad was constructed . . . Caliente has been a key town on the railroad. It is true, the town owed its inception to the

railroad, but it has paid this back in becoming one of the most attractive communities on the system. With nice homes, streets and parks, good school . . . good city government . . . Caliente offers advantages that most big corporations would be gratified to have for their employees—a homey spot where they could live their lives of contentment, happiness and security.

Caliente's strategic location, midway of some of the toughest road on the entire system has been a lifesaver for the road several times when floods have wrecked havoc on the roadbed in the canyon above and below Caliente. This has been possible through storage in Caliente of large stocks of repair material and equipment—and not overlooking man-power—which has thus become available on short notice.

. . . But (the railroad) or at least one of its big officials appearing to be almost completely divorced from policies which made this railroad great, has ordered changes which are about as inconsiderate as anything of which "Big Business" has ever been accused! Employees who have given the best years of their lives to this railroad are cut off without anything to which they can turn, many of them with homes in which they have taken much pride; while others, similarly with nice homes, are told to move elsewhere and are given runs that only a few will be able to endure from a physical standpoint, according to common opinion.

Smart big corporations the country over encourage their employees to own their own homes—and loud are their boasts when the percentage of such employees is favorable! But in contrast, a high (company) official is reported to have said only recently that "a railroad man has no business owning a home!" Quite a departure from what has appeared to be (company) tradition.

It is difficult for the *Herald* to believe that this official, however "big" he is, speaks for the . . . (company) . . . when he enunciates a policy that, carried to the latter, would make tramps of (company) employees and their families!

No thinking person wants to stand in the way of progress, but true progress is not made when it is overshadowed by cold-blooded disregard for the loyalty of employees, their families, and the communities which have developed in the good American way through the decades of loyal service and good citizenship.

This editorial, written by a member of all the service clubs, approved by Caliente business men, and quoted with approbation by the most conservative members of the community, is significant of changing sentiment.

The people of Caliente continually profess their belief in "The American Way," but like the editor of the *Herald* they criticize decisions made solely in pursuit of profit, even though these decisions grow out of a clear-cut case of technological "progress." They feel that the company should have based its decision upon consideration for loyalty, citizenship, and community morale. They assume that the company should regard the seniority rights of workers as important considerations, and that it should consider significant the effect of permanent unemployment upon old and faithful employees. They look upon community integrity as an important community asset. Caught between the support of a "rational" system of "economic" forces and laws, and sentiments which they accept as significant values, they seek a solution to their dilemma which will at once permit them to retain their expected rewards for continued adherence to past norms and to defend the social system which they have been taught to revere but which now offers them a stone instead of bread.

IMPLICATIONS

We have shown that those in Caliente whose behavior most nearly approached the ideal taught are hardest hit by change. On the other hand, those seemingly farthest removed in conduct from that ideal are either rewarded or pay less of the costs of change than do those who follow the ideal more closely. Absentee owners, completely anonymous, and consumers who are not expected to co-operate to make the gains possible are rewarded most highly, while the local people who must cooperate to raise productivity pay dearly for having contributed.

In a society run through sacred mysteries whose rationale it is not man's privilege to criticize, such incongruities may be explained away. Such a society may even provide some "explanation" which makes them seem rational. In a secular society, supposedly defended rationally upon scientific facts, in which the pragmatic test "Does it work?" is continually applied, such discrepancy between expectation and realization is difficult to reconcile.

Defense of our traditional system of assessing the costs of technological change is made on the theory that the costs of such change are more than offset by the benefits to "society as a whole." However, it is difficult to show the people of Caliente just why *they* should pay for advances made to benefit others whom they have never known and who, in their judgment, have done nothing to justify such rewards. Any action that will permit the people of Caliente to levy the costs of change upon those who will benefit from them will be morally justifiable to the people of Caliente. Appeals to the general welfare leave them cold and the compulsions of the price system are not felt to be self-justifying "natural laws" but are regarded as being the specific consequence of specific bookkeeping decisions as to what should be included in the costs of change. They seek to change these decisions through social action. They do not consider that the "American Way" consists primarily of acceptance of the market as the final arbiter of their destiny. Rather they conceive that the system as a whole exists to render "justice," and if the consequences of the price system are such as to produce what they consider to be "injustice" they proceed to use some other institution as a means to reverse or offset the effects of the price system. Like other groups faced with the same situation, those in Caliente seize upon the means available to them. The operating employees had in their unions a device to secure what they consider to be their rights. Union practices developed over the years make it possible for the organized workers to avoid some of the costs of change which they would otherwise have had to bear. Featherbed rules, make-work practices, restricted work weeks, train length legislation and other similar devices were designed to permit union members to continue work even when "efficiency" dictated that they be disemployed. Members of the "Big Four" in Caliente joined with their fellows in demanding not only the retention of previously existing rules, but the imposition of new ones such as that requiring the presence of a third man in the diesel cab. For other groups there was available only the appeal to the company that it establish some other facility at Caliente, or alternatively a demand that "government" do something. One such demand took the form of a request to the Interstate Commerce Commission that it require inspection of rolling stock at Caliente. This request was denied.

It rapidly became apparent to the people of Caliente that they could not gain their objectives by organized community action nor individual endeavor but there was hope that by adding their voices to those of others similarly injured there might be hope of solution. They began to look to the activities of the whole labor movement for succor. Union strategy which forced the transfer of control from the market to government mediation or to legislation and operation was widely approved on all sides. This was not confined to those only who were currently seeking rule changes but was equally approved by the great bulk of those in the community who had been hit by the change. Cries of public outrage at their demands for make-work rules were looked upon as coming from those at best ignorant, ill-informed or stupid, and at worst as being the hypocritical efforts of others to gain at the workers' expense. When the union threat of a national strike for rule changes was met by government seizure, Caliente workers like most of their compatriots across the country welcomed this shift in control, secure in their belief that if "justice" were done they could only be gainers by government intervention. These attitudes are not "class" phenomena purely nor are they merely occupational sentiments. They result from the fact that modern life, with the interdependence that it creates, particularly in one-industry communi-

ties, imposes penalties far beyond the membership of the groups pre-
sumbly involved in industry. When make-work rules contributed to the
livelihood of the community, the support of the churches, and the taxes
which maintain the schools; when featherbed practices determine the
standard of living, the profits of the businessman and the circulation of
the press; when they contribute to the salary of the teacher and the
preacher; they can no longer be treated as accidental, immoral, deviant
or temporary. Rather they are elevated into the position of emergent
morality and law. Such practices generate a morality which serves them
just as the practices in turn nourish those who participate in and preserve
them. They are as firmly a part of what one "has a right to expect" from
industry as are parity payments to the farmer, bonuses and pensions to
the veterans, assistance to the aged, tariffs to the industrialist, or the
sanctity of property to those who inherit. On the other hand, all these
practices conceivably help create a structure that is particularly vulnerable to changes such as that described here.

Practices which force the company to spend in Caliente part of what
has been saved through technological change, or failing that, to reward
those who are forced to move by increased income for the same service,
are not, by the people of Caliente, considered to be unjustifiable. Confronted by a choice between the old means and resultant "injustice"
which their use entails, and the acceptance of new means which they
believe will secure them the "justice" they hold to be their right, they are
willing to abandon (insofar as this particular area is concerned) the
liberal state and the omnicompetent market in favor of something that
works to provide "justice."

The study of the politics of pressure groups will show how widely the
reactions of Caliente people are paralleled by those of other groups.
Amongst them it is in politics that the decisions as to who will pay and
who will profit are made. Through organized political force railroaders
maintain the continuance of rules which operate to their benefit rather
than for "the public good" or "the general welfare." Their defense of
these practices is found in the argument that only so can their rights be
protected against the power of other groups who hope to gain at their
expense by functioning through the corporation and the market.

We should expect that where there are other groups similarly affected
by technological change, there will be similar efforts to change the operation of our institutions. The case cited is not unique. Not only is it
duplicated in hundreds of railroad division points but also in other
towns abandoned by management for similar reasons. Changes in the
location of markets or in the method of calculating transportation costs,
changes in technology making necessary the use of new materials, changes

due to the exhaustion of old sources of materials, changes to avoid labor costs such as the shift of the textile industry from New England to the South, changes to expedite decentralization to avoid the consequences of bombing, or those of congested living, all give rise to the question, "Who benefits, and at whose expense?"

The accounting practices of the corporation permit the entry only of those costs which have become "legitimate" claims upon the company. But the tremendous risks borne by the workers and frequently all the members of the community in an era of technological change are real phenomena. Rapid shifts in technology which destroy the "legitimate" expectations derived from past experience force the recognition of new obligations. Such recognition may be made voluntarily as management foresees the necessity, or it may be thrust upon it by political or other action. Rigidity of property concepts, the legal structure controlling directors in what they may admit to be costs, and the stereotyped nature of the "economics" used by management make rapid change within the corporation itself difficult even in a "free democratic society." Hence while management is likely to be permitted or required to initiate technological change in the interest of profits, it may and probably will be barred from compensating for the social consequences certain to arise from those changes. Management thus shuts out the rising flood of demands in its cost-accounting only to have them reappear in its tax accounts, in legal regulations or in new insistent union demands. If economics fails to provide an answer to social demands then politics will be tried.

It is clear that while traditional morality provides a means of protecting some groups from the consequences of technological change, or some method of meliorating the effects of change upon them, other large segments of the population are left unprotected. It should be equally clear that rather than a quiet acquiescence in the finality and justice of such arrangements, there is an active effort to force new devices into being which will extend protection to those hitherto expected to bear the brunt of these costs. A good proportion of these inventions increasingly call for the intervention of the state. To call such arrangements immoral, unpatriotic, socialistic or to hurl other epithets at them is not to deal effectively with them. They are as "natural" as are the "normal" reactions for which we have "rational" explanations based upon some pre-scientific generalization about human nature such as "the law of supply and demand" or "the inevitability of progress." To be dealt with effectively they will have to be understood and treated as such.

44. The Decline and Fall
of the Small Town

WILLIAM SIMON
JOHN H. GAGNON

It is a fact of our twentieth century life that as the centers of economic, social, and political power have shifted from farm and countryside to city and suburb, those small communities that are not absorbed by some metropolitan complex come under threat (if not actual sentence) of decline and decay. But why do some small towns wither and not others? And is there long term hope for any?

Actually, this Darwinian life and death struggle of American small towns is not confined to modern times. During the nineteenth century the petering out of natural resources or the demand for them (gold in California, coal in parts of the Midwest) and the considerations that determined whether a railroad went through one area rather than another often determined whether a village would prosper or become a ghost town. Today, decisions about where to place highways, intersections, dams, or where to move an industry can have similar effects— revitalizing or building one community, sentencing another to senescence.

SOURCE: Reprinted with permission of the authors and publisher from *Transaction*, Vol. 4, No. 5 (April, 1967), Copyright 1967 by Washington University, St. Louis, Mo.

But in the nineteenth century decline or vitalization were considered to result from the natural workings of *laissez-faire*. The fittest survived. The economic success grew and the failure faded away—a process that was not to be interfered with and that made for progress. Today the state and federal governments are actively intervening to try to maintain the small town—which they perceive to be a useful way of life, a balancing force against the rise of megalopolis.

But is it enough to simply inject redevelopment funds into a community to assure its health? For that matter, what do we learn from using medical terms to describe a town's economic vitality—a robust community, a sick or moribund community? What really determines a town's viability? Is it different with each town?

This article attempts detailed analyses of three neighboring rural towns in southern Illinois, to determine why, despite many similarities in location, economic problems, and history, they developed differently after World War II.

The three communities—which we will call East Parrish, Clyde, and Spiresburg—are in an area distinctly "southern" in many characteristics and values. It was originally settled in the first half of the nineteenth century by migrants from the southern hill country. They rapidly exhausted a land as inhospitable, if not more so, than what they had originally left. Its barren, clay-ridden soil did not, and will not in the future, support more than meager subsistence farming.

At the turn of the century coal was discovered in the area, and large-scale mining brought a new, unprecedented, and profoundly uncertain prosperity. Coal camps appeared, and rail lines connecting them to each other and to the outside world began to crisscross the region. Typical of the influence of the railroads, in a very few years entire town sites moved to the nearby rail lines.

The growing coal industry brought in a few Negroes and many immigrants, largely from eastern Europe. Though farming continued, it increasingly became a part-time venture, and everything became tied to a highly unstable, single industry—coal. Typical of coal mining areas, a culture full of strong contrasts developed (as Herman Lantz described it in his *The People of Coaltown*). Side by side there was violence and resignation, Bible-belt religion and hard-drinking, serious gambling, and (at least historically) no small amount of whoring. All three communities are within 40 miles of what has, with full justification, become known as "Bloody Williamson County."

By the mid-1920's, the local coal boom reached its peak, and from then on, except for a brief period during World War II, went into continuous decline. East Parrish, the largest of the three towns, declined from almost

25,000 to its present 9000. From 1950 to 1960 East Parrish declined by 21 percent, Clyde by 11 percent, and Spiresburg by six percent. People continue to leave in large numbers—primarily the younger, healthier, and better educated. Nor has there been (especially as far as mining is concerned) any substantial leveling off of employment. Between 1950 and 1960 the number of persons employed in mining in East Parrish decreased by 71 percent, in Clyde by 72 percent, and in Spiresburg by 61 percent. And there were substantial, if smaller, declines in such things as railroad carloadings. All during the preceding decade the immediate area has been defined by government agencies as "chronically depressed" and "surplus labor."

By the early 1950's people in all three communities began to realize that the very survival of their towns was at stake. Responding to this realization, and prodded by federal and state governments and a nearby state university, community leaders became very adept at the rhetoric of community redevelopment.

But the consequences of both rhetoric and action have been markedly different among the three. East Parrish (population 9000) has had virtually no change or improvement—nor does any appear even remotely likely. Clyde (population 7000) has been able to check its decline somewhat and expects in the near future to derive the benefits of a federal water and land redevelopment project. Spiresburg, the smallest (population 3000), has in the last six years attracted four new industries and thereby largely reconstituted its economic base.

EAST PARRISH

East Parrish first recognized its problem openly in the early 1950's when the East Parrish Industrial Fund was created with working capital of $100,000 raised from over 2000 public contributors. This fund was deposited in the local bank where it remained untouched for eight years. Its first expenditure was to rebuild a dress factory that had burned down. This factory, typical of industry attracted by such communities, is "labor-intensive," paying low wages and primarily employing women.

But while the basic fund was put to restricted use, the accumulated interest was more freely available. Much of it went to subsidize the local Chamber of Commerce; and this in turn strengthened the hold of the community conservatives over the Chamber.

Rarely was any money used in realistic scouting for new industry. As one member of the development board put it:

> We didn't run around like some of the towns around here wining and dining company officials or taking junkets around the country looking

for companies. And we weren't going to offer the moon to some of these companies. Industry that you get that way either won't stay or won't pay off. Sure, there are companies that we might have looked at, but they are out for what they can get. They don't want to pay taxes, want free water, gas, and free land. It is just like raping a community. And then they move on. If you can get them on this basis, so can another town get them from you on the same basis. Hell, they have no ties to the community; they could move tomorrow. Besides, our real problem is labor. For all the talk around here, most of the people really don't want to work—they're content on public assistance. And those that do want to work have been spoiled by the unions; they won't work for wages that the kind of industry that would come here would pay—they [the workers] think that they can only work for the $16 and $17 a day they used to make when the mines were running.

The next big economic event was the discovery of exploitable oil within the corporate limits of the community. However, the oil industry is highly automated. The oil ownership was concentrated among a very few, and additional employment was barely noticeable. To this day the endlessly see-sawing, black, squat-pumps constantly remind the population of still another disappointment.

To date no federal funds have been requested—except for some public housing and clearance—and on at least two occasions they were rejected by community leaders when offered.

When we look at East Parrish's formal political structure one thing stands out: since 1947, no mayor of the community succeeded himself (although two tried), and only two city commission members won re-election. This would suggest considerable political instability. Curiously, however, as one makes inquiries of community residents about community events during this period, one finds that essentially the same names appear. These names virtually never appear in contests for major political office (mayor or city commission), although roughly half of them have participated in one or more public commissions. Formal government apparently became the target for the expression of the frustrations of community residents, but rarely the framework within which serious solutions for community problems could be approached.

What, then, is the political life of East Parrish? Of the three communities, East Parrish is the only one with a strong tradition of working-class involvement in politics. This probably developed out of the high level of social solidarity characteristic of coal mining communities.

There is a basic cleavage going back for a number of decades between the miners (for whom the merchants remain those "bastards on Main

Street") and the professional merchant group (for whom the miner remains the hillbilly or hunkie to whom they once sold silk shirts at highly inflated prices). As the medical director of the United Mine Workers Association hospital remarked, it was still almost impossible to get a Main Street merchant to serve on the hospital board. One effect of this cleavage was a historic pattern of miner representation in city government. One mayor, deposed in a recent election, was employed as a miner concurrently with his occupancy of the mayor's office.

The effects of this traditional cleavage became intensified because the middle-class elite (if this term is at all applicable) is itself badly split. Among the merchants a split occurs between those whose operations serve a broad area and those whose business centers entirely upon local retail trade. One cost of this second cleavage has been the inability—despite successive attempts—to have Main Street broadened and repaved with state funds and turned over to state maintenance because the local retail merchants refuse to surrender angle parking.

Typical of self-centered communities, there is no local industrial elite —even in the heyday of the coal boom most operations were absentee-owned.

With the decline of mining, its importance to the community and the number of people it employs, the effectiveness of the miners and their ability to organize has lessened. In addition, a relatively high proportion of miners or their families are on welfare. In towns like East Parrish, welfare is handled very informally through the township supervisor, a very political office. Further, people generally know who is on relief. Both these factors make welfare recipients feel very vulnerable, and this tends to undermine their political participation. Also, the more promising young people, potential political leaders, leave in large numbers.

This does not mean that working-class politics has eroded in East Parrish. There has been considerable miner participation. In 1959, for instance, three of four city commissioners were miners, and one of these was later appointed mayor upon the death of the incumbent. But it does mean that their effectiveness and independence has been undermined. Election rhetoric centers heavily on class politics—but the election of miners has not given rise to working-class programs. The miners in politics have been largely coopted by the "politicos" of the community.

Between the larger, more affluent merchants and the lower-class community a small but crucial group of professional, or near professional, politicians has developed—a group whose basic constituency is greatly enhanced by a large number of dependent and chronic welfare recipients. As with government in an underdeveloped country, an amazing amount of money can be made by manipulating the local political structure, particularly in playing with taxes and land speculation, even where land itself is not worth much.

Significantly absent from political life are the community's hired professionals—schoolteachers and ministers. Local school systems, because they are small and split among several authorities, are highly vulnerable. Moreover, the staff in such school systems—either women tied to families that in turn are tied to the community, or men of rather low competence —are not likely to seek involvement. Ministers, at least Protestant ministers, move around a great deal and are at the mercy of lay leaders who are primarily drawn from the community conservatives. They tend to avoid speaking out on community issues because there is rarely a community issue that would not find competing factions within the same church, and it is a rare minister who, in the context of East Parrish's long history of community conflicts, would invite such a conflict into his church.

While churches seem to be nearly totally estranged from power and community decision-making in all three communities, in East Parrish the social and fraternal organizations have also tended to withdraw. A recent reform movement has taken control of city hall, and it reflects primarily the needs of local merchants. Ostensibly it is committed to industrial renewal, but little is expected to come of it. The professional politicians know all too well that they, despite this temporary setback, control access to county and state politicans, without whom little can be done.

As a result, the recent political history of East Parrish is one of apathy and distrust punctuated by episodes of scandal and conflict. Where decisions have to be made—such as providing a new library or even something as trivial as paying for a local production of an opera produced by a nearby university—they are made by a very small number of citizens operating in a completely nonpublic way. This nonpublic process —which turns out to be the only way to get something done because it does not invoke some form of community cleavage—only further feeds community paranoia and resentment. During our interview with one of the city fathers who showed us the drawings for a projected new library, he turned to his secretary and jokingly asked: "How much have we made on it so far?"

CLYDE

Economically, Clyde, aside from its new dress factory, has seen no substantial change. Its biggest step forward came when a small group of community leaders, in the mid-1950's, created a tax-raising administration with special bond-issuing powers under some long obscure state law. About $250,000 were raised in taxes that went into a local water development based on a nearby lake. After considerable lobbying, the federal government took over the project. The leaders hope that this development will attract new industry, and lead to expanded development of Clyde and environs into a prosperous and pleasant recreation center and resort.

Politically, Clyde differs considerably from East Parrish. It has no real tradition of lower-class action. As a county seat, it has a higher proportion of middle-class people working for, or involved in, county and courthouse activities. This is also the reason why the main political focus in Clyde is on county, rather than civic, affairs. It does not even have the same "coal-camp" appearance of East Parrish. To the innocent urban eye it looks very much like any small town in Illinois; one has to go to the unincorporated fringe, or to a tavern in an obscure alley off the square, to see what almost 20 years of poverty will do to human beings. Of the three towns, only in Clyde does one hear frequent and almost compulsive talk of "white trash."

Also, probably because it is a county seat, a number of industry executives live there. The town's previous mayor was a retired railroad vice president; its present mayor is a retired coal company president—in manner and style very much resembling his famous brother who led the miner's union. One of the last major coal companies—the one reputed to be the most ruthlessly exploitative—maintains offices in Clyde. This small executive group has left its mark on the politics of Clyde.

If the politics of East Parrish resemble in a strange way the politics of France before DeGaulle, the politics of Clyde resemble the politics of DeGaulle. There have been a series of strong mayors who have not "sought" public office, but who have demanded that the community offer it to them. The present mayor in his first election cautioned supporters that, if campaign posters were put up, he would decline the office. These strong mayors have given the community its neat, clean appearance; they have also sapped the political vitality of the people.

The present upper-middle class, which might ordinarily have been expected to provide considerable leadership, will obviously bring little change. It has split into two elements. The more conservative element was described by one citizen:

> There is definitely a group of inheritors—doctors, lawyers, those running insurance agencies, stores, garages. For the most part a very unaggressive lot. . . . These people are in no great hurry to see things change.

One conservative spoke about his group this way:

> True, we might lack some spirit. For most of us, it is a matter of getting out of school and inheriting your father's business. This is what

happened in my case. I'm not sure I really wanted to come back. . . . But, as I say, it is a life with many compensations.

To the extent that they take an interest in politics, they are Republican and concentrate on town affairs.

The other element mostly consists of the recently prosperous—including those who rose from Italian or Slavic coal mining families. They—with a few mavericks from the older elites—tend to dominate county politics which are largely Democratic. They are more concerned with the decline of the community than the older group, possibly because they are more vulnerable—yet they accept, with little quibble, the present structure of control.

Clyde has experienced none of the turbulence of East Parrish politics—but that is probably because it has not evinced as much interest as East Parrish—the interest caused by frustration. It developed no new community organizations, engaged in no campaigns to raise funds from community residents, and rarely did economic redevelopment become a political issue.

It is thus not unexpected that Clyde's major bid for renewal came not from some broad, popular campaign, but from an administrative unit of government; that it did not seek funds through public appeal, but through taxation. Despite the fact that, as one resident put it, "for years the merchants have been hanging on by their teeth hoping for a miracle to save them," and that the pressures of poverty are such that the state's attorney (the Illinois name for county prosecutor) complains that he "can only do a small part of what the state requires because I spend 90 percent of my time doing social work," this community feels it can afford to take the long view. But even at this point, the brightest estimate of the transformations to be wrought by the new lake development offers a promise for only a small section of the community.

The only public opposition, an angry typographer employed by the community's daily newspaper, can be seen on occasional Saturdays parading around the town square, carrying now familiar sandwich boards that decry the community's domination by a small and selfish group and that challenge the community to undertake its own program of revival. And just as this single, isolated figure is accepted with good humor but not much thought by the residents of Clyde, so there appears to be a somewhat thoughtless and casual acceptance of an unchanging drift.

SPIRESBURG

Spiresburg clearly has been the most successful of the three towns. In a sense, the crisis caused by the decline of the coal industry came to it first.

Spiresburg lost its two major mines during the early years of the great depression and, while it retained a number of persons employed in mining, it served essentially as a dormitory for miners of the general area.

Like Clyde, it is a county seat and the core of the community is located around the courthouse. Also, like Clyde, Spiresburg is a second city in its county, subordinate in industry, retail, and service activity to a nearby town.

In these respects, as well as in general location, types of industry, natural resources and so on, it has some similarity to the other two. If anything, it has more disadvantages. It has not been nearly as successful as Clyde in attracting potentially prominent, capable, and educated people to live there. It is markedly smaller than either—less than half the population of Clyde, a third that of East Parrish. But it is the character and activity of the political and community leaders of Spiresburg that is most dramatically different.

They are a fairly well-integrated group of small merchants and independent professionals and semiprofessionals. Even schoolteachers and ministers, in contrast to Clyde and East Parrish, are included. Reading a roster of offices for social clubs, official and semiofficial boards, and local government offices for a period of years, one quickly detects an interweaving and reoccurrence of names that suggests nothing so much as a well-rehearsed square dance. To the middle class, high or low, a lot of sociability is most of what is required for access to community life. The pattern of integrated community leadership is so great that lower-class participation is all but impossible. (Its dormitory status, which meant a dispersal of its workers over the countryside, obviously weakened class solidarity, unlike East Parrish where residential and work populations overlapped.)

Social contacts among Spiresburg's upper group are the highest for all three communities—while social participation for its workers and reliefers is the lowest for all three. The frequent and easy contacts among influentials are facilitated by Spiresburg's size—it is small enough so that its community leadership can take a collective daily coffee break. While sitting in a restaurant in early afternoon for less than an hour with the mayor, the senior author met most of the town's leading merchants, a local insurance agent, the police chief, postmaster, state senator, optometrist, and the newspaper publisher.

In three of the cases of successful plant relocation in Spiresburg government aid was sought and utilized; in the fourth the community provided its own resources. The wages in all four plants are at best marginal, and there are few white collar or managerial positions.

However, the limits of Spiresburg's recovery have been set by the shopkeeper mentalities of its leadership. By these standards the town has recovered. But in Spiresburg's lower class there is a continuing, if ineffectual, discontent. And in the upper class the most promising young people leave, usually for college, and seldom return. Spiresburg's situation is best symbolized by the contrast between its four almost brand-new factories—on its outskirts—and its town square which looks today much as it must have about 1925.

THE ISSUE OF LEADERSHIP

From this comparison of the three towns it seems obvious that the quality of community leadership—particularly political leadership—is a crucial determinant of the course of development. The picture is amazingly consistent with that thesis. And it is also reflected in the feelings and attitudes of the citizens of each town.

The depressed spirit in East Parrish and Clyde, and the unrealistic attitudes toward their problems, is revealed by the answers people had to questions about events that had occurred recently. (For example, what was "the biggest thing that happened in the community during the last year?") The ones they emphasized were on the horizon rather than of immediate importance. Very prominent were a major interstate highway due to pass close to both towns and the federal lake resort project—both due for completion well in the future. Seventy-three percent of the citizens of Clyde, the town most directly involved, mentioned one or the other. Even though East Parrish was not as closely concerned, 27 percent also referred to them.

Similar results came from the more specific question that asked people to describe the "most important problem facing the community." Almost 80 percent of Clyde's respondents spoke of unemployment or poor business conditions, as did 66 percent from East Parrish. (The continuing political conflict in East Parrish, not present in Clyde, accounted for 17 percent, and so kept the score for economic depression from being even higher.) Spiresburg, too, registered a 47 percent vote for unemployment and poor business which indicated that its recovery was also far from complete. On the other hand, 36 percent of Spiresburg's respondents listed problems associated with growth—the taxing of existing community facilities or the financing of improvements—as being the "most important."

Would the picture get "better or worse in the next few months?" Fifty percent of East Parrish votes went for worse; in Clyde 26 percent felt this way; but in optimistic Spiresburg, only 12 percent.

How attached the respondents were to their communities and how they felt about them are described in the table.

Spiresburg is the easiest to single out. Its economic improvement has had an effect on (and perhaps also was affected by) the attitude of its citizens. A majority thought it no place for a young man just starting out (63 percent); but that is considerably lower than the 78 and 83 percent who felt that way about East Parrish and Clyde. They also show the highest community identification and commitment—68 percent selected it as their ideal community of residence; 84 percent felt their fellow residents "really care" about it.

The differences between the depressed communities, Clyde and East Parrish, were not great; but such as they were, they emphasized the greater magnitude of East Parrish's decline.

CHANGE—BUT DON'T UPSET ANYTHING

In these three towns different traditions and different political structures have led to three essentially different modes of adjustment to similar crises. What these modes do have in common however—despite a prevailing rhetoric of community renewal—is a deep-seated resistance to social change of any real significance. And in this respect they resemble hundreds of other declining communities too far from urban centers in an urban society.

This resistance to change has many causes. Most important perhaps, community leaders do not really believe enough in the futures of their towns to be willing to commit their own children to them. (The lower classes have little choice.) There was only one professional or semi-professional in all those we interviewed in all three communities who did not sometime boast about how well his children were doing somewhere else. The only middle-class group whose children, generally, did not leave, are the marginal retail merchants who often had little to bequeath except their businesses.

And it is precisely this element, notably in East Parrish, that is most committed to community renewal. The mayor of Spiresburg talked—as most people did—about the loss of young people to the community; each new plant was referred to as having taken care of the graduating class of the community high school of this year or that year. But the reference was not to the entire graduating class, only that part of it primarily, if not exclusively, lower class. That is, that portion not going on to college. The son of the mayor himself, obviously, had no future in a plant with few managerial or professional jobs.

Since the leaders are not really committed to the future of the towns—except in the most abstract way—there is little incentive to undertake community renewal that might rock their boats; and any genuine community renewal would have to rock it. The president of East Parrish's only bank was most explicit:

> This community has lost population and it may have to lose more. But things have settled down quite nicely and everything operates smoothly. East Parrish has a pretty stable economy. Of course there are no new industries. But when I started this bank in 1943 there was a mine payroll of over one million dollars a month, now it is down to one hundred and fifty thousand. Then there were three banks with combined assets of about four million, now there is only one (his), but it has assets of over twelve million. . . . The town may get smaller instead of bigger. For a community, like a man, things have to balance out.

The town might die, but he was doing nicely. Things balanced out.

This banker was a leading member of the East Parrish Industrial Fund; it is easy to see why it was so cautious about spending its $100,000 to attract new industry. Even in Spiresburg, though everyone was in favor of prosperity in general, some did not want too much—too much being defined as the point at which it might bring competition to established businesses and established allocations of power.

TABLE 1.

Perception Of And Attachment To Community

Items:	E. Parrish (%)*	Clyde (%)*	Spiresburg (%)*
Most of the important decisions in _____ are made by a small group of people who are on "the inside."....	82	72	78
There have been so many changes in _____ that it is hardly the same town.	24	12	15
Most people in _____ really care about what happens to the community.	68	62	84
_____ is no place for a young man just starting out. ...	78	83	63
It is better to live in a small town than a big city.	80	88	90
Percent selecting present community in free choice of ideal community in which to live.	58	53	68

* Percent agreeing.

The present high level of integration of leadership in Spiresburg is sustained by systematic back-scratching. For example, the town's optometrist makes it perfectly clear that none of the town's four practicing physicians would dream of giving an eye examination. Unfortunately, economic back-scratching cannot survive where there is extensive economic and social growth, vital to community renewal. You can't have everything. Despite the rhetoric, the choice has been made.

Further, whether as rationalization or compensation, or because those who might think otherwise have already flown to the cities, a strongly anti-urban system of values has emerged. One community resident observed:

> When I or my wife want to take a walk we can do it without being robbed or assaulted. You can't say that in St. Louis or Chicago.

This is an overstatement, but not without some truth. However, he does not ask what the young people of the community ask continually: Where in town is there anything to walk to?

Since for most the money lies in the cities, those who stay must believe, or profess, a rejection of purely mercenary values. A young returnee to East Parrish commented:

> This is a friendly town. I know 'most everyone. When I walk down the street, everyone says hello. Here I am my own boss. I make less, but I also worry less. In St. Louis, at GM, everyone was worried that the guy at the next desk would get a promotion before you did—I could have stayed, they called from Flint and offered me a promotion. You have to grow up sometimes, a person has to learn to walk a straight road.

Or a young publisher in Clyde:

> You might say that we here in Clyde have learned to settle for second best. But I prefer to think that we just value things differently. . . . I have ten minutes from my house what the big city businessman has to travel hundreds of miles to get and then for only a few days a year.

The lessons are plain. First, superficial indicators are not the accurate predictors of community health they are often conceived to be. Whether a town will climb, slow its decline, or go under altogether is determined often very largely by the character and activity of its middle and upper-middle class political leadership.

But there is an even more important lesson hovering ominously in the background. The economic progress of each of the three southern Illinois towns studied is different, and they have responded differently to crisis; but none represents a substantial—certainly not permanent—comeback in the face of increased urbanization.

Their approach to the future is one of improvisation. Their horizons must remain limited—for redevelopment is not only a promise but a threat to the ideologies of small town life. They must lose their best people and business concerns to the larger towns because of greater opportunities, education, and satisfactions there. Those who return will be failures—or be willing, for whatever reason, to settle for what represents second-best in our competitive society.

It is impossible for any similar small town to maintain a first-rate school system—and the children, and the future, must suffer for it. The fundamental character of the leadership of these communities will limit the nature and direction of growth—because they do not want to face real competition. If they had been willing and prepared to face it, they would have moved out long before. They cannot be expected to deliberately make their own worst fears come true.

The land and the economy of the United States will not support as many small towns as they did before. It is very difficult not to see the future as a long drawn-out struggle for community survival, lasting for half a century, in which some battles may be won but the war will be lost. A future in which most such towns will become isolated or decayed, in which the local amenities must deteriorate, and in which there will finally be left only the aged, the inept, the very young—and the local power elite.

Index of Subjects

Index of Names

THE BOOK MANUFACTURE

The Community: A Comparative Perspective was composed and offset printed by Webb Publishing Company. Binding was by A. J. Dahl Co. The paper is Perkins & Squier Company's Glatfelter Old Forge. Internal and case design was by the art department of F. E. Peacock Publishers, Inc. The type in this book is Baskerville.